D0631673

Tyranny on Trial

TYRANNY *on* TRIAL

THE TRIAL OF THE MAJOR GERMAN WAR CRIMINALS
AT THE END OF WORLD WAR II
AT NUREMBERG, GERMANY, 1945–1946

WHITNEY R. HARRIS

REVISED EDITION

with new
PART SEVEN: JUSTICE AFTER NUREMBERG
containing updated chapter on
PRINCIPLES AND PRECEDENT
and new chapter on
THE INTERNATIONAL CRIMINAL COURT

Foreword by
Robert G. Storey

Introduction by
Robert H. Jackson

SOUTHERN METHODIST UNIVERSITY PRESS
Dallas

ALEXANDRIA LIBRARY
ALEXANDRIA, VA 22

Copyright © 1954 (renewed 1982), 1995, 1999 by Whitney R. Harris
All rights reserved
First Southern Methodist University Press edition published 1954
A LOU REDA BOOK edition published by Barnes & Noble, Inc., 1995
Revised Southern Methodist University Press edition 1999

Requests for permission to reproduce material from this work should be sent to:
Rights and Permissions
Southern Methodist University Press
PO Box 750415
Dallas, Texas 75275-0415

The quotation from *Decision in Germany*, by Lucius D. Clay, is reprinted by permission of Doubleday & Company, Inc.

Cover design by Tom Dawson Graphic Design

LIBRARY OF CONGRESS CATALOGING IN PUBLICATION DATA

Harris, Whitney R.
    Tyranny on trial : the trial of the major German war criminals at the end of World War II at Nuremberg, Germany, 1945–1946 / Whitney R. Harris ; foreword by Robert G. Storey ; introduction by Robert H. Jackson. — Rev. ed.
        p.   cm.
    "With new part seven, Justice after Nuremberg, containing updated chapter on Principles and precedent, and new chapter on the International Criminal Court."
    Includes bibliographical references (p.   ) and index.
    ISBN 0-87074-436-4. — ISBN 0-87074-437-2 (pbk.)
    1. Nuremberg Trial of Major German War Criminals, Nuremberg, Germany.   2. War crimes—History—20th century.   I. Title.
D804.G42H36   1999
341.6'9'0268—dc21   98-46376

Printed in the United States of America on acid-free paper

10   9   8   7   6   5   4   3   2   1

Tyranny on Trial *is dedicated to the memory of
Mr. Justice Robert H. Jackson, the United States Chief of Counsel
at the trial of the Major German War Criminals before the
International Military Tribunal at Nuremberg, Germany, 1945–46.*

TO THE MEMORY OF JANE HARRIS

Contents

Illustrations

The illustrations listed below will be found in a group following page 34

Mr. Justice Robert H. Jackson
Shattered Nuremberg
Adolf Hitler Platz
The Palace of Justice
Prisoners' Row
Courtroom Scene as the Tribunal Enters
The International Military Tribunal
United States Judges
British Judges
French Judges
Soviet Judges
Robert G. Storey
United States Prosecution Staff
Sir Hartley Shawcross
Sir David Maxwell Fyfe
Thomas J. Dodd
General R. A. Rudenko
The Author Cross-examining a Gestapo Witness
Pressroom
French Chief Prosecutors
Prosecution Staffs at Close of Trial
Defendants in the Dock

Above illustrations are United States Army photographs

*Above illustrations, except as otherwise noted, are United States Army
photographs; the three photographs of scenes during Hitler's
"Days of Triumph" were Nazi propaganda pictures*

Foreword

THE TRIAL of the major Axis war criminals at the end of World War II was the most significant criminal action in history. It was my honor to serve as the Executive Trial Counsel to Mr. Justice Jackson in that proceeding until completion of the presentation of the affirmative case. Among the lawyers drawn from the several branches of the military to assist in the prosecution was a young naval officer who, because of his expertness on the German intelligence system, was assigned to the preparation and presentation of the case against Ernst Kaltenbrunner, the chief of the principal repressive agencies of the Hitler regime—the Gestapo and the SD. He served as a member of the prosecution staff until the end of the trial, after which he went to Berlin where he was Chief of the Legal Advice Branch, Legal Division, United States Office of Military Government. From there he came to the faculty of Southern Methodist University School of Law, of which I am the Dean. This former Lieutenant Commander in the Navy, and present professor of law, is Whitney R. Harris, the author of this book.

The purpose of the Nuremberg trial was not merely, or even principally, to convict the leaders of Nazi Germany and affix a punishment upon them commensurate with their guilt. Of far greater importance, it seemed to me from the outset, was the making of a record of the Hitler regime which would withstand the test of history. I set about, therefore, to assemble the maximum number of German documents which had relevance to the crimes charged to the defendants. To distinguish them from similar evidence collected by other persons and authorities, these documents carried the designator "PS" (Paris-Storey), and ultimately constituted the basic documentary evidence introduced by the American prosecution staff.

We were greatly aided by teams of the United States Army in the collection and preliminary screening of these documents. But it was necessary for us to establish our own records center to which were assigned analysts and translators. The documents which we considered useful, upon final screening, were translated and duplicated for use by the teams of lawyers assigned to the preparation of the several aspects of the affirmative case.

In the few weeks we had to work before the commencement of the trial we were able to assemble a surprising number of documents establishing criminality of the Hitler regime. This was partly the result of the maintenance of records by all German offices and departments, and partly due to the fact that when the war drew to a close no general order was issued for the destruction of documents, decisions in that regard being left up to individuals, offices, and departments. Not infrequently attempts were made to hide, rather than to destroy, important documents. And sometimes we were able to recover entire caches of invaluable written evidence.

The complete records of the wordy Nazi philosopher, Alfred Rosenberg, were found in an abandoned castle in eastern Bavaria. They had been hidden behind a false wall eighteen inches thick. The total mass of the documents weighed several tons. Included were important letters involving Hitler, Goering, Goebbels, and other top leaders of the Hitler state. Even original correspondence from the Norwegian traitor, Quisling, turned up in this special collection. Likewise discovered in an abandoned castle were the invaluable records of the German Foreign Office. This collection weighed four hundred and eighty-five tons and contained a great many secret documents pertaining to plans for aggression.

The personal files of Heinrich Himmler were recovered. In them were found the terrible reports of the activities of Einsatz groups in the eastern territories, and the mass murder of Jews and other peoples by roving bands of Gestapo, SD, and SS personnel.

The Reich Main Security Office moved its documents to Prague toward the end of the war, and virtually all its headquarters records were burned in the basement of the Prague headquarters. All that was recovered by the United States prosecution staff there was a charred order by RSHA chief Kaltenbrunner for the murder of a concentration camp inmate. The RSHA could not, however, destroy the many copies of incriminating documents which had been distributed, and local Gestapo offices proved to be valuable sources of some of the most important evidence against the repressive agencies.

There were, of course, numerous other "finds" of documents, but the above illustrate sources of the incriminating documentary evidence. While the affirmative case was thus established primarily out of these German documents, the Tribunal did hear a number of important witnesses. Thirty-three persons testified for the prosecution. Sixty-one defense witnesses, in addition to nineteen of the defendants, testified for the defense. The prosecution introduced into evidence a number of affidavits taken from witnesses, subject, however, to the witnesses being called to testify in court if the defense demanded. The testimony of 143 witnesses was given for the defense in the form of written answers to interrogatories.

The Tribunal appointed commissioners to hear evidence relating to the organizations named as criminal in the indictment. The commissioners heard 101 witnesses for the defense and received 1,809 affidavits signed by other witnesses. Thirty-eight thousand affidavits, signed by 155,000 people, were filed for the Leadership Corps of the Party, 136,215 for the SS, 10,000 for the SA, 7,000 for the SD, 3,000 for the General Staff and High Command, and 2,000 for the Gestapo.

This tremendous volume of evidence constitutes the record of the Hitler regime in Germany as received by the International Military Tribunal. The official record is now in custody of the International Court of Justice at The Hague, under arrangements made with the United Nations. An exact duplicate of the record has been filed with the National Archives of the General Services Administration, Washington, D. C. Photostatic copies were substituted for many original documents introduced as United States exhibits, and these original documents, together with photostats of British, French, and Soviet documents, have been deposited with the Departmental Records Branch of the Adjutant General's Office, Department of the Army.

From this great quantity of evidence, Professor Harris has drawn this story of Hitler's Germany. He has performed a remarkable feat in reducing the unco-ordinated mass of documents and testimony into logical form in a single volume. His work is the first comprehensive study made of the Nuremberg record. The story he tells within these pages is in every respect verified by citation to authority. It is a record of fact, and of truth. And if it is sometimes harsh reading—that is only because the Hitler regime was an evil era in world history.

ROBERT G. STOREY

Dallas, Texas
April, 1954

Preface

THIS IS A BOOK OF TRAGEDY. It is a story of what dictatorship really is, and what tyranny and terror really mean. It tells of incredible crimes and unbelievable events. The Third Reich of Hitler, promised by him to last a thousand years, was destroyed because of him in twelve years. Hitler led Germany into the abyss, and the people of Germany followed him, believing and enchanted, until the end. In his brief hour upon history's stage, he caused the commission of crimes of the greatest magnitude ever endured by suffering humanity. By their own misery the German people have come to know the penalty of following a false prophet. But false prophets have arisen in other lands.

World War II is now an event of history. Germany, free of Nazism, is once more a respected member of the world community. Russia, free of Communism, strongly supports the principles of democracy. As never before in history the prospect has opened for the establishment of a world of peace and justice, under the rule of law. The opportunity is here to end war on this planet and turn to the exploration of new worlds in the unfolding universe. Man's vision will turn from the horrors of the mid-twentieth century to the visions of the twenty-first century. That is as it should be, provided that in shunning the evil of yesterday we do not forget the wrongs to which it led—and having forgotten them, believe them never to have happened. Sir David Maxwell Fyfe, the British Deputy Chief Prosecutor at Nuremberg, has written:

> After exhausting wars men tend to suffer from a certain weariness of mind. This lassitude can make men shrink from facing unpleasant facts. It exhibits itself in an easy-going skepticism as to how much was truth, and

xv

how much propaganda. Escapism as to gas chambers today might let the
gas chambers escape from history tomorrow.[1]

Apologists for the Hitler regime may be heard from, challenging
truths which in the absence of positive proofs might successfully be
denied. Fortunately, for history's sake, and for the sake, too, of many
men of many lands who gave their lives to rectify the wrongs of
Hitler's Germany, the proofs are permanently of record in the proceedings of the Nuremberg trial.

The Nuremberg record shows, of course, only the evil side
of Hitler's Germany. It does not recount the building of great
highways, the erection of buildings and monuments, the recovery of
business and industry, nor the resurgence of patriotism, which Hitler
may have brought to Germany and its people in the dark years of the
fourth decade of this century. But no one can doubt, after reading the
pages which follow, that whatever merits the Hitler tyranny may
have had were all blacked out by the wrongs of his regime.

For twelve years Germany was ruled by the tyrant Adolf Hitler.
While he had willing collaborators and accomplices, Hitler alone
made the major decisions for Germany. It was Hitler who ordered
the German armies into aggressive war; it was Hitler who commanded that the war in the East be conducted with extreme cruelty;
it was Hitler who ordered the decimation of European Jewry.
Germany was in his hands.

At a situation report in the final hours of the war, Hitler
discussed the spirit of ruthlessness in war with his top military leaders and referred to stern measures taken by Frederick William I:

> If people think that I am so brutal, I would recommend all dignified gen-
> tlemen to read this. It has always been that way. These things ought to be read
> by our officers. They have absorbed only the spirit of Schlieffen, not the spirit
> of Moltke, Frederick the Great, Frederick William I, Bluecher, et cetera. That
> was also a good spirit.[2]

The spirit of Hitlerism was one of the greatest factors for evil in
history. For Hitler had the incomparable advantage, over tyrants of
earlier times, of modern technology through which his propaganda
could be constantly pounded into the German people and his war
machine could be made to strike with terrible force upon his enemies.

The consequence of that spirit was the commission of crimes against humanity which stagger belief. The people of Europe and America understood that the Hitler regime had committed acts of great wickedness; but not until these wrongs had been exposed to the searching light of truth in an open judicial forum did the world gain comprehension of their enormity. This trial took place in Nuremberg.

An unkind fate had led Hitler to select this ancient walled city of commerce and culture as the center of National Socialism. Nuremberg was a city of noble traditions. In medieval times it achieved greatness as a commercial center where the riches of Italy and the East were traded for the goods of northern Europe. It was a popular residence of German monarchs, and in 1219 Frederick II conferred upon it the privileges of an imperial city. Nuremberg was the home of the painters Duehrer and Wohlgemuth, the sculptors Adam Krafft, Veit Stoss, and Peter Vischer, and Hans Sachs and the Meistersingers.

In this city of quaint mills, gabled houses, and stone bridges passing over the peaceful river Pegnitz, the annual September celebrations of the Nazi Party were held——enlivened by parades of storm troopers and soldiers and the Hitler Youth, bombastic speeches of the Nazi hierarchy, and tumultuous crowds screaming Nazi slogans. Here Hitler planned and began construction of the gigantic stadium dedicated to Nazism and the Party. And here, in 1935, he decreed the infamous "Nuremberg Laws" which swept away the rights of German Jews.

In 1945 the medieval beauty of Nuremberg was shattered by the scourge of war. Pitiless bombing and shelling left only gaunt remains of buildings, crumbled bridges, and great piles of rubble tumbling into the Pegnitz river which still tranquilly coursed its way through the city center. The destruction of the city marked the end of an epoch in its long history, dating from the building of the great castle in 1050 A.D. At war's end the Kaiserschloss, standing on a rock to the north of the city, towered over the devastation wrought by modern men. Ancient walls and bastions showed the pockmarks of rifle fire and the gaping holes of artillery shells. And in many places the moat was filled with the debris of war.

The end of Hitlerism in Germany resulted in new fame for Nuremberg, for in this city of ruined beauty the first attempt in history was made to bring to justice men who brought aggression to the world. In these pages is recorded the story of that trial—of the case against Hitler and those who conspired with him for the military conquest of Europe.

The German attack upon Poland in September, 1939, ignited World War II. Like a raging fire borne upon high winds, the flames of war leaped from Europe, to Africa, to Asia, and to every sea. At one time more than seventy million men were under arms. Thirty-four million were wounded; twenty-two million were killed. The total military cost exceeded one trillion dollars. In lives lost and in property destroyed World War II was the greatest calamity ever to befall mankind.

Moreover, in Europe particularly, the war was characterized by crimes against the laws of war and of humanity unparalleled in history. Five million persons were deported to Germany for slave labor; six million Jews were slaughtered; hundreds of thousands of persons were imprisoned in concentration camps; thousands of war prisoners were killed. For these crimes, as well as for that of starting the conflagration, the world asked retribution at war's end.

The responsibility for determining where war guilt lay, and for imposing commensurate punishments, was placed upon eight men who comprised the International Military Tribunal. On the basis of the evidence which the Tribunal heard and received it found that crimes against peace, the laws of war, and of humanity, had been committed. Of twenty-two defendants, selected as the principal leaders of the Nazi state, it convicted nineteen and acquitted three.

Writing in 1950, General Lucius D. Clay declared of these trials:

They were conducted in solemn dignity and with a high sense of justice. The mass of evidence, which exposed not only the relentless cruelty of the Nazi regime but also the grasping rapacity of its leaders, was convincing to the German people. They may have known something of the crimes committed by their own leaders, but they did not know the full extent of the mass extermination of helpless human lives, of the ruthless cruelty of the concentration camp. The trials completed the destruction of Nazism in Germany.[3]

The people of Germany can look back upon the Hitler era today with an objectivity totally beyond them in the first years after the war. All they wished at that time was to forget Hitler and to set about repairing the destruction that Nazism had wrought. Nor could other peoples then readily evaluate the Hitler regime. The travail of those fearful years was yet too close upon the world. It is only now, after the passions of war have cooled, that Adolf Hitler's Germany may be frankly and dispassionately judged in the light of all the facts. It is vital that any such appraisal be based upon an unimpeachable record. The proceeding at Nuremberg, conducted according to the judicial method of presentation and challenge, examination and cross-examination, proof and rebuttal, has provided just that record.

Dr. Hans Ehard, Minister-President of Bavaria, wrote:

In my opinion it is now the duty and the gratifying task of German legal science and politics to investigate the voluminous material of the trial and to make use of it. This task must, if it is to have permanent value, be performed without any preconceived ideas, in the spirit of law and of justice, which cannot be the task of a single people or of individual power groups, but must be the concern of the entire human race.[4]

What Dr. Ehard so eloquently proposes, this volume modestly attempts to achieve. It is but a sampling of the great content of factual evidence received at Nuremberg. But it purports to describe, as faithfully as the facts speak for themselves, the wrongs of the Hitler regime.

The Nuremberg trial marked the close of the Hitler era, but it did not mark the end of the struggle for freedom. The case of Tyranny versus Justice has been pending in the courts of mankind since the dawn of history. It is the oldest and most bitterly contested of all controversies. The basic issue is whether the dignity of the individual shall prevail, or whether man shall be scourged through time by the lash of autocratic power. Adolf Hitler is dead. But his passing has not brought an end to tyrants or to despotism. As with Theseus, so it is in modern times:

Naught is more hostile to a city than a despot; where
he is, there are first no laws common to all, but one man is tyrant
in whose keeping and in his alone the law resides, and
in that case equality is at an end.[5]

At Nuremberg, for the first time in history, absolute rulers were brought to account before the law. There is no longer any state, or any ruler of any state, who can claim total immunity from the law. However feebly articulated, basic principles of international law, derived from the common sense of suffering mankind, now govern the would-be despots of the world. Indeed, despotism no longer has any place in civil society. It is archaic, and of another time—another world. The age of empires has passed. And the time of emperors is gone. At Nuremberg we put Tyranny on Trial. It is our duty to keep Tyrants forever under the Law.

The story of Hitler's Germany is recorded here—a lesson for all humanity.

WHITNEY R. HARRIS

St. Louis, Missouri
February 1999

Acknowledgments

Most of the factual material in this book was drawn from three basic sources. Foremost is the official transcript of the proceedings of the International Military Tribunal. This transcript was published in Nuremberg, Germany, 1947–49, under the direction of the Tribunal, as *Trial of the Major War Criminals Before the International Military Tribunal.* The forty-two volumes in the set constitute the official text of the proceedings in the English, French, and German languages. Documents received in evidence were printed in their original languages. The official transcript was checked against stenographic notes and the electric sound recording taken of the oral proceedings. Reviewing personnel verified citations, statistics, and other data in the three languages. The final text was certified for publication by Colonel John E. Ray for the United States, Mr. Mercer for the United Kingdom, M. Serge Fuster for France, and Major A. Poltorak for the Soviet Union. The record was not published in the Russian language because the Soviets failed to pay their contribution toward publication costs. The editor was Lieutenant Colonel Lawrence D. Egbert, and the director of printing was Captain Sigmund Roth.

The second source is the eight-volume work, with two supplements, prepared by the Office of the United States Chief of Counsel for the Prosecution of Axis Criminality, under the title *Nazi Conspiracy and Aggression.* This work contains briefs prepared by members of the prosecution staff of the United States and the English translations of a very large number of documents, many of which were not read in full into evidence and therefore appear in complete form only in this set. It was published in 1946 by the

United States Government Printing Office. The editors were Captain Roger W. Barrett and Lieutenant (j.g.) William E. Jackson. The work was approved by the United States Chief of Counsel, Mr. Justice Robert H. Jackson.

The third important source is the record of the negotiations conducted by Mr. Justice Jackson as the representative of the United States at the London Conference, June 26 to August 8, 1945, leading to the adoption of the Charter of the International Military Tribunal. This record was based principally upon the stenographic notes of the conference deliberations taken by Mrs. Elsie L. Douglas for Mr. Justice Jackson and the United States delegation. The book was published in 1947 as Department of State Publication 3080 under the title *International Conference on Military Trials*.

In addition to these sources the author has had access to the daily transcript of the proceedings upon which the official transcript was based. In some cases, such as the Katyn Forest massacre, it has been necessary to go outside the official record in order to complete the account of the subject.

The author wishes to express his appreciation to Mr. Justice Jackson for his Introduction and to Mr. Storey for his Foreword. Both of them are now deceased. He wishes likewise to thank Mr. Alfred Hill, Mr. Fredo Dannenbring, and Mr. William E. Jackson for their helpful suggestions.

International Military Tribunal

LORD JUSTICE LAWRENCE, Member for the United Kingdom of Great Britain and North Ireland, *President*

MR. JUSTICE BIRKETT, Alternate Member

MR. FRANCIS BIDDLE, Member for the United States of America

JUDGE JOHN J. PARKER, Alternate Member

M. LE PROFESSEUR DONNEDIEU DE VABRES, Member for the French Republic

M. LE CONSEILLER R. FALCO, Alternate Member

MAJOR GENERAL I. T. NIKITCHENKO, Member for the Union of Soviet Socialist Republics

LIEUTENANT COLONEL A. F. VOLCHKOV, Alternate Member

Prosecution Counsel

United States of America

MR. JUSTICE ROBERT H. JACKSON, Chief of Counsel

COLONEL ROBERT G. STOREY, Executive Trial Counsel

MR. THOMAS J. DODD, Executive Trial Counsel

MR. SIDNEY S. ALDERMAN

COLONEL JOHN HARLAN AMEN

COLONEL LEONARD WHEELER, JR.

LT. COLONEL WILLIAM H. BALDWIN

LT. COMDR. WHITNEY R. HARRIS, U.S.N.R.

MAJOR WILLIAM F. WALSH

MAJOR HARTLEY MURRAY

CAPTAIN DREXEL A. SPRECHER

LT. THOMAS F. LAMBERT, JR., U.S.N.R.

LT. BERNARD D. MELTZER, U.S.N.R.

MR. WALTER W. BRUDNO

BRIGADIER GENERAL TELFORD TAYLOR

MR. RALPH G. ALBRECHT

COMDR. JAMES BRITT DONOVAN, U.S.N.R.

LT. COLONEL SMITH W. BROOKHART, JR.

MAJOR FRANK B. WALLIS

MAJOR WARREN F. FARR

CAPTAIN SAMUEL HARRIS

LT. HENRY K. ATHERTON

LT. BRADY O. BRYSON, U.S.N.R.

DR. ROBERT M. KEMPNER

United Kingdom of Great Britain and Northern Ireland

SIR HARTLEY SHAWCROSS, K.C., M.P., H.M. Attorney-General,
Chief Prosecutor

SIR DAVID MAXWELL FYFE, P.C., K.C., M.P., Deputy Chief Prosecutor

MR. G. D. ROBERTS, K.C., O.B.E., Leading Counsel

LT. COLONEL J. M. G. GRIFFITH-JONES, M.C.

COLONEL H. J. PHILLIMORE, O.B.E.

MAJOR F. ELWYN JONES, M.P.

MAJOR J. HARCOURT BARRINGTON

Union of Soviet Socialist Republics

GENERAL R. A. RUDENKO, Chief Prosecutor

COLONEL Y. V. POKROVSKY, Deputy Chief Prosecutor

L. R. SHENIN, State Counsellor of Justice, 2nd Class

M. Y. RAGINSKY, State Counsellor of Justice, 2nd Class

N. D. ZORYA, State Counsellor of Justice, 3rd Class

L. N. SMIRNOV, Chief Counsellor of Justice

COLONEL D. S. KAREV   CAPTAIN V. V. KUCHIN

LT. COLONEL J. A. OZOL

French Republic

M. FRANCOIS DE MENTHON, Chief Prosecutor

M. AUGUSTE CHAMPETIER DE RIBES, Chief Prosecutor

M. CHARLES DUBOST, Deputy Chief Prosecutor

M. EDGAR FAURE, Deputy Chief Prosecutor

M. PIERRE MOUNIER   M. CHARLES GERTHOFFER

M. DELPHIN DEBENEST   M. JACQUES B. HERZOG

M. HENRY DELPECH   M. SERGE FUSTER

M. CONSTANT QUATRE   M. HENRI MONNERAY

Defendants

Individuals

HERMANN WILHELM GOERING . Commander-in-Chief of the Air Force and successor designate to Hitler

RUDOLF HESS .... Deputy to the Fuehrer and successor designate to Hitler after Goering

JOACHIM VON RIBBENTROP..... Reich Minister for Foreign Affairs

ROBERT LEY .... Leader of the German Labor Front

WILHELM KEITEL .... Chief of the High Command of the Armed Forces

ERNST KALTENBRUNNER ...... Chief of the Security Police and the Security Service

ALFRED ROSENBERG .... Reich Minister for the Occupied Eastern Territories

HANS FRANK .... Governor General of Occupied Poland

WILHELM FRICK .... Reich Minister of the Interior

JULIUS STREICHER .... Editor-in-Chief of the anti-Semitic newspaper *Der Stuermer*

WALTER FUNK .... President of the Reichsbank

HJALMAR SCHACHT .... Reich Minister of Economics

GUSTAV KRUPP VON BOHLEN
  UND HALBACH .... Head of the Krupp Works

KARL DOENITZ .... Commander-in-Chief of U-Boats and actual successor of Hitler

ERICH RAEDER .... Commander-in-Chief of the Navy

BALDUR VON SCHIRACH........ Leader of Youth

FRITZ SAUCKEL .... Plenipotentiary for the Employment of Labor

ALFRED JODL .... Chief of the Operations Staff of the High Command of the Armed Forces

MARTIN BORMANN .... Head of the Party Chancery

FRANZ VON PAPEN.......... Vice Chancellor under Hitler

ARTHUR SEYSS-INQUART ...... Reich Commissar for Occupied Netherlands

ALBERT SPEER .... Plenipotentiary for Armaments

CONSTANTIN VON NEURATH... Reich Protector for Occupied Czechoslovakia

HANS FRITZSCHE .... Head of the Radio Division of the Propaganda Department of the Party

Organizations

THE REICH CABINET.......... Leadership in Government

LEADERSHIP CORPS OF NAZI PARTY .... Leadership in the Nazi Party

SS (SCHUTZSTAFFELN)........ Elite Corps under Himmler

SD (SICHERHEITSDIENST)...... Security Service

GESTAPO (GEHEIME STAATSPOLIZEI) .... Secret State Police

SA (STURMABTEILUNGEN) .... Para-Military Organization

GENERAL STAFF AND HIGH COMMAND OF THE ARMED FORCES .... Leadership in the Military

Defense Counsel

Individuals

Counsel	*Defendant*
DR. OTTO STAHMER	Hermann Wilhelm Goering
DR. GUENTHER VON ROHRSCHEIDT AND DR. ALFRED SEIDL..........	Rudolf Hess
DR. FRITZ SAUTER AND DR. MARTIN HORN	Joachim von Ribbentrop
DR. OTTO NELTE	Wilhelm Keitel
DR. KURT KAUFFMANN	Ernst Kaltenbrunner
DR. ALFRED THOMA	Alfred Rosenberg
DR. ALFRED SEIDL	Hans Frank
DR. OTTO PANNENBECKER.....	Wilhelm Frick
DR. HANNS MARX	Julius Streicher
DR. FRITZ SAUTER	Walter Funk
DR. RUDOLF DIX AND PROF. DR. HERBERT KRAUS..	Hjalmar Schacht
FLOTTENRICHTER OTTO KRANZBUEHLER	Karl Doenitz
DR. WALTER SIEMERS	Erich Raeder
DR. FRITZ SAUTER	Baldur von Schirach
DR. ROBERT SERVATIUS	Fritz Sauckel
PROF. DR. FRANZ EXNER AND PROF. DR. HERMANN JAHREISS	Alfred Jodl
DR. FRIEDRICH BERGOLD	Martin Bormann (in absentia)
DR. EGON KUBUSCHOK	Franz von Papen
DR. GUSTAV STEINBAUER	Arthur Seyss-Inquart
DR. HANS FLAECHSNER	Albert Speer

DR. OTTO FREIHERR VON
  LUEDINGHAUSEN . . . .   Constantin von Neurath

DR. HEINZ FRITZ AND
  DR. ALFRED SCHILF . . . .   Hans Fritzsche

DR. THEODOR KLEFISCH AND
  DR. WALTER BALLAS . . . .   Gustav Krupp von Bohlen
                                        und Halbach

Organizations

Counsel	Organization
DR. EGON KUBUSCHOK	The Reich Cabinet
DR. ROBERT SERVATIUS	Leadership Corps of the Nazi Party
LUDWIG BABEL, HORST PELCK-MANN, DR. CARL HAENSEL, AND DR. HANS GAWLIK.	The SS and SD
GEORG BOEHM AND DR. MARTIN LOEFFLER	The SA
DR. RUDOLF MERKEL	The Gestapo
PROF. DR. FRANZ EXNER AND DR. HANS LATERNSER	The General Staff and High Command

Introduction

IF MANKIND really is to master its destiny or control its way of life, it must first find means to prevent war. So long as it cannot, war demands will dictate the course of our collective and individual lives. And if we are to come to grips with the problem of preventing war, it is important that we know how wars are made, to what extent they result from impersonal pressures and tensions, and how far they are due to blunders or pugnacity of individual statesmen or political factions.

Never have the archives of a belligerent nation been so completely exposed as were those of Nazi Germany at the Nuremberg trial. In its preparation over a hundred thousand captured documents were screened, about five thousand were translated, and over four thousand were used in evidence. Some of these ran to several volumes. They were not old records dragged to light by a subsequent generation which knew not how to value them. They were laid out in a courtroom before the very highest of their surviving authors, who, with able counsel and firsthand knowledge, subjected them to correction, explanation, and attempted justification. The result is a documentation unprecedented in history as to any major war.

Lord Acton, in his inaugural lecture as professor of history at Cambridge, said, "We are still at the beginning of the documentary age, which will tend to make history independent of historians. . . ." It may be doubted whether we are more independent of historians, however, when such an avalanche of documents descends upon the world that their meaning and import can be learned only from fair and intelligent arrangement, condensation, and interpretation. This, in a hurried and partisan way, both the prosecution and the defense attempted to do as part of the trial. But its record of forty-two volumes is too vast, detailed, and disjointed for general study. Now, Professor Harris—by scholarship and experience admirably qualified —in the calm of intervening years has prepared a factual summary of the evidence that is objective, accurate, and comprehensive. It constitutes a report of the Nuremberg post-mortem examination of the Nazi regime and its part in causing World War II.

Our enlightened century twice has seen the Western peoples array themselves into hostile camps, each dedicated to the exhaustion and destruction of the other. Each side has been more successful in the infliction of injury on the enemy than in improving its own position. They have bled each other to such low vitality that the East has been left ascendant in the world balance of power. Certainly that mixture of legal principles and diplomatic practices which we call international law has demonstrated to Western statesmen by successful experiences that arbitration can be an honorable and civilized alternative, better even for the losing party than a successful war.

Why, then, did we have to have a second World War? The Nuremberg trial record answers that Hitler, along with some grievances that might have been adjusted peacefully, had as his major policy such ruthless and aggressive objectives that they could not be submitted to any civilized tribunal with the slightest hope it could approve them. He had to win by war, if at all, because he could never win by appeal to reason.

Not until the Nuremberg trial disclosed the German archives was it known how cynical and brazen was the Nazi conspiracy for aggression. Of course, in *Mein Kampf* Hitler openly declared his aim to acquire more territory, and to do it by war; but these only impressed the world as the mad daydreams of one then a prisoner. By April, 1939, however, he had seized supreme power in the German state and ordered final preparations for war to begin from September 1, 1939, onward. On May 23, 1939, Hitler secretly reiterated to his high officials his purpose to expand "our living space in the East" and to "attack Poland at the first suitable opportunity." His pact with the Soviet Union made him feel safe in going ahead. On August 22, Hitler again harangued his top civilian and military officials:

> Destruction of Poland is in the foreground. The aim is elimination of living forces, not the arrival at a certain line.... I shall give a propagandistic cause for starting the war,—never mind whether it be plausible or not. The victor shall not be asked later on whether we told the truth or not. In starting and making a war, not the right is what matters but victory.

Thus the conflagration was set. The rapidity with which the German armies swept away opposition showed that Germany was in no danger of attack, for it alone was prepared for modern war.

Moreover, the Nazi regime, in driving Germany toward war and in conducting it, had waged the most frightful of the world's persecutions against Jews, Catholics, Protestants, Freemasons, organized labor, and all suspected of pacifist tendencies. It had exterminated human beings by gas chambers, gas wagons, medical means, firing squads, overwork, and undernourishment, to the appalling number of six million. It had seized, transported to Germany, and impressed into forced labor five million more. The magnitude of this planned reversion to barbarism taxes the civilized imagination and the cruelty of its execution taxes credulity.

Few Americans seem now to appreciate that only by the narrowest margin, and largely because of his own blunders, did Hitler lose his war for supremacy of all Europe. But when the war did end successfully, the surviving planners and executioners of this policy were prisoners in our custody or that of our allies.

The interests of the United States in the problem of the Nazi war criminals were put in my hands on May 2, 1945. What we should have done with these men is a question always evaded by those who find fault with what we did do. To expect the Germans to bring these Germans to justice was out of the question. That was proved by the farcical experiment after World War I. But after World War II, organized society in Germany was in a state of collapse. There was no authoritative judicial system except remnants of the violently partisan judiciary set up by Hitler. And German law had been perverted to be a mere expression of the Nazi will.

To have turned the men over to the anti-Nazi factions in Germany would have been a doubtful benevolence. Even a year and a half later, when Schacht, Von Papen, and Fritzsche were acquitted by the Tribunal, they begged to remain within the protection of the American jail lest they be mobbed by the angry and disillusioned elements of the German population. They knew the fate of Mussolini.

Where in the world were neutrals to take up the task of investigation and judging? Does one suggest Spain? Sweden? Switzerland? True, these states as such were not engaged in the war, but powerful elements of their society and most leading individuals were reputed not to be impartial but to be either for or against the Nazi order. Only the naïve or those forgetful of conditions in 1945 would contend that we could have induced "neutral" states to assume the duty of doing justice to the Nazis.

Of course, we might have refused all responsibility for either their safety or their punishment and turned them out scot free. But in 1945 what we had to fight against was an insistent and worldwide demand for immediate, unhesitating, and undiscriminating vengeance.

Stalin, according to Churchill's account, proposed to line up and shoot fifty thousand high-ranking German leaders. Churchill says he indignantly refused. But Judge Samuel Rosenman, who was in Europe representing President Roosevelt when the latter died, reported of the British officials in his *Working with Roosevelt:* "They wanted to take the top Nazi criminals out and shoot them without warning one morning and announce to the world that they were dead." Churchill, he says, agreed, for he thought long-drawn-out trials would be a mistake.

Proposal of a long, tedious hearing-process was not popular at that time, even among high officials of the United States. Secretary Hull's memoirs recite: "If I had my way, I would take Hitler and Mussolini and Tojo and their arch-accomplices and bring them before a drumhead court-martial. And at sunrise on the following day there would occur an historic incident." Treasury sources seriously proposed to turn over as many as a half-million young Germans, regardless of personal guilt, to the Soviet Union for "labor reparations," and when I protested vigorously I was accused of being "soft" with the Nazis.

The demand for summary action infected ordinarily calm sources of public opinion. The *Chicago Tribune* gave wide currency to an interview with Professor Hans J. Morgenthau, of the University of Chicago, in which he was quoted as saying:

I am doubtful of the whole setup under which these trials will be conducted. . . . What, in my opinion, they should have done is to set up summary courts-martial. Then they should have placed these criminals on trial before them within 24 hours after they were caught, sentenced them to death, and shot them in the morning.

The *Nation,* which bears at its masthead the legend "America's Leading Liberal Weekly Since 1865," said as the trial started:

In our opinion the proper procedure for this body would have been to identify the prisoners, read off their crimes with as much supporting data as seemed useful, pass judgment upon them quickly, and carry out the judgment without any delay whatever.

Chief Justice Stone, who had his own personal reasons for disliking the trial, writing about "the power of the victor over the vanquished" said, "It would not disturb me greatly if that power were openly and frankly used to punish the German leaders for being a bad lot, but it disturbs me some to have it dressed up in the habiliments of the common law and the Constitutional safeguards to those charged with crime." (Mason, "Extra-Judicial Work for Judges: The Views of Chief Justice Stone," 67 Harv. L. Rev. 193.) It is hard to find a statement by a law-trained man more inconsistent with the requirements of elementary justice. When did it become a crime to be one of a "bad lot"? What was the specific badness for which they should be openly and frankly punished? And how did he know what individuals were included in the bad lot? Can it be less right to punish for specific acts such as murder, which has been a crime since the days of Adam, than to punish on the vague charge always made against an enemy that he is "bad"? If it would have been right to punish the vanquished out of hand for being a bad lot, what made it wrong to have first a safeguarded hearing to make sure who was bad, and how bad, and of what his badness consisted?

It must be admitted that such summary action as would have been acceptable to Stone was consistent with what was going on in Europe. The French Minister of Justice has reported that 8,348 collaborators were summarily executed without trial by members of the French Resistance and 1,325 were executed by decisions of nonlegal committees. The Nuremberg Judgment showed that something over 10 per cent of those we accused, on what was believed to be reliable information, were not proved guilty when the evidence was put to judicial test; for three of those indicted by the prosecution were wholly acquitted, and several others were not found guilty on some of the charges. There is little doubt that any policy of punishment by political decision in a time of passion and confusion will condemn persons against whom it is impossible to prove guilt by the standards we set and followed.

The only course, in my view, was for the victors to behave as civilized victors and take the responsibilities implicit in demanding and accepting capitulation of the whole German state and population. Unless history was to lay the war guilt and the guilt for organized programs of atrocities upon the whole German people, some process must identify those individuals who were in fact responsible and make an authentic record of their deeds.

President Roosevelt had steadily and insistently favored a speedy but fair trial for these men, fearful that if they were punished without public proof of their crimes and opportunity to defend themselves there would always remain a doubt of their guilt that might raise a myth of martyrdom. Secretary Stimson, and those associated with him in the War Department, had strongly supported President Roosevelt's policy of no punishment except for those proved guilty at a genuine good-faith trial. They gave unfailing support to me in trying to carry out that policy. The British and French were persuaded eventually to that view and did their utmost to co-operate in carrying the difficult task to successful execution. The Soviet reluctantly joined. Rosenman says that later Churchill acknowledged to him, "Now that the trials are over, I think the President was right and I was wrong."

The policy decision to give a hearing raised problems of the technique to be followed. There was no precedent in legal history, and no lawyer had experience in conducting such a trial. Most lawyers thought it impossible of success. The trial must be conducted by five groups of attorneys, each trained in a different system of law and practice. The defense would be in the hands of German lawyers, and their procedure was derived largely from Roman law. The prosecution would be divided among the British, American, French, and Soviet, the two former being practitioners of common-law traditions and the two latter both roughly following the Roman system but with important variations between them. Moreover, the trial required the simultaneous use of four languages —German, Russian, French, and English—and none of the lawyers was competent in all these tongues, few in more than one. Because no one insisted that his own practices be wholly adopted, but all agreed that the best features of each system be used, we worked out an amalgamation of Continental and common-law procedures which enabled the trial to proceed with fair speed and with less bickering over evidence and procedure than is common in most American criminal trials. The German lawyers, too, deserve to have it said that while they objected strongly to the idea of Germans being tried by anybody but Germans, or judged by any law except German law, they took a professional attitude toward the trial on the whole and did not endeavor to break up the hearings or cause disorder.

The prosecution early was confronted with two vital decisions of policy about which there were strong disagreements among members of the American staff. One was whether chiefly to rely upon living witnesses or upon documents for proof of our case. The decision, supported by most of the staff, was to use and rest on documentary evidence to prove every point possible. The argument against this was that documents are dull, the press would not report them, the trial would become wearisome and would not get across to the people. There was much truth in this position, I must admit. But it seemed to me that witnesses, many of them persecuted and hostile to the Nazis, would always be chargeable with bias, faulty recollection, and even perjury. The documents could not be accused of partiality, forgetfulness, or invention, and would make the sounder foundation, not only for the immediate guidance of the Tribunal, but for the ultimate verdict of history. The result was that the Tribunal declared, in its judgment, "The case, therefore, against the defendants rests in a large measure on documents of their own making, the authenticity of which has not been challenged except in one or two cases."

The other question was whether to take advantage of the readiness of some defendants to testify against others in return for concessions to themselves as to their penalty, if convicted. When a defendant is convicted on the testimony of an accomplice who "turns state's evidence" as we say in this country, it always gives the conviction a bad odor. We decided it would be better to lose our case against some defendants than to win by a deal that would discredit the judgment. We did lose our case against Schacht, against whom testimony might have been obtained by concession; but still I think we made the better choice.

During the almost year-long trial, it was not practicable for the daily press to present American readers with more than occasional, sketchy, and sometimes inaccurate accounts of the evidence and proceedings, nor was there in this country the wide and sustained reader-interest felt by the peoples of Europe, whose countries had been occupied. As a result, no sound and general foundation of public information about the trial was laid. This has made it easy for those hostile to the policy of holding a trial to stigmatize it with slogans which required no information to utter and none to understand.

Whatever else one may think of the policy of holding the Nuremberg trial or of the way in which it was carried out, no one can deny that turning to the techniques of trial to determine who of the enemy deserved punishment is a significant development in the practice of nations. It can be appraised intelligently only with a background of accurate information which it would be a tedious and long-drawn task to acquire from original sources. If there is to be any general understanding of the trial, the importance of a summary of its policy, proceedings, and evidence in a single readable and reliable volume is apparent.

We are much too near the event to pass judgment on the ultimate influence of the Nuremberg trial on the development of international law and policy. Procedurally, we know it demonstrated that there is enough fundamental harmony and likeness in our Western systems of law, including the Soviet, so that five separate professions can join in the conduct of a legal proceeding. This means that the nations, if they will to do so, can utilize legal techniques in a much wider field than had heretofore been deemed possible. Many mistakes were made—no critic knows that as well as we who were responsible for them. But in an effort so unprecedented the profession may learn as much from our failures and mistakes as from our accomplishments.

The contribution to substantive law may not yet be discernible. The United Nations has given general approval to the Nuremberg principles, though it has not been able to progress with their codification beyond the point to which they already were codified by the London Agreement and Charter. Meanwhile, these principles are taking their place in the scholarship of international law. It is perhaps significant that, despite German dislike for the war crimes trials, Western Germany has embodied in the Bonn Constitution its most basic principles. The London Agreement and the trial pursuant to it started a movement in the world of thought that is deep and enduring.

Professor Harris is one of a large staff of men and women who were inspired by the ideals of the Nuremberg effort and whose loyalty and hard work are to be credited with their success in practice. He has not felt bound to praise or approve all that he recites, and his views of the law and procedure are his own. One may take issue with his views, but none can question that he has set forth the whole subject with objectivity, learning, and insight. His manuscript teaches me that the hard months at Nuremberg were well spent in the most important, enduring, and constructive work of my life.

ROBERT H. JACKSON

Washington, D. C.
February, 1954

Tyranny on Trial

PART ONE

The Background

CHAPTER 1

Negotiations

THIS STORY begins with Exodus: "And if any mischief follow, then thou shalt give life for life, eye for eye, tooth for tooth, hand for hand, foot for foot, burning for burning, wound for wound, stripe for stripe." It is the nature of man that, shocked and revolted by acts of wanton cruelty, he shall strike back at the perpetrator. That the end of World War II did not lead to reprisals against the German people—a life taken for a life destroyed—is a tribute to the calm judgment of men trained in law who channeled the fury of the hurt and the oppressed into a judicial forum. There the record of Nazi crimes was published and preserved for history, the responsibility of those who committed those crimes was judicially established and declared, and a punishment was visited upon the guilty commensurate with civilized standards of criminal accountability.

From the inception, Hitler's wars were waged fiercely. The Nazis had perfected the concept of "total war," and Hitler's police forces committed incredible crimes against humanity in the course of military conflict. As word of these offenses spread about the world, warnings to Hitler and his clique were repeated again and again.

On October 25, 1941, President Roosevelt referred specifically to Nazi execution of hostages in France and warned that these acts of frightfulness would "only sow the seeds of hatred which will one day bring fearful retribution."[1] On the same day, Prime Minister Churchill associated his government with the President's declaration and stated that "the punishment of these crimes should now be counted among the major goals of the war."[2] These statements were followed by the St. James Declaration of January 13, 1942, in which the London governments-in-exile of nine enemy-occupied countries affirmed their determination to punish through the judicial process the Nazi war criminals found guilty of ordering or perpetrating acts of violence against civilian populations.

President Roosevelt declared on August 21, 1942:

When victory has been achieved, it is the purpose of the Government of the United States, as I know it is the purpose of each of the United Nations, to make appropriate use of the information and evidence in respect to these barbaric crimes of the invaders in Europe and in Asia. It seems only fair that they should have this warning that the time will come when they shall have to stand in courts of law in the very countries which they are now oppressing and answer for their acts.[3]

The United States and Great Britain issued simultaneous declarations on October 7, 1942, that a United Nations War Crimes Commission would be established to affix the responsibility of individuals guilty of war crimes and to collect and evaluate all the available evidence pertaining thereto. It was also stated that upon capitulation the enemy would be required to surrender war criminals within its jurisdiction. The announcement pointed out that it was not the intention of the United Nations to resort to mass reprisals but to punish "ringleaders responsible for the organized murder of thousands of innocent persons and the commission of atrocities which have violated every tenet of the Christian faith."[4] Corresponding declarations were communicated to the Dominions and India, and to China and the Soviet Union, with the view of obtaining their concurrence and co-operation. The Allied governments-in-exile in London and the French National Committee approved and adopted the convention. The Soviet Union alone declined to participate in the United Nations War Crimes Commission. Instead, on October 15 the U.S.S.R. issued a unilateral declaration urging the extradition, prosecution, and stern punishment of "Hitlerites and their accomplices guilty of organization, encouragement, or perpetration of crimes in occupied countries."[5] On November 2 the Soviet Union established its own war crimes investigative agency, the Soviet Extraordinary State Commission to Investigate War Crimes.

On December 17, 1942, the Allied powers, including the Soviet

Union, took official notice of the reports of pogroms against the Jews and condemned "in the strongest possible terms this bestial policy of cold-blooded extermination,"[6] reaffirming "their solemn resolution to insure that those responsible for these crimes shall not escape retribution and to press on with the necessary practical measures to this end."[7]

Congress, too, reflected the rising indignation of the American people at the atrocities inflicted upon the civilian populations in the countries occupied by Germany and on March 9, 1943, by resolution of the Senate, the House of Representatives concurring, resolved:

That the dictates of humanity and honorable conduct in war demand that this inexcusable slaughter and mistreatment shall cease and that it is the sense of this Congress that those guilty, directly or indirectly, of these criminal acts shall be held accountable and punished in a manner commensurate with the offenses for which they are responsible.[8]

The United Nations War Crimes Commission was officially established in London on October 20, 1943, with authorization to compile lists of war criminals and to receive evidence against them submitted by the State Commissions of the participating countries. Member nations were to co-operate by reporting all crimes committed against nationals of any of the United Nations, deciding what war crimes should be brought before the Commission, and supplying the Commission with the proofs required for prosecution. The Commission itself was not empowered to prefer charges.

The foreign secretaries of the United States, Great Britain, and the Soviet Union conferred at Moscow from the nineteenth to the thirtieth of October, 1943. At the conclusion of the conference they published a statement signed by President Roosevelt, Prime Minister Churchill, and Premier Stalin affirming the joint determination of the three powers to hold Germans individually responsible for crimes committed by them in the course of the war. The statement warned that at the time of the granting of any armistice to any German government, those German officers and men and members of the Nazi Party who were responsible for or took a consenting part in atrocities, massacres, or executions would be sent back to the countries in which their deeds had been committed in order that they might be judged and punished according to the laws of the liberated countries and of the free governments established therein. Excepted were those whose offenses had no particular geographical localization and who would be punished by joint decision of the governments of the Allies. The statement concluded: "Most assuredly the three Allied Powers will pursue them to the uttermost ends of the earth and will deliver them to their accusers in order that justice may be done."[9] The Moscow Declaration was the first official pronouncement of Allied intention jointly to punish top German war criminals.

Stalin's declaration on the eve of the twenty-sixth anniversary of the Socialist Revolution, November 6, 1943, that "Fascist criminals, guilty instigators of the present war and the suffering of peoples, must be dealt stern punishment, in whatever countries they may hide themselves,"[10] was followed by the Soviet war crimes trial at Kharkov, December 15 and 18. Three German prisoners of war and one Russian were tried before a three-man military tribunal on an indictment which charged them "with having directly participated in the atrocities, executions and tortures by which 30,000 citizens of Kharkov, including the aged, and women and children, had been exterminated by the Nazi German occupationists."[11] The trial was conducted under a Soviet decree of April 19, 1943, which effectively barred the defenses of superior orders and *ex post facto* prosecution. True to the Soviet pattern, the accused confessed their crimes. The defendant Retslaw is quoted as testifying:

Wholesale executions by hanging and shooting appeared to the German Command to be too bothersome and slow a means of fulfilling the task set the punitive organizations, and it was therefore deemed necessary to devise simpler means of exterminating the population; and it must be said that these means were found.[12]

According to Colonel Heinsch, the method used was gassing—by gas van and by gas chamber.

By the following year reports of Nazi exterminations of the Jews had risen to a horrendous crescendo. On March 24, 1944, President Roosevelt declared:

In one of the blackest crimes of all history — begun by the Nazis in the day of peace and multiplied by them a hundred times in time of war — the wholesale systematic murder of the Jews of Europe goes on unabated every hour.... It is therefore fitting that we should again proclaim our determination that none who participate in these acts of savagery shall go unpunished. The United Nations have made it clear that they will pursue the guilty and deliver them up in order that Justice be done. That warning applies not only to the leaders but also to their functionaries and subordinates in Germany and in the satellite countries. All who knowingly take part in the deportation of Jews to their death in Poland, or Norwegians and French to their death in Germany, are equally guilty with the executioner. All who share the guilt shall share the punishment.[13]

These crimes of which the Germans were accused caused a wave of resentment to spread over the American continent. On September 6, 1944, Secretary of the Treasury Henry Morgenthau delivered a memorandum to President Roosevelt in which he proposed that the Ruhr and surrounding industrial areas should be stripped of all industries, and that all mines in the area should be wrecked, so that Germany could be reduced to a purely agricultural state. Reflecting this viewpoint, President Roosevelt and Prime Minister Churchill initialed on September 16 a memorandum which called for elimination of the warmaking industries in the Ruhr and in the Saar, "looking forward to converting Germany into a country primarily agricultural and pastoral in its character."[14] While the plan was never put into effect, the fact that it received this initial approval indicates the high sense of outrage felt at that time against Germany.

In his September 6 memorandum, Secretary Morgenthau called for the preparation of a list of "German arch-criminals"—men whose obvious guilt was generally recognized by the United Nations —who, upon capture and identification, should be shot at once. There were, of course, many persons who felt, under the exigencies of the time, that the leaders of Hitler's Germany did not deserve a fair trial but only prompt execution.

Opposing Morgenthau in the Cabinet were Secretary of War Henry L. Stimson and, subsequently, Secretary of State Hull. Stimson sought to convince President Roosevelt that the enforced impoverishment of seventy million Germans was not possible, but that even if it were possible "it would be just such a crime as the Germans themselves hoped to perpetrate upon their victims—it would be a crime against civilization itself."[15] And he contended that punishment of those Germans who were responsible for crimes and depredations should follow a well-defined procedure which embodied "at least the rudimentary aspects of the Bill of Rights, namely, notification to the accused of the charge, the right to be heard, and within reasonable limits, to call witnesses in his defense."[16] He contended that the top Nazis should be tried before "an international tribunal constituted to try them,"[17] and he advocated the theory of conspiracy as the best means of establishing the complete record of Nazi criminality.

In the end Stimson, and those with him who favored judicial action, won out in America over Morgenthau and others who favored on-the-spot executions.

On September 25, 1944, Secretary Stimson, with the concurrence of the Department of State and the Navy Department, designated the Office of the Judge Advocate General, War Department, as the central agency for taking preliminary measures to assure punishment of individuals guilty of atrocities against military and civilian personnel of the United States. The duties of this agency, as defined in several directives, included the collection and evaluation of "war crimes" evidence, arrangement for apprehension, and prompt trial of those against whom a prima facie case could be made. The Judge Advocate General created a War Crimes Office under the direction of Brigadier General John M. Weir to carry out these orders. Announcement of the establishment of the War Crimes Office was made to the commanding generals in the European and Pacific theaters by a secret directive of December 25, 1944, from the Acting Adjutant General. Each theater headquarters was ordered to establish a War Crimes Branch for the investigation of evidence, including information relating to crimes against nationals of other countries, for transmission to the governments concerned. After Germany's unconditional surrender, the Judge Advocate, European Theater, tried numerous cases involving ordinary war crimes, such as the killing or mistreating of American prisoners of war, as well as cases against officials of concentration camps, such as Dachau, Mauthausen, Hadamar, and Buchenwald. The screening teams of the army assisted tremendously in collecting documentary evidence used by the prosecution at Nuremberg.

On January 22, 1945, a memorandum initialed by Stimson, as Secretary of War, Edward R. Stettinius, Jr., as Secretary of State, and Francis Biddle, as Attorney General, was delivered to the President as an aid to him at the forthcoming Yalta conference in discussing the trial and punishment of Nazi war criminals. This "Yalta memorandum" strongly urged use of the judicial method. "Condemnation of these criminals after a trial, moreover, would command maximum public support in our own times and receive the respect of history. The use of the judicial method will, in addition, make available for all mankind to study in future years an authentic record of Nazi crimes and criminality."[18] It was recommended that German leaders and repressive organizations such as the SS and the Gestapo should be charged with the commission of particular crimes, "and also with joint participation in a broad criminal enterprise which included and intended these crimes, or was reasonably calculated to bring them about."[19] The allegation of the criminal enterprise was to be drawn to permit

full proof of the entire Nazi plan from its inception and the means used in its furtherance and execution, including the prewar atrocities and those committed against their own nationals, neutrals, and stateless persons, as well as the waging of an illegal war of aggression with ruthless disregard for international law and the rules of war.[20]

The charge was to be based on the legal concept of conspiracy, "that those who participate in the formulation and execution of a criminal plan involving multiple crimes are jointly liable for each of the offenses committed and jointly responsible for the acts of each other."[21] It was proposed that the highest ranking German leaders fairly representative of the groups and organizations charged with complicity in the common plan should first be brought to trial before occupation courts, as well as lesser ranking criminals who were not sent to occupied countries for trial under the Moscow Declaration. The international trial was to be conducted by a military tribunal established by executive agreement of the heads of state of the interested United Nations. It was suggested that the court might consist of seven members, one each to be appointed by the British Commonwealth, the United States, the Soviet Union, and France, and three to be appointed by agreement among the other United Nations who became parties to the plan. Finally, it was proposed that a full-time executive group be established consisting of representatives from the United States, the British Commonwealth, the Soviet Union, and France, to prepare charges and assemble proofs for presentation to the international military tribunal. This historic document, inspired chiefly by Secretary Stimson, became the working basis for the London Agreement which established the International Military Tribunal and defined its jurisdiction. Attorney General Biddle, a sponsor of the memorandum, later was named the United States member of that Tribunal.

Former Secretary of State Byrnes has described the conference at Yalta, which ended on February 12, 1945, as marking the "high tide of Big Three Unity."[22] It was there that Premier Stalin uttered his prophetic warning that while it is relatively easy to maintain unity in time of war, "the difficult task will come after the war when diverse interests tend to divide the Allies."[23] The representatives declared that it was their inflexible purpose to destroy German militarism and Nazism and to insure that Germany would never again be able to disturb the peace of the world, and they agreed that one of the means to that end would be to "bring all war criminals to just and swift punishment."[24] But no definitive action was taken upon the American memorandum.

After the Yalta conference President Roosevelt sent Judge Samuel Rosenman to Europe as his personal representative with the mission to obtain agreement of the United Kingdom for the trial of war criminals in general conformity with the Yalta proposal. Judge Rosenman was in Europe on this mission at the time of President Roosevelt's death. President Truman requested Judge Rosenman to continue his efforts in San Francisco at the time of the United Nations Conference on International Organization. To assist him in this task a draft protocol was prepared by the State, War, and Justice Departments, with the assistance of Mr. Justice Robert H. Jackson, Associate Justice of the Supreme Court. Judge Rosenman took the draft with him to San Francisco and, after minor revisions, presented it to Foreign Ministers Eden of the United Kingdom, Molotov of the Soviet Union, and Bidault of France. Informal discussions with the Foreign Ministers in San Francisco between May 2 and May 10 resulted in general agreement upon trial of the major war criminals by an international military tribunal and the establishment of a committee of representatives from each of the four governments to prepare and prosecute the case. It was agreed that meetings of the representatives would be held to draft a formal protocol.

By an Executive Order of May 2, 1945, President Truman formally designated Mr. Justice Jackson to act as the representative of the United States in drafting the protocol, and as its chief of counsel in preparing and prosecuting charges of atrocities and war crimes against such of the leaders of the European Axis powers as the United States might agree with any of the United Nations to bring to trial before an international military tribunal. He was authorized to select personnel from offices and agencies of the government to assist him, and was directed to co-operate with any foreign government to the extent deemed necessary by him to carry out the duties delegated to him.

On May 22, 1945, Mr. Justice Jackson went to Europe for the purpose of conferring with American military authorities concerning availability of evidence against the major German war criminals, and with French, British, and Soviet officials concerning the steps to be taken to establish the tribunal and define the procedures to be followed in the prosecution. By chance, Foreign Minister Bidault was returning to Europe by the same plane, and this afforded Mr. Justice Jackson an opportunity to explain to him the basic American proposal. Foreign Minister Bidault assured Mr. Justice Jackson that the Provisional Government agreed in principle with the American plan and that a representative would be promptly appointed to assist in the coming negotiations.

In London, Mr. Justice Jackson called upon Lord Chancellor John Viscount Simon, who declared that the British government had become convinced of the merit of the American proposals. The

negotiations were conducted for the British chiefly by Sir David
Maxwell Fyfe, the Attorney General in the Churchill Coalition
Cabinet, with the assistance of Sir Thomas Barnes, the Solicitor of
the Treasury. Mr. Patrick Dean represented the Foreign Office and
Mr. George Coldstream the Lord Chancellor. On May 29 Prime
Minister Churchill announced in the House of Commons that Sir
David Maxwell Fyfe had been appointed the British representative
for drafting the protocol to establish an international tribunal for
the trial of the major war criminals. The Soviet ambassador to the
United Kingdom was not able to advise Mr. Justice Jackson of the
Soviet position at that time. Thus, while Mr. Justice Jackson had
obtained assurances of co-operation from the French and British
Governments, he was still in doubt as to Soviet participation in the
forthcoming negotiations, and in the trial itself.

Upon his return to the United States Mr. Justice Jackson submitted on June 6, 1945, a formal report to President Truman
which met with the complete approval of the President and was
widely published throughout the United States and Europe. It was
later presented to the representatives at the London Conference as
the official statement of the position of the United States. The report
was the first comprehensive analysis of the problem of bringing to
trial the major war criminals of the Axis powers:

The American case is being prepared on the assumption that an
inescapable responsibility rests upon this country to conduct an inquiry,
preferably in association with others, but alone if necessary, into the
culpability of those whom there is probable cause to accuse of atrocities
and other crimes. We have many such men in our possession. What
shall we do with them? We could, of course, set them at large without
a hearing. But it has cost unmeasured thousands of American lives to
beat and bind these men. To free them without a trial would mock the
dead and make cynics of the living. On the other hand, we could
execute or otherwise punish them without a hearing. But undiscriminating executions or punishment without definite findings of guilt, fairly
arrived at, would violate pledges repeatedly given, and would not set
easily on the American conscience or be remembered by our children
with pride. The only other course is to determine the innocence or
guilt of the accused after a hearing as dispassionate as the times and
horrors we deal with will permit, and upon a record that will leave
our reasons and motives clear.[25]

Mr. Justice Jackson observed that while fair hearings must be assured the accused, they could not be permitted to delay the proceedings by obstructive and dilatory tactics. He contended that neither the defense of sovereign immunity to heads of states, or of superior orders to subordinates, could be recognized. "It will be noticed that the combination of these two doctrines means that nobody is responsible."[26] He stated that a large number of persons in authority in the German state would be prosecuted, and that several voluntary organizations would be named with them for the purpose of establishing their criminal character and purposes. Findings in the principal trial that an organization was criminal in nature would be conclusive in subsequent proceedings against individual members who would, however, be permitted to advance personal defenses:

Our case against the major defendants is concerned with the Nazi master plan, not with individual barbarities and perversions which occurred independently of any central plan. The groundwork of our case must be factually authentic and constitute a well-documented history of what we are convinced was a grand, concerted pattern to incite and commit the aggressions and barbarities which have shocked the world. We must not forget that when the Nazi plans were boldly proclaimed they were so extravagant that the world refused to take them seriously. Unless we write the record of this movement with clarity and precision, we cannot blame the future if in days of peace it finds incredible the accusatory generalities uttered during the war. We must establish incredible events by credible evidence.[27]

On June 1 the British Ambassador in Washington informed the State Department by *aide-memoire* that His Majesty's government had accepted in principle the American proposal as a basis for discussion by the representatives of the Allied governments. On June 3 he presented the Secretary of State with an *aide-memoire* inviting the United States to send representatives to London for conferences to begin on or about June 25. Similar invitations were sent to the Soviet and French governments. The United States accepted at once, and France and the U.S.S.R. shortly after. In advance of the meeting a revised American draft agreement was submitted to the other three countries through their embassies in Washington.

On June 19, Mr. Justice Jackson arrived in London with his nucleus staff, to begin informal conversations with the British. Mr. Justice Jackson's staff at that time consisted of Sidney S. Alderman, Associate Counsel; William Dwight Whitney, Associate Counsel; Colonel Murray C. Bernays; Francis M. Shea, Assistant Attorney General; Lieutenant James Donovan, U.S.N.R., General Counsel of the Office of Strategic Services; Major General William J. Donovan, Director of the Office of Strategic Services (who arrived later); Lieutenant Gordon Dean, U.S.N.R.; and Major Lawrence Coleman. Personal aides to Mr. Justice Jackson then and throughout the negotiations and the trial were his son, Ensign William E. Jackson, U.S.N.R., and his secretary, Mrs. Elsie L. Douglas.

The first informal preliminary meeting took place on June 20. The British stated that they hoped the trial might be completed within three weeks. While this was optimistic, even the American representatives did not then foresee that it would require nearly ten months of actual trial time. It was reported that M. Donnedieu de Vabres had been appointed the French representative. At a second informal meeting on the following day the British chief negotiator, Sir David Maxwell Fyfe, suggested Munich as a possible site for the trial, and stated that he hoped the proceedings could begin by the first of September. On June 24 the British reported that the Soviets had agreed to participate in the negotiations, and that Robert Falco, Judge, Cour de Cassation, would represent the French in the place of M. Donnedieu de Vabres.

The first formal meeting of the negotiators took place on June 26, 1945. The Soviet representatives were General I. T. Nikitchenko, Vice-President of the Supreme Court of the Soviet Union, and Professor A. N. Trainin, member of the Soviet Academy of Sciences. The French representatives were Judge Robert Falco and Professor Andre Gros, French member of the United Nations War Crimes Commission. The larger American and British staffs were respectively headed by Mr. Justice Jackson and Sir David Maxwell Fyfe. This meeting was the beginning of a difficult and, for Mr. Justice Jackson, a frequently frustrating period of negotiations which, in spite of all the preparatory work, continued for many weeks.

Pursuant to a Soviet suggestion, it was early agreed that two instruments should be prepared, one to declare the basic agreement of the participating nations, and the other to define the jurisdiction and powers of the proposed international tribunal. On July 4 a subcommittee was appointed to begin the drafting of these instruments. The representatives on the drafting subcommittee were Mr. Alderman for the United States, Sir Thomas Barnes for the United Kingdom, Judge Falco for France, and Professor Trainin for the Soviet Union. The subcommittee completed and filed its draft on July 11, reserving, however, numerous points of difference for the chief representatives.

The first problems in negotiating the London Agreement and the Charter of the Tribunal arose out of basic differences in Anglo-American and Continental criminal procedure. Under the civil law, in criminal cases, defendants are subjected to a preliminary examination by a magistrate who prepares a dossier which contains the record of interrogations and documents. This dossier is presented by the prosecutor to the trial judges. At the trial, the defendants are questioned on various points by the judges, and are examined only to a minor extent by the prosecutor and defense counsel, whose principal functions are summation and argument. Defendants are not permitted to testify under oath but may make an unsworn final statement. Under the Anglo-American system, no evidence is received by the court in advance of the hearing. Evidence is introduced in the course of the trial, witnesses are examined and cross-examined, and defendants are permitted to testify under oath in their own behalf subject to cross-examination by the prosecution. These procedural differences never were wholly eliminated. In general, however, it was agreed to follow the Anglo-American rather than the Continental approach. Where differences could be accommodated by adopting features of both legal systems this was done, as by permitting defendants to testify in their own behalf in accordance with the Anglo-American practice, and allowing them to make a final statement to the court in accordance with Continental practice. Of course, technical rules of evidence applicable to

Anglo-American jury trials could not be insisted upon. There was some confusion, until the opening of the trial, as to whether documentary evidence would be submitted along with the indictment. This problem was resolved largely by the impossibility of translating the vast amount of evidence by the date set for filing the indictment.

There was disagreement as to the basic purpose of the trial. This was understandable, since there had been considerable resistance by some of the participants to the use of the judicial system in the first place. General Nikitchenko, for example, seemed to consider the trial essentially as a judicial fulfilment of the political agreements which had been reached at the Moscow and Yalta conferences. These views were disclosed to the other negotiators by General Nikitchenko when he explained four basic propositions concerning the proposed trial at the June 29 meeting:

The first is with regard to the character of the trial. We are not dealing here with the usual type of case where it is a question of robbery, or murder, or petty offenses. We are dealing here with the chief war criminals who have already been convicted and whose conviction has been already announced by both the Moscow and Crimea declarations by the heads of the governments, and those declarations both declare to carry out immediately just punishment for the offenses which have been committed.

Second, the procedure that we want to work out should be such as to insure the speediest possible execution of the decisions of the United Nations, and the regulations that we set down for this Tribunal must be worked out with that in view. In this connection the Soviet Delegation is in complete agreement with statements made by the French Delegation with regard to the formulation of rules and regulations to achieve maximum speed. The object should not be to select any individual national system of trial. All these systems have good points. In the British and American there is probably too much latitude allowing the possibility to the accused of dragging out the process of the trial and causing unnecessary delay. As we now have to deal with something completely new, it is necessary for us to select the best of the different systems with a view to achieving speed in arriving at a decision.

Third, with regard to the position of the judge—the Soviet Delegation considers that there is no necessity in trials of this sort to accept the principle that the judge is a completely disinterested party with no previous knowledge of the case. The declaration of the Crimea Conference is quite clear that the objective is to bring these criminals to a just and speedy trial. Therefore, the judge, before he takes his seat in court, already knows what has been quoted in the press of all countries, and it is well known about the criminal as accused and the general outline of the case against him. The case for the prosecution is undoubtedly known to the judge before the trial starts and there is, therefore, no necessity to create a sort of fiction that the judge is a disinterested person who has no legal knowledge of what has happened before. If such procedure is adopted that the judge is supposed to be impartial, it would only lead to unnecessary delays and offer opportunity for the accused to bring delays in the action of the trial.

Fourth, the Soviet Delegation points out that, at the time when the declaration was made by the leaders of the United Nations on the question that the chief criminals should be tried, it was not certain whether these criminals would actually be tried by a court or would be punished by some purely political action. That is to say, they might have been dealt with by means other than a trial. Since then it has been decided that they shall go through a process of trial, but the object of that trial is, of course, the punishment of the criminals, and therefore the role of the prosecutor should be merely a role of assisting the court in the actual cases. That is the role of either the investigation committee or Chiefs of Counsel as proposed in these drafts. The difference is that the prosecution would assist the judge, and there would be no question that the judge has the character of an impartial person. Only rules of fair trial must, of course, apply because years and centuries will pass and it will be to posterity to examine these trials and to decide whether the persons who drew up the rules of the court and carried out the trials did execute their task with fairness and with justice but subject to giving the accused an opportunity for defense to that extent. The whole idea is to secure quick and just punishment for the crime.[28]

General Nikitchenko requested that the charge against named organizations be deleted because the criminality of the organizations, to his mind, already had been established:

The Soviet Delegation explains this point by the fact that organizations such as the SS or the Gestapo have already been declared criminal by authorities higher than the Tribunal itself, both in the Moscow and the Crimea declarations, and the fact of their criminality has definitely been established. We cannot imagine any position arising in which the Tribunal might possibly bring out a verdict that any one of these organizations was not criminal when it has most definitely been labeled so by the governments.[29]

On the afternoon of that day Mr. Justice Jackson replied to
General Nikitchenko in the following words:

I think we are in a philosophical difference that lies at the root of
a great many technical differences and will continue to lie at the root
of differences unless we can reconcile our basic viewpoints. As the statement of our Soviet colleague said, they proceed on the assumption that
the declarations of Crimea and Moscow already convict these parties and
that the charges need not be tried before independent judges empowered
to render an independent decision on guilt. Now that underlies a great
deal of their position, and we don't make that assumption. In the first
place, the President of the United States has no power to convict anybody. He can only accuse. He cannot arrest in most cases without
judicial authority. Therefore, the accusation made carries no weight in
an American trial whatever. These declarations are an accusation and
not a conviction. That requires a judicial finding. Now we could not
be parties to setting up a mere formal judicial body to ratify a political
decision to convict. The judges will have to inquire into the evidence
and reach an independent decision. There is a great deal of realism in
Mr. Nikitchenko's statement. There could be but one decision in this
case—that we are bound to concede. But the reason is the evidence and
not the statements made by heads of state with reference to these cases.
That is the reason why, at the very beginning, the position of the United
States was that there must be trials rather than political executions. The
United States feels we could not make political executions. I took that
position publicly. I have no sympathy with these men, but, if we are
going to have a trial, then it must be an actual trial.[30]

This conceptual difference toward the trial actually never was
reconciled. At the sessions of the Conference held on July 19,
toward the close of the negotiations, General Nikitchenko restated
his views in these words: "The fact that the Nazi leaders are
criminals has already been established. The task of the Tribunal is
only to determine the measure of guilt of each particular person and
mete out the necessary punishment—the sentences."[31]

The Soviet negotiators, apprehensive of the judgment of world
public opinion upon their own aggressions against Finland and
Poland, consistently contended that any definition of crimes against
peace should be restricted to aggressive acts committed by the European Axis. As late in the negotiations as July 23, they presented a
draft definition of the crimes which were to be within the jurisdic-

tion of the proposed tribunal, in which aggressive war was defined as "aggression against or domination over other nations carried out by the European Axis in violation of the principles of international law and treaties."[32] In discussing this Soviet proposal, Mr. Justice Jackson said:

We would think that had no place in any definition because it makes an entirely partisan declaration of law. If certain acts in violation of treaties are crimes, they are crimes whether the United States does them or whether Germany does them, and we are not prepared to lay down a rule of criminal conduct against others which we would not be willing to have invoked against us. Therefore, we think the clause "carried out by the European Axis" so qualifies that statement that it deprives it of all standing and fairness as a juridical principle.[33]

Nevertheless, the Soviets continued to persist in their determination to limit the definition to the Axis. At the meeting of July 25 General Nikitchenko asked: "Is it supposed then to condemn aggression or initiation of war in general or to condemn specifically aggressions started by the Nazis in this war? If the attempt is to have a general definition, that would not be agreeable."[34] And on July 28 the Soviets were still insisting upon this limitation in definition. The dispute ultimately was resolved on the last day of the meeting by using general definitions of crimes while limiting the jurisdiction of the International Military Tribunal to the trial of major war criminals "of the European Axis."[35] The result was that the Charter stated basic principles of international law binding upon all signatories, but restricted the jurisdiction of the Tribunal to the trial of the alleged major war criminals of the Axis powers. As it turned out, only Germans were tried by the International Military Tribunal.

A dispute arose over the determination of the American negotiators to obtain a declaration that the initiating of wars of aggression is criminal, without regard to whether such wars are launched in violation of specific treaties, agreements, or assurances. In the course of the debate on this subject, Professor Gros declared:

I should think that in consequence our differences are more or less this: the Americans want to win the trial on the ground that the Nazi war was illegal, and the French people and other people of the occupied countries just want to show that the Nazis were bandits. It is not very difficult to show. There has been an organized banditry in Europe for many years. The result was crimes, and we want to show that those crimes have been executed by a common plan. The result of that will be to show that the Nazis have launched and conducted an illegal war; so it is really a difference of wording, but the results will be shown to the world as you want to show them.[36]

Contrary to the French position, Mr. Justice Jackson contended for the proposition that the initiating and waging of aggressive war is, and should be declared to be, illegal:

It is probably very difficult for those of you who have lived under the immediate attack of the Nazis to appreciate the different public psychology that those of us who were in the American Government dealt with. Our American population is at least 3,000 miles from the scene. Germany did not attack or invade the United States in violation of any treaty with us. The thing that led us to take sides in this war was that we regarded Germany's resort to war as illegal from its outset, as an illegitimate attack on the international peace and order. And throughout the efforts to extend aid to the peoples that were under attack, the justification was made by the Secretary of State, by the Secretary of War, Mr. Stimson, by myself as Attorney General, that this war was illegal from the outset and hence we were not doing an illegal thing in extending aid to peoples who were unjustly and unlawfully attacked. Now we believed, and the American people believed, just the doctrine that I have put into this definition. No one excuses Germany for launching a war of aggression because she had grievances, for we do not intend entering into a trial of whether she had grievances. If she had real grievances, an attack on the peace of the world was not her remedy. Now we come to the end and have crushed her aggression, and we do want to show that this war was an illegal plan of aggression. We want this group of nations to stand up and say, as we have said to our people, as President Roosevelt said to the people, as members of the Cabinet said to the people, that launching a war of aggression is a crime and that no political or economic situation can justify it. If that is wrong, then we have been wrong in a good many things in the policy of the United States which helped the countries under attack before we entered the war. Now it may be that we were mistaken in our attitude and philosophy and that what Germany has done is legal and right, but I am not here to confess the error nor to confess that the United States was wrong in regarding this as an illegal war from the beginning and in believing that the great crime of crimes of our century was the launching of a needless war in Europe.[37]

Over this issue Mr. Justice Jackson, at the July 26 meeting, suggested the possibility of giving up the plan to hold an international trial:

I do not consider that I would be authorized to abandon the American position, and, if I were so authorized and it were left to my discretion, I would not be willing to do it. I think there are four possible courses here: one is to set up the international Four Power trials we have been considering; another is to refer the war-criminal matter back to the Potsdam Conference for a political decision as to what they will do with these prisoners; another is for the United States, whose interests and views in the matter do not seem to be in accordance with those of the European Allies, to turn over its prisoners to the three Allies and permit their trial or disposition by such method as you three agree upon; and the fourth course would be for each of us, by separate trials, to proceed to try those we have as criminals. I am willing to recommend sending the question to Potsdam for a political decision if we cannot agree on a judicial disposition of it, and certainly a definition is necessary to any judicial disposition of it. I am willing to recommend to my Government that we turn these prisoners over, willing to recommend separate trials, and willing to recommend international trial on any basis which seems to assure a reasonably successful trial and which preserves our position.[38]

On that very day Mr. Justice Jackson left London for Potsdam where he conferred with Secretary of State Byrnes on the unsatisfactory progress and prospects of the London Conference. The result was the incorporation of Article VII in the Potsdam Agreement, a factor which must greatly have facilitated the negotiations which subsequently took place in London. Article VII provided:

The Three Governments have taken note of the discussions which have been proceeding in recent weeks in London between British, United States, Soviet and French representatives with a view to reaching agreement on the methods of trial of those major war criminals whose crimes under the Moscow Declaration of October 1943 have no particular geographical localization. The three Governments reaffirm their intention to bring those criminals to swift and sure justice. They hope that the negotiations in London will result in speedy agreement being reached for this purpose, and they regard it as a matter of great importance that the trial of those major criminals should begin at the earliest possible date. The first list of defendants will be published by 1 September.[39]

While Mr. Justice Jackson was in Potsdam the Churchill Government, in which Sir David Maxwell Fyfe had served as Attorney General and as His Majesty's representative to the London Conference, had been voted out of office. For the new Labor government Lord Chancellor Sir William Jowitt assumed the responsibilities formerly assigned to Sir David Maxwell Fyfe. He named Sir Hartley Shawcross, the new Attorney General, as Chief Prosecutor for the British government, with Sir David Maxwell Fyfe as his first deputy. Sir David Maxwell Fyfe undertook the full burden of actual prosecution of the case for Great Britain at Nuremberg, and his great skill as advocate was a major factor in the success of the trial. It was indeed fortunate that he was continued in this position and was able to devote his entire energies to the difficult task which lay ahead.

For all the delays and difficulties in its drafting, the London Agreement was neither elaborate nor complicated. It consisted of two parts: the Agreement proper, and the Charter. The Agreement called for establishing an International Military Tribunal for the trial of war criminals whose offenses had no particular geographical location and provided that the constitution, jurisdiction, and functions of the Tribunal should be those set out in the annexed Charter. Provision was made for other governments of the United Nations to adhere to the Agreement, and by the date judgment was handed down nineteen such nations had expressed their adherence.

The Charter created the International Military Tribunal "for the just and prompt trial and punishment of the major war criminals of the European Axis."[40] The Tribunal was to consist of four members, each with an alternate. One member and one alternate were to be appointed by each of the original signatories. The presence of all four members or the alternate for any absent member was necessary to constitute a quorum. The members of the Tribunal were to agree among themselves upon the selection from their number of a president. Decisions were to be by majority vote, with the vote of the president deciding in case of ties, except that convictions and sentences were to require the affirmative votes of at least three members.

The following acts were declared crimes within the jurisdiction of the Tribunal for which there was to be individual responsibility:

(a) *Crimes Against Peace:* namely, the planning, preparation, initiating, or waging of a war of aggression, or a war in violation of international treaties, agreements, or assurances, or the participation in a common plan or conspiracy for the accomplishment thereof.

(b) *War Crimes:* namely, violations of the laws or customs of war, including the murder, ill-treatment, or deportation to slave labor of civilian populations of occupied territories, the murder or ill-treatment of prisoners of war or persons on the seas, the killing of hostages, the plunder of public or private property, and the wanton destruction of cities, towns, or villages not justified by military necessity.

(c) *Crimes Against Humanity:* namely, the murder, extermination, enslavement, deportation, or other inhumane treatment of any civilian populations before or during the war, or persecutions on political, racial, or religious grounds in execution of or in connection with any crime within the jurisdiction of the Tribunal.

Leaders, organizers, instigators, and accomplices participating in the formulation or execution of a common plan or conspiracy to commit the crimes so specified were declared responsible for all acts performed by any persons in execution of such plan.

The official positions of defendants as head of state or holder of high government office were not to free them from responsibility or mitigate their punishment; nor was the fact that a defendant acted pursuant to an order of a superior to excuse him from responsibility, although it might be considered by the Tribunal in mitigation of punishment.

At the trial of any individual member of any group or organization the Tribunal was authorized to declare (in connection with any act of which the individual was convicted) that the group or organization to which he belonged was a criminal organization. And where a group or organization was so declared criminal the competent national authority of any signatory was given the right to bring individuals to trial for membership in that organization, in which trial the criminal nature of the group or organization was to be taken as proved.

Each original signatory was to appoint a chief prosecutor, and the prosecutors were directed to act as a committee to decide upon the persons to be tried, and for approving an indictment and lodging it with the Tribunal. The chief prosecutors individually were charged with investigating and assembling evidence and prosecuting the defendants.

To ensure a fair trial for the accused it was provided that they should be served with a copy of the indictment in a language understood by them, that preliminary examinations should be conducted in such language, that defendants should have the right to conduct their own defense or to have the assistance of counsel, and that they should have the right to present evidence in their own behalf and to cross-examine any witnesses called by the prosecution.

The Tribunal was given powers essential for the proper conduct of the trial and was directed to apply to the greatest possible extent expeditious and nontechnical procedures and to admit any evidence which it deemed to have probative value. Berlin was named the permanent seat of the Tribunal and Nuremberg as the place of trial. All official documents were to be produced, and all court proceedings conducted, in English, French, and Russian, and in the language of the defendant.

The judgment of the Tribunal as to the guilt or innocence of any defendant was to be final and not subject to review, and the Tribunal was authorized to impose sentences of death or such other punishment as it deemed just upon persons convicted. In cases of guilt, sentences were to be carried out in accordance with the orders of the Control Council for Germany, which was empowered to reduce or otherwise alter the sentences, but not to increase the severity thereof.

With the signing of the London Agreement the legal basis for the trial was laid. The next tasks were finding a suitable place to hold the trial, drawing the indictments, assembling the evidence, and preparing for trial.

CHAPTER 2

Accusations

The problem of where the first trial should be held had proved a major point of difference in the London discussions. The Soviets were firmly of the opinion that Berlin should be the site of the trial. But the unsatisfactory physical conditions in Berlin dissuaded Mr. Justice Jackson from that view. During the course of the London negotiations he flew to Germany for the purpose of discussing the problem with General Lucius D. Clay, the military governor of the portion of Germany under United States command. General Clay suggested Nuremberg. The tremendous Palace of Justice in that city, together with the adjoining prison, afforded fully adequate space for the actual trial. Although the city had been badly damaged by bombing and shellfire, it was not being used for other governmental purposes and could provide housing for the personnel who would be required for the proceedings.

On July 21, at the invitation of Mr. Justice Jackson, the other delegations, except the Soviets who declined at the last moment, flew to Nuremberg for a tour of inspection. All agreed that the historic city offered the best available facilities, although it was apparent that a great deal of work would be required to put the Palace of Justice and the prison into condition suitable for the actual trial. Subsequently the Soviets agreed to Nuremberg as the site for the first international trial with Berlin serving as the permanent seat for the Tribunal.

The Palace of Justice had been struck by Allied bombs, and extensive repairs had to be made to the building before it could be occupied. Moreover, there was no courtroom available in the building large enough to accommodate the personnel required to conduct the trial and also to provide galleries for visitors and for the press. One wall was torn out of the courtroom finally selected and galleries were built in the adjoining room. A bench for the four judges and their alternates was built along the west wall. The witness box and the interpreters' booth were installed along the south wall. To the east was the prisoners' dock, with a special entrance from the elevator which brought the prisoners from the prison. In front of the prisoners' dock were tables for their counsel. To the north of the room were four tables for the prosecution staffs, and before them the lectern from which counsel examined witnesses and addressed the court. Behind the prosecution tables was the press gallery and, above it, the visitors' gallery. The room was redecorated, but the massive symbols adorning the lintel on the inside of the main entrance, consisting of three bronze plaques supported by pillars of green marble, were not removed. The center plaque represented human frailty, in the offering by Eve of the apple to Adam; on one side were the Roman fasces, for Authority; and on the other side was a kneeling figure holding a sword, representing Justice.

Most of the leaders of Hitler's Germany who had been arrested as probable defendants had been taken to Mondorf, Luxembourg, for confinement. Arrangements had to be made promptly for bringing them to Nuremberg for detention. A special cell block was set aside and put into shape to receive the prisoners who were to be tried. Each prisoner-defendant was assigned his own cell. Precautions were taken to prevent suicides. Furniture was made of flimsy material, and objects were removed which might be used by defendants to inflict injuries upon themselves. Even so, Ley succeeded in strangling himself with a noose fashioned from the edges of an army towel which he had formed into a rope and had tied to the toilet pipe. After Ley's suicide the commandant of the prison, Colonel B. C. Andrus, stationed guards for round-the-clock observations at each prisoner's cell, under instructions to watch the prisoners closely for any attempts at suicide. The prisoners had their own cell block yard in which they were permitted to take exercise. Their block was connected by a covered passageway to the wing of the courthouse in which the courtroom was located and from which the elevator took them directly to the courtroom.

The most pressing practical problem facing the combined prosecution staffs was the translation of documents and the interpreting of testimony. A large number of expert translators and interpreters was assembled. But difficulties did not end with their arrival. In the ordinary trial in which a witness is called to testify in a foreign language a court interpreter translates the questions put to the witness and the answers of the witness, with consequent slowness of examination. Threat of delay for this reason was far greater at Nuremberg since every document offered into evidence, and every statement made in court, had to be put into German, French, English, and Russian. The time which traditional court interpreting would have consumed under the circumstances was appalling to Mr. Justice Jackson. Accordingly, he sent Brigadier General Gill and Ensign Jackson to the United States to consult with Charles Horsky and John Briggs of the Washington office on the feasibility of using an instantaneous translation system. They found that International Business Machines had the equipment and would install it without charge.

The other prosecuting staffs agreed to give the system a trial, but unexpected opposition developed among the professional translators, who disliked being relegated to the anonymity of an interpreters' cage, and many of whom found it impossible to interpret accurately at the speeds required. The Chief of Interpreters, Colonel Leon Dostert, believed in the system, however, and he set about to train the necessary interpreters. Even the judges and the lawyers had to have some preliminary training.

The plan called for an elaborate telephonic installation. From the microphones at the lawyers' lectern, the witness box, and the judges' bench, wires ran to the central interpreters' booth. Whatever was said on an incoming line was instantaneously translated into the other languages by wonderfully skilled interpreters. The interpretations then went out to every chair in the courtroom by other telephonic wires, to be picked up through headphones for which a switch was provided to enable the listener to select the preferred language. Flashing red and yellow lights cautioned speakers to give interpreters more time or warned of temporary breakdowns. After participants had become accustomed to it, the instantaneous translation system worked admirably. It was the first time in history that such a system had been used in a judicial proceeding—or, for that matter, in any hearing of such length and complexity. The same arrangement was later installed under the direction of Colonel Dostert in the United Nations. It has greatly facilitated the holding of international conferences and conventions.

A nucleus trial staff had been assembled in the London offices of the United States Chief of Counsel, where the work of gathering evidence and outlining the plan of prosecution began. The writer joined that staff in July. On the Continent, Colonel John Harlan Amen, assisted by Lieutenant Colonel Smith W. Brookhart, Jr., established an interrogation center, and Colonel Robert G. Storey, assisted by Lieutenant Colonel William H. Baldwin, established a document center. The United States prosecution staff was brought to Nuremberg in August and September, 1945, and offices were assigned in the Palace of Justice. The staff was divided into teams of lawyers for the purpose of assembling evidence and preparing briefs. A document center was established under the direction of Captain Roger A. Barrett where documents were received, photostated, translated, mimeographed, and filed for the use of the prosecuting attorneys. Interrogations of key witnesses were conducted by the interrogation staff. The work of preparing the affirmative case went forward swiftly.

Of first importance, of course, was the naming of the accused persons and organizations. A provisional list of defendants submitted by Sir David Maxwell Fyfe at the informal meeting of representatives on June 21 named Hans Frank, Wilhelm Frick, Hermann Goering, Rudolf Hess, Ernst Kaltenbrunner, Wilhelm Keitel, Robert Ley, Joachim von Ribbentrop, Alfred Rosenberg, and Julius Streicher. On June 23 the American staff proposed a list including, in addition to those already named by the British, Adolf Hitler, Hjalmar Schacht, Arthur Seyss-Inquart, Karl Doenitz, Walter Funk, and Albert Speer. According to Mr. Alderman, "Both the British and we were somewhat doubtful as to the wisdom of including Gross-Admiral Doenitz in the list."[1] Doenitz did remain under accusation, however, and was a defendant at Nuremberg.

At a meeting held on August 21, additional names were proposed by the Soviet and French representatives. The Soviets had captured Gross-Admiral Raeder, who, as former Chief of the German Navy, was a not-illogical defendant-counterpart to Keitel. They also held a relatively obscure individual by the name of Hans Fritzsche, a radio commentator, whose subsequent trial was to prove of some embarrassment to them. The French also held two prisoners, Franz von Papen and Constantin von Neurath, who they thought should be indicted. The result of this meeting was that Hitler was eliminated from the list and the following nine persons were added: Martin Bormann, Hans Fritzsche, Alfred Jodl, Gustav Krupp von Bohlen und Halbach, Constantin von Neurath, Franz von Papen, Erich Raeder, Fritz Sauckel, and Baldur von Schirach.

The defendants had been selected not only because of their prominence in the Hitler movement but also because they represented important aspects of the Nazi conspiracy. The two political leaders second to Hitler were Goering and Hess. Chief diplomats were Ribbentrop, Papen, and Neurath. Military leaders were Keitel, Jodl, Raeder, and Doenitz. Bormann and Rosenberg were top Party members. Kaltenbrunner and Frick were responsible for interior police control. Ley and Sauckel were in charge of labor. Speer and Krupp represented armaments and industry. Finance was the principal work of Schacht and Funk. Schirach was the leader of German youth. Occupational commissioners were Seyss-Inquart, Neurath, Frank, and Rosenberg. Official propaganda was represented by Fritzsche; anti-Jewish propaganda, by Streicher.

Organizations were selected which the prosecution sought to have named as criminal by the Tribunal in order to facilitate subsequent trials of individual members. The SA, the SS, the Gestapo, and the SD were named as the principal repressive agencies of Hitler's Germany. The Reich Cabinet was selected as the top political instrumentality of the Nazi government. Hitler's position had been maintained by two other powerful forces—the Party and the Army—and an attempt was made to define the leading elements of both groups. While this was done only with considerable difficulty, definitions were finally agreed upon under which the Leadership Corps of the Party and the General Staff and High Command of the German Armed Forces were named as criminal organizations.

All of these organizations were accused, along with the individual defendants, of perpetrating the acts charged as criminal in the several counts of the indictment.

At the first informal meeting of the negotiators in London on June 21 a working committee of British and United States members was appointed to begin work on the drafting of an indictment. A first draft, prepared by the British, was very short and, in the American view, quite inadequate. Alternatively, the American staff presented a planning memorandum, containing a large amount of descriptive and evidentiary matter, which was entirely too long to serve as an indictment. In the course of the negotiations General Nikitchenko suggested a division of the case which was largely incorporated into later drafts of the indictment. It called for presentation by the Americans of the general conspiracy theory and the crime of aggressive war, presentation by the British of crimes on the high seas and treaty violations, and for division by the French and Soviets of war crimes and crimes against humanity committed in the East and the West, respectively. Under this proposal each prosecution staff became charged with drafting that portion of the indictment for which it was to be chiefly responsible for the proofs. When finally completed by the several staffs, the indictment contained four counts.

Count One charged the defendants, during a period of years preceding May 8, 1945, with participating in a common plan or conspiracy to commit crimes against peace, war crimes, and crimes against humanity, as defined in the Charter. Particulars of the nature and development of the alleged common plan were specified and the Nazi Party was described as the central core of the plan.

Count Two charged the defendants, during a period of years preceding May 8, 1945, with participating in the planning, preparation, initiating, and waging of wars of aggression. The actions against Austria and Czechoslovakia were not specified as aggressive wars; but it was charged that wars of aggression were waged against Poland, the United Kingdom and France, Denmark and Norway, Belgium, the Netherlands and Luxembourg, Yugoslavia and Greece, the U.S.S.R., and the United States of America.

Count Three charged the defendants with the commission of

war crimes between September, 1939, and May 8, 1945, including the murder and ill-treatment of civilian populations of occupied territory and on the high seas, deportation for slave labor of the civilian populations of occupied territories, murder and ill-treatment of prisoners of war, killing of hostages, plunder of public and private property, exaction of collective penalties, wanton destruction not justified by military necessity, conscription of civilian labor, and Germanization of occupied territories.

Count Four charged the defendants with the commission of crimes against humanity in Germany, Austria, and Czechoslovakia, and on the high seas, prior to May 8, 1945, and in all countries and territories occupied by German armed forces after September 1, 1939, including murder, extermination, enslavement, deportation, and other inhumane acts committed against civilian populations before and during the war, and persecutions of political, racial, and religious groups in connection with the common plan in Count One.

Attached to the indictment, as Appendix A, was a statement of the individual responsibility of the defendants for the crimes set out in the four counts; and incorporated, as Appendix B, was a similar statement of the criminality of the groups and organizations named in the indictment.

The final draft of the indictment was signed in Berlin on October 6, 1945, by Mr. Justice Jackson for the United States, Sir Hartley Shawcross for the United Kingdom, M. de Menthon for France, and General Rudenko for the Union of Soviet Socialist Republics. In view of a Soviet definition of the U.S.S.R. which included the Baltic states as Soviet Republics, Mr. Justice Jackson took the precaution in signing the indictment on behalf of the United States of notifying the other signers in writing that his action in so doing was not to be construed as a recognition by the United States of the asserted Soviet sovereignty over the Baltic states or as indicating any attitude on the part of the United States or on his part toward any claim to recognition.

The following days were spent in reconciling the German language version of the indictment with the English, French, and Russian texts. At the last moment, over strong United States opposition, the Soviet prosecutor insisted on inserting in the indictment a charge that the Nazis were responsible for the killing of 1,000 Polish officer prisoners of war in the Katyn Forest massacre. The indictment, as thus amended, was officially deposited with the International Military Tribunal in Berlin on October 18, 1945.

The indictment was promptly served upon all individual defendants and upon counsel appointed to represent the named organizations. Each defendant was permitted to have German counsel of his choice, irrespective of whether the lawyer selected had been a member of the Nazi Party or might himself be subject to indictment for war crimes.

On November 4, 1945, Krupp's attorney filed a motion to defer the proceedings against the seventy-five-year-old Krupp, because of his illness, until he might again be fit for trial; and it was further moved that Krupp be not prosecuted *in absentia*. In spite of the strong opposition of the prosecution, the Tribunal granted both motions, and further denied a subsequent prosecution motion to substitute Krupp's son, Alfried Krupp von Bohlen, as a primary defendant. These rulings of the Tribunal eliminated the only defendant who represented the German armament industry.

A similar motion was filed on behalf of Rudolf Hess. From the time he had been brought to Nuremberg Hess claimed to be suffering from "progressive amnesia"; that is, he could remember only things which had occurred during the preceding two weeks. The Tribunal appointed a psychiatric commission to examine Hess and report its findings. The members of the commission were not able to agree in detail, but in substance they concurred that Hess was suffering from loss of memory. At the conclusion of the hearing at which the medical reports were received, Hess was invited to make a statement, and he responded:

In order to forestall the possibility of my being pronounced incapable of pleading, in spite of my willingness to take part in the proceedings and to hear the verdict alongside my comrades, I would like to make the following declaration before the Tribunal, although, originally, I intended to make it during a later stage of the trial:

Henceforth my memory will again respond to the outside world. The reasons for simulating loss of memory were of a tactical nature. Only my ability to concentrate is, in fact, somewhat reduced. But my capacity to follow the trial, to defend myself, to put questions to witnesses, or to answer questions myself is not affected thereby.

I emphasize that I bear full responsibility for everything that I did, signed or co-signed. My fundamental attitude that the Tribunal is not competent is not affected by the statement I have just made. I also simulated loss of memory in consultations with my officially appointed defense counsel. He has, therefore, represented it in good faith.[2]

Needless to say, the motion to dismiss as to Hess was denied. And yet on August 17, 1946, Dr. G. M. Gilbert, the prison psychologist, found on later examination that Hess had suffered a recurrence of amnesia such that his memory span had dropped to "about one-half day."[3]

On November 19, 1945, the attorneys for the defendants filed with the Tribunal a joint motion that the Tribunal "direct that an opinion be submitted by internationally recognized authorities on international law on the legal elements of this Trial under the Charter of the Tribunal."[4] The principal contentions were that the trial was *ex post facto* in charging aggressive war as criminal and that the proceeding was not proper because the judges represented only the victorious powers in the war. As to the first point the motion recited:

Two frightful world wars and the violent collisions by which peace among the States was violated during the period between these enormous and world embracing conflicts caused the tortured peoples to realize that a true order among the States is not possible as long as such State, by virtue of its sovereignty, has the right to wage war at any time and for any purpose. During the last decades public opinion in the world challenged with ever increasing emphasis the thesis that the decision of waging war is beyond good and evil. A distinction is being made between just and unjust wars and it is asked that the Community of States call to account the State which wages an unjust war and deny it, should it be victorious, the fruits of its outrage. More than that, it is demanded that not only should the guilty State be condemned and its liability be established, but that furthermore those men who are responsible for unleashing the unjust war be tried and sentenced by an International Tribunal. In that respect one goes now-a-days further than even the strictest jurists since the early middle ages. This thought is at the basis of the first three counts or the Indictment, which have been put forward in this Trial, to-wit, the Indictment for

Crimes against Peace. Humanity insists that this idea should in the future be more than a demand, that it should be valid international law. However, today it is not yet valid international law....[5]

On November 21 the Tribunal ruled that insofar as the motion of the German defense counsel constituted a plea to the jurisdiction of the Tribunal it conflicted with Article 3 of the Charter and could not be entertained, and that insofar as it contained other arguments, the defendants could advance them at a later stage in the proceedings. The motion was therefore denied.

The trial opened on Tuesday, November 20, 1945, with the convening of the International Military Tribunal for its first regular session. The members of the Tribunal were Lord Justice Geoffrey Lawrence for Great Britain, with Mr. Justice Norman Birkett, alternate; Mr. Francis Biddle for the United States, with Judge John J. Parker, alternate; M. le Professeur Donnedieu de Vabres for France, with M. le Conseiller R. Falco, alternate; and Major General I. T. Nikitchenko for the Soviet Union, with Lieutenant Colonel A. F. Volchkov, alternate. The President of the Tribunal, Lord Justice Lawrence, set the tone for the proceedings of that day, and all the days to follow, when he said:

The Trial which is now about to begin is unique in the history of the jurisprudence of the world and it is of supreme importance to millions of people all over the globe. For these reasons, there is laid upon everybody who takes any part in this Trial a solemn responsibility to discharge their duties without fear or favor, in accordance with the sacred principles of law and justice. The four Signatories having invoked the judicial process, it is the duty of all concerned to see that the Trial in no way departs from those principles and traditions which alone give justice its authority and the place it ought to occupy in the affairs of all civilized states.[6]

The indictment was read at length into the record, after which the defendants were called upon to enter their pleas. Ley was dead by his own hand, and the Tribunal had postponed proceedings against Krupp von Bohlen because of his physical incapacity. Bormann was absent and a not guilty plea was entered for him; Kaltenbrunner was hospitalized and later made his personal plea of

Mr. Justice Robert H. Jackson
United States Chief of Counsel

SHATTERED NUREMBERG—The river Pegnitz flows
through the wreckage of the medieval city.

ADOLF HITLER PLATZ in the center of the Old City with the
remains of the Frauen Kirche in the background.

THE PALACE OF JUSTICE—Defendants were confined in the prison to the rear.
The trial took place in the building at the extreme right.

PRISONERS' ROW—After Ley committed suicide, guards maintained
a constant vigil at the cell of each defendant.

COURTROOM SCENE as the Tribunal enters. To left of lawyers' lectern (with microphone) are Lt. (j.g.) Jackson and Mrs. Douglas; behind her is Sir David Maxwell Fyfe. At the U.S. prosecution table in the center are Mr. Dodd and Col. Amen on the left, and on the right, Mr. Justice Jackson, Air Secretary Symington (a visitor), and the author. General Rudenko stands at the table to the right.

THE INTERNATIONAL MILITARY TRIBUNAL—Lt. Col. A. F. Voлchkov, Maj. Gen. I. T. Nikitchenko, Mr. Justice Norman Birkett, Lord Justice Geoffrey Lawrence, Mr. Francis Biddle, Judge John J. Parker, M. le Professeur Donnedieн de Vabres, and M. le Conseiller R. Falco.

(Above, left) UNITED STATES JUDGES—Mr. Francis Biddle (member)
and Judge John J. Parker (alternate).
(Above, right) BRITISH JUDGES—Mr. Justice Norman Birkett (alternate)
and Lord Justice Geoffrey Lawrence (member and presiding judge).

(Below, left) FRENCH JUDGES—M. le Professeur Donnedieu de Vabres (member)
and M. le Conseiller R. Falco (alternate).
(Below, right) SOVIET JUDGES—Lt. Col. A. F. Volchkov (alternate)
and Maj. Gen. I. T. Nikitchenko (member).

ROBERT G. STOREY—United States Executive Trial Counsel.

UNITED STATES PROSECUTION STAFF—From left around table: Thomas J. Dodd, who succeeded Mr. Storey as Executive Trial Counsel at conclusion of the affirmative case, Sidney S. Alderman, Col. John H. Amen, Ralph G. Albrecht, Capt. Samuel Harris, Robert Kempner, the author, Mrs. Elsie Douglas, and Mr. Justice Jackson. At rear: Lt. Bernard Meltzer, Maj. Hartley Murray, Capt. John Auchincloss, and Brig. Gen. Robert Gill; member of Russian staff at right.

Sir Hartley Shawcross—British Chief Prosecutor.

Sir David Maxwell Fyfe—British Deputy Chief Prosecutor at the lawyers' lectern between Major J. Harcourt Barrington (seated) and a German defense counsel.

THOMAS J. DODD—United States Executive Trial Counsel.
Mr. Dodd holds the shrunken head of a concentration camp victim.

GENERAL R. A. RUDENKO—Soviet Chief Prosecutor at the lectern. At British
counsel table to the left, Sir David Maxwell Fyfe, Messrs. J. M. G. Griffith-Jones
and F. Elwyn Jones; facing them, Messrs. J. Harcourt Barrington, G. D. Roberts,
and H. J. Phillimore. At extreme right, Messrs. Dodd and Alderman, Col. Amen,
and Lt. (j.g.) William E. Jackson.

THE AUTHOR cross-examining a Gestapo witness; British prosecutors in background.

PRESSROOM—In addition to the gallery at the rear of the courtroom members
of the press were provided this room for preparing news releases.
Testimony was carried to the pressroom by loud-speaker.

FRENCH CHIEF PROSECUTORS—M. Auguste Champetier de Ribes at lectern;
M. Charles Dubost at lower left.

PROSECUTION STAFFS AT CLOSE OF TRIAL—In second row from the bottom are
Mr. Justice Jackson, Mr. Storey, Brig. Gen. Gill, Lt. (j.g.) Jackson, and
Lt. Col. Jay Nimtz; in third row, Mr. Dodd, Brig. Gen. Telford Taylor,
the author, Mr. Kempner, Maj. Murray, and Capt. Drexel A. Sprecher.
Members of Russian prosecution staff are in foreground.

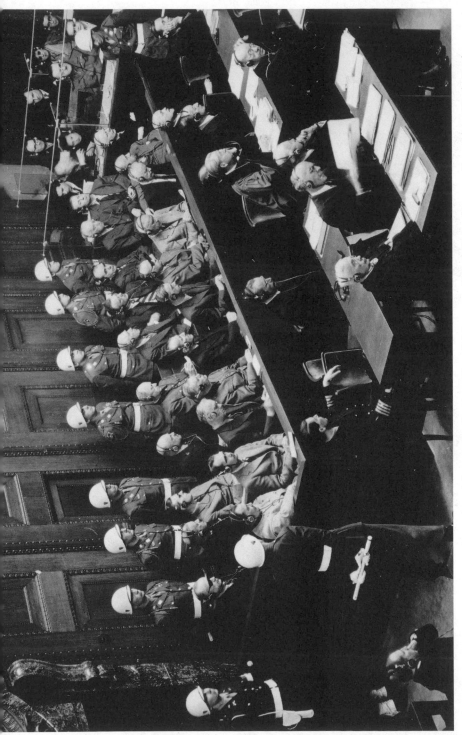

DEFENDANTS IN THE DOCK—Front row: left to right, Goering, Hess, Ribbentrop, Keitel, Kaltenbrunner, Rosenberg, Frank, Frick, Streicher, Funk, Schacht. Back row: Doenitz, Raeder, Schirach, Sauckel, Jodl, Papen, Seyss-Inquart, Speer, Neurath, Fritzsche.

not guilty. All other defendants were present in court and entered not guilty pleas, many of them "not guilty to the indictment."[7]

In his opening statement, which already has become a jurisprudential classic, Mr. Justice Jackson began:

> The privilege of opening the first trial in history for crimes against the peace of the world imposes a grave responsibility. The wrongs which we seek to condemn and punish have been so calculated, so malignant, and so devastating, that civilization cannot tolerate their being ignored because it cannot survive their being repeated. That four great nations, flushed with victory and stung with injury, stay the hands of vengeance and voluntarily submit their captive enemies to the judgment of the law is one of the most significant tributes that Power ever has paid to Reason.[8]

Mr. Justice Jackson described the gigantic conspiracy of crime which the prosecution would prove. He declared that the evidence would show the defendants uniting in a plan which could be accomplished only by war in Europe—"Their seizure of the German State, their subjugation of the German people, their terrorism and extermination of dissident elements, their planning and waging of war, their calculated and planned ruthlessness in the conduct of warfare, their deliberate and planned criminality toward conquered peoples."[9] He stated that the prosecution had "no purpose to incriminate the whole German people,"[10] but that it wanted to reach "the planners and designers, the inciters and leaders without whose evil architecture the world would not have been for so long scourged with the violence and lawlessness, and wracked with the agonies and convulsions, of this terrible war."[11] And he concluded:

> While the defendants and the prosecutors stand before you as individuals, it is not the triumph of either group alone that is committed to your judgment. Above all personalities there are anonymous and impersonal forces whose conflict makes up much of human history. It is yours to throw the strength of the law back of either the one or the other of these forces for at least another generation. What are the real forces that are contending before you?

No charity can disguise the fact that the forces which these defendants represent, the forces that would advantage and delight in their acquittal, are the darkest and most sinister forces in society — dictatorship and oppression, malevolence and passion, militarism and lawlessness. By their fruits we best know them. Their acts have bathed the world in blood and set civilization back a century. They have subjected their European neighbors to every outrage and torture, every spoliation and deprivation that insolence, cruelty, and greed could inflict. They have brought the German people to the lowest pitch of wretchedness, from which they can entertain no hope of early deliverance. They have stirred hatreds and incited domestic violence on every continent. These are the things that stand in the dock shoulder to shoulder with these prisoners.

The real complaining party at your bar is Civilization. In all our countries it is still a struggling and imperfect thing. It does not plead that the United States, or any other country, has been blameless of the conditions which made the German people easy victims to the blandishments and intimidations of the Nazi conspirators.

But it points to the dreadful sequence of aggressions and crimes I have recited, it points to the weariness of flesh, the exhaustion of resources, and the destruction of all that was beautiful or useful in so much of the world, and to greater potentialities for destruction in the days to come. It is not necessary among the ruins of this ancient and beautiful city with untold numbers of its civilian inhabitants still buried in its rubble, to argue the proposition that to start or wage an aggressive war has the moral qualities of the worst of crimes. The refuge of the defendants can be only their hope that international law will lag so far behind the moral sense of mankind that conduct which is crime in the moral sense must be regarded as innocent in law.

Civilization asks whether law is so laggard as to be utterly helpless to deal with crimes of this magnitude by criminals of this order of importance. It does not expect that you can make war impossible. It does expect that your juridical action will put the forces of international law, its precepts, its prohibitions and, most of all, its sanctions, on the side of peace, so that men and women of good will, in all countries, may have "leave to live by no man's leave, underneath the law."[12]

The negotiations and the accusations were done. The hard task of determining truth, and proving facts as only courts require that they be established, lay ahead. The world watched the unfolding of the story of Hitler's Germany.

CHAPTER 3

The Rise to Power

Hitler was not the founder of the Party through which he gained control of Germany. The German Labor Party, forerunner of National Socialism, was formed shortly after the Armistice ending World War I. Hitler became a member of this party on September 12, 1919. His prominence was soon evident in his announcement of the program of the German Labor Party at its first public meeting in Munich on February 24, 1920. The political objectives then outlined were taken over by the NSDAP (National Socialist German Labor Party) of which Hitler became "First Chairman" on July 29, 1921. Of the twenty-five points set out in the 1920 program, the first four defined principles which led to Hitler's wars of aggression and crimes against humanity. They were:

1. A demand for the unification of all Germans in a Greater Germany, on the basis of the right of self-determination of peoples.

2. A demand for equality of rights for the German people in respect to other nations and abrogation of the peace treaties of Versailles and Saint Germain.

3. A demand for land and territory for the sustenance of the German people, and the colonization of surplus German population.

4. A statement that only a member of the race can be a citizen; that a member of the race can only be one who is of German blood, without consideration of creed; and that consequently no Jew could be a member of the German race.

In the beginning neither the program nor Hitler found favor with more than a handful of followers. The Party therefore became essentially conspiratorial. A para-military organization, the SA (*Sturmabteilung*), was created to fight against political opposition.

One of the first acts of the Party, under Hitler, was an attempt to seize political power by force.

On the evening of November 8, 1923, the Bavarian Commissioner General, Von Kahr, was addressing a political gathering in the Buergerbraeukeller in Munich. Hitler, supported by his storm troopers, broke into the meeting and announced that a Nationalist Revolution setting up a dictatorship had taken place. A conference followed at which, under pressure of Hitler's armed escort, Von Kahr agreed to co-operate with Hitler in setting up a Provisional National Government with Hitler as Reich Chancellor. As soon as he was able to leave, Von Kahr informed the police, and troops were brought to Munich to suppress the putsch.

On the afternoon of the next day, November 9, Hitler, Ludendorff, and their supporters attempted to march into the center of Munich. At the Feldherrnhalle they met a patrol of police and were ordered to disband. As they continued to advance, shots were exchanged, and some men were killed on both sides. Hitler fled, and the putsch was put down. Goering was wounded and shortly after escaped abroad. However, Hitler, Frick, Roehm, and other leaders were arrested and brought to trial for high treason.

The trial of Hitler took place in the spring of 1924. In his concluding statement to the court Hitler declaimed: "May you pronounce us guilty a thousand times, the Goddess of the eternal court of history will smilingly tear up the accusation of the prosecutor and the sentence of the court; because she pronounces us free."[1] But the court ruled otherwise, and Hitler was convicted of high treason and sentenced to five years' confinement in a fortress. That same day he was transferred to the fortress Landsberg. The Party had been outlawed on November 23, 1923, but it held together as an underground movement under Rosenberg and others during the enforced absence of its leader.

While in Landsberg, Hitler worked on the book which was to become the Bible of National Socialism—*Mein Kampf.* The first part of the autobiography appeared in 1925; the second part in 1927. While it would scarcely be fair to hold later followers of Hitler to the letter of all views expressed by him in his statement of political principles, the book was a clear warning to the world of Hitler's determination to subjugate other peoples in the interest of the new racial state which he envisioned for Germany. Over six million copies of *Mein Kampf* were distributed.

Wrote Hitler:

The soil on which we now live was not a gift bestowed by Heaven on our forefathers. They had to conquer it by risking their lives. So also in the future our people will not obtain territory and therewith the means of existence as a favor from any other people, but will have to win it by the power of a triumphant sword.[2]

As to the manner of waging war, he said: "In regard to the part played by humane feeling, Moltke stated that in time of war the essential thing is to get a decision as quickly as possible and that the most ruthless methods of fighting are at the same time the most humane."[3] He praised the "peace that would be guaranteed by the triumphant sword of a people endowed with the power to master the world and administer it in the service of a higher civilization."[4]

Hitler was not satisfied with the boundaries of Germany even as they existed before World War I:

To demand that the 1914 frontiers should be restored is a glaring political absurdity that is fraught with such consequences as to make the claim itself appear criminal. The confines of the Reich as they existed in 1914 were thoroughly illogical because they were not really complete, in the sense of including all the members of the German nation. Nor were they reasonable in view of the geographical exigencies of military defense. They were not the consequences of a political plan which had been well considered and carried out, but they were temporary frontiers established in virtue of a political struggle that had not been brought to a finish; and, indeed, they were partly the chance result of circumstances.[5]

And later—"For the future of the German nation the 1914 frontiers are of no significance."[6]

He sought the union of all racial Germans:

German Austria must be restored to the great German motherland; and not, indeed, on any grounds of economic calculation whatsoever.

No, no. Even if the union were a matter of economic indifference, and even if it were to be disadvantageous from the economic standpoint, still it ought to take place. People of the same blood should be in the same Reich. The German people will have no right to engage in a colonial policy until they shall have brought all their children together in one state. When the territory of the Reich embraces all the Germans and finds itself unable to assure them a livelihood, only then can the moral right arise from the need of the people, to acquire foreign territory. The plough is then the sword; and the tears of war will produce the daily bread for the generations to come.[7]

The determination of Hitler to expand German territorial control was stated repeatedly by him in *Mein Kampf:* "We National Socialists must stick firmly to the aim that we have set for our foreign policy, namely, that the German people must be assured the territorial area which is necessary for it to exist on this earth."[8] And he added: "Germany will either become a world power or will not continue to exist at all. But, in order to become a world power, it needs that territorial magnitude which gives it the necessary importance today and assures the existence of its citizens."[9] These announced objectives led to definitive political aims:

From the past we can learn only one lesson, and this is that the aim which is to be pursued in our political conduct must be twofold, namely: (1) the acquisition of territory as the objective of our foreign policy, and (2) the establishment of a new and uniform foundation as the objective of our political activities at home, in accordance with our doctrine of nationhood.[10]

Nor did Hitler leave his readers in doubt as to where the new territory he desired would be sought:

Therefore, the only possibility which Germany had of carrying a sound territorial policy into effect was that of acquiring new territory in Europe itself. Colonies cannot serve this purpose so long as they are not suited for settlement by Europeans on a large scale. . . . The political leadership of the German Empire should then have been directed exclusively to this goal. No political step should have been taken in response to considerations other than this task and the means of accomplishing it. Germany should have been alive to the fact that such a goal could have been reached only by war, and the prospect of war should have been faced with calm and collected determination.[11]

Not Europe generally, but Russia, specifically, was his announced victim:

If new territory were to be acquired in Europe, it must have been mainly at Russia's cost, and once again the new German Empire should have set out on its march along the same road as was formerly trodden by the Teutonic knights, this time to acquire soil for the German plough by means of the German sword and thus provide the nation with its daily bread.[12]

And toward the end of *Mein Kampf*, Hitler wrote:

Therefore we National Socialists have purposely drawn a line through the line of conduct followed by pre-war Germany in foreign policy.... We put an end to the perpetual Germanic march toward the South and West of Europe and turn our eyes towards the lands of the East. We finally put a stop to the colonial and trade policy of the pre-war times, and pass over to the territorial policy of the future. But when we speak of new territory in Europe today we must think principally of Russia and the border states subject to her.[13]

Hitler appreciated the importance of France to the stability of Europe and as a block to these bold objectives:

Only when the Germans have taken all this fully into account will they cease allowing the national will-to-live to wear itself out in merely passive defense and will rally together for a last decisive contest with France. And in this contest the essential objective of the German nation will be fought for.... Of course it is here presumed that Germany sees in the suppression of France nothing more than a means which will make it possible for our people finally to expand to another quarter. Today there are 80 million Germans in Europe. And our foreign policy will be recognized as rightly conducted only when, after barely a hundred years, there will be 250 million Germans living on this continent, not packed together as the coolies in the factories of another continent, but as tillers of the soil and workers whose labor will be a mutual assurance for their existence.[14]

The world read, but did not heed, Hitler's warnings.

After his release from prison in December, 1924, Hitler vigorously renewed his political activities. In 1925 the SS *(Schutzstaffeln)* was created as an elite guard. It soon rivaled the SA in acts of violence, and under Himmler ultimately replaced the SA as the primary strong-arm instrumentality of the Party. During this period, however, the storm troopers of the SA principally waged the struggle in the streets in behalf of National Socialism, as shown by official reports of SA activities:

As an example of a seemingly impossible deed, the 11th of February, 1927 should be firmly preserved. It is the day on which the SA broke the Red Terror, with heavy sacrifice, in the hall battle at the Pharoah's Hall in Berlin, the stronghold of the Communists, and thereby established itself decisively in the capitol city of the Reich. In considering the badly wounded SA men, Dr. Goebbels coined the phrase "unknown SA Man," who silently fights and bleeds, obeying only his duty.[15]

Under the leadership of Goebbels in Berlin the Nazis formed units called *Rollkommandos* for the purpose of disrupting the meetings of political opponents. These groups not only heckled the speakers, but they also created disturbances which made it impossible to conduct meetings at all. Frequently the result was a riot. During the campaign preceding the 1930 Reichstag elections the Nazis interrupted, and frequently took over, the meetings of their political adversaries. After these elections, the acts of violence increased until almost every day several riots were reportedly instigated by the Nazis. Direct action was used not only to frustrate the opposition, but also to demonstrate the strength of the Nazi movement. The situation became so critical in Berlin, shortly before Hitler obtained political control, that it was necessary to utilize most of the police force in the attempt to control the Nazis.

Possibly, in spite of the terror-tactics of his storm troopers, Hitler would never have gained the power of government in Germany if it had not been for the depression of the early thirties. Disturbed by the distressing economic conditions of the times, and swayed by the violent struggle for power waged by the antiparliamentarian movements, the German people fled to the poles of extremism. Both Communist and National Socialist representation in the Reichstag increased from nominal to substantial minorities.

The Nazis gained the support of thousands of Germans who saw in Hitler the only answer to the Communist threat.

In 1928 the National Socialists received only 2.6 per cent of the total vote and only 12 out of 491 seats in the Reichstag. In 1930 they obtained 18.3 per cent of the total vote and 107 out of 577 seats. They received their largest vote in July, 1932, gaining 37.3 per cent of the total vote and 230 of 608 seats. Thereafter, their popular strength declined. By November, 1932, they held only 196 of 584 seats in the Reichstag. Yet two months later, on January 30, 1933, Hitler's political maneuvering led to his appointment as Chancellor of the Reich by the aged and ailing Reich President, Field Marshal von Hindenburg.

The election of July 31, 1932, made it impossible for any German government to form a majority without the co-operation of the NSDAP. From that time forward, Hitler was able to frustrate the formation of a government by refusing to participate in it, or to support it. The November election, while weakening Hitler's power in the Reichstag, did not fundamentally affect this strategic position.

Von Papen resigned as Reich Chancellor on November 17, 1932, but agreed to continue in office until a new government was formed. On November 19 Reich President von Hindenburg directed Hitler to form a majority government. Four days later Hitler replied, through Goering, that he "could not undertake the formation of a majority government."[16] It was impossible to form a coalition government with Hitler, or without him.

On December 2 Von Schleicher was appointed Chancellor upon the strength of his assertion that he would be able to force a split in the NSDAP. Von Schleicher failed in this attempt principally because of a resurgence of Nazi political power in the Lippe elections of January 15, 1933. Von Schleicher resigned on January 28. On that day, Von Hindenburg instructed Papen to seek the formation of a government under Hitler, but with limited National Socialist cabinet representation and control. The government was formed on January 30 with Hitler as Chancellor, Frick as Reich Minister of the Interior, and Goering as Minister without Portfolio.

National Socialism had triumphed politically at last.

CHAPTER 4

The Consolidation of Power

THE DAY Adolf Hitler became Chancellor of the German Reich, January 30, 1933, was called by the National Socialists the *Machtergreifung,* or the rise to power. It was the beginning of the tyranny—the springboard to absolutism. The immediate tasks were the elimination of all political enemies and the welding of Germany into a totalitarian state. The larger plans of world conquest could not be undertaken until Germany had been unified. In this purpose Hitler succeeded remarkably.

On February 20, 1938, in the course of a political statement to the Reichstag, Hitler said:

National Socialism... possesses Germany entirely and completely since the day when, five years ago, I left the house in Wilhelmsplatz as Reich Chancellor. There is no institution in this State which is not National Socialist. Above all, however, the National Socialist Party in these five years has not only made the nation National Socialist but also has given itself that perfect organizational structure which guarantees its preservation for all the future. The greatest guarantee of the National Socialist revolution lies in the complete domination of the Reich and all of its institutions and organizations, internally and externally, by the National Socialist Party.[1]

The domination of Germany by National Socialism was the result of bold planning and ruthless measures. The spirit of democratic resistance was broken and the natural idealism and aspirations of the people were corrupted and abused. The consolidation of power by the Nazis was a perfect demonstration of totalitarian technique.

Of first importance was the vesting of the absolute power of government in Hitler. This could be accomplished only by obtaining an enabling act from the Reichstag which would place legislative power in Hitler's cabinet. Such an act would require an amendment to the constitution. Under the Weimar Constitution acts of the Reichstag amending the basic law could take effect only if two-thirds of the regular number of members were present and at least two-thirds of those present voted in favor of the amendment. While the Communists remained in the Reichstag passage of such legislation would not be possible. At the first meeting of the Cabinet, the day Hitler took office, it was suggested that the Communist Party be suppressed in order to eliminate its votes in the Reichstag, so that the necessary two-thirds vote might be obtained.

Suppression of the Communist Party raised certain complications. The Weimar Constitution contained positive guarantees of basic civil rights. Chief among these were personal freedom (Article 114), inviolability of the home (Article 115), secrecy of letters and other communications (Article 117), freedom of speech and of the press (Article 118), freedom of assembly (Article 123), and freedom of association (Article 124). While these constitutional safeguards remained in effect suppression of the Communists and other political enemies would be difficult because the courts could release them almost as promptly as they were arrested. However, the constitution contained a special provision (Article 48(2)) under which the Reich President was authorized to suspend basic civil rights "if the public safety and order in the German Reich are considerably disturbed or endangered."[2] The purpose of Article 48(2) was to enable the state to protect itself against revolutionists who might seek to destroy the state while claiming the protection of constitutional rights. Hitler saw in that article the Achilles' heel of the Weimar Republic, and the legal basis for imprisoning hostile Communist and Social Democratic deputies while the enabling act was under consideration. But Hitler did not at that hour have the power of suspending the bill of rights of the Weimar Constitution. Von Hindenburg was Reich President. Furthermore, such rights could be suspended only if public safety and order were considerably disturbed or endangered. A conflagration was needed. And it was plain that the Nazis themselves would have to set the fire.

The plan finally agreed upon was the burning of the Reichstag. The world will probably never learn the complete and accurate facts concerning this first action of Nazi violence after the rise to power. So many versions have been published, including a purported confession of SA-leader Karl Ernst, who was shot in the Roehm purge the following year, that it is not possible to state authentically just what happened.[3] Nor was any effort made to establish the facts of this episode in the Nuremberg trial.

One fact of importance is that there was an underground passage to the Reichstag from the palace of the President of the Reichstag. The occupant of the palace was Hermann Goering. A second unquestioned fact is that a half-witted Dutch Communist, Marinus van der Lubbe, was involved in the act of burning the building. The circumstance which makes it reasonably certain that Van der Lubbe was used by the Nazis to accomplish this deed, with Goering's knowledge and consent, is that lists of Communist functionaries to be arrested were prepared in advance of the fire, and the round-up of these political opponents was swiftly carried out during the next day. Goering and Hitler arrived that night to see the Reichstag building—symbol of German democratic liberties—thus consumed in flames.[4]

General Franz Halder averred at Nuremberg that in 1942, at a birthday party for Hitler, Goering boasted that he had set fire to the Reichstag. In denying this accusation at the trial, Goering testified:

> The accusation that I had set fire to the Reichstag came from a certain foreign press. That could not bother me because it was not consistent with the facts. I had no reason or motive for setting fire to the Reichstag. From the artistic point of view I did not at all regret that the assembly chamber was burned; I hoped to build a better one. But I did regret very much that I was forced to find a new meeting place for the Reichstag and, not being able to find one, I had to give up my Kroll Opera House, that is, the second State Opera House, for that purpose. The opera seemed to me much more important than the Reichstag.[5]

Of course a better assembly chamber never was built by Goering, or by anyone. The fire marked the end of legislative government in

Germany. There was no longer any need for a building to house the national legislative assembly. The infrequent meetings of the Reichstag thereafter were called to provide a captive audience for Hitler's statements of policy and his pronouncements of political propaganda. Never again was there to be a Reichstag building, old or new, in which could be heard the debates, the votes, and the processes of democratic government. In Germany, democracy was dead, awaiting only burial.

The morning after the fire Hitler obtained from Von Hindenburg the decree of the Reich President suspending the bill of rights of the Weimar Constitution, on the representation that the building had been burned by Communists and a national emergency had resulted. The decree was signed by Von Hindenburg, Reich Chancellor Hitler, Reich Minister of the Interior Frick, and Reich Minister of Justice Guertner. It provided in part:

> Sections 114, 115, 117, 118, 123, 124 and 153 of the Constitution of the German Reich are suspended until further notice. Thus, restrictions on personal liberty, on the right of free expression of opinion, including freedom of the press, on the right of assembly and the right of association, and violations of the privacy of postal, telegraphic, and telephonic communications, and warrants for house-searchers, orders for confiscations as well as restrictions on property, are also permissible beyond the legal limits otherwise prescribed.[56]

This decree made possible the seizure of political opponents without danger of judicial interference. It was utilized to destroy all effective political opposition. Hundreds of persons were taken into custody. Among those arrested were Communist and Social Democratic deputies in the Reichstag. The single blow broke the strength of all organized resistance to the tyranny and assured the Nazis of the two-thirds control of the Reichstag which they required for the passage of the enabling act. In the elections of March 5, 1933, they received only 288 seats out of a total of 647. But it was a meaningless vote. The voice of the people had been stilled. Neither constitutional liberties nor power of government would be returned to them under Hitler.

On March 9 Frick announced that the Communists would be

prevented from participating in the first session of the Reichstag called for March 21. He declared: "When the Reichstag meets the 21st of March, the Communists will be prevented by urgent labor elsewhere from participating in the session. In concentration camps they will be re-educated for productive work. We will know how to render permanently harmless sub-humans who do not want to be re-educated."[7]

In the course of his statement to the Reichstag on March 23 in favor of the proposed enabling act, Hitler said:

The Government insists on the passage of this law. It expects a clear decision in any case. It offers to all the Parties in the Reichstag the possibility of a peaceful development and a possible conciliation in the future. But it is also determined to consider a disapproval of this law as a declaration of resistance. It is up to you, gentlemen, to make the decision now. It will be either peace or war.[8]

With the recent purge fresh in their minds, and the knowledge that many empty seats belonged to deputies who even then were suffering detention and humiliation in concentration camps, it is remarkable that as many as 94 deputies had the courage to vote against the enabling act. Their votes were not enough; on March 24, 1933, 441 deputies gave Hitler the power he asked to impress the rule of decree upon a broken nation.

In brief, the Law for the Protection of People and State,[9] as it was euphoniously styled, provided that the Reich Cabinet could enact Reich laws, that such laws could deviate from the constitution, and that they would be prepared by the Reich Chancellor. Thus, legislative as well as executive powers were lodged in Hitler. Parliamentary laws were replaced by executive decrees. Subject only to the authority of the President of the Reich, Hitler was the absolute ruler of Germany. And when Von Hindenburg passed away the following year Hitler assumed his powers and prerogatives, too, under a Cabinet decree of August 1, 1934.

In *Mein Kampf* Hitler had described the Nazi movement as essentially antiparliamentarian. "Its participation in the activities of a parliament has only the purpose to contribute to its destruction, to the elimination of an institution which we consider as one of the gravest symptoms of decay of mankind...."[10] From 1933 until 1937 the Reichstag enacted only four laws: the Reconstruction Law of January 30, 1934, and the three Nuremberg laws of September 15, 1935. These enactments were, of course, demanded by Hitler. All other legislation was in the form of decrees issued by the Cabinet, by Hitler, or by Cabinet ministers. The Reichstag had been reduced to a facsimile parliament.

With absolute power in his hands, Hitler set about to complete the nazification of the nation. Of first importance was the elimination of other political organizations. The Communist Party had been broken and practically destroyed after the Reichstag fire. Communist deputies were in protective custody. Some Social Democratic deputies were under similar detention. In May, 1933, the Nazis smashed the Social Democrats in their principal stronghold—the free trade unions. In July, Social Democrats were eliminated from the Reichstag, and, as in the case of the Communists, the property of the Social Democratic Party was seized. Under this pressure, other political organizations joined the Nazis or dissolved. By July 6 Hitler could say: "The political parties have finally been abolished. This is an historical occurrence, the meaning and implications of which one cannot yet be fully conscious. Now we must set aside the last vestige of democracy...."[11] The statement became the law eight days later in the form of a decree declaring the National Socialist Party the only political party in Germany and making it criminal to maintain any other political party or to form a new political party.

On December 1, 1933, the position of the Party was further strengthened by the promulgation of a Law for Securing the Unity of Party and State. Under this law the National Socialist Party was declared the bearer of the concept of the German state and "inseparably the State."[12] While the form of elections was continued, freedom of political choice was effectively frustrated. By 1938 only one list of candidates could be submitted legally to the vote of the people.

Having gained control of the Reich and broken the power of the Reichstag, Hitler next sought to reduce state and local governments to impotence. On March 31, 1933, the Provisional Law

Integrating the Laender with the Reich was promulgated. Under this law all state and local self-governing bodies were dissolved and reconstituted according to the number of votes cast for each party in the March 5 Reichstag elections. A Second Law Integrating the Laender with the Reich followed soon after. This law created the office of Reich Governor, who had power to appoint the members of Land governments and higher officials and to reconstruct Land legislatures according to the law of March 31. But it was the Law for the Reconstruction of the Reich, promulgated on January 31, 1934, which effectively reduced the Laender to administrative departments. Under that act popular assemblies of the Laender were abolished and their sovereign powers were transferred to the Reich. Governors were placed under the administrative supervision of the Reich Minister of the Interior. As to this, Minister of the Interior Frick declared:

The reconstruction law abolished the sovereign rights and the executive powers of the Laender and made the Reich the sole bearer of the rights of sovereignty. The supreme powers of the Laender did not exist any longer. The natural result of this was the subordination of the Land governments to the Reich government and the Land ministers to the corresponding Reich ministers.[13]

With the abolishment of the Reichsrat by the law of February 14, 1934, all representation by Laender in the administration of the Reich was ended. And finally, by the Reich Governor Law of January 30, 1935, the Reich Governors were declared the official representatives of the Reich subject to the direct orders of Hitler. In the words of Frick: "The German Reich became one state."[14]

Under the Weimar Constitution (Article 102) judges were declared independent "and subject only to the law." While the attack upon the courts was less direct than upon the parliament and Land governments, it took only a short time for Hitler to undermine the independence of the judiciary in all matters of political importance. Judges who openly opposed the regime were removed. The Law for the Restoration of the Professional Civil Service of April 7, 1933, under which officials of non-Aryan descent or whose previous political activity rendered them "security risks" were retired, was made expressly applicable to judges.[15]

Apart from the dismissal of judges, the attack upon the judiciary took the form of establishing parallel courts subject to direct executive control. An aftermath of the Reichstag fire was the treason trial of Van der Lubbe and two well-known Communists, Torgler and Dimitroff. The celebrated case was heard by the Supreme Court of the Reich. Much to the embarrassment of the real conspirators, the court acquitted Torgler and Dimitroff. Only Van der Lubbe, who had confessed, was convicted. Hitler's reaction to the decision was to establish a "People's Court," consisting of two judges and five Party officials, with exclusive jurisdiction over treason cases.[16] The definition of treason was then broadened to include almost every type of "political" crime.[17] No appeal was allowed from decisions of the People's Court.

Special courts known as *Sondergerichte* were established to take jurisdiction over certain types of criminal cases having political ramifications. These courts were under the Party and constituted a criminal system, separate and apart from the ordinary courts. Members of the Party, rather than professional judges, were appointed to them. Appeals to the ordinary courts were not allowed from the decisions of the special courts. Only select defense counsel were permitted to represent accused persons brought to trial in these courts. Prosecutors, appointed by the Nazis, had the choice of filing cases in the ordinary or in the special courts. The ordinary courts were usually by-passed in cases having political significance.

The Nazis could not entrust to the ordinary courts the trials of persons charged with crimes against the state; neither could they permit the ordinary courts to try members of the Party who committed crimes in aid of state-approved purges and pogroms. To handle such cases, a special system of courts was established within the Party itself with jurisdiction to hear cases involving infractions of Party orders. It was relatively simple to find that a charge of brutality brought against a member of the Party involved a breach of discipline rather than an ordinary crime. Where the acts complained of were committed pursuant to Party orders, the trials were little more than formalities. Justice was meted according to Party policy and not according to law.

In these ways the independence of the judiciary, the only sure safeguard against arbitrary action, was utterly destroyed. Minister of Justice Thierack described the judge under National Socialism as the direct assistant in the administration of government, responsible to the leadership of the nation for the preservation of the community. The concept of the independence of the judiciary was swept away, and the courts were made absolutely subordinate to Hitler, as the head of the German state.

Of particular significance were the extralegal methods used by the Hitler government to maintain its position. The world will long remember that branch of the Reich Main Security Office known as the Gestapo (*Geheime Staatspolizei*). While political police had not been unknown previously in Germany, the Gestapo was purely a Nazi invention. It was established first in Prussia on April 26, 1933, by Goering. Shortly afterward Himmler created similar units in other parts of Germany. Unification was accomplished with the appointment of Himmler as Deputy Chief of the Prussian Gestapo in 1934.

The basic law for the Gestapo was promulgated on February 10, 1936, by Goering as Prussian Prime Minister. The Gestapo was given "the duty to investigate and to combat in the entire territory of the State, all tendencies inimical to the State."[18] A decree of that date authorized the Gestapo to administer the concentration camps, and it was given authority to make police investigations in treason, espionage, and sabotage cases, and in other cases of criminal attacks on Party and State. The Gestapo was thus established as the principal political police of the Nazi state.

Closely allied with the Gestapo and associated with it in the Reich Main Security Office was the special intelligence service of the Party, the SD (*Sicherheitsdienst*). This agency, likewise under the control of Himmler, maintained offices for internal and external intelligence. It was the political information office of the Nazi government. In 1944 even military intelligence functions were transferred to the SD. Close working relations between the SD and the Gestapo provided excellent means for obtaining information concerning political or racial opponents, and effective methods for liquidating such opposition.

The great power of the Gestapo in consolidating the hold of the Nazi tyranny over the German people was *Schutzhaft*, or protective custody. Persons who were politically objectionable were apprehended by the Gestapo, taken into custody, and frequently confined in concentration camps—the special prisons of the Gestapo. Those who were thus apprehended and imprisoned were denied the right to counsel. Detention under *Schutzhaft* was not subject to review in the ordinary or in the administrative courts. The only possibility of relief was by appeal to higher authority within the Gestapo itself.

Protective custody as generally applied in modern legal systems is the furnishing of police protection to persons in danger of violence by others. The purpose is to protect the person taken into custody. The Nazis perverted the doctrine so as to permit arrest and imprisonment not for protection of the person but for the protection of the state. This concept was well stated in the 1936 issue of *Das Archiv:*

The most effective preventive measure is without doubt the withdrawal of freedom, which is accomplished in the form of protective custody, if it is to be feared that the free activity of the persons in question might endanger the security of the state in any way. While protective arrest of short duration is carried out in police and court prisons, the concentration camps under the secret state police admit those taken into protective custody who have to be withdrawn from public life for a longer time.[19]

Through this power to arrest and confine in concentration camps without recourse to law the Gestapo quickly became the strong arm of the dictatorship. Diels, Deputy Chief of the Gestapo in Prussia, described it in these words:

...From [1934] on the Gestapo was responsible for all deprivations of freedom and breaches of law and killings in the political field which took place without court verdict.... As for deprivation of freedom, there was no legal reason any more for protective custody orders after 1934, which had still been the case before that date, since from 1934 on the power of the totalitarian state was so stabilized that the arrest of a person for his own protection was only an excuse for arbitrary arrest — without court verdict and without legal measures for him. The terroristic measures, which led to the development of the pure force system and punished to an increasing degree each critical remark and each impulse of freedom with the concentration camp, took on more and more arbitrary and cruel forms. The Gestapo became the symbol of the regime of force.[20]

The SD, operating furtively through a vast network of informants, spied upon the German people in their daily lives, on the streets, in the shops, and even within the sanctity of the churches. In this atmosphere of suspense and terror the German citizen learned to pull down the blinds against the glances of the passer-by, to listen to footsteps in the hall outside his door, and to speak in whispers. His casual remark, repeated to the police, might lead to the call in the night, the terror of Gestapo inquisition, and the horror of the concentration camp. In the Nazi government, where the rule of law was replaced by a tyrannical rule of men, the Gestapo and the SD were primary instrumentalities of oppression.

Although thousands of individual citizens were thus deprived of basic rights, until the war came Hitler found it necessary to carry out mass reprisals in only three cases. The first of these was the imprisonment of Communist and Social Democratic leaders in concentration camps following the Reichstag fire. The second was the Roehm purge. This murderous action, on June 30, 1934, was in reality the climax to a struggle for power between Himmler as head of the SS and Roehm as head of the SA. The defendant Frick, who was then Reich Minister of the Interior, described the events in the following words:

Heinrich Himmler, in June of 1934, was able to convince Hitler that Roehm wanted to start a putsch. The Fuehrer ordered Himmler to suppress the putsch, which was supposed to take place at the Tegernsee, where all of the SA leaders were coming to a meeting. For northern Germany, the Fuehrer gave the order to Goering to suppress the putsch. On account of this order many, many people were arrested; and, as was heard in the course of time, little by little, something like a hundred, even more, who were accused of high treason, were killed.

All of this was done without resort to legal proceedings. They were just killed on the spot.[21]

The third mass reprisal was a pogrom against German Jewry on the night of November 9, 1938. The excuse for the action was the report that an obscure secretary in the German Embassy in Paris by the name of Von Rath had been killed by a Jew. The reaction was a State-planned and Party-executed pogrom of extreme cruelty and viciousness. The police were directed to protect non-Jewish property but to take no action against the participants in the pogrom. Synagogues were to be burned down only when there was no danger of fire to surrounding buildings. The destruction of Jewish business houses and dwellings was approved but private looting was forbidden.

During the night political leaders, with the protection of the police, broke into the homes of sleeping Jews, pulled them from their beds, and placed them under arrest. Those who resisted were beaten and in some cases were killed. Jewish shops were smashed and looted, synagogues were burned, and Jewish cemeteries were desecrated. In almost every city of Germany that night, flames shot into the sky from burning buildings—the flames of racial hatred and Nazi bigotry.

The next day, November 10, Heydrich, as chief of the Gestapo, reported by express letter to Goering on the measures which had been taken against the Jews:

The extent of the destruction of Jewish shops and houses cannot yet be verified by figures. The figures given in the reports—815 shops destroyed, 29 department stores set on fire or destroyed, 171 dwelling houses set on fire or destroyed—indicate only a fraction of the actual damage caused, as far as arson is concerned. Due to the urgency of the reporting, the reports received to date are entirely limited to general statements such as "numerous" or "most shops destroyed." Therefore the figures given will be considerably augmented.

One hundred and ninety-one synagogues were set on fire and another 76 completely destroyed. In addition, 11 parish halls, cemetery chapels, and similar buildings were set on fire and three more completely destroyed.

Twenty thousand Jews were arrested, also seven Aryans and three foreigners. The latter were arrested for their own safety.

Thirty-six deaths were reported and those seriously injured were also numbered at 36. Those killed and injured are Jews. One Jew is still missing. The Jews killed include one Polish national, and those injured include two Poles.[22]

On the following day Heydrich reported to Goering: "Altogether there are 101 synagogues destroyed by fire, 76 synagogues demolished, and 7,500 stores ruined in the Reich."[23] When Goering later commented, "I wish you had killed 200 Jews instead of destroying such values," Heydrich replied, "There were 35 killed."[24] The Jews who had been arrested during the pogrom were for the most part sent to the Dachau concentration camp, which had been enlarged to accommodate 20,000 new prisoners shortly before the pogrom began.

Three months later the Supreme Party Court of the NSDAP submitted its report on the pogrom and the punishments which it had imposed upon those found guilty of murder and other major crimes that night. The report summarized the general occurrences in the following words:

On the evening of 9 November 1938, Reich Propaganda Director Party Member Dr. Goebbels told the Party leaders assembled at a reunion in the old town hall in Munich that in the districts of Kurhessen and Magdeburg-Anhalt anti-Jewish demonstrations had taken place, during which Jewish shops were demolished and synagogues were set on fire.... It was probably understood by all the Party leaders present, from the oral instructions of the Reich Propaganda Director, that the Party should not appear outwardly as the originator of the demonstrations but in reality should organize and execute them. Instructions in this sense were telephoned immediately...to the headquarters of their districts by a large part of the Party members present."[25]

The report stated that, according to the conception of justice in the National Socialist State, the Supreme Party Court rather than the ordinary courts of justice should determine the guilt of the accused and assess the punishments. The Party Court, in fact, found that several Party members had committed serious crimes during the anti-Jewish riots. Those who committed offenses against morals and "race violations" upon Jewish women were in most cases expelled from the Party and turned over to the ordinary courts.

But murder was not considered as serious an offense as "race violation." Thus, Party member Franz "was given a warning and sentenced to three years deprivation of ability to hold public office because of disciplinary violation, namely, killing of the Jewish couple Seelig in Heilsberg contrary to orders."[26] Party member Rudolf "was given a warning and sentenced to three years deprivation of ability to hold public office because of shooting of the sixteen-year old Jew Herbert Stein contrary to orders after completion of the drive."[27] In other cases involving the killing of Jews, proceedings were suspended or minor punishments were pronounced.

In explaining the reasons for its rulings, the Supreme Party Court said:

The public, down to the last man, realizes that political drives like those of 9 November were organized and directed by the Party, whether this is admitted or not. When all the synagogues burn down in one night, it must have been organized in some way and can only have been organized by the Party.... Also in such cases as when Jews were killed without an order or contrary to orders, ignoble motives could not be determined. At heart the men were convinced that they had done a service to their Fuehrer and to the Party. Therefore, exclusion from the Party did not take place.... According to the statement by the deputy district leader of Munich, Upper Bavaria, Party member Dr. Goebbels replied that the informer should not get excited about one dead Jew, that in the next few days thousands of Jews would perforce see the point. At that time most of the killings could still have been prevented by a supplementary decree. Since this did not happen it must be deduced from this fact as well as from the remark itself that the final success was intended, or at least considered as possible and desirable.[28]

These were episodes in the rise of National Socialism—the burning of the Reichstag, the Roehm purge, and the anti-Jewish pogrom of November, 1938. They were manifestations of the power which Hitler had consolidated. They proved that Nazism meant a regime of gangster government, of viciousness and violence. The Nazis marched at night to the light of torches. They ignited fires of hatred within Germany, and soon they set the world aflame.

PART TWO

Aggressive War

CHAPTER 5

The Blood of Our Sons

F<small>ROM THE</small> beginning, Hitler intended war. He has been called a clever diplomat who won out time and again by bluffing. But his bluffing was incidental; he always wanted war. The victories gained by peaceful negotiations only whetted the more his desire for bloodshed. After each political triumph Hitler promised he would press no further demands, and his political gains were thus made principally because of the hope, and even the belief, of men of good faith that he would stand behind his word. But men of good faith should have remembered Hitler's words in *Mein Kampf:*

"The territory on which one day our German peasants will be able to bring forth and nourish their sturdy sons will justify the blood of the sons of the peasants that has to be shed today."[1]

Secret Preparations for War

On April 4, 1933, the Reich Cabinet passed a resolution establishing the Reich Defense Council with the power to prepare secret plans for the mobilization for war. Keitel was the chairman at the second meeting of the Working Committee of the Council, which met on May 22, 1933. At that meeting, Keitel stated that the Reich Defense Council would immediately undertake to prepare for war emergency. He stressed the urgency of the task of organizing a war economy, and announced that the Council stood ready to brush aside all obstacles. Such activity was in flagrant violation of the Treaty of Versailles, and Keitel warned: "No document must be lost since otherwise the enemy propaganda would make use of it. Matters communicated orally cannot be proven; they can be denied by us in Geneva."[2] Hitler caused Germany to withdraw from the International Disarmament Conference and the League of Nations on October 14, 1933.

On January 23-24, 1934, at the sixth meeting of the Working Committee of the Reich Defense Council, plans were projected for providing 240,000 plants with mobilization orders and a mobilization calendar for war. It was agreed that these industrial preparations should be kept secret, and again that nothing should be reduced to writing which might make possible the tracing of the military purpose behind the plans.

Surreptitious rearmament began almost at once after the seizure of power. In 1934 secret construction of U-boats and of warships over the 10,000-ton limit was begun. Similar measures were taken to create an air force and an army. And only two years after he became Reich Chancellor Hitler felt bold enough to announce publicly that Germany was rearming. On March 10, 1935, Goering declared that Germany was building an air force. Six days later, a decree was issued imposing compulsory military service for a peacetime army of 500,000. Recognition of the German Navy was given by Great Britain in a 1935 agreement which restricted the German Navy to one-third the tonnage of the British Navy — except for U-boats, for which Germany was allowed a larger percentage. While thus breaking the military clauses of the Versailles Treaty, Hitler sought to reassure other nations that his intentions were not aggressive and that he would respect the other clauses of the Treaty. On May 21, 1935, he declared that Germany would continue to observe the Locarno Pacts and the territorial limitations of the Treaty of Versailles.

The tenth meeting of the Working Committee of the Reich Defense Council took place on June 26, 1935. It was announced that the occasion marked a turning point in the regaining of military forces and the reintroduction of universal compulsory military service. Moreover, Major General von Reichenau declared that all principal legal measures for the preparation and conducting of war had been drawn and put into effect, although they were not then to be publicly announced. These measures consisted of a Reich Defense Law which provided for the office of Plenipotentiary General for the War Economy, to which Schacht was named, a Law Providing Total Mobilization for War which placed the person and property of every German at the service of Reich defense, and the National Service Law which made possible the drafting of all Reich citizens between the ages of fifteen and sixty-five who had not been called up for military duty. By these measures Hitler's Germany was thus preparing for total war in 1935. Promulgation of the laws was to be postponed until further notice; but, although unproclaimed, they were declared to constitute the basis for military and civil preparations. Jodl emphasized that the plans for mobilization in the demilitarized areas were to be kept in strictest secrecy, and he warned against reducing directives to writing. In the demilitarized zone, in contrast to the rest of the Reich, Jodl emphasized the principle that "concealment is more important than results."[3]

Thus, only a few days after Hitler's assurance that Germany would respect the territorial limitations of the Versailles Treaty, the Working Committee of the Reich Defense Council was already projecting the remilitarization of the Rhineland. And ten months later, on March 7, 1936, Hitler ordered his new German army into the demilitarized zone. He sought to justify this first aggressive move in a speech delivered that day to the Reichstag:

Men of the German Reichstag: France has replied to the repeated friendly offers and peaceful assurances made by Germany by infringing on the Rhine Pact through a military alliance with the Soviet Union, exclusively directed against Germany. In this manner, however, the Locarno Rhine Pact has lost its inner meaning and ceased in practice to exist. Consequently, Germany regards herself for her part as no longer bound by this dissolved treaty. The German Government are now constrained to face the new situation created by this alliance, a situation which is rendered more acute by the fact that the Franco-Soviet Treaty has been supplemented by a Treaty of Alliance between Czechoslovakia and the Soviet Union, exactly parallel in form. In accordance with the fundamental right of a nation to secure its frontiers and insure its possibilities of defense, the German Government have today restored the full and unrestricted sovereignty of Germany in the demilitarized zone of the Rhineland....

We have no territorial claims to make in Europe. We know above all that all the tensions resulting either from false territorial settlements or from the disproportion of the numbers of inhabitants to their living spaces cannot, in Europe, be solved by war.[4]

Hitler was not prepared for general war at that time. The remilitarization of the Rhineland was pure bluff. Hitler did not then have the military strength to make good his action, if faced by a British-French-Soviet ultimatum to withdraw. But the other powers were not prepared to call his hand. And later on, when they finally sought to do so, Hitler was no longer bluffing.

This was the turning point in the aggressions of Adolf Hitler. A firm stand would have denied him the first success. Sir Winston Churchill has written that to prevent the occupation of the Rhineland would have required only a police action. At Munich, two years later, Hitler could have put only thirteen divisions into action against the West. But after the defeat of Poland the combined military forces of Britain and France were outnumbered three to two. As Sir Winston Churchill wrote: "All this terrible superiority had grown up because at no moment had the once victorious Allies dared to take any effective step, even when they were all-powerful, to resist repeated aggressions by Hitler and breaches of the Treaties."[5]

Hitler could have been stopped in this incipient act of aggression, and the later war might thereby have been averted. But the will to stop him was not then present. Emboldened by this first challenge, Hitler gathered strength for the greater demands of which he had forewarned in *Mein Kampf*.

From time to time, under the chairmanship of Goering, the Council of Ministers met to discuss plans for financing the war economy. At the meeting of May 12, 1936, Goering said: "If we have war tomorrow we must help ourselves by substitutes. Then money will not play any role at all."[6] At the meeting of May 27, 1936, he said: "All measures are to be considered from the standpoint of an assured waging of war.... A common front of China with Japan against Soviet Russia can probably be produced."[7] Goering was named Commissioner for the Four Year Plan on October 18, 1936, with the mission, as he said, "within four years to put the entire economy in a state of readiness for war."[8] The appointment led to a certain rivalry with Schacht, who had similar responsibilities as the Plenipotentiary General for War Economy. During war the functions of the Commissioner for the Four Year Plan were to be suspended, and the Plenipotentiary General for the War Economy was to have the centralized direction of the war economy, excluding the armament industry. But in peacetime their functions were somewhat overlapping, and it was provided that any conflict which might arise would be resolved by Hitler after consultation with the Reich Minister for War.

The outbreak of civil war in Spain provided Hitler the opportunity to test his new military machine under actual war conditions. He was motivated only partially by ideological considerations in making the decision to intervene on behalf of Franco shortly after the civil war began. Goering stated quite frankly these purposes of German participation in the Spanish conflict:

When the Civil War broke out in Spain, Franco sent a call for help to Germany and asked for support, particularly in the air. One should not forget that Franco with his troops was stationed in Africa and that he could not get the troops across, as the fleet was in the hands of the Communists, or, as they called themselves at the time, the competent Revolutionary Government....

The Fuehrer thought the matter over. I urged him to give support under all circumstances, firstly, in order to prevent the further spread of communism in that theatre and, secondly, to test my young Luftwaffe at this opportunity in this or that technical respect.

With the permission of the Fuehrer, I sent a large part of my transport fleet and a number of experimental fighter units, bombers, and anti-aircraft guns; and in that way I had an opportunity to ascertain, under combat conditions, whether the material was equal to the task. In order that the personnel, too, might gather a certain amount of experience, I saw to it that there was continuous flow, that is, that new people were constantly being sent and others recalled.[9]

In June, 1937, Marshal von Blomberg, War Minister and Commander in Chief of the Armed Forces, issued a directive in which he said that Germany need not consider danger of an attack from any side. Yet, only a few months later, on November 5, 1937, Hitler declared to his top political and military leaders, in a secret meeting held at the Reich Chancellery, his intention to wage war. Goering, Raeder, and Von Neurath were among those present. The minutes of the meeting were faithfully recorded by Hitler's adjutant, Colonel Hoszbach, and they prove that at that early date the question of "war" had been reduced simply to "when" and "where." Hoszbach's minutes provided in part:

The Fuehrer stated initially that the subject matter of today's conference was of such high importance that its detailed discussion would certainly in other states take place before the Cabinet in full session. However, he, the Fuehrer, had decided not to discuss this matter in the larger circle of the Reich Cabinet, because of its importance. His subsequent statements were the result of detailed deliberations and of the experiences of his four and one-half years in government; he desired to explain to those present his fundamental ideas on the possibilities and necessities of expanding our foreign policy, and in the interests of a far-sighted policy he requested that his statements be looked upon, in the case of his death, as his last will and testament.

The Fuehrer then stated: The aim of German policy is the security and the preservation of the nation and its propagation. This is consequently a problem of space. The German nation comprises 85 million people, which, because of the number of individuals and the compactness of habitation, form a homogeneous European racial body, the like of which cannot be found in any other country. On the other hand, it justifies the demand for larger living space more than for any other nation. . . .

The question for Germany is where the greatest possible conquest could be made at the lowest cost.

German politics must reckon with its two hateful enemies, England and France, to whom a strong German colossus in the center of Europe would be intolerable. Both these states would oppose a further reinforcement of Germany, both in Europe and overseas, and in this opposition they would have the support of all parties. . . .

The German question can be solved only by way of force, and this is never without risk. The battles of Frederick the Great for Silesia, and Bismarck's wars against Austria and France had been a tremendous risk and the speed of Prussian action in 1870 had prevented Austria from participating in the war. If we place the decision to apply force with risk at the head of the following expositions, then we are left to reply to the questions "when" and "how." . . .

If the Fuehrer is still living, then it will be his irrevocable decision to solve the German space problem not later than 1943-45.[10]

Final Plans

On July 8, 1938, Goering called together a number of the leading German aircraft manufacturers, explained to them the political situation which then prevailed, and laid the groundwork for a vast increase in aircraft production. After stating that war with Czechoslovakia was imminent, and boasting that the German air force was already superior in quality and quantity to the British air force, he said that if Germany should win the coming world conflict she

will be the greatest power in the world; then it is Germany who dominates the world market, then will be the hour when Germany is a rich nation. For this goal, however, we have to undertake risks....And even if you know what you are doing now may mean that within three years your firm will collapse, you will have to do it all the same. For if Germany collapses, who will dare to tell me to my face that his shop will go on?...It does not matter if someone says: I disapprove entirely of the National Socialistic system. I don't care, let him disapprove, it is still the system which at this moment decides Germany's fate. That is why he has willy-nilly to co-operate. Therefore I repeat once more: Only that nation which stakes everything on its armaments and draws all consequences from this fact, will be able to continue its existence....Beyond this, gentlemen, I want you to be perfectly clear, today already, how you will run your business when war comes.[11]

Goering exhorted the manufacturers to produce aircraft in great quantities in anticipation of the coming war. He said that there was a small 10 to 15 per cent possibility that the war would be a relatively small-scale action, but that he was convinced that an 80, 85, or 90 per cent chance existed for a great war. He called upon the manufacturers to produce a stratosphere bomber and rocket motors. Finally he complained, "I completely lack the bombers capable of round trip flights to New York with a five-ton bomb load. I would be extremely happy to possess such a bomber which would at last stuff the mouth of arrogance across the sea."[12]

Two weeks after Mr. Chamberlain returned to England from Munich, in September, 1938, holding in his hand the signed document which was to bring "peace for our time," Goering called a further conference to accelerate German plans for war:

Everybody knows from the press what the world situation looks like and therefore the Fuehrer has issued an order to him [Goering] to carry out a gigantic program compared to which previous achievements are insignificant. There are difficulties in the way which he will overcome with the utmost energy and ruthlessness.

The amount of foreign exchange has completely dwindled on account of the preparation for the Czech enterprise and this makes it necessary that it should be strongly increased immediately. Furthermore, the foreign credits have been greatly overdrawn, and thus the strongest export activity — stronger than up to now — is in the foreground.... These gains made through the export are to be used for increased armament. The armament should not be curtailed by the export activity. He received the order from the Fuehrer to increase the armament to an abnormal extent, the air force having first priority. Within the shortest time the air force is to be increased five-fold, also the navy should get armed more rapidly and the army should procure large amounts of offensive weapons at a faster rate, particularly heavy artillery pieces and heavy tanks. Along with this, manufactured armaments must go, especially fuel, powder and explosives are moved into the foreground. It should be coupled with the accelerated construction of highways, canals, and particularly of the railroads....

The recommitment of youth into industry will be organized by him on a very large scale. Large state apprenticeships are to be created; besides, the plants will be obliged to hire a certain number of apprentices. A retraining of hundreds of thousands of people will have to take place. Much more work will have to be performed by women than until now. Above all, the young women have to be employed much more. Work periods of eight hours do not exist any more; wherever necessary, overtime is to be performed; double and triple shifts are a matter of course. Where the workers will protest, as in Austria for example, General Field Marshal Goering will proceed with forced labor; he will create camps for forced labor. The Labor Front should not carry false social ideas among the workers. It is a fact that one generation has driven the cart into the mud through the mutiny of the workers, and by being guilty of not having shot those workers on the spot. Therefore, we had to put the thing in order again....

The Sudetenland has to be exploited with all means. General Field Marshal Goering counts upon a complete industrial assimilation of Slovakia. Czechia and Slovakia would become German dominions. Everything possible must be taken out....

The Jewish problem had to be tackled now with all methods, because they have to get out of the economy.... However, he could not release foreign exchange for shipping away the Jews. In an emergency situation ghettos should be erected in the individual large cities.[13]

The certainty that Germany was heading for world conflict was reflected in the observations of Admiral Carls made in September, 1938, in a "Draft Study of Naval Warfare against England":

There is full agreement with the main theme of the study.

1. If according to the Fuehrer's decision Germany is to acquire a position as a world power, she needs not only sufficient colonial possessions but also secure naval communications and secure access to the ocean.

2. Both requirements can be fulfilled only in opposition to Anglo-French interests and will limit their positions as world powers. It is unlikely that they can be achieved by peaceful means. The decision to make Germany a world power therefore forces upon us the necessity of making the corresponding preparations for war.

3. War against England means at the same time war against the Empire, against France, probably against Russia as well, and a large number of countries overseas; in fact, against one-half to one-third of the whole world.[14]

By June, 1939, plans had been perfected for the armed conflict for which preparations had been so feverishly made, and Germany was ready to attack. The Reich Defense Council met, with Goering, Keitel, Raeder, Frick, and Funk in attendance, among others, to perfect mobilization details. It was assumed that five million servicemen would be called up, and the allotment of the remaining labor force was under consideration. It was said to be important not only that every German possess his mobilization orders but also that he be thoroughly prepared for his wartime activity. Women were to be compelled to work in wartime. The General Plenipotentiary for Economy was assigned the task of settling what work would be given to prisoners of war and to concentration camp inmates. Orders to workers to report for war tasks were said to be "ready and tied up in bundles at the labor offices," and 727,000 applications for indispensability of key workers had already been approved. "Hundreds of thousands of workers" were to be brought to Germany from the Protectorate to be "housed together in hutments" while their labor was exploited for the German economy.[15]

Armed Aggression

Hitler led Germany into war on September 1, 1939. On November 23, 1939, flushed with his swift victory over Poland, he confided his planning of aggression to his military leaders:

The purpose of this conference is to give you an idea of the world of my thoughts, which takes charge of me, in the face of future events, and to tell you my decisions. The building up of our Armed Forces was only possible in connection with the ideological "education of the German people by the Party."

When I started my political task in 1919, my strong belief in final success was based on a thorough observation of the events of the day and the study of the reasons for their occurrence. Therefore, I never lost my belief in the midst of setbacks which were not spared me during my period of struggle. Providence has had the last word and brought me success. Moreover, I had a clear recognition of the probable course of historical events, and the firm will to make brutal decisions. The first decision was in 1919 when, after long internal conflict, I became a politician and took up the struggle against my enemies. That was the hardest of all decisions. I had, however, the firm belief that I would arrive at my goal. First of all, I desired a new system of selection. I wanted to educate a minority which would take over the leadership. After 15 years I arrived at my goal, after strenuous struggles and many setbacks. When I came to power in 1933, a period of the most difficult struggle lay behind me. Everything existing before that had collapsed. I had to reorganize everything, beginning with the mass of the people and extending it to the Armed Forces. First, reorganization of the interior, abolishment of appearances of decay and defeatist ideas, education to heroism. While reorganizing the interior, I undertook the second task: to release Germany from its international ties. Two particular characteristics are to be pointed out: secession from the League of Nations and denunciation of the Disarmament Conference. It was a hard decision. The number of prophets who predicted that it would lead to the occupation of the Rhineland was large, the number of believers was very small. I was supported by the nation, which stood firmly behind me when I carried out my intentions. After that the order for rearmament. Here again there were numerous prophets who predicted misfortunes, and only a few believers. In 1935 the introduction of compulsory armed service. After that, militarization of the Rhineland, again a process believed to be impossible at that time. The number of people who put trust in me was very small. Then, beginning of the fortification of the whole country, especially in the West.

One year later, Austria came. This step also was considered doubtful. It brought about a considerable reinforcement of the Reich. The next step was Bohemia, Moravia and Poland. This step also was not possible to accomplish in one campaign. First of all, the western fortifications had to be finished. It was not possible to reach the goal in one effort. It was clear to me from the first moment that I could not be satisfied with the Sudeten-German territory. That was only a partial solution. The decision to march into Bohemia was made. Then followed the erection of the Protectorate, and with that the basis for the action against Poland was laid, but I wasn't quite clear at that time whether I should start first against the East and then in the West, or vice-versa.[16]

This was a confession of aggression, planned and consummated with malice aforethought. Hitler had wanted war; now he had war. The peasant took the scythe out of the hands of his son, and Hitler gave the boy a gun. German blood was spilled—"the blood of our sons."

Hitler's private interpreter, Paul Schmidt, who attended almost every important conference in the brief diplomatic history of National Socialist Germany, summarized the objectives of the Hitler clique in these words: "The general objectives of the Nazi leadership were apparent from the start—namely, the domination of the European continent, to be achieved first, by the incorporation of all German speaking groups into the Reich, and secondly, by territorial expansion under the slogan of 'Lebensraum.' "[17]

Under cross-examination by Mr. Justice Jackson, the man whose financial wizardry made possible the rebuilding of Germany's military machine, Hjalmar Schacht, testified:

Question: You knew of the invasion of Poland?
Answer: Yes.
Question: ... As an unqualified act of aggression on Hitler's part? ...
Answer: Absolutely.
Question: The same was true of the invasion of Luxembourg, was it not?
Answer: Absolutely.
Question: And of Holland?
Answer: Absolutely.
Question: And of Denmark?
Answer: Absolutely.

Question: And of Norway?
Answer: Absolutely.
Question: And of Yugoslavia?
Answer: Absolutely.
Question: And of Russia?
Answer: Absolutely, sir; and you have left out Belgium.
Question: ... The entire course was a course of aggression?
Answer: Absolutely—to be condemned.[18]

The Swedish businessman, Dahlerus, who knew Hitler well, wrote that "the essence of National Socialism was bellicose and aggressive and completely devoid of all moral scruples in its dealings with other nations. Hitler . . . thirsted after conquest."[19]

Before striking with his war club, Hitler handed every intended victim an olive branch. He made the breaking of a promise the first step in the crushing of a nation as the case by case story of his aggressions clearly shows.

CHAPTER 6

Case Otto

Hitler, Austrian-born, might be expected to have had a particular affection for his homeland and a desire to see it within the Third Reich. On the first page of *Mein Kampf,* he had written: "German Austria must return to the Great German Motherland."[1] The establishment of political unity between Germany and Austria had long been a declared objective of the Nazi government. But on May 21, 1935, Hitler said in a speech to the Reichstag, "Germany neither intends nor wishes to interfere in the international affairs of Austria, to annex Austria, or to conclude an Anschluss."[2]

Dollfuss is Murdered

A year earlier, on July 25, 1934, the Austrian Chancellor Dollfuss had been murdered by Austrian Nazis seeking to overthrow the government. About noon on that day, one hundred men, dressed in uniforms of the Austrian army, attacked the Chancellery, shot Dollfuss, and took possession of the government offices. The putsch failed, and at about 7:00 P.M. they yielded the building. Chancellor Dollfuss had died an hour before.

The United States Minister to Austria at that time, Mr. George Messersmith, stated by affidavit:

The events of the putsch of July 25, 1934, are too well known for me to repeat them in this statement. I need say here only that there can be no doubt that the putsch was ordered and organized by the Nazi officials from Germany through their organization in Austria made up of German Nazis and Austrian Nazis. Dr. Reith, the German Minister in Vienna, was fully familiar with all that was going to happen and that was being planned.[3]

In the evening of the day of the assassination, the German government issued formal statements to the newspapers rejoicing at the fall of Dollfuss and proclaiming the greater Germany that would follow. But when it became evident that the Austrian people were unwilling to support the insurgents the releases were withdrawn, and Hitler removed his Minister, Dr. Reith, on the ground that he had offered safe conduct to the rebels without making inquiry of the German government. This was only the second year of the Nazi revolution—Germany was not yet ready to defy the world.

Four years later, after the Anschluss had been effected, the Nazis celebrated this first Nazi action in festive fashion. On July 24, 1938, a memorial assembly was held at Klagenfurt where in 1934 the revolt found its widest response. Hess addressed the assemblage, which included the families of the Nazis who had been hanged for their part in the 1934 putsch. On the following day, the surviving members of the SS group which had made the attack on the Chancellery in 1934 marched again over the route they had then taken. They were met at the Chancellery by Seyss-Inquart, who addressed them and unveiled a memorial tablet. On the tablet the following words were inscribed: "One hundred and fifty-four German men of the 89th SS Standarte stood up here for Germany on July 25, 1934. Seven found death at the hands of the hangman."[4]

In describing this celebration of the assassination of Dollfuss prosecutor Thomas J. Dodd declared: "We call celebrating a murder four years later 'murder by ratification.' "[5]

Undermining the Austrian Government

After the dismissal of Dr. Reith, Hitler sent Von Papen to Austria as his special plenipotentiary, with the mission, as Von Papen told Messersmith, "to undermine and weaken the Austrian government."[6] On July 27, 1935, Von Papen wrote to Hitler: "The Third Reich will be with Austria, or it will not be at all. National

Socialism must win it or perish if it is unable to solve this task."[7]

On July 11, 1936, the governments of Germany and Austria entered into an agreement in which Austria declared that in her foreign policy, especially with regard to Germany, she would regard herself as a German state, and in which Germany recognized the full sovereignty of Austria and declared that her inner political system, including the question of the future status of National Socialism, was solely the concern of Austria and that Germany would exercise no influence in the matter, either directly or indirectly. Contemporaneously with the publication of the official communiqué, an informal understanding was reached in which Austria agreed to appoint to the Cabinet a number of persons friendly to Germany, to give the National Socialist opposition a role in the political life of Austria, and to provide a general amnesty for Nazis other than those convicted of the most serious offenses. At the cost of a promise, the Nazis thus gained further penetration into the Austrian government. And promises were of no real cost—they were freely given to be readily broken.

Five days after he had signed the pact, Hitler violated it. He called the leaders of the Austrian National Socialist party to Obersalzberg where, on July 16, 1936, he issued instructions to them for carrying on revolutionary activities. The plan contemplated the formation of an organization through which subversive operations could be conducted with legal sanction in Austria.

In the meantime the military plans for "Case Otto" went forward. On June 24, 1937, General von Blomberg, as Minister of War and Commander in Chief of the Armed Forces, described the events upon which the operation would be put into effect: "The special Case Otto," wrote Von Blomberg, is "armed intervention in Austria in the event of her restoring the Monarchy. The object of this operation will be to compel Austria by armed force to give up a restoration. Making use of the domestic political divisions of the Austrian people, the march in will be made in the general direction of Vienna, and will break any resistance."[8]

In November, 1937, Mr. Bullitt, the American Ambassador to France, had a conversation with Goering, the memorandum of which contained the following passages:

I asked Goering if he meant that Germany was absolutely determined to annex Austria to the Reich. He replied that this was an absolute determination of the German government. The German government, at the present time, was not pressing this matter because of certain momentary political considerations, especially in their relations with Italy. But Germany would tolerate no solution of the Austrian question other than the consolidation of Austria in the German Reich.

He then added a statement which went further than any I have heard on this subject. He said:

"There are schemes being pushed now for a union of Austria, Hungary and Czechoslovakia, either with or without a Hapsburg at the head of the union. Such a solution is absolutely unacceptable to us, and for us the conclusion of such an agreement would be an immediate casus belli."[9]

Goering testified before the Tribunal: "I personally have always stated that I would do everything to make sure that the Anschluss should not disturb the peace, but that in the long run if this should be denied us forever, I personally might resort to war in order to reach this goal, that these Germans return to their fatherland—a war for Austria, not against Austria."[10]

By November, 1937, Hitler was prepared to announce to his military commanders that he was determined to seek more space for Germany in Europe; that such space would be obtained by force if necessary; and that for the improvement of Germany's military and political position, it must be the first aim of the Nazis, in every case of war, to conquer Czechoslovakia and Austria simultaneously, in order to remove any threat from the flanks in case of a possible advance westward.

The Entrapment of Schuschnigg

The wily Von Papen took Chancellor Schuschnigg to Hitler's lair at Berchtesgaden in February, 1938. Von Papen convinced Schuschnigg that it was essential to the best interests of Austria that he meet Hitler face to face and discuss all problems of mutual concern to Austria and to Germany, while, at the same time, a member of Schuschnigg's own cabinet, Seyss-Inquart, secretly conferred with Hitler, as disclosed in Seyss-Inquart's cross-examination:

Question: Actually, isn't it a fact that you prepared notes, or if you prefer to call it, a memorandum for Hitler which he used as the basis of his discussions with Schuschnigg in Berchtesgaden?

Answer: I made a written proposal for clearing up the matter; and I gave it to Zernato, on the one hand, and Dr. Rainer on the other. It is perfectly possible that Rainer passed it on to the Reich....

Question: Why in the world were you notifying the head of another state about your conversation with the head of your own state, to which you owed allegiance?

Answer: I do not see that this is a breach of faith. It was giving information to heads of two parties to an agreement, for whom I was negotiating.

Question: Would you say that you could negotiate between your country and Germany at that time without notifying your own Chancellor? Schuschnigg didn't know that you'd sent that note on to Hitler, did he? Now be frank about it.

Answer: Yes, it is certain that Dr. Schuschnigg did not know.[11]

Dr. Schuschnigg did not know that a member of his own government was in secret communication with Hitler before he arrived at Berchtesgaden, but shortly after his arrival he learned that the conference had not been called in the interest of Austria's betterment.

Schuschnigg and his Foreign Minister, Guido Schmidt, were brought at once into the presence of Hitler's military staff. Among the commanders present were Admiral Canaris and Generals Keitel, Jodl, von Reichenau, and Sperrle. Hitler's plan in giving the military leaders a prominent part in the conference was to convince Schuschnigg that he was prepared to send his army against Austria if Schuschnigg did not agree to all of his demands. Jodl's diary discloses the tremendous pressure exerted upon Schuschnigg:

11 February: In the evening and on 12 February General K [Keitel] with General von Reichenau and Sperrle at the Obersalzberg. Schuschnigg together with G. Schmidt are being put under heaviest political and military pressure. At 2300 hours Schuschnigg signs protocol.

13 February: In the afternoon General K [Keitel] asks Admiral C. [Canaris] and myself to come to his apartment. He tells us that the Fuehrer's order is to the effect that military pressure, by shamming military action, should be kept up until the 15th. Proposals for these

deceptive maneuvers are drafted and submitted to the Fuehrer by telephone for approval.

14 February: At 2:40 o'clock the agreement of the Fuehrer arrives. Canaris goes to Munich to the Counter-Intelligence Office VII and initiates the different measures.

The effect is quick and strong. In Austria the impression is created that Germany is undertaking serious military preparations.[12]

Keitel's order for the intimidation of Austria contained the following directive: "Spread false but quite credible news which may lead to the conclusion of military preparations against Austria."[13]

Guido Schmidt testified as follows concerning the demands that Hitler made at the conference:

Question: Did Schuschnigg tell you that Hitler demanded that Seyss-Inquart should be made Minister of Security of the Government?

Answer: That was one of the demands on the program....

Question: Were there also demands made with regard to currency exchange and customs unions?

Answer: Yes, economic demands of this kind were discussed....

Question: All right; now, Hitler told you that you had until 15 December to accept his terms, did he not? I mean, 15 February.

Answer: Yes.

Question: And he told you that if you did not do so, he would use force?

Answer: The ultimatum was—yes, it was an ultimatum—to the effect that Hitler intended to march into Austria as early as February, and was still prepared to make one last attempt.[14]

At a conversation with Schuschnigg on February 26, 1938, Von Papen recorded that he asked Schuschnigg whether, without pressure, he would have been ready to make the concession he made at Berchtesgaden, to which Schuschnigg answered, "To be honest, no."[15]

Significant results of the conference were the reorganization of the Austrian Cabinet in which the betrayer of free Austria, Seyss-Inquart, was appointed Minister of Security and Interior, so that he had full control of the Austrian police; the granting of a general political amnesty to Austrian Nazis convicted of crime; and the incorporation of Austrian Nazis into the Fatherland Front, the single legal political party of Austria.

The day after his appointment as Minister of the Interior, Seyss-Inquart flew to Berlin for a conference with Hitler.

The Plebiscite

On March 9, 1938, Schuschnigg announced that he would hold a plebiscite throughout Austria on the following Sunday, March 13, 1938, on the question: "Are you for an independent and social, a Christian, German and united Austria?"[16] Hitler felt that he could not permit any expression of confidence in the Schuschnigg government on the basis of such a plebiscite. He treated the call for a plebiscite as an act of defiance and used it as the excuse for overthrowing the Austrian government and subordinating Austria to the German Reich.

On March 10 Jodl made the following entry in his diary describing developments in Berlin:

By surprise and without consulting his ministers, Schuschnigg ordered a plebiscite for Sunday, 13 March, which would bring strong majority for the Legitimists in the absence of plan or preparation. The Fuehrer is determined not to tolerate it. This same night, March 9 to 10, he calls for Goering.... General Keitel communicates the facts at 9:45. He drives to the Reich Chancellery at 10 o'clock. I follow at 10:15, according to the wish of General von Viebahn, to give him the old draft: "Prepare Case Otto."

1300 hours: General K. [Keitel] informs Chief of Operational Staff and Admiral Canaris. Ribbentrop is being detained in London. Neurath takes over the Foreign Office. Fuehrer wants to transmit ultimatum to the Austrian Cabinet. A personal letter is dispatched to Mussolini and the reasons are developed which force the Fuehrer to take action.

1830 hours: Mobilization order is given to the Commander of the 8th Army (Corps Area 3), 7th and 13th Army Corps, without Reserve Army.[17]

The Austrian Nazis were alerted for immediate revolutionary action. The report of Gauleiter Rainer stated in part:

On 10 March all the preparations for future revolutionary actions had already been made...and the necessary orders given to all unit leaders.... During the night of the 10th and 11th, Globocnik returned from the Fuehrer with the announcement that the Fuehrer gave the Party freedom of action ... and that he would back it in everything it did.[18]

On March 11, 1938, Hitler issued a top secret directive, initialed by Keitel and Jodl, referring to "Case Otto" and providing in part:

1. If other measures prove unsuccessful I intend to invade Austria with armed force to establish constitutional conditions and to prevent further outrages against the pro-German population....

4. The forces of the Army and Air Force detailed for this operation must be ready for invasion and/or ready for action on 12 March 1938 at the latest from 1200 hours. I reserve the right to give permission for crossing and flying over the frontier and to decide the actual moment for invasion.

5. The behavior of the troops must give the impression that we do not want to wage war against our Austrian brother; it is in our interest that the whole operation shall be carried out without any violence, but in the form of a peaceful entry welcomed by the population. Therefore any provocation is to be avoided. If, however, resistance is offered it must be broken ruthlessly by force of arms.[19]

On the same day Jodl issued a directive stating the policy toward Czechoslovakian and Italian troops or militia units which might be encountered on Austrian soil. Czechoslovakian troops were to be regarded as hostile; but Italian troops were to be treated as friendly.

Taking Austria by Telephone

The political events in the afternoon of that day, March 11, 1938, were largely directed from Berlin by Hitler and Goering, and the complete top secret transcriptions of the telephone conversations with Vienna have been preserved.

At 2:45 P.M. Goering called Seyss-Inquart in Vienna. The plan was for Seyss-Inquart to resign from the Austrian government and to bring about its collapse, after which he was to assume the Chancellorship and invite German troops to enter Austria. Seyss-Inquart informed Goering that Schuschnigg had called off the plebiscite and had taken extensive precautionary measures. Goering replied that he saw in this only a postponement, not a change, in "the present situation which had been brought about by the behavior of Chancellor Schuschnigg in breaking the Berchtesgaden agreement."[20]

After discussing the matter with Hitler, Goering again telephoned Seyss-Inquart at 3:05 P.M. Goering instructed Seyss-Inquart and other National Socialist members of the government to hand in their resignations to the Chancellor at once, and to demand that the Chancellor resign. "As a matter of course, an immediate commission by the Federal President for Seyss-Inquart to form a new cabinet would follow Schuschnigg's resignation."[21] Seyss-Inquart should send a telegram to the Fuehrer requesting intervention of German troops.

At 3:55 P.M. Seyss-Inquart telephoned Goering to inform him that Chancellor Schuschnigg was on his way to Federal President Miklas to hand in his resignation, as well as that of the whole cabinet. At 5:00 P.M. Goering spoke on the telephone with Dombrowski at the German Embassy in Vienna. Dombrowski stated that Schuschnigg had advised Seyss-Inquart that it was technically impossible to dissolve the cabinet by 5:30. Goering replied that the cabinet must be dissolved by 7:30 and a new cabinet, entirely National Socialist, established. Dombrowski reported that the SA and the SS were fully mobilized and had been on duty for half an hour. Goering said that he would talk with Hitler and then advise what men were to be appointed to cabinet posts. His brother-in-law was to have the Ministry of Justice; Kaltenbrunner was to have the Department of Security; Fischboeck was to have the Department of Economy and Commerce; and Seyss-Inquart was to take control of the Austrian Army.

At 5:26 Goering spoke again with Seyss-Inquart, who informed him that President Miklas had not after all agreed to appoint Seyss-Inquart Chancellor. When he received this information Goering instructed Seyss-Inquart as follows:

Now remember the following: You go immediately, together with Lieutenant General Muff, and tell the Federal President that if the conditions which are known to you are not accepted immediately, the troops who are already stationed at and advancing to the frontier will march in tonight along the whole line, and Austria will cease to exist. Lieutenant General Muff should go with you and demand to be admitted for conference immediately. Please inform us immediately about Miklas' position. Tell him there is no time now for any joke. Just through the false report we received before, action was delayed, but now the situation is such that tonight the invasion will begin from all the corners of Austria. The invasion will be stopped and the troops will be held at the border only if we are informed by 7:30 that Miklas has entrusted you with the Federal Chancellorship. . . . And then call out all the National Socialists all over the country. They should now be in the streets; so remember, report must be given by 7:30. Lieutenant General Muff is supposed to come along with you. I shall inform him immediately. If Miklas could not understand it in 4 hours, we shall make him understand it now in 4 minutes.[22]

To which Seyss-Inquart replied, "All right."

At 8:00 P.M. Seyss-Inquart called Goering:

Seyss-Inquart: Dr. Schuschnigg will give the news over the radio that the Reich Government has given an ultimatum.

Goering: I heard about it.

Seyss-Inquart: And the Government itself has abdicated, General Schiwaski is in command of the military forces and he will draw the troops back. The gentlemen pointed out that they are waiting for the troops to march in.

Goering: Well, they were appointed by you?

Seyss-Inquart: No.

Goering: Did you dismiss them from their office?

Seyss-Inquart: No one was dismissed from his office, but the Government itself has pulled back and let matters take their course.

Goering: And you were not commissioned, it was refused?

Seyss-Inquart: Now like before it was refused. They expect that they are taking a chance with the invasion and expect that, if the invasion will actually take place the executive power will be transferred to other people.

Goering: O.K. I shall give the order to march in and then you make sure that you get the power. Notify the leading people about the following which I shall tell you now: Everyone who offers resistance or organizes resistance, will immediately be subjected to our court-martial, the court-martial of our invading troops. Is that clear?

Seyss-Inquart: Yes.

Goering: Including leading personalities, it does not make any difference.

Seyss-Inquart: Yes, they have given the order, not to offer any resistance.

Goering: Yes, it does not matter; the Federal President will not authorize you, and that also can be considered as resistance.

Seyss-Inquart: Yes.

Goering: Well, now you are officially authorized.

Seyss-Inquart: Yes.

Goering: Well, good luck, Heil Hitler.[23]

At 8:48 P.M. Goering spoke with Keppler:

Goering: Well, I do not know yet. Listen, the main thing is that if Inquart takes over all powers of Government he keeps the radio stations occupied. . . .

Keppler: Well, we represent the Government now.

Goering: Yes, that's it. You are the Government. Listen carefully. The following telegram should be sent here by Seyss-Inquart: Take the notes:

"The provisional Austrian Government which, after the dismissal of the Schuschnigg Government, considered it its task to establish peace and order in Austria, sends to the German Government the urgent request for support in its task of preventing bloodshed. For this purpose, it asks the German Government to send German troops as soon as possible." . . .

Then our troops will cross the border today.

Keppler: Yes.

Goering: Well, and he should send the telegram as soon as possible. . . . Please show him the text of the telegram and do tell him that we are asking him—well, he does not even need to send the telegram—all he needs to do is to say, "Agreed."

Keppler: Yes.

Goering: He should call me at the Fuehrer's or at my place. Well, good luck, Heil Hitler![24]

At 9:45 P.M. a conversation took place between Dr. Dietrich in Berlin and Keppler in Vienna:

Dietrich: I need the telegram urgently.

Keppler: Tell the General Field Marshal that Seyss-Inquart agrees

Dietrich: This is marvelous. Thank you.

Keppler: Listen to the radio. News will be given.

Dietrich: Where?
Keppler: From Vienna.
Dietrich: So Seyss-Inquart agrees?
Keppler: Certainly.[25]

An hour before this word was received from Austria, Hitler had already given the order for German troops to execute "Case Otto." The top secret directive provided:

(1) The demands of the German ultimatum to the Austrian Government have not been fulfilled.

(2) The Austrian armed forces have been ordered to withdraw before the entry of German troops and to avoid fighting. The Austrian Government has ceased to function of its own accord.

(3) To avoid further bloodshed in Austrian towns, the entry of the German armed forces into Austria will commence, according to Directive No. 1, at daybreak on 12.3.

I expect the set objectives to be reached by exerting all forces to the full as quickly as possible.[26]

Co-operation from Italy

At 10:25 that night, Hitler conferred with Von Hessen, his ambassador to Rome, concerning conversations of the latter with Mussolini about the Austrian affair:

Hessen: I have just come back from Pallazzo Venezia. Il Duce accepted the whole thing in a very friendly manner. He sends you his regards. He has been informed from Austria; Schuschnigg gave him the news. He had then said it would be a complete impossibility; it would be a bluff; such a thing could not be done. So he was told that it was unfortunately arranged thus, and it could not be changed any more. Then Mussolini said that Austria would be immaterial to him.
Hitler: Then, please tell Mussolini I will never forget him for this.
Hessen: Yes.
Hitler: Never, never, never, whatever happens. I am still ready to make a quite different agreement with him.
Hessen: Yes, I told him that, too.
Hitler: As soon as the Austrian affair has been settled, I shall be ready to go with him through thick and thin; nothing matters.
Hessen: Yes, my Fuehrer. . . .

Hitler: I will never forget it, whatever will happen. If he should ever need any help or be in any danger, he can be convinced that I shall stick to him whatever might happen, even if the whole world were against him.

Hessen: Yes, my Fuehrer.[27]

Explanations

On Sunday, March 13, the day after the invasion, Goering telephoned Ribbentrop in London for the purpose of officially and falsely denying the reports that Hitler had issued an ultimatum to Miklas. Goering supposed that the conversation would be intercepted by the British, and what he said was partly for British benefit.

Goering began by saying: "Now, I mainly want to talk about political things. Well, this story that we had given an ultimatum is just foolish gossip. From the very beginning the National Socialist Ministers and the representatives of the people [Volksreferenten] have presented the ultimatum."[28] A little later in the conversation he further expounded on this point:

I want you . . . to tell the following to Halifax and Chamberlain: It is not correct that Germany has given an ultimatum. This is a lie by Schuschnigg, because the ultimatum was presented to him by Seyss-Inquart, Glaise-Horstenau, and Jury. Furthermore, it is not true that we have presented an ultimatum to the Federal President, but that it also was given by the others, and as far as I know, just a military attaché came along, asked by Seyss-Inquart, because of a technical question. . . . He was supposed to ask whether in case Seyss-Inquart would ask for the support of German troops, Germany would grant this request. Furthermore, I want to state that Seyss-Inquart asked us expressly, by phone and by telegram, to send troops because he did not know about the situation in Wiener-Neustadt, Vienna, and so on; because arms had been distributed there. And then he could not know how the Fatherland Front might react since they always had had such a big mouth.[29]

The conversation was concluded by Goering on the following idyllic note:

The weather is wonderful here—blue sky. I am sitting here on my balcony—all covered with blankets—in the fresh air, drinking my coffee. Later on I have to drive in. I have to make the speech. And the birds are twittering, and here and there I can hear over the radio the enthusiasm which must be wonderful over there.

And Ribbentrop replied: "This is marvelous."[30]

When questioned about these conversations with Ribbentrop, Goering excused himself on the basis of "artful diplomacy."

In the conversation which I had with Foreign Minister von Ribbentrop, who was in London at that time, I pointed out that the ultimatum had not been presented by us but by Seyss-Inquart. That was absolutely true *de jure; de facto,* of course, it was my wish. But this telephone conversation was being listened to by the English and I had to conduct a diplomatic conversation, and I have never heard yet that diplomats in such cases say how matters are *de facto;* rather they always stress how they are *de jure.* And why should I make a possible exception here?[31]

"Case Otto" had largely been engineered by the No. 2 Nazi. Before the Tribunal, Goering took the full credit for bringing about the subjugation of Austria. He said: "And I close with the statement that in this matter not so much the Fuehrer as I, personally, bear the full and entire responsibility for everything that has happened."[32]

The End of Austria

As a result of the invasion of Austria, Miklas was forced to resign as President, and Seyss-Inquart became both Chancellor and President. Seyss-Inquart signed a "Federal Constitutional Law,"[33] effective March 13, 1938, which approved the incorporation of Austria into the German Reich, and on the same day Germany enacted the Reich Statute of Reunion, which provided for the incorporation of Austria. So ended free Austria.

In his telephone conversation with Ribbentrop in London, Goering had spoken again and again of the great joy of the Austrians over the arrival of the German troops. He said:

Yesterday I landed hundreds of airplanes with some companies, in order to secure the airfields, and they were received with joy. Today the advance unit of the 17th division marches in, together with the Austrian troops. Also, I want to point out that the Austrian troops did not withdraw, but that they got together and fraternized immediately with the German troops, wherever they were stationed.[34]

Goering's statement could hardly be relied on as an impartial appraisal of the reception by the Austrian people of the German invaders. But in spite of this initial enthusiasm the Austrians displayed, the people soon became thoroughly disillusioned about the purposes and benefits of union with Germany. Schirach, who was appointed the Gauleiter of Vienna, testified before the Tribunal:

... in Vienna the population had sobered considerably after the first wave of enthusiasm over the Anschluss had subsided. Herr Buerckel, my predecessor, had brought many officials to Vienna from the outside; and the German system of administration, which was in no wise more practicable or efficient than the Austrian, was introduced there. This resulted in a certain over-organization in the administrative field, and Buerckel had started on a church policy which was more than unsatisfactory. Demonstrations took place under his administration. On one occasion the palace of the archbishop was damaged. Theaters and other places of culture were not taken care of as they should have been. Vienna was experiencing a feeling of great disillusionment. Before I got there I was informed that if one spoke in the streetcars with a North-German accent, the Viennese took an unfriendly attitude.[35]

If the Viennese soon lost their enthusiasm for Hitler, it was equally the case that Hitler soon came to have little use for the Viennese. Schirach recounted the occasion of a conference with Goebbels and Hitler:

Then the Fuehrer began with, I might say, incredible and unlimited hatred to speak against the people of Vienna.... At 4:00 o'clock in the morning, among other things, Hitler suddenly said something which I should now like to repeat for historical reasons. He said, "Vienna should never have been admitted into the union of Greater Germany." Hitler never loved Vienna. He hated its people.[36]

Events were to prove that Hitler had a similar feeling toward the people of Czechoslovakia.

CHAPTER 7

Case Green

By A FORMAL treaty signed at Locarno on October 16, 1925, Germany and Czechoslovakia agreed to refer to an arbitration tribunal or to the Permanent Court of International Justice "all disputes of every kind between Germany and Czechoslovakia with regard to which the parties are in conflict as to their respective rights, and which it may not be possible to settle amicably by the normal methods of diplomacy."[1]

The preamble to this treaty stated:

The President of the German Reich and the President of the Czechoslovak Republic, equally resolved to maintain peace between Germany and Czechoslovakia by assuring the peaceful settlement of differences which might arise between the two countries, declaring that respect for the rights established by treaty or resulting from the law of nations is obligatory for international tribunals, agreeing to recognize that the rights of a state cannot be modified save with its consent, and considering that sincere observance of the methods of peaceful settlement of international disputes permits of resolving, without recourse to force, questions which may become the cause of divisions between states, have decided to embody in a treaty their common intention in this respect.[2]

This solemn treaty, which had been entered into without compulsion of any kind upon either party, was openly violated on the morning of March 15, 1939, when the German Wehrmacht stormed into Czechoslovakia. The attack had been conceived as early as June, 1937, in connection with plans against other nations, and thereafter was secretly prepared under the code-name "Case Green."

Initial Preparation

On June 24, 1937, the High Command of the Wehrmacht issued under the signature of Von Blomberg a top secret directive which stated in part:

The war in the East can begin with a surprise German operation against Czechoslovakia in order to parry the imminent attack of a superior enemy coalition. The necessary conditions to justify such an action politically, and in the eyes of international law, must be created beforehand. . . . The task of the German armed forces is to make their preparations in such a way that the bulk of all forces can break into Czechoslovakia quickly, by surprise, and with the greatest force, while in the West the minimum strength is provided as rear-cover for this attack.

The aim and object of this surprise attack by the German armed forces should be to eliminate from the very beginning and for the duration of the war, the threat by Czechoslovakia to the rear of the operations in the West, and to take from the Russian Air Force the most substantial portion of its operational base in Czechoslovakia. This must be done by the defeat of the enemy armed forces and the occupation of Bohemia and Moravia.[3]

Hitler discussed the proposal to attack Czechoslovakia at a meeting of his military commanders on November 5, 1937. "For the improvement of our military political position," he said,

it must be our first aim, in every case of entanglement by war, to conquer Czechoslovakia and Austria, simultaneously, in order to remove any threat from the flanks in case of a possible advance westward. . . . Once Czechoslovakia is conquered—and a mutual frontier, Germany-Hungary is obtained—then a neutral attitude by Poland in a German-French conflict could more easily be relied upon.[4]

Even at that date, Hitler believed that no Western nation would come to the aid of little Czechoslovakia.

The Fuehrer believes personally, that in all probability England and perhaps also France, have already silently written off Czechoslovakia, and that they have got used to the idea that this question would one day be cleaned up by Germany. . . . Naturally, we should in every case have to bar our frontier during the operation of our attacks against Czechoslovakia and Austria. It must be taken into consideration here that Czechoslovakia's defense measures will increase in strength from year to year and that a consolidation of the inside values of the Austrian army will also be effected in the course of years. Although the population of Czechoslovakia in the first place is not a thin one, the embodiment of Czechoslovakia and Austria would nevertheless constitute the conquest of food for five to six million people, on the basis that a compulsory emigration of two million from Czechoslovakia, and of one million from Austria, could be carried out.[5]

Czechoslovakia and Austria were not merely to be conquered and defeated militarily; they were to be incorporated into the Greater German Reich.

The annexation of the two states to Germany, militarily and politically, would constitute a considerable relief, owing to shorter and better frontiers, the freeing of fighting personnel for other purposes, and the possibility of reconstituting new armies up to a strength of about twelve divisions, representing a new division per one million population.

No opposition to the removal of Czechoslovakia is expected on the part of Italy. . . .[6]

General military strategy having been outlined, it became necessary to consider political aspects of the proposed invasion and particularly the reaction of other countries bordering Czechoslovakia. On March 4, 1938, Ribbentrop wrote Keitel concerning a conference with Sztojay, the Hungarian Ambassador: "I have many doubts about such negotiations. In case we should discuss with Hungary possible war aims against Czechoslovakia, the danger exists that other parties as well would be informed about this. I would greatly appreciate it if you would notify me briefly whether any commitments were made here in any respect."[7]

A few days later Austria was invaded, and the Nazis hurriedly made assurances to the Czech Government that no hostile actions would be taken against Czechoslovakia. Goering promised M. Mastny, then Czechoslovak Minister in Berlin, on behalf of the German Government, that German-Czech relations were not adversely affected by the development in Austria and that Germany had no hostile intentions toward Czechoslovakia. Goering emphasized this pledge with the words: "I give you my word of honor."[8]

And Von Neurath, the acting Foreign Minister in Ribbentrop's absence, assured Mastny that Germany still considered herself bound by the arbitration treaty of 1925.

The Strategy of Surprise Attack

Scarcely a month later, Hitler and Keitel were plotting the destruction of Czechoslovakia. Hitler's adjutant, Schmundt, prepared a summary of their discussion of "Case Green" held on April 21, 1938:

A. Political Aspect.

1. Strategic surprise attack, out of a clear sky without any cause or possibility of justification, has been turned down, as result would be hostile world opinion which can lead to a critical situation. Such a measure is justified only for the elimination of the last opponent on the mainland.

2. Action after a time of diplomatic clashes, which gradually come to a crisis and lead to war.

3. Lightning-swift action as the result of an incident (for example, the assassination of German ambassador in connection with an anti-German demonstration).

B. Military Conclusions.

1. The preparations are to be made for the political possibilities (2 and 3). Case 2 is the undesired one since "Green" will have taken security measures.

2. The loss of time caused by transporting the bulk of the divisions by rail—which is unavoidable, but should be cut down as far as possible—must not impede a lightning-swift blow at the time of the action.

3. "Separate thrusts" are to be carried out immediately with a view to penetrating the enemy fortification lines at numerous points and in a strategically favorable direction. The thrusts are to be worked out to the smallest detail (knowledge of roads, of targets, composition of the columns according to their individual tasks). Simultaneous attacks by the Army and Air Force. The Air Force is to support the individual columns (for example, dive-bombers, sealing off installations at penetration points, hampering the bringing up of reserves, destroying signal communications traffic, thereby isolating the garrisons).

4. Politically, the first four days of military action are the decisive ones. If there are no effective military successes, a European crisis will certainly arise. Accomplished facts must prove the senselessness of foreign military intervention, draw Allies into the scheme (division of

spoils), and demoralize "Green." Therefore: bridging the time gap between the first penetration and employment of the forces to be brought up, by a determined and ruthless thrust by a motorized army (for example, via Pilsen, Prague).[9]

By May 30, 1938, Keitel was able to provide the commanders in chief of the Army, Navy, and Air Force with a Fuehrer directive in these words:

1. *Political prerequisites:*
It is my unalterable decision to smash Czechoslovakia by military action in the near future. It is the job of the political leaders to await or bring about the politically and militarily suitable moment.

An inevitable development of conditions inside Czechoslovakia or other political events in Europe, creating a surprisingly favorable opportunity and one which may never come again, may cause me to take early action.

The proper choice and determined and full utilization of a favorable moment is the surest guarantee of success. Accordingly the preparations are to be made at once. . . .

2. *Political possibilities for the commencement of the action.* The following are necessary prerequisites for the intended invasion: a. suitable obvious cause and with it, b. sufficient political justification, and c. action unexpected by the enemy which will find him prepared in the least possible degree.

From a military as well as a political standpoint the most favorable course is a lightning-swift action as the result of an incident through which Germany is provoked in an unbearable way and for which at least part of world opinion will grant the moral justification of military action.

But even a period of tension, more or less preceding a war, must terminate in sudden action on our part, which must have the elements of surprise as regards time and extent, before the enemy is so advanced in military preparedness that he cannot be surpassed.

3. *Conclusions for the preparation of Case Green.*
a. For the "armed war" it is essential that the surprise element, as the most important factor contributing to success, be made full use of by appropriate preparatory measures already in peacetime and by an unexpectedly rapid course of the action. Thus it is essential to create a situation within the first two or three days which plainly demonstrates to hostile nations, eager to intervene, the hopelessness of the Czechoslovakian military situation and which, at the same time, will give nations with territorial claims on Czechoslovakia an incentive to

intervene immediately against Czechoslovakia. . . . If concrete successes are not achieved by the land operations within the first few days, a European crisis will certainly result. This knowledge must give commanders of all ranks the impetus to decided and bold action.

b. The propaganda war must on the one hand intimidate Czechoslovakia by threats and wear down her power of resistance; on the other hand, issue directions to national groups for support in the "armed war" and influence the neutrals into our way of thinking. I reserve further directions and determination of the date.

4. *Tasks of the Armed Forces.*

Armed forces preparations are to be made on the following basis:

a. The mass of all forces must be employed against Czechoslovakia.

b. For the West, a minimum of forces are to be provided as rear cover which may be required, the other frontiers in the East against Poland and Lithuania are merely to be protected, the southern frontiers to be watched.

c. The sections of the Army which can be rapidly employed must force the frontier fortifications with speed and decision and must break into Czechoslovakia with the greatest daring in the certainty that the bulk of the mobile army will follow them with the utmost speed. Preparations for this are to be made and timed in such a way that the sections of the army which can be rapidly employed cross the frontier at the appointed time, simultaneously with the penetration by the Air Force, before the enemy can become aware of our mobilization. For this, a timetable between Army and Air Force is to be worked out in conjunction with OKW and submitted to me for approval.[10]

Of first importance, under these plans, was the manufacture of an incident suitable as a simulated casus belli. On August 24, 1938, Jodl made clear in a memorandum for Hitler's consideration that the "incident" which Hitler had proposed would be useful for blitz attack if properly timed. He wrote:

"Operation Green" will be set in motion by means of an "incident" in Czechoslovakia which will give Germany provocation for military intervention. The fixing of the exact time for this incident is of the utmost importance.

It must come at a time when the over-all meteorological conditions are favorable for our superior air forces to go into action and at an hour which will enable authentic news of it to reach us on the afternoon of X minus 1. . . .

Even a warning of diplomatic representatives in Prague is impossible before the first air attack, although the consequences could be very grave in the event of their becoming victims of such an attack (that is the death of representatives of friendly or confirmed neutral powers). . . .

It is the purpose of these notes to point out what a great interest the Wehrmacht has in the incident and that it must be informed of the Fuehrer's intentions in good time. . . .[11]

By the middle of the summer the plans for the absorption of Czechoslovakia had progressed so far that Hitler felt it necessary to inform his allies, Italy and Hungary. Toward the end of August, 1938, Hungary sent a delegation headed by Admiral Horthy to Germany to discuss mutual problems with Hitler. A boat trip was arranged on the SS *Patria,* and the Italian ambassador, Attolico, was also invited. Ribbentrop made the following notes concerning his conversation with Mussolini's representative:

On the voyage of the Patria, Ambassador Attolico explained to me that he had instructions to request the notification of a contemplated time for German action against Czechoslovakia from the German Government. In case the Czechs should again cause a provocation against Germany, Germany would march. This would be tomorrow, in six months, or perhaps in a year. However, I could promise him that the German Government, in case of an increasing gravity of the situation or as soon as the Fuehrer made his decision, would notify the Italian Chief of Government as rapidly as possible. In any case, the Italian Government will be the first one who will receive such a notification.[12]

Both Hitler and Ribbentrop conferred with Horthy and his delegates, Imredy and Kanya, aboard the SS *Patria.* Ribbentrop suggested that a German attack on Czechoslovakia would provide Hungary a good opportunity to seize some land for herself, and Hitler said, allegorically: "Whoever wants to join the meal would have to participate in the cooking as well."[13]

The report of this conference showed that considerable persuasion was applied to the Hungarian representatives. "Von Ribbentrop then explained to the Hungarians that the Yugoslavs would not dare to march while they were between the pincers of the Axis Powers. Rumania alone would therefore not move. England and France would also remain tranquil. England would not recklessly risk her Empire. She knew our newly-acquired power."[14]

From August to the eve of the intended invasion and its temporary postponement by the Munich agreement, Hitler and his top military advisers, Keitel, Jodl, and Von Brauchitsch, planned the tactics of the surprise attack to be made against Czechoslovakia. The day and hour were to be set well in advance of the "incident" which was to be used as justification to the Western powers. According to the Schmundt notes:

At 1300 hours 27 September, the Fuehrer and Supreme Commander of the Armed Forces ordered the movement of the assault units from their exercise areas to their jumping off points. The assault units (about 21 reinforced regiments, or 7 divisions) must be ready to begin the action against "Green" on September 30, the decision having been made one day previously by 1200 noon.[15]

How nearly the world came to being plunged into war in the fall of 1938 is dramatically demonstrated by the fact that the Munich Pact was signed at 0230 hours in the morning of September 30 — the day selected for the attack.

Pause at Munich

War was averted at the eleventh hour by Czechoslovakia's forced surrender of the Sudetenland and her natural geographical defenses to Germany. After Munich, Czechoslovakia lay virtually defenseless before the armies of Hitler's Germany. Czechoslovakia had exchanged her best means of self-defense for a belief in the support of powerful nations in the West against any further German demands. In this the Czechs were soon to suffer bitter disillusionment.

In the intense political negotiations from September 15 to 30, Hitler had based his claim to the Sudetenland upon the contention that it was largely inhabited by Volksdeutsche, people of German descent, who were alleged to be persecuted by the Czechs. And he assured Prime Minister Chamberlain that his only desire in asserting such territorial claims was to provide protection for these German people. He told Chamberlain in private conversation, and he told the world publicly, that this was his final territorial claim to be made in Europe.

On September 26, in a speech delivered at the Sportspalast in Berlin, Hitler had said:

And now we are confronted with the last problem which must be solved and will be solved. . . . It is the last territorial claim which I have to make in Europe, but it is a claim from which I will not swerve and which I will satisfy, God willing. . . . I have little to explain. I am grateful to Mr. Chamberlain for all his efforts, and I have assured him that the German people want nothing but peace; but I have also told him that I cannot go back beyond the limits of our patience. I assured him, moreover, and I repeat it here, that when this problem is solved there will be no more territorial problems for Germany in Europe. And I further assured him that from the moment when Czechoslovakia solves its other problems—that is to say, when the Czechs have come to an arrangement with their other minorities peacefully and without oppression—I will no longer be interested in the Czech State. And that, as far as I am concerned, I will guarantee it. We don't want any Czechs![16]

Yet, ten days after Munich, Hitler propounded the following four questions to the High Command of the Wehrmacht:

Question 1. What reinforcements are necessary in the present situation to break all Czech resistance in Bohemia and Moravia?

Question 2. How much time is required for the regrouping or moving up of new forces?

Question 3. How much time will be required for the same purpose if it is executed after the intended demobilization and return measures?

Question 4. How much time would be required to achieve the state of readiness of 1 October?[17]

Plans for the Final Liquidation

On October 21, 1938, the same day on which the administration of the Sudetenland was handed over to the civilian authorities, a directive outlining plans for the conquest of the remainder of Czechoslovakia was signed by Hitler and initialed by Keitel:

The future tasks for the armed forces and the preparations for the conduct of war resulting from these tasks will be laid down by me in a later directive. Until this directive comes into force, the armed forces must be prepared at all times for the following eventualities:

1. The securing of the frontiers of Germany and the protection against surprise air attacks.

2. The liquidation of the remainder of Czechoslovakia.

3. The occupation of Memel.

Liquidation of the remainder of Czechoslovakia: It must be possible to smash at any time the remainder of Czechoslovakia if her policy should become hostile towards Germany.

The preparations to be made by the armed forces for this contingency will be considerably smaller in extent than those for Green; they must, however, guarantee a continuous and considerably higher state of preparedness, since planned mobilization measures have been dispensed with. The organization, order of battle, and state of readiness of the units earmarked for that purpose are in peacetime to be so arranged for a surprise assault that Czechoslovakia herself will be deprived of all possibility of organized resistance. The object is the swift occupation of Bohemia and Moravia and the cutting off of Slovakia. . . .[18]

This directive then set forth the detailed missions of the Army and Air Force. It was signed by Hitler, authenticated by Keitel, and distributed to the High Command of the Army, to Goering's Air Force, and to Raeder's Navy. Two months later, Keitel issued a further directive to the effect that by command of the Fuehrer the preparations for the liquidation of Czechoslovakia were to continue:

Reference "Liquidation of the Rest of Czechoslovakia." The Fuehrer has given the following additional order:

"The preparations for this eventuality are to continue on the assumption that no resistance worth mentioning is to be expected.

"To the outside world, too, it must clearly appear that it is merely an action of pacification, and not a warlike undertaking." . . .[19]

While Germany thus feverishly prepared for the strike against what Munich had left of Czechoslovakia, the mendacious Ribbentrop sought to beguile the Czechs into unpreparedness. Referring to his conversation with the Czechoslovakian Foreign Minister, Chvalkovsky, in Berlin on January 21, 1939, Ribbentrop wrote: "I mentioned to Chvalkovsky especially that a quick reduction in the Czech army would be decisive in our judgment."[20]

During this same period, the Nazis sought to separate Slovakia from the rest of Czechoslovakia to weaken even further the resistance of the intended victim. The minutes of a conversation between Goering and Durcansky, a leader of the Slovak extremist group, recorded the following: "The Field Marshal [Goering] considers that the Slovak negotiations towards independence are to be supported in a suitable manner. Czechoslovakia without Slovakia is still more at our mercy. Air bases in Slovakia are of great importance to the German Air Force for use against the East."[21]

On February 12, 1939, at a conference with Hitler in the Reich Chancellery in Berlin, another Slovak extremist, Tuka, speaking for the "Slovak nation," told Hitler that future association with the Czechs had become an impossibility for the Slovaks. He concluded, "I entrust the fate of my people to your care."[22]

The efforts of the Nazis to bring about the revolt of Slovakia from Czechoslovakia were reflected in the dismissal by the Czech government on March 10, 1939, of the members of the Slovak cabinet who had refused to continue negotiations. Within twenty-four hours, Seyss-Inquart, Buerckel, and five German generals appeared at a cabinet meeting in progress in Bratislava and told the Slovak cabinet that it should proclaim the independence of Slovakia.

The final "liquidation" was a matter of days. Hitler decided once again to invite Horthy to the banquet table, and the dictator of Hungary wrote to him on March 13, 1939, that he had made the necessary dispositions and was "going into this affair with eager enthusiasm."[23] Horthy said that on the sixteenth "a frontier incident will take place which will be followed by the big blow on Saturday."[24]

On March 13, the Slovakians Tiso, Durcansky, and Meissner arrived in Berlin, in response to a summons from Hitler, and were told that within a matter of hours they must proclaim the independence of Slovakia, or Hitler could promise them no protection from Hungary, which even then had deployed troops on the Slovakian borders. Keitel was a participant in this round of bluff. The plan succeeded. Tiso was flown back to Bratislava on the night of the thirteenth, and on the following day the Slovakian Diet proclaimed the independence of Slovakia.

The Hacha Conference

All was in readiness for the final assault upon little Czechoslovakia. On the evening of the fourteenth, at the suggestion of the German legation in Prague, the aged President of the Czechoslovak Republic, Monsieur Hacha, and his Foreign Minister, Chvalkovsky, arrived in Berlin for discussions with Hitler. At 1:15 on the morning of the fifteenth, they were brought to the Reich Chancellery, where they were confronted by Hitler, Ribbentrop, Goering, Keitel, and other top Nazi officials and generals.

The minutes of this conference began: "State President Hacha greets the Fuehrer and expresses his thanks for being received by him. . . . He was convinced that the fate of Czechoslovakia lay in the hands of the Fuehrer, and he believed that her fate was safe in the Fuehrer's hands."[25] Hacha then briefly discussed the Slovakian crisis. "Now he came to the point which concerned him most, the fate of his people. He believed that the Fuehrer, especially, would understand him when he expressed his opinion that Czechoslovakia had the right to wish to live her own national life. . . ."[26]

Hitler is then recorded as having replied:

He regretted that he had been forced to ask Hacha to come to Berlin, particularly because of the great age of the President, . . . But this journey could be of great advantage to his country because it was only a matter of hours until Germany would intervene. . . . For the other countries, Czechoslovakia was nothing but a means to an end. London and Paris were not in a position to really stand up for Czechoslovakia. . . .[27]

Hitler continued:

He had given the order to the German troops to march into Czechoslovakia and to incorporate Czechoslovakia into the German Reich. . . . At 6:00 o'clock in the morning the German Army would invade Czechoslovakia from all sides and the German Air Force would occupy the Czech air fields. There existed two possibilities. The first one would be that the invasion of the German troops would lead to a battle. In this case, the resistance will be broken by all means with physical force. The other possibility is that the invasion of the German troops occurs in bearable form. In that case, it would be easy for the Fuehrer to give Czechoslovakia in the new organization of Czech life a generous life of her own, autonomy, and a certain national liberty. . . . At 6:00 o'clock the troops would march in. He was almost ashamed to say that there was one German division to each Czech battalion. The military action was no small one, but planned with all generosity. He would advise him now to retire with Chvalkovsky in order to discuss what should be done.[28]

Upon Hacha's return the following conversation took place, as shown by the minutes:

Hacha says that the situation is completely clear to him and that any resistance to this would be foolish. . . . Hacha asks whether the whole purpose of the invasion is to disarm the Czech army. This might, perhaps, be done in some other way. The Fuehrer says that his decision is irrevocable. Everyone knows what a decision by the Fuehrer means. He could see no other practical method of disarmament and asks the others present whether they agree with him, which they confirm. The only possibility of disarming the Czech army would be by the German army.[29]

After Goering stated that he would be sorry if he had to "bomb beautiful Prague,"[30] the weary and frightened Hacha, at four-thirty on the morning of March 15, signed the document which surrendered his country to the Nazis.

At the trial, Ribbentrop was asked by Sir David Maxwell Fyfe whether he was present at the meeting between President Hacha and Hitler on March 15, 1939.

Answer: Yes, I was present. . . .
Question: Will you agree with me that that agreement was obtained through a threat of aggressive action by the German army and air force?
Answer: It is certain, since the Fuehrer told President Hacha that the Germans would march in, that naturally this instrument was written under that impression. That is correct. . . .
Question: What further pressure could you put on the head of a country except to threaten him that your army would march in, in overwhelming strength, and your air force would bomb his capital?
Answer: War, for instance.
Question: What is that but war?[31]

Czechoslovakia Ceases to Exist

In point of fact, while President Hacha was being thus intimidated, the Wehrmacht had in some areas already crossed the Czech border. Bloody fighting depended only upon the determination of the Czech forces to oppose the great might of the German military machine, a machine that would in any case, as Goering rightly stated, roll over and crush Czechoslovakia in a matter of hours.

At dawn on March 15, 1939, the main forces of the German army struck Czechoslovakia from all sides, and Hitler issued a proclamation to the German people which stated cynically and succinctly, "Czechoslovakia has ceased to exist."[32] On the following day, the Republic of Czechoslovakia was rubbed out and Bohemia and Moravia were incorporated into the German Reich as the Protectorate of Bohemia and Moravia.[33]

On March 17, 1939, Sumner Welles, the Acting Secretary of State, issued the following statement:

> The Government of the United States has on frequent occasions stated its convictions that only through international support of a program of order based upon law can world peace be assured.
>
> This Government, founded upon and dedicated to the principles of human liberty and of democracy, cannot refrain from making known this country's condemnation of the acts which have resulted in the temporary extinguishment of the liberties of a free and independent people with whom, from the day when the Republic of Czechoslovakia attained its independence, the people of the United States have maintained specially close and friendly relations.
>
> The position of the Government of the United States has been made consistently clear. It has emphasized the need for respect for the sanctity of treaties and of the pledged word, and for non-intervention by any nation in the domestic affairs of other nations; and it has on repeated occasions expressed its condemnation of a policy of military aggression.
>
> It is manifest that acts of wanton lawlessness and of arbitrary force are threatening the world peace and the very structure of modern civilization. The imperative need for the observance of the principles advocated by this Government has been clearly demonstrated by the developments which have taken place during the past three days.[34]

But by then "Case Green" was closed, and the stage was being set for Poland.

CHAPTER 8

Case White

THE PLAN for the invasion and subjugation of Poland was perfected under the code name "Case White."

Germany and Poland had entered into an arbitration treaty at Locarno on October 16, 1925, similar to the arbitration treaty between Germany and Czechoslovakia. Moreover, on January 26, 1934, Hitler entered into a ten-year nonaggression pact with Poland.[1] On May 21, 1935, Hitler said of this agreement:

Without taking the past into account, Germany has concluded a non-aggression pact with Poland. This is more than a valuable contribution to European peace, and we shall adhere to it unconditionally. We only hope that it will be renewed and continued uninterruptedly and that it will deepen the friendly relations between the two countries. With the understanding and heartfelt friendship of genuine nationalists we recognize Poland as the home of a great and nationally conscious people.[2]

In the course of a speech delivered in the Reichstag on February 20, 1938, Hitler said:

In the fifth year following the first great foreign political agreement with the Reich, it fills us with sincere gratification to be able to state that in our relations with the state with which we had had perhaps the greatest differences, not only has there been a *détente,* but in the course of these years there has been a constant improvement in relations. This good work, which was regarded with suspicion by so many at the time, has stood the test, and I may say that since the League of Nations finally gave up its continual attempts to unsettle Danzig and appointed a man of great personal attainments as the new commissioner, this most dangerous spot from the point of view of

European peace has entirely lost its menacing character. The Polish state respects the national conditions of this state, and both the city of Danzig and Germany respect Polish rights. And so the way to friendly understanding has been successfully paved, an understanding which beginning with Danzig has today, in spite of the attempts of certain mischief-makers, succeeded in finally taking the poison out of the relations between Germany and Poland and transforming them into a sincere, friendly co-operation. Relying on her friendships, Germany will not leave a stone unturned to save that ideal which provides the foundation for the task which is ahead of us—peace.[3]

The reason for such conciliatory statements made at a time when Germany was frantically preparing for war is disclosed in a memorandum addressed to Ribbentrop as Reich Foreign Minister on August 26, 1938:

The fact is that after the liquidation of the Czech question, it will be generally assumed that Poland will be the next in turn.
But the later this assumption sinks in in international politics as a firm factor, the better. In this sense, however, it is important for the time being to carry on the German policy under the well-known and approved slogans of "the right to autonomy" and "racial unity." Anything else might be interpreted as pure imperialism on our part and provoke resistance by the Entente at an earlier date and more energetically than our forces could stand up to.[4]

Hitler continued the deception by stating, four days before the Munich Agreement, with reference to his conversation with Prime Minister Chamberlain: "I assured him, moreover, and I repeat it here, that when this problem is solved there will be no more international problems for Germany in Europe."[5]

The First Demands

On October 25, 1938, Ribbentrop conferred with Lipski, the Polish ambassador to Germany, at Berchtesgaden. Ribbentrop proposed that Danzig be reunited with the Reich and suggested, in exchange, a possible extension of the Polish-German Agreement by twenty-five years and a guarantee of Polish-German frontiers. Lipski advised Ribbentrop that he could see no possibility of an agreement involving the reunion of the Free City of Danzig with the Reich.

The Polish Foreign Minister, Beck, instructed Lipski to inform the German Government that Poland was quite willing to enter into a bilateral Polish-German agreement which would guarantee the existence of the Free City of Danzig so as to assure freedom of national and cultural life to its German majority and also to guarantee all Polish rights. Beck further instructed Lipski to inform the German Government that he was ready to have final conversations personally with the governing circles of the Reich.

A few days later, Keitel issued a top secret order on behalf of the Supreme Command of the Armed Forces stating that Hitler had ordered preparations to be made to enable the Free City of Danzig to be occupied by German troops by surprise.

On January 5, 1939, the Polish Foreign Minister conferred with Hitler. Hitler assured Beck that he had always followed the policy laid down by the 1934 German-Polish Agreement. He discussed the Danzig question and emphasized that in the German view it must sooner or later return to Germany. The notes of the conversation recite the following exchange of views:

Mr. Beck replied that the Danzig question was a very difficult problem. He added that in the Chancellor's suggestion he did not see any equivalent for Poland, and that the whole of Polish opinion, and not only people thinking politically but the widest spheres of Polish society, were particularly sensitive on this matter.

In answer to this the Chancellor stated that to solve this problem it would be necessary to try to find something quite new, some new form, for which he used the term "Koerperschaft," which on the one hand would safeguard the interests of the German population, and on the other, the Polish interests. In addition, the Chancellor declared that the Minister could be quite at ease, there would be no *faits accomplis* in Danzig, and nothing would be done to render difficult the situation of the Polish Government.[6]

Three weeks later Ribbentrop delivered a speech in Warsaw in which he said:

In accordance with the resolute will of the German National Leader, the continual progress and consolidation of friendly relations between Germany and Poland, based upon the existing agreement between us, constitute an essential element in German foreign policy. The political foresight and the principles worthy of true statesmanship, which induced both sides to take the momentous decision of 1934, provide a guarantee that all other problems arising in the course of the future evolution of events will also be solved in the same spirit, with due regard to the respect and understanding of the rightful interest of both sides. Thus Poland and Germany can look forward to the future with full confidence in the solid basis of their mutual relations.[7]

On January 30, 1939, Hitler stated in the course of a speech to the Reichstag:

We have just celebrated the fifth anniversary of the conclusion of our non-aggression pact with Poland. There can scarcely be any difference of opinion today among the true friends of peace as to the value of this agreement. One only needs to ask oneself what might have happened to Europe if this agreement, which brought such relief, had not been entered into five years ago. In signing it the great Polish marshal and patriot rendered his people just as great a service as the leaders of the National Socialist State rendered the German people. During the troubled months of the past year the friendship between Germany and Poland has been one of the reassuring factors in the political life in Europe.[8]

Friendship proved a fragile thing after the seizure of Czechoslovakia by Germany on March 15, 1939. For by that action a military basis for war against Poland had been established.

On March 21, 1939, Lipski conferred with Ribbentrop, who pressed Hitler's suggestion of a guarantee of Poland's frontiers in exchange for a motor road across the Corridor and the incorporation of Danzig into the Reich. Ribbentrop indicated that he was under the impression "that difficulties arising between us were also due to some misunderstanding of the Reich's real aims."[9] At the conclusion of the discussion Lipski asked whether Ribbentrop could tell him anything about his conversation with the Foreign Minister of Lithuania. Ribbentrop answered vaguely "that he had seen Mr. Urbszys on the latter's return from Rome, and that they had discussed the Memel question, which called for a solution."[10] The next day German armed forces occupied Memel.

On March 31, 1939, Prime Minister Chamberlain, speaking in the House of Commons, declared:

As the House is aware, certain consultations are now proceeding with other governments. In order to make perfectly clear the position of His Majesty's Government in the meantime, before those consultations are concluded, I now have to inform the House that during that period, in the event of any action which clearly threatened Polish independence and which the Polish Government accordingly considered it vital to resist with their national forces, His Majesty's Government would feel themselves bound at once to lend the Polish Government all support in their power. They have given the Polish Government an assurance to this effect.

I may add that the French Government has authorized me to make it plain that they stand in the same position in this matter as do His Majesty's Government.[11]

On April 3, 1939, Keitel issued another directive on behalf of the Supreme Command of the Armed Forces:

The Fuehrer has added the following directives to Case White:

1. Preparations must be made in such a way that the operations can be carried out at any time from 1st September 1939 onwards.

2. The High Command of the Armed Forces has been directed to draw up a precise time-table for Case White and to arrange by conferences the synchronized timings among the three branches of the armed forces.

3. The plan of the branches of the armed forces and the details for the time-table must be submitted to the OKW by the 1st of May.[12]

A few days later, the remarks of Prime Minister Chamberlain in the House of Commons were formalized in a provisional British understanding with Poland, to be replaced by a permanent agreement, in which each country agreed to support the other in the event of an attack against either. The German reaction was a declaration issued April 28, 1939, that the Anglo-Polish understanding was incompatible with the 1934 Agreement between Germany and Poland, and that Poland had thereby unilaterally renounced the 1934 Agreement.

When interrogated concerning "Case White," Goering was asked whether he had not thought that a peaceful solution of the Polish question was impossible at the time of the preliminary Anglo-Polish agreement in March, 1939, and he replied:

Yes, it seemed impossible . . . according to my conviction . . . but not according to the convictions of the Fuehrer. When it was mentioned to the Fuehrer that England had given her guarantee to Poland, he said that England was also guaranteeing Rumania, but then when the Russians took Bessarabia nothing happened; and this made a big impression on him. I made a mistake here. At this time Poland only had the promise of a guarantee. The guarantee itself was only given shortly before the beginning of the war. On the day when England gave her official guarantee to Poland, the Fuehrer called me on the telephone and told me that he had stopped the planned invasion of Poland. I asked him then whether this was just temporary or for good. He said, "No, I will have to see whether we can eliminate British intervention." . . .[13]

In an annex to a directive of April 11, 1939, Hitler stated that if Poland should adopt a threatening attitude toward Germany a "final settlement" would be necessary, notwithstanding the nonaggression pact. In such an event, he declared that the object would be to destroy the Polish army. Danzig would be incorporated into the Reich at the outbreak of the conflict.

While preparations for the invasion of Poland progressed according to the Keitel directive of April 3, Hitler, on April 28, discussed the renunciation of the 1934 Agreement with Poland in a speech to the Reichstag in which he used these words:

I have regretted greatly this incomprehensible attitude of the Polish Government. But that alone is not the decisive fact. The worst is that now Poland, like Czechoslovakia, a year ago, believes under the pressure of a lying international campaign, that it must call up troops although Germany, on her part, has not called up a single man and had not thought of proceeding in any way against Poland.[14]

On May 5, 1939, the Polish Government issued a memorandum in reply to the German declaration in which it rejected the accusation that the Anglo-Polish agreement was incompatible with the 1934 German-Polish agreement, alleged that Germany herself had entered into similar arrangements with other nations, and declared that it was still willing to entertain a new pact with Germany. The Polish Government further stated: "It is clear that negotiations in which one state formulates demands and the other is to be obliged to accept those demands unaltered, are not negotiations in the spirit of the declaration of 1934 and are incompatible with the vital interests and dignity of Poland."[15]

Not Danzig, but Poland, Itself

All along Hitler had said publicly that all he wanted was the return of Danzig and a motor road across the Corridor. But on May 23, 1939, he confided his true intentions in a secret conference with his top military advisors. "Danzig," he said,

is not the subject of the dispute at all. It is a question of expanding our living space in the East and of securing our food supplies, of the settlement of the Baltic problem. Food supplies can be expected only from thinly populated areas. Over and above the natural fertility, thoroughgoing German exploitation will enormously increase the surplus. There is no other possibility for Europe.[16]

He quickly arrived at this conclusion: "There is therefore no question of sparing Poland, and we are left with the decision *to attack Poland at the first suitable opportunity*."[17]

"We cannot expect a repetition of the Czech affair. There will be fighting. Our task is to isolate Poland. The success of the isolation will be decisive."[18] He added, "The isolation of Poland is a matter of skilful politics."[19]

Hitler said that if the German-Polish conflict resulted in war in the West, "then the fight must be primarily against England and France."[20] He described England as Germany's enemy and said, "the conflict with England will be a life and death struggle."[21] And later he said again, "The war with England and France will be a life and death struggle."[22]

Secret mobilization got under way in June. On June 22, 1939, the Supreme Command of the Armed Forces submitted to Hitler a preliminary timetable for "Case White," to which Hitler made the following comment:

In order not to disquiet the population by calling up of reserves on a larger scale than usual for the maneuvers scheduled for 1939, as is intended, civilian establishments, employers or other private persons who make inquiries should be told that men are being called up for the autumn maneuvers and for the exercise units it is intended to form for these maneuvers.[23]

By July 27, 1939, orders had been issued for the occupation of Danzig. "The Fuehrer and Supreme Commander of the Armed Forces has ordered the reunion of the German Free State of Danzig with the Greater German Reich. The armed forces must occupy Danzig Free State immediately in order to protect the German population."[24]

Germany's U-boats were alerted for the impending attack. On August 2, 1939, operational orders were issued for the submarines to be sent out to the Atlantic, by way of precaution, if the intention to carry out "Case White" remained unchanged.

On August 12 and 13, 1939, Hitler, for the first time, divulged to his Italian ally his intention to attack Poland and endeavored to persuade the Italians, through Ciano, to come into the war with him. Ciano was surprised at the speed with which Hitler proposed to begin the war, and stated that Italy was not yet prepared. At this conference Hitler discussed at considerable length the struggle with England and France which he knew would follow from an unpremeditated attack upon Poland: "At sea, England had for the moment no immediate reinforcements in prospect. Some time would elapse before any of the ships now under construction could be taken into service." Hitler sought to belittle England's troops and air strength:

If England kept the necessary troops in her own country she could send to France, at the most, two infantry divisions and one armored division. For the rest she could supply a few bomber squadrons, but hardly any fighters since, at the outbreak of war, the German Air Force would at once attack England and the English fighters would be urgently needed for the defense of their own country.

With regard to the position of France, the Fuehrer said that in the event of a general war, after the destruction of Poland—which would not take long—Germany would be in a position to assemble a hundred divisions along the West Wall and France would then be compelled to concentrate all her available forces from the colonies, from the Italian frontier and elsewhere, on her own Maginot Line, for the life and death struggle which would then ensue. The Fuehrer also thought that the French would find it no easier to overrun the Italian fortifications than to overrun the West Wall. Here Count Ciano showed signs of extreme doubt.

The Polish Army was most uneven in quality. Together with a few parade divisions, there were large numbers of troops of less value. Poland was very weak in anti-tank and anti-aircraft defense and at the moment neither France nor England could help her in this respect.

If, however, Poland were given assistance by the Western powers over a longer period, she could obtain these weapons, and German superiority would thereby be diminished. In contrast to the fanatics of Warsaw and Krakow, the population of their areas is indifferent. Furthermore, it was necessary to consider the position of the Polish State. Out of 34 million inhabitants, one and one-half million were German, about four million were Jews, and approximately nine million were Ukrainians, so that genuine Poles were much less in number than the total population and, as already said, their striking power was not to be valued highly. In these circumstances Poland could be struck to the ground by Germany in the shortest time.

Since the Poles, through their whole attitude, had made it clear that in any case, in the event of a conflict they would stand on the side of the enemies of Germany and Italy, a quick liquidation at the present moment could only be of advantage for the unavoidable conflict with the western democracies. If a hostile Poland remained on Germany's eastern frontier, not only would the 11 East Prussian divisions be tied down, but also further contingents would be kept in Pomerania and Silesia. This would not be necessary in the event of a previous liquidation. . . .

Coming back to the Danzig question, the Fuehrer said to Count Ciano that it was impossible for him to go back now. He had made an agreement with Italy for the withdrawal of the Germans from South Tyrol, but for this reason he must take the greatest care to avoid giving the impression that this Tyrolese withdrawal could be taken as a precedent for other areas. Furthermore, he had justified the withdrawal by pointing to a general easterly and northeasterly direction of German policy. The east and northeast, that is to say the Baltic countries, had been Germany's undisputed sphere of influence since time immemorial, as the Mediterranean had been the appropriate sphere for Italy. For economic reasons also, Germany needed the foodstuffs and timber from these eastern regions.

In the case of Danzig, German interests were not only material, although the city had the greatest harbor in the Baltic. . . . Danzig was a Nuremberg of the North, an ancient German city awaking sentimental feelings for every German, and the Fuehrer was bound to take account of this psychological element in public opinion. To make a comparison with Italy, Count Ciano should suppose that Trieste was in Yugoslav hands and that a large Italian minority was being treated brutally on Yugoslav soil. It would be difficult to assume that Italy would long remain quiet over anything of this kind.

Count Ciano, in replying to the Fuehrer's statement, first expressed the great surprise on the Italian side over the completely unexpected seriousness of the position. Neither in the conversations in Milan nor in those which took place during his Berlin visit had there been any sign, from the German side, that the position with regard to Poland was so serious. On the contrary, the Minister of Foreign Affairs had said that in his opinion the Danzig question would be settled in the course of time. On these grounds, the Duce, in view of his conviction that a conflict with the Western powers was unavoidable, had assumed that he should make his preparations for this event; he had made plans for a period of two or three years. If immediate conflict were unavoidable, the Duce, as he had told Ciano, would certainly stand on the German side, but for various reasons he would welcome the postponement of a general conflict until a later time. Ciano then showed, with the aid of a map, the position of Italy in the event of a general war. Italy believed that a conflict with Poland would not be limited to that country but would develop into a general European war. . . . For these reasons the Duce insisted that the Axis Powers should make a gesture which would reassure people of the peaceful intentions of Italy and Germany.[25]

And Hitler replied:

The Fuehrer answered that for a solution of the Polish problem no time should be lost; the longer one waited until the autumn, the more difficult would military operations in eastern Europe become. From the middle of September weather conditions made air operations hardly possible in these areas, while the condition of the roads, which were quickly turned into a morass by the autumn rains, would be such as to make them impossible for motorized forces. . . .[26]

Ciano asked how soon, according to the Fuehrer's view, the Danzig question must be settled. Hitler answered that a settlement must be made one way or another by the end of August. Hitler made clear to Ciano that he recognized Italy's proper sphere of expansion to be the Mediterranean area whereas Germany would have to expand to the East.

The Mediterranean was obviously the most ancient domain for which Italy had a claim to predominance. The Duce himself . . . had summed up the position to him in the words that Italy . . . was already the dominant power in the Mediterranean. On the other hand, the Fuehrer said that Germany must take the old German road eastwards and that this road was also desirable for economic reasons, and that Italy had geographical and historical claims to permanency in the Mediterranean. Bismarck had recognized it and had said as much in his well-known letter to Mazzini. The interests of Germany and Italy went in quite different directions and there never could be a conflict between them.[27]

Ribbentrop pointed out in the course of the conversation that settlement of differences with Poland would free Italy and Germany for action against the West, and Hitler said that Poland must be struck down so that "matters in the west could be settled."[28]

To Ciano's request for the date by which Poland must meet Germany's demands, Hitler's reply was recorded as follows:

The Fuehrer answered that the decision of Poland must be made clear at the latest by the end of August. Since, however, the decisive part of the military operations against Poland could be carried out within a period of 14 days, and the final liquidation would need another . . . four weeks, it could be finished at the end of September or the beginning of October. These could be regarded as the dates. It followed, therefore, that the last date on which he could begin to take action was the end of August.

Finally, the Fuehrer assured Ciano that since his youth he had favored German-Italian cooperation, and that no other view was expressed in his publications. He had always thought that Germany and Italy were naturally suited for collaboration, since there were no conflicts of interest between them. He was personally fortunate to live at a time in which, apart from himself, there was one other statesman who would stand out great and unique in history; that he could be this man's friend was for him a matter of great personal satisfaction, and if the hour of common battle struck, he would always be found on the side of the Duce.[29]

The Black Pact

The German-Soviet nonaggression pact of August 22, 1939, made World War II a certainty. Had Hitler been restrained at all it could only have been by a demonstration of unity and of superior might of other European nations. Hitler had always striven to separate his intended victims from their allies. He had succeeded in these efforts in the cases of Austria and Czechoslovakia. That had been his initial strategy in Poland. But the English agreement to stand by Poland made it clear that Hitler would have to fight in the West. He had now to isolate the West from the East. The conclusion of a nonaggression pact with the Soviet Union eliminated the last hindrance to Hitler's plan for war.

The understanding reached between Hitler and Stalin was more than an agreement of nonaggression. It constituted an affirmative military alliance, set out in a secret protocol which was not incorporated in the treaty itself. This secret protocol defined the respective spheres of interest of Germany and Russia in Europe, and provided for an agreed partition of Poland in case of any conflict involving that small land so unhappily situated between large and hungry neighbors.

Ribbentrop testified as follows concerning the execution of the Black Pact:

On the evening of 22 August I arrived in Moscow. The reception given me by Stalin and Molotov was very friendly. We had at first a two-hour conversation. During this conversation the entire complex of Russo-German relations was discussed. The result was, first, the mutual will of both countries to put their relations on a completely new basis. This was to be expressed in a pact of non-aggression. Secondly, the spheres of interests of the two countries were to be defined; this was done by a secret supplementary protocol. . . .

I talked very frankly during the negotiations with Stalin and Molotov, and the Russian gentlemen also used plain language with me. I described Hitler's desire that the two countries should reach a definite agreement, and, of course, I also spoke of the critical situation in Europe. I told the Russian gentlemen that Germany would do everything to settle the situation in Poland and to settle the difficulties peacefully in order to reach a friendly agreement despite everything. However, I left no doubt that the situation was serious and that it was possible that an armed conflict might break out. That was clear anyway. For both statesmen, Stalin as well as Hitler, it was a question of territories which both countries had lost after an unfortunate war. It is, therefore, wrong to look at these things from any other point of view. And just as Adolf Hitler was of the opinion which I expressed in Moscow, that in some form or other this problem would have to be solved, so also the Russian side saw clearly that this was the case.

We then discussed what should be done on the part of the Germans and on the part of the Russians in the case of an armed conflict. A line of demarcation was agreed upon, as is known, in order that in the event of intolerable Polish provocation, or in the event of war, there should be a boundary, so that the German and Russian interests in the Polish theater could and would not collide. The well known line was agreed upon along the line of the Rivers Vistula, San, and Bug in Polish territory. And it was agreed that in the case of conflict the territories lying to the west of these rivers would be the German sphere of interest, and those to the east would be the Russian sphere of interest. . . .

Over and above that, it is also known that other spheres of interest were defined with reference to Finland, the Baltic States, and Bessarabia. This was a great settlement of the interests of two great powers providing for a peaceful solution as well as for solution by war.[30]

On the very day the announcement was made of the pact, Hitler called his top military commanders to Obersalzberg, where he gave them their final briefing for the impending clash. In the course of two speeches delivered that day Hitler made the following remarks:

It was clear to me that a conflict with Poland had to come sooner or later. I had already made this decision in the spring. But I thought that I would first turn against the West in a few years, and only afterwards against the East. But the sequence cannot be fixed. . . . For us it is easy to make decisions. We have nothing to lose—we can only gain. . . .

All these fortunate circumstances will no longer prevail in two or three years. No one knows how long I shall live. Therefore, better the conflict now.

The creation of Greater Germany was a great achievement politically, but militarily it was questionable, since it was achieved through a bluff of the political leaders. It is necessary to test the military, if at all possible, not by general settlement, but by solving individual tasks.[31]

Hitler spoke about the support which England and France could give to Poland, and dismissed it as entirely insufficient. "Actually England cannot help Poland," he said.

He discussed the pact with the Soviet Union:

Four days ago, I took a special step, which brought about Russia's answer yesterday that she is ready to sign. Personal contact with Stalin has been established. The day after tomorrow Von Ribbentrop will conclude the treaty. Now Poland is in the position in which I wanted her. . . . Today's publication of the non-aggression pact with Russia hit like a shell. The consequences cannot be over-emphasized. Stalin also said that this course will be of benefit to both countries. The effect on Poland will be tremendous.[32]

In a second speech that afternoon, Hitler made the following statements:

Everybody shall have to make a point of it that we were determined from the beginning to fight the western powers. . . .
Destruction of Poland is in the foreground. The aim is elimination of living forces, not the arrival at a certain line. Even if war should break out in the West, the destruction of Poland shall be the primary objective. . . .
I shall give a propagandistic cause for starting the war,—never mind whether it be plausible or not. The victor shall not be asked later on whether we told the truth or not. In starting and making a war, not the right is what matters but victory.[33]

On that fateful day Prime Minister Chamberlain transmitted a message to Hitler which provided in part:

Your Excellency will have already heard of certain measures taken by His Majesty's Government, and announced in the press and on the wireless this evening.
These steps have, in the opinion of His Majesty's Government, been rendered necessary by the military movements which have been reported from Germany, and by the fact that apparently the announcement of a German-Soviet agreement is taken in some quarters in Berlin to indicate that intervention by Great Britain on behalf of Poland is no longer a contingency that need be reckoned with. No greater mistake could be made. Whatever may prove to be the nature of the German-Soviet agreement, it cannot alter Great Britain's obligation to Poland, which His Majesty's Government have stated in public repeatedly and plainly and which they are determined to fulfill.[34]

On the following day, August 23, 1939, Hitler replied to the British note. He began by asserting that Germany had always sought England's friendship; but, he said,

the unconditional assurance given by England to Poland that she would render assistance to that country in all circumstances regardless of the causes from which a conflict might spring, could only be interpreted in that country as an encouragement thenceforward to unloosen, under cover of such a charter, a wave of appalling terrorism against the one and a half million German inhabitants living in Poland.[35]

Hitler complained that the resulting atrocities were intolerable, and he accused Poland of numerous breaches of legal obligations toward Danzig, of issuing ultimata, and of instituting a process of economic strangulation. He insisted that the questions of the Corridor and of Danzig must be solved. The fact that the British Government had given assurances of assistance to Poland in the event of intervention on the part of Germany would make no change in the determination of the Reich Government to safeguard its interests. "I have already more than once declared before the German people and the world that there can be no doubt concerning the determination of the new German Reich rather to accept, for however long it might be, every sort of misery and tribulation than to sacrifice its national interests, let alone its honor."[36]

Hitler then accused the British Government of threatening hostile actions against Germany:

The German Reich Government has received information to the effect that the British Government has the intention to carry out measures of mobilization which, according to the statements contained in your own letter, are clearly directed against Germany alone. This is said to be true of France as well. Since Germany has never had the intention of taking military measures other than those of a defensive character against England or France and, as has already been emphasized, has never intended, and does not in the future intend, to attack England or France, it follows that this announcement as confirmed by you, Mr. Prime Minister, in your own letter, can only refer to a contemplated act of menace directed against the Reich. I, therefore, inform your Excellency that in the event of these military announcements being carried into effect, I shall order immediate mobilization of German forces. . . .

The question of the treatment of European problems on a peaceful basis is not a decision which rests on Germany, but primarily on those who, since the crime committed by the Versailles *Diktat,* have stubbornly and consistently opposed any peaceful revision. Only after a change of spirit on the part of the responsible powers can there be any real change in the relationship between England and Germany. I have all my life fought for Anglo-German friendship. The attitude adopted by British diplomacy—at any rate up to the present—has, however, convinced me of the futility of such an attempt. Should there be any change in this respect in the future, nobody could be happier than I.[37]

Pleas for Peace

On August 24, 1939, President Roosevelt wrote to Hitler in part:

To the message which I sent you last April I have received no reply, but because my confident belief that the cause of world peace— which is the cause of humanity itself—rises above all other considerations, I am again addressing myself to you, with the hope that the war which impends, and the consequent disaster to all people, may yet be averted.

I therefore urge with all earnestness—and I am likewise urging the President of the Republic of Poland—that the Governments of Germany and Poland agree by common accord to refrain from any positive act of hostility for a reasonable, stipulated period; and that they agree, likewise by common accord, to solve the controversies which have arisen between them by one of the three following methods:

First, by direct negotiation; second, by the submission of these controversies to an impartial arbitration in which they can both have confidence; third, that they agree to the solution of these controversies through the procedure of conciliation.[38]

On August 25, no reply having been forthcoming from the German Government, President Roosevelt wrote to Hitler again:

I have this hour received from the President of Poland a reply to the message which I addressed to your Excellency and to him last night....

Your Excellency has repeatedly publicly stated that the aims and objects sought by the German Reich were just and reasonable.

In his reply to my message the President of Poland has made it plain that the Polish Government are willing, upon the basis set forth in my message, to agree to solve the controversy which has arisen between the Republic of Poland and the German Reich by direct negotiation or the process of conciliation.

Countless human lives can yet be saved, and hope may still be restored that the nations of the modern world may even now construct the foundation for a peaceful and happier relationship, if you and the Government of the German Reich will agree to the pacific means of settlement accepted by the Government of Poland. All the world prays that Germany, too, will accept.[39]

On August 25, 1939, the Anglo-Polish agreement of mutual assistance was formally signed in London. On the following day Prime Minister Daladier of France addressed an eloquent plea for peace to Hitler:

In the hours in which you speak of the greatest responsibility which two heads of the Governments can possibly take upon themselves, namely, that of shedding the blood of two great nations who long only for peace and work, I feel I owe it to you, personally, and to both our peoples, to say that the fate of peace still rests in your hands alone.

You cannot doubt but what are my own feelings toward Germany, nor France's peaceful feelings toward your nation. No Frenchman has done more than myself to strengthen between our two nations not only peace but also sincere co-operation in their own interests as well as in those of Europe and of the whole world. Unless you credit the French people with a lower sense of honor than I credit to the German nation, you cannot doubt that France loyally fulfills her obligations toward other powers, such as Poland, which, as I am fully convinced, wants to live in peace with Germany.

These two convictions are fully compatible.

Till now there has been nothing to prevent a peaceful solution of the international crisis with all honor and dignity for all nations, if the same will for peace exists on all sides.

Together with the good will of France I proclaim that of all her allies. I take it upon myself to guarantee Poland's readiness, which she has always shown, to submit to the mutual application of a method of open settlement as it can be imagined between the governments of two sovereign nations. With the clearest conscience I can assure you that, among the differences which have arisen between Germany and Poland over the question of Danzig, there is not one which could not be submitted to such a method with a purpose of reaching a peaceful and just solution.

Moreover, I can declare on my honor that there is nothing in France's clear and loyal solidarity with Poland and her allies, which could in any way prejudice the peaceful attitude of my country. This solidarity has never prevented us, and does not prevent us today, from keeping Poland in the same friendly state of mind.

In so serious an hour I sincerely believe that no high minded human being could understand it if a war of destruction were started without a last attempt being made to reach a peaceful settlement between Germany and Poland. Your desire for peace could, in all certainty, work for this aim without any prejudice to German honor. I, who desire good harmony between the French and the German people, and who am, on the other hand, bound to Poland by bonds of friendship and by a promise, am prepared, as head of the French Government, to do everything an upright man can do to bring this attempt to a successful conclusion.

You and I were in the trenches in the last war. You know, as I do, what horror and condemnation the devastations of that war have left in the conscience of the people without any regard to its outcome. The picture I can see in my mind's eye of your outstanding role as the leader of the German people on the road of peace, toward the fulfillment of its task in the common work of civilization, leads me to ask for a reply to this suggestion.

If French and German blood should be shed again as it was shed 25 years ago in a still longer and more murderous war, then each of the two nations will fight, believing in its own victory. But the most certain victors will be destruction and barbarity.[40]

Final Negotiations

In the course of his interrogation, Goering was asked whether it was not a fact that the start of the campaign against Poland was ordered for August 25 but was postponed until September 1 to await the results of diplomatic maneuvers with the British, and he answered, "Yes."[41]

On August 25, 1939, Hitler issued a verbal communiqué to Sir Neville Henderson in which he played the first card in this five-day game of strategy the object of which was "to isolate Poland" by "skillful politics," as he had said to his military advisors at the meeting in May. He began by saying that he was anxious to make one more effort to avert war, but that Poland's provocations had become unbearable. "Germany was in all circumstances determined to abolish these Macedonian conditions on her eastern frontier and, what is more, to do so in the interest of quiet and order, and also in the interest of European peace."[42] With finality he declared, "The problem of Danzig and the Corridor must be solved."[43]

Hitler then threatened England, emphasizing the freedom of action and the additional strength which Germany had gained through the pact with the Soviet Union:

The British Prime Minister has made a speech which was not in the least calculated to induce any change in the German attitude. At the most, the result of this speech could be a bloody and incalculable war between Germany and England. Such a war would be bloodier than that of 1914 to 1918. In contrast to the last war, Germany would no longer have to fight on two fronts. Agreement with Russia was unconditional and signified a change in foreign policy of the Reich which would last a very long time. Russia and Germany would never again take up arms against each other. Apart from this, the agreements reached with Russia would also render Germany secure economically for the longest possible period of war.[44]

Hitler apparently even thought that England could be bribed.

The Fuehrer declared the German-Polish problem must be solved and will be solved. He is, however, prepared and determined, after the solution of this problem, to approach England once more with a large, comprehensive offer. He is a man of great decisions; and in this case also, he will be capable of being great in his action. He accepts the British Empire and is ready to pledge himself personally for its continued existence and to place the power of the German Reich at its disposal on condition that his colonial demands, which are limited, should be negotiated by peaceful means.[45]

After again expressing the irrevocable determination of Germany never again to enter into conflict with Russia, he concluded: "If the British Government would consider these ideas, a blessing for Germany and also for the British Empire might result. If they reject these ideas, there will be war. In no case will Great Britain emerge stronger; the last war proved it."[46]

On August 28, 1939, the British Government replied to the *note verbale*, stating that it was prepared to enter into discussions. This reply declared in part:

His Majesty's Government have said enough to make their own attitude plain in the particular matters at issue between Germany and Poland. They trust that the German Chancellor will not think that, because His Majesty's Government are scrupulous concerning their obligations to Poland, they are not anxious to use all their influence to assist the achievement of a solution which may commend itself both to Germany and to Poland.[47]

Hitler's answer to this offer of the British Government to enter into discussions was handed to Sir Neville Henderson at 7:15 P.M. on August 29, 1939. In this document, for the first time, Hitler enlarged his demands to include the whole Corridor, rather than the highway which he had previously been seeking, and stated that the German Government was prepared to enter into the proposed discussions only on the basis that the Corridor as well as Danzig be returned to the Reich. The document said in part:

The demands of the German Government are in conformity with the revision of the Versailles Treaty which has always been recognized as being necessary in regard to this territory; namely, return of Danzig and the Corridor to Germany, the safeguarding of the existence of the German national group in the territories remaining to Poland....

Though sceptical as to the prospects of a successful outcome, they are nevertheless prepared to accept the English proposal and to enter into direct discussions. They do so, as has already been emphasized, solely as the result of the impression made upon them by the written statement received from the British Government that they, too, desire a pact of friendship in accordance with the general lines indicated to the British ambassador....

For the rest, in making these proposals, the German Government have never had any intention of touching Poland's vital interests or questioning the existence of an independent Polish State.

The German Government, accordingly, in these circumstances agree to accept the British Government's offer of their good offices in securing the despatch to Berlin of a Polish emissary with full powers. They count on the arrival of this emissary on Wednesday, the 30th August 1939.

The German Government will immediately draw up proposals for a solution acceptable to themselves and will, if possible, place these at the disposal of the British Government before the arrival of the Polish negotiator.[48]

At midnight on August 30 Sir Neville Henderson handed
to Ribbentrop the British reply, in which it was stated that the
British Government made a reservation to the demands that the
German Government put forward in the last letter; that the British
Government was informing the Polish Government of the contents
of the note immediately; and that the British Government understood that the German Government was drawing up definite proposals. Sir Neville Henderson reported his conversation with
Ribbentrop that night in part as follows:

I told Herr von Ribbentrop this evening that His Majesty's Government found it difficult to advise the Polish Government to accept
the procedure adumbrated in the German reply and suggested that he
should adopt normal contact, i.e., that when German proposals were
ready, to invite the Polish ambassador to call and to hand him proposals for transmission to his Government with a view to immediate
opening of negotiations. I added that if this basis afforded prospect
of settlement, His Majesty's Government could be counted upon to do
their best in Warsaw to temporize negotiations.

Ribbentrop's reply was to produce a lengthy document which he
read out in German, aloud, at top speed. Imagining that he would
eventually hand it to me, I did not attempt to follow too closely the
sixteen or more articles which it contained. . . .

When I asked Ribbentrop for the text of these proposals in accordance with the understanding in the German reply of yesterday, he
asserted that it was now too late as the Polish representative had not
arrived in Berlin by midnight.

I observed that to treat the matter in this way meant that the
request for the Polish representative to arrive in Berlin on the 30th
of August constituted in fact an ultimatum, in spite of what he and
Herr Hitler had assured me yesterday. This he denied, saying that the
idea of an ultimatum was a figment of my imagination. Why then, I
asked, could he not adopt normal procedure and give me a copy of the
proposals, and ask the Polish ambassador to call on him, just as Hitler
had summoned me a few days ago, and hand them to him for communication to the Polish Government? In the most violent terms Ribbentrop said that he would never ask the ambassador to visit him. He
hinted that if the Polish ambassador asked him for an interview it
might be different. I said that I would, naturally, inform my Government so at once. Whereupon he said, while those were his personal
views, he would bring all that I had said to Hitler's notice. It was for
the Chancellor to decide.

We parted on that note, but I must tell you that Von Ribbentrop's demeanor during an unpleasant interview was aping Herr Hitler at his worst. He inveighed incidentally against Polish mobilization, but I retorted that it was hardly surprising since Germany had also mobilized as Herr Hitler himself had admitted to me yesterday.[49]

On the following day, August 31, at 6:30 in the evening, the Polish ambassador, Lipski, conferred with Ribbentrop, and reported his conversation as follows:

I carried out my instructions. Ribbentrop asked if I had special plenipotentiary powers to undertake negotiations. I said, "No." He then asked whether I had been informed that on London's suggestion the German Government had expressed their readiness to negotiate directly with a delegate of the Polish Government, furnished with the requisite full powers, who was to have arrived on the preceding day, the 30th of August. I replied that I had no direct information on the subject. In conclusion, Ribbentrop repeated that he had thought I would be empowered to negotiate. He would communicate my *démarche* to the Chancellor.[50]

But by that hour Hitler had already completed the final orders for war. His top secret order of August 31, 1939, called Directive No. 1 for the Conduct of the War, provided in part:

(1) Now that all the political possibilities of disposing by peaceful means of a situation on the eastern frontier, which is intolerable for Germany, are exhausted, I have determined on a solution by force.

(2) The attack on Poland is to be carried out in accordance with the preparations made for Case White with the alterations which result, where the Army is concerned, from the fact that it has in the meantime almost completed its dispositions.

Allotment of tasks and the operational target remain unchanged.

The date of attack: 1st of September 1939; time of attack: 4:45 [insert in red pencil]—this time also applies to the operation at Gdynia, Bay of Danzig and the Dirschau Bridge.

(3) In the West it is important that the responsibility for the opening of hostilities should rest unequivocally with England and France. At first, purely local action should be taken against insignificant frontier violations.[51]

At nine o'clock in the evening of that day the German proposals, of which a written copy had not up to that hour been furnished the Polish Government or the British Government, or their accredited representatives, were broadcast to the German people. The broadcast stated that instead of sending an envoy with special plenipotentiary powers, as requested by the German Government, the Polish Government had ordered mobilization.

While these "negotiations" were being carried on through normal diplomatic channels, Goering was conducting private negotiations with the British through a sincere and peace-minded Swedish businessman by the name of Dahlerus. Dahlerus testified at length concerning the negotiations carried on by Goering through him as intermediary. When he finished his testimony he was asked on cross-examination: "Did you say 'I then realized . . . that his,'— that is, Goering's—'aim had been to split Poland and Great Britain and to occupy Poland with the consent of Great Britain'? Is that right?" And Dahlerus answered: "Yes, it is correct, but I should like to say it was the German Government including Goering."[52]

The "skilful politician" had failed to "isolate Poland." He was left with no alternative but to attack Poland and to fight England and France as well. Still he had no excuse for war. The Poles were not threatening Germany with military force; it was Germany who was rattling the saber. Lacking an excuse, Hitler proceeded to fabricate one.

Framing the Excuse

Early in August, 1939, a plan had been conceived for this purpose by the Chief of the Security Police and SD, Heydrich, to stage simulated border raids by personnel of the Gestapo and SD dressed as Poles. To add authenticity, it was planned to take certain prisoners from concentration camps, kill them by use of hypodermic injections, and leave their bodies, clad in Polish uniforms, at the various places where the incidents supposedly were to occur. On August 31 these "border incidents" were staged at Beuthen, Hindenburg, Gleiwitz, and elsewhere.

Alfred Naujocks, the leader of the Gleiwitz incident, described that action:

On or about 10 August 1939, the chief of the Sipo and SD, Heydrich, personally ordered me to simulate an attack on the radio station near Gleiwitz, near the Polish border, and to make it appear that the attacking force consisted of Poles. Heydrich said, "Actual proof of these attacks of the Poles is needed for the foreign press as well as for German propaganda purposes." I was directed to go to Gleiwitz with five or six SD-men and wait there until I received a code word from Heydrich indicating that the attack should take place. My instructions were to seize the radio station and to hold it long enough to permit a Polish-speaking German, who would be put at my disposal, to broadcast a speech in Polish. Heydrich told me that this speech should state that the time had come for the conflict between the Germans and the Poles and that Poles should get together and strike down any Germans from whom they met resistance. Heydrich also told me at this time that he expected an attack on Poland by Germany in a few days.

I went to Gleiwitz and waited there a fortnight. Then I requested permission of Heydrich to return to Berlin but was told to stay in Gleiwitz. Between the 25th and 31st of August I went to see Heinrich Mueller, head of the Gestapo, who was then nearby at Oppeln. In my presence, Mueller discussed with a man named Mehlhorn plans for another border incident, in which it should be made to appear that Polish soldiers were attacking German troops.... Germans in the approximate strength of a company were to be used. Mueller stated that he had 12 or 13 condemned criminals who were to be dressed in Polish uniforms and left dead on the ground at the scene of the incident to show that they had been killed while attacking. For this purpose they were to be given fatal injections by a doctor employed by Heydrich. Then they were also to be given gunshot wounds. After the assault, members of the press and other persons were to be taken to the spot of the incident. A police report was subsequently to be prepared.

Mueller told me that he had an order from Heydrich to make one of those criminals available to me for the action at Gleiwitz. The code name by which he referred to these criminals was "Canned Goods."

The incident at Gleiwitz in which I participated was carried out on the evening preceding the German attack on Poland. As I recall, war broke out on the 1st of September 1939. At noon on the 31st of August I received by telephone from Heydrich the code word for the attack which was to take place at 8 o'clock that evening. Heydrich said, "In order to carry out this attack, report to Mueller for 'Canned Goods.'" I did this and gave Mueller instructions to deliver the man near the radio station. I received this man and had him laid down at the entrance to the station. He was alive but he was completely unconscious. I tried to open his eyes. I could not recognize by his eyes that he was alive, only by his breathing. I did not see the shot wounds but a lot of blood was smeared across his face. He was in civilian clothes.

We seized the radio station as ordered, broadcast a speech of three to four minutes over an emergency transmitter, fired some pistol shots, and left.[53]

The Attack

Having created an "excuse" for invading Poland, and with full knowledge that such invasion would bring the horror and bloodshed of war to the world, Hitler gave his troops the signal to march. On September 1, 1939, while his soldiers moved across the Polish frontier and his aircraft bombed Polish towns and cities, Hitler issued to the people of Germany a proclamation conceived in mendacity and uttered in hypocrisy:

The Polish Government, unwilling to establish good neighborly relations as aimed at by me, want to force the issue by war of arms.

The Germans in Poland are being persecuted by bloody terror and driven from their homes. Several acts of frontier violation, which cannot be tolerated by a great power, show that Poland is no longer prepared to respect the Reich's frontiers. To put an end to these mad acts, I can see no other way but from now onwards to meet force with force.

The German armed forces will with firm determination take up the struggle for the honor and the vital rights of the resuscitated German people.

I expect every soldier to be conscious of the high tradition of the eternal German soldierly qualities and to do his duty to the last.

Remember always and in any circumstance that you are the representatives of National Socialist Greater Germany.

Long live our people and the Reich.[54]

Hitler had no reason to expect, or even to hope, that under these circumstances England and France would fail to stand by their commitments to Poland. Yet Britain gave him two further chances to avert a world cataclysm. On September 1 the British ambassador submitted a communication to the German Government, the last paragraph of which stated:

I am accordingly to inform your Excellency that unless the German Government are prepared to give His Majesty's Government satisfactory assurances that the German Government have suspended all aggressive action against Poland and are prepared promptly to withdraw their forces from Polish territory, His Majesty's Government in the United Kingdom will without hesitation fulfill their obligations to Poland.[55]

No reply having been received to this communication, at nine o'clock on the morning of September 3, 1939, a final ultimatum was handed to the German Foreign Minister:

Although this communication was made more than 24 hours ago, no reply has been received but German attacks upon Poland have continued and intensified. I have accordingly the honor to inform you that, unless not later than 11 o'clock, British summer time today the 3rd of September, satisfactory assurances to the above effect have been given by the German Government and have reached His Majesty's Government in London, a state of war will exist between the two countries as from that hour.[56]

Even Mussolini sought to intervene and terminate the bloody struggle which had begun. But Hitler was adamant to ally and enemy alike. His reply, addressed simply "Duce," stated in part:

I have not given in to the English because, Duce, I do not believe that peace could have been maintained for more than one-half year or a year. Under these circumstances I thought that, in spite of everything, the present moment was better for resistance. At present the superiority of the German armed forces in Poland is so overwhelming in all fields that the Polish Army will collapse in a very short time. I doubt whether this fast success could have been achieved in one or two years. England and France would have armed their allies to such an extent that the crushing technical superiority of the German armed forces could not have become so apparent anymore. I am aware, Duce, that the fight which I enter is one for life and death. My own fate does not play any role in it at all. But I am also aware that one cannot avoid such a struggle permanently and that one has to choose, after cold deliberation, the moment for resistance in such a way that the probability of success is guaranteed; and I believe in this success, Duce, with the firmness of a rock.[57]

Hitler acted in "cold deliberation" and with utter disregard for humanity. He had been determined to wage war at some time, and he sought in waging war at this time to take advantage of the "crushing technical superiority of the German armed forces." He said his own fate was not a factor but that he believed in his success "with the firmness of a rock." Less than six years later, the rock of his success had crumbled into rubble, and his fate was ignominious death by suicide. These six years were to witness the greatest struggle of armed forces in history. Poland was only the beginning.

CHAPTER 9

The Weser Exercise

WESER EXERCISE was the code name for the attack upon Denmark and Norway. As in the cases of Austria, Czechoslovakia, and Poland, these invasions were founded in deceit and in deliberate disregard of solemn covenants.

On June 2, 1926, Germany had entered into a Treaty of Arbitration and Conciliation with Denmark which provided in the first article:

> The contracting parties undertake to submit to the procedure of arbitration or conciliation, in conformity with the present treaty, all disputes of any nature whatsoever which may arise between Germany and Denmark, and which it has not been possible to settle within a reasonable period by diplomacy or to bring with the consent of both parties before the Permanent Court of International Justice.[1]

On April 28, 1939, Hitler stated in the course of a speech:

> I have given binding declarations to a large number of states. None of these states can complain that even a trace of a demand contrary thereto has ever been made to them by Germany. None of the Scandinavian statesmen, for example, can contend that a request has ever been put to them by the German Government or by German public opinion which was incompatible with the sovereignty and integrity of their States.[2]

On May 31, 1939, Germany entered into a ten-year treaty of nonaggression with Denmark, which provided that: "The German Reich and the Kingdom of Denmark shall in no case resort to war or to any other use of force, one against the other."[3]

The day after the invasion of Poland, September 2, 1939, the German Minister to Norway handed the Norwegian Foreign Minister an *aide memoire* which provided in part: "The German Reich Government are determined, in view of the friendly relations which exist between Norway and Germany, under no circumstances to prejudice the inviolability and integrity of Norway, and to respect the territory of the Norwegian State."[4]

And in the course of a speech delivered by Hitler on October 6, 1939, he said: "Germany has never had any conflicts of interest or even points of controversy with the Northern States; neither has she any today. Sweden and Norway have both been offered non-aggression pacts by Germany and have both refused them solely because they did not feel themselves threatened in any way."[5]

Planning the Attack in the North

But on October 3, 1939, plans for the invasion of Norway had already been taken under advisement. An entry in the War Diary of that date disclosed:

The Chief of the Naval Operations Staff considers it necessary that the Fuehrer be informed as soon as possible of the opinions of the Naval Operations Staff on the possibilities of extending the operational base to the North. It must be ascertained whether it is possible to gain bases in Norway under the combined pressure of Russia and Germany, with the basic aim of improving our strategic and operational position. The following questions must be given consideration:

(a) What places in Norway can be considered as bases?

(b) Can bases be gained by military force against Norway's will, if it is impossible to carry this out without fighting?

(c) What are the possibilities of defense after occupation?

(d) Will the harbors have to be developed completely as bases or have they already decisive advantages suitable for supply position? (The Commander of the U-Boat Fleet considers such harbors already extremely useful as equipment and supply bases at which Atlantic U-Boats can call temporarily.)

(e) What decisive advantages would exist for the conduct of the war at sea in gaining bases in North Denmark, e.g. Skagen?[6]

On October 10 Raeder submitted proposals to Hitler for the

invasion of Norway. In a confidential memorandum to Admiral Assmann, written in January, 1944, Raeder recounted these early developments:

> During the weeks preceding the report on the 10th of October 1939, I was in correspondence with Admiral Carls, who, in a detailed letter to me, first pointed out the importance of an occupation of the Norwegian coast to Germany. I... prepared some notes based on this letter... for my report to the Fuehrer, which I made on the 10th of October 1939, since my opinion was identical with that of Admiral Carls.... In these notes I stressed the disadvantages which an occupation of Norway by the British would have for us: control of the approaches of the Baltic, outflanking of our naval operations and of our air attacks on Britain, pressure on Sweden. I also stressed the advantages for us of the occupation of the Norwegian coast: outlet to the North Atlantic, no possibility of a British mine barrier as in the years 1917-18. Naturally, at the time, only the coast and bases were considered; I included Narvik, though Admiral Carls, in the course of our correspondence, thought that Narvik could be excluded.... The Fuehrer saw at once the significance of the Norwegian problem; he asked me to leave the notes and stated that he wished to consider the question himself.[7]

Quisling

In the meantime, the Nazis were negotiating with the Norwegian traitor, Vidkun Quisling. In reporting upon political preparations for the military occupation of Norway during the years 1939-40, Rosenberg's Foreign Affairs Bureau of the Nazi Party disclosed:

> As previously mentioned, of all political groupings in Scandinavia only Nasjonal Samling, led in Norway by the Former Minister of War and retired major, Vidkun Quisling, deserved serious political attention. This was a fighting political group possessed by the idea of a Greater Germanic Community. Naturally all ruling powers were hostile and attempted to prevent by any means its success among the population. The bureau maintained constant relations with Quisling and attentively observed the attacks he conducted with tenacious energy on the middle class, which had been taken in tow by the English. From the beginning, it appeared probable that without revolutionary events

which would stir the population from their former attitude no successful progress of Nasjonal Samling was to be expected. During the winter 1938-1939 Quisling was privately visited by a member of the bureau. When the political situation in Europe came to a head in 1939,
Quisling made an appearance at the convention of the Nordic Society
in Luebeck in June. He expounded his conception of the situation and
his apprehensions concerning Norway. He emphatically drew attention to the geopolitically decisive importance of Norway in the Scandinavian area and to the advantages that would accrue to the power
dominating the Norwegian coast in case of a conflict between the
Greater German Reich and Great Britain.

Assuming that his statement would be of special interest to the
Marshal of the Reich, Goering, for aero-strategical reasons, Quisling
was referred to State Secretary Koerner by the bureau. The Staff Director of the bureau handed the Chief of the Reich Chancellory a memorandum for transmission to the Fuehrer.... [8]

In his memorandum to Admiral Assmann, Raeder had written:

In the further developments, I was supported by Commander
Schreiber, Naval Attache in Oslo and the M-Chief personally—in conjunction with the Rosenberg Organization. Thus we got in touch with
Quisling and Hagelin, who came to Berlin at the beginning of December and were taken to the Fuehrer by me—with the approval of Reichsleiter Rosenberg. [9]

A report from Rosenberg to Raeder on the activities of Quisling
at this time disclosed:

A plan has been put forward which deals with the possibility of
a coup, and which provides for a number of selected Norwegians to
be trained in Germany with all possible speed for such a purpose,
being allotted their exact tasks and provided with experienced and die-
hard National Socialists who are practiced in such operations. These
trained men should then proceed with all speed to Norway where details would then have to be further discussed. Some important centers
in Oslo would have to be taken over forthwith, and at the same time
the German Fleet together with suitable contingents of the German
Army would go into operation when summoned specially by the new
Norwegian Government in a specified bay at the approaches to Oslo.
Quisling has no doubts that such a coup, having been carried out with
instantaneous success, would immediately bring him the approval of
those sections of the army with which he at present has connections,

and thus it goes without saying that he has never discussed a political fight with them. As far as the King is concerned, he believes that he would respect it as an accomplished fact.

Quisling gives figures of the number of German troops required which accord with German calculations.[10]

On December 12, 1939, Hitler met with Raeder, Keitel, Jodl, and others on the "Norwegian Question." The report began: "Commander-in-Chief Navy has received Quisling and Hagelin. Quisling creates the impression of being reliable."[11] It continued:

The Fuehrer thought of speaking to Quisling personally so that he might form an impression of him. He wanted to see Rosenberg once more beforehand, as the latter has known Quisling for a long while. Commander-in-Chief Navy suggests that if the Fuehrer forms a favorable impression, the OKW should obtain permission to make plans with Quisling for the preparation and carrying out of the occupation: (a) By peaceful means—that is to say, German forces summoned by Norway, or (b) to agree to do so by force.[12]

Two days later Hitler met Quisling, and soon thereafter he issued orders for preparation of the Norwegian campaign. Raeder's memorandum to Assmann continued: "On the grounds of the Fuehrer's discussion with Quisling and Hagelin on the afternoon of the 14th of December 1939, the Fuehrer gave the order that the preparations for the Norwegian operation were to be made by the Supreme Command of the Armed Forces."[13]

Final Preparations

On January 27, 1940, Keitel issued a top secret memorandum on "Study 'N'." The memorandum recited in part:

The Fuehrer and Supreme Commander of the Armed Forces wishes that Study "N" should be further worked on under my direct and personal guidance, and in the closest conjunction with the general war policy. For these reasons the Fuehrer has commissioned me to take over the direction of further preparations.

A working staff has been formed at the Supreme Command of the Armed Forces Headquarters for this purpose, and this represents at the same time the nucleus of a future operational staff....

All further plans will be made under the cover name Weser Exercise.[14]

Jodl made the following entry in his diary on February 28, 1940: "I propose first to the Chief of OKW and then to the Fuehrer that Case Yellow [invasion of the Lowlands] and Weser Exercise must be prepared in such a way that they will be independent of one another as regards both time and forces employed. The Fuehrer completely agrees, if this is in any way possible."[15]

On March 1, 1940, Hitler issued a top secret directive for the Weser Exercise in which it was disclosed clearly that the purpose of the operation was not merely to forestall possible British intervention but rather to provide additional bases for later German military actions:

The development of the situation in Scandinavia requires the making of all preparations for the occupation of Denmark and Norway by a part of the German armed forces—Weser Exercise. This operation should prevent British encroachment on Scandinavia and the Baltic; further, it should guarantee our ore base in Sweden and give our Navy and Air Force a wider starting line against Britain.

In view of our military and political power in comparison with that of the Scandinavian states, the force to be employed in the Weser Exercise will be kept as small as possible. The numerical weakness will be balanced by daring actions and surprise execution. On principle we will do our utmost to make the operation appear as a peaceful occupation, the object of which is the military protection of the neutrality of the Scandinavian states. Corresponding demands will be transmitted to the Governments at the beginning of the occupation. If necessary, demonstrations by the Navy and Air Force will provide the necessary emphasis. If, in spite of this, resistance should be met with, all military means will be used to crush it.

I put in charge of the preparations and the conduct of the operation against Denmark and Norway the Commanding General of the 21st Army Corps, General von Falkenhorst.

The crossing of the Danish border and the landings in Norway must take place simultaneously. I emphasize that the operations must be prepared as quickly as possible. In case the enemy seizes the initiative against Norway, we must be able to apply immediately our own counter measures.

It is most important that the Scandinavian states as well as the western opponents should be taken by surprise by our measures. All preparations, particularly those of transport and of readiness, drafting, and embarkation of the troops, must be made with this factor in mind.

In case the preparations for embarkation can no longer be kept secret, the leaders and the troops will be deceived with fictitious objectives.[16]

The directive outlined the tasks of the special groups which were to carry out the invasions. The occupation of Denmark was to be called Weser Exercise South, and the occupation of Norway, Weser Exercise North. A principal objective in the plans was shown by the following order to the Luftwaffe: "The Air Force, after the occupation has been completed, will ensure air defense and will make use of Norwegian bases for air warfare against Britain."[17]

The only sour note in the German battle song for the Scandinavian invasion was the result of the overlooking of the chief of the Luftwaffe, Hermann Goering, in formulating the plans. On March 5, 1940, Jodl entered in his diary: "Big conference with the three commanders-in-chief about Weser Exercise; Field Marshal in a rage because not consulted till now. Won't listen to anyone and wants to show that all preparations so far made are worthless."[18]

The plans for invasion of these countries, whose neutrality had been guaranteed by Germany, nevertheless went forward. And, as they proceeded to finality, Hitler once again sought an incident which might afford outward justification for the action. A March 14 entry in Jodl's diary stated: "Fuehrer does not give order yet for 'W'. He is still looking for justification."[19] And on the next day Jodl wrote: "Fuehrer has not yet decided what reason to give for Weser Exercise."[20]

On April 2, 1940, Jodl entered in his diary: "Commander-in-Chief of the Air Force, Commander-in-Chief of the Navy, and General von Falkenhorst with the Fuehrer. All confirm preparations completed. Fuehrer orders carrying out of the Weser Exercise for April 9th."[21] Two days later Jodl made a further entry showing that Quisling was a prominent factor to the last moment in bringing about the military subjugation of his native land: "Fuehrer drafts the proclamations. Pieckenbrock, Chief of Military Intelligence I, returns with good results from the talks with Quisling in Copenhagen."[22]

In accordance with the objectives thus decided upon, Doenitz issued a top secret operational order:

The day and hour are designated as Weser-Day and Weser-Hour, and the whole operation is known as Weser Exercise.
The operation ordered by the codeword has as its objective the rapid surprise landing of troops in Norway. Simultaneously, Denmark will be occupied from the Baltic and from the land side.... The naval forces will, as they enter the harbor, fly the British flag until the troops have landed except, presumably, at Narvik.[23]

Thrust in the North

In September, 1939, the First Lord of the Admiralty, Winston Churchill, proposed to the British cabinet a technical violation of Norwegian neutrality. He recommended that Norwegian territorial waters be strategically mined so as to force ships bringing iron ore from the port of Narvik to Germany to pass out upon the high seas where they would run the risk of capture as enemy prizes. It was considered important that this traffic in iron ore, coming from Sweden to Germany, be denied secure passage in sheltered Norwegian territorial waters. It was not until April 3, 1940, however, that approval was given to the plan. The mines were laid on April 8, 1940, even as German forces were maneuvering for the assault upon Norway. This action was carried out under the name "Operation Wilfred." The laying of mines by the British in Norwegian territorial waters was an undoubted violation of Norwegian neutrality, but it was far removed from actual invasion and occupation. It was not to frustrate this laying of mines that Hitler attacked Norway, but rather to secure Norway for Germany and to provide superior bases for future operations against Great Britain.

The "Weser Exercise" began early in the morning of April 9, 1940, with simultaneous thrusts against Denmark and Norway. A memorandum was delivered to the Norwegian and Danish Governments on that day claiming justification for the attacks on the alleged ground that France and England were plotting such an occupation themselves for the purpose of obtaining bases for an attempted penetration of the Continent from the north. Hitler denied that his attack had similar purposes: "The German troops, therefore, do not set foot on Norwegian soil as enemies. The German High Command does not intend to make use of the points occupied by German troops as bases for operations against England."[24] This, of course, was a lie, for Hitler had given direct orders to the Luftwaffe some five weeks before that Norwegian bases were to be used for air warfare against England.

It was the old game of force and deception. But in this case the victims were neither deceived nor did they surrender at show of force. Hitler had aptly described his aggression in the north as an "exercise" against these tiny neighbors. But he thought in terms of physical strength, not in terms of moral fiber. On April 19, 1940, Jodl entered in his diary the alarm felt at the unexpected resistance of Norway: "Renewed crisis. Envoy Brauer is recalled. Since Norway is at war with us, the task of the Foreign Office is finished. In the Fuehrer's opinion force has to be used."[25]

Norway had her Quisling and Denmark her Klausen. But traitors cannot deliver a brave people. The Danish King stubbornly remained at Amelienborg Palace in Copenhagen, at considerable personal danger, a symbol of the unwavering determination of the Danish people never to surrender to the conqueror. The Norwegian King and members of his government made good their escape to England, from which they carried on active resistance in exile. Thousands of young Danes and Norwegians left their homelands, and by perilous journeys reached free lands and free forces, there to begin the long hard fight for liberation.

In the meantime Hitler and his minions held sway in the north. Hardly had that campaign ended when he took the next step of aggression against small neutral nations of Europe.

CHAPTER 10

Case Yellow

THE CODE name "Case Yellow" was selected for the attack upon the Netherlands, Belgium, and Luxembourg.

The frequency of the assurances given to the three little countries on Germany's northwestern border made the ultimate violation of their neutrality the more reprehensible. Germany had entered into treaties of arbitration with Holland in 1926, with Luxembourg in 1929, and with Belgium in 1935.

On January 30, 1937, Hitler said: "The German Government has further given the assurance to Belgium and Holland that it is prepared to recognize and to guarantee the inviolability and neutrality of these territories."[1]

On April 24, 1937, France and England released Belgium from her obligations under the Locarno Pact and Belgium published an open statement in which she asserted her traditional position of strict independence and neutrality. On October 13, 1937, the German Government issued a direct guarantee of the territorial integrity and political independence of Belgium:

The German Government have taken cognizance with particular interest of the public declaration in which the Belgian Government define the international position of Belgium. For their part they have repeatedly given expression, especially through the declaration of the Chancellor of the German Reich in his speech of the 30th of January 1937, to their own point of view. The German Government have also taken cognizance of the declaration made by the British and French Governments on the 24th of April 1937.

Since the conclusion of a treaty to replace the Treaty of Locarno may still take some time and being desirous of strengthening the peaceful aspirations of the two countries, the German Government regard it as appropriate to define now their own attitude towards Belgium. To this end they make the following declaration:

First: The German Government have taken note of the views which the Belgian Government have thought fit to express. That is to say, (a) of the policy of independence which they intend to exercise in full sovereignty; (b) of their determination to defend the frontiers of Belgium with all their forces against any aggression or invasion and to prevent Belgian territory from being used for purposes of aggression against another state as a passage or as a base of operation by land, by sea, or in the air, and to organize the defense of Belgium in an efficient manner to this purpose.

Second: The German Government consider that the inviolability and integrity of Belgium are common interests of the Western Powers. They confirm their determination that in no circumstances will they impair this inviolability and integrity, and that they will at all times respect Belgian territory except, of course, in the event of Belgium's taking part in a military action directed against Germany in an armed conflict in which Germany is involved.

Third: The German Government, like the British and French Governments, are prepared to assist Belgium should she be subjected to an attack or to invasion.[2]

Less than a year later, consideration was already being given by Hitler to violation of the territorial integrity of Belgium and the Netherlands. In planning "Case Green" the following entry was made:

Belgium and the Netherlands would, in German hands, represent an extraordinary advantage in the prosecution of the air war against Great Britain as well as against France. Therefore it is held to be essential to obtain the opinion of the Army as to the conditions under which an occupation of this area could be carried out and how long it would take. And in this case it would be necessary to reassess the commitment against Great Britain.[3]

On the diplomatic front, hypocritical assurances were still the order of the day. On April 28, 1939, shortly after the absorption of Czechoslovakia, Hitler declared in a speech:

I have given binding declarations to a large number of states. None of these states can complain that even a trace of a demand con-

trary thereto has ever been made to them by Germany. . . . I was
pleased that a number of European states availed themselves of these
declarations by the German Government to express and emphasize
their desire too for absolute neutrality. This applies to the Netherlands,
Belgium, Switzerland, Denmark, *et cetera.*[4]

Less than a month later, on May 23, 1939, however, Hitler
secretly declared his intention to break his pledge to the Low Countries and to violate their neutrality. In the course of a military planning conference on "Case White," attended by Raeder, Brauchitsch,
Keitel, Goering, and others, Hitler said: "The Dutch and Belgian
air bases must be occupied by armed forces. Declarations of neutrality must be ignored."[5] Later he added: "Therefore, if England
intends to intervene in the Polish war, we must occupy Holland
with lightning speed. We must aim at securing a new defense line
on Dutch soil up to the Zuyder Zee."[6]

At the meeting of his top commanders on August 22, 1939,
Hitler said: "Another possibility is the violation of Dutch, Belgian,
and Swiss neutrality. I have no doubts that all these states as well
as Scandinavia will defend their neutrality by all available means.
England and France will not violate the neutrality of these countries."[7]

Hitler thus plotted the invasion of Belgium and the Netherlands on the basic assumption that they would defend themselves
and that England and France would live up to their treaty commitments to observe the neutrality of the Low Countries.

On August 26, 1939, in connection with the planned invasion
of Poland, Germany gave explicit assurances to Belgium, Holland,
and Luxembourg that under no circumstances would Germany
impair the inviolability and integrity of those countries and that
at all times Germany would respect their territories in the expectation that they in turn would observe attitudes of strict neutrality.

After the subjugation of Poland, Hitler gave further assurances
to Belgium and Holland on October 6, 1939:

Immediately after I had taken over the affairs of the state I tried
to create friendly relations with Belgium. I renounced any revision
or any desire for revision. The Reich has not made any demands which
would in any way be likely to be considered in Belgium as a threat.

The new Reich has endeavored to continue the traditional friend-ship with the Netherlands. It has not taken over any existing differ-ences between the two countries and has not created any new ones.[8]

Preparations

On the next day, Von Brauchitsch stated in a communication to various Army Groups: ". . . Army Group B has to make all preparations according to special orders for immediate invasion of Dutch and Belgian territory if the political situation so demands."[9]

And on October 9, only three days after his latest public assur-ances to Holland and Belgium, Hitler declared in an order to Keitel, Raeder, and Goering:

Preparations should be made for offensive action on the northern flank of the Western Front crossing the area of Luxembourg, Belgium and the Netherlands. This attack must be carried out as soon and as forcefully as possible.

The object of this attack is... to acquire as great an area of Hol-land, Belgium and Northern France as possible.[10]

On October 15 Keitel issued an implementation of this order in which he directed: "It must be the object of the Army's prepara-tions to occupy—on receipt of a special order—the territory of Holland in the first instance as far as the Grebbe-Maas line."[11]

At the conference on November 23, 1939, Hitler had said to his military leaders:

We have an Achilles heel: The Ruhr. The progress of the war depends on the possession of the Ruhr. If England and France push through Belgium and Holland into the Ruhr, we shall be in the greatest danger. That could lead to the paralyzing of the German power of resistance. Every hope of compromise is childish: Victory or defeat! The question is not the fate of a national-socialistic Germany, but who is to dominate Europe in the future. The question is worthy of the greatest efforts. Certainly England and France will assume the offensive against Germany when they are armed. England and France have means of pressure to bring Belgium and Holland to request English and French help. In Belgium and Holland the sympathies are all for France and England.... If the French army marches into Belgium in order to attack us, it will be too late for us. We must anticipate them. One more thing. U-boats, mines, and Luftwaffe (also for mines) can strike England effectively if we have a better starting point.... The permanent sowing of mines on the English coasts will bring England to her knees. However, this can only occur if we have occupied Belgium and Holland.... My decision is unchangeable. I shall attack France and England at the most favorable and earliest moment. Breach of the neutrality of Belgium and Holland is meaningless. No one will question that when we have won. We shall not bring about the breach of neutrality as idiotically as it was in 1914. If we do not break the neutrality, then England and France will. Without attack the war is not to be ended victoriously.[12]

The numerous operational plans for the coming offensive in the west were thereafter all predicated upon the planned invasion of Luxembourg, Holland, and Belgium. Jodl wrote in his diary on February 26: "Fuehrer raises the question whether it is better to undertake the Weser Exercise before or after Case Yellow." On March 3 that final detail had been decided, for Jodl wrote: "Fuehrer decides to carry out Weser Exercise before Case Yellow with a few days' interval."[13]

The Assault

On the morning of May 10, 1940, just a month after the invasions of Denmark and Norway, war came to the Low Countries. The mammoth German military machine rolled over their frontiers, crashed through their defenses, laid waste their lands, and killed their people. Rotterdam was bombed from the air and burned.

No warning was given of the attacks. Germany struck with all the fury of mechanized warfare, and soldiers and civilians alike of these little countries suffered the bloody impact of a war which Hitler had promised time and again he would never bring to their lands—promises made to be broken, nations intended to be deceived.

The invasion began at 4:30 A.M. Later in the morning the German ambassadors called upon representatives of the three countries and handed them a memorandum which stated:

In order to forestall the invasion of Belgium, Holland, and Luxembourg, for which Great Britain and France have been making preparations clearly aimed at Germany, the Government of the Reich are compelled to ensure the neutrality of the three countries mentioned by means of arms. For this purpose the Government of the Reich will bring up an armed force of the greatest size so that resistance of any kind will be useless.[14]

At 8:30 in the morning of that day, the German ambassador appeared with his paper in his hand before M. Spaak, the Belgian Foreign Minister. M. Spaak abruptly forestalled the remarks of the German ambassador. "I beg your pardon, Mr. Ambassador, I will speak first."[15] Indignantly he stated the protest of the Belgian Government:

Mr. Ambassador, the German Army has just attacked our country. This is the second time in twenty-five years that Germany has committed a criminal aggression against a neutral and loyal Belgium. What has just happened is perhaps even more odious than the aggression of 1914. No ultimatum, no note, no protest of any kind has ever been placed before the Belgian Government. It is through the attack itself that Belgium has learned that Germany has violated the undertakings given by her on October 13, 1937 and renewed spontaneously at the beginning of the war. The act of aggression committed by Germany for which there is no justification whatever will deeply shock the conscience of the world. The German Reich will be held responsible by history. Belgium is resolved to defend herself. Her cause, which is the cause of Right, cannot be vanquished.[16]

In thus speaking for Belgium, M. Spaak spoke as well for Belgium's neighbors, Luxembourg and Holland, and for the people of all small countries who were to face the might of Germany's armies—people like the Greeks and the Yugoslavs.

The German armed forces moved over Belgium and into northern France. They drove the British divisions to the beaches at Dunkirk from which the English troops were evacuated to the island fortress. In forty-two days the war on the western front was over. Belgium, Holland, and Luxembourg were the way to France. Hitler accepted surrender in the railway car at Compiègne. And when he came out, he joyously rubbed his hands together and danced a little jig.

CHAPTER 11

Case Marita

Case Marita was the code name for the attack on Greece. The invasion of Yugoslavia was co-ordinated with it.

Pledge

On April 28, 1938, following the seizure of Austria, the German Foreign Office issued a release to the countries bordering Austria in which assurances were given to Yugoslavia and other named nations:

As a consequence of the re-union of Austria with the Reich we have now new frontiers with Italy, Yugoslavia, Switzerland, Liechtenstein, and Hungary. These frontiers are regarded by us as final and inviolable. . . .

The Yugoslav Government have been informed by authoritative German quarters that German policy has no aims beyond Austria, and that the Yugoslav frontier would in any case remain untouched.[1]

At a dinner given in honor of the Prince Regent of Yugoslavia on June 1, 1939, Hitler added his personal pledge in these words:

The German friendship for the Yugoslav nation is not only a spontaneous one. It gained depth and durability in the midst of the tragic confusion of the World War. The German soldier then learned to appreciate and respect his extremely brave opponent. I believe that this feeling was reciprocated. This mutual respect finds confirmation in common political, cultural and economic interests. We therefore look upon your Royal Highness's present visit as a living proof of the accuracy of our view, and at the same time, on that account we derive from it the hope that German-Yugoslav friendship may continue further to develop in the future and to grow ever closer.

In the presence of your Royal Highness, however, we also perceive a happy opportunity for a frank and friendly exchange of views which —and of this I am convinced—in this sense can only be fruitful to our two peoples and States. I believe this all the more because a firmly established reliable relationship of Germany and Yugoslavia, now that owing to historical events we have become neighbors with common boundaries fixed for all time, will not only guarantee lasting peace between our two peoples and countries, but can also represent an element of calm to our nerve-wracked continent. This peace is the goal of all who are disposed to perform really constructive work.[2]

Hitler's real attitude toward Yugoslavia was disclosed in his conference with Ciano of August 12, 1939, in which he urged Italy to dispose of Yugoslavia as he intended to dispose of Poland. "Generally speaking," Hitler said, "the best thing to happen would be for uncertain neutrals to be liquidated one after the other. This process could be carried out more easily if on every occasion one partner of the Axis covered the other while it was dealing with an uncertain neutral. Italy might well regard Yugoslavia as a neutral of this kind."[3]

Yet, two months later, on October 6, 1939, Hitler continued his game of deception by publicly renewing his assurances to Yugoslavia: "Immediately after the completion of the Anschluss I informed Yugoslavia that from now on the frontier with this country would also be an unalterable one and that we desire only to live in peace and friendship with her."[4]

Italy was ready to follow Hitler's lead in dealing with "uncertain neutrals" after the German armies had defeated France and England on the Continent in the summer of 1940. At three o'clock in the morning of October 28, 1940, the Italian Minister handed the Greek Government a three-hour ultimatum, upon the expiration of which Italian troops began their ill-fated attack upon the noble little country. Like other "uncertain neutrals," the Greeks fought back with the determination and sacrifice which have added a page of glory to Greek history. Unaided, Mussolini's legions were not able to defeat the forces of embattled Greece.

Shortly after the Italian attack upon Greece, Hitler, who was displeased with the ineptness of Mussolini, wrote the Italian dictator a letter in which he discussed the strategic difficulties of German participation in a campaign against the Balkan states. And he paid particular regard to Yugoslavia:

> Without assurances from Yugoslavia, it is useless to risk any successful operation in the Balkans. Unfortunately I must stress the fact that waging a war in the Balkans before March is impossible. Therefore any threatening move towards Yugoslavia would be useless since the impossibility of a materialization of such threats before March is well known to the Serbian General Staff. Therefore, Yugoslavia must, if at all possible, be won over by other means and other ways.[5]

Preparing to Destroy Greece

Nevertheless, by the next month Hitler's military staff was busily preparing plans for coming operations in the Balkans. Hitler's top secret directive of November 12, 1940, initialed by Jodl, provided:

> The Commander-in-Chief of the Army will make preparations for occupying the Greek mainland north of the Aegean Sea in case of need, entering through Bulgaria, and thus make possible the use of German Air Force units against targets in the eastern Mediterranean, in particular against those English air bases which are threatening the Rumanian oil area.[6]

Hitler issued a directive on December 13, 1940, in which he stated that after the coming of favorable weather, probably in March, he intended to send a military force by way of Bulgaria to occupy the north coast of the Aegean and, if necessary, the entire Greek mainland.

Military plans continued to be laid, and on January 20, 1941, Hitler conferred with Mussolini on the action to be taken against Greece. At the conclusion of the conference Hitler said: "Desirable that this deployment is completed without interference from the enemy. Therefore, disclose the game as late as possible. The tendency will be to cross the Danube at the last possible moment and to line up for the attack at the earliest possible moment."[7]

Bulgaria was brought into the conspiracy. On February 8, 1941, representatives of the German and Bulgarian general staffs conferred and arrived at certain conclusions:

The Bulgarian and the German General Staffs will take all measures in order to camouflage the preparation of the operations and to assure in this way the most favorable conditions for the execution of the German operations as planned.

The representatives of the two general staffs consider it to be suitable to inform their governments that it will be advisable out of necessity to take secrecy and surprise into consideration when the Three Power Treaty is signed by Bulgaria, in order to assure the success of the military operations.[8]

By February 19, 1941, military arrangements had reached the point where dates for "Case Marita" could be set. In a top secret directive Keitel fixed the date for issuance of final orders as February 26, for laying the bridge across the Danube as February 28, and for the crossing of the Danube as March 2. On March 1, 1941, Bulgaria signified her adherence to the three-power pact. Two days later British troops landed in Greece to repel the Italian invaders.

Eliminating Yugoslavia

Hitler was ready to take action against Greece, but he decided to get Yugoslavia out of the way first. For this purpose he invited the Yugoslavian Premier, Cvetkovic, and the Foreign Minister, Cinkar-Markovic, to a meeting at Berchtesgaden. Responding to German pressure, at Vienna a few days later, the intimidated representatives of the Yugoslavian Government signified the adherence of their country on March 25, 1941, to the three-power pact, whereupon Ribbentrop wrote Premier Cvetkovic: "On the occasion of the Yugoslavian entry today into the Tri-Partite Pact the German Government confirm their determination to respect the sovereignty and territorial integrity of Yugoslavia at all times."[9]

At this point, German troops were already in Bulgaria moving toward the Greek frontier, and Yugoslavia had been successfully isolated. Hitler had succeeded in making Yugoslavia for the moment outwardly "positively interested in our point of view." But on the night of March 26, when the two duped Ministers returned to Belgrade, they were removed by the coup d'état of General Simo-witsch. On the following day, without consideration of the attitude of the new Yugoslav government and without regard to his frequent pledges of peace, Hitler determined upon the immediate liquidation of Yugoslavia.

At a meeting with Goering, Keitel, Jodl, Ribbentrop, and others Hitler declared on March 27:

The Fuehrer describes Yugoslavia's situation after the *coup d'état.* Statement that Yugoslavia was an uncertain factor in regard to the coming Marita action and even more in regard to the Barbarossa under-taking later on. Serbs and Slovenes were never pro-German....

The Fuehrer is determined, without waiting for possible loyalty declarations of the new government, to make all preparations in order to destroy Yugoslavia militarily and as a national unit. No diplomatic inquiries will be made nor ultimatums presented. Assurances of the Yugoslav Government which cannot be trusted anyhow in the future will be taken note of. The attack will start as soon as the means and troops suitable for it are ready.

It is important that actions will be taken as fast as possible. An attempt will be made to let the bordering states participate in a suit-able way. An actual military support against Yugoslavia is to be re-quested of Italy, Hungary, and in certain respects of Bulgaria too. Rumania's main task is the protection against Russia. The Hungarian and the Bulgarian Ministers have already been notified. During the day a message will still be addressed to the Duce.

Politically, it is especially important that the blow against Yugo-slavia is carried out with unmerciful harshness and that the military destruction is done in a lightning-like undertaking. In this way Turkey would become sufficiently frightened and the campaign against Greece later on would be influenced in a favorable way. It can be assumed that the Croats will come to our side when we attack. A corresponding political treatment (autonomy later on) will be assured to them. The war against Yugoslavia should be very popular in Italy, Hungary and Bulgaria, as territorial acquisitions are to be promised to these states; the Adriatic coast for Italy, the Banat for Hungary, and Macedonia for Bulgaria.

This plan assumes that we speed up the schedule of all prepara-tions and use such strong forces that the Yugoslav collapse will take place within the shortest time....

The main task of the Air Force is to start as early as possible with the destruction of the Yugoslavian Air Force ground installations and to destroy the capital, Belgrade, in attacks by waves....[10]

Jodl confirmed these decisions by entries made at the time in his diary:

The Fuehrer is determined, without waiting for loyalty declarations from the new government, to make all preparations in order to destroy Yugoslavia militarily and as a national unit. No diplomatic inquiries will be made; no ultimatum presented. Assurances of the Yugoslav Government which cannot be trusted for the future will be taken note of. The attack will start as soon as the means and the troops suitable are ready. It is important that action is taken as fast as possible.... Politically it is especially important that the blow against Yugoslavia is carried out with unmerciful harshness and military destruction is done in a lightning-like undertaking.[11]

Jodl was asked, on the witness stand, the following question concerning these entries in his diary: "Do you approve as an honorable soldier, of attacking a city crowded with civilians without a declaration of war or even half an hour's warning?" And he answered, "I do not hold that view."[12]

The first paragraph of the order issued after the meeting provided: "The military putsch in Yugoslavia has altered the political situation in the Balkans. Yugoslavia must, in spite of her protestation of loyalty, for the time being be considered as an enemy and therefore crushed as speedily as possible."[13]

Hitler proceeded at once to issue orders to his Italian flag lieutenant:

Duce, events force me to give you, Duce, by this the quickest means, my estimation of the situation and the consequences which may result from it.

(1) From the beginning I have regarded Yugoslavia as the most dangerous factor in the controversy with Greece. Considered from the purely military point of view, German intervention in the war in Thrace would not be at all justified as long as the attitude of Yugoslavia remains ambiguous, and she could threaten the left flank of the advancing columns on our enormous front.

(2) For this reason I have done everything and honestly have endeavored to bring Yugoslavia into our community bound together by

mutual interests. Unfortunately these endeavors did not meet with success, or they were begun too late to produce any definite result. Today's reports leave no doubt as to the imminent turn in the foreign policy of Yugoslavia.

(3) I do not consider this situation as being catastrophic, but nevertheless it is a difficult one, and we on our part must avoid any mistake if we do not want in the end to endanger our whole position.

(4) Therefore I have already arranged for all necessary measures in order to meet a critical development with necessary military means. The change in the deployment of our troops has been ordered also in Bulgaria. Now I would cordially request you, Duce, not to undertake any further operations in Albania in the course of the next few days. I consider it necessary that you should cover and screen the most important passes from Yugoslavia into Albania with all available forces. These measures should not be considered as designed for a long period of time, but as auxiliary measures designed to prevent for at least 14 days to 3 weeks a crisis arising. I also consider it necessary, Duce, that you should reinforce your forces on the Italian-Yugoslav front with all available means and with utmost speed.

(5) I also consider it necessary, Duce, that everything which we do and order be shrouded in absolute secrecy and that only personalities who necessarily must be notified know anything about them. These measures will completely lose their value should they become known....[14]

On the morning of April 6, 1941, Hitler launched his long-prepared attack against Greece and his precipitate assault upon Yugoslavia. On that morning bombs fell on Belgrade in one of the most terrible and devastating bombardments of any city during the war—planes flying out of the dawn over unsuspecting people in their homes and shops and on the streets. Blood ran in the gutters of Belgrade. But though brave little Greece, which had fought off the Italians for better than half a year, was to succumb to German might, the gallant Yugoslavians were to fight on in their mountain hideouts until war ended in Hitler's defeat.

Hitler had broken France and overrun most of the small countries of Europe. His troops stood on the warm shores of the Mediterranean and on the icy banks of Norwegian fiords. Only his lately acquired friend, and partner in the partition of Poland, Soviet Russia, stood between him and the absolute domination of the whole of Europe.

CHAPTER 12

Case Barbarossa

CASE BARBAROSSA was the code name for the invasion of the Union of Soviet Socialist Republics.

On January 31, 1939, a few months before the signing of the German-Soviet Pact, Himmler conferred with Oshima, the Japanese ambassador to Berlin. They discussed the conclusion of a treaty to consolidate further the tripartite understanding among Germany, Italy, and Japan. The conversation turned to Russia. Oshima told Himmler that he was undertaking long-range projects aimed at the disintegration of Russia and emanating from the Caucasus and Ukraine:

> However, this organization was to become effective only in case of war.... Furthermore, he had succeeded up to now in sending ten Russians with bombs across the Caucasian frontier. These Russians had the mission to kill Stalin. A number of additional Russians, whom he had also sent across, had been shot at the frontier.[1]

Efforts to assassinate Stalin having failed, several weeks later Hitler commenced negotiations with him for the ostensible purpose of creating the basis for an enduring friendship between the two dictators. For Hitler, the understanding was essential to the success of his coming campaign against Poland, England, and France; for Stalin, it afforded an opportunity to gain a slice of Poland and to turn Hitler against the West. Just a week before the attack upon Poland, the Nonaggression Treaty of August 23, 1939, was entered into between Hitler and Stalin. By Article 1 of the treaty the contracting parties undertook to refrain from any act of violence, any aggressive action, or any attack against each other, whether individually or jointly with other powers. Article 5 provided that should disputes or conflicts arise between the parties regarding questions of any kind whatsoever, they should be settled solely by friendly exchanges of views or if necessary by arbitration commissions. The treaty was supplemented by a trade agreement between the two countries.

The making of this alliance constituted an abrupt reversal in both the Nazi and the Communist propaganda lines. In attempting to explain this departure from established policy to the German people, Hitler said in a speech delivered on October 6, 1939:

> The Soviet Union is the Soviet Union, National Socialist Germany is National Socialist Germany. But one thing is certain: from the moment when the two states mutually agreed to respect each other's distinctive regime and principles, every reason for any mutually hostile attitude had disappeared. Long periods in the history of both nations have shown that the inhabitants of these two largest states in Europe were never happier than when they lived in friendship with each other. ... Germany and Russia together will relieve one of the most acute danger spots in Europe of its threatening character, and will, each in her own sphere, contribute to the welfare of the peoples living there, thus aiding European peace in general.[2]

Whatever motives Stalin may have had in entering into this pact which led to the destruction of Poland by the combined might of the German and Soviet war machines, Hitler's purposes were entirely opportunistic. On February 23, 1941, Ribbentrop used these words in explaining the pact to the Japanese ambassador, Oshima: "Then when it came to war the Fuehrer decided on a compromise with Russia—as a necessity for avoiding a two-front war."[3] But in a speech to Reichsleiter and Gauleiter in November, 1943, Jodl said, speaking retrospectively:

> Parallel with all these developments realization was steadily growing of the danger drawing constantly nearer from the Bolshevik East —that danger which had been only too little perceived in Germany and of late, for diplomatic reasons, had deliberately to be ignored. However, the Fuehrer himself has always kept this danger steadily in view and even as far back as during the Western Campaign had informed me of his fundamental decision to take steps against this danger the moment our military position made it at all possible.[4]

The Franco-German armistice was signed at Compiègne on June 22, 1940, and the campaign on the Continent of Europe was brought to a temporary termination. Having eliminated one front, Germany was free to fight on another. In August, 1940, Goering informed General Thomas that Hitler desired punctual deliveries to the Soviets, under the Soviet-German trade agreement of 1939, only until the spring of 1941.

In a High Command directive of September 6, 1940, Jodl stated that the eastern territory would be manned more strongly in the weeks to come, but that the "regrouping must not create the impression in Russia that we are preparing an offensive in the East."[5] In the same directive Jodl specifically ordered: "The respective total strength of the German troops in the East is to be veiled as far as possible by giving news about a frequent change of the army units there. This change is to be explained by movements into training camps, regroupings, *et cetera.*"[6]

On November 12, 1940, Hitler issued a top secret directive on preparatory measures for the prosecution of the war in the near future. Regarding the Soviet Union he said:

Political discussions have been initiated with the aim of clarifying Russia's attitude for the time being. Irrespective of the results of these discussions all preparations for the East which have already been verbally ordered will be continued

Instructions on this will follow as soon as the general outline of the Army's operational plans has been submitted to and approved by me.[7]

The Chief of the General Staff of the Army, General Halder, reported to Hitler on December 5, 1940, on the progress of plans for the coming operations against the U.S.S.R. He observed that the principal industrial centers of military importance were in the Ukraine, in Moscow, and in Leningrad. Hitler expressed agreement with the operational plans. He then added:

The most important goal is to prevent the Russians from withdrawing on a closed front. The eastward advance should be continued until the Russian Air Force will be unable to attack the territory of the German Reich and on the other hand the German Air Force will be enabled to conduct raids to destroy Russian war industrial territory.

In this way we should be able to achieve the annihilation of the Russian Army and to prevent its regeneration. The first commitment of the forces should take place in such a way as to make the annihilation of strong enemy units possible....It is essential that the Russians should not take up positions in the rear again. The number of 130 to 140 divisions as planned for the entire operation is sufficient.[8]

Decision to Destroy the U.S.S.R.

On December 18, 1940, top secret Directive No. 21, of which only nine copies were prepared, was issued from Hitler's headquarters. This directive, signed by Hitler and initialed by Keitel and Jodl, provided in part:

The German armed forces must be prepared to crush Soviet Russia in a quick campaign before the end of the war against England. (Case Barbarossa.) For this purpose the Army will have to employ all available units with the reservation that the occupied territories will have to be safeguarded against surprise attacks.

For the Eastern campaign the Air Force will have to free such strong forces for the support of the Army that a quick completion of the ground operations may be expected and that damage of the eastern German territories will be avoided as much as possible. This concentration of the main effort in the East is limited by the following reservation: That the entire battle and armament area dominated by us must remain sufficiently protected against enemy air attacks and that the attacks on England, and especially the supply for them, must not be permitted to break down.

Concentration of the main effort of the Navy remains unequivocally against England also during an Eastern campaign.

If occasion arises I will order the concentration of troops for action against Soviet Russia eight weeks before the intended beginning of operations.

Preparations requiring more time to start are—if this has not yet been done—to begin presently and are to be completed by 15 May 1941.

Great caution has to be exercised that the intention of an attack will not be recognized.

The preparations of the High Command are to be made on the following basis:

1. General Purpose:

The mass of the Russian Army in Western Russia is to be destroyed in daring operations by driving forward deep wedges with tanks, and the retreat of intact battle-ready troops into the wide spaces of Russia is to be prevented.

In quick pursuit, a line is to be reached from where the Russian Air Force will no longer be able to attack German Reich territory. The first goal of operations is the protection from Asiatic Russia from the general line Volga-Archangel. In case of necessity, the last industrial area in the Urals left to Russia could be eliminated by the Luftwaffe.

In the course of these operations the Russian Baltic Sea Fleet will quickly erase its bases and will no longer be ready to fight.

Effective intervention by the Russian Air Force is to be prevented through powerful blows at the beginning of the operations.[9]

Keitel and Goering both testified that the plan to attack the Soviet Union was decided upon in December, 1940. Goering testified that after he had been informed of Hitler's intention to invade Soviet territory he attempted to dissuade him from the decision because, among other reasons, it made impossible Goering's own plan of attacking Gibraltar through Spain. Goering said on cross-examination: "At that particular time I was of the opinion that this attack should be postponed in order to carry through other tasks which I considered more important."[10]

By February 3, 1941, preparations had progressed to the point where Hitler was able to declare confidently to his top commanders: "When Barbarossa commences the world will hold its breath...."[11] At this conference Hitler stated that on the whole he was in agreement with the operational plan, the main purpose of which was to gain possession of the Baltic States and Leningrad. The strategic concentration for Barbarossa was to be camouflaged as a feint for other actions.

On March 13, 1941, Keitel signed an operational supplement to Hitler's Directive No. 21, in which the division of administrative responsibility for territories to be absorbed under Case Barbarossa was outlined. This order provided that in the area of operations Himmler, as Reichsfuehrer SS, was to be entrusted, on behalf of Hitler, with special tasks for the preparation of the political administration, "tasks which result from the struggle which has to be carried out between two opposing political systems."[12] In executing these tasks Himmler was to act independently and upon his own responsibility. The newly occupied territory in the rear of the area of operations was to be given its own political administration, divided according to genealogic conceptions into three major groupings, North (Baltic countries), Center (White Russia), and South (Ukraine). In these territories the political administration was to be under Commissioners of the Reich who received their orders directly from Hitler. The uniform direction of the administration of economy in the area of operations and in the territories of political administration was to be entrusted to the Reich Marshal, Goering.

The beginning of "Case Barbarossa" was delayed by the actions against Greece and Yugoslavia. An entry of April 3, 1941, in the Naval War Staff War Diary stated: "Balkan operations delay; Barbarossa now in about 5 weeks. All measures which can be construed as offensive actions are to be stopped according to the Fuehrer's order."[13] But by April 30, 1941, the actual time for the invasion had been set. A top secret report of a military conference of that date stated that Hitler had ordered action Barbarossa to begin on June 22, 1941.

Hitler succeeded in acquiring allies to assist in the projected action. Finland, which had suffered grievously from the Soviet attack the year before, needed little urging. Hungary agreed as early as December, 1940, to enter the conflict provided she received certain Yugoslavian territories. And the Rumanian Prime Minister, Antonescu, promised to participate in exchange for Bessarabia, northern Bukovina, and the right to Soviet territory to the river Dnieper.

The Invasion

Meanwhile, as reports from the German ambassador to Moscow clearly indicated, the Soviet Union was doing everything within its power to preserve good relations with Germany under the non-aggression and trade pacts to which the U.S.S.R. was committed. On June 4, 1941, the ambassador reported: "Outwardly, no change in the relationship Germany-Russia; Russian deliveries continue to full satisfaction. Russian Government is endeavoring to do everything to prevent a conflict with Germany."[14] And on June 7, the German ambassador reported:

All observations show that Stalin and Molotov, who alone are responsible for Russian foreign policy, are doing everything to avoid a conflict with Germany. The entire behavior of the Government, as well as the attitude of the press, which reports all events concerning Germany in a factual, indisputable manner, supports this view. The loyal fulfillment of the economic treaty with Germany proves the same thing.[15]

Nonetheless, the secret plans for military aggression against the Soviet Union went on, and by June 6, 1941, the plotters had reached the final stage. A top secret report was issued from Hitler's headquarters on that date enclosing the timetable on Barbarossa, giving the state of preparations on June 1, 1941. The first entry noted that "the timetable was put into operation on the 22nd of May."[16] An elaborate chart accompanying the report gave the day by day responsibilities of the Army, Air Force, Navy, and the OKW. Across the Army and Air Force columns for June 22 was the item, "Invasion Day," followed by, "H-hour for the start of the invasion by the Army and crossing of the frontier by the Air Force: 0330 hours."[17]

And at 3:30 o'clock in the morning of June 22, 1941, German troops began, in fact, the assault in the East which Hitler had urged in the days before his rise to power. On that morning Hitler said in a proclamation to his troops: "I have decided to give the fate of the German people and of the Reich and of Europe again into the hands of our soldiers."[18]

All principal European nations were now directly involved in the titanic struggle. Of the large countries of the world, only Japan and the United States remained neutral.

CHAPTER 13

Alliance for Aggression

Hitler's diplomatic success was due in part to his ability to enter into some kind of pact with each of his intended victims. It is a tribute to his duplicity and a testimony to the weakness of others that he was able to gain new friends after he had betrayed old ones. Through all his machinations and trickery he retained the slavish loyalty of two other countries who also wanted to become big by eating up their neighbors. These were Italy and Japan.

Japan was the first to identify her destiny and fundamental interest with Hitler's Germany. On November 25, 1936, Japan joined with Germany in the Anti-Comintern Pact, an agreement which on the printed sides of the pages was directed against the Communist International but which on the unprinted sides was pointed against the future enemy, Russia. Italy adhered to the Pact on November 6, 1937.

The Tri-Partite Pact

Four years later, on September 27, 1940, after German troops had overrun Western Europe, the Tri-Partite Pact, a ten year military-economic agreement, was signed on behalf of Germany Japan, and Italy in Berlin. Some of the more significant portions of this document stated:

> The Governments of Germany, Italy and Japan consider it as a condition precedent of a lasting peace, that each nation of the world be given its own proper place. They have, therefore, decided to stand

together and to co-operate with one another in their efforts in Greater East Asia and in the regions of Europe, wherein it is their prime purpose to establish and maintain a new order of things calculated to promote the prosperity and welfare of the peoples there. Furthermore, it is the desire of the three Governments to extend this co-operation to such nations in other parts of the world as are inclined to give to their endeavors a direction similar to their own, in order that their aspirations towards world peace as the ultimate goal may thus be realized. Accordingly, the Governments of Germany, Italy and Japan have agreed as follows:

Article 1. Japan recognizes and respects the leadership of Germany and Italy in the establishment of a New Order in Europe.

Article 2. Germany and Italy recognize and respect the leadership of Japan in the establishment of a New Order in Greater East Asia.

Article 3. Germany, Italy and Japan agree to co-operate in their efforts on the aforesaid basis. They further undertake to assist one another with all political, economic and military means, if one of the three contracting parties is attacked by a power at present not involved in the European war or in the Chinese-Japanese conflict.[1]

Negotiations Vis-à-vis Great Britain

Even before the attack on Soviet Russia Ribbentrop, on January 23, 1941, had strongly urged Japan to enter the war as Germany's ally against Great Britain. The minutes of the conference read in part:

The Fuehrer will beat England wherever he encounters her. Besides, our strength is not only equal but superior to a combined English-American air force at any time. The number of pilots at our disposal is unlimited. The same is true of our airplane production capacity. As far as quality is concerned, ours always has been superior to the English—to say nothing about the American—and we are on the way to enlarge even this lead. Upon order of the Fuehrer the anti-aircraft defense, too, will be greatly reinforced. Since the Army has been supplied far beyond its requirements and enormous reserves have been piled up—the ammunition plants have been slowed down because of the immense stock of material—production now will be concentrated on submarines, airplanes and anti-aircraft guns.

Every eventuality has been provided for; the war has been won today, militarily, economically and politically. We have the desire to end the war quickly, and to force England to sue for peace soon. The Fuehrer is vigorous and healthy, fully convinced of victory, and determined to bring the war as quick as possible to a victorious close. To this end the co-operation with Japan is of importance. However, Japan, in her own interest, should come in as soon as possible. This would destroy England's key position in the Far East. Japan, on the other hand, would thus secure her position in the Far East, a position which she could acquire only through war. There are three reasons for quick action.

1. Intervention by Japan would mean a decisive blow against the center of the British Empire (threat to India, cruiser-warfare, et cetera). The effect upon the morale of the British people would be very serious and this would contribute toward a quick ending of the war.

2. A surprise intervention by Japan is bound to keep America out of the war. America, which at present is not yet armed and would hesitate greatly to expose her Navy to any risks west of Hawaii, could then less likely do this. If Japan would otherwise respect the American interests, there would not even be the possibility for Roosevelt to use the argument of lost prestige to make war plausible to the Americans. It is very unlikely that America would declare war if she then would have to stand by helplessly while Japan takes the Philippines without America being able to do anything about it.

3. In view of the coming New World Order it seems to be in the interest of Japan also to secure for herself, even during the war, the position she wants to hold in the Far East at the time of a peace treaty....

If America should declare war because of Japan's entry into the war, this would mean that America had the intention to enter the war sooner or later anyway. Even though it would be preferable to avoid this, the entry into the war would, as explained above, be by no means decisive and would not endanger the final victory of the countries of the Three Power Pact. The Foreign Minister further expressed his belief that a temporary lift of the British morale caused by America's entry into the war would be cancelled by Japan's entry into the war. If, however, contrary to all expectations, the Americans should be careless enough to send their navy, in spite of all, beyond Hawaii and to the Far East, this would represent the biggest chance for the countries of the Three Power Pact to bring the war to an end with the greatest rapidity. He—the Foreign Minister—is convinced that the Japanese fleet would then do a complete job. Ambassador Oshima replied to this that unfortunately he does not think the Americans would do it, but he is convinced of a victory of his fleet in Japanese waters.[2]

A few days after this meeting Keitel, as Chief of the High Command, issued a top secret order under date of March 5, 1941, which stated that Hitler had issued the following instructions regarding collaboration with Japan:

1. It must be the aim of the collaboration based on the Three Power Pact to induce Japan, as soon as possible, *to take active measures in the Far East.* Strong British forces will thereby be tied down, and the center of gravity of the interests of the United States of America will be diverted to the Pacific. The sooner she intervenes, the greater will be the prospects of success for Japan in view of the still undeveloped preparedness for war on the part of her adversaries. The Barbarossa operation will create particularly favorable political and military prerequisites for this.

2. To prepare the way for the collaboration it is essential to strengthen the Japanese military potential with all means available. For this purpose the high commands of the branches of the armed forces will comply in a comprehensive and generous manner with Japanese desires for information regarding German war and combat experience, and for assistance in military economics and in technical matters. Reciprocity is desirable, but this factor should not stand in the way of negotiations. Priority should naturally be given to those Japanese requests which would have the most immediate application in waging war. In special cases the Fuehrer reserves the decisions for himself.

3. The harmonizing of the operational plans of the two parties is the responsibility of the naval high command. This will be subject to the following guiding principles:

a. The common aim of the conduct of war is to be stressed as forcing England to the ground quickly and thereby keeping the United States out of the war. Beyond this Germany has no political, military, or economic interests in the Far East which would give occasion for any reservations with regard to Japanese intentions.

b. The great successes achieved by Germany in mercantile warfare make it appear particularly suitable to employ strong Japanese forces for the same purpose. In this connection every opportunity to support German mercantile warfare must be exploited.

c. The raw material situation of the pact powers demands that Japan should acquire possession of those territories which it needs for the continuation of the war, especially if the United States intervenes. Rubber shipments must be carried out even after the entry of Japan into the war, since they are of vital importance to Germany.

d. The seizure of Singapore as the key British position in the Far

East would mean a decisive success for the entire conduct of the war of the Three Powers....

5. The Japanese must not be given any intimation of the Barbarossa operations.[3]

On March 18, 1941, at a meeting with Hitler, Keitel, and Jodl, Raeder urged that Japan intervene immediately in the war against Great Britain:

Japan must take steps to seize Singapore as soon as possible, since the opportunity will never again be as favorable: (tie-up of the whole English Fleet; unpreparedness of U.S.A. for war against Japan; inferiority of United States Fleet in comparison with the Japanese). Japan is indeed making preparations for this action; but according to all declarations made by Japanese officers, she will only carry it out if Germany proceeds to land in England. Germany must, therefore, concentrate all her efforts on spurring Japan to act immediately. If Japan has Singapore, all other East Asiatic questions regarding the U.S.A. and England are thereby solved (Guam, Philippines, Borneo, Dutch East Indies).[4]

Ribbentrop met the Japanese Foreign Minister, Matsuoka, on March 29, 1941, and took advantage of the opportunity to urge him to bring Japan into the war against Great Britain, but without divulging the coming action against the Soviet Union. The conversation is reported, in part:

The RAM [viz., Ribbentrop] resumed, where they had left off, the preceding conversation with Matsuoka about the latter's impending talks with the Russians in Moscow. He expressed the opinion that it would probably be best, in view of the whole situation, not to carry the discussions with the Russians too far. He did not know how the situation would develop. One thing was certain, however, namely that Germany would strike immediately, should Russia ever attack Japan. He was ready to give Matsuoka this positive assurance so that Japan could push forward to the south on Singapore without fear of possible complications with Russia. The largest part of the German Army was on the Eastern frontiers of the Reich anyway and fully prepared to open the attack at any time. However, he believed that Russia would try to avoid developments leading to war. Should Germany, nevertheless, enter into a conflict with Russia, the U.S.S.R. would be finished off within a few months. In this case, Japan would have, of course, even less reason to be afraid than ever, if she wants to advance on Singapore. Consequently, she need not refrain from such an undertaking because of possible fears of Russia.

He could not know, of course, just how things with Russia would develop. It was uncertain whether or not Stalin would intensify his present unfriendly policy against Germany. He wanted to point out to Matsuoka in any case that a conflict with Russia was at least within the realm of possibility. In any case, Matsuoka could not report to the Japanese Emperor, upon his return, that a conflict between Russia and Germany was impossible. On the contrary, the situation was such that a conflict, even if it were not probable, would have to be considered possible. . . .

Next, the RAM turned again to the Singapore question. In view of the fears expressed by the Japanese of possible attacks by submarines based on the Philippines, and of the intervention of the British Mediterranean and home fleets, he had again discussed the situation with Grossadmiral Raeder. The latter had stated that the British Navy during this year would have its hands so full in the English home waters and in the Mediterranean that it would not be able to send even a single ship to the Far East. Grossadmiral Raeder had described the United States submarines as so poor that Japan need not bother about them at all.

Matsuoka replied immediately that the Japanese Navy had a very low estimate of the threat from the British Navy. It also held the view that, in case of a clash with the American Navy, it would be able to smash the latter without trouble. However, it was afraid that the Americans would not take up the battle with their fleet; thus the conflict with the United States might perhaps be dragged out to five years. This possibility caused considerable worry in Japan.

The RAM replied that America could not do anything against Japan in case of the capture of Singapore. Perhaps for this reason alone, Roosevelt would think twice before deciding on active measures against Japan. For while on the one hand he could not achieve anything against Japan, on the other hand, there was the probability of losing the Philippines to Japan; for the American President, of course, this would mean a considerable loss of prestige, and because of the inadequate rearmament he would have nothing to offset such a loss.

In this connection Matsuoka pointed out that he was doing everything to reassure the English about Singapore. He acted as if Japan had no intention at all regarding this key position of England in the East. Therefore it might be possible that his attitude toward the British would appear to be friendly in words and in acts. However, Germany should not be deceived by that. He assumed this attitude not only in order to reassure the British, but also in order to fool the pro-British and pro-American elements in Japan just so long, until one day he would suddenly open the attack on Singapore.

In this connection Matsuoka stated that his tactics were based on the certain assumption that the sudden attack against Singapore would unite the entire Japanese nation with one blow.... He followed here the example expressed in the words of a famous Japanese statesman addressed to the Japanese Navy at the outbreak of the Russo-Japanese war: "You open fire, then the nation will be united." The Japanese need to be shaken up to awaken. After all, as an Oriental, he believed in the fate which would come, whether you wanted it or not.[5]

Negotiations Vis-à-vis America

The negotiations with Japan had, up to this time, been largely directed against Great Britain. But the Japanese were well aware that any attack by them against British interests in the Far East would probably bring the United States into the war. And Matsuoka, at least, was quite prepared to anticipate this contingency and plan accordingly. At a meeting with Hitler and Ribbentrop on April 4, 1941, Matsuoka pointed out the undesirability of conflict with the United States, and yet the acute possibility that Japanese action in the Far East might lead to such involvement.

The Fuehrer ... pointed out that Germany, too, considered a conflict with the United States undesirable, but that it had already made allowances for such a contingency. In Germany one was of the opinion that America's contributions depended upon the possibilities of transportation, and that this again is conditioned by the available tonnage. Germany's war against tonnage, however, means a decisive weakening, not merely against England, but also against America. Germany has made her preparations so that no American could land in Europe. She would conduct a most energetic fight against America with her U-boats and her Luftwaffe, and due to her superior experience, which would still have to be acquired by the United States, she would be vastly superior, and that quite apart from the fact that the German soldiers naturally rank high above the Americans.

In the future course of the discussion, the Fuehrer pointed out that Germany, on her part, would immediately take the consequences if Japan would get involved with the United States. It did not matter with whom the United States would first get involved, whether with Germany or with Japan.... Therefore Germany would strike, as already mentioned, without delay in case of a conflict between Japan and America, because the strength of the tripartite powers lies in their joint action; their weakness would be if they would let themselves be beaten individually.

Matsuoka once more repeated his request that the Fuehrer might give the necessary instructions, in order that the proper German authorities would place at the disposal of the Japanese the latest improvements and inventions, which are of interest to them because the Japanese Navy had to prepare immediately for a conflict with the United States.

As regards Japanese-American relationship, Matsuoka explained further that he has always declared in his country that sooner or later a war with the United States would be unavoidable if Japan continued to drift along as at present. In his opinion this conflict would happen rather sooner than later. His argumentation went on, why should Japan, therefore, not decisively strike at the right moment and take the risk upon herself of a fight against America? Just thus would she perhaps avoid a war for generations, particularly if she gained predominance in the South Seas. There are, to be sure, in Japan many who hesitate to follow those trends of thought. Matsuoka was considered in those circles a dangerous man with dangerous thoughts. He, however, stated that if Japan continued to walk along her present path, one day she would have to fight anyway and this would then be under less favorable circumstances than at present.

The Fuehrer replied that he could well understand the situation of Matsuoka because he himself had been in similar situations (the clearing of the Rhineland, declaration of sovereignty of armed forces). He, too, was of the opinion that he had to exploit favorable conditions and accept the risk of an anyhow unavoidable fight at a time when he himself was still young and full of vigor. How right he was in his attitudes was proven by events. Europe now was free. He would not hesitate a moment to reply instantly to any widening of the war, be it by Russia, be it by America. Providence favors those who will not let dangers come to them, but who will bravely face them.

Matsuoka replied that the United States, or rather their ruling politicians, had recently still attempted a last maneuvre towards Japan by declaring that America would not fight Japan on account of China or the South Seas, provided that Japan gave free passage to the consignment of rubber and tin to America to their place of destination. However, America would war against Japan the moment she felt that Japan entered the war with the intention to assist in the destruction of Great Britain. Such an argument naturally did not miss its effect upon the Japanese, because of the education oriented on English lines which many had received.

The Fuehrer commented on this that this attitude of America did not mean anything, but that the United States had the hope that, as long as the British world empire existed, one day they could advance against Japan together with Great Britain, whereas, in case of the collapse of the world empire, they would be totally isolated and could not do anything against Japan.

The Reich Foreign Minister interjected that the Americans, precisely under all circumstances, wanted to maintain the powerful position of England in East Asia, but that on the other hand it is proved by this attitude, to what extent she fears a joint action of Japan and Germany.

Matsuoka continued that it seemed to him of importance to give to the Fuehrer an absolutely clear picture of the real attitude inside Japan. For this reason he also had to inform him regretfully of the fact that he, Matsuoka, in his capacity as Japanese Minister for Foreign Affairs could not utter in Japan a single word of all that he had expounded before the Fuehrer and the Reich Foreign Minister regarding his plans. This would cause him serious damage in political and financial circles. Once before he had committed the mistake, before he became Japanese Minister for Foreign Affairs, of telling a close friend something about his intentions. It seems that the latter had spread these things, and thus brought about all sorts of rumors, which he, as Foreign Minister had to oppose energetically, though as a rule he always tells the truth. Under these circumstances, he also could not indicate how soon he could report on the questions discussed to the Japanese Premier or to the Emperor. He would have to study exactly and carefully, in the first place, the development in Japan, so as to make his decision at a favorable moment, to make a clear breast of his proper plans to Prince Konoye and the Emperor. Then the decision would have to be made within a few days because the plans would otherwise be spoiled by talk.[6]

Seven weeks later, on May 24, 1941, the German military attaché in Tokyo informed the Intelligence Division of the High Command: "The preparations for attack on Singapore and Manila stand."[7]

Negotiations Vis-à-vis Russia

The German attack upon Soviet Russia changed abruptly the tenor of the negotiations with Japan. If an attack by Japan on

Singapore had been desirable before, an attack by Japan on Russia's far eastern territories seemed indispensable now.

On July 10, 1941, Ribbentrop cabled the following instructions to the German ambassador in Tokyo:

Please take this opportunity to thank the Japanese Foreign Minister for conveying the cable report of the Japanese ambassador in Moscow. It would be convenient if we could keep on receiving news from Russia this way. In summing up, I should like to say I have now, as in the past, full confidence in the Japanese policy and in the Japanese Foreign Minister; first of all because the present Japanese Government would really act inexcusably toward the future of their nation if they would not take this unique opportunity to solve the Russian problem, as well as to secure for all time its expansion to the south and settle the Chinese matter. Since Russia, as reported by the Japanese ambassador in Moscow, is in effect close to collapse—a report which coincides with our own observations as far as we are able to judge the present war situation—it is simply impossible that Japan should not settle the matter of Vladivostok and the Siberian area as soon as her military preparations are completed....

However, I ask you to employ all available means in further insisting upon Japan's entry into the war against Russia at the earliest possible date, as I have mentioned already in my note to Matsuoka. The sooner this entry is effected, the better. The natural objective still remains that we and Japan join hands on the trans-Siberian railroad before winter starts. After the collapse of Russia however, the position of the Three Power-Pact States in the world will be so gigantic that the question of England's collapse or the total destruction of the British Isles will be only a matter of time. An America totally isolated from the rest of the world would then be faced with our taking possession of the remaining portions of the British Empire which are important for the Three-Power-Pact countries. I have the unshakeable conviction that a carrying through of the New Order as desired by us will be a matter of course, and there will be no insurmountable difficulties if the countries of the Three Power Pact stand close together and encounter every action of the Americans with the same weapons. I ask you to report in the near future, as often as possible and in detail, on the political situation there.[8]

The German ambassador replied by secret message on July 13, 1941:

I am trying with all means to work toward Japan's entry into the war against Russia as soon as possible, especially using arguments of the personal message of the Foreign Minister and the telegram cited above to convince Matsuoka personally, as well as the Foreign Office, military elements, nationalists, and friendly businessmen. I believe that according to military preparations, Japanese participation will soon take place. The greatest obstacle to this against which one has to fight is the disunity within the activist group which, without unified command, follows various aims and only slowly adjusts itself to the changed situation.[9]

But Japan had her own plans. With Great Britain and the Soviet Union tied down by Germany, only the United States of America stood in the way of her ambition to establish, through military action, the Greater East Asia Co-Prosperity Sphere, the trade name for Japanese aggression in the Orient. She was encouraged in this direction by the advice which Ribbentrop gave to the Japanese ambassador in Berlin during a conversation on the night of November 28. Ribbentrop warned that if Japan hesitated to enter the war and Germany established her new order in Europe Japan might be faced with the combined military strength of Britain and the United States. And he said that if the negotiations then pending between Japan and the United States should break down, as seemed probable, and Japan then reached a decision to fight Great Britain and the United States, he was confident that the consequent enlargement of the war would be to the interest of both Germany and Japan. And Ribbentrop gave his unconditional promise that if Japan became engaged in a war against the United States, Germany would enter immediately.

Thus strengthened by unconditional German promises of help in case of war with the United States, the Japanese planned their attack under cover of the then pending negotiations. The worsening situation was reported by the German ambassador in a telegram of November 30, 1941, to Berlin in which he commented upon a recent conversation with the Japanese Foreign Minister:

The progress of the negotiations so far confirms his viewpoint that the difference of opinion between Japan and the U.S. is very great. The Japanese Government, since they sent Ambassador Kurusu, has taken a firm stand as he told me. He is convinced that this position is in our favor, and makes the United States think that her entry into the European war would be risky business....

Japan is not afraid of a breakdown of negotiations, and she hopes that if occasion arises Germany and Italy, according to the Three Power Pact, would stand at her side. I answered that there could be no doubt about Germany's future position. The Japanese Foreign Minister thereupon stated that he understood from my words that Germany, in such a case, would consider her relationship to Japan as that of a union by fate. I answered, according to my opinion, Germany was certainly ready to have mutual agreement between the two countries over this situation.

The Minister of Foreign Affairs answered that it was possible that he would come back to this point soon. The conversation with the Minister of Foreign Affairs confirmed the impression that the United States note, in fact, is very unsatisfactory even for the compromise-seeking politicians here. For these circles, America's position, especially in the China question, is very disappointing. The emphasis upon the Three Power Pact as being the main obstacle between successful Japanese-United States negotiations seems to point to the fact that the Japanese Government are becoming aware of the necessity of close co-operation with the Axis Powers.[10]

By the first of December it had become clear, from the Japanese viewpoint, that these negotiations had reached an impasse. Japanese enmity was thus diverted from her historical enemy, Russia, to her historical friend, the United States.

On December 3, 1941, Count Ciano made the following entry in his diary:

Sensational move by Japan. The Ambassador asks for an audience with the Duce and reads him a long statement on the progress of negotiations with America, concluding with the assertion that they have reached a dead end. Then invoking the appropriate clause in the Tripartite Pact, he asks that Italy declare war on America immediately after the outbreak of hostilities and proposes the signing of an agreement not to conclude a separate peace. The interpreter translating this request was trembling like a leaf. The Duce gave fullest assurances, reserving the right to confer with Berlin before giving a reply. The Duce was pleased with the communication and said, "We are now on the brink of the inter-continental war which I predicted as early as September 1939." What does this new event mean? In any case it means that Roosevelt has succeeded in his maneuvre. Since he could not enter into the war immediately and directly, he entered it indirectly by letting himself be attacked by Japan. Furthermore, this event also means that every prospect of peace is becoming further and further removed, and that it is now easy—much too easy—to predict a long war. Who will be able to hold out longest?[11]

On December 4, 1941, Ciano wrote: "Berlin's reaction to the Japanese move is extremely cautious. Perhaps they will accept because they cannot get out of it, but the idea of provoking America's intervention pleases the Germans less and less. Mussolini, on the other hand, is pleased about it."[12]

The December 5 entry in Ciano's diary disclosed that Germany and Italy had agreed with Japan to stand by their tripartite agreement in the event of a Japanese attack upon the United States:

A night interrupted by Ribbentrop's restlessness. After delaying 2 days, now he cannot wait a minute to answer the Japanese; and at three in the morning he sent Mackensen to my house to submit a plan for a triple agreement relative to Japanese intervention and the pledge not to make a separate peace. He wanted me to awaken the Duce, but I did not do so, and the latter was very glad I had not.[13]

Pearl Harbor

On Sunday, December 7, 1941, Japanese planes attacked and destroyed the major units of the United States fleet at Pearl Harbor and simultaneously attacked the British in the southwest Pacific. Four days later Germany, faced with the *fait accompli* of her protégé in trickery and aggression, declared war upon the United States, and the military struggle became world-wide.

On the day after the Japanese attack on Pearl Harbor, Ciano made the following entry in his diary:

A night telephone call from Ribbentrop. He is overjoyed about the Japanese attack on America. He is so happy about it that I am happy with him, though I am not too sure about the final advantage of what has happened. One thing is now certain, that America will enter the conflict and that the conflict will be so long that she will be able to realize all her potential forces. This morning I told this to the King who had been pleased about the event. He ended by admitting that in the long run, I may be right. Mussolini was happy, too. For a long time he has favored a definite clarification of relations between America and the Axis.[14]

On the fourteenth of December, 1941, in presenting Japanese Ambassador Oshima with the Grand Cross of the Order of Merit of the German Eagle, Hitler said:

You gave the right declaration of war. This method is the only proper one. Japan pursued it formerly and it corresponds with his own system, that is, to negotiate as long as possible. But if one sees the other is interested only in putting one off, in shamming and humiliating one, and is not willing to come to an agreement, then one should strike as hard as possible, indeed, and not waste time declaring war. It was heart-warming to him to hear of the first operations of the Japanese. He, himself, negotiated with infinite patience at times, for example, with Poland and also with Russia. When he then realized that the other did not want to come to an agreement, he struck suddenly and without formality. He would continue to go on this way in the future.[15]

But the future led only to Stalingrad, Rome, Normandy, Berlin, and Hiroshima

PART THREE

War Crimes

CHAPTER 14

Let the Prisoners Perish

THE BASIC crime of the leaders of Nazi Germany was the initiating and waging of wars of aggression, with the consequent killing of millions of people and the wastage of billions of dollars in property. Death and devastation are the inevitable accompaniments of war. As Mr. Justice Jackson said: "Any resort to war—to any kind of war—is a resort to means that are inherently criminal. War inevitably is a course of killings, assaults, deprivations of liberty, and destruction of property."[1] Moreover, war crimes are committed on both sides in every war. While recorded here are the most serious offenses chargeable to the Nazis during World War II, it must be appreciated that in all they involved but a very small percentage of German military forces. Indeed, most of these crimes were executed by police forces and not by military personnel at all. In recounting these crimes, therefore, the writer has no purpose of indicting the German armed forces, which, in the main, lived up to standards of humane warfare observed by the armies they were pitted against.

Nor is it always possible, in the course of war, even with optimum good faith, to provide the care contemplated by international conventions for prisoners of war. General von Manstein gave this explanation for mass casualties of Soviet war prisoners during the first winter of the German-Soviet war:

During the large battles of encirclement in 1941 which took place within the Army Group Center and near Kiev, where the prisoners ran into many hundreds of thousands, the situation was different. When the Russian soldiers came out of the encircled areas in which they had held out to the last, they were already half-starved, and in this case, an army with its transportation space cannot possibly bring with it the means to feed 500,000 prisoners at once, and accommodate them in central Russia.[2]

The inevitable result was that thousands of prisoners died from starvation.

But the suffering and dying of soldiers who were taken prisoner by German military forces was not due alone to the circumstances of war. For in certain territories, in the East particularly, and with certain troops, especially Himmler's SS formations, specific crimes against prisoners were ordered by Hitler and executed by his subordinates. Insofar as those who carried out these orders had power of moral choice, they were properly charged with the commission of war crimes. In the words of Sir Hartley Shawcross: "Political loyalty, military obedience are excellent things, but they neither require nor do they justify the commission of patently wicked acts. There comes a point where a man must refuse to answer to his leader if he is also to answer to his conscience."[3]

Some crimes against the laws of war were based upon mistreatment of civilians of occupied territories, particularly in connection with reprisals, the taking and killing of hostages, and secret arrests and deportations. Other crimes, such as the killing of escaped war prisoners, the murder of "undesirable" prisoners screened out of prisoner of war cages, and the killing of commandos and captured flyers, were inexcusable violations of fundamental rights of prisoners of war. These specific crimes are dealt with in the chapters that follow. This chapter considers only the general mistreatment of war prisoners, and their utilization in war work contrary to the Geneva Convention.

Mistreatment of Prisoners of War

In the year 1902, the German General Staff published these instructions concerning the rights of prisoners of war: "The only purpose in capturing prisoners of war is to prevent their further participation in the war. Although prisoners of war lose their freedom, they do not lose their rights. In other words, captivity is not an act of mercy on the part of the conqueror. It is the right of the disarmed soldier."[4] This humane doctrine, which had long governed the conduct of war by the German military, was utterly rejected by Hitler in wàging war in the East.

By order of General Reinecke, head of the prisoner of war department, the Chief of the Supreme Command of the Armed Forces issued on September 8, 1941, regulations for the treatment of Soviet prisoners of war which rejected these long-held principles governing captured enemy soldiers:

Bolshevism is the deadly enemy of National Socialist Germany. For the first time, the German soldier is encountering not only a military opponent, but one, at the same time, steeped in the ideas of Bolshevism so pernicious to the people. The fight against National Socialism has become part of his system. He conducts it by every means in his power: sabotage, seditious propaganda, incendiarism, murder. The Bolshevist soldier has therefore lost all claim to treatment as an honorable opponent in accordance with the Geneva Convention....

The order for ruthless and energetic action must be given at the slightest indication of insubordination, especially in the case of Bolshevistic fanatics. Insubordination, active or passive resistance, must *immediately* be broken completely by force of arms (bayonets, butts and firearms)....Anyone carrying out an order, who does not use his weapons or does so with insufficient energy, is punishable.

Prisoners of war attempting to escape are to be fired on without previous challenge. No warning shot must ever be fired....On the other hand, no arbitrary action is permitted. Prisoners of war who are obedient and willing to work are to be treated correctly. However, caution and mistrust must never lapse when dealing with prisoners of war. The use of arms against prisoners of war is, as a rule, legal.[5]

Exactly one week later, Admiral Canaris, as Chief of Military Intelligence, submitted a reply memorandum to Keitel on the legal aspects of the Reinecke directive for the treatment of Soviet war prisoners. He conceded that the Geneva Convention was not binding between Germany and the Soviet Union, and that therefore only the principles of general international law on the treatment of prisoners of war applied to the eastern theater of operations.

Since the 18th century these have gradually been established along the lines that war captivity is neither revenge nor punishment, but solely protective custody the only purpose of which is to prevent the prisoners of war from a further participation in the war. This principle was developed in accordance with the view held by all armies that it is contrary to military tradition to kill or injure helpless people; this is also in the interest of all belligerents in order to prevent mistreatment of their own soldiers in case of capture.

The decrees for the treatment of Soviet prisoners of war enclosed as supplement No. 1 are based on a fundamentally different viewpoint, as is shown in the opening phrases. According to this viewpoint military service for the Soviets is not considered military duty but, because of the murders committed by the Russians, is characterized in its totality as a crime. Hence the validity of international legal standards in wartime is denied in the war against Bolshevism.... The instructions are very general. But if one considers their basic principles the expressly approved measures will result in arbitrary mistreatments and killings, the formal prohibition of arbitrary actions notwithstanding.[6]

Canaris then expounded in detail the several aspects of the regulations which he considered to be both contrary to international law and unwise as a matter of military policy. Keitel's reaction to the memorandum was indicated by his notation of September 23: "The objections arise from the military concept of chivalrous warfare! This is the destruction of an ideology! Therefore I approve and back the measures."[7]

Just five months after the war began with the Soviet Union, Foreign Minister Molotov published a note charging the Germans with terrible acts of atrocity. He asserted that Soviet soldiers had been "nailed to stakes, and on their bodies five-pointed stars had been cut with red-hot knives,"[8] and that German soldiers had committed other equally gruesome acts of torture. In April, 1942, Molotov published a second, and similar, note on atrocities. These reports, and others which followed, were based upon information collected by the Soviet Extraordinary State Commission for the investigation of atrocities in various eastern territories which had been under occupation by German military and police forces. Undoubtedly they were primarily propagandistic, designed to work the Soviet people into a frenzy of resistance. To what extent truth was in them can scarcely be judged.

From time to time, however, complaints of German officials were raised against the mistreatment of Soviet prisoners of war. Such complaints had the merit of being against interest and are, therefore, of undoubted authenticity. A complaint of this kind was made by the Reich Ministry for the Occupied Eastern Territories on February 28, 1942. It was addressed to Field Marshal Keitel, as Chief of the High Command.

The fate of the Soviet prisoners of war in Germany is on the contrary a tragedy of the greatest extent. Of 3,600,000 prisoners of war, only several hundred thousand are still able to work fully. A large part of them has starved, or died, because of the hazards of the weather. Thousands also died from spotted fever. It is understood, of course, that there are difficulties encountered in the feeding of such a large number of prisoners of war. Anyhow, with a certain amount of understanding for goals aimed at by German politics, dying and deterioration could have been avoided in the extent described. For instance, according to information on hand, the native population within the Soviet Union are absolutely willing to put food at the disposal of the prisoners of war. Several understanding camp commanders have successfully chosen this course. However, in the majority of the cases the camp commanders have forbidden the civilian population to put food at the disposal of the prisoners and they have rather let them starve to death. Even on the march to the camps, the civilian population was not allowed to give the prisoners of war food. In many cases, when prisoners of war could no longer keep up on the march because of hunger and exhaustion, they were shot before the eyes of the horrified civilian population, and the corpses were left. In numerous camps, no shelter for the prisoners of war was provided at all. They lay under the open sky during rain or snow. Even tools were not made available to dig holes or caves. A systematic delousing of the prisoners of war in the camps and of the camps themselves has apparently been missed. Utterances such as these have been heard: "The more of these prisoners die, the better it is for us." The consequence of this treatment is now this, that spotted fever is spreading due to the escape and discharge of prisoners and has claimed its victims among the armed forces as well as among the civilian population, even in the old part of Germany. Finally, the shooting of prisoners of war must be mentioned; these were partly carried out according to view-points which ignore all political understanding. For instance, in various camps, all the "Asiatics" were shot, although the inhabitants of the areas, considered belonging to Asia, of Transcaucasia and Turkestan especially, are among those people in the Soviet Union who are most strongly opposed to Russian subjugation and to Bolshevism....

It was a basic mistake that no difference was made between real prisoners of war and deserters. It is known that German propaganda deposited millions of leaflets beyond the lines, and encouraged the Red soldiers to desert, whereby good treatment and sufficient food were specifically assured to them. These promises were not kept. The deserters were beaten and left to starve the same as so many prisoners of war. A natural consequence of this politically and militarily unwise treatment was not only a paralyzing of the will to desert, but a plain deadly fear to get into German captivity. It would be naive to assume that the occurrences in the prisoner of war camps could be kept hidden from the Soviet Government. As can be seen in Molotov's circular, the Soviets have in fact an excellent knowledge of the conditions described above, and naturally they have done everything in their power to influence the Soviet population and Red Soldiers accordingly. It can be said without exaggeration that the mistakes in the treatment of prisoners of war are to a great extent the cause for the stiffening power of resistance of the Red Army, and therefore also cause for the deaths of thousands of German soldiers.[9]

In Yugoslavia, all who resisted the invading German forces were treated as "bandits" and were denied the rights of soldiers.[10] By this ruse, Hitler sought to excuse the killing of prisoners of war and the imposition of repressive measures upon noncombatants who gave aid to Yugoslavian troops. A secret report signed by Major General Kuebler under date of May 12, 1943, provided that anyone who participated openly in the fight against the German armed forces and was taken prisoner was "to be shot after interrogation."[11]

Mistreatment of Allied prisoners of war in the West was sporadic, and not to be compared with actions taken against Soviet and Yugoslavian troops. On some occasions, however, fanatical SS troops did commit acts in deliberate violation of principles of humane warfare. During the course of a speech to his commanding officers in Kharkov in April, 1943, Himmler had said: "We will never let that excellent weapon, the dread and terrible reputation which preceded us in the battle of Kharkov, fade, but will constantly add new meaning to it."[12] That reputation was founded on the principle of war without quarter.

A court of inquiry of the Supreme Headquarters, Allied Expeditionary Force, found that between the seventh and seventeenth of June, 1944, the 12th SS Panzer Division in Normandy, France, was responsible for seven cases of shooting unarmed Allied prisoners, involving sixty-four soldiers, all in uniform, many wounded, and none of whom had resisted arrest or attempted to escape. The killings were based upon secret orders that SS troops should take no prisoners and that captives were to be executed after having been interrogated for information against the enemy.

During the Battle of the Bulge a massacre of 129 American prisoners of war took place on December 17, 1944, in a field near Baignez in Belgium.

Some of these tanks stopped when they came opposite the field in which the unarmed American prisoners were standing in a group, with their hands up or clasped behind their heads. A German soldier, either an officer or a noncommissioned officer, in one of these vehicles which had stopped, got up, drew his revolver, took deliberate aim and fired into the group of American prisoners. One of the American soldiers fell. This was repeated a second time and another American soldier in the group fell to the ground. At about the same time, from two of the vehicles on the road fire was opened on the group of American prisoners in the field. All, or most, of the American soldiers dropped to the ground and stayed there while the firing continued for 2 or 3 minutes. Most of the soldiers in the field were hit by this machine gun fire. The German vehicles then moved off toward the south and were followed by more vehicles which also came from the direction of Weismes. As these latter vehicles came opposite the field in which the American soldiers were lying, they also fired with small arms from the moving vehicles at the prostrate bodies in the field.... Some German soldiers, evidently from the group of those who were on guard at the crossroad, then walked to the group of the wounded American prisoners who were still lying on the ground in the field ... and shot with pistol or rifle, or clubbed with a rifle butt or other heavy object, any of the American soldiers who still showed any sign of life. In some instances, American prisoners were evidently shot at close range, squarely between the eyes, in the temple, or the back of the head....[13]

The Malmedy massacre was entirely exceptional. Certain categories of Allied prisoners were subjected to mistreatment, as will be shown in later chapters. In general, however, prisoners of war in the West were properly cared for.

Labor in War Industries

As the manpower shortage became increasingly acute in Germany, prisoners of war were transported to the Reich in huge numbers to work in the coal mines, in the fields and factories, and even in armament industries in violation of the Geneva Convention. In August, 1941, Goering personally ordered 100,000 French prisoners of war to be assigned to the armament industry as part of a plan to transfer all French prisoners to war factories, replacing them in the nonmilitary industries with Soviet prisoners.

On October 31, 1941, Hitler ordered that Soviet prisoners of war likewise should be utilized to a large extent in war industries. And on November 7, 1941, at a conference at the Air Ministry, Goering said: "The Fuehrer's point of view as to employment of prisoners of war in war industries has changed basically. So far, a total of five million prisoners of war—employed so far, two million.... In the interior and the Protectorate it would be ideal if entire factories could be manned by Russian prisoners of war except the employees necessary for directing."[14] With respect to armament industries, Goering suggested: "Preferably factories of armor and guns. Possibly also construction of parts for aircraft engines. Suitable complete sections of factories to be manned exclusively by Russians if possible."[15]

Sauckel's labor mobilization program contained a provision that "all prisoners of war now in Germany, from the territories of the West as well as of the East, must be completely incorporated into the German armament and food industries."[16] At a meeting of the Central Planning Board, Field Marshal Milch said: "Our best new engine is made 88% by Russian prisoners of war and the other 12% by German men and women."[17] And Speer, the Reich Minister for Armaments and Munitions, complained to the same Board that a greater percentage of Soviet prisoners of war was not employed in the armament industry: "There is a detailed statement showing in what sectors the Russian prisoners of war have been distributed. This statement is quite interesting. It shows that the armament industry only received 30%. I constantly complained about this."[18]

Prisoners of war were not only compelled to make the guns to be fired against their countrymen—they were also required in some instances to fire the guns. At a meeting of the Central Planning Board of February 19, 1943, Field Marshal Milch was recorded as saying: "We have made a request for an order that a certain percentage of men in the anti-aircraft artillery must be Russians. Fifty thousand will be taken altogether; thirty thousand are already employed as gunners. It is an amusing thing that Russians must work the guns."[19]

French war prisoners were not required to engage in actual combat, but they were assigned to military work on the eastern front. They were employed to transport munitions, to load bombs on aircraft, to repair aviation camps, and to construct fortifications.

In spite of the need for war prisoners for the armament industry, Keitel issued on July 8, 1943, a directive carrying out a Hitler order that manpower requirements for coal production were to be filled out of prisoners of war. Of the Soviet war prisoners in German hands, 200,000 fit for coal mining were to be transferred immediately; and the coal mining industry was to have absolute priority on new Soviet war prisoners. But by then the tide of battle had turned, and prisoners were being taken principally by the other side.

In a speech to SS-Generals at Posen on October 4, 1943, Himmler admitted that the killing and mistreatment of prisoners of war was responsible for the shortage of prisoners for labor:

At that time we did not value the mass of humanity as we value it today as raw material, as labor. What, after all, thinking in terms of generations, is not to be regretted, but is now deplorable by reason of the loss of labor, is that the prisoners died in tens and hundreds of thousands of exhaustion and hunger.[20]

For Hitler, war was part conquest and part extermination. Prisoners of war taken in the East were exploited for their labor until they died. They were frequently denied warm clothing, habitable shelter, medical treatment, and living food rations. They did die—by the thousands and the tens of thousands. It had been Hitler's policy in the East to let the prisoners perish. In Germany's hour of crisis that policy contributed to her collapse—and to Hitler's downfall.

CHAPTER 15

The Fight Behind the Lines

HITLER, HIMSELF, was largely responsible for the guerrilla problem in eastern territories. When the German armies invaded the Ukraine they found at first an outward willingness on the part of the people to accept the occupation without serious opposition. But mistreatment of Ukrainians who volunteered for labor in Germany and harsh measures imposed by the occupying forces soon led to disillusionment and ultimately inflamed the people to resistance. Thousands fled to forest areas behind the lines from which they marauded against the occupying forces and their supplies. Action against them was unparalleled in severity.

Draconian Measures

On May 13, 1941, more than a month before the attack upon the Soviet Union, Keitel published an order concerning certain "military" measures to be taken in the area "Barbarossa." This order provided in part:

1. Until further notice the military courts and the courts-martial will not be competent for crimes committed by enemy civilians.
2. Guerrillas should be disposed of ruthlessly by the military, whether they are fighting or in flight.
3. Likewise all other attacks by enemy civilians on the armed forces, its members, and employees, are to be suppressed at once by the military, using the most extreme methods, until the assailants are destroyed.
4. Where such measures have been neglected or were not at first possible, persons suspected of criminal action will be brought at once before an officer. This officer will decide whether they are to be shot.

On the orders of an officer with the powers of at least a battalion commander, collective drastic measures will be taken without delay against localities from which cunning or malicious attacks are made on the armed forces, if circumstances do not permit of a quick identification of individual offenders.[1]

An amplification of this order was issued by Keitel on July 23, 1941, in which it was stated that security could not be maintained in the East by legal prosecutions, but only "by the spreading of such terror by the occupying forces" as would remove every inclination of the population to resist. Military commanders were directed to find the means of keeping order not by demanding more security forces, but "by applying suitable, Draconian measures."

Notwithstanding these directives, less than three months after the attack upon the Soviet Union the resistance of the civilians had become so serious to German military operations that Keitel issued even more severe orders. On September 16, 1941, he directed:

Since the beginning of the campaign against Soviet Russia, Communist insurrection movements have broken out everywhere in the area occupied by Germany. The type of action taken is growing from propaganda measures and attacks on individual members of the armed forces into open rebellion and widespread guerrilla warfare....

The measures taken up to now to deal with this general Communist insurrection movement have proved inadequate. The Fuehrer has now given orders that we take action everywhere with the most drastic means in order to crush the movement in the shortest possible time....

In order to nip these machinations in the bud, the most drastic measures should be taken immediately on the first indication, so that the authority of the occupying forces may be maintained and further spreading prevented. In this connection it should be remembered that a human life in the countries concerned frequently counts for nothing, and a deterrent effect can be attained only by unusual severity. The death penalty for 50-100 Communists should generally be regarded in these cases as suitable atonement for one German soldier's death. The way in which sentence is carried out should still further increase the deterrent effect.[2]

Keitel was interrogated by the Soviet prosecutor on this order:

Question: ... You remember this basic idea of the order, that human life absolutely does not amount to anything.... Do you remember this sentence?

Answer: Yes.

Question: You signed the order containing this statement?

Answer: Yes....

Question: I shall interrogate you, defendant Keitel, only on one question in connection with this order. In sub-paragraph one of this order, paragraph three, it is stated, and I would draw your attention to the following sentence: "The troops are therefore authorized and ordered in this struggle to take any measures without restriction even against women and children, if that is necessary to achieve success." Have you found this passage?

Answer: Yes.

Question: Have you found the order calling for the application of any kind of measures you like without restriction, also against women and children?

Answer: "To employ without restriction any means, even against women and children, if it is necessary." I have found that.[3]

On October 10, 1941, Field Marshal von Reichenau, Commander in Chief of the German Sixth Army, operating on the Eastern front, issued the following implementing instructions to his troops:

Regarding the conduct of troops towards the Bolshevistic system, vague ideas are still prevalent in many cases. The most essential aim of war against the Jewish-Bolshevistic system is a complete destruction of their means of power and the elimination of Asiatic influence from the European culture. In this connection the troops are facing tasks which exceed the one-sided routine of soldiering. The soldier in the Eastern territories is not merely a fighter according to the rules of the art of war, but also a bearer of ruthless national ideology and the avenger of bestialities which have been inflicted upon German and racially related nations.

Therefore, the soldier must have full understanding for the necessity of a severe but just revenge on subhuman Jewry. The army has to aim at another purpose, that is, the annihilation of revolts in the hinterland, which, as experience proves, have always been caused by Jews....

The fear of the German counter-measures must be stronger than the threats of the wandering Bolshevistic remnants. Being far from all political considerations of the future, the soldier has to fulfill two tasks:

1. Complete annihilation of the false Bolshevistic doctrine of the Soviet state and its armed forces.

2. The pitiless extermination of alien treachery and cruelty and thus the protection of the lives of German military personnel in Russia.

This is the only way to fulfill our historic task to liberate the German people once and for ever from the Asiatic-Jewish danger.[4]

During the course of a conversation with Mussolini in the Palazzo Venezia on October 23, 1942, Goering commented upon Germany's method of fighting partisans:

... The Reich Marshal then described Germany's method in fighting the partisans. To begin with, all livestock and food-stuffs were taken away from the areas concerned, so as to deny the partisans all sources of supply. Men and women were taken away to labor camps, the children to children's camps, and the villages burned down. It was by the use of these methods that the railways in the vast wooded areas of Bialowiza had been safeguarded. Whenever attacks occurred, the entire male population of the villages was lined up on one side and the women on the other. The women were told that all the men would be shot, unless they—the women—pointed out which men did not belong to the village.[5]

When asked if this was a correct description of the German method of fighting partisans Goering replied, "Yes, certainly."[6]

During cross-examination by Mr. Justice Jackson, Goering was confronted with his antipartisan order of October 26, 1942:

Simultaneously with the intensified combating of guerrilla activity ordered by the Fuehrer, and the cleaning up of the land behind the lines, in particular that behind the Army Group Center, I request that the following points be taken into consideration, and the conclusions drawn therefrom be put into practice:

1. Simultaneously with the combating of the underground forces and the combing out of the areas contaminated by them, all available livestock must be driven off to safe areas. Similarly, food supplies are to be removed and brought into safety, so that they will no longer be available to the guerrillas.

2. All male and female labor suitable for any kind of employment must be forcibly recruited and allocated to the Plenipotentiary General for Labor, who will then employ them in safe areas behind the lines or in the Reich. Separate camps must be organized behind the lines for the children.[7]

Goering was asked whether he had issued this order, and he answered, "Absolutely."[8]

Antipartisan Warfare

The chief of the antipartisan units operating in the eastern territories was SS Obergruppenfuehrer von dem Bach. In a speech to his SS Generals at Posen on October 4, 1943, Himmler gave credit to Von dem Bach for fulfilling this responsibility as a member of the SS, subject to Himmler's orders. "I considered it necessary," said Himmler, "for the Reichsfuehrer SS to be in authoritative command in all these battles, for I am convinced that we are best in a position to take actions against this enemy struggle, which is a decidedly political one."[9]

The activities of Von dem Bach were referred to in a report of June 5, 1943, by SS Brigadefuehrer von Gottberg in which he described an antipartisan action called "Cottbus":

The figures mentioned above indicate that again a heavy destruction of the population must be expected. If only 492 rifles are taken from 4,500 enemy dead, this discrepancy shows that among these enemy dead were numerous peasants from the country. The Battalion Dirlewanger especially has a reputation for destroying many human lives. Among the 5,000 people suspected of belonging to bands, there were numerous women and children. By order of the Chief of Antipartisan Combat, SS Obergruppenfuehrer von dem Bach, units of the armed forces have also participated in the operation.[10]

Upon direct examination, Von dem Bach himself confessed that antipartisan warfare was carried out ruthlessly and resulted in the unnecessary killing of large numbers of civilians:

Question: What proportion of Wehrmacht troops was used in anti-partisan operations as compared to Police and SS troops?
Answer: Since the number of Police and SS troops was very small, anti-partisan operations were undertaken mainly by Wehrmacht formations.
Question: Were the anti-partisan troops usually commanded by Wehrmacht officers or by SS Officers?
Answer: It varied, depending mostly on the individual area; in the operational areas Wehrmacht officers nearly always commanded, but an order existed to the effect that the formation, be it Wehrmacht, Waffen-SS or Police, which supplied the most troops for a particular operation, had command of it.

Question: Did the highest military leaders issue instructions that anti-partisan operations were to be conducted with severity?

Answer: Yes.

Question: Did the highest military authorities issue any detailed instructions as to the methods to be used in anti-partisan operations?

Answer: No.

Question: What was the result, in the occupied territories, of this lack of detailed directives from above?

Answer: This lack of detailed directives resulted in a wild state of anarchy in all anti-partisan operations....

Question: Did these measures result in the unnecessary killing of large numbers of the civilian population?

Answer: Yes.[11]

Von dem Bach confirmed the existence of an order that German soldiers who committed offenses were not to be subject to military discipline.

Question: Was an order ever issued by the highest authorities that German soldiers who committed offenses against the civilian population were not to be punished in the military courts?

Answer: Yes, this order was issued.

Question: Was this order an obstacle to correcting the excesses of the troops?

Answer: Yes, in my opinion, this order prevented the orderly conduct of operations, since one can train troops only if one has adequate disciplinary powers and jurisdiction over them and is able to check excesses.[12]

To encourage more ruthless action against guerrillas, Goering conceived the idea of using convicts against partisans in the occupied territories. The following extract from the Plans of the Reich Marshal, dated September 24, 1942, describes this plan:

The Reich Marshal is looking for daring fellows, who will be employed in the East as Sonderkommandos and who will be able to carry out the task of creating confusion behind the lines. They are to be formed into bands under leadership, and with interpreters assigned to them. For this purpose the Reich Marshal is considering convicts who are first offenders, who have committed not particularly heinous offenses for which there can be some human understanding.

The Reich Marshal first of all mentioned persons convicted of poaching.... The Reich Marshal also mentioned fanatical members of smuggling gangs, who take part in gun battles on the frontiers and whose passion it is to outwit the customs at the risk of their own lives. ...In the regions assigned for their operations, these bands, whose first task should be to destroy the communications of the partisan groups, could murder, burn, and ravish; in Germany, they would once again come under strict supervision.[13]

Von dem Bach admitted that Goering's plan to use common criminals in the fight against partisans was actually put into practice:

Question: Do you know anything about the existence of a special brigade consisting of smugglers, poachers, and persons released from prison?

Answer: When all the troops really suitable for anti-partisan warfare had been withdrawn, an anti-partisan battalion under the command of Dirlewanger was formed and attached to Army Group Center at the end of 1941 or the beginning of 1942. This battalion was gradually strengthened by the addition of reserve units until it reached the proportions, first, of a regiment, and later, of a brigade. This "Dirlewanger Brigade" consisted for the most part of previously convicted criminals; officially it consisted of so-called poachers, but it did include real criminals convicted of burglary, murder, *et cetera.*

Question: How do you explain the fact that the German Army Command so willingly strengthened and increased its forces by adding criminals to them and then using these criminals against the partisans?

Answer: I am of the opinion that this step was closely connected with a speech made by Heinrich Himmler at Weselsburg at the beginning of 1941, prior to the campaign against Russia, when he spoke of the purpose of the Russian campaign, which was, he said, to decimate the Slav population by 30 million, and that it was in order to achieve this purpose that troops of such inferior caliber were introduced....

Question: Do you believe that Himmler's speech, in which he demanded the extermination of 30 million Slavs, expressed only his personal opinion; or do you consider that it corresponded to the National Socialist ideology?

Answer: Today I believe that it was the logical consequence of our ideology.

Question: Today?... What was your own opinion at that time?

Answer: It is difficult for a German to fight through to this conviction. It took me a long time.... I am of a different opinion. If for years, for decades, a doctrine is preached to the effect that the Slav race is an inferior race, that the Jews are not even human beings, then an explosion of this sort is inevitable."[14]

The underlying principle in antipartisan warfare was the killing of all partisans, including even women and children. While asserting that prisoners were taken in antipartisan actions, Jodl admitted that "it was the Fuehrer's view that in their fight against the partisans the troops should in no way be restricted."[15] During the course of a conversation at Hitler's headquarters on December 19, 1942, attended by Field Marshal Keitel, Foreign Minister von Ribbentrop, Count Ciano, and Marshal Cavallero, the partisan problem in Croatia came under discussion. Keitel declared that "every village in which partisans were found had to be burned down."[16] And Ribbentrop added: "These partisan gangs had to be exterminated, including men, women, and children...."[17]

While the killing of all partisans was clearly permissible, and even required, under the basic orders issued by Hitler and Keitel, less clearly defined was the action authorized against those who assisted partisans. The punishment for such collaboration was fixed at punitive labor in concentration camps. An entry in the War Diary of the Deputy Chief of the Armed Forces Operational Staff as of March 14, 1943, stated:

> The treatment of captured partisans has been laid down in the combat directive for the combating of partisans in the East of 27 November 1942 and Hitler's order of 16 December 1941. On the basis of the foregoing the Reichsfuehrer SS ordered on 30 December that persons suspected of being partisans or their assistants, who are not to be executed, are to be transferred to concentration camps in Germany.
>
> This order, which corresponds to the terms of reference already decreed, differs from an order already given on 30 October 1942 by the Commander in Chief of the 18th Army, which calls for the shooting without discrimination of all members of partisan groups....
>
> The High Command of the Armed Forces therefore orders that partisan helpers and suspects who are not to be executed should be handed over to the competent Higher SS and Police Leader and orders that the difference between "punitive work" and "work in Germany" is to be made clear to the population.[18]

Antipartisan warfare thus provided Himmler with the means to destroy some elements of the Slav population and to enslave others. General Adolf Heusinger, who was Chief of the Operations Section at Army headquarters from 1940 to 1944, averred:

It had always been my personal opinion that the treatment of the civilian population and the methods of antipartisan warfare in operational areas presented the highest political and military leaders with a welcomed opportunity of carrying out their plans, namely, the systematic extermination of Slavism and Jewry. Entirely independent of this, I always regarded these cruel methods as military insanity, because they only helped to make combat against the enemy unnecessarily more difficult.[19]

Antipartisan warfare was severe, and it was cruel, but at least it was quasi-military. From the German viewpoint, the roving bands of guerrillas had to be dealt with by positive action if the invading German armies were to be protected from assaults against their occupying troops and lines of supply. Of course, the actions in many cases, particularly in the East, far exceeded reasonable retaliation. And it should not be overlooked that antipartisan warfare was a product of the aggressive course of war upon which Hitler led the German nation.

Reprisals

The world will long remember the word "Lidice." The name of a tiny Czechoslovakian village, it has acquired secondary meaning as an act of extreme and wanton reprisal. For the alleged offense of harboring two persons involved in the murder of Reinhard Heydrich, the former chief of the Reich Main Security Office, the village was razed to the ground, all the male inhabitants were murdered, the women were taken to concentration camps, and the children were dispersed. Lidice was literally plowed under. It was so completely destroyed that it was left an empty field, now marked by a cross to signify the place of the crime.

The Czechoslovakian government reported as follows on the events of Lidice:

On 9 June 1942 the village of Lidice was surrounded, on the order of the Gestapo, by soldiers who arrived from the hamlet of Slany in ten large trucks. They allowed anyone to enter the village, but no one was permitted to leave. A 12-year-old boy tried to escape; a soldier shot him on the spot. A woman tried to escape; a bullet in the back mowed her down, and her corpse was found in the fields after the harvest....

The 10th of June was the last day of Lidice and of its inhabitants. The men were locked up in the cellar, the barn, and the stable of the Horak family farm.... The men were led out of the Horak farm into the garden behind the barn, in batches of 10, and shot. The murders lasted from early morning until 4 o'clock in the afternoon.... One hundred seventy-two adult men and youths from 16 years upwards were shot on 10 June 1942. Nineteen men who worked on 9 and 10 June in the Kladno mines were arrested later on in the collieries or nearby woods, taken to Prague, and shot.

Seven women from Lidice were shot in Prague as well. The remaining 195 women were deported to the Ravensbrueck concentration camp. Forty-two died of ill treatment; seven were gassed; three disappeared. Four of these women were taken from Lidice to a maternity hospital in Prague where their newly born infants were murdered; then the mothers were sent to Ravensbrueck.

The children of Lidice were taken from their mothers a few days after the destruction of the village. Ninety children were sent to Lodz, in Poland, and thence to Gneisenau concentration camp, in the so-called Wartheland. So far no trace of these children has been found. Seven of the youngest, less than a year old, were taken to a German hospital in Prague. After examination by "racial experts" they were sent to Germany, there to be brought up as Germans and under German names. Every trace of them has been lost.[20]

Lidice was more than an action of reprisal. It was Gestapo-revenge for the murder by Czechoslovaks of Gestapo chief Heydrich. But even if it had been an authentic reprisal, its effect would have been only to bring about more determined resistance on the part of the people of Czechoslovakia. As Hans Fritzsche testified: "Outrages always called for reprisals and reprisals always called forth new outrages."[21] Lidice was the most notorious of the actions taken against occupied territories, but it was by no means the only such action. Even in Czechoslovakia there were other cases of villages razed to the ground. "Lezhaky, like Lidice, was totally destroyed and the ground where it stood is now covered over with rubble."[22] And the crime of Lidice was repeated in other occupied countries.

On November 24, 1942, Seyss-Inquart issued the following notice in the Netherlands:

> For the destruction or the damaging of railway installations, telephone cables, and post offices I shall make responsible all the inhabitants of the community on whose territory the act is committed. The population of these communities must expect that reprisals will be taken against private property and that houses or whole blocks will be destroyed.[23]

Illustrating the consequence of such orders was the case of the village of Putten. Toward the end of the war an attempt was made by members of the Dutch resistance to harm two German officers. Concluding that Putten was a refuge of the partisans, the Germans searched the houses of the inhabitants. In the course of the search they learned that a German officer had been taken prisoner. They announced that if the officer was released within twenty-four hours there would be no reprisals. The officer was released, after having been medically cared for by the soldiers of the Dutch resistance who had captured him. In spite of the pledge given, however, reprisals were taken against the inhabitants of the village of Putten. The report of the Dutch Government stated:

> The population gathered in the church was informed that the men would be deported and the women would have to leave the village because it would be destroyed. 150 houses were burned down (the total amount of houses in the built-up area being about 2,000). Eight people, among them a woman who tried to escape, were shot.
>
> The men were taken to the concentration camp at Amersfoort. Among them were many accidental passers-by who had been admitted into the closed village but who had been prevented from leaving the place.... Six hundred twenty-two men were eventually deported to Auschwitz. The majority of those died after two months. Of the 622 deported men, only 32 inhabitants of the village of Putten and 10 outsiders returned after the liberation.[24]

The report of the Belgian Government contained numerous cases of the killing of civilians and the burning of their homes:

At Arendonck, on the 3rd, 80 men were killed, five houses were burned. At St. Hubert, on the 6th, three men killed and four houses burned. At Hody, on the 6th, systematic destruction of the village, 40 houses destroyed, 16 people killed. At Marcourt 10 people were shot, 35 houses were burned. At Neroeteren, on the 9th, 9 people were killed. At Oost-Ham, on the 10th, 5 persons were killed. At Balen-Neet, on the 11th, 10 persons were shot....

At Hechtel, the Germans having withdrawn before the British vanguard, the inhabitants hung out flags. But fresh German troops came in to drive out the British vanguard and reprisals were taken; 31 people were shot, 80 houses were burned, and general looting took place. At Helchteren, 34 houses were set on fire and 10 persons were killed under similar circumstances....

At Lommel, the unexpected return of the German soldiers found the village with flags out. Seventeen persons who had sought refuge in a shelter were noticed by a German. He motioned to a tank which ran against the shelter, crushing it and killing 12 people.[25]

In Norway, to avenge the death of two German policemen killed at Televaag on April 26, 1942, the entire town of 344 buildings was destroyed. In reporting upon this action to Goering on May 1, 1942, the Reich Commissioner for Norway, Gauleiter Terboven, stated:

On the same day the entire village which had harbored the sabotage unit was burned down and the population deported. All the males were taken to a German concentration camp without any notification being sent to their families. The women were sent to a female forced labor camp in Norway, and those children who were not capable of working went to a children's camp. Heil Hitler![26]

Destruction of property was extensive in France. A large section of Marseilles was demolished by the German engineers corps. Approximately 1,200 buildings were razed, and about 20,000 people were deported, many of them to the concentration camp of Compiègne.

Extremely severe reprisals were taken by the Gestapo and SD against suspected members of the Maquis, and their sympathizers:

On 8 April 1944 German soldiers of the Gestapo arrested young Andre Bézillon, 18 years of age, dwelling at Oyonnax (Ain), whose brother was in the Maquis. The body of this young man was discovered on 11 April 1944 at Sièges (Jura) frightfully mutilated. His nose and tongue had been cut off. There were traces of blows over his whole body and of slashes on his legs. Four other young men were also found at Sièges at the same time as Bézillon. All of them had been mutilated in such a manner that they could not be identified. They bore no trace of bullets, which clearly indicates that they died from the consequences of ill-treatment....

Having been attacked at Presles by several groups of Maquis in the region, by way of reprisal this Mongolian detachment, as usual commanded by SS, went to a farm where two French members of the resistance had been hidden. Being unable to take them prisoners, those soldiers then took the proprietors of that farm (the husband and wife), and after subjecting them to numerous atrocities, rape, et cetera, they shot them with submachine guns. Then they took the son of these victims, who was only 3 years of age; and, after having tortured him frightfully, they crucified him on the gate of the farmhouse....

On the night of 6 to 7 June last, in the course of an operation in the region of Montpeat-de-Quercy, German troops set fire to four farmhouses which formed the hamlet called "Perches." Three men, two women, and two children, 14 and 4 years old, were burned alive. Two women and a child of ten who disappeared probably suffered the same fate.

On 7 June a large group of francs-tireurs attacked the French forces employed in the maintenance of order and succeeded in seizing the greater part of the town of Tulle, after a struggle which lasted until dawn.... The same day, at about 2000 hours, important German armored forces came to the assistance of the garrison.... The victims were selected without any inquiry, without even any questioning, haphazardly, workmen, students, professors, industrialists. There were even among them some militia sympathizers and candidates for the Waffen SS. The 120 corpses which were hanged from the balconies and lampposts of the Avenue de la Gare, along a distance of 500 meters, were a horrible spectacle that will remain in the memory of the unfortunate population of Tulle for a long time.

On Saturday, 10 June, having been fired at by two recalcitrants at the village of Marsoulas, German troops killed these two men. Moreover, they massacred, without any explanation, all the other inhabitants of the village that they could lay their hands on. Thus 7 men, 6 women, and 14 children were killed, most of them still in their beds at the early hour when this happened.[27]

The United Nations War Crimes Commission reported a reprisal action at Civitella, Italy, on June 18, 1944:

Two German soldiers were killed and a third wounded in a fight with partisans in the village of Civitella. Fearing reprisals, the inhabitants evacuated the village, but when the Germans discovered this, punitive action was postponed. On June 29 when the local inhabitants were returned and were feeling secure once more, the Germans carried out a well-organized reprisal, combing the neighborhood. Innocent inhabitants were often shot on sight. During that day 212 men, women, and children in the immediate district were killed. Some of the dead women were found completely naked. In the course of investigations a nominal roll of the dead has been compiled and is complete with the exception of a few names whose bodies could not be identified. Ages of the dead ranged from 1 year to 84 years. Approximately one hundred houses were destroyed by fire. Some of the victims were buried alive in their homes.[28]

Oradour-sur-Glane

The massacre of Oradour-sur-Glane, by troops of the SS "Das Reich" Division, was the worst atrocity committed by Germans in France. The Vichy Government sent the following report of this crime to the Commander-in-Chief West:

On Saturday, 10 June, a detachment of SS belonging very likely to the "Das Reich" division which was present in the area, burst into the village, after having surrounded it entirely, and ordered the population to gather in the central square. It was then announced that it had been reported that explosives had been hidden in the village and that a search and the checking of identity were about to take place. The men were asked to make four or five groups, each of which was locked into a barn. The women and children were taken to the church and locked in. It was about 1400 hours. A little later machine-gunning began and the whole village was set on fire, as well as the surrounding farms. The houses were set on fire one by one. The operation lasted undoubtedly several hours, in view of the extent of the locality.

In the meantime the women and the children were in anguish as they heard the sound of the fires and of the shootings. At 1700 hours, German soldiers entered the church and placed upon the communion table an asphyxiating apparatus which comprised a sort of box from which lighted fuses emerged. Shortly after the atmosphere became unbreathable. However someone was able to break open the vestry door which enabled the women and children to regain consciousness. The German soldiers then started to shoot through the windows of the church, and they came inside to finish off the last survivors with machine guns. Then they spread upon the soil some inflammable material. One woman alone was able to escape, having climbed out the window to run away. The cries of a mother who tried to give her child to her, drew the attention of one of the guards who fired on the would-be fugitive and wounded her seriously. She saved her life by simulating death and she was later cared for in a hospital at Limoges.

At about 1800 hours the German soldiers stopped the local train which was passing in the vicinity. They told passengers going to Oradour to get off, and, having machine-gunned them, threw their bodies into the flames. At the end of the evening, as well as the following day, a Sunday morning, the inhabitants of the surrounding hamlets, alarmed by the fire or made anxious because of the absence of their children who had been going to school at Oradour, attempted to approach, but they were either machine-gunned or driven away by force by German sentinels who were guarding the exits of the village. However, on the afternoon of Sunday some were able to get into the ruins, and they stated that the church was filled with the corpses of women and children, all shrivelled up and calcinated.

An absolutely reliable witness was able to see the body of a mother holding her child in her arms at the entrance of the church, and in front of the altar the body of a little child kneeling, and near the confessional the bodies of two children in each other's arms.[29]

The dead of Oradour numbered 190 men, 245 women, and 207 children. The town was destroyed and its inhabitants were decimated. No attempt was made to restore life in the village. Instead, Oradour, like Lidice, has been permitted to remain a monument to bestiality. The gutted church stands, gaunt and still against the sky. Beneath a paneless window there is the notice: "Madame Rouffance, only escapee from the church, escaped through this window." Elsewhere, signs refer to the barns in which the men were slaughtered as "place of agony." Wrecked homes and empty market place complete a scene of utter desolation. The only sound is the murmuring of the quiet stream, the Glane, a symbol of purity passing through the remnants of horror. And there is one other symbol—outside the church, the figure of Christ affixed to a rusty iron cross.

The men who participated in the massacre, and who could be found after the war, were brought to trial in Bordeaux in 1953. Judge Marcel Nussy Saint-Saëns announced the verdict of death for

SS Sergeant Georges-René Boos (a Frenchman) and Karl Lenz
(a German), and sentences of from five to twelve years for eighteen
others, most of whom were Alsatians who, as youths, had entered
or had been impressed into the German military service. The leader
of the SS "Das Reich" Division, responsible for the massacre, SS
Major Otto Dickmann, was not brought to trial. A few days after
the crime, Otto Dickmann was killed at Normandy.

Kalavryta

Hitler attacked Greece on April 6, 1941. His soldiers swept
across the plains of Thessaly and down the valleys beside Olympus
and the Pindus range to Delphi, Thebes, Marathon, and Athens.
They crossed the Isthmus of Corinth to the Peloponnesus and the
ancient cities of Corinth and Sparta. And on June 1, 1941, they
completed the conquest of Crete.

Deep in the rugged interior of the Peloponnesian peninsula
Hitler's soldiers took control of the village of Kalavryta. Toward
the end of 1943 Greek guerrillas, striking from mountain hide-outs,
captured eighty German soldiers. They took the captives into the
mountains and pushed them over a precipice. Only three of the
eighty survived. Nazi retribution was swift and terrible. It was
mistakenly directed against the townspeople rather than against the
guerrillas. The Germans slaughtered every able-bodied man and
youth in the village, and burned all houses to the ground. The
women found the bodies of their sons and husbands where they had
been killed upon an escarpment overlooking the town. They buried
the bodies in a grove of black cypress. There were twelve hundred
graves.

This action was not proved at Nuremberg. It is included here
as a further striking example of extreme reprisal.[30]

Destruction of Warsaw

The leader of the Polish underground army in Warsaw was
General Bor Komorowski. When, in July, 1944, Soviet troops
crashed through crumbling German defenses to the edge of the
Vistula River, Bor was authorized by the Polish government in exile

in London to commence an insurrection against the German occupying forces. The Soviets, however, were eager to establish the
Communist Committee of National Liberation in control of Poland,
and were not at all willing to have Poland's capital city freed by
the insurgent forces under General Bor.

Consequently, when the insurrection began on August 1, Soviet
help was not forthcoming, even though on the day previous it had
been reported that Soviet forces were then less than ten miles from
the city. The counterattack by the German forces under the command of SS General von dem Bach-Zelewski began on August 4.
The Polish insurgents did not receive Soviet help then, nor for
weeks after, while Warsaw went through a torment of fighting,
from house to house and from hand to hand, unparalleled in the
history of the entire war. Not until the revolt had been crushed, at
the cost of thousands of Polish lives—the lives of women and
children, as well as of fighting men—did the Soviets, three months
later, enter the broken city.

During this period of agony, Prime Minister Churchill and
President Roosevelt sent message after message to Premier Stalin
beseeching him for humanity's sake to come to the aid of the stricken
Poles. Notwithstanding these pleas the Soviets not only refused to
give their own military assistance so close at hand, but even frustrated the attempts of the Allied air forces to fly in supplies to the
beleaguered Polish forces by denying the Allies use of Soviet airfields for shuttle flights. Writing of the martyrdom of Warsaw,
Prime Minister Churchill quoted one of the final Polish broadcasts
before the surrender to the Germans in which these words were
used: "May God, Who is just, pass judgment on the terrible injustice
suffered by the Polish nation, and may He punish accordingly all
those who are guilty." Hitler was guilty of the destruction of
Wasarw. What was Stalin's guilt in standing by while the Poles,
his allies, suffered and died?

The German reprisal against Warsaw was cruel to the point of
inhumanity. In his diary, Hans Frank quoted the following telegram
which he had sent to Reich Minister Dr. Lammers on August 5,
1944: "The city of Warsaw is, for the most part, engulfed in
flames. Burning of the houses is the surest way to rob the insurgents

of any shelter.... After this uprising and its suppression, Warsaw will justly be committed to its deserved fate of being completely destroyed."[31]

With that objective announced on the second day of the German counterattack, it is more easily to be understood why the forces under Von dem Bach-Zelewski were pitiless in their measures against the insurgents and other inhabitants of the city, as well. Postwar investigations by the Central Commission for the Investigation of German Crimes in Poland disclosed that the principal forces used by the Germans "consisted of a police brigade in which criminals and Volksdeutsche served, and of the Vlassov army composed of Soviet prisoners of war"[32] which the Warsaw population usually called Ukrainians. These miserable and impoverished troops welcomed the opportunities for looting offered by orders to destroy the city. Eyewitness accounts indicate the severity of the countermeasures taken by these forces.

RECORD NO. 63. I lived at No. 18, Dzialdowska Street, Wola. The insurgents had built two barricades near our house, at the corner of Wolska and Gorczewska Streets, with the help of the inhabitants, including even children. Machine-guns, ammunition and grenades were placed in the neighboring house. On August 1 at 3 p.m. heavy fighting broke out in our district. The situation had been difficult from the beginning, all the more because the Volksdeutsche, who were numerous here, shot covertly at the insurgents and betrayed their whereabouts to the Germans. Tiger tanks were brought up, houses were broken into, and many people were killed; our house was hit several times. The tanks attacked from Wolska and Gorczewska Streets. The Germans broke in; they dragged the men out and ordered them to demolish the barricades. They then began to set the houses on fire. I saw Nos. 35 and 8 in our street being set on fire; bottles of petrol were thrown into the flats without warnings, and so it was impossible for the inhabitants to escape. I stayed in the cellar of No. 18 until August 5, when, between 11 and 12 noon, the Germans ordered all of us to get out, and marched us to Wolska Street. This march was carried out in dreadful haste and panic. My husband was absent, taking an active part in the Rising, and I was alone with my three children, aged 4, 6 and 12, and in the last month of pregnancy. I delayed my departure, hoping they would allow me to remain, and left the cellar at the very last moment. All the inhabitants of our house had already been escorted to the "Ursus" works in Wolska Street at the corner of Skierniewicka Street, and I too was ordered to go there. I went alone, accompanied only by my three children. It was difficult to pass, the road being full of wire, cable, remains of barricades, corpses, and rubble. Houses were burning on both sides of the street; I reached the "Ursus" works with great difficulty. Shots, cries, supplications and groans could be heard from the factory yard. We had no doubt that this was a place for mass executions. The people who stood at the entrance were led, no, pushed in, not all at once but in groups of 20. A boy of twelve, seeing the bodies of his parents and of his little brother through the half-open entrance door, fell in a fit and began to shriek. The Germans and Vlassov's men beat him and pushed him back, while he was endeavoring to get inside. He called for his father and his mother. We all knew what awaited us here; there was no possibility of escape or of buying one's life; there was a crowd of Germans, Ukrainians (Vlassov's men), and cars. I came last and kept in the background, continuing to let the others pass, in the hope that they would not kill a pregnant woman, but I was driven in with the last lot. In the yard I saw heaps of corpses three feet high, in several places. The whole right and left side of the big yard (the first yard) was strewn with bodies. We were led through the second. There were about 20 people in our group, mostly children of 10 to 12. There were children without parents, and also a paralyzed old woman whose son-in-law had been carrying her all the time on his back. At her side was her daughter with two children of 4 and 7. They were all killed. The old woman was literally killed on her son-in-law's back, and he along with her. We were called out in groups of four and led to the end of the second yard to a pile of bodies. When the four reached this point, the Germans shot them through the backs of their heads with revolvers. The victims fell on the heap, and others came. Seeing what was to be their fate, some attempted to escape; they cried, begged, and prayed for mercy. I was in the last group of four. I begged the Vlassov's men around me to save me and the children, and they asked if I had anything with which to buy my life. I had a large amount of gold with me and gave it to them. They took it all and wanted to lead me away, but the German supervising the execution would not allow them to do so, and when I begged him to let me go he pushed me off, shouting "Quicker!" I fell when he pushed me. He also hit and pushed my elder boy, shouting "hurry up, you Polish bandit." Thus I came to the place of execution, in the last group of four, with my three children. I held my two younger children by one hand, and my elder boy by the other. The children were crying and praying. The elder boy, seeing the mass of bodies, cried out: "They are going to kill us" and called for his father. The first shot hit him, the second me; the next two killed the two younger children. I fell on my right side. The shot was not fatal. The bullet penetrated the back of my head from the right side and went out through my cheek. I spat out several teeth; I felt the left side of my body growing numb, but I was still conscious and saw everything that was going on around me. I witnessed other executions, lying there among the dead; more groups of men were led in. I heard cries, supplications, moaning, and shots. The bodies of these men fell on me. I was covered by four bodies. Then I again saw a group of women and children; thus it went on with group after group until late in the evening. It was already quite, quite dark when the executions stopped....[33]

RECORD NO. 57. I lived in the Wola district at No. 8, Elekcyjna Street. At 10 a.m. on August 5, 1944 a detachment of SS-men and Vlassov's men entered. They drove us from the cellars and brought us near the Sowinski Park at Ulrychow. They shot at us when we passed. My wife was killed on the spot; our child was wounded and cried for his mother. Soon a Ukrainian approached and killed my two-year-old child like a dog; then he approached me together with some Germans and stood on my chest to see whether I was alive or not.—I shammed dead, lest I should be killed too. One of the murderers took my watch; I heard him reloading his gun. I thought he would finish me off, but he went on further, thinking I was dead. I lay thus from 10 a.m. until 9 p.m. pretending to be dead, and witnessing further atrocities. During that time I saw further groups being driven out and shot near the place where I lay. The huge heap of corpses grew still bigger. Those who gave any sign of life were shot. I was buried under other corpses and nearly suffocated. The executions lasted until 5 p.m. At 9 p.m. a group of Poles came to take the corpses away. I gave them a sign that I was alive. They helped me to get up and I regained sufficient strength to carry with them the body of my wife and child to the Sowinski Park, where they took all the dead. After this sad duty had been performed they took me to St. Laurence's Church at Wola, where I remained till the next day. I cannot state the exact number of the victims, but I estimate that those among whom I lay amounted to some 3,000 (three thousand). I met a friend in the church who had gone through the same experience as I, having lost a boy of 8, who had been wounded and died calling for his father. I am still in the hospital and the image of death is constantly before my eyes.[34]

RECORD NO. 58. When I was endeavoring to get outside the town from Wola, I passed through Gorczewska Street. This was on August 7, 1944. When we passed No. 9, Gorczewska Street (a house which belonged to nuns), we were called into the house and ordered to carry out and bury the corpses which were there. The courtyard was a dreadful sight. It was an execution place. Heaps of corpses were lying there; I think they must have been collecting there for some days, for some were already swollen and others quite freshly killed. There were bodies of men, women and children, all shot through the backs of their heads.

It is difficult to state exactly how many there were. There must have been several layers carelessly heaped up. The men were ordered to carry away the bodies—we women to bury them. We put them in anti-tank trenches and then filled these up. In this way we filled up a number of such trenches in Gorczewska Street. I had the impression that during the first days of the Rising everybody was killed. Later on women and children were sometimes left alive, but the killing of men still went on. I watched all this until August 7, when I succeeded some-how in getting away out of this hell, having been saved by a miracle.[35]

RECORD NO. 117. On August 7, at 9 p.m., they hunted us out of the Ministry of Commerce and Industry building, No. 2, Elektoralna Street. There were several hundreds of us, driven here from various burning houses. They drove us through the cellars of the Ministry. In the passage, a German dragged me aside and tried to violate me, but after a moment he chose a new victim from another group. Wanting to get rid of me, he took out his revolver and aimed it at my forehead. At this moment someone else passed, and he ran after that person, shooting. I took advantage of this and ran up to the Ministry of Finance, and then through the burning streets to No. 5, Solna Street where they kept us the whole night until 11 the next morning. They then robbed us of all our watches and valuables, and drove us on through Mirowski Square and Elektoralna Street towards the suburb of Wola. In the Square I saw huge bomb-craters, and also burning corpses. The streets all round were on fire. At the intersection of Chlodna and Wolska Streets, and Towarowa Street, and Kercelli Place we stopped. From Kercelli Place the insurgents were firing towards Towarowa Street. The Germans who were going into the fighting stopped us and made of us a living barricade; under threats of being shot, they ordered us to lie down across the street from one side to the other. With our backs turned to the insurgents, we knelt or crouched and the Germans placed themselves on the ground behind us, or knelt on one knee, firing over our heads towards Kercelli Place. There were 23 of us including two children, mostly young women. It is difficult to describe what we felt during the two hours the fighting lasted. We were all prepared to die and said the Rosary aloud. Bullets whistled over our heads, or past our ears. The noise of the German guns nearly deafened us. As if by some miracle, the bullets only hit the Germans. When the first German fell we were paralyzed with fear. My mother told me: "If I am shot remember not to shed one tear; do not complain, preserve the dignity of a Polish woman. Show no weakness in their presence." Only the children wept bitterly and were greatly afraid.[36]

RECORD NO. 506. I was taken from Dlugosz Street (as a civilian) at 6 a.m. on August 6, 1944, and led to Sokolowska Street to the so-called Arbeitskommando headquarters. Next day I volunteered for work with 50 others thinking that in this way I should be better off. We were sent to a house opposite St. Adalbert's Church in Wolska Street, where about six hundred bodies of men, women and children were lying in heaps. Near by were a few dozen more, which we added to the heap. Then we went to No. 60, Wolska Street, where, on both sides of the courtyard, lay the bodies of more than 100 men, as far as we could judge, victims of a mass execution. In the garden of this same house we found in a thicket the bodies of more than a dozen women, children, and babies, shot through the back of the head. We carried out from the house at the corner of Plocka and Wolska Street (a large yellow house) several dozens of bodies of men, women and children, partly burnt, who had been shot through the back of the head. From a house in Plocka Street, between Wolska and Gorczewska Streets, we carried out about 100 bodies. In one of the houses we found the half-burnt body of a man, holding two children in the arms. When we returned to No. 60, Wolska Street, we made a wooden platform on which we laid the dead; and then we cleared the ground of all traces of the German crimes, such as documents, clothes, or linen, which we placed on the pile of dead, sprinkled with petrol, and set alight. While we were thus burning the bodies, a drunken SD officer arrived in a car. He picked out three men of about 20 or 30 from a group of refugees passing by. He shot them through the back of the head in the course of a "friendly" conversation. After having murdered the first man he ordered us to throw him on the burning pyre before the eyes of the remaining two.[37]

The Polish insurgents surrendered to the Germans early in October. Immediately thereafter orders for the complete destruction of Warsaw and the deportation of its population to concentration camps were issued out of Berlin. On October 11, 1944, a telegram was sent by the Governor of the Warsaw District, Dr. Fischer, to Hans Frank, the Governor General of Poland, on the subject, "New Policy with Regard to Poland":

As a result of the visit of SS Obergruppenfuehrer von dem Bach to the Reichsfuehrer SS, I wish to inform you of the following: ... Obergruppenfuehrer von dem Bach again received an order to pacify Warsaw—that is, to raze Warsaw to the ground while the war is still on, if there is nothing against this from the military point of view (construction of fortresses). Prior to destruction, all raw materials, textiles, and furniture should be taken out of Warsaw. The main role in performing this task should be assumed by the civilian administration. I am informing you of these facts because this new order of the Fuehrer regarding the destruction of Warsaw is of the greatest importance for the future policy toward Poland.[38]

As to this retributive action against the remaining inhabitants of Warsaw, Frank testified:

The part played by the civil administration began only after the capitulation of General Bòr, when the most atrocious orders for vengeance came from the Reich. A letter came to my desk one day in which Hitler demanded the deportation of the entire population of Warsaw into German concentration camps. It took a struggle of three weeks, from which I emerged victorious, to avert that act of insanity and to succeed in having the fleeing population of Warsaw, which had no part in the revolt, distributed throughout the Government General.[39]

In spite of the alleged efforts of Frank to prevent wholesale removal of the Poles to German concentration camps, between 50,000 and 60,000 persons were so incarcerated. When, later in the year, efforts were made to obtain their release, the Chief of the Reich Main Security Office, Kaltenbrunner, refused on the ground that these people "were being used in the secret manufacture of armaments in the Reich and that therefore a general release was out of the question."[40]

All cases of reprisal were for the purpose of preventing or avenging acts of resistance by inhabitants of the occupied territories. In most of them, particularly those involving severe cruelties, German military forces did not play a significant part. The reprisals were inflicted by SS and police units which sometimes utilized non-Germans in support. Frenchmen and Alsatians participated in the massacre at Oradour-sur-Glane; Russians and Polish Volksdeutsche fought against Bor in Warsaw. The reprisals were, of course, ordered or approved by Hitler, and they were directed by Himmler as chief of the SS and the German police. They were a product of Hitler's wars and a reflection of Hitler's personal code of cruelty.

CHAPTER 16

One Hundred for One

A<small>T A</small> <small>MEETING</small> of political leaders on January 15, 1944, at Krakow, Hans Frank said: "I have not hesitated to declare that when a German is shot, up to 100 Poles shall be shot too...."[1]

The hostage system used by Hitler to control the territories occupied by his troops actually was a form of reprisal. It was not enough to deprive persons of their liberty as a deterrent to the commission of acts of resistance by others; the unfortunate ones taken hostage were frequently killed, although they were themselves entirely innocent of any opposition to the occupying forces.

In a secret report to Goering on February 15, 1940, the Supreme Commander of the Army stated:

According to the opinion of the OKW, the arrest of hostages is justified in all cases in which the security of the troops and the carrying out of their orders demand it.... In selecting hostages it must be borne in mind that their arrest shall take place only if the refractory sections of the population are anxious for the hostages to remain alive. The hostages shall therefore be chosen from sections of the population from which a hostile attitude may be expected. The arrest of hostages shall be carried out among persons whose fate, we may suppose, will influence the insurgents.[2]

It was not until the invasion of the Soviet Union, however, that hostage-law was widely employed by the Germans in governing occupied territories. On September 16, 1941, Keitel issued the basic order concerning Communist insurrections in the occupied areas. He noted that after the opening of the campaign against the Soviet Union, insurrections had broken out in all the areas occupied by

Germany. He stated that this condition indicated "a mass movement, centrally directed by Moscow" and that it should be inferred thereafter "in every case of resistance to the German occupation forces, no matter what the individual circumstances, that it is of Communistic origin."[3] On this reasoning he ordered severe reprisals to be taken against the populations of the occupied territories.

This basic decree was complemented by Keitel's order of October 1, 1941, dealing particularly with the taking and killing of hostages:

Attacks committed on members of the armed forces lately in the occupied territories give reason to point out that it is advisable that military commanders always have at their disposal a number of hostages of different political tendencies, namely:
(1) Nationalists,
(2) Democratic-bourgeois, and
(3) Communists.
It is important that these should include well-known leading personalities, or members of their families whose names are to be made public.
Hostages belonging to the same group as the culprit are to be shot in case of attacks.
It is asked that commanders be instructed accordingly.[4]

This order was addressed to the Military Commander, South-East, and stated that it already had been complied with in France and Belgium.

Hostage-law in the West

Three months after the beginning of the occupation of France, on September 12, 1940, a directive was issued by the administrative section, Commander in Chief of the Army in France, defining hostages for the information of occupying authorities:

Hostages are inhabitants of a country who guarantee with their lives the impeccable attitude of the population. The responsibility for their fate is thus placed in the hands of their compatriots. Therefore, the population must be publicly threatened that the hostages will be held responsible for hostile acts of individuals. Only French citizens may be taken as hostages. The hostages can be held responsible only for actions committed after their arrest and after the public proclamation.[5]

This directive was amplified by General Staff ordinances of November 2, 1940, and February 13, 1941:

...The population is to be treated as jointly responsible for individual acts of sabotage, if by its attitude in general toward the German armed forces it has favored hostile or unfriendly acts of individuals, or if by its passive resistance against the investigation of previous acts of sabotage, it has encouraged hostile elements to similar acts, or otherwise created a favorable atmosphere for opposition to the German occupation. All measures must be taken in a way that it is possible to carry out. Threats that cannot be realized give the impression of weakness.[6]

General von Stuelpnagel, who was head of the German Armistice Commission in France, issued the following announcement on August 22, 1941:

On the morning of 21 August 1941, a member of the German armed forces was killed in Paris as a result of a murderous attack. I therefore order that:

1. All Frenchmen held in custody of whatever kind, by the German authorities or on behalf of German authorities in France, are to be considered as hostages as from 23 August.

2. If any further incident occurs, a number of these hostages are to be shot, to be determined according to the gravity of the attempt....[7]

On September 19, 1941, General von Stuelpnagel directed that as from that date all French males under arrest of any kind by the French authorities or who were taken into custody because of Communist agitation were to be kept under arrest by the French authorities on behalf of the Military Commander in France.

General von Stuelpnagel issued a further order on September 30, 1941, in which hostages were defined as persons held by German authorities in any kind of detention, such as police custody, imprisonment on remand, or penal detention, and persons held in any kind of detention by French authorities on behalf of German authorities. This order provided that whenever an incident occurred which necessitated the shooting of hostages under the announcement of August 22, 1941, the execution was to follow immediately. District commanders were therefore instructed to select for their districts from the total number of hostages "those who, from a practical point of view, may be considered for execution and enter them on a list of hostages."[8] It was noted that "the better known the hostages to be shot, the greater will be the deterrent effect on the perpetrators, themselves, and on those persons who, in France or abroad, bear the moral responsibility—as instigators or by their propaganda—for acts of terror and sabotage."[9] The following categories of persons were to be placed at the head of lists of hostages held for execution:

(1) Former officials or deputies of Communist or anarchist organizations.

(2) Intellectuals who supported the spreading of Communist ideas in speech or by writing.

(3) Persons who proved by their attitude to be dangerous.

(4) Persons who assisted in the distribution of leaflets.

Each district was to enter the names of about 150 persons on its hostage list. About 300 or 400 people were to be listed for the Greater Paris command. Lists were to be kept up to date. And finally, "when the bodies are buried, the burial of a large number in a common grave in the same cemetery is to be avoided, in order not to create places of pilgrimage which, now or later, might form centers for anti-German propaganda. Therefore, if necessary, burials must be carried out in various places."[10]

Compliance with these orders was made manifest by the subsequent publication of notices of the killing of hostages. One such notice was published in the October 22, 1941, edition of the newspaper *Le Phare:*

Notice. Cowardly criminals in the pay of England and of Moscow killed, with shots in the back, the Feldkommandant of Nantes on the morning of 20 October 1941. Up to now the assassins have not been arrested.

As expiation for this crime I have ordered that 50 hostages be shot to begin with. Because of the gravity of the crime, 50 more hostages will be shot in case the guilty should not be arrested between now and 23 October 1941 by midnight.[11]

During the occupation of France the Germans converted the Fort of Romainville, in the suburbs of Paris, into a hostage depot.

From this depot hundreds of persons were taken to be shot for the alleged crimes of others. In September, 1942, some German soldiers were assaulted at a motion picture theater in Paris. Shortly thereafter the Military Commander issued a proclamation stating that he had caused 116 hostages to be shot in reprisal. In all, it was estimated that 29,660 persons were executed as hostages in France alone.

The German military commander in Belgium and northern France was General von Falkenhausen. In compliance with Keitel's basic order for hostage-law, General von Falkenhausen authorized reprisal killings of hostages in Belgium by an order of September 19, 1941:

In the future, the population must expect that if attacks are made on members of the German army or the German police and the culprits cannot be arrested, a number of hostages proportionate to the gravity of the offense, five at a minimum, will be shot if the attack causes death. All political prisoners in Belgium are, with immediate effect, to be considered as hostages.[12]

After the experience of one year in applying this hostage-law to the Belgian people, General von Falkenhausen complained to Keitel of its ineffectiveness. On September 16, 1942, he wrote:

Enclosed is a list of the shootings of hostages which have taken place until now in my area and the incidents on account of which these shootings took place.

In a great number of cases, particularly in the most serious, the perpetrators were later apprehended and sentenced.

This result is undoubtedly very unsatisfactory. The effect is not so much deterrent as destructive of the feeling of the population for right and security; the cleft between the people influenced by Communism and the remainder of the population is being bridged; all circles are becoming filled with a feeling of hatred toward the occupying forces and effective inciting material is given to enemy propaganda. Thereby, military danger and general political reaction of an entirely unwanted nature....[13]

Notwithstanding this complaint, the hostage system was not discontinued in Belgium. Thus, the following notice was published in the April 25, 1944, edition of the newspaper *Nouveau Journal:*

The perpetrators of the assassination on 6 April of the members of the SS Sturmbrigade Wallonie, Hubert Stassen and Francois Musch, who fought at Tcherkassy, have so far not been apprehended. Therefore, in accordance with the communication dated 10 April 1944, the 20 terrorists whose names follow have been executed....[14]

In the Netherlands, Seyss-Inquart issued similar orders for the taking and killing of hostages. In that country the actions were more nearly absolute reprisals. Even after the commission of acts of resistance, innocent persons were sometimes arrested and held for execution as hostages. This evil practice was disclosed in the August, 1942, report of the Commander of the Wehrmacht in the Netherlands:

On the occasion of an attempt against a train of soldiers on furlough due to arrive in Rotterdam, a Dutch railway guard was seriously wounded by touching a wire connected with an explosive charge, thus causing an explosion. The following repressive measures were announced in the Dutch press:
"The deadline for the arrest of the perpetrators, with collaboration of the population, is fixed at 14 August, midnight. A reward of 100,000 florins will be made for a denunciation, which will be treated confidentially. If the culprits are not arrested within the time appointed, arrests of hostages are threatened; railway lines will be guarded by Dutchmen."
Since, despite this summons, the perpetrator did not report and was not otherwise discovered, the following hostages, among whom some had already been in custody for several weeks as hostages, were shot on the order of the Higher SS and Police Leader.[15]

Among the "hostages" murdered on this occasion were leading citizens of the Netherlands, including noblemen and men of high position. The officer who made the report commented upon the instantaneous reaction of the Dutch people to this outrage:

From the bitterest insults to apparently pious petitions and prayers not to resort to extremes, no nuance was lacking which did not in one way or another indicate, to say the least, complete disapproval and misunderstanding, first of the threat, and secondly of the actual execution of the hostages.... In short, such disapproval even in the ranks of the very few really pro-German Dutch had never before been noticed, so much hatred at one time had never been felt.[16]

But the killing of hostages continued, unabated, and with like disregard for basic principles of humane conduct. Thus, as late as March 7, 1945, an order was given to shoot eighty hostages, and the officer who gave the order stated: "I don't care where you get your prisoners."[17] More than two thousand persons were killed as hostages in the Netherlands.

The hostage system was, of course, utilized in Denmark and Norway. On April 26, 1942, two German policemen were killed on an island off the west coast of Norway while attempting to arrest two Norwegian citizens. Four days later eighteen young men were killed in revenge. The German report stated: "All these eighteen Norwegians had been in prison since the 22 February of the same year and therefore had nothing to do with this affair."[18]

In Italy, the commander of the German forces, Field Marshal Kesselring, issued the following order on June 17, 1944:

The partisan situation in the Italian theater, particularly central Italy, has recently deteriorated to such an extent that it constitutes a serious danger to the fighting troops and their supply lines as well as to the war industry and economic potential. The fight against the partisans must be carried on with all means at our disposal and with the utmost severity. I will protect any commander who exceeds our usual restraint in the choice of severity of the methods he adopts against partisans. In this connection the old principle holds good, that a mistake in the choice of methods in executing one's orders is better than failure or neglect to act.[19]

And three days later he ordered the shooting of hostages:

It is the duty of all troops and police in my command to adopt the severest measures. Every act of violence committed by partisans must be punished immediately. Reports submitted must also give details of countermeasures taken. Wherever there is evidence of considerable numbers of partisan groups a proportion of the male population of the area will be arrested; and in the event of an act of violence being committed, these men will be shot.[20]

The daily situation report of the commander in chief of southwest Italy for June 26, 1944, carried the notation that a Colonel von Gablenz had been captured by bandits and that the entire male population of the villages on the stretch of road where he disappeared had been taken into custody under an announcement that all would be shot if the captured colonel was not set free within forty-eight hours. The report of June 28 disclosed that 560 persons were taken into custody as hostages, the majority of whom were women and children.

Following the bomb plot in Rome on March 23, 1944, Hitler ordered that ten or twenty Italians were to be killed for every German. In fact 382 people who had been found guilty of entirely unrelated offenses were executed in reprisal. The SD official in charge of the operation reported that "later the number of victims rose to 325 and I decided to add 57 Jews."[21]

In Poland the taking and killing of hostages reached a blood-curdling climax. From October, 1943, until the popular uprising in August, 1944, approximately eight thousand civilians were killed as hostages in Poland, most of them taken in manhunts in Warsaw. During the uprising, hostage law was replaced by the orgy of killings previously described.[22]

Family Reprisals

Family reprisals were a variation of the Hitler hostage system. In a document concerning measures to be taken against French officers, this order was set out:

As a measure of reprisal, families of suspected persons who have already shown themselves to be resistants or who might become so in the future, will be transferred as internees to Germany or to the territory of eastern France. For these, questions of billeting and surveillance must first of all be solved. Afterwards we contemplate as a later measure the deprivation of their French nationality and the confiscation of property, already carried out in other cases by Laval.[23]

High-ranking military officers were involved in this cruel measure of repression, as shown by a report of June 5, 1943:

General Warlimont had asked the Commander-in-Chief of the Western front to raise the question of reprisal measures against the relatives of persons who had joined the resistance and to submit any proposals. President Laval declared himself ready, not long ago, to take measures of this kind on behalf of the French Government; but to limit himself to the families of some particularly distinguished persons....

We must wait and see whether Laval is really willing to apply reprisal measures in a practical way. All those present at the meetings were in agreement that such measures should be taken in any event, as rapidly as possible, against families of well-known personages who had become resistants. (For example, members of the families of General Giraud, Juin, Georges, the former Minister of the Interior Pucheu, Inspector of Finance Couvre de Murville, Leroy-Beaulieu and others.)

The measures may also be carried out by the German authorities since the persons who have become resistants are to be considered as foreigners belonging to an enemy power and the members of their families are also to be considered as such. In the opinion of those present, the members of these families should be interned; the practical carrying out of this measure and its technical possibilities must be carefully examined....

We might also study the question of whether these families should be interned in regions particularly exposed to air attacks; for instance in the vicinity of dams or in industrial regions which are bombed often.

A list of families who are considered liable for internment will be compiled in collaboration with the Embassy.[24]

The Reich Commissioner for Norway, in a report for the "information of the Fuehrer," stated that he had received a cable from Field Marshal Keitel in which Keitel demanded the issuance of a regulation under which "members of the personnel, and, if necessary their relatives," were to be made collectively responsible for cases of sabotage occurring in their establishments. "This demand," said Terboven, "serves a purpose and promises success only if I am actually allowed to perform executions by firing squads."[25] To this comment Keitel entered a notation: "Yes, that is best."[26] And shortly thereafter, Keitel replied by telegram: "In the matter of checking sabotage in Norway, I agree with the view of the Reich Commissioner for Occupied Norwegian Territory, to the extent that I expect results from reprisals only if they are carried out ruthlessly and if Reich Commissioner Terboven is authorized to carry out shootings."[27]

Family reprisals were applied in extreme measure in the East during the summer of 1944. On June 28, 1944, the Higher SS and Police Leader East issued the following order:

The security situation in the General Government has in the last months grown worse to such an extent, that from now on the most radical means and the harshest measures must prevail against the alien assassins and saboteurs. The Reichsfuehrer SS in agreement with the General Government has ordered, in all cases of attack and attempted assassination against Germans, or where saboteurs have destroyed installations essential to life, that not only the seized perpetrators be shot but that all male kin also be executed and their female relatives over 16 years of age be put into concentration camps.[28]

It is hard to imagine anything more wicked than to mistreat a man's wife and children for his misconduct. But that became, in some cases, permissible practice under the family reprisal system.

The Clearing Murders

A clearing transaction is one in which claims are balanced to achieve a settlement. A unique settlement of claims was achieved by the Nazis in Denmark through the use of murder to offset acts of resistance. These transactions were known as the "clearing murders." For every act against German occupying forces a secret reprisal action was taken against some Dane. A few of the reprisals were acts of terrorism, such as the bombing of homes; but most of them were premeditated murders planned and executed by the German police forces.

The chief political officer in occupied Denmark was Dr. Werner Best, the Reich Plenipotentiary for Denmark. Other officials were Guenther Pancke, the Higher SS and Police Leader, and General Hermann von Hannecken, the Military Commander. The clearing murders were ordered and carried out during the time when these men were the responsible German officials of occupied Denmark.

On December 30, 1943, complaints having been made by Himmler to Hitler that insufficiently stern measures had been taken against Danish resistance leaders, Hitler called these top German representatives in Denmark to a conference in Berlin to consider actions of reprisal which should be taken against the Danish people. Present at the conference, in addition to these officials, were Himmler, as head of the SS and the German police, Kaltenbrunner, as chief of the Reich Main Security Office, and Hitler's principal military advisers, Generals Keitel and Jodl. The minutes of the meeting were recorded by Hitler's adjutant, Colonel Schmundt; and Dr. Best made complete notes which he entered in his diary.

The participants in the meeting discussed the growing acts of resistance by the Danes, many of which were directed against the occupying police forces. It was decided that the best way to check the opposition thus manifested would be to counter each act of resistance with an act of terror against the Danish people. To make the countermeasures more frightening, it was agreed that they should be carried out in secret. The Danes would learn, through association, that any act of resistance would be followed in due course by an act of violence against some Danish person. While it was observed that it would be desirable for the clearing action to be taken against a person suspected of having a part in the resistance movement, of greater importance was the selection of a person of prominence whose violent death would be sure to attract the attention of the people. Hitler "demanded compensatory murders in the proportion of at least five to one."[29]

After the meeting, police leader Pancke conferred with Himmler concerning the methods of implementing Hitler's order. Himmler evidently agreed at that time to order special agents sent from Gestapo headquarters in Berlin for the purpose of directing and executing the countermeasures to be taken. These experts in murder and sabotage were to be selected by the chief of the Gestapo in Berlin, Heinrich Mueller, whose immediate superior was the defendant Kaltenbrunner.

Meanwhile, Dr. Best had seen fit to consult Foreign Minister Ribbentrop about the decisions reached at the conference. According to Dr. Best: "Ribbentrop shared his opinion that some protest should be made against such methods but that, after all, nothing could be done."[30] Under cross-examination by the writer, Dr. Best was asked whether he knew that pursuant to the order issued at the conference murders and wilful destruction of property were carried out in Denmark, and he replied: "This general fact is known to me, yes."[31]

The official report of the Danish government on the German

occupation of Denmark contained the following entry describing the occurrences which took place in Denmark shortly after Hitler's order for clearing murders was made at the meeting of December 30, 1943:

> From New Year 1944 onwards, a large number of persons, most of them well-known, were murdered at intervals which grew steadily shorter. The doorbell would ring, for instance, and one or two men would ask to speak to them. The moment they appeared at the door they were shot by these unknown persons. Or, someone would pretend to be ill and go to a doctor during the latter's consulting hour. When the doctor entered the room, the unknown shot him. At other times, unknown men would force their way into a house and kill the owner in front of his wife and children, or else a man would be ambushed in the street by civilians and shot.... As the number of victims increased it was borne in upon the Danes, to their amazement, that there was a certain political motive behind all these murders; for they realized that in one way or another the Germans were the instigators.[32]

The clearing murders were carried out by bands of terrorists formed and acting under the direction of professional killers. Among the men brought from Berlin to head these gangs, for example, was the notorious Alfred Naujocks who had faked the Polish attack upon the radio station at Gleiwitz which Hitler used as one of the "justifications" for the German assault upon Poland. In some cases, Danish hoodlums were induced to join the gangs and carry out acts of terror against their own people.

One of the most outrageous of the Danish clearing murders was the killing of the renowned Danish poet, Kaj Munk, who was also the pastor of a parish. Kaj Munk was forcibly taken from his home, thrust into an automobile, and driven into the country, where he was murdered and his body left on the side of the highway. The corpse was found the following day with a sign pinned to the coat: "Swine, you worked for Germany just the same."[33]

Under cross-examination by the writer, Dr. Best recalled a number of these acts of Gestapo-directed gangsterism. One case involved the dynamiting of a row of houses; another, involving the murder of four physicians, turned out to be a serious error of judgment:

Question: Now, Dr. Best, you also remember the murder of four doctors in Odense, against which you protested because these doctors had been pointed out to you by National Socialist circles as being German sympathizers, don't you?

Answer: Yes, and apart from that, that was not the only reason. I called attention to the growing senselessness of these measures, for I had found out that some of these physicians were friendly to Germany.

Question: Yes, and that was a terrible thing for the Gestapo to murder German sympathizers in Denmark, wasn't it? There were so few....[34]

The Danish government report stated: "After the capitulation of the German forces in Denmark, investigations by the Danish police established the fact that all these murders, running into hundreds, were in reality committed on the direct orders of the supreme authorities and with the active collaboration of Germans who occupied the highest positions in Denmark."[35]

The Danish authorities were able to prove 267 different acts of retaliatory murder or sabotage. All members of the bandit gangs who carried out the depredations received commendatory letters from Reichsfuehrer SS Heinrich Himmler.

The Danish "clearing murders" were a Himmler-conceived and Hitler-ordered form of reprisal, in which innocent persons were assassinated by their captors as a method of rule by terror. Although these murders were not to be compared in numbers with the reprisal actions in the East, they were unique, and peculiarly wicked, violations of international law.

The taking of hostages is an almost inevitable consequence of aggression waged against patriotic peoples who refuse to surrender to the invader. Aggression leads to resistance—and resistance results in reprisals. Leaders of states who initiate wars of aggression may not be heard to plead that resistance of the peoples whose lands have been invaded justifies the indiscriminate seizure of innocent persons as hostages and the cruel mistreatment or killing of such persons in reprisal.

CHAPTER 17

The Night and Fog Decree

ONE OF THE most bizarre of the Nazi repressive measures against the inhabitants of territories overrun by the German armies was the *Nacht und Nebel Erlass,* or the Night and Fog Decree, which derived its name from the fact that under it people were taken away from their homes, never to be heard of again—kidnapped by night and disappearing forever into the fog of the unknown.

The Worst Crime

Under cross-examination by Sir David Maxwell Fyfe, Keitel was reminded of a statement he had made in a preliminary interrogation:

"In carrying out these thankless and difficult tasks, I had to fulfill my duty under the hardest exigencies of war, often acting against the inner voice of my conscience and against my own convictions. The fulfillment of urgent tasks assigned by Hitler, to whom I was directly responsible, demanded complete self-abnegation."[1]

Keitel was then asked: "Can you tell the Tribunal the three worst things you had to do which were against the inner voice of your conscience? What do you pick out as the three worst things you had to do?"[2]

And he answered:

Perhaps to start with the last, the orders given for the conduct of the war in the East, insofar as they were contrary to the acknowledged usages of war; then something which particularly concerns the British delegation, the question of the 50 R.A.F. officers, the question which weighed particularly heavy on my mind, that of the terror-fliers, and, worst of all, the *Nacht und Nebel Erlass* and the actual consequences it entailed at a later stage and about which I did not know. Those were the worst struggles which I had with myself.[3]

Orders for Secret Deportation

The basic Night and Fog Decree was the Hitler order of December 7, 1941. This order stated that within the occupied territories the adequate punishment of persons for offenses committed against the German State or the occupying power which endangered security or state of readiness was on principle the death penalty. Where it did not appear in any case that a sentence of death would be passed upon the offender within a very short time, he was to be taken to Germany and no information was to be given concerning the disappearance of the accused.

Keitel's instructions to implement the decree explained Hitler's reasons for it as follows: "In such cases penal servitude or even a hard labor sentence for life will be regarded as a sign of weakness. An effective and lasting deterrent can be achieved only by the death penalty or by taking measures which will leave the family and the population uncertain as to the fate of the offender. The deportation to Germany serves this purpose."[4]

On February 2, 1942, Keitel issued explanatory orders providing that offenses committed by civilians in the occupied territories of the type covered by the decree of December 7, 1941, would be dealt with by the military courts only if the death sentence were pronounced within eight days of the prisoner's arrest. "In all other cases the prisoners are, in the future, to be transported to Germany secretly, and further dealings with the offenses will take place here; these measures will have a deterrent effect because (a) the prisoners will vanish without leaving a trace, and (b) no information may be given as to their whereabouts or their fate."[5]

Secrecy under this decree was maintained even after death of the persons deported to Germany. A letter written on June 24, 1942, by the Chief of the Security Police and SD, into whose custody the victims were transferred, provided that, since the purpose of the decree was to create uncertainty over the fate of prisoners among their relatives and acquaintances, "this goal would be jeopardized if the relatives were to be notified in cases of death," and "release of the body for burial at home is inadvisable for the same reason...."[6]

Keitel was asked whether he considered these decrees to be cruel and brutal, and he answered: "I said both at the time and yesterday that I personally thought that to deport individuals secretly was very much more cruel than to impose a sentence of death."[7]

The Night and Fog Decree was a subtly woven fabric of fear cast by Hitler over the territories occupied by his military forces. The dread apprehension of the silent removal of loved ones made life a torment of anxiety. The lad on his way to school, the man in his workshop, the wife at home, mysteriously disappeared, never to be seen or heard of again. Frantic inquiries at Gestapo offices met with silence. Those left behind feared constantly that the missing ones would suffer torture, confinement in the concentration camp— or even death. Not until liberation did they gain knowledge of when, or how, or where members of their families had disappeared save the haunting wonder that in some way, for some reason, Hitler had caused them to be spirited away "by night and by fog."

The harshness of this decree was increased as the war progressed in Germany's disfavor. By an order of July 30, 1944, Hitler directed that acts of violence by non-German civilians in the occupied territories against members of the German armed forces, the SS, or the police were to be punished by death to all persons caught in the act, and by the handing over to the SD of all other apprehended persons. Accomplices, especially women, who did not participate directly in the actions were to be put to forced labor. Only children were to be spared.

On August 18, 1944, this order was extended to non-German civilians who "endanger the security or tactical preparedness of the occupying power otherwise than through acts of terrorism and sabotage."[8] Under this order any nominal act of resistance by the people of the occupied territories could be punished by death or the secret penalties of the Night and Fog Decree. There was no longer any purpose in legal proceedings against persons accused of resistance. On the same day Keitel ordered that legal proceedings against non-German civilians in the occupied territories for crimes imperiling the security or war-preparedness of the occupying power were to be suspended and the accused were to be handed over to the SD, except in those cases in which death sentences had already been imposed.

Keitel further ordered on September 4, 1944, that persons who had been sentenced under the decree of December 7, 1941, and were not therefore to be allowed to have any contact with the outer world, were "to be given a distinguishing mark."[9]

On September 21, 1944, the commander of the German armed forces in the Netherlands, while complaining of a strike of railwaymen in that country, pointed out that the troops were permitted to use armed force only against persons who committed acts of violence as terrorists or saboteurs, whereas persons who endangered the security or war-preparedness of the occupation power in any other way were to be handed over to the SD, and he asked that the troops again receive authority to shoot with or even without summary trial such persons "who endanger the fighting forces by passive resistance."[10]

Keitel was asked: "Now, defendant, will you agree that shooting, with or even without trial, railway men who will not work, is about as brutal and cruel a measure as could be imagined by the mind of man? Do you agree?"[11] And he replied: "That is a cruel measure, yes."[12] Yet the fact was that three days after this complaint by the commander of the armed forces in the Netherlands, Keitel gave him the authority which he had requested:

According to the Fuehrer's order of 30 July 1944 non-German civilians in the occupied territories who attack us in the rear in the crisis of our battle for existence deserve no consideration.... If the military situation and the state of communications make it impossible to hand them over to the SD, other effective measures are to be taken ruthlessly and independently. There is naturally no objection to passing and executing death sentences by summary court-martial under such circumstances.[13]

Keitel was asked what he considered the fate would be of non-German civilians surrendered to the SD under these decrees. "It means a concentration camp and gas chamber usually, does it not? That is what it meant in fact, whether you knew it or not?"[14] Keitel answered: "I did not know it, but it obviously led to the concentration camp in the end. I consider it possible; in any case, I cannot say that it was not."[15]

What actually happened to the "Night and Fog" prisoners who were not shot at once, but were handed over to the SD, was told by a Norwegian prisoner, Hans Cappelen:

Well, the Moellergata 19, in Oslo, the prison where I was for about 25 months, was a house of horror. I heard every night—nearly every night—people screaming and groaning. One day, it must have been in December, 1943, about the 8th of December, they came into my cell and told me to dress. It was in the night. I put on my ragged clothes, what I had. Now I had recovered, practically. I was naturally lame on the one side, could not walk so well, but I could walk; and I went down in the corridor and there they placed me as usual against the wall, and I waited that they would bring me away and shoot me. But they did not shoot me; they brought me to Germany together with lots of other Norwegians. I learned afterwards...we were so-called "Nacht und Nebel" prisoners, "Night and Mist" prisoners. We were brought to a camp called Natzweiler, in Alsace. It was a very bad camp, I must say....

Well, we saw many cruel things there, so cruel that they need— they are well-known. The camp had to be evacuated in September, 1944. We were then brought to Dachau near Munich, but we did not stay long there; at least I didn't stay long there. I was sent to a Kommando called Aurich in East Friesland, where we were about...fifteen hundred prisoners. We had to dig tank traps.... The work was so strong and so hard and the way they treated us so bad, that most of them died there. I suppose about half of the prisoners died of dysentery or of ill-treatment in the five or six weeks we were there. It was too much even for the SS, who had to take care of the camp, so they gave it up, I suppose; and I was sent...to a camp called Gross-Rosen, in Silesia; it is near Breslow. That was a very bad camp, too. We were about 40 Norwegians there; and of those 40 Norwegians we were about 10 left after four to five weeks.[16]

Only a small percentage of "Night and Fog" prisoners survived imprisonment and returned safely to their families at the end of the war.

CHAPTER 18

To Certain Death

To HITLER, the success of any military action depended in large part upon the factor of surprise. All of his invasions were undeclared. They were gigantic attacks out of the night, the very swiftness of which brought terror to the people whose homes were bombed and whose lands were laid waste. They were not merely the small raids of armies feeling out the strength of their opponents. They were raids in force—the full force of the powerful German Wehrmacht. The result of each of these surprise attacks was the death of thousands of noncombatants who had no chance to gain protection before the onslaughts.

After the fall of France the English began to carry the fight to Hitler in the only way they could—in the air and by daring forays of infantrymen across the Channel. The commandos, who dared to strike against German installations guarded by troops of overwhelming superiority in arms and in numbers, bravely put their lives on a table of odds which by the normal risk of war meant death within a year. Little did they know that Hitler had given orders which meant that, in addition, even capture would mean execution. Later in the war, parachutists and soldiers captured behind enemy lines were likewise made subject to this decree for certain death.

Order to Kill Commandos

The first to draw Hitler's wrath were the commandos. On October 18, 1942, he issued the top secret Commando Order:

From now on all enemies on so-called commando missions in Europe or Africa, challenged by German troops, even if they are to all appearances soldiers in uniform or demolition troops, whether armed or unarmed, in battle or in flight, are to be slaughtered to the last man. It does not make any difference whether they are landed from ships and airplanes for their actions, or whether they are dropped by parachute. Even if these individuals, when found, should apparently be prepared to give themselves up, no pardon is to be granted them on principle. In each individual case full information is to be sent to the OKW for publication in the communiqué of the armed forces.

If individual members of such commandos, such as agents, saboteurs, et cetera, fall into the hands of the armed forces by some other means, through the police in occupied territories, for instance, they are to be handed over immediately to the SD. Army imprisonment under military guard, in PW stockades, for instance, et cetera, is strictly prohibited, even if this is only intended for a short time....

I will hold responsible under military law, for failing to carry out this order, all commanders and officers who either have neglected their duty of instructing the troops about this order, or acted against this order when it was to be executed.[1]

The reasons for the commando decree were stated by Hitler in a supplementary order issued on the same day:

I have been compelled to issue strict orders for the destruction of enemy sabotage troops and to declare non-compliance with these orders severely punishable. I deem it necessary to announce to the competent commanding officers and commanders the reasons for this decree.

As in no previous war, a method of destruction of communications behind the front, intimidation of the populace working for Germany, as well as the destruction of war-important industrial plants in territories occupied by us, has been developed in this war....

The consequences of these activities are of extraordinary weight. I do not know whether each commander and officer is cognizant of the fact that the destruction of one single electric power plant, for instance, can deprive the Luftwaffe of many thousands of tons of aluminum, thereby eliminating the construction of countless aircraft that will be missed in the fight at the front and so contribute to serious damage of the homeland as well as bloody losses of the fighting soldiers....

If the German conduct of war is not to suffer grievous damage through these incidents, it must be made clear to the adversary that all sabotage troops will be exterminated, without exception, to the last man.

This means that their chance of escaping with their lives is nil.

Under no circumstances can it be permitted, therefore, that a dynamite, sabotage, or terrorist unit simply allows itself to be captured, expecting to be treated according to rules of the Geneva Convention. It must, under all circumstances, be ruthlessly exterminated.

The report on this subject appearing in the armed forces communiqué will briefly and laconically state that a sabotage, terror, or destruction unit has been encountered and exterminated to the last man.... If it should become necessary, for reasons of interrogation, to initially spare one man or two, then they are to be shot immediately after interrogation.[2]

The explanation of the top secret classification of the order was given in a memorandum, dated February 11, 1943, which was circulated within the Naval War Staff in order to clear up certain misunderstandings as to the scope of the order:

The first Fuehrer order concerning this matter of 18 October 1942 was given the protection of top secret merely because it stated therein (1) that according to the Fuehrer's views, the spreading of military sabotage organizations in the East and West may have portentous consequences for our whole conduct of the war, and (2) that the shooting of uniformed prisoners acting on military orders must be carried out even after they have surrendered voluntarily and asked for pardon.

On the other hand, the annihilation of sabotage units in battle is not at all to be kept secret; but on the contrary, to be currently published in the OKW report. The purpose of these measures to act as a deterrent will not be achieved if those taking part in enemy commando operations do not learn that certain death and not safe imprisonment awaits them. As the saboteurs are to be annihilated immediately, unless their statements are first needed for military reasons, it is necessary that not only all members of the armed forces must receive instructions that these types of saboteurs, even if they are in uniform, are to be annihilated but also all departments of the home staff, dealing with this kind of question, must be informed of the course of action which has been ordered.[3]

Among the many cases in which soldiers in uniform who had been captured on commando raids were shot and killed by the Germans were the following:

During the night of November 19-20, 1942, a British freight glider crashed near Egersund, while carrying a British commando unit of seventeen men, all in uniform. Fourteen survivors of the crash were executed on the evening of November 20 in compliance with the order. During the next several days the members of commando units in raids upon the Norwegian coast at Glomfjord, in the two-man torpedo Drontheim, and the glider plane Stavanger, were killed after interrogation.

When two commandos were put to death by the German Navy at Bordeaux on December 10, 1942, the Naval War Staff commented that the action was "in accordance with the Fuehrer's special order, but is nevertheless something new in international law, since these soldiers were in uniform."[4]

In May, 1943, a cutter sent from the Shetland Islands by the Norwegian Navy was blown up in Toftefjord, Norway, and ten prisoners taken, all of whom were executed after capture. The report of the Wehrmacht was, "In northern Norway an enemy sabotage unit was engaged and destroyed on approaching the coast."[5] Three British commandos who were taken prisoner near Pascara, Italy, on November 2, 1943, were killed.

Killing of Parachutists and Troops Behind the Lines

The commando order was enlarged in practice to cover any military units of the enemy operating behind the established lines of combat. On the night of March 22, 1944, two officers and thirteen enlisted men of the 267th Special Reconnaissance Battalion of the United States Army disembarked from Navy boats and landed on the Italian coast near Stasione di Framura. They were in field uniform and carried no civilian clothes. Their mission was to demolish a railroad tunnel on the main line between La Spezia and Genoa which was being used by the Germans to supply their fighting forces on the Cassino and Anzio beachhead fronts. The entire group was captured and placed under interrogation in La Spezia. They were held there until the morning of the twenty-sixth of March, when they were all executed by a firing squad. General Dostler, who ordered the executions and who was convicted of the crime, testified in his defense that the killings were carried out pursuant to the Hitler order of October 18, 1942.

Even after the Allied landing in Normandy in June, 1944, the commando order remained in effect and was carried out by the Germans. On June 17, 1944, the Chief of the Gestapo addressed a letter to the Supreme Command of the Armed Forces in which he reported the arrest of members of the De Gaulle army who had parachuted in English uniforms into France. He stated that he had instructed the commander of the Security Police and the SD in Paris to treat such parachutists as commandos under the order of October 18, 1942, and continued: "I consider it essential that the necessary orders should also be given from there, in order that the lesser units of the armed forces may not—as has often been the case recently—interpret them wrongly and turn the commando troops over to the Security Police instead of slaughtering them in combat as they retreat."[6]

A reaction to this request was an order of Supreme Command West of June 24, 1944, which provided:

Accordingly, the paratroop saboteurs dropped by the enemy over Britanny will be treated as commando personnel, since this area is not at present an immediate combat zone. It is immaterial in this case whether the paratroopers wear uniforms or civilian clothes. The number of paratroopers captured in Britanny will be included in the daily report currently. In this respect an annex... has already been published to the effect that such criminal elements should be massacred in combat.[7]

The next day, June 25, 1944, Keitel signed the following order on behalf of the High Command:

1. Even after the landing of Anglo-Americans in France, the order of the Fuehrer on the annihilation of terror and sabotage units of 18 October 1942 remains fully in force.

Enemy soldiers in uniform in the immediate combat area of the bridgehead, that is, in the area of the divisions fighting in the most forward lines as well as of the reserves up to the corps commands, according to number 5 of the basic order of 18 October 1942, remain exempted.

2. All members of terror and sabotage units, found outside the immediate combat area, who include fundamentally all parachutists, are to be killed in combat. In special cases, they are to be turned over to the SD.

3. All troops committed outside the combat area of Normandy are to be informed about the duty to destroy enemy terror and sabotage

units briefly and succinctly, according to the directives issued for it.

4. Supreme Commander West will report immediately daily how many saboteurs have been liquidated in this manner. This applies especially also to undertakings by the military commanders. The number is to be published daily in the armed forces communiqué to exercise a frightening effect, as had already been done toward previous commando undertakings in the same manner.[8]

On cross-examination by Sir David Maxwell Fyfe, Keitel was asked whether he approved of the order that all commandos should be shot. He answered:

I no longer opposed it, firstly on account of the punishment threatened, and secondly because I could no longer alter the order without personal orders from Hitler.[9]

Question: Did you think that that order was right?

Answer: According to my inner convictions I did not consider it right, but after it had been given I did not oppose it or take a stand against it in any way.[10]

In July, 1944, the commando order was extended to members of British, American, and Soviet military missions operating in southeastern Europe. The Keitel order of July 30, 1944 provided for the summary execution of combat teams found operating behind the lines:

In the areas of the High Command Southeast and Southwest, members of foreign so-called "Military Missions" (Anglo-American as well as Soviet-Russian) captured in the course of the struggle against partisans shall not receive the treatment as specified in the special orders regarding the treatment of captured partisans. Therefore they are not to be treated as prisoners of war but in conformity with the Fuehrer's order concerning the annihilation of terror and sabotage troops of 18 October 1942.[11]

Anglo-American Slovakian Mission

Pursuant to this order approximately fifteen members of an Allied military mission to Slovakia, consisting of uniformed soldiers and one civilian—a news reporter of the Associated Press—were murdered in Mauthausen concentration camp. The adjutant of Mauthausen confessed to the killings in the following words:

Concerning the American military mission, which landed behind the German front in the Slovakian or Hungarian area in January, 1945, I remember when these persons were brought to Camp Mauthausen. I suppose the number of the arrivals was about 12 to 15 men. They wore a uniform which was American or Canadian, brown-green color shirt and tunic and cloth cap. Eight or 10 days after their arrival the execution order came in by telegraph or teletype. Standartenfuehrer Ziereis came to me into my office and told me, "Now Kaltenbrunner has given the permission for the execution." This letter was secret and had the signature "signed, Kaltenbrunner." Then these people were shot according to martial law and their belongings were given to me by Oberscharfuehrer Niedermeyer.[12]

Behind this matter-of-fact report of an execution carried out under orders of the Gestapo is the story of one of the most heinous Nazi crimes. The members of the mission were sent to Mauthausen concentration camp rather than to a prisoner of war camp for the purpose, as they understood, of being interrogated by special Gestapo officials sent from Berlin. The commandant, Ziereis, arranged for the interrogations to be carried out in small rooms. Torture was frequently used, the favorite method being to hang the men by their wrists tied behind their backs. The guards sometimes pulled the legs of the hanging men to add excruciating pain to the strain upon their arms. When the interrogations were finished, the men were told that they were to be turned over to a prisoner of war camp, and they were required to sign a statement that they had received proper treatment at Mauthausen. They were then taken to a basement room, one at a time, and told to stand before a measuring device. When they backed against the device, a bullet was discharged into their necks. Each member of this British-American mission was murdered in this barbaric fashion. Their bodies were cremated.

The heroic commandos and the volunteers for special military missions behind the enemy lines, courageous soldiers of Britain, America, Norway, and other countries overrun by Hitler's armies, faced not only the danger of death in combat but, under these orders, of death in capture.

CHAPTER 19

The Sagan Incident

Of the three branches of the armed services in World War II, on both sides, not the least in gallantry were the men of the air forces. The young flyers, daring the storms of the skies, the deadly flak, and the challenge of enemy fighters, were not afraid of the risks of battle. They took those risks in the confident belief that even if they lost their aircraft they might still save their lives by parachuting into enemy territory, there to be interned as prisoners of war, with the rights guaranteed them by the Geneva Convention, until the war's end.

The Commander in Chief of the Luftwaffe, from the inception of the war until the end, was Hermann Goering. In a speech to a thousand of his young Air Force officers in 1935 he said: "I intend to create a Luftwaffe which, if the hour should strike, will burst upon the foe like an avenging host. The enemy must feel that he has lost even before he has started fighting."[1] The men of the Luftwaffe were taught to fight hard and bravely. It would have been thought that the man who led that air force would have had a high respect for all airmen, irrespective of nationality.

Goering's attitude toward enemy flyers was betrayed by his remarks in a secret discussion of the war situation by the top military commanders in Hitler's headquarters on January 27, 1945. At that time the German troops were retreating rapidly in the East. There was danger that the prisoner of war camp at Sagan, in which ten thousand Allied flyers were imprisoned, might be overrun by the advancing Soviet troops. When Hitler ordered that the prisoners be transported to the West, Goering suggested that their trousers and shoes be taken away so that there would be no danger of escape in the snow.

The Escape from Camp Sagan

It was at Camp Sagan that one of the most outrageous crimes against prisoners of war occurred during the latter part of the war. Between March 25 and April 23, 1944, fifty flyers who had escaped from Sagan and had been recaptured were murdered by the Gestapo in wanton disregard of international law. The officers escaped from Sagan on the night of March 24-25. They had spent many weeks in digging a tunnel to freedom. Their success in the enterprise was one of the dramatic sagas of the war.

The order to kill the flyers upon recapture was given by Hitler after consultation with Himmler. On March 27 representatives of the Air Force, the High Command, the Gestapo, and the Criminal Police met at the headquarters of the Security Police in Berlin to work out the details. Colonel Ernst Walde described this conference in the following words:

... We were informed about a conference, which had taken place on the previous day, that is Sunday, at the Fuehrer's headquarters in connection with the mass escape from Sagan, in the course of which heated discussions had taken place between the participants. In this connection the names of Himmler, Goering and Keitel were mentioned. Whether Ribbentrop's name was also mentioned I do not remember. The Fuehrer was not mentioned. At this conference appropriate measures were said to have been discussed, or taken, to check any such mass escape in the future. The nature of these measures was not disclosed. Later and more or less in conclusion Gruppenfuehrer Mueller [Chief of the Gestapo] declared that requisite orders had already been given and put into effect the previous morning. Regarding the search for escaped prisoners, he could or would not make any statement; he merely declared that according to reports so far received, shootings had taken place at some points for attempted escapes. I think he said that the number was 10 or 15.

After these remarks by Gruppenfuehrer Mueller, which unmistakably caused a shattering effect, it became clear to me that a decision had been made by the highest authority, and that therefore any intervention by subordinate departments was impossible and pointless.[2]

General Westhoff recalled a conversation which he had with Keitel concerning the matter. He quoted Keitel as saying nervously:

Gentlemen, this is a bad business.... This morning Goering reproached me in the presence of Hitler for having let some more prisoners of war escape.... Gentlemen, these escapes must stop. We must set an example. We shall take very severe measures. I can only tell you that the men who have escaped will be shot; probably the majority of them are dead already.[3]

Keitel testified that in the course of a situation report at the Berghof, Himmler reported the escape of the flyers from Sagan, and that after a heated discussion Hitler ordered that the prisoners were not to be returned to the armed forces but were to remain with the police. Keitel admitted he told Generals von Graevenitz and Westhoff that an example must be made and that he probably said something like: "You will see what a disaster this is, perhaps many of them have been shot already."[4] When Graevenitz protested that under the rules of land warfare escape was not a dishonorable offense punishable by execution, Keitel said that it was a matter of indifference to him.[5]

The actual killings were carried out by the Gestapo. The bodies were burned and the ashes put into urns and returned to the prisoner of war camp. Keitel stated that in his opinion the cremation of officer prisoners of war was "horrible."[6]

After the murders were carried out the German government sent an official note to England saying that the flyers had been shot while resisting arrest during an attempt to escape. Goering admitted that in any other service of the world an attempt to escape is considered the duty of an officer. He testified that he "considered it the most serious incident of the whole war," and that later he knew that the note to the British government "was not in accordance with the truth."[7]

Jodl was questioned by Mr. Roberts of the British prosecution staff concerning his knowledge of the Sagan incident:

You said yesterday that after the incident of the Sagan shooting, you thought Hitler was no longer "humane." Did you say that?
Answer: I said yesterday, I had the impression then that he was disavowing all humane concepts of right....

Question: ... Would you agree with me—the word is not too strong
—that this was sheer murder of these 50 airmen?

Answer: I completely agree with you: I consider it sheer murder.[8]

Sagan was an incident—the incident of fifty murdered flyers.
But it was by no means an isolated atrocity. It was part of a larger
policy to encourage the killing of captured flyers.

Lynching Allied Flyers

While the Luftwaffe was dominant in the skies over Europe,
the Nazis were quite willing that the Geneva Convention be observed with respect to captured flyers, for their men parachuted to
English soil. But as the war went on and the vaunted Luftwaffe had
been reduced to little more than fighter squadrons battling the
Allied bombers over German-occupied Europe, the Nazis became
less chivalrous in their outlook and more willing to overlook, for
themselves, the covenants of international law which guaranteed
the life of a soldier taken as a prisoner of war.

There were two stages in this metamorphosis. The first was the
protection of civilians who, under the incitement of the propaganda
of Goebbels, and motivated by the personal sense of suffering from
the raids of the Allied airmen, lynched, shot, or beat to death
captured flyers who had been forced to parachute to earth behind
the German lines. The second was the direct order to kill flyers.

On August 10, 1943, Himmler issued an order to the Security
Police stating that it was "not the task of the police to interfere
in clashes between Germans and English and American terror flyers
who have bailed out."[9] This order subsequently was reissued by
Kaltenbrunner to the heads of the Gestapo, the SD, and the Criminal
Police in these words: "All offices of the SD and the Security Police
are to be informed that pogroms of the populace against English
and American terror flyers are not to be interfered with. On the
contrary, this hostile mood is to be fostered."[10] And in a letter dated
April 5, 1944, Kaltenbrunner gave detailed instructions to the
various police offices as to the treatment of flyers who had parachuted down, stating that they were to be handcuffed as a rule,
that crews who resisted arrest or wore civilian clothes under their
uniforms were to be shot immediately after capture, and that

civilians who lynched Allied flyers were to be protected by the police.

The result of these orders was an indiscriminate lynching of flyers who fell into the hands of the civilian populace. Party leaders not only murdered flyers who surrendered to civilians; they frequently demanded and obtained the release of flyers who had surrendered to the police. Revenge for Allied bombings was thus taken against the Allied flyers personally. The airman who was lucky enough to bail out of a shot-down plane, and who surrendered himself as a prisoner, might be taken into a near-by field, disarmed and helpless, and there shot or beaten to death. The majority of the war crimes trials conducted by the Theater Judge Advocate in Germany were the trials of civilians, usually petty Party officials, who lynched Allied airmen.

But the indiscriminate killings which resulted from the incitement of the population under police protection were not enough. Lynching had to be put on a scientific basis. By May, 1944, the Allied superiority in the air had become intolerable to the head of the Luftwaffe. In a conference on the sixteenth day of that month Goering agreed to "propose to the Fuehrer that American and English crews who fire indiscriminately on towns, on civilian trains in motion, or on soldiers dropping by parachute, shall be shot immediately on the spot."[11]

Within five days Hitler acted upon the Goering proposal. A memorandum dated May 21, 1944, initialed by Keitel, and directing the drafting of an order, stated that "after a report of the Reichsmarshal,"[12] Hitler had ordered that downed Anglo-American airmen were to be shot without court-martial proceedings if they shot German air crews parachuting to earth, attacked German planes which had made emergency landings, attacked railway trains engaged in civilian transportation, or strafed individual civilians. Jodl commented on the memorandum that he considered an attack upon an airplane which had made an emergency landing to be "in complete agreement with the strictest standards of civilized warfare."[13]

A further conference on the matter was held on June 6, 1944, attended by Goering, Kaltenbrunner, Ribbentrop, and Himmler. The memorandum describing this meeting stated:

Contrary to the original suggestion made by the Reich Foreign Minister who wished to include every type of terror attack on the German civilian population, that is, also bombing attacks on cities, it was agreed in the above conference that merely those attacks carried out with A/C armament, aimed directly at the civilian population and their property, should be taken as the standard for the evidence of a criminal action in this sense. Lynch law would have to be the rule. On the contrary, there has been no question of court martial sentence or handing over to the police.[14]

When Kaltenbrunner was asked at the conference to provide an instance of such a "terror" attack by an Allied flyer, which Goebbels could use in the press in advance of the distribution of the new order, he confessed that no such case was known to the SD. On the bottom of this memorandum Keitel made the notation: "Min. Dir. Berndt got out and then shot the enemy aviators on the road. I am against *legal* procedure! It doesn't work out!"[15]

It was even planned to turn over captured flyers in military custody to the German secret police for execution. On June 15, 1944, Keitel wrote a letter to Goering which specified acts "to be considered the acts of terror, which are to be taken into consideration upon the publication of an instance of lynching and which will justify the transfer of enemy aviators from the Air Force (P.W.) Reception Camp Oberursel to the SD for special treatment."[16] Referring to this statement Keitel was asked: "We know, defendant, that 'special treatment' means death. Didn't you know, in 1944, what 'special treatment' meant?" and Keitel replied: "Yes, I know what 'special treatment' meant. I do know that."[17]

On June 23, 1944, Keitel requested that Goering agree to the description of the acts to be considered as terroristic for the purpose of the lynch law, and that he give the necessary verbal instructions to the commandant of the Air Force reception camp at Oberursel to surrender such flyers to the SD for execution. On June 26, 1944, the reply came back: "The Reichsmarshal approves the definition of terror flyer communicated by the OKW, as well as the procedure which is proposed."[18]

The witness Lampe testified to the brutal murder of forty-seven British, American, and Dutch flying officers at Mauthausen concentration camp while he was interned there during the last months of the war:

During September, I think it was on the 6th of September 1944, there came to Mauthausen a small convoy of 47 British, American, and Dutch officers. They were airmen who had come down by parachute. They had been arrested after having tried to make their way back to their own lines. Because of this they were condemned to death by a German tribunal. They had been in prison about a year and a half and were brought to Mauthausen for execution.

On their arrival they were transferred to the bunker, the camp prison. They were made to undress and had only their pants and a shirt. They were barefooted. The following morning they were at the roll call at seven o'clock. The work gangs went to their tasks. The 47 officers were assembled in front of the office and were told by the commanding officer of the camp that they were all under sentence of death.

I must mention that one of the American officers asked the commander that he should be allowed to meet his death as a soldier. In reply he was lashed with a whip. The 47 were led barefoot to the quarry.

For all the prisoners at Mauthausen the murder of these men has remained in their minds like a scene from Dante's Inferno. This is how it was done: At the bottom of the steps they loaded stones on the backs of these poor men and they had to carry them to the top. The first journey was made with stones weighing 25 to 30 kilos and was accompanied by blows. Then they were made to run down. For the second journey the stones were still heavier; and whenever the poor wretches sank under their burden, they were kicked and hit with a bludgeon, even stones were hurled at them.

...In the evening when I returned from the gang with which I was then working, the road which led to the camp was a path of blood. I almost stepped on the lower jaw of a man. Twenty-one bodies were strewn along the road. Twenty-one had died on the first day. The twenty-six others died the following morning.[19]

The witness Jean Frederic Veith gave additional testimony on this atrocity:

Those officers, those parachutists, were shot in accordance with the usual systems used whenever prisoners had to be done away with. That is to say, they were forced to work to excess, to carry heavy stones.

Then they were beaten until they took heavier ones; and so on and so forth until, finally driven to extremity, they turned towards the barbed wire. If they did not do it of their own accord they were pushed there; and they were beaten until they did so; and the moment they approached it and were perhaps about one meter away from it, they were mown down by machine guns fired by the SS guards in the watchtowers. This was the usual system for the "killing for attempted escape" as they afterwards called it.[20]

As the Allied bombings became more severe, it was even proposed that captured enemy flyers should be moved into camps in the large cities, unprotected by air-raid shelters, where they might be killed by the bombs of their flying comrades. This proposal was made on August 18, 1943, to the High Command of the Wehrmacht by the Commander in Chief, Air General Staff:

> The Commander in Chief, Air General Staff, proposes to erect prisoner of war camps in the residential quarters of cities, in order to obtain a certain protection thereby....In view of the above reason, consideration should be given to the immediate erection of such camps in a large number of cities which appear to be endangered by air attacks....So far, there are in Germany about 8,000 prisoners of war of the British and American air forces (without counting those in hospitals). By evacuating the camps actually in existence, which might be used to house bombed-out people, we should immediately have at our disposal prisoners of war for a fairly large number of such camps.[21]

On September 3, 1943, the Supreme Commander of the Wehrmacht, Chief of War Prisoners, approved this project in principle.[22]

Thus was the fate of American and British flyers decreed. If they were caught by civilians, they might be lynched under protection of the police. If they were suspected of attacking civilians they could be turned over to the SD for "special treatment,"[23] without trial or chance for defense. If they escaped from the prisoner of war camps and were recaptured by the SD, they could be shot. Under these rules the concept of the "chivalrous war"[24] lost ground rapidly to the idea of war without quarter.

CHAPTER 20

Special Treatment

H ITLER'S military and police state had several pseudonyms for murder. The most popular was the phrase "special treatment."[1] It was in connection with the screening of prisoner of war camps for politically "undesirable"[2] prisoners that the term came into its widest use. Categories of Soviet prisoners of war were taken from the camps and turned over to the Gestapo and the SD for "special treatment." The story of these murders is one of the most atrocious of all the Hitler crimes against soldiers.

Design for Murder

General Warlimont, Deputy Chief of Staff of the Wehrmacht Leading Operations Staff, described the Hitler decision to commit this crime:

Shortly before the beginning of this campaign I was present in a group composed of the commanders in chief (with their chiefs of staff) of the three armed forces, of the army groups, of armies, and of the corresponding groups in the air forces and navy. Hitler made an announcement to this group that special measures would have to be taken against political functionaries and commissars of the Soviet Army. He said that this would not be an ordinary campaign but would be the clash of conflicting ideologies. He further said that the political functionaries and commissars were not to be considered as prisoners of war but were to be segregated from other prisoners immediately after their capture and were to be turned over to special detachments of the SD which were to accompany the German troops to Russia. He further said that when it was not possible to turn over the political functionaries and commissars to the SD, they were to be eliminated by the German troops.[3]

The Chief of the SD, Otto Ohlendorf, testified by affidavit:

In 1941, shortly after the start of the campaign against Russia, an agreement was entered into between the Chief of the Security Police and SD and the OKW (supreme command of the armed forces) and OKH (supreme command of the army) to the effect that operative detachments of the security police and SD were to go to the prisoner of war camps on the Eastern front to screen the prisoners of war. All Jews and Communist functionaries were to be removed from the prisoner of war camps by the operative detachments and were to be executed outside of the camps. To my knowledge, this action was carried out throughout the entire Russian campaign.

In the other occupied territories and in the Reich—to my knowledge —the Gestapo had been made responsible for this program in the Russian prisoner of war camps. This action was, to my knowledge, carried on throughout the greater part of the war.[4]

Plans for this unbelievable action having been laid prior to the attack upon the Soviet Union, the Gestapo issued instructions to its field commandos on July 17, 1941. These instructions provided in part:

The mission of the Commandos is the political investigation of all camp inmates, the separation and further treatment of:

a) All political, criminal, or in some other way, intolerable elements among them;

b) Those persons who could be used for the reconstruction of the occupied countries....

Further, the Commandos must make efforts from the beginning to seek out among the prisoners elements which would appear reliable, regardless of whether they are Communists or not, in order to use them for intelligence purposes inside the camp and, if advisable, later in the occupied territories also.

By use of such informers and by use of all other existing possibilities, the discovery of all elements to be eliminated among the prisoners must proceed, step by step, at once....Above all, the following must be discovered:

All important functionaries of State and Party, especially professional revolutionaries.

Functionaries of the Komintern.

All policy forming party functionaries of the KPdSU [Communist Party of the Soviet Union] and its fellow organizations in the central committees and the regional and district committees.

All Peoples-Commissars and their deputies.

All former political commissars in the Red Army.

Leading personalities of the state authorities of central and middle regions.

The leading personalities of the business world.

Members of the Soviet-Russian intelligence.

All Jews.

All persons who are found to be agitators or fanatical Communists....

Executions are not to be held in the camp or in the immediate vicinity of the camp. If the camps in the General-Government are in the immediate vicinity of the border, then the prisoners are to be taken for special treatment, if possible, into the former Soviet-Russian territory....[5]

Murder in the Field

A description of a case of "special treatment"[6] carried out in the field appeared in a report of December 24, 1942, submitted by the commander of the Security Police and SD in Zhitomir in the course of an inquiry into the death of two SS-men. The report contained the sworn testimony of the police official in charge of the action:

As from the middle of August, I was head of the Berditchev field office of the Commander of the Security Police and SD in the town of Zhitomir. On 23 December 1942 the Deputy Commander, Hauptsturm-fuehrer of the SS Kallbach, inspected the local office and also the Educational Labor Camp which was supervised by my office. In this Educational Labor Camp, as from the end of October or in the beginning of November, there were 78 former prisoners of war who had been dismissed from the permanent camp (Stalag) in Zhitomir as being unfit for work....

The 78 prisoners of war in the local camp were, one and all, severely wounded men. Some had lost both legs; others both arms; others again had lost one or the other of their limbs. Only a few of them had all their arms and legs, although they were so mutilated by other kinds of wounds that they were totally unfit for work. The latter had to nurse the former.

At the time he was inspecting the Educational Labor Camp, on 23 December 1942, SS Haupsturmfuehrer Kallbach issued an order to the effect that the surviving 68 or 70 prisoners of war, the others having died in the meantime, should that very day be subjected to "special treatment." For this purpose he assigned a motor truck, driven by SS-man Schaefer, from the command division, who arrived here today at 1130 hours. I entrusted the preparations for the execution early that morning to my colleagues in the local administration, SS Unterscharfuehrer Paal, SS Rottenfuehrer Hesselbach, and SS Sturmmann Vollprecht....

For this particular execution I issued orders to choose a site outside on a terrain behind the permanent camp. Concerning the three above-mentioned persons whom I entrusted with the shooting of the prisoners of war, I knew that they had, in Kiev, participated in the mass executions of many thousands of persons and that they had before, that is during my time of service, been entrusted by the local administration with the shooting of many hundreds of victims.[7]

Murder in the Camps

Whenever it was equally convenient the commandos of the Security Police and SD preferred to send prisoners of war screened out of prisoner of war cages to near-by concentration camps for execution rather than to conduct the killings in the field. On October 23, 1941, the commandant of the Gross Rosen concentration camp reported to the Chief of the Gestapo a list of twenty prisoners who had been executed the preceding day.

On November 9, 1941, the Chief of the Gestapo ordered that diseased prisoners of war should be excluded from transports to concentration camps for execution:

The commanders of the concentration camps are complaining that five to ten percent of the Soviet Russians destined for execution are arriving in the camps dead or half dead. Therefore the impression has arisen that the Stalags are getting rid of such prisoners in this way.

It was particularly noted that, when marching, for example, from the railroad station to the camp, a rather large number of prisoners of war collapsed on the way from exhaustion, either dead or half dead, and had to be picked up by a truck following the convoy. It cannot be prevented that the German people take notice of these occurrences.[8]

Tens of thousands of Soviet prisoners of war were transported to Germany for forced labor in special labor camps under the direct control of the Gestapo. The prisoners were removed to Germany in such numbers and with such rapidity that it was impossible for the special teams of Gestapo and SD personnel to complete their screening of prisoners in the transit cages for selection of those to be given special treatment. It therefore fell to the Gestapo offices located in Germany to screen the labor camps, remove the objectionable prisoners, and send them to a near-by concentration camp which had gassing and crematorial facilities for killing them and disposing of their bodies. That such killings were routinely conducted in numerous camps was disclosed by a file of documents relating to a certain Major Meinel, who complained of the manner in which the murders were carried out by the Gestapo.

A report in this file from the Gestapo office in Munich, dated November 15, 1941, listed 18 labor camps visited by the Gestapo, and a total of 3,088 Soviet prisoners of war screened, of which 410 were screened out as intolerable. The 410 Russians sorted out belonged to the following categories: officials and officers, Jews, members of intelligentsia, fanatical Communists, agitators and others, runaways, and incurably sick. At the date of the report, 301 had already been executed in the Dachau concentration camp. These 410 Russians constituted 13 per cent of the total, whereas the Gestapo offices at Nuremberg, Furth, and Regensburg screened out an average of 15 to 17 per cent. The report concluded: "The complaints of the High Command of the Armed Forces that the screening of the Russians had been carried out in a superficial manner must be most emphatically refuted."[9] This percentage becomes the more significant when it is considered that presumably the prisoners had already been subjected to preliminary screening in prisoner of war cages from which objectionable prisoners had been removed for killing in the field by the special commandos of the Gestapo and SD.

When Major Meinel mentioned that it weighed heavily on the conscience of the officers to hand over the prisoners to the Gestapo, the cynical reply was that "the hearts of some of the SS-men who were charged with executing prisoners were all but breaking."[10] The results of Major Meinel's efforts to prevent the murder of "objectionable" Soviet prisoners of war were a sharp complaint against him lodged with the High Command, and his removal from his post.

Slaughter

The number of Soviet prisoners of war who were screened out of prisoner of war cages and labor camps by the Gestapo and SD and who received "special treatment" by SS-men in the field or in the concentration camps can never be determined. The documents on the Meinel case show that the following were killed: (1) officials and officers, (2) Jews, (3) members of intelligentsia, (4) fanatical Communists, (5) agitators and ringleaders, (6) runaways, and (7) incurably sick.

In effect, this program left alive of the Soviet prisoners of war only those whose health was able to withstand the disease and semi-starvation of the labor camps and who were accepted as uneducated and nonpolitical. All others were killed. In Auschwitz concentration camp alone, according to the testimony of the commandant of that camp, Hoess, twenty thousand Soviet prisoners of war, who had previously been screened out of prisoner of war cages and had been delivered to Auschwitz for extermination, were gassed and cremated.

Of special significance in this terrible action is the fact that it was in no sense a retaliation for cruelties which the Soviets might have inflicted upon German troops. The plans were all laid before the attack upon the Soviet Union had begun. Keitel was asked whether he denied that as early as May, 1941, at least a month before the attack on the Soviet Union, plans were under way "for the annihilation of Russian political commissars and military personnel?" He replied: "No, that I do not deny. That was the result of the directive which had been communicated and which had been worked out here in writing by the generals."[11]

The "special treatment" of selected prisoners of war was thus planned by Hitler and Himmler, with the assistance of general officers, as a part of the war plan for the invasion of the Soviet Union; the "selection" of those to be killed was conducted by the Gestapo and the SD; the killings were carried out in the field by Gestapo commandos and in the concentration camps by the SS guards. A more perfect indictment of the Hitler military-police state could scarcely be found.

CHAPTER 21

The Bullet Decree

Goering testified that in his conception of legal warfare the worst matter in the whole war was the shooting of the fifty Allied officer-flyers who were recaptured after their escape from the prisoner of war camp at Sagan. How relatively trivial in the Nazi scale of criminality this incident really was is evident from consideration of the venal *Kugel Erlass,* the Bullet Decree.

Step III

On March 4, 1944, the Chief of the Gestapo issued instructions to local Gestapo offices enclosing the following order of the Supreme Command of the Army:

1. Every captured escaped prisoner of war who is an officer or a not-working, non-commissioned officer, except British and American prisoners of war, is to be turned over to the Chief of the Security Police and of the Security Service under the classification "Step III" regardless of whether the escape occurred during a transport, whether it was a mass escape or an individual one.

2. Since the transfer of the prisoners of war to the security police and security service may not become officially known to the outside under any circumstances, other prisoners of war may by no means be informed of the capture. The captured prisoners are to be reported to the Army Information Bureau as "escaped and not captured." Their mail is to be handled accordingly. Inquiries of representatives of the Protective Power, of the International Red Cross, and of other aid societies will be given the same answer.

3. If escaped British and American prisoners of war who are officers or not-working non-commissioned officers, respectively, are captured

they are to be detained at first outside the prisoner of war camps and out of sight of prisoners of war; if Army owned buildings are unavailable they are to be placed in police custody. In every instance the Corps Area Command will request speedily the Supreme Command of the Army (Chief, Prisoner of War Section) for a decision as to whether they are to be turned over to the Chief of the Security Police and the Security Service.[1]

In reference to this order the Chief of the Gestapo issued the following instructions:

The State Police Directorates will accept the captured escaped officer prisoners of war from the prisoner of war camp commandants and will transport them to the Concentration Camp Mauthausen following the procedure previously used, unless the circumstances render a special transport imperative. The prisoners of war are to be put in irons on the transport—not on the way to the station if it is subject to view by the public. The camp commandant at Mauthausen is to be notified that the transfer occurs within the scope of the action "Kugel."[2]

On July 27, 1944, the Commander of Military District VI issued a summary of all decrees requiring the delivery of prisoners of war to the Gestapo and consequent dismissal from prisoner of war status. This summary listed, in addition to attempted escape, several other circumstances which required the surrender of prisoners of war to the Gestapo for handling under the Bullet Decree:

(a) Soviet prisoners of war who committed offenses for which the camp commander did not believe he could take adequate disciplinary measures.

(b) Recaptured Soviet prisoners of war who committed offenses during the escape.

(c) Recaptured Soviet officers.

(d) Soviet officer prisoners of war who refused to work or who had "unfavorable influence" upon the willingness to work of the other prisoners.

(e) Soviet enlisted prisoners of war who refused to work and were ringleaders in influencing other prisoners not to work.

Concerning the Bullet Decree, a high Gestapo official averred:

As far as I remember, the subjects of this decree were Russian prisoners of war, who had escaped from prisoner of war camps and had been recaptured by the SIPO. These prisoners of war were not to be put into a prisoner of war camp after their recapture, but into a concentration camp. For the outside world they were to be considered dead. To my knowledge there was to be no court martial procedure. I furthermore remember certain executive orders for this decree, regarding the certification of the alleged death of these prisoners of war.[3]

Murder Macabre

What actually happened to the prisoners of war who were transported to Mauthausen concentration camp under the Bullet Decree was described by two French officer prisoners confined in Mauthausen, Lieutenant Colonel Guivante de Saint Gast and Lieutenant Jean Veith.

In Mauthausen existed several treatments of prisoners, amongst them the "action K or Kugel" (Bullet Action). Upon the arrival of transports, prisoners with the mark "K" were not registered, got no numbers, and their names remained unknown except to the officials of the Political Department. Lt. Veith had the opportunity of hearing upon the arrival of a transport the following conversation between the Untersturmfuehrer Streitwieser and the chief of the convoy: "How many prisoners?" "15, but two K." "Well, that makes 13."

The K prisoners were taken directly to the prison where they were unclothed and taken to the "bathroom." This bathroom in the cellars of the prison building near the crematory was specially designed for execution (shooting and gassing).

The shooting took place by means of a measuring apparatus—the prisoner being backed towards a metrical measure with an automatic contraption releasing a bullet in his neck as soon as the moving plank determining his height touched the top of his head.

If a transport consisted of too many "K" prisoners, instead of losing time for the "measurement" they were exterminated by gas sent into the shower room instead of water....[4]

The witness Lampe testified to the killing of a group of fifty Soviet officers at Mauthausen concentration camp—a killing witnessed personally by Himmler:

The execution which Himmler himself witnessed—at least the beginning of it, because it lasted throughout the afternoon—was another particularly horrible spectacle.... The Soviet Army officers were called one by one, and there was a sort of human chain between the group which was awaiting its turn and that which was in the stairway listening to the shots which killed their predecessors. They were all killed by a shot in the neck.

Question: You witnessed this personally?

Answer: I repeat that on that afternoon I was in Block 11, which was situated opposite the crematorium; and although we did not see the execution itself, we heard every shot; and we saw the condemned men who were waiting on the stairway opposite us embrace each other before they parted.

Question: Who were these men who were condemned?

Answer: The majority of them were Soviet officers, political commissars, or members of the Bolshevik party.[5]

In his death statement, the commandant of Mauthausen concentration camp, Ziereis, confessed that shooting in the back of the neck was a form of execution used in the camp.[6]

The affiant Waldmann, a member of the SS, described the execution of Soviet prisoners of war under the Bullet Decree at Sachsenhausen concentration camp:

The Russian prisoners of war had to walk about one kilometer from the station to the camp. In the camp they stayed one night without food. The next night they were led away for execution. The prisoners were constantly being transferred from the inner camp on three trucks, one of which was driven by me. The inner camp was approximately one and three-quarters of a kilometer from the execution grounds. The execution itself took place in the barracks which had recently been constructed for this purpose.

One room was reserved for undressing and another for waiting; in one of them a radio played rather loudly. It was done purposely so that the prisoners could not guess that death awaited them. From the second room they went, one by one, through a passage into a small fenced-in room with an iron grid let into the floor. Under the grid was a drain. As soon as a prisoner of war was killed, the corpse was carried out by two German prisoners while the blood was washed off the grid.

In this small room there was a slot in the wall, approximately 50 centimeters in length. The prisoner of war stood with the back of his head against the slot and a sniper shot at him from behind the slot. In practice, this arrangement did not prove satisfactory, since the sniper often missed the prisoner. After 8 days a new arrangement was made. The prisoner, as before, was placed against the wall; an iron plate was then slowly lowered onto his head. The prisoner was under the impression that he was being measured for height. The iron plate contained a ramrod which shot out suddenly and pole-axed the prisoner with a blow on the back of the head. He dropped dead. The iron plate was operated by a foot lever in a corner of the room. The personnel working in the room belonged to the above-mentioned Sonderkommando.

By request of the execution squad, I was also forced to work this apparatus. I shall refer to the subject later. The bodies of the prisoners thus murdered were burned in four mobile crematories transported in trailers and attached to motor cars. I had to ride constantly from the inner camp to the execution yard. I had to make 10 trips a night with 10 minutes' interval between trips. It was during these intervals that I witnessed the executions.[7]

This was Hitler's *Kugel Erlass*. It was not murder on the grand scale, but it was vile killing nonetheless of totally helpless, unarmed prisoners of war. The pseudoscientific method used—the measuring device with the hidden pistol—was perfectly suited to the crime. For it was, after all, the "Bullet Decree" under which the prisoners of war were murdered.

CHAPTER 22

The Katyn Massacre

THE GERMAN armies moved against Poland on the first day of September, 1939. They quickly overran the Polish armies and put them to flight. The Polish ambassador to the Soviet Union received a note on September 17, 1939, declaring that the Soviets regarded the Polish government as disintegrated and the Polish state as having in fact ceased to exist; that consequently, all agreements between the Soviet Union and Poland were rendered invalid; that Poland, without leadership, constituted a threat to the Soviet Union; that the Soviet government could not view with indifference the fate of the Ukrainians and White Russians living on Polish territory; that, accordingly, the Soviet government had ordered its troops to cross the Polish border, and that the Soviet government proposed to extricate the Polish people from the unfortunate war into which they were dragged by their unwise leaders and enable them to live a peaceful life. On that day Soviet troops marched into Poland from the east.

When the Russian troops crossed the Polish-Soviet border orders were given many Polish units not to resist because it was thought (or at least hoped) that the Red Army was entering Poland for the purpose of joining in the fight against the Germans. Of course, the action actually was a comradeship in arms between Germany and the Soviet Union against the weak and helpless Poles. Soviet troops quickly captured and disarmed Polish soldiers and drove them as prisoners across the Soviet frontier. During the early period all officers and men were gathered together in several transit camps, but later the majority of commissioned officers and a considerable number of noncommissioned officers were removed to three camps:

Starobielsk, near Voroshilovgrad; Kozielsk, near Smolensk; and Ostaszkov, near Kalinin—all within Soviet territory. There were approximately 4,000 Polish prisoners of war in Starobielsk; 5,000 in Kozielsk; and 6,500 in Ostaszkov. Out of the entire group of approximately 15,000 officers only about 400, who had been transferred to the prison camp at Pavlishev Bor and thence to a camp at Gryazonets, survived. Of the remainder, the corpses of 4,000 were found in mass graves at Katyn Forest near Smolensk. Nothing was ever heard of the rest.

These Polish officers either were killed while in Soviet custody or were captured by invading German armies and destroyed by them. When the Germans announced the discovery of the bodies of the 4,000 officers killed and buried in Katyn Forest, they blamed the Soviets for the crime. Subsequently the Soviets accused the Germans.

No mention was made of the Katyn Forest massacre in the negotiations leading to the drafting of the indictment until the final meeting of the prosecution staffs in London. At that meeting the Soviet representatives sought for the first time to include in the indictment a charge that the defendants were responsible for the killing of 925 Polish officers in the Katyn Forest. While both British and United States representatives were against it, this accusation was nevertheless included.

Subsequently, at Berlin, the Soviet representatives insisted upon amending this count by raising the number of the slain from 925 to 11,000. As finally worded, the charge stated: "In September, 1941, 11,000 Polish officers, prisoners of war, were killed in the Katyn Forest near Smolensk."[1]

Mr. Justice Jackson strongly opposed the insertion of this charge in the indictment, and when the Soviets remained adamant he took the position that "we would keep hands off and leave the entire contest to the Soviet and German lawyers."[2] This opposition was not founded upon any positive evidence then in his possession establishing that the Germans were not responsible for the crime. "It was not based upon any conviction in my own mind about the truth or falsity of the charge. I knew that the Nazis and the Soviets accused each other, that both were capable of the offense, that perhaps both had opportunity to commit it, and that it was perfectly consistent with the policy of each toward Poland."[3]

But Mr. Justice Jackson realized that to attempt to prove the truth about the Katyn massacre would require departure from the basic plan to develop the case by authentic German documents. The complete story could be established only by witnesses, and the American prosecutors at that time knew of no witnesses to the crime whose testimony "would meet the high standards of credibility required in a criminal trial."[4]

On January 21, 1946, General Lucius D. Clay, the United States Military Governor for Germany, sent to Mr. Justice Jackson a strictly confidential report from the United States Embassy in Warsaw that certain Polish circles did not consider the Germans to have been responsible for the atrocity. Yet two years later the American ambassador to Poland was unable to state that the perpetrators of the massacre had been definitely established. Other information subsequently received from United States military intelligence was not in evidentiary form. As Mr. Justice Jackson later said: "Whatever the facts were, they had become overlaid with deep layers of Nazi and Soviet propaganda and counterpropaganda, and it seemed we could not at the international trial wisely undertake or satisfactorily achieve the long task of separating truth from falsehood."[5]

Moreover, proof of this atrocity was unnecessary to sustain the prosecution's case. For in Poland the Nazis had committed their gravest crimes against humanity. The expulsion of the Jews from the Warsaw Ghetto and the murders committed at Chelmno, Treblinka, Auschwitz, and elsewhere sufficed to establish an irrefutable case. It was fully appreciated that, unlike these clear cases of criminality, the Katyn Forest massacre would be bitterly contested by the German defense counsel and the trial considerably prolonged in resolving this single and, from the over-all viewpoint, relatively unimportant fact issue.

The key to the solution of the crime, in the absence of reliable eyewitness testimony, was the approximate date of the executions. German troops reached Smolensk on July 17, 1941. The Katyn Forest itself was occupied by Signal Regiment 537 shortly thereafter, the principal staff arriving about September 20, 1941. Consequently, if the executions took place before July, 1941, the responsibility must have been upon the Soviets, who had first taken the Polish officers prisoner. If the executions took place after that date the Germans were accountable.

The highway east of Smolensk toward Vitebsk passes through the Katyn Forest. A road branching off this highway to the north runs to a large house on the bank of the river Dneiper. This road passes through the lesser Katyn Forest, and it was there that the mass graves of the slain Polish officers were discovered. The house was first occupied by a Soviet detachment, and later by a German signal regiment.

The Soviet Case

In an attempt to establish German responsibility, the Soviet prosecutor offered to the Tribunal the report of a special commission which investigated the crime in accordance with a directive of the Soviet Extraordinary State Commission. No direct evidence on the issue was submitted by the Soviet prosecution. This hearsay report contained the following conclusions:

According to the estimates of medico-legal experts, the total number of bodies amounts to over 11,000. The medico-legal experts carried out a thorough examination of the bodies exhumed, and of the documents and material evidence found on the bodies and in the graves. During the exhumation and examination of the corpses, the commission questioned many witnesses among the local inhabitants. Their testimony permitted the determination of the exact time and circumstances of the crimes committed by the German invaders. . . .

On perusal of the material at the disposal of the special commission, that is, the depositions of over 100 witnesses questioned, the data of the medico-legal experts, the documents and the material evidence and belongings taken from the graves in Katyn Forest, we can arrive at the following definite conclusions:

1. The Polish prisoners of war imprisoned in the three camps west of Smolensk and engaged in railway construction before the war, remained there after the occupation of Smolensk by the Germans, right up to September, 1941.

2. In the autumn of 1941, in Katyn Forest, the German occupa-

tional authorities carried out mass shootings of the Polish prisoners of war from the above-mentioned camps.

3. Mass shootings of the Polish prisoners of war in Katyn Forest were carried out by German military organizations disguised under the specific name, "Staff 537, Engineer Construction Battalion," commanded by Oberleutnant Arnes (sp.) and his colleagues, Oberleutnant Rex and Leutnant Hottl (sp.).

4. In connection with the deterioration, for Germany, of the general military and political machinery at the beginning of 1943, the German occupational authorities, with a view to provoking incidents, undertook a whole series of measures to ascribe their own misdeeds to organizations of the Soviet authorities, in order to make mischief between the Russians and the Poles.

5. For these purposes:

a. The German fascist invaders, by persuasion, attempts at bribery, threats, and by barbarous tortures, endeavored to find "witnesses" among the Soviet citizens from whom they obtained false testimony, alleging that the Polish prisoners of war had been shot by organizations of the Soviet authorities in the spring of 1940.

b. The German occupational authorities, in the spring of 1943, brought from other places the bodies of Polish prisoners of war whom they had shot, and laid them in the turned up graves of Katyn Forest, with the dual purpose of covering up the traces of their own atrocities and of increasing the numbers of "victims of Bolshevist atrocities" in Katyn Forest.

c. While preparing their provocative measures, the German occupational authorities employed up to 500 Russian prisoners of war for the task of digging up the graves in Katyn Forest. Once the graves had been dug, the Russian prisoners of war were shot by the Germans in order to destroy thus all proof and material evidence on the matter.

6. The data of the legal and medical examinations determined, without any shadow of doubt:

a. That the time of shooting was autumn 1941.

b. The application by the German executioners, when shooting Polish prisoners of war, of the identical method—a pistol shot in the nape of the neck—as used by them in the mass murders of Soviet citizens in other towns, especially in Orel, Voronetz, Krasnodar, and Smolensk itself....

7. The conclusions reached, after studying the affidavits and medicolegal examinations concerning the shooting of Polish military prisoners of war by Germans in the autumn of 1941, fully confirmed the material evidence and documents discovered in the Katyn graves.

8. By shooting the Polish prisoners of war in Katyn Forest, the

German fascist invaders consistently realized their policy for the physical extermination of the Slav peoples.[6]

The German Defense

The defense called as a witness the officer, Friedrich Ahrens, who had been accused in the Soviet report of directing the mass shooting. Ahrens testified that he was the commanding officer of Signal Regiment 537 with headquarters in the Katyn woods. He said that he took command of the regiment on November 30, 1941, and that never during the entire time he served in Russia did he see a single Polish prisoner or even hear of Poles. He denied that he had ever given an order for the shooting of Polish prisoners and stated that he had never heard any rumor that his predecessor had caused such shooting to be carried out, or that he considered it possible that such a crime could have been perpetrated by his predecessor or any other member of the regiment. As to the discovery of the grave and the disinterment, Ahrens testified:

Question: After your arrival at Katyn, did you notice that there was a grave mound in the woods at Katyn?

Answer: Shortly after I arrived—the ground was covered by snow—one of my soldiers pointed out to me that at a certain spot there was some sort of mound, which one could hardly describe as such, on which was a birch cross. I have seen that birch cross. In the course of 1942 my soldiers kept telling me that here in our woods shootings were supposed to have taken place, but at first I didn't pay any attention to it. However, in the summer of 1942 this topic was referred to in an order of the army group later commanded by General von Harsdorff. He told me that he had also heard about it.

Question: Did these stories prove true later on?

Answer: Yes, they did turn out to be true and I was able to confirm quite by accident that there was actually a grave here. During the winter of 1943—I think either January or February—quite accidentally I saw a wolf in this wood and at first I did not believe that it was a wolf; when I followed the tracks with an expert, we saw that there were traces of scratchings on the mound with the cross. I had investigations made as to what kind of bones these were. The doctors told me "human bones." Thereupon, I informed the officer responsible for war graves in the area of this fact, because I believed that it was a soldier's grave, as there were a number of such graves in our immediate vicinity.

Question: Then, how did the exhumation take place?

Answer: I do not know about all the details. Professor Dr. Butz arrived one day on orders from the army group, and informed me that following the rumors in my little wood, he had to make exhumations, and that he had to inform me that these exhumations would take place in my wood.

Question: Did Professor Butz later give you details of the results of his exhumations?

Answer: Yes, he did occasionally give me details and I remember that he told me that he had conclusive evidence regarding the date of the shootings. Among other things, he showed me letters of which I cannot remember much now; but I do remember some sort of diary which he passed over to me in which there were dates followed by some notes which I could not read because they were written in Polish. In this connection he explained to me that these notes had been made by a Polish officer regarding events of the past months, and that at the end—the diary ended with the spring of 1940—the fear was expressed in these notes that something horrible was going to happen. I am giving only a broad outline of the meaning.

Question: Did he give you any further indication regarding the period he assumed the shootings had taken place?

Answer: Professor Butz, on the basis of the proofs which he had found, was convinced that the shootings had taken place in the spring of 1940 and I often heard him express these convictions in my presence, and also later on, when commissions visited the grave and I had to place my house at the disposal of these commissions to accommodate them. I personally did not have anything to do whatsoever with the exhumations or the commissions. All I had to do was to place the house at their disposal and act as host.

Question: It was alleged that in March 1943 lorries had transported bodies to Katyn from outside and that bodies were buried in the little wood. Do you know anything about that?

Answer: No, I know nothing about that.

Question: Would you have had to take notice of it?

Answer: I would have had to take notice of it—at least my officers would have reported it to me, because my officers were constantly at the regimental battle headquarters, whereas I, as a regimental commander, was of course frequently on the way. The officer who, in those days, was there constantly was First Lieutenant Hodt, whose address I got to know last night from a letter.

Question: Were Russian prisoners of war used for these exhumations?

Answer: As far as I remember, yes.

Question: Can you tell us the number?

Answer: I cannot say exactly as I did not concern myself any further with these exhumations on account of the dreadful and revolting stench around our house, but I should estimate the number as being forty to fifty men.

Question: It has been alleged that they were shot afterwards; have you any knowledge of that?

Answer: I have no knowledge of that and I also never heard of it.

Question: Colonel, did you yourself ever discuss the events of 1940 with any of the local inhabitants?

Answer: Yes. At the beginning of 1943 a Russian married couple were living near my regimental headquarters; they lived 800 meters away and they were bee-keepers. I, too, kept bees, and I came into close contact with this married couple. When the exhumations had been completed, approximately in May 1943, I told them that, after all, they ought to know when these shootings had taken place, since they were living in close proximity to the graves. Thereupon, these people told me it had occurred in the spring of 1940, and that at the Gnjesdova station, more than two hundred Poles in uniform had arrived in railway trucks of fifty tons each and were taken to the woods in lorries. They had heard lots of shots and screams, too.[7]

A second defense witness, Von Eichborn, who was also attached to Signal Regiment 537, stated that Smolensk fell to the Germans on July 17, 1941, and that the advance unit arrived shortly thereafter, most of the staff coming about September 20, 1941. He denied that in the area west of Smolensk Soviet prisoner of war camps, containing captured Polish officers, had fallen into German hands. He testified on direct examination:

Question: Was there ever at any time an order given out by your office to shoot Polish prisoners of war?

Answer: Such an order was neither given to the regiment by our office or by any other office. Neither did we receive a report to this effect, nor did we hear about things like that through any other channel.

Question: If an order like that came through official channels, it could come only through you?

Answer: This order would have necessitated a great many members of the regiment being taken away from their own duties, which were to safeguard the system of communications. As we were very short of signallers, we had to know what almost every man in the regiment was doing. It would have been quite out of the question for any member of the regiment to have been taken away from such a duty without our knowledge.[8]

On cross-examination of Von Eichborn the Soviet prosecutor produced evidence that German Commandos of Special Action Group B of the Security Police and SD were operating in the autumn of 1941 in Smolensk, under orders to carry out executions of prisoners of war screened out of prisoner of war camps. A top secret order dated October 29, 1941, which referred specifically to the Smolensk region, stated that the Soviet civilian and prisoner of war camps and transient camps in the rear army territories were to be evacuated under directives worked out by the Security Police and SD in collaboration with the High Command of the Army, the actual evacuations to be carried out by the Special Action Groups of the Security Police and SD.

General Oberhauser, signal commander of the Army Group of which Regiment 537 was a part, and a third defense witness, testified that he had never heard of the three Soviet camps near Smolensk in which Polish prisoners were allegedly held, that he was not aware of any order to destroy these or other Polish prisoners of war, and that he considered it entirely impossible that the signal regiment or any of the officers thereof could have carried out such an action:

Question: Did you or Regiment 537 have the necessary technical means, pistols, ammunition, and so on, at your disposal which would have made it possible to carry out shootings on such a scale?

Answer: The regiment, being a signal regiment in the rear area, was not equipped with weapons and ammunition as well as the actual fighting troops. Such a task, moreover, would have been something unusual for the regiment; first, because a signal regiment has completely different tasks, and secondly it would not have been in a position technically to carry out such mass executions.

Question: Do you know the place where these graves were discovered later on?

Answer: I know the site because I drove past it a great deal....

Question: In view of your knowledge of the place, would you consider it possible that 11,000 Poles could have been buried at that spot, people who may have been shot between June and September, 1941?

Answer: I consider that it is out of the question, for the mere reason that if the commander had known it at the time he would certainly never have chosen this spot for his headquarters, next to 11,000 dead.[9]

The Soviet Rebuttal

The Soviet deputy mayor of Smolensk was called in rebuttal. His testimony was largely hearsay and of very little probative value:

Question: Do you know that in the vicinity of Smolensk there were Polish prisoners of war?
Answer: Yes, I do very well.
Question: Do you know what they were doing? ...
Answer: In the spring of 1941 and at the beginning of the summer they were working on the restoration of the roads, Moscow-Minsk and Smolensk-Vitebsk.
Question: What do you know about the further fate of the Polish prisoners of war?
Answer: Thanks to the position that I occupied, I learned very early about the fate of the Polish prisoners of war....
Question: Please be short and tell us what Menschagin told you when he came back from the German Kommandantur....
Answer: As to Polish prisoners of war, he told me that Russians would at least be allowed to die in the camps while there were proposals to exterminate the Poles.
Question: What else was said?
Answer: I replied, "What do you mean? What do you want to say? How do you understand this?" And Menschagin answered: "You should understand this in the very literal sense of these words." He asked me not to tell anybody about it, since it was a great secret.
Question: When did this conversation of yours take place with Menschagin? In what month, and on what day?
Answer: This conversation took place at the beginning of September. I cannot remember the exact date.
Question: But you remember it was the beginning of September?
Answer: Yes.
Question: Did you ever come back again to the fate of Polish prisoners of war in your further conversation with Menschagin?
Answer: Yes.... Two weeks later—that is to say, at the end of September—I could not help asking him, "What was the fate of the Polish prisoners of war?" At first Menschagin hesitated, and then he told me haltingly, "They have already died. It is all over for them."
Question: Did he tell you where they were killed?
Answer: He told me that they had been shot in the vicinity of Smolensk, as Von Schwetz told him.[10]

A Bulgarian citizen, Dr. Marko Markov, was called by the

Soviet prosecution. He had been appointed a member of the International Medical Commission organized by the Germans in April, 1943, for the purpose of examining the graves of the Polish officers buried in the Katyn woods. The Commission arrived in Smolensk on April 28, remained there two days for work, and departed on May 1.

Question: How many times did the members of the Commission personally visit the mass graves in the Katyn woods?

Answer: We were twice in the Katyn wood, that is, in the forenoon of 29 and 30 April.

Question: I mean, how many hours did you spend each time at the mass graves?

Answer: I consider not more than three or four hours each time.

Question: Were the members of the Commission present at least once during the opening of one of the graves?

Answer: No new graves were opened in our presence. We were shown only several graves which had already been opened before we arrived.

Question: Therefore, you were shown already opened graves, near which the corpses were already laid out, is that right?

Answer: Quite right. Near these opened graves were exhumed corpses already laid out there. . . .

Question: I would like you to answer the following question. Did the medico-legal investigators testify to the fact that the corpses had been in the graves already for three years?

Answer: As to that question I could judge only from the corpse on which I myself had held a post mortem. The condition of this corpse, as I have already stated, was typical of the average condition of the Katyn corpses. These corpses were far removed from the stage of disintegration of the soft parts, since the fat was only beginning to turn into wax. In my opinion these corpses were buried for a shorter period of time than three years. I considered that the corpse which I dissected had been buried for not more than one year or eighteen months.[11]

On cross-examination the witness admitted signing the report of the Commission which contained this entry:

The Commission interrogated several indigenous Russian witnesses personally. Among other things, these witnesses confirmed that in the months of March and April, 1940, large shipments of Polish officers arrived almost daily at the railroad station Gnjesdova near Katyn. These trains were emptied, the inmates were taken in lorries to the woods of Katyn and never seen again. Furthermore, official notice was taken of the proofs and statements, and the documents containing the evidence were inspected.[12]

As to this statement the witness said that during the questioning which occurred on the spot two witnesses spoke to a member of the Commission and told him that they saw how Polish officers were brought to the railroad station of Gnjesdova and thereafter disappeared.

The Commission report contained the following entry: "The documents found with the corpses (diaries, letters, and newspapers) were dated from the fall of 1939 until March and April, 1940. The latest date which could be ascertained was the date of a Russian newspaper of 22 April, 1940."[13]

As to this Markov testified: "Such letters and newspapers were indeed in the glass cases and were shown to us. Some such papers were found by members of the Commission who were dissecting the bodies, and if I remember rightly they described the contents of these documents, but I did not do so."[14]

The report concluded: "From statements made by witnesses, from the letters and correspondence, diaries, newspapers, and so forth, found on the corpses, it may be seen that the shootings took place in the months of March and April, 1940. The following are in complete agreement with the findings made with regard to the mass graves and the individual corpses of the Polish officers, as described in the report."[15] Signatures of the members of the Commission were then affixed.

The witness attempted to explain away his own signature to the report:

I have already indicated that this statement regarding the condition of the corpses is based on the data resulting from testimony by the witnesses and from the available documents, but it is in contradiction to the observations I made on the corpse which I dissected. That means I did not consider that the results of the autopsies corroborated the presumable date of death taken from the testimonies or the documents. If I had been convinced that the condition of the corpse did indeed correspond to the date of the decease mentioned by the Germans, I would have given such a statement in my individual protocol....[16]

He was not able to explain the signatures of the other ten scientists who joined in the report:

I cannot say on what considerations the other delegates signed the protocol. But they also signed it under the same circumstances as I did. However, when I read their individual protocols, I noticed that they also refrained from stating the precise date of the killing of the man whose corpse they had dissected. There was one exception only, as I have already said. That was Professor Miloslavich, who was the only one who asserted that the corpse which he had dissected was that of a man buried for at least three years. After the signing of the protocol, I did not have any contact with any of the persons who had signed the collective protocol.[17]

The final Soviet witness was the president of the "Special Commission for the Investigation and Ascertaining of the Circumstances of the Shootings by the German Fascist Aggressors of Polish Officers."[18] He testified that in the Katyn Forest the Soviet medical commission of experts exhumed and examined, from various graves and from various layers, a total of 925 corpses. And he asserted that documents found on the corpses were dated as late as June 20, 1941. As to cause of death, the witness testified: "The cause of death of the Polish officers was bullet wounds in the nape of the neck. In the tissue of the brain or in the bone of the skull we discovered bullets which were more or less deformed. As to cartridge cases, we did indeed discover, during the exhumation, cartridge cases of German origin, for on their bases we found the mark G-e-c-o, Geco."[19]

A secret telegram to the Government General corroborated this statement: "Part of the Polish Red Cross returned yesterday from Katyn. The employees of the Polish Red Cross have brought with them the cartridge cases which were used in shooting the victims of Katyn. It appears that these are German munitions. The caliber is 7.65. They are from the firm Geco."[20]

The witness testified that in his opinion, based upon the experience of exhuming more than five thousand corpses of victims shot by Germans during the war, the Katyn murders were perpetrated in the fall of 1941 and certainly not as early as 1940.

On the basis of this evidence the International Military Tribunal declined to make a finding in its judgment as to responsibility for the Katyn atrocity.

Congressional Investigation

During the Eighty-second Congress, the House of Representatives created a select committee composed of seven members of the House, appointed by the speaker, to conduct a full and complete investigation and study of the facts, evidence, and circumstances surrounding the Katyn massacre. This committee held hearings in the United States and abroad and reviewed and published a large amount of evidence upon this crime.

It was conclusively established by this evidence that the camps in which the Polish officer prisoners of war had been imprisoned by the Soviets were cleared of prisoners during the period from April 5, 1940, to May 12, 1940. The witness Bronislaw Mylnarski testified that he was the first Polish officer to arrive at Starobielsk and the last to leave—the time being from September 30, 1939, until May 12, 1940. He was one of the small number taken to Pavlishev Bor and to Gryazovets, ultimately to be liberated on September 2, 1941.[21]

Another witness testified that after her father, an officer in the Polish army, had been captured by the Soviets, she and her mother were deported to Siberia. From time to time they received letters from her father until June, 1940, when they received his last letter, written on April 4, 1940. Her mother wrote a letter to him in June, 1940, which was returned with the cryptic notation: "You will not find him again."[22]

The diary of Major Adam Solski, identified as one of the Polish prisoners in Kozielsk, laconically recorded the events by the hour to the very moment of his execution:

April 8, 3:30 a.m. Departure from Kozielsk station to the west. 9:45 a.m. at Jelnia station.
April 8, 1940. From 12 noon we are standing at Smolensk on a railway siding.

April 9, 1940. A few minutes before 5 in the morning reveille in the prison cars and preparation for departure.... We are to go somewhere by car, and what then?

April 9, 5 a.m.

April 9. From the very dawn, the day started somewhat peculiarly. Departure by prison van in little cells (terrible); they brought us somewhere into the woods—some kind of summer resort. Here a detailed search. They took the watch, on which time was 6:30 a.m. (8:30) asked me for my wedding ring, which they took, roubles, my main belt, and pocket knife.[23]

Evidence of the actual killings by Soviet authorities was given by a former Soviet citizen who testified to a conversation with a Captain Borisov, chief of a unit of the Soviet military police establishment. Borisov had admitted to the witness that his unit killed over 400 Polish officers in Katyn in April, 1940. The prisoners were said to have been led to the edge of a mass grave and there shot.[24]

On March 18, 1941, the director of the Polish Red Cross sent a letter to the Committee of the International Red Cross War Prisoner Agency in Geneva concerning the status of Polish prisoners detained in Soviet Russia. The Polish Red Cross stated that whereas it had received a large volume of letters from prisoners detained at Starobielsk, Kozielsk, and Ostaszkov, all such correspondence ceased completely in the spring of 1940. From information received from families of the prisoners and other sources it was concluded that the camps were slowly liquidated from March until the end of May, 1940.[25]

After discovery of the mass graves was announced by the Germans in April, 1943, representatives of the Polish Red Cross were invited to inspect the scene of the crime. Casimer Skarzynski, the general secretary of the Polish Red Cross, visited the graves. About 300 bodies had been exhumed. All prisoners had been shot through the back of the neck. The bodies were clad in winter clothes, and in some cases the coats were pulled over the heads and then tied with a rope. Skarzynski talked to Russian peasants who told him that in April and May, 1940, cars of Polish prisoners arrived at the station. The prisoners were taken by special trucks, called Black Raven, to the Katyn Forest.[26]

Dr. Edward Miloslavich, to whom reference had been made by the Soviet witness Markov, appeared in person before the committee. He testified in detail to the exhumation of the body which he examined and affirmed his previous estimate that the bodies had been buried for more than three years. Contrary to Markov's testimony, Dr. Miloslavich testified that Professor Orsos, who was also a medical-legal expert, reached the same conclusion and that no other members of the Commission "objected to the interpretation or the findings."[27]

Shortly after the German attack upon Russia in June, 1941, the Soviets declared an amnesty for Polish prisoners of war so that they might join in the struggle against Germany. General Anders was put in charge of the Polish army in Russia. Assigned to his staff was Captain Joseph Czapski, whom he ordered to assemble the Polish officers who had been taken prisoner by the Soviets. Captain Czapski himself had been a prisoner at Starobielsk and was one of the small number of prisoners removed to Gryazovets. In spite of all investigations he was able to make, Captain Czapski was unable to discover the whereabouts of the almost fifteen thousand prisoners of war who had been in the three camps. The Polish ambassador, Kot, conferred with Stalin, and later General Anders himself spoke to Stalin. On both occasions Stalin promised complete co-operation, but the prisoners were never produced. Further attempts to locate them were frustrated at every turn. As early as October, 1940, it had been suggested by the NKVD to senior Polish officers that it might be possible to form a Polish army on Soviet soil. But when reference was made to the officers imprisoned in the three camps, one security officer is reported to have replied: "We have committed an error. These men are not available. We will give you others."[28] And Beria himself is said to have confessed: "We have committed a great blunder. We have made a great mistake."[29]

In April, 1943, Colonel Szymanski of the United States army was ordered to investigate the Katyn affair. He proceeded to Palestine and thence to Iraq, where General Anders supplied him with all available information which had been obtained on the massacre from former Polish prisoners of war and other sources. His report was submitted to United States Military Intelligence on May 29,

1943. On the basis of his investigation Colonel Szymanski concluded that the crime was committed by the Soviets. He reached that conclusion for several reasons, among which were the following: (1) In all the discussions by General Anders and other Polish leaders with Stalin and other Soviet officials concerning the disappearance of the Polish officers, never once was it suggested by the latter that the prisoners had been captured by the advancing German forces; (2) only four thousand prisoners were buried in the mass graves at Katyn, and the Soviets were never able to account for the disappearance of the approximately eleven thousand others; (3) none of the relatives of the deceased prisoners received any mail from them written after May, 1940; (4) Polish officers in German prison camps did not all disappear, whereas substantially all of the officer prisoners in Soviet prison camps did disappear.[30]

The final report of the Select Committee for the Investigation of the Katyn Forest Massacre was submitted to the Committee of the Whole House on the State of the Union and ordered to be printed on December 22, 1952. The Select Committee incorporated the recommendations of its interim report which it had filed on July 2, 1952. In that report the committee concluded:

No one could entertain any doubt of Russian guilt for the Katyn massacre when the following evidence is considered:

1. The Russians refused to allow the International Committee of the Red Cross to make a neutral investigation of the German charges in 1943.

2. The Russians failed to invite any neutral observers to participate in their own investigation in 1944, except a group of newspaper correspondents taken to Katyn who agreed "the whole show was staged" by the Soviets.

3. The Russians failed to produce sufficient evidence at Nuremberg —even though they were in charge of the prosecution—to obtain a ruling on the German guilt for Katyn by the International Military Tribunal.

4. This committee issued formal and public invitations to the Government of the U.S.S.R. to present any evidence pertaining to the Katyn massacre. The Soviets refused to participate in any phase of this committee's investigation.

5. The overwhelming testimony of prisoners formerly interned at the three camps, of medical experts who performed autopsies on the

massacred bodies, and of observers taken to the scene of the crime conclusively confirms this committee's findings.

6. Polish Government leaders and military men who conferred with Stalin, Molotov, and NKVD chief Beria for a year and a half attempted without success to locate the Polish prisoners before the Germans discovered Katyn. This renders further proof that the Soviets purposely misled the Poles in denying any knowledge of the whereabouts of their officers when, in fact, the Poles already were buried in the mass graves at Katyn.

7. The Soviets have demonstrated through their highly organized propaganda machinery that they fear to have the people behind the iron curtain know the truth about Katyn. This is proven by their reaction to our committee's efforts and the amount of newspaper space and radio time devoted to denouncing the work of our committee. They also republished in all newspapers behind the iron curtain the allegedly "neutral" Russian report of 1944. The world-wide campaign of slander by the Soviets against our committee is also construed as another effort to block this investigation.

8. This committee believes that one of the reasons for the staging of the Soviet "germ warfare" propaganda campaign was to divert attention of the people behind the iron curtain from the hearings of the committee.

9. Our committee has been petitioned to investigate mass executions and crimes against humanity committed in other countries behind the iron curtain. The committee has heard testimony which indicates there are other "Katyns." We wish to impress with all the means at our command that the investigation of the Katyn massacre barely scratches the surface of numerous crimes against humanity perpetrated by totalitarian powers. This committee believes that an international tribunal should be established to investigate willful and mass executions wherever they have been committed. The United Nations will fail in their obligation until they expose to the world that "Katynism" is a definite and diabolical totalitarian plan for world conquest.[31]

Relation of the Katyn Forest Massacre to the AB Action

Ausserordentliche Befriedigungsaktion, better known as the "AB Action," was the Nazi code-name for the extermination of the intelligentsia of Poland. This "extraordinary pacification action" had been contemplated from the beginning of the Polish occupation. At a conference on October 2, 1939, concerning the Government General, Hitler said: "There should be one master only for the Poles—the Germans. Two masters side by side cannot exist. All representatives of the Polish intelligentsia are to be exterminated. This sounds cruel; but such is the law of life."[32]

The responsibility for executing this plan of extermination fell upon Hans Frank, who was present at the conference in the capacity of Governor General of occupied Poland. The following day Frank stated that the task which had been entrusted to him by Hitler called for the prevention of the growth of a "new" Polish intelligentsia. "Poland," he said, "shall be treated as a colony; the Poles shall be the slaves of the Greater German World Empire."[33] Shortly after, on October 20, 1939, Hitler confirmed his intention to eliminate Polish leadership in instructions which he gave to Keitel: "The Polish intelligentsia must be prevented from forming a ruling class. The standard of living in the country is to remain low. We want only to draw labor forces from there."[34]

The actual extermination of the intelligentsia of Poland by the Nazis was delayed until the outbreak of the western offensive in May, 1940. Frank felt relatively secure in ordering this action while world attention was focused upon the military struggle in the West. On May 16, 1940, he decreed that the "extraordinary pacification action" should be undertaken by the Chief of the Security Police and that a detailed report should be made to him on May 30. On the latter date Frank made the following statement:

The offensive in the West began on 10 May. On that day the center of interest shifted from the events taking place here. It would be a matter of complete indifference to me whether the deeds attributed by atrocity propaganda and lying reports all over the world to the National Socialist authorities in these districts worried the Americans, the French, the Jews, or the Pope in Rome for that matter. But it was terrible for me and for all of them to be told unceasingly during all these months by the Ministry of Propaganda, the Ministry of Foreign Affairs, the Ministry of the Interior, and even the Army, that ours was a regime of murder, and that these crimes of ours were to cease and so forth. And we had to say, of course, we would no longer do it. It was equally clear that up to that moment, under the cross-fire of the whole world, we could not do anything of the kind on a large scale. But since 10 May we are completely indifferent to this atrocity propaganda. We must use the opportunity in our hands....

I frankly admit that it will cost the lives of some thousands of Poles and that these will be taken mainly from leading members of the Polish intelligentsia.... I pray you, gentlemen, to take the most rigorous measures possible to help us in this task. For my own part, I will do everything in my power in order to facilitate its execution. I appeal to you as the champions of National Socialism, and I need surely say nothing further. We will carry out this measure and I may tell you in confidence that we shall be acting on the Fuehrer's orders.... He expressed himself in this way: The men capable of leadership whom we have found to exist in Poland must be liquidated. Those following men must... be eliminated in their turn. There is no need to burden the Reich and the Reich police organization with this. There is no need to send these elements to Reich concentration camps, and by so doing involve ourselves in disputes and unnecessary correspondence with their relations. We will liquidate our difficulties in the country itself, and we will do it in the simplest way possible.[35]

The Chief of the Security Police, Strechenbach, reported at the conference, according to Frank's diary notes, in part as follows:

About 2,000 men and several hundred women were in the hands of the Security Police at the beginning of the extraordinary pacification action; they had been taken into custody as functionaries of some repute of the Polish resistance movement. In fact, they represented the intellectual class of leaders of the resistance movement. This class of leaders was, of course, not limited to the 2,000 persons. In the documents and files of the SD there were the names of approximately another 2,000 persons, who were to be reckoned in this class. These were persons who, because of their activities and behavior came without exception under the decree on summary procedure which was valid for the Government General. The summary sentencing of these people began simultaneously with the order for the extraordinary pacification action. The summary sentencing of the 2,000 prisoners was approaching its end, and there were only a few still to be sentenced. After this summary court procedure had been carried out, a series of arrests had now already begun, which should also bring into the hands of the Security Police a number of people for summary sentencing, who were known to the SD, but had not yet been arrested. The result of these arrests had not yet been ascertained. He reckoned with a 75 percent result. Altogether, the action would therefore include a circle of about 3,500 persons, who were actually the politically most dangerous section of the resistance movement in the Government General.[36]

The determination to prevent a revival of Polish leadership by killing potential Polish leaders was stated by Frank at a conference of Party heads at Krakow on March 18, 1942:

Incidentally, the struggle for the achievement of our aims will be pursued cold-bloodedly. You see how the state agencies work. You see that we do not hesitate before anything, and stand whole dozens of people up against the wall. This is necessary because here simple consideration says that it cannot be our task at this period when the best German blood is being sacrificed to show regard for the blood of another race. . . . Therefore, everything revealing itself as a Polish power of leadership must be destroyed again and again with ruthless energy. This does not have to be shouted abroad, it will happen silently.[37]

The parallelism between the AB Action ordered by Frank and the Katyn Forest massacre is evident. The actions took place about the same time and for the same purpose—to destroy the intelligentsia of Poland. Referring to the Polish officer prisoners who had been imprisoned by the Soviets, Captain Joseph Czapski declared in his statement to the Select Committee of the House of Representatives: "I can affirm here in all certitude that it was the flower of the Polish 'Intelligentsia.' "[38]

The Post-Trial Admission That the Katyn Forest Massacre Was a Soviet Crime

Fifty years after the event, an electrifying broadcast from Moscow Radio declared that, in truth, the massacre of Polish officers in the Katyn Forest had been a Soviet crime. On April 12, 1990, the official Soviet press agency, Tass, announced that the NKVD, predecessor of the KGB secret police, was responsible for the Katyn Forest massacre. The Polish officers were declared killed in the spring of 1940 when Soviet troops held the territory near Smolensk, long before the arrival of German forces in 1941. Soviet responsibility has since been confirmed by Russian presidents Mikhail Gorbachev and Boris Yeltsin. Gorbachev told me that after he came to power in 1977, President Brezhnev was advised by KGB chief Shelepin that Katyn was, in truth, a Soviet crime. It was kept a State secret until Gorbachev decided that the truth should be revealed. Speaking of the reason for the murder of the Polish officers by the Soviets, the witness Mylnarski stated to the Select Committee of the House of Representatives "that they had to destroy the bulk of the Polish intelligentsia."[39]

Gestapo or NKVD, Hitler or Stalin, Nazi or Communist—by any name *tyranny* is the same.

CHAPTER 23

The Mesny Murder

In the winter of 1940 Hitler and Keitel determined to assassinate French Marshal Weygand, who was then in North Africa, because it was feared that Weygand might form a center of resistance in North Africa with the unconquered part of the French Army. The killing was to be performed by the Abwehr. Canaris, as chief of the Abwehr and a constant opponent of Hitlerian atrocities, succeeded in forestalling the plan; and it failed.

After General Giraud escaped from imprisonment at Koenigstein in 1942 similar orders were issued for his assassination. Canaris was able to convince Keitel that the ugly task should be performed by the SD rather than by the Abwehr. It was left to Canaris to inform the Chief of the SD, who then was Heydrich. Canaris, of course, deliberately "neglected" to do so. Sometime later Keitel demanded of Canaris what had happened to the plan to murder Giraud. Heydrich had been assassinated in Prague in the meantime, and it was easy for Canaris to say that he had informed Heydrich but that evidently Heydrich had not been able to complete the task before his death. When this information reached Hitler, he indignantly complained of this miserable failure of the SD to carry out such a simple execution.

The French generals, Weygand and Giraud, escaped the plan of Hitler and Keitel to assassinate them. Another French general, less well known, was less fortunate. His name was General Mesny, and his death was the joint result of a bizarre plan for murder and his own incredible misfortune.

In the first part of November, 1944, an act of resistance evidently having taken place in France against a German officer, Hitler ordered that a French general—any French general—in German custody should be murdered. The killing was to be carried out by Kaltenbrunner, who had succeeded Heydrich as Chief of the SD. Since the fact of the general's death would soon be known, it was necessary to plan in advance the explanations to be offered to Switzerland as the protecting power of French prisoners of war in German prison camps.

It was reported to Ribbentrop that the preliminary plan provided for the murder of one of the French generals in Camp Koenigstein. There were seventy-five French generals in the camp in November, 1944, and for some time it had been planned that they should be transferred to a different prison. The killing could thus be accomplished under cover of their removal. According to preliminary plan, five or six French generals were to be taken in the first group removed from Camp Koenigstein, each in a special automobile with a driver and guard in Wehrmacht uniforms. On the way, General De Boisse was to be killed.

During the drive, General De Boisse's car will have a breakdown in order to separate him from the others. This will provide the opportunity to have the General shot in the back "while attempting to escape." The time proposed is twilight. It will be made certain that no rural inhabitants are in the vicinity. To ensure against later investigation, it is planned to burn the body and to send the urn to the cemetery of the fortress Koenigstein. A decision has yet to be reached whether or not the burial of this urn should be carried out with military honors.[1]

This was in November, 1944. The crime had not been completed by December 13, when a further progress report was made to Ribbentrop. Germany was reeling, then, from the Soviet and Allied blows in the East and in the West, and the military situation was desperate. Yet Germany's highest leaders took time from the serious task of defending the country for the morbid job of devising the method by which a single captive and helpless French general was to be slain. The calculated murder at which they connived is one of the ugliest of Nazi crimes.

The report of December 13 stated that the French general— De Boisse, as noted above—would be transferred, together with four other younger generals, from Camp Koenigstein to a new prisoner of war camp. The transfer was to be carried out in three automobiles. Two of the younger ranking generals were to enter the first two cars, while De Boisse, as senior general, was to drive alone in the last car as befitted his rank. The drivers and guards were to be SS personnel in Wehrmacht uniforms. The method of assassination had not definitely been determined. Two alternatives were proposed: (1) On the way the automobile carrying General De Boisse was to stop as for a breakdown while the others continued on their way. The General was then to be killed "by well-aimed bullets from behind."[2] Examination of the body, even a possible later autopsy, would then only confirm the "fact" that the General had been fatally shot while attempting to escape. (2) En route the General would be poisoned by carbon monoxide gas. A car, specially designed for this type of murder, had already been constructed. The General was to sit alone in the back seat. The doors were to be locked in order to prevent him from jumping out during the drive. On account of the cold winter weather all windows, including the special window between the front and back seats, were to be closed. Odorless carbon monoxide gas was to be introduced into the closed area where the General was riding, a special apparatus having been installed for that purpose under the front seat. It was believed that the General would be killed after a couple of breaths of the deadly gas. As the gas is odorless, it was not felt that the General would become suspicious in time to break a window in order to let in fresh air. The cause of death would, in this event, be easily ascertainable through the change in skin color resulting from the action of the gas, and it was proposed to represent that the General died unnoticed as the result of a leakage of gas from the exhaust pipe.

Even by December 30, 1944, this elaborate scheme to terminate the life of a single prisoner of war had not been consummated. On that date Kaltenbrunner reported the status of the operation to Himmler. He said that killing would be accomplished by shooting or by gas. "Other possibilities, such as poisoning of food or drink, have been considered but have been discarded again as too unsafe."[3] He said that provisions had been made for the completion of subsequent details, such as reports, documentation, and burial. As to press notices, arrangements had been made with Geheimrat Wagner of the Foreign Office. Ribbentrop was insistent that the action be co-ordinated in every detail. Then came the fateful proposal for a last-minute substitution of victims:

In the meantime it has been learned that the name of the man in question has been mentioned in the course of various long distance calls between Fuehrer Headquarters and the Chief of Prisoners of War Matters; therefore, the Chief of Prisoners of War Matters now proposes the use of another man with the same qualifications. I agree with this and propose that the choice be left to the Chief of Prisoners of War Matters.[4]

It was not until January 18, 1945, that the plans had been brought to the state of readiness for action. On that day six French generals in Camp Koenigstein were advised that on the morning of the following day they were to be transported to a new and un-identified destination. They were to leave at fifteen-minute intervals, commencing at 6:00 A.M. In the first car were to be Generals Daine and De Boisse; in the second car, Generals Flavigny and Buisson; and in the third car, Generals Mesny and Vauthier.

On the morning of January 19 the first car left at the appointed time, but departure of the others was delayed. At 7:00 A.M. General Mesny left in the second car alone, for it was reported that during the night an order had arrived from the German High Command canceling the departure of General Vauthier. The third car departed at 8:00 A.M.

As later reported by General Louis Buisson to the French Minister of War: "The orders for the journey were Draconian; destination unknown; it was strictly forbidden to make any stop on the way; the door handles were taken off the cars; there was a German officer in each car with an automatic pistol on his knees and his finger on the trigger."[5]

The four generals who had left in the first and third cars arrived at Colditz toward noon. General Mesny did not arrive. His comrades thought that he had been sent to another camp, although they noticed that his luggage was in the truck which carried the luggage of the other generals. But on the morning of the following day the camp commandant, Prawitt, came to their rooms and made the following announcement: "I inform you officially that General Mesny was shot yesterday in Dresden while trying to escape. He was buried in Dresden with military honors by a detachment of the Wehrmacht."[6]

Thus, finally, all the elaborate plans came to their fruition. After two months of feverish work the Gestapo had accomplished what the Abwehr previously had prevented—it managed to fulfil Hitler's order to murder a French general prisoner of war. In commenting upon the strange circumstances under which Mesny had disappeared, General Buisson stated in his report:

Two facts remain obscure in the sombre tragedy: (1) The transport of General Mesny *alone* in the second car. The choice of General Vauthier, then the cancelling of the order, seemed very suspicious to us given the attitude of the general, who was a volunteer for work in Germany, and whose transfer to a reprisal camp seemed inexplicable. (2) General Mesny, whose eldest son is in a camp for political deportees in Germany, said to me several times during the course of our conversation: "If up to 1944 I always tried to prepare my escape, afterwards I gave up trying altogether, even if I had every chance of succeeding.—First of all, the end of the war is only a question of weeks; moreover, and especially, I should be much too afraid that my flight would cost my eldest son his life."

An hour before his departure from Koenigstein on January 19, General Mesny repeated these words to me again. And how can one imagine that a general in *uniform* would attempt to escape, given the transport conditions described above?

If it is true that General Mesny was shot during the transport from Koenigstein to Colditz, it could not be for trying to escape. Premeditation or the terrified act of a German officer (after a discussion or a request for a halt of a few minutes), these are, we think, the only explanations for this tragic drama.[7]

On April 5, 1945, the International Red Cross Committee, General Agency for Prisoners of War, notified Madame Mesny of the death of her husband and of the fact that the Germans had reported that he was shot near Dresden "while trying to escape."[8]

Keitel said that the worst war crime was the Night and Fog Decree, Goering contended that the killing of the fifty airmen who escaped from Stalag Luft III was the worst, and "special treatment" of the screened Soviet prisoners of war was wicked mass murder. But of all these crimes the one which best illustrates the degeneracy of Hitler's coterie was this organized scheme to murder a single innocent, unsuspecting, and totally helpless French general, a prisoner of war awaiting only liberation and reunion with son and wife. While Germany reeled under the assault of Allied armies, Hitler took one more life even as the sands in the hourglass of his own span on earth were swiftly running out.

PART FOUR

Crimes Against Humanity

CHAPTER 24

The Final Solution

A PRINCIPAL OBJECTIVE of the National Socialist movement, as disclosed by Hitler in *Mein Kampf*, was the struggle against the Jews:

> It [anti-Semitism] must open the eyes of the people with regard to foreign nations and must remind them again and again of the true enemy of our present day world. In the place of hate against Aryans— from whom we may be separated by almost everything but to whom, however, we are tied by common blood or the great tie of a common culture—it must dedicate to the general anger the evil enemy of mankind as the true cause of all suffering. It must see to it, however, that at least in our country he be recognized as the most mortal enemy and that the struggle against him may show, like a flaming beacon of a better era, to other nations too, the road to salvation for a struggling Aryan mankind.[1]

The elimination of German Jewry—and of world Jewry—was fundamental to Hitler's program and philosophy. Anti-Semitism was a political device to unite the German people in a common antagonism; but to Hitler it was more than that. The fight against the Jews was the direct and inescapable result of Hitler's belief in the blood dogma, and in the impurity of Jewish blood. The Jews were absolutely unacceptable in any state or empire ruled by Hitler. In his mind there was always the determination, when opportunity provided itself, to annihilate the Jews of Germany, and of Europe.

In his speech to the Reichstag on January 30, 1939, Hitler, well knowing that war was soon to commence in Europe, assumed the role of fateful prophet: "If the international Jewish financiers within and without Europe, succeed in plunging the nations once

more into a world war, then the result will be not the Bolshevisa-
tion of the world and thereby the victory of Jewry—but the
annihilation of the Jewish race in Europe...."[2]

In a discussion which took place between Hitler, Reich Foreign
Minister Ribbentrop, and Hungarian Regent Horthy in Klessheim
Castle on April 17, 1943, Ribbentrop was reported to have told
Horthy "that the Jews must either be exterminated or taken to
concentration camps."[3] And Hitler followed with this explanation:

> Where the Jews were left to themselves, as for instance in Poland,
> the most terrible misery and decay prevailed. They are just pure para-
> sites. In Poland this state of affairs had been fundamentally cleared up.
> If the Jews there did not want to work, they were shot. If they could
> not work, they had to succumb. They had to be treated like tuberculosis
> bacilli, with which a healthy body may become infected. This was not
> cruel, if one remembered that even innocent creatures of nature, such
> as hares and deer, have to be killed, so that no harm is caused by them.
> Why should the beasts who wanted to bring us Bolshevism be spared
> more? Nations which did not rid themselves of Jews, perished.[4]

When asked whether Hitler made such statements at that time,
Ribbentrop replied: "The Fuehrer did express himself in some such
way at that time. That is true."[5]

In these three statements of Adolf Hitler is the full exposition
of the German struggle against the Jewish race in Europe. There
was first the conviction that Jewry was the enemy of mankind;
there was secondly the determination to annihilate the Jews should
opportunity be provided; there was finally that opportunity in the
course of the Hitler wars of aggression in Europe.

This struggle against the Jews was, in truth, a second war—
which was waged as implacably and efficiently as the armed struggle
against other nations. This second war began in relatively isolated
actions against the Jews, increasing in scope and tempo until it
reached the crescendo of fury which horrified the world. The persecution took the form of a series of "solutions" of the "Jewish
problem." The first "solution" was the elimination of the Jews from
the political and economic life of Germany; the second "solution"
was their forced deportation and isolation in ghettos; the third, and

"final solution" was the actual extermination of the Jews through slave labor and mass murder.

Anti-Semitic Propaganda

The initial step, and yet one which continued of necessity until the end, was the propaganda campaign against the Jewish race and religion and against the Jewish people, by which the Nazis sought to revile and degrade the Jews, to inflame the people to hatred against them, and thus to enlist ordinary persons in conduct against Jewish people which they otherwise would instantly recognize and abjure as indecent, or criminal.

In this campaign of calumny, the defendant Streicher was the prototype of Evil. He had called for the annihilation of the Jews as early as 1925. Promptly upon the Nazi rise to power Streicher, in a speech delivered on April 1, 1933, stated the premises of the gigantic program of anti-Semitism which was to take place under the Nazi regime:

Never since the beginning of the world and the creation of man has there been a nation which dared to fight against the nation of blood-suckers and extortioners who, for a thousand years, have spread all over the world.... It was left to our Movement to expose the eternal Jew as a mass murderer.... As long as I stand at the head of the struggle, this struggle will be conducted so honestly that the eternal Jew will derive no joy from it.[6]

In September, 1937, on the occasion of the dedication of the Wilhelm Gustloff bridge in Nuremberg, Streicher said:

The man who murdered Wilhelm Gustloff had to come from the Jewish people, because the Jewish text-books teach that every Jew has the right to kill a non-Jew; and indeed, that it is pleasing to the Jewish God to kill as many non-Jews as possible.

Look at the road the Jewish people have been following for thousands of years past; everywhere murder, everywhere mass murder! Neither must we forget that behind present-day wars there stands the Jewish financier who pursues his aims and interests. The Jew always lives on the blood of other nations; he needs such murder and such victims. For us who know, the murder of Wilhelm Gustloff is the same as ritual murder.

The Jew no longer shows himself among us openly as he used to. But it would be wrong to say that victory is ours. Full and final victory will have been achieved only when the whole world is rid of Jews.[7]

In the course of a speech delivered on November 10, 1938, at the time of the anti-Jewish pogrom, Streicher said:

From the cradle the Jew is not taught, as we are, such texts as "Thou shalt love thy neighbor as thyself" or "Whosoever shall smite thee on the right cheek, turn to him the other also." No, he is told "With the non-Jew you can do whatever you like." He is even taught that the slaughtering of a non-Jew is an act pleasing to God. For 20 years we have been writing about this in Der Stuermer; for 20 years we have been preaching it throughout the world, and we have made millions recognize the truth.[8]

It was in the pages of Der Stuermer that Streicher carried on most effectively his propaganda war against the oppressed Jews of Germany. Der Stuermer was not a Party publication; but it succeeded because it conformed to Party policy and because its owner was a leading member of the Party. When Streicher bought the paper in 1935 it had a circulation of only about 28,000 copies. Soon thereafter the circulation increased to well over 200,000; and this figure was more than doubled at a later date. In the pages of Der Stuermer there constantly appeared slanders against the Jews. Streicher's purpose in this calumny was stated by him:

Der Stuermer's 15 years of work of enlightenment has already led an army of initiated—millions strong—to National Socialism. The continued work of Der Stuermer will help to ensure that every German down to the last man will, with heart and hand, join the ranks of those whose aim it is to crush the head of the serpent Pan-Juda beneath their heels. He who helps to bring this about helps to eliminate the devil, and this devil is the Jew.[9]

Most vicious of all Streicher libels against the Jewish people was the charge of "ritual murder."[10] Against such wicked aspersions the Archbishop of Canterbury and other religious leaders spoke out sharply. Der Stuermer replied:

The Archbishop of Canterbury therefore sides with the money bags, with the lying world press, with the Jewish crooks and financial hyenas, with the Jewish-Bolshevist mass-murderers. It is a fine company which the Archbishop of Canterbury has joined. They are flayers of mankind, criminals, gangsters, murderers. In short, they are Jews. By choosing their side, the Archbishop of Canterbury committed a further, even more contemptible crime. He committed the crime of betraying Christianity. The crime of betraying non-Jewish mankind.[11]

After the beginning of war in September, 1939, the propaganda in *Der Stuermer,* while not less vicious, became increasingly violent. The following are excerpts from articles published during the first months of the war.

September, 1939: "The Jewish people ought to be exterminated root and branch. Then the plague of pests would have disappeared in Poland also at one stroke."[12]

December, 1939: "The day will come some time when the French will awake. Then they will slay the Jews in masses."[13]

January, 1940: "... The time is near when a machine will go into motion which is going to prepare a grave for the world's criminal—Judah—from which there will be no resurrection."[14]

February, 1940: "At the end of this Jewish war the extermination of the Jewish people will have been brought about."[15]

March, 1940: "The Jew is a devil in human form. It is fitting that he be exterminated root and branch."[16]

September, 1940: "Not for nothing did the Fuehrer say: 'A war in Europe will bring about the complete extermination of the Jews in this part of the world.'"[17]

November, 1940: "The Jewish rabble will be exterminated like weeds and vermin so that it can never again disturb the bloodily fought for peace of the European peoples."[18]

January, 1941: "Now judgment has begun and it will reach its conclusion only when knowledge of the Jews has been erased from the earth."[19]

July, 1941: "The end of this day, however, will bring the annihilation of these murderers of humanity."[20]

August, 1941: "The cemeteries in which people are buried who were destroyed by Jews will only have become places of rest when the last trace of the eternal Jew has been obliterated from this earth."[21]

August, 1941: "Behind the German Wehrmacht, however, a new, awakened Europe is marching. And this new Europe will see to it that the Jewish devils of the Soviet hell are annihilated for all time."[22]

September, 1941: "The source of the world's disaster will be done away with forever only when Jewry in its entirety has been annihilated."[23]

December, 1941: "If the danger of the reproduction of that curse of God in the Jewish blood is to finally come to its end, then there is only one way: The extermination of that people whose father is the devil."[24]

Meanwhile, what Streicher and *Der Stuermer* had so constantly called for actually was taking place in the East—the mass killing of the Jews of Europe. By November 4, 1943, on the basis of these annihilation actions, Streicher was able to report to the German people in the pages of *Der Stuermer* the final result of his propaganda:

It is actually true that the Jews have so to speak disappeared from Europe and that the Jewish "Reservoir of the East," from which the Jewish pestilence has for centuries beset the peoples of Europe, has ceased to exist. But the Fuehrer of the German people at the beginning of the war prophesied what has now come to pass.[25]

Through the pages of *Der Stuermer* Streicher sought constantly to inflame the people of Germany against the Jews. But he was not content merely to poison the adult mind. He sought similarly to pollute the minds of youths and children. The *Fraenkische Tageszeitung* reported on March 19, 1934, a talk given by Streicher to girls upon graduation from a vocational school:

...Then Julius Streicher spoke about his life and told them about a girl who at one time went to his school and who fell for a Jew and was finished for the rest of her life.

"German girls," the Frankenfuehrer continued, "when you go out into the world you are in great danger. The Jew, to whom according to his laws you are free game, will try to approach you in various ways. Repulse him, stay honest and good. It is not beautiful frocks, lipstick and the powder-box that make you into German women. See that you remain clean spiritually and eventually become good German mothers."

...Then Julius Streicher gave a few typical examples of how the Jew carefully plans to break up the lives of the people; how he tries, by violating German women and girls, to lower the level of a race so as to render it unable to offer any resistance and thus helps to establish his world domination.[26]

Streicher spoke to children at every opportunity upon his basic theme, hatred of the Jew, and his single overture—Hitler had been sent to redeem Germany from Jewish oppression. Such a talk was reported as given by him to the children of Nuremberg at Christmastime, 1936: " 'Do you know who the Devil is?' he asked his breathlessly listening audience. 'The Jew, the Jew,' resounded from a thousand children's voices."[27]

Streicher demanded that anti-Jewish propaganda be disseminated in the public schools. In the course of a 1935 speech he said: "I repeat, we demand the transformation of the school into an ethno-German institution of education. If German children are taught by German teachers, then we shall have laid the foundations for the ethno-German school. This ethno-German school must teach racial doctrine."[28]

From the offices of Der Stuermer Streicher published a book for teachers entitled The Jewish Question and School Instruction, in which his anti-Semitic doctrines were expounded. In the introduction to the book Streicher wrote: "No one should be allowed to grow up in the midst of our people without this knowledge of the frightfulness and dangerousness of the Jew."[29] The purpose of the book, which was of course directed against the Jews at every page, was summarized in this sentence: "One who has reached this stage of understanding will inevitably remain an enemy of the Jews all his life and will instill this hatred into his own children."[30]

Had Streicher been recognized as the perverted person he was, and ignored by the responsible elements of the Nazi Party, his vicious propaganda might have gone virtually unnoticed. But the contrary was true. On Streicher's fiftieth birthday, February 13, 1935, Adolf Hitler himself came to Nuremberg to congratulate and to praise him. In April, 1937, Reichsfuehrer SS Himmler wrote Streicher:

When in future years the history of the reawakening of the German people is written and the next generation is already unable to understand that the German people were once friendly to the Jews, it will be recognized that Julius Streicher and his weekly paper *Der Stuermer* contributed a great deal toward the enlightenment regarding the enemy of mankind.[31]

And the leader of the Hitler Youth, Baldur von Schirach, wrote a letter, published in *Der Stuermer* of March, 1938, in which he praised Streicher's anti-Semitism:

It is the historical merit of *Der Stuermer* to have enlightened the broad masses of our people in a popular way as to the Jewish world danger. *Der Stuermer* is right in not carrying out its task in a purely aesthetic manner, for Jewry has shown no regard for the German people. We have, therefore, no reason for being considerate toward our worst enemy. What we fail to do today, the youth of tomorrow will have to suffer for bitterly.[32]

Streicher lost favor with the Party leadership after 1938. He never again saw Hitler. And in 1940 he was relieved of his position as Gauleiter of Franconia. But his propaganda against the Jews was never stopped. He was, of course, on the lunatic fringe of the anti-Semitic movement. Others, in higher and more important posts, echoed his strident cries.

Goebbels, as Minister of Propaganda, was perhaps the most extreme advocate of Jewish persecution in the Nazi government. Each week he gave several anti-Jewish releases to the German press. These articles, while not of the base nature of the Streicher publications, undoubtedly were of greater influence, since they were published in more than three thousand dailies and illustrated papers throughout Germany. The Department of Propaganda, within the Propaganda Ministry, had a special branch for the "enlightenment of the German people and of the world as to the Jewish question, fighting with propagandistic weapons against enemies of the State and hostile ideologies."[33]

On August 8, 1940, the editor of the *Black Corps,* the official publication of the SS, wrote: "Just as the Jewish question will be solved for Germany only when the last Jew has been deported, so the rest of Europe should also realize that the German peace which awaits it must be a peace without Jews."[34]

In the issue of the publication *World Struggle* for April, 1941, the defendant Rosenberg wrote: "The Jewish question will be solved only when the last Jew has left the European continent."[35]

On Heroes' Day, March 12, 1944, Grossadmiral Doenitz talked to the German people by radio. In the course of the speech, the Commander in Chief of the Navy referred to the "poison of Jewry":

What would have become of our country today, if the Fuehrer had not united us under National-Socialism! Split into parties, beset with the spreading poison of Jewry and vulnerable to it, and lacking, as a defense, our present uncompromising ideology, we would long since have succumbed to the burdens of this war and been subject to the merciless destruction of our adversaries....[36]

Before the war there were only 500,000 Jews in Germany out of a total population of 70,000,000 persons—or a mere seven-tenths of one per cent. Against this hapless minority the full weight of the Hitler state was brought to bear. Calumny was laid upon calumny; abuse upon abuse; terror upon terror. It became a mark of loyalty to manifest unremitting hatred of the oppressed Jewish minority. Racial prejudice provided the fertile ground for anti-Jewish propaganda. Because of it the most transparent lies were widely believed. Propaganda led to the pogrom; and the pogrom led to genocide.

The arch-killer of Hitler's Germany, Rudolf Hoess, explained to prison psychologist G. M. Gilbert that Himmler's order to exterminate thousands of people "fitted in with all that had been preached to me for years. The problem itself, the extermination of Jewry, was not new—but only that *I* was to be the one to carry it out, frightened me at first. But after getting the clear direct order and even an explanation with it—there was nothing left but to carry it out."[37]

When asked whether he had participated in the annihilation of the Jews, Hans Frank replied:

I myself have never installed an extermination camp for Jews, or promoted the existence of such camps; but if Adolf Hitler personally has laid that dreadful responsibility on his people, then it is mine too, for we have fought against Jewry for years; and we have indulged in the most horrible utterances—my own diary bears witness against me. Therefore, it is no more than my duty to answer your question in this connection with "yes."[38]

And then he added: "A thousand years will pass and still this guilt of Germany will not have been erased."[39]

Discrimination, Boycotts, and Pogroms

The principle of racial supremacy was incorporated as Point 4 of the Party program of February 24, 1920:

"Only a member of the race can be a citizen. A member of the race can only be one who is of German blood without consideration of confession. Consequently, no Jew can be a member of the race."[40]

Full effect was given to this doctrine by the Nuremberg Laws of 1935. And legally promulgated discriminations against the Jews were continuous after Hitler's rise to power:

1933: Jews were denied the right to hold public office or civil service positions; they were excluded from farming; they were denied employment by press or radio; and Jewish immigrants were denaturalized.

1934: Jews were excluded from stock exchanges and stock brokerage.

1935: Jews were precluded from citizenship; they were forbidden to live in marriage or to have extramarital relations with persons of German blood, or to employ female nationals of German blood; they were forbidden the right to raise the Reich or national flag.

1936: Jews were denied the right to vote; the death penalty was imposed for transferring or leaving property outside Germany.

1938: Jews were excluded from certain city areas, sidewalks, transportation, places of amusement, and restaurants; they were denied the right to practice law or medicine; they were excluded from business in general, and were required to pay discriminatory taxes and huge atonement fines; they were ordered to register all property; disposal of Jewish enterprises was made subject to permission of the authorities.

1939: Jews were ordered to surrender all objects of precious metals and jewels which they had purchased; they were excluded from the practice of dentistry.

1940: Jews were denied compensation for damages to property caused by enemy attacks or German forces.

1943: Jews were placed beyond the protection of any judicial process, and the police were given complete discretion in imposing punishments, including even death.

All these decrees were officially and publicly recorded in the *Reichsgesetzblatt.* They were open discriminations imposed by Hitler upon the Jewish people of Germany. Of course, nonpublished measures were far more extreme. And the removal of basic legal protection led to boycotts and pogroms not infrequently initiated by Party and state.

The first anti-Jewish boycott was approved by the entire Hitler cabinet on March 29, 1933, and became effective on April 1. Many acts of violence were visited upon the Jews. Raids were made on synagogues by uniformed Nazis; worshipers were molested and religious symbols desecrated. The synagogue in Nuremberg was demolished on August 11, 1938. On November 10, 1938, the anti-Jewish pogrom took place in which thousands of Jews were put into concentration camps, their stores and places of business destroyed, their synagogues burned to the ground, and their homes invaded by marauding Party leaders.

On the following day, November 11, 1938, Goering met with Hitler and Goebbels for the purpose of discussing measures to be taken in furtherance of the action. There was no thought of compensation for the miserable people who had been driven from their homes, beaten, and thrust into concentration camps, but only consideration of ways in which they could be further exploited for the enrichment of the state. It was particularly desired to confiscate all insurance which the Jews were entitled by law to collect on account of the destruction of their places of business and thefts of merchandise. To this end it was agreed that a fine of one billion

Reichsmarks would be levied upon the Jews, with insurance payments going to the state in liquidation of the fine.

A meeting was called on November 12, 1938, at the Reich Air Ministry to consider the details of these measures. Goering, Goebbels, Funk, Heydrich, and others met with representatives of the insurance companies. Goering presided and opened the meeting:

> Gentlemen!—Today's meeting is of a decisive nature. I have received a letter written on the Fuehrer's orders by the Stabsleiter of the Fuehrer's deputy Bormann requesting that the Jewish question be now, once and for all, co-ordinated and solved one way or another. And yesterday once again did the Fuehrer request by phone for me to take co-ordinated action in the matter....
>
> The fundamental idea in this program of elimination of the Jew from the German economy is first, the Jew being ejected from the economy transfers his property to the State. He will be compensated. The compensation is to be listed in the debit ledger and shall bring a certain percentage of interest. The Jew shall have to live out of this interest....
>
> The trustee of the State will estimate the value of the property and decide what amount the Jew shall receive. Naturally, this amount is to be set as low as possible. The representative of the State shall then turn the establishment over to the "Aryan" proprietor, that is, the property shall be sold according to its real value....
>
> We must agree on a clear action that shall be profitable to the Reich.[41]

The broad subject of the treatment of Germans who were Jews was opened in this fashion:

> Goebbels: I am of the opinion that this is our chance to dissolve the synagogues. All these not completely intact shall be razed by the Jews. The Jews shall pay for it. There in Berlin, the Jews are ready to do that. The synagogues which burned in Berlin are being leveled by the Jews themselves. We shall build parking lots in their places or new buildings. That ought to be the criterion for the whole country, the Jews shall have to remove the damaged or burned synagogues, and shall have to provide us with ready free space.... I deem it necessary to issue a decree forbidding the Jews to enter German theaters, movie houses, and circuses. I have already issued such a decree under the authority of the law of the chamber for culture. Considering the present situation of the theaters, I believe we can afford that. Our theaters are overcrowded, we have hardly any room. I am of the opinion that it

is not possible to have Jews sitting next to Germans in the movies and
theaters. One might consider, later on, to let the Jews have one or
two movie houses here in Berlin, where they may see Jewish movies.
But in German theaters they have no business any more.

Furthermore, I advocate that the Jews be eliminated from all positions in public life in which they may prove to be provocative. It is
still possible today that a Jew shares a compartment in a sleeping car
with a German. Therefore, we need a decree by the Reich Ministry
for Communications stating that separate compartments for Jews shall
be available; in cases where compartments are filled up, Jews cannot
claim a seat. They shall be given a separate compartment only after
all Germans have secured seats. They shall not mix with Germans, and
if there is no more room, they shall have to stand in the corridor....

It'll also have to be considered if it might not become necessary to
forbid the Jews to enter the German forests. In the Grunewald, whole
herds of them are running around. It is a constant provocation and we
are having incidents all the time. The behavior of the Jews is so
inciting and provocative that brawls are a daily routine.

Goering: We shall give the Jews a certain part of the forest, and
the Alpers shall take care of it that various animals that look damned
much like Jews—the Elk has such a crooked nose—get there also and
become acclimated.

Goebbels: I think this behavior is provocative. Furthermore, Jews
should not be allowed to sit around in German parks. I am thinking
of the whispering campaign on the part of Jewish women in the
public gardens at Fehrbelliner Platz. They go and sit with German
mothers and their children and begin to gossip and incite. I see in
this a particularly grave danger. I think it is imperative to give the
Jews certain public parks, not the best ones—and tell them: "You may
sit on these benches," these benches shall be marked "For Jews only."
Besides that they have no business in German parks. Furthermore,
Jewish children are still allowed in German schools. That's impossible.
It is out of the question that any boy should sit beside a Jewish boy
in a German gymnasium and receive lessons in German history. Jews
ought to be eliminated completely from German schools; they may take
care of their own education in their own communities.[42]

At this point the discussion turned to the question of insurance
on Jewish properties damaged in the pogrom.

Goering: Are they insured against damages caused by public disturbances?

Hilgard: No, no more. May I show this by an example. The most
remarkable of these cases is the case of Margraf Unter Den Linden.

The Jewelry store of Margraf is insured with us through a so-called combined policy. That covers practically any damage that may occur. This damage was reported to us as amounting to $1,700,000 because the store was completely stripped.

Goering: Daluge and Heydrich, you'll have to get me this jewelry through raids, staged on a tremendous scale! ...

Heydrich: The insurance may be granted, but as soon as it is to be paid, it'll be confiscated. That way we'll have saved face.

Hilgard: I am inclined to agree with what General Heydrich has just said. First of all, use the mechanism of the insurance company to check on the damage, to regulate it and even pay, but give the insurance company the chance to...

Goering: One moment! You'll have to pay in any case because it is the Germans who suffered the damage. But there'll be a lawful order forbidding you to make any direct payments to the Jews. You shall also have to make payment for the damage the Jews have suffered, but not to the Jews, but to the Minister of Finance. (Hilgard: Aha!) What he does with the money is his business. ...

Hilgard: I wonder to what extent insurance companies in foreign countries might be involved in this.

Goering: Well, they'll have to pay. And we'll confiscate that. ... Like the Fuehrer says, we'll have to find a way to talk this over with the countries which also do something against their Jews. That every dirty Polish Jew has a legal position here and we have to stand him— that ought to cease. The Fuehrer was not very happy about the agreement that was made with the Poles. He thinks we should take a few chances and just tell the Poles; all right, we are not going to do that; let's talk over what we may be able to accomplish together; you are doing something against your own Jews in Poland but the minute the Itzig has left Poland, he should suddenly be treated like a Pole! I'd like to disregard these stories from foreign countries a little.

Woermann: It ought to be considered whether or not the U.S. might take measures against German property. This question cannot be handled equally for all countries. I have to make a formal and general reservation.

Goering: I have always said and I'd like to repeat it that our steamship companies and German companies in general should finally catch on and liquidate their investments in the U.S., sell them, *et cetera*. That country of scoundrels does not do business with us according to any legal rules. Once before they stole everything from us, that is why I don't understand how we could do it again, just for some temporary profit. It is dangerous. You can do it with a regular country but not with one that cares for the Right as little as the U.S. The other day I had the American ambassador with me, we talked about the zeppelin and I told him: "We don't need any helium, I fly without helium but the prerequisite will have to be that this ship will be flying to civilized countries where the Right prevails. It goes without saying that one cannot fly to such gangster-states." He had a rather silly look on his face. One ought to tell these Americans. But you are right, Mr. Woermann, it ought to be considered....

Funk: The decisive question is: Are the Jewish stores to be reopened or not?

Goering: That depends on how big a turnover these Jewish stores have. If it is big, it is an indication that the German people are compelled to buy there, in spite of its being a Jewish store, because a need exists. If we'd close all Jewish stores which are not open right now, altogether before Christmas, we'd be in a nice mess.

Fischboeck: Your Excellency, in this matter we have already a very complete plan for Austria.... Out of 17,000 stores 12,000 or 14,000 would be shut down and the remainder aryanized or handed over to the bureau of trustees which is operated by the State.

Goering: I have to say that this proposal is grand. This way, the whole affair would be wound up in Vienna, one of the Jewish capitals, so to speak, by Christmas or by the end of the year.... Of course, I too am of the opinion that these economic measures ought to be strengthened by a number of Police-action-Propaganda-measures and cultural displays so that everything shall be fixed now and the Jewry will be slapped this week right and left.

Heydrich: In spite of the elimination of the Jew from the economic life, the main problem, namely to kick the Jew out of Germany, remains. May I make a few proposals to that effect?

Following a suggestion by the Commissioner of the Reich, we have set up a center for the Emigration of Jews in Vienna, and that way we have eliminated 50,000 Jews from Austria while from the Reich only 19,000 Jews were eliminated during the same period of time; we were so successful because of the co-operation on the part of the competent Ministry for Economic Affairs and of the foreign charitable organizations.... As for the isolation, I'd like to make a few proposals regarding police measures which are important also because of their psychological effect on public opinion. For example, who is Jewish according to the Nuremberg laws shall have to wear a certain insignia. That is a possibility which shall facilitate many other things. I don't see any danger of excuses, and it shall make our relationship with the foreign Jew easier....

Goering: But, my dear Heydrich, you won't be able to avoid the creation of ghettos on a very large scale, in all the cities. They shall have to be created....

Heydrich: As an additional measure, I'd propose to withdraw from the Jews all personal papers such as permits and drivers' licenses. No Jew should be allowed to own a car, neither should he be permitted to drive because that way he'd endanger German life. By not being permitted to live in certain districts, he should be further restricted to move about so freely. I'd say the Royal Square in Munich, the Reichsweihestätte, is not to be entered any more within a certain radius by Jews. The same would go for establishments of culture, border fences, military installations. Furthermore, like Minister Dr. Goebbels has said before, exclusion of the Jews from public theaters, movie houses, et cetera....

Goering: One more question, gentlemen: What would you think the situation would be if I'd announce today that Jewry should have to contribute this 1 billion as a punishment?

Buerckel: The Viennese would agree to this whole-heartedly.

Goebbels: I wonder if the Jews would have a chance to pull out of this, and to put something on the side.

Brinkmann: They'd be subject to punishment....

Goering: I shall close the wording this way; that German Jewry shall, as punishment for their abominable crimes *et cetera, et cetera.*, have to make a contribution of 1 billion. That'll work. The pigs won't commit another murder. Incidentally, I'd like to say again that I would not like to be a Jew in Germany.... If in the near future, the German Reich should come into conflict with foreign powers, it goes without saying that we in Germany should first of all let it come to a showdown with the Jews....[43]

The war came, not a war begun or instigated by the Jewish people, but a war designed and initiated by Adolf Hitler. And that conflict gave Hitler the opportunity which he, and Goering, and others in top leadership of the Nazi state had sought for the final solution of the Jewish problem in Europe.

The Chief of the Gestapo and SD, Reinhard Heydrich, had previously been given the responsibility of driving the Jews out of Germany. In a letter dated July 31, 1941, shortly after the invasion of the Soviet Union, Goering, as Reich Marshal of the Greater German Reich and Commissioner for the Four Year Plan, charged Heydrich with the complete solution of the Jewish problem in all of Europe:

Complementing the task that was assigned to you on the 24th of January 1939, which dealt with arriving at a thorough furtherance of emigration and evacuation, a solution of the Jewish problem, as advantageously as possible, I hereby charge you with making all necessary preparations in regard to organizational and financial matters for bringing about a complete solution of the Jewish question in the German sphere of influence in Europe.

Wherever other governmental agencies are involved, these are to co-operate with you.

I charge you furthermore to send me, before long, an overall plan concerning the organizational, factual, and material measures necessary for the accomplishment of the desired solution of the Jewish question.[44]

The steps leading to the "complete solution" had been these: (1) intensive and increasingly vicious anti-Jewish propaganda; (2) exclusion of the Jews from the political life of Germany—deprivation of the right to hold office, to hold civil service positions, to vote, and to enjoy other rights incident to citizenship; (3) removal of the Jews from the economic life of Germany—Aryanization of their properties and confiscation of their wealth; (4) constant pogroms, persecutions, and anti-Jewish agitation, designed to drive the Jews out of Germany.

Thousands fled to the West before the war with England and France began; and thousands more sought escape through the Balkans before war began with the Soviet Union. But with military operations in both East and West, the elimination of the Jews could no longer be considered in terms of emigration. A "complete solution" came to mean a "final solution"—the biological extermination of the race.

The carrying out of the final solution of the Jewish problem was performed systematically. It called for registration of all European Jews, transportation of Jews to ghettos set up in the East, and deportation from ghettos to annihilation centers.

Segregation

Registration of the Jews in Germany was required by a decree issued in 1938. Elsewhere registration followed quickly after conquest. In Poland it was 1939; in Austria and France, 1940; and in Holland, 1941. Registration measures for the eastern occupied territories were described by the defendant Rosenberg:

The first main goal of the German measures must be strict segregation of Jewry from the rest of the population. In the execution of this, first of all is the seizing of the Jewish populace by the introduction of a registration order and similar appropriate measures.... Then, immediately, the wearing of the recognition sign consisting of a yellow Jewish star is to be brought about and all rights of freedom for Jews are to be withdrawn. They are to be placed in ghettos and at the same time are to be separated according to sexes. The presence of many more or less closed Jewish settlements in White Ruthenia and in the Ukraine makes this mission easier. Moreover, places are to be chosen which make possible the full use of the Jewish manpower in case labor needs are present. These ghettos can be placed under the supervision of a Jewish self-government with Jewish officials. The guarding of the boundaries between the ghettos and the outer world, is, however, the duty of the police.

Also in the cases in which a ghetto could not yet be established, care is to be taken through strict prohibitions and similar suitable measures that a further intermingling of blood of the Jews and the rest of the populace does not continue....

The entire Jewish property is to be seized and confiscated with exception of that which is necessary for a bare existence. As far as the economic situation permits, the power of disposal of their property is to be taken from the Jews as soon as possible through orders and other measures given by the commissariat, so that the moving of property will quickly cease.

Any cultural activity will be completely forbidden to the Jews. This includes the outlawing of the Jewish press, the Jewish theaters and schools.[45]

A report to Himmler of October 15, 1941, described the setting up of ghettos in the East in response to this directive:

Apart from organizing and carrying out measures of execution, the creation of ghettos was begun in the larger towns at once during the first days of operations. This was especially urgent in Kovno because there were 30,000 Jews in a total population of 152,400.... In Riga the so-called "Moscow suburb" was designated as a ghetto. This is the worst dwelling district of Riga, already now mostly inhabited by Jews. The transfer of the Jews into the ghetto district proved rather difficult because the Latvian dwellings in that district had to be evacuated and residential space in Riga is very crowded. Of the 28,000 Jews living in Riga 24,000 have been transferred into the ghetto so far.[46]

At a cabinet meeting on December 16, 1941, Hans Frank, the Governor General of Poland, said:

The Jews represent for us also extraordinarily malignant gluttons. We have now approximately 2,500,000 of them in the Government General, perhaps with the Jewish mixtures and everything that goes with it, 3,500,000 Jews. We cannot shoot or poison those 3,500,000 Jews; but we shall nevertheless be able to take measures which will lead, somehow, to their annihilation, and this in connection with the gigantic measures to be determined in discussions in the Reich. The Government General must become free of Jews, the same as the Reich. . . .

As an old National Socialist I must also say: This war would be only a partial success if the whole lot of Jewry would survive it, while we would have shed our best blood in order to save Europe. My attitude towards the Jews will, therefore, be based only on the expectation that they must disappear. They must be done away with. I have entered negotiations to have them deported to the East. A large conference concerning that question, to which I am going to delegate the State Secretary Dr. Buehler, will take place in Berlin in January. That discussion is to take place in the Reich Security Main Office with SS Lieutenant General Heydrich. A great Jewish migration will begin, in any case. . . .

Gentlemen, I must ask you to rid yourselves of all feeling of pity. We must annihilate the Jews, wherever we find them and wherever it is possible, in order to maintain there the structure of the Reich as a whole. . . .[47]

It was true that three and a half million Polish Jews could not be shot or poisoned, as Frank said; but even as he spoke, plans were under way for establishing the gassing facilities which would lead "to their annihilation." And if, in the beginning, the Jews really believed the propaganda that deportation meant only resettlement, it was not long before they understood quite well the true fate in store for them. Hiding in their caves and hovels, they resisted every attempt at removals, which had to be accomplished by force and violence, if at all.

Frank's orders led to many acts of extreme cruelty in the enforced deportation of Polish Jews. One such action was described in a German report of June 30, 1943, on the clearing of the Jews from Galicia, a district of Poland on the northern slopes of the Carpathian Mountains:

The influence of this Galician Jewry, being considerable already under Austrian and Polish rule, increased to an almost incredible extent when the Soviets occupied this district in 1939. Every important appointment within the country was filled by them. This explains the fact that in July 1941, after the occupation by German troops, Jews were found everywhere. Hence it was considered to be also our most urgent task to find a solution for this problem as soon as possible.

Our first measure consisted of marking every Jew by a white armlet bearing the star of David in blue. . . . In the course of this action again thousands of Jews were caught who were in possession of forged certificates or who had obtained surreptitiously certificates of labor by all kinds of pretexts. These Jews also were exposed to special treatment. . . .

Despite all these measures concerning the employment of Jews, their evacuation from the district of Galicia was commenced in April 1942, and executed step by step. When the Higher SS and Police Leader once again intervened in the solution of the Jewish problem by his Decree Concerning the Formation of Districts Inhabited by Jews of 10 November 1942 already 254,989 Jews had been evacuated or resettled. . . .

In the meantime further evacuation was executed with energy, so that with effect from 23 June 1943 all Jewish residence districts could be dissolved. Therewith I report that the district of Galicia, with the exception of those Jews living in the camps under the control of the SS and Police Leader, is: *Free from Jews.*

Jews still caught in small numbers are given special treatment by the competent detachments of police and gendarmerie.

Up to 27 June 1943 altogether 434,329 Jews have been evacuated.[48]

The extremities to which the harried people were driven in their efforts to hide from the German police were described:

Nothing but catastrophical conditions were found in the ghettos of Rawa-Ruska and Rohatyn. The Jews of Rawa-Ruska, fearing the evacuation, had concealed those suffering from spotted fever in underground holes. When evacuation was to start, the Police found that 3,000 Jews suffering from spotted fever lay about in this ghetto. . . . At once every police officer innoculated against spotted fever was called into action. Thus we succeeded in destroying this plague-boil, losing thereby only one officer. . . .

On the occasion of these actions, many more difficulties occurred owing to the fact that the Jews tried every means to evade evacuation. Not only did they try to flee, but they concealed themselves in every imaginable corner, in pipes, chimneys, even in sewers, *et cetera.* They built barricades in passages of catacombs, in cellars enlarged to dug-outs, in underground holes, in cunningly contrived hiding places in attics and sheds, within furniture, *et cetera.*

Since we received more and more alarming reports on the Jews becoming armed in an ever increasing manner, we started during the last fortnight in June 1943 an action throughout the whole of the district of Galicia with the intent to use strongest measures to destroy the Jewish gangsterdom. Special measures were found necessary during the action to dissolve the ghetto in Lwow where the dugouts mentioned above had been established. Here we had to act brutally from the beginning, in order to avoid losses on our side; we had to blow up or to burn down several houses. On this occasion the surprising fact arose that we were able to catch about 20,000 Jews instead of 12,000 Jews who had registered. We had to pull at least 3,000 Jewish corpses out of every kind of hiding places; they had committed suicide by taking poison....[49]

Jews of western Europe were brought to staging camps from which they were shipped by boxcar to the ghettos and extermination centers of the East. Such deportations were justified on "cultural grounds" by Baldur von Schirach in addressing the European Youth Conference in Vienna on September 14, 1943:

Every Jew who exerts influence in Europe is a danger to European culture. If anyone reproaches me with having driven from this city, which was once the European metropolis of Jewry, tens of thousands upon tens of thousands of Jews into the ghetto of the East, I feel myself compelled to reply: I see in this an action contributing to European culture.[50]

A Dutch witness, Vorrink, testified to the deportation of Jews from the Netherlands:

The Green Police sealed off whole sections of cities, went into houses, even went on the roofs, and drove out young and old and took them off in their trucks. No difference was made between young and old. We have seen old women of over 70, who were lying ill at home and had no other desire than to be allowed to die quietly in their own home, put on stretchers and carried out of their home, to be sent to Westernborg and from there to Germany, where they died.

I myself remember very well how a mother, when she was dragged from her home, gave her baby to a stranger, who was not a Jewess, and asked her to look after her child. At this moment there are still hundreds of families in Holland where these small Jewish children are being looked after and brought up as their own.[51]

The head of the Jewish bureau in France was SS-Obersturm-fuehrer Dannecker. Following methods used elsewhere, his office compiled lists of Jews and, as orders were received, assigned them to transports moving to the concentration camps and extermination centers in the East. By the end of October, 1942, it was estimated that over 50,000 Jews had been evacuated from occupied France, and demands for a like number had been made of French authorities in unoccupied France. It was noted that "most of the European countries are much nearer to a final solution of the Jewish problem than France."[52] The traffic in French Jews continued unabated until almost the war's end. On April 6, 1944, a home for Jewish children in Ain was raided, "and a total of 41 children, aged from 3 to 13, were apprehended."[53] The report stated that the Jewish personnel in charge of the home, ten in number, had also been arrested, and it concluded: "The convoy for Drancy will leave on April 7, 1944."[54]

The rounding up of Jews from Czechoslovakia, Greece, and Hungary was described by the Gestapo official Wisliceny under examination by Lieutenant Colonel Brookhart:

Question: Considering the case of Slovakia, you have already made reference to the 17,000 specially selected Jews who were sent from Slovakia. Will you tell the Tribunal of the other measures that followed concerning Jews in Slovakia? . . . What happened to the first group of 17,000 specially selected workers?

Answer: This group was not annihilated, but all were employed for enforced labor in the Auschwitz and Lublin Concentration Camps. . . .

Question: What happened to the approximately 35,000 members of the families of the Jewish workers that were also sent to Poland?

Answer: They were treated according to the order which Eichmann had shown me in August 1942. Part of them were left alive if they were able to work; the others were killed. . . .

Question: Referring now to the 25,000 Jews that remained in Slovakia until September of 1944, do you know what was done with those Jews? . . .

Answer: I assume that they also met with the so-called final solution, because Himmler's order to suspend this action was not issued until several weeks later.

Question: Considering now actions in Greece about which you have personal knowledge, will you tell the Tribunal of the actions there in chronological sequence?

Answer: In January 1943 Eichmann ordered me to come to Berlin and told me that I was to proceed to Salonika to solve the Jewish problem there.... In Salonika the Jews were first of all concentrated in certain quarters of the city. There were in Salonika about 50,000 Jews of Spanish descent. At the beginning of March, after this concentration had taken place, a teletype message from Eichmann to Brunner ordered the immediate evacuation of all Jews from Salonika and Macedonia to Auschwitz. Armed with this order, Brunner and I went to the Military Administration. No objections were raised by the Military Administration, and measures were prepared and executed. Brunner directed the entire action in Salonika in person. The trains necessary for the evacuation were requisitioned from the Transport Command of the Armed Forces. All Brunner had to do was to indicate the number of railway cars needed and the exact time at which they were required.... The cash which the Jews possessed was taken away and put into a common account at the Bank of Greece. After the Jews had been evacuated from Salonika this account was taken over by the German Military Administration. About 280,000,000 Drachmas were involved.

Question: When you say the Jews taken to Auschwitz were submitted to the final solution, what do you mean by that?

Answer: By that I mean what Eichmann had explained to me under the term "final solution," that is, they were annihilated biologically. As far as I could gather from my conversations with him, this annihilation took place in the gas chambers and the bodies were subsequently destroyed in the crematories....

Question: ... Turning to actions in Hungary, will you briefly outline the actions taken there and your participation?

Answer: After the entry of the German troops in Hungary Eichmann went there personally with a large command. By an order signed by the head of the Security Police, I was assigned to Eichmann's command. Eichmann began his activities in Hungary at the end of March 1944. He contacted members of the then Hungarian Government, especially State Secretaries Endre and Von Baky. The first measure adopted by Eichmann in co-operation with these Hungarian Government officials was the concentration of the Hungarian Jews in special places and special localities. These measures were carried out according to zones, beginning in Ruthenia and Transylvania. The action was initiated in mid-April 1944.... This operation affected some 450,000 Jews....

Question: What became of the Jews to whom you have already referred—approximately 450,000?

Answer: They were, without exception, taken to Auschwitz and brought to the final solution....[55]

Details of the deportation of Hungarian Jews to Auschwitz were given by the affiant Dr. Rudolf Kastner:

19 March 1944: Together with the German military occupation there arrived in Budapest a "Special Section Commando" of the German Secret Police with the sole object of liquidating the Hungarian Jews. It was headed by Adolf Eichmann.... They arrested, and later deported to Mauthausen, all the leaders of Jewish political and business life and journalists, together with the Hungarian democratic and anti-Fascist politicians; ...

15 May 1944: General and total deportation begins. On day before the evacuation, all hospital cases, newly born babies, blind and deaf, all mental cases and prison inmates of Jewish origin were transferred to the ghettos. About 80-100 Jews were placed in each cattle-car with one bucket of water; the car was then sealed down. At Kassa the deportation trains were taken over from the escorting Hungarian gendarmerie by the SS. While searching for "hidden valuables" the gendarmerie squads tortured the inmates with electric current and beat them mercilessly. Hundreds committed suicide. Those who protested or resisted were shot at once (as for instance Dr. Rosenfeld, solicitor of Marosvasarhely). The Hungarian press and radio kept quiet about the deportations. The Hungarian Government denied in the foreign press that Jews were tortured.

Between 5 June and 8 June 1944 Eichmann told me: "We accepted the obligation toward the Hungarians that not a single deported Jew will return alive!"

Up to 27 June 1944, 475,000 Jews were deported. The Pope and the King of Sweden intervened with Horthy. Then followed the ultimatum-like appeal of President Roosevelt to stop the brutal anti-Jewish persecutions. Thereupon Horthy has forbidden the deportation of the Jews from the capitol which was already fixed to take place on July 5....

But on 15 October 1944 a German coup ended the Horthy regime and Szalasy took over power. On 17 October Eichmann returned to Budapest by air. On his orders the Arrow-Cross Party and the police began the deportation of all Jews locked into the houses marked by yellow-stars; 25,000 Jewish people, mostly women, were made to walk over 100 miles in rain and snow without food to the Austrian border;

hundreds died on the way, more died in Austria through exhaustion and dysentery....[56]

The deportations of Jews from the ghettos in Radom, Poland, to the extermination center at Treblinka were described by the affiant David Wajnapel:

A few weeks after the entry of the German troops into Radom, Police and SS arrived. Conditions became immediately worse. The house in the Zermoskist, where their headquarters were, became a menace to the entire population.... Later on two ghettos were established in Radom. In August 1942 the so-called "deportations" took place. The ghettos were surrounded by many SS units who occupied all the street exits. People were driven out to the streets, and those who ran away were fired on. Sick people at home or in hospitals were shot on the spot, among others also the inmates of the hospital where I was working as a doctor. The total number of people killed amounted to about 4,000. About 3,000 people were spared and the rest—about 20,000 people—were sent to Treblinka.... After the "deportation" the remaining people were crowded into a few narrow lanes and we came under the exclusive rule of the SS and became the private property of the SS who used to hire us out for payment to various firms. I know that these payments were credited to a special SS account at the Radom Bank Emisyjny. We had to deal with SS-men only. Executions carried out by the SS in the ghetto itself were a frequent occurrence. On 14 January 1943 another "deportation" to Treblinka took place.

On 21 March 1943 there took place throughout the whole district the so-called action against the intelligentsia, which action, as far as I know, was decided upon at an SS and Police Leaders' meeting in Radom. In Radom alone about 200 people were shot at that time; among others, my parents, my brother, and his 9-month-old child met their deaths.

On 9 November of the same year all Jewish children up to 12 years of age as well as the old and sick were gathered from Radom and from camps situated near Radom and shot in the Biala Street in Radom. SS officers as well as SS-men participated in this.

... The SS-men were certainly well-informed about the bloody deeds which were committed by the SS in Poland; in particular they told me personally about mass murders of Jews in Maidanek (in November 1943). This incident is an open secret. It was common knowledge among the civil population as well as among the lowest-ranking SS-men.[57]

The Warsaw Ghetto

The clearing of the Warsaw ghetto was an action of climactic cruelty. The complete report of this crime was made by SS Brigade-fuehrer Stroop who directed the combined SS, Police, and Wehrmacht forces which drove the Jews from the ghetto. Stroop called his report "The Warsaw Ghetto is no more,"[58] and he began it with a historical justification of the abuse of the Jewish people:

The creation of special areas to be inhabited by Jews, and the restriction of the Jews with regard to residence and trading is nothing new in the history of the East. Such measures were first taken far back in the Middle Ages; they could be observed as recently as during the last few centuries. These restrictions were imposed with the intention of protecting the Aryan population against the Jews....

In October 1940, the Governor ordered the Commissioner of the District, President for the City of Warsaw, to complete the resettlement necessary for establishing the ghetto within the City of Warsaw by 15 November 1940. The ghetto thus established in Warsaw was inhabited by about 400,000 Jews. It contained 27,000 apartments with an average of two and one-half rooms each. It was separated from the rest of the city by partition and other walls and by walling-up of thoroughfares, windows, doors, open spaces, et cetera.

It was administered by the Jewish Board of Elders, who received their instructions from the Commissioner for the ghetto, who was immediately subordinated to the Governor. The Jews were granted self-administration in which the German supervising authorities intervened only where German interests were touched. In order to enable the Jewish Board of Elders to execute its orders, a Jewish police force was set up, identified by special armbands and a special beret and armed with rubber truncheons. This Jewish police force was charged with maintaining order and security within the ghetto and was subordinated to the German and Polish police.

It soon became clear, however, that not all dangers had been removed by this confining the Jews to one place. Security considerations required removing the Jews from the city of Warsaw altogether. The first large resettlement action took place in the period from 22 July to 3 October 1942. In this action 310,322 Jews were removed. In January 1943, a second resettlement action was carried out by which altogether 6,500 Jews were affected.

When the Reichsfuehrer SS visited Warsaw in January 1943 he ordered the SS and Police Leader for the District of Warsaw to transfer to Lublin the armament factories and other enterprises of military importance which were installed within the ghetto, including their personnel and machines. The execution of this transfer order proved to be very difficult, since the managers as well as the Jews resisted in every possible way. The SS and Police Leader thereupon decided to enforce the transfer of the enterprises in a large-scale action which he intended to carry out in three days. The necessary preparations had been taken by my predecessor, who also had given the order to start the large-scale action. I myself arrived in Warsaw on 17 April 1943 and took over the command of the action on 19 April 1943, 0800 hours, the action itself having started the same day at 0600 hours.[59]

Stroop then described in general terms the clearing of the ghetto:

Before the large-scale action began, the limits of the former ghetto had been blocked by an external barricade in order to prevent the Jews from breaking out. This barricade was maintained from the start to the end of the action and was especially reinforced at night.

When we invaded the ghetto for the first time, the Jews and the Polish bandits succeeded in repelling the participating units, including tanks and armored cars, by a well-prepared concentration of fire. When I ordered a second attack, about 0800 hours, I distributed the units, separated from each other by indicated lines, and charged them with combing out the whole of the Ghetto, each unit for a certain part. Although firing commenced again, we now succeeded in combing out the blocks according to plan. The enemy was forced to retire from the roofs and elevated bases to the basements, dug-outs, and sewers. In order to prevent their escaping into the sewers, the sewerage system was dammed up below the Ghetto and filled with water, but the Jews frustrated this plan to a great extent by blowing up the turning off valves. Late the first day we encountered rather heavy resistance, but it was quickly broken by a special raiding party. In the course of further operations we succeeded in expelling the Jews from their prepared resistance bases, sniper holes, and the like, and in occupying during the 20 and 21 April the greater part of the so-called remainder of the Ghetto to such a degree that the resistance continued within these blocks could no longer be called considerable....

The number of Jews forcibly taken out of the buildings and arrested was relatively small during the first few days. It transpired that the Jews had taken to hiding in the sewers and in specially erected dug-outs. Whereas we had assumed during the first days that there were only scattered dug-outs, we learned in the course of the large-scale action that the whole Ghetto was systematically equipped with cellars, dug-outs and passages. In every case these passages and dug-outs were connected with the sewer system. Thus, the Jews were able to maintain undisturbed subterranean traffic....

The resistance put up by the Jews and bandits could be broken only by relentlessly using all our force and energy by day and night. On 23 April 1943 the Reichsfuehrer SS issued through the Higher SS and Police Leader East at Cracow his order to complete the combing out of the Warsaw Ghetto with the greatest severity and relentless tenacity. I therefore decided to destroy the entire Jewish residential area by setting every block on fire, including the blocks of residential buildings near the armament works. One concern after the other was systematically evacuated and subsequently destroyed by fire. The Jews then emerged from their hiding places and dug-outs in almost every case. Not infrequently, the Jews stayed in the burning buildings until, because of the heat and the fear of being burned alive they preferred to jump down from the upper stories after having thrown mattresses and other upholstered articles into the street from the burning buildings. With their bones broken, they still tried to crawl across the street into blocks of buildings which had not yet been set on fire or were only partly in flames. Often Jews changed their hiding places during the night, by moving into the ruins of burnt-out buildings, taking refuge there until they were found by our patrols. Their stay in the sewers also ceased to be pleasant after the first week. Frequently from the street, we could hear loud voices coming through the sewer shafts. Then the men of the Waffen SS, the Police or the Wehrmacht Engineers courageously climbed down the shafts to bring out the Jews and not infrequently they then stumbled over Jews already dead, or were shot at. It was always necessary to use smoke candles to drive out the Jews. Thus one day we opened 183 sewer entrance holes and at a fixed time lowered smoke candles into them, with the result that the bandits fled from what they believed to be gas to the center of the former Ghetto where they could then be pulled out of the sewer holes there. A great number of Jews who could not be counted, were exterminated by blowing up sewers and dug-outs....

Only through the continuous and untiring work of all involved did we succeed in catching a total of 56,065 Jews whose extermination can be proved. To this should be added the number of Jews who lost their lives in explosions or fires but whose numbers could not be ascertained....

The large-scale action was terminated on 16 May 1943 with the blowing up of the Warsaw synagogue at 2015 hours.[60]

Appended to Stroop's report were copies of daily statements, from which the following excerpts are taken:

April 21, 1943:...I resolved therefore to blow up these passages which we had discovered and subsequently to set the entire block on fire. Not until the building was well aflame did screaming Jews make their appearance, and they were evacuated at once....[81]

April 22, 1943: Our setting the block on fire achieved the result in the course of the night that those Jews whom we had not been able to find despite all our search operations left their hideouts under the roofs, in the cellars, and elsewhere, and appeared at the outside of the buildings, trying to escape the flames. Masses of them—entire families —were already aflame and jumped from the windows or endeavored to let themselves down by means of sheets tied together or the like. Steps had been taken so that these Jews as well as the remaining ones were liquidated at once....[82]

April 23, 1943: The whole operation is rendered more difficult by the cunning way in which the Jews and bandits act; for instance, we discover that the hearses which were used to collect the corpses lying around, at the same time bring living Jews to the Jewish cemetery, and thus they are enabled to escape from the Ghetto. Now this way of escape also is barred by continuous control of the hearses.[63]

April 25, 1943:...As in the preceding days uncounted Jews were buried in blown up dug-outs and, as can be observed time and again, burned with this bag of Jews today. We have, in my opinion, caught a very considerable part of the bandits and lowest elements of the Ghetto. Intervening darkness prevented immediate liquidation. I am going to try to obtain a train for T II [Treblinka II] tomorrow. Otherwise liquidation will be carried out tomorrow....[64]

April 26, 1943:...During today's operations several blocks of buildings were burned down. This is the only and final method which forces this trash and subhumanity to the surface.[65]

April 27, 1943:...SS-men who descended into the sewers discovered that a great number of corpses of perished Jews are being washed away by the water.[66]

May 15, 1943:...A special unit once more searched the last block of buildings which was still intact in the Ghetto and subsequently destroyed it. In the evening the chapel, mortuary, and all other buildings on the Jewish cemetery were blown up or destroyed by fire.[67]

May 16, 1943:...The former Jewish quarter of Warsaw is no longer in existence.[68]

There had been four hundred thousand Jews in the Warsaw ghetto. By May 16, 1943, all had been removed to extermination centers, or had been killed while evading deportation. The pitiful and fanatical resistance of the final sixty thousand demonstrated that they knew that "resettlement" meant, for them, transfer to Treblinka—and death. The terror of death showed in their faces.

Huge amounts of property were expropriated from Jewish evacuees. In Poland, a special organization was created for this purpose under the name Action Reinhardt. This single action group amassed Jewish properties exceeding 100 million Reichsmarks in value. The properties consisted of carloads of clothing, currency from all principal countries of the world, precious metals, watches, jewelry, and other valuables. In the Galicia action it was reported that the following items, among others, were taken from the Jews: 20,952 kilograms of gold wedding rings, 97,581 kilograms of gold coins, 11,730 kilograms of gold dentures, 343,100 kilograms of silver cigarette boxes, 261,589 U.S. dollars, and 35 wagons of furs.

Much of the property thus stolen from the Jewish people was transferred to the Reichsbank for deposit. The head of the SS office responsible for these collections, Oswald Pohl, testified to the arrangements for that purpose:

The second business deal between Walter Funk and the SS concerned the delivery of articles of value of dead Jews to the Reichsbank. It was in the year 1941 or 1942, when large quantities of articles of value, such as jewelry, gold rings, gold fillings, spectacles, gold watches, and such had been collected in the extermination camps. These valuables came packed in cases to the WVHA in Berlin. Himmler had ordered us to deliver these things to the Reichsbank. I remember that Himmler explained to me that negotiations concerning this matter had been conducted with the Reichsbank, that is, Herr Funk. As a result of an agreement which my chief had made, I discussed with the Reichsbank Director Emil Puhl, the manner of delivery. In this conversation no doubt remained that the objects to be delivered were the jewelry and valuables of concentration camp inmates, especially of Jews, who had been killed in extermination camps. The objects in question were rings, watches, eyeglasses, ingots of gold, wedding rings, brooches, pins, frames of glasses, foreign currency, and other valuables. Further discussions concerning the delivery of these objects took place between my subordinates and Puhl and other officials of the Reichsbank. It was an enormous quantity of valuables, since there was a steady flow of deliveries for months and years.[69]

Annihilation

In December, 1941, Hans Frank had observed that there were approximately two and a half million Jews in the General Government.[70] On January 25, 1944, three years later, he noted in his diary: "At the present time we still have in the General Government perhaps 100,000 Jews."[71] The percentages were about the same in every country occupied by the Germans. Practically all Jewish men, women, and children who could be found were put into ghettos, concentration camps, or extermination centers—or they were killed in the field.

Those who were physically able to work were used as slave labor until they became too weak and, unable further to perform what was demanded of them, were sent to the gas chambers. The American Jewish Committee estimated the Jewish population of Europe in 1939 at 9,739,200. In 1949 it estimated that population at 3,505,800. Over six million Jews thus disappeared from Europe in the ten years after the beginning of the war with Poland.

The extermination of the Jews of Europe was a carefully planned and thoroughly organized action. Ordered by Hitler, it was directed by the Reichsfuehrer SS and Chief of the German Police, Heinrich Himmler. In a speech to his SS Generals at Posen on October 4, 1943, Himmler said:

I also want to talk to you, quite frankly, on a very grave matter... I mean the clearing out of the Jews, the extermination of the Jewish race. It's one of those things it is easy to talk about—"The Jewish race is being exterminated," says one party member, "that's quite clear, it's in our program—elimination of the Jews, and we're doing it, exterminating them." And they come, 80 million worthy Germans, and each one has his decent Jew. Of course the others are vermin, but this one is an A-1 Jew. Not one of all those who talk this way has witnessed it, not one of them has been through it. Most of *you* must know what it means when 100 corpses are lying side by side, or 500 or 1000. To have stuck it out and at the same time—apart from exceptions caused by human weakness—to have remained decent fellows, that is what has made us hard. This is a page of glory in our history which has never been written and is never to be written, for we know how difficult we should have made it for ourselves, if—with the bombing raids, the burdens and the deprivations of war—we still had Jews today in every town as secret saboteurs, agitators and trouble-mongers. We would now probably have reached the 1916/17 stage when the Jews were still in the German national body.

We have taken from them what wealth they had. I have issued a strict order, which SS-Obergruppenfuehrer Pohl has carried out, that this wealth should, as a matter of course, be handed over to the Reich without reserve.... We had the moral right, we had the duty to our people, to destroy this people which wanted to destroy us.... Altogether, however, we can say, that we have fulfilled this most difficult duty for the love of our people. And our spirit, our soul, our character has not suffered injury from it.[72]

Under Himmler, as Reichsfuehrer SS and Chief of the German Police, was the Reich Main Security Office, or RSHA, which included the Gestapo and the SD as principal components. Until his assassination in Czechoslovakia on June 4, 1942, Reinhard Heydrich was the Chief of the RSHA; he was succeeded in that position by the defendant Ernst Kaltenbrunner who took office on January 30, 1943.

The Gestapo was Office IV of the RSHA, and was under the direct command of Heinrich Mueller. Section B of the Gestapo dealt with political churches, sects, and Jews, and B4 was responsible for Jewish affairs, matters of evacuation, means of suppressing enemies of the people and state, and dispossession of rights of German citizenship. The head of B4 of the Gestapo was Adolf Eichmann. It was he who had direct operational responsibility for the extermination of European Jewry.

Eichmann's primary function was to round up the Jews and deport them to the great extermination centers established under Himmler's orders. He was assisted by special task forces of the Gestapo and SD, known as Einsatzgruppen, which carried out exterminations in the field. The witness Dieter Wisliceny testified to conversations he had with Eichmann relative to the number of Jews killed in the extermination centers:

Question: In your meetings with the other specialists on the Jewish problem and Eichmann did you gain any knowledge or information as to the total number of Jews killed under this program?

Answer: Eichmann personally always talked about at least 4 million Jews. Sometimes he even mentioned 5 million. According to my own estimate I should say that at least 4 million must have been destined for the so-called final solution. How many of those actually survived, I am not in a position to say.

Question: When did you last see Eichmann?

Answer: I last saw Eichmann toward the end of February 1945 in Berlin. At that time he said that if the war were lost he would commit suicide.

Question: Did he say anything at that time as to the number of Jews that had been killed?

Answer: Yes, he expressed this in a particularly cynical manner. He said he would leap laughing into the grave because the feeling that he had 5 million people on his conscience would be for him a source of extraordinary satisfaction.[73]

SS-Sturmbannfuehrer Wilhelm Hoettl was a reporter and deputy in Office VI of the RSHA. As such, he came into contact with Adolf Eichmann. In August, 1944, Eichmann informed Hoettl of a report which he had made to Himmler on the approximate number of Jews who had been killed pursuant to Himmler's orders for the extermination of European Jewry: "Approximately four million Jews had been killed in the various extermination camps while an additional two million met death in other ways, the major part of which were shot by operational squads of the Security Police during the campaign against Russia."[74]

As to the accuracy of this estimate Hoettl further averred:

I have to believe that this information, given to me by Eichmann, was correct, as he, among all the persons in question, certainly had the best survey of the figures of the Jews who had been murdered. In the first place, he "delivered" so to speak the Jews to the extermination camps through his special squads and knew, therefore, the exact figure and, in the second place, as deputy leader in Office IV (the Gestapo) of the RSHA, which was also responsible for Jewish matters, he knew indeed better than anyone else the number of Jews who had died in other ways.

In addition to that, Eichmann was at that moment in such a state of mind as a result of the events, that he certainly had no intention of telling me something that was not true.[75]

The estimate bears out the statement of Eichmann to Dieter Wisliceny that four or possibly five million Jews had been killed in the extermination centers. The over-all total of six million is slightly less than the loss of life reported by the American Jewish Committee. This slight difference may be accounted for by the number of Jews who succeeded in escaping from Europe even after the war began.

Responsibility

The defendants, almost without exception, denied personal knowledge of the annihilation of the Jews. Even the defendant Frank, in whose administrative territory the most dreadful extermination centers—Maidanek, Auschwitz, and the Treblinka complex—were established, pretended that he did not know until 1943 or 1944 that Jews were being slaughtered there.

Funk, whose Reichsbank received the gold and jewels and other loot taken from the murdered Jews, testified that "up to the day of this trial no one told me anything, not a soul told me that Jews were being murdered in concentration camps."[76]

The Jew-baiting Streicher pleaded ignorance of the killings, although in November, 1943, he quoted verbatim in Der Stuermer an article from the Israelitisches Wochenblatt which stated that the Jews had virtually disappeared from Europe, and on which he commented, "This is not a Jewish lie."[77]

And Goering, who had given Heydrich the order to work out the program for the complete solution of the Jewish problem in Europe, denied that he had been informed what that solution ultimately was.

Yet the smallest in importance of all the defendants, the radio commentator who assisted Goebbels in anti-Jewish propaganda, Hans Fritzsche, a man who had no responsibilities for the carrying out of the program, confessed knowledge of the extermination measures put into operation after the attack upon the Soviet Union:

Question: I should like to ask you, if, as you stated here to the High Tribunal, at the beginning of 1942 you received information that in one of the regions in the Ukraine, which was at the time occupied by the Germans, an extermination of the Jews and the Ukrainian intelligentsia was being prepared, simply because they were Jews and members of the Ukrainian intelligentsia? Did you receive such information? Is that correct?

Answer: That is correct.[78]

But Fritzsche could not believe that the ordinary people of Germany really knew, or believed, that the Jews of Europe were mass-exterminated:

> If the German people had learned of these mass murders, they would certainly no longer have supported Hitler. They would probably have sacrificed five million for a victory, but never would the German people have wished to bring about victory by the murder of five million people.
>
> I should like to state further that this murder decree of Hitler's seems to me the end of every race theory, every race philosophy, every kind of race propaganda, for after this catastrophe any further advocacy of race theory would be equivalent to approval in theory of further murder. An ideology in the name of which five million people were murdered is a theory which cannot continue to exist.[79]

One of the most striking features of this crime, as disclosed by the evidence, is that it was perpetrated by an amazingly small number of Nazi police officials and SS guards. As far as the German people themselves were concerned, the secret was very well kept. Lutheran Bishop Hanns Lilje, who was a foe of Hitler, wrote: "When occasionally we had heard stories of this kind during the Nazi days, they seemed so incredible that even the most implacable German enemies of the Nazis refused to believe them."[80]

This, then, was the end of Hitlerian anti-Semitism. It began with prejudice; it was inflamed by propaganda; it led to persecution; and it resulted in mass murder. Adolf Hitler added "genocide" to language, and with it he introduced to law a new concept of "crimes against humanity."

CHAPTER 25

The Murder Marts

IN PERFECTING the totalitarian Third Reich, Hitler had first of all to dispense with the rights of the people under the law. The Bill of Rights of the Weimar Constitution was repealed, and a system of "protective custody" was inaugurated, which gave the political police power to imprison without trial. Since people could be confined in state prisons only upon order of court, it became necessary to create special prisons for those who were taken into protective custody by the police. These special prisons were the concentration camps.

In the beginning the concentration camps were prisons for the confinement of political prisoners. Goering established the first concentration camps under the control of the Gestapo, and said of them: "Therefore the concentration camps have been created, where we have first confined thousands of Communist and Socialist Democratic functionaries."[1] Dachau, Oranienburg, and Buchenwald were among the first concentration camps in Hitler's Germany.

The ever mounting persecution of the Jews and other minorities in the Hitler police state led to a demand for increased space for political prisoners. In the anti-Jewish pogrom of 1938, twenty thousand Jews were taken into protective custody and confined in Gestapo jails, or sent to concentration camps, particularly Dachau. Concentration camps were guarded by SS-units known as Totenkopf Verbaende—the Death's Head Battalions.

At the outbreak of the war, Oranienburg had been converted to an administrative headquarters, and the principal concentration camps were Dachau, Sachsenhausen, Buchenwald, Mauthausen, Flossenbuerg, and Ravensbrueck, where escaped prisoners of war, or Jews, or persecutees from the occupied territories could be confined. And as the need for more concentration camps increased, so, by a strange turn of events, did the need for more inmates arise.

Concentration Camp Labor

The cheapest labor is slave labor, and Himmler was soon called upon to furnish slaves from the concentration camps to work in the Reich armament industries. To provide this labor he ordered the Gestapo to round up thousands of persons for incarceration in concentration camps, not because they had committed crimes, but simply because he needed more workers in the satellite labor camps which he established around the concentration camps.

In a report to Himmler on April 30, 1942, SS Obergruppenfuehrer Pohl, who was in charge of the administration of the concentration camps, noted that while at the outbreak of the war there were only six concentration camps, in the years 1940 to 1942 nine more camps had been established: Auschwitz, Neuengamme, Gusen, Natzweiler, Gross-Rosen, Lublin, Niederhagen, Stutthof, and Arbeitsdorf.

Pohl observed that the war had brought about a marked change in the structure of the concentration camps and the employment of prisoners. "The custody of prisoners for the sole reasons of security, education, or as a preventive measure is no longer the main consideration.... The mobilization of all prisoner labor for purposes of the war (increase of armament) now, and for purposes of construction in the forthcoming peace, is coming more and more to the foreground."[2]

Attached to the report was an order which Pohl had issued on the same date to the commanders of the several concentration camps. The order stated that camp commanders were alone responsible for the employment of labor.

This utilization must be, in the true meaning of the word, complete, in order to obtain the greatest measure of performance.... There is no limit to working hours. Their duration depends upon the kind of working establishments.... Any circumstances which may result in a shortening of working hours (for example, meals, roll-calls, et cetera), have therefore to be restricted to an irreducible minimum. Time-wasting walks and noon intervals, except for the purpose of taking meals, are forbidden.[3]

It was openly contemplated that concentration camp inmates would work as slaves until they died. This principle was expressed in a memorandum of Minister of Justice Thierack, dated September 18, 1942, in which he commented upon a conference with Himmler:

Transfers of asocial elements from prisons to the Reichsfuehrer SS are to be made for extermination through work. To be transferred without exception are persons under protective arrest, Jews, Gypsies, Russians and Ukrainians, Poles with more than 3-year sentences, Czechs, and Germans with more than 8-year sentences, according to the decision of the Reich Minister for Justice. First of all the worst asocial elements amongst those just mentioned are to be handed over. I shall inform the Fuehrer of this through Reichsleiter Bormann.[4]

A few days after this meeting between Thierack and Himmler, Speer conferred with Hitler on the methods by which concentration camp labor could be most effectively exploited. This conference extended over September 20, 21, and 22. Speer's notes stated:

The Fuehrer agrees to my proposal that the numerous factories set up outside towns for reasons of air raid protection should release their workers to supplement the second shift in town factories and should in turn be supplied with labor from the concentration camps—also two shifts.

I pointed out to the Fuehrer the difficulties which I expect to encounter if Reichsfuehrer SS Himmler should be able, as he requests, to exercise authoritative influence over these factories. The Fuehrer, too, does not consider such an influence necessary.

The Fuehrer, however, agrees that Reichsfuehrer SS Himmler should derive advantage from making his prisoners available; he should get equipment for his division.

I suggested giving him a share in kind (war equipment) in ratio to the man hours contributed by his prisoners. A three to five per cent share is being discussed, the equipment also being calculated according to man hours. The Fuehrer would agree to such a solution.[5]

An agreement having been made under which Himmler could obtain special weapons for his Armed SS, he immediately began a recruitment campaign to increase the number of concentration camp inmates. On December 17, 1942, the chief of the Gestapo notified the regional offices that Himmler had given an order that at least thirty-five thousand persons who were fit for work had to be put into concentration camps not later than the end of January. The order further provided that the Eastern or foreign workers who had escaped or had broken labor contracts were to be sent to the nearest concentration camp as quickly as possible, and that inmates of detention rooms and educational work camps who were fit for work should be transferred to concentration camps.

The chief of the Gestapo issued a supplementary directive on March 23, 1943, in which he stated that these measures were to be carried out until April 30, 1943. He added: "Care has to be taken that only prisoners who are fit for work are sent to concentration camps, and adolescents only in accordance with the provisions issued; otherwise, contrary to the purpose, the concentration camps become overburdened."[6] On June 25, 1943, the chief of the Gestapo reported that the objectives of these decrees had been satisfactorily attained.

The Reich Minister of Justice instructed public prosecutors on April 21, 1943, that all Jews who were released from prison were to be handed over to the Gestapo for imprisonment in the concentration camps at Auschwitz and Lublin for the rest of their lives. Poles released after an imprisonment of over six months were to be transferred for imprisonment in a concentration camp for the duration of the war.

On February 14, 1944, Goering sent a teletype to Himmler in which he asked that concentration camp prisoners be turned over to him for aircraft production:

At the same time I ask you to put at my disposal as great a number of KZ [concentration camp] convicts as possible for air armament, as this kind of manpower proved to be very useful according to previous experience. The situation of the air war makes subterranean transfer of industry necessary. For work of this kind KZ convicts can be especially well concentrated at work and in the camp.[7]

In a conference of December 11, 1944, Doenitz said: "Furthermore, I propose reinforcing of the ship-yard crews by prisoners from the concentration camps.... Twelve thousand concentration camp prisoners will be employed in the shipyards as additional man-power...."[8]

The exploitation of the inmates was not confined to the labor of their hands. They were even used to grow hair for the German economy. An order of August 6, 1942, to the thirteen principal concentration camps provided:

The chief of the SS Economic and Administrative Main Office, SS Obergruppenfuehrer Pohl, on the basis of a report submitted to him, has ordered that all human hair cut in concentration camps be appropriately utilized. Human hair is to be used for the manufacture of industrial felt and to be spun into yarn. Out of combed and cut hair of women, hair-yarn socks for U-boat crews are to be made, as well as hair felt stockings for employees of the Reich railways.

Therefore, I order that the hair of women prisoners after due disinfection be collected. Cut hair of male prisoners can only be utilized beginning with a length of at least twenty millimeters....[9]

Working conditions for concentration camp laborers were very severe. A report of an investigator of the War Crimes Branch, Judge Advocate Section, Third United States Army, into conditions at Flossenbuerg stated:

The work at these camps mainly consisted of underground labor, the purpose being the construction of large underground factories, storage rooms, *et cetera*. This labor was performed completely underground and as a result of the brutal treatment, working and living conditions, a daily average of 100 prisoners died. To the one camp Oberstaubling 700 prisoners were transported in February 1945, and on the 15 April 1945 only 405 of these men were living. During the twelve months preceding the liberation, Flossenburg and the branch camps under its control accounted for the death of 14,739 male inmates and 1,300 women.... Flossenburg concentration camp can best be described as a factory dealing in death.[10]

Thousands of persons died in the course of transit to the concentration camps. The witness Franz Blaha testified that out of a single transport of two thousand persons brought from Compiègne, eight hundred died on the way and were disposed of, and upon arrival after twelve days more than five hundred were dead on the train:

> The deaths were caused by the fact that too many people were packed into the cars, which were then locked, and that they did not get anything to eat or drink for several days. Usually they starved or suffocated. Many of those who survived were brought to the camp hospital, and of these a large number died from various complications and diseases.[11]

The witness Lampe described his personal experience in a convoy of French prisoners deported to Mauthausen:

> I was arrested on 8 November 1941. After two years and a half of internment in France, I was deported on 22 March 1944 to Mauthausen in Austria. The journey lasted three days and three nights under particularly vile conditions—104 deportees in a cattle truck without air. I do not believe that it is necessary to give all the details of this journey, but one can well imagine the state in which we arrived at Mauthausen on the morning of the 25th of March 1944, in weather 12 degrees below zero. I mention, however, that from the French border we traveled in the trucks, naked.[12]

The witness DuPont described precisely the same conditions in transports of prisoners to Buchenwald:

> In other cases the extermination was carried out by progressive stages. It had already begun when the convoy arrived. For instance, in the French convoy which left Compiègne on 24 January 1944 and arrived on 26 January, I saw one van containing 100 persons, of which 12 were dead and 8 insane. During the period of my deportation I saw numerous transports come in. The same thing happened every time; only the numbers varied. In this way the elimination of a certain proportion had already been achieved when the convoy arrived.[13]

The commandant of Mauthausen, Franz Ziereis, said in his dying statement that thousands of prisoners died while en route to Mauthausen. He spoke of an order of Himmler under which 60,000 Jews employed in border fortifications were to be sent on foot to Mauthausen. Only a small fraction of the number actually arrived. "As an example I mention that out of one convoy of 4,500

Jews which started out from somewhere in the country, only 180 arrived. . . . Women and children had been without shoes and were in rags and were very verminous. In that convoy were complete families of which due to weakness an immense number had been shot on the way."[14]

All this was preliminary to murder in the camps. And the prelude to that was the state-directed extermination of the sick and feeble.

Euthanasia

Shortly after the beginning of the war, Hitler instituted a program of euthanasia, under which the insane, feeble-minded, and epileptic inmates of hospitals were taken to institutions where they were killed and their bodies cremated. While this crime was directed primarily against Germans, a U.S. Military Commission at Wiesbaden found that more than four hundred Poles and Russians were exterminated at one of these places, Hadamar castle, during the period from about July 1, 1944, to April 1, 1945. The practice became widely known and caused considerable uneasiness among the German populace.

On July 19, 1940, for example, the Provincial Bishop of the Wuerttemberg Evangelical Provincial Church complained of the action in a letter to Reich Minister of the Interior Frick:

> For some months past, insane, feeble-minded and epileptic patients of state and private medical establishments have been transferred to another institution on the orders of the Reich Defense Council. Their relatives, even when the patient was kept at their cost, are not informed of the transfer until after it has taken place. Mostly they are informed a few weeks later that the patient concerned had died of an illness, and that, owing to the danger of infection, the body had had to be cremated. On a superficial estimate several hundred patients from institutions in Wuerttemberg alone must have met their death in this way, among them war-wounded of the Great War.
>
> Owing to numerous inquiries from town and country and from the most variegated circles, I consider it my duty to point out to the Reich Government that this affair is causing a particular stir in our small province. Firstly because one of the institutions concerned, Grafeneck

DAYS OF TRIUMPH . . .

MAUTHAUSEN CONCENTRATION CAMP—Reichsfuehrer SS Heinrich Himmler;
Franz Ziereis, camp commander; and Ernst Kaltenbrunner, chief of the
Reich Main Security Office, standing together in quarry.

JEWS MARCHING UNDER GUARD from the burning Warsaw Ghetto to the
"transit camp" from which they were taken to the extermination center at Treblinka.
"The terror of death showed in their faces."

CARNAGE—Bodies in concentration camp piled up
preparatory to cremation in furnaces.

A CREMATING OVEN used in the small Struthof concentration camp, France.

DEFENDANTS—Hermann Goering, Erich Raeder, Baldur von Schirach.

KARL DOENITZ—Chief of the German Navy, named by Adolf Hitler
as his successor in the last hours of the war.

DEFENDANTS—Rudolf Hess and Joachim von Ribbentrop in front row. Behind them, a German defense counsel, and Karl Doenitz, Erich Raeder, and Baldur von Schirach.

DEFENDANTS—Wilhelm Keitel, Fritz Sauckel, Alfred Rosenberg.

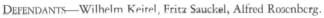

DEFENDANTS—Hjalmar Schacht, center, looks toward Von Neurath. Next to Von Neurath with his arms on the bench is Fritzsche. Seated beside Schacht is Walter Funk.

DEFENDANTS—Alfred Jodl, Hans Frank, Alfred Rosenberg.

MR. JUSTICE JACKSON assisted by the author, right, during the cross-examination
of Hermann Goering. Between them is Mrs. Elsie L. Douglas,
secretary to Mr. Justice Jackson.

JOACHIM VON RIBBENTROP—Foreign Minister of Hitler's Germany.

DEFENDANTS—Wilhelm Frick, Arthur Seyss-Inquart, Albert Speer.

JULIUS STREICHER—Chief propagandist of anti-Semitism in Hitler's Germany.

ERNST KALTENBRUNNER—The author presented the case against this defendant who, under Heinrich Himmler, was in charge of the principal repressive agencies of the Nazi government—the Gestapo and the SD.

Hermann Goering, left, under examination by his counsel, Dr. Otto Stahmer, at lawyers' lectern, lower right corner.

Franz von Papen, Hjalmar Schacht and Hans Fritsche immediately after acquittal by the Tribunal.

"Heil Hitler! Now I go to God, Purim Festival 1946. And now to God. The Bolshevists will one day hang you. I am now by God my father. Adele, my dear wife."

"I served the German people and my Fatherland with willing heart. I did my duty according to its laws. I am sorry that in her trying hour she was not led only by soldiers. I regret that crimes were committed in which I had no part. Good luck Germany."

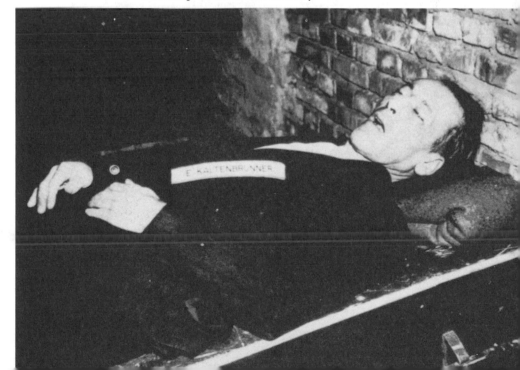

ONLY GOERING . . .

CHEATED THE HANGMAN

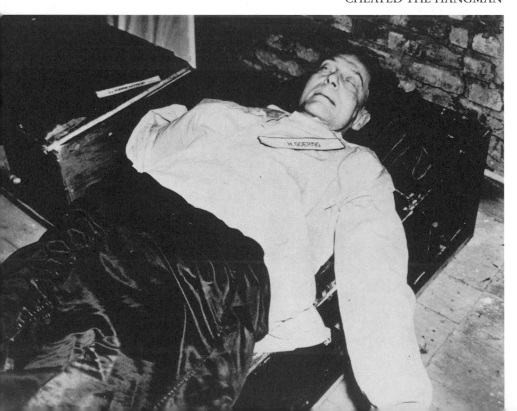

castle, to which the patients are delivered and where a crematorium and registrar's office have been set up, is in Wuerttemberg.... The castle lies on a height on the Swabian Alb in a sparsely populated forest district. With all the more attention does the population of the surrounding area follow the events that take place there. The transports of sick persons who are unloaded at the small railway station of Marbach a.L., the buses with opaque windows which bring sick persons from more distant railway stations or directly from the institutions, the smoke which rises from the crematorium and which can be noticed even from a considerable distance—all this gives all the more rise to speculation as no one is allowed into the castle.... The *manner* of action is already sharply criticized in these circles; there is much talk, in particular, of deceptions which occur in this connection. Everybody is convinced that the causes of deaths which are published officially are selected at random. When, to crown everything, regret is expressed in the obituary notice that all endeavors to preserve the patient's life were in vain, this is felt as a mockery. But it is, above all, the air of mystery which gives rise to the thought that something is happening that is contrary to justice and ethics and cannot therefore be defended by the Government with full publicity like other necessary and severe war measures. This point is continually stressed—by simple people as well—in numerous written and oral statements which come to us. It also appears that very little care was taken, at first at any rate, in the selection of the patients destined for annihilation. They did not limit themselves to insane persons, but included also persons capable of work, especially among the epileptics....

I can imagine, Mr. Minister, that this protest will be regarded as embarrassing. Hardly dare I express the hope, either, that my voice will be heard. If, nevertheless, I have made this declaration, I have done so primarily because the relations of the compatriots affected expect such action from the leaders of a church. I am also, however, moved by the thought that this action may perhaps give rise to a serious examination and to the abandonment of this path. *Dixi et salvari animam meam!*[15]

The Bishop's complaint fell upon deaf ears. On September 5, 1940, he again wrote to Interior Minister Frick:

On the 19th of July I sent you a letter about the systematic extermination of lunatics, feeble-minded and epileptic persons. Since then this practice has reached tremendous proportions; recently the inmates of old-age homes have also been included. The basis for this practice seems to be the opinion that in an efficient nation there should be no room for weak and frail people. It is evident from the many reports which we are receiving that the people's feelings are being badly hurt by the measures ordered and that a feeling of legal insecurity is spreading which is regrettable from the point of view of national and state interests. If the leadership of the state is convinced that it is a question of an inevitable war measure, why does it not issue a decree with legal force, which would at least have this good point that official quarters would not have to seek refuge in lies? But if—as can be assumed with certainty—Germany is in a position to feed these members of the nation as well, why then these rigorous steps? Is it necessary that the German nation should be the first civilized nation to return, in the treatment of weak people, to the habits of primitive races? Does the Fuehrer know about this matter? Has he approved it? I beg you not to leave me without a reply in this tremendously serious matter.[16]

On the following day, September 6, 1940, the supervisor of the sanatorium for mental patients and epileptics at Stettin expressed like concern about these killings in a letter to the Reich Minister of Justice:

The measures which are at present being applied to mental patients of all kinds have led to the rise of a feeling of absolute legal insecurity among wide circles of the population. Such patients are transferred from the institutions, without obtaining the consent of their relations or guardians, to other institutions from which after a short time the notification follows that the persons concerned have died of some kind of disease. In view of the multitude of death notifications, the people are convinced that these patients are done away with....

Because of the absolute secrecy and impenetrability in which these measures are carried out, not only the wildest rumours arise among the people (for instance, that people who cannot work because of old age or wounds received in the Great War, have been done away with or are also to be done away with), but also they get the impression that the selection of the persons affected by this measure is done in a completely arbitrary manner.

If the State really wants to carry out the extermination of these patients or certain kinds of mental diseases, should not a clear law—openly accounted for to the people—be published, a law which would give every single person the guarantee of a careful examination of his liability to die or right to live, and would also give relatives the chance to be heard, as in the case of the law for the prevention of the transmission of hereditary diseases?

With regard to the other patients entrusted to our institutions, I urgently beg you to do all you can to get the execution of these measures suspended, at least until a clear legal position has been created.[17]

To these earnest complaints, there was no reported reply. And the dreadful practice continued. On August 13, 1941, the Bishop of Limburg also wrote to the Reich Minister of Justice:

About 8 kilometers from Limburg, in the little town of Hadamar, on a hill overlooking the town, there is an institution which had formerly served various purposes and of late had been used as a nursing home; this institution was renovated and furnished as a place in which, by consensus of opinion, the above mentioned euthanasia has been systematically practiced for months—approximately since February 1941. The fact has become known beyond the administrative district of Wiesbaden, because death certificates from a Registry Hadamar-Moenchberg are sent to the home communities. (Moenchberg is the name of this institution because it was a Franciscan monastery prior to its secularization in 1803.)

Several times a week buses arrive in Hadamar with a considerable number of such victims. School children of the vicinity know this vehicle and say: "There comes the murder-box again." After the arrival of the vehicle, the citizens of Hadamar watch the smoke rise out of the chimney and are tortured with the ever-present thought of the miserable victims, especially when repulsive odors annoy them, depending on the direction of the wind.

The effect of the principles at work here are: Children call each other names and say, "You're crazy; you'll be sent to the baking oven in Hadamar." Those who do not want to marry, or find no opportunity, say, "Marry, never! Bring children into the world so they can be put into the bottling machine!" You hear old folks say, "Don't send me to a state hospital! After the feeble-minded have been finished off, the next useless eaters whose turn will come are the old people."

All God-fearing men consider this destruction of helpless beings as crass injustice. And if anybody says that Germany cannot win the war, if there is yet a just God, these expressions are not the result of a lack of love of fatherland but of a deep concern for our people. The population cannot grasp that systematic actions are carried out which in accordance with Par. 211 of the German criminal code are punishable with death! High authority as a moral concept has suffered a severe shock as a result of these happenings. The official notice that N. N. had died of a contagious disease and that for that reason his body has to be burned, no longer finds credence, and such official notices which are no longer believed have further undermined the ethical value of the concept of authority.

Officials of the Secret State Police, it is said, are trying to suppress discussion of the Hadamar occurrences by means of severe threats. In the interest of public peace, this may be well intended. But the knowledge and the conviction and the indignation of the population cannot be changed by it; the conviction will be increased with the bitter realization that discussion is prohibited with threats but that the actions themselves are not prosecuted under penal law.

Facta loquuntur.

I beg you most humbly, Herr Reich Minister, in the sense of the report of the Episcopate of July 16 of this year, to prevent further transgressions of the Fifth Commandment of God.[18]

Such pleas were unavailing, and the actions continued against Germans who were considered to be "useless eaters." The man who instituted the methods of killing in furtherance of the euthanasia program was Kriminalkommissar Wirth. When it was decided to erect extermination centers in the East this man was first selected, on the basis of his experience in euthanasia, to undertake that task.

Mass Murder

The world was horrified, at the end of the war, to discover that in almost every major concentration camp overrun by Allied forces in Germany there were thousands of dead and dying inmates, and to learn from the stark evidence at hand that these institutions had been used for mass killings. Gas chambers and crematoria were visible proof of these terrible deeds.

The concentration camps in Germany were not, however, primarily for extermination. They had been established originally as detention centers. During the war they became slave labor camps. The heavy attrition in human lives was due mainly to excessive labor requirements, poor and inadequate food, and disease. The deliberate taking of life was incidental to these other purposes of the camps. Of course, in some, such as Mauthausen, special killing functions were performed. There, for example, Soviet prisoners of war were murdered under the Bullet Decree. And in all the larger concentration camps in Germany killings of inmates went on constantly and for a variety of reasons, principally the inability of inmates to continue effective work.

A witness called on behalf of the SS, Georg Konrad Morgen,

testified that he had been detailed by Himmler to investigate charges of corruption in concentration camps. In the course of his investigations he made personal inspections of several camps. His favorable impression of most of them was illustrated by his description of Buchenwald.

> The installations of the camp were in good order, especially the hospital. The camp authorities, under Commander Diester, aimed at providing the prisoners with an existence worthy of human beings. They had regular mail service. They had variety shows, motion pictures, sporting contests and even had a brothel. Nearly all the other concentration camps were similar to Buchenwald.[19]

But even Morgen became aware of the fact that killings were commonplace:

> The prisoners were taken to a secret place and were killed there, mostly in a cell of the camp prison, and sick reports and death certificates were prepared for the files. They were made out so cleverly that any unprejudiced reader of the documents would get the impression that the prisoner concerned had actually been treated and had died of the serious illness which was indicated.[20]

The Death's Head Battalions, which guarded the concentration camps, had the absolute power of life and death over inmates. Murdered prisoners could always be reported as "shot while trying to escape." Various killings were described by Morgen:

> The procedure was very simple. The prisoners in question were called, without being given reasons, and had to report at the gate of the camp. That was nothing striking, because almost every hour prisoners were picked up there for questioning, for removal to other camps, and so forth. These prisoners, without the other prisoners becoming aware of it, came to the so-called Kommandantur prison, which was outside the camp. There they were held for a few days, often one or two weeks, and then the jailer had them killed, mostly in the form of a sham inoculation; actually, they were given an injection of phenol into the arteries.
> Another possibility of secret killing was the occasional transfer to the hospital. The doctor simply stated that a man needed treatment. He brings him in and after some time he puts him into a single room and

kills him there. In all these cases the record showed that the prisoner died of such and such a normal illness.

Another case: The prisoner was assigned to a detail of hard work, generally the so-called "quarry detail." The Kapo of this detail is given a hint and makes the life of the prisoner more and more unbearable by making him work incessantly and vexing him in every respect. Then the day arrives when the prisoner loses patience and in order to escape this torture, breaks through the cordon of sentries, whereupon the guard, whether he wants to or not, has to shoot him.

These different forms of killing varied from case to case. By that very fact they were outwardly unrecognizable, because they took place in secret places by various methods at various times.[21]

The facts were, of course, that the inmates of all concentration camps knew very well that killings took place. And camps having gas chambers, such as Mauthausen and Dachau, were notorious for exterminations.

The practice of concealing murders of concentration camp inmates, as testified by SS witness Morgen, was corroborated by one of the most amazing documents placed in evidence—a set of books in which deaths at Mauthausen concentration camp were systematically recorded. Each book had on its cover the words "Totenbuch [Death Book]—Mauthausen." These books, which covered a five-year period, contained entries of 35,318 deaths, exclusive of prisoners of war. The ledgers were a confession of murder. For example, on March 19, 1945, the names of 203 persons were entered as having died between 1:15 A.M. and 2:00 P.M. All persons were recorded as expiring from the same disease—heart trouble. They died at close intervals. And they all passed away in alphabetical order. The first man who died was named Ackerman, and the last who died was Zynger. Killings of prisoners of war were similarly entered in separate death books.

In some cases prisoners of war were actually and literally worked to death. The witness Boix described the mistreatment of Soviet war prisoners who were brought to Mauthausen concentration camp. For a few weeks they were merely deprived of sufficient clothing and food. "Then began the process of elimination. They were made to work under the most horrible conditions; they were beaten, hit, kicked, insulted; and out of the 7,000 Russian prisoners of war who came from almost everywhere, only 30 survivors were left at the end of three months."[22]

The witness Lampe, who was an inmate of Mauthausen, testified that upon the arrival of a convoy of 1,200 Frenchmen, of whom he was one, the SS officer who received them into the camp stated: "Germany needs your arms. You are, therefore, going to work; but I want to tell you that you will never see your families again. When one enters this camp, one leaves it by the chimney of the crematorium."[23]

Conditions in the concentration camps in Germany were bad enough. But it was in Poland that the frightful centers for mass killing were established by order of Reichsfuehrer SS Himmler. Poland was a dumping ground for the unwanted peoples of the Reich and the various occupied territories. It was here that the horrible destruction of the Jewish people of Europe largely took place. Poland itself had a large Jewish population, and these people were among the first to be destroyed. Then came the shipments of Jews from France, and Belgium, and Holland, and Germany, and Hungary—frequently via other concentration camps. Russian Jews were killed principally in the field by Special Task Forces of the Gestapo and the SD. But those who were shipped to Poland were exterminated in the gas chambers.

The concentration camp system in Poland consisted of transit and labor camps, concentration camps, and extermination centers. There were eighteen transit camps and evacuation centers and 435 labor camps, nearly one hundred of which had over a thousand workers each. The inmates were used principally in the building of fortifications and roads. Labor was likewise the principal commodity in the four major concentration camps: (1) Maidanek, near Lublin in the southeast, (2) Auschwitz, near Cracow in the south; (3) Gross-Rosen, near Breslau in the west; and (4) Stutthof, near Danzig in the north.

These concentration camps were complex institutions, consisting of numerous branch camps. Auschwitz had forty-four and Stutthof thirty supplementary labor camps. Three of the concentration camps, Maidanek, Auschwitz, and Stutthof, were likewise extermination centers. Only Gross-Rosen was exclusively a concentration camp.

In addition to the three extermination centers united with concentration camps, there were in Poland four extermination centers which were used solely for mass murder: (1) Belzec, in the southeast; (2) Sobibor, in the east; (3) Treblinka, in the northeast; and (4) Chelmno, in the west central.

Most of the prisoners brought to the extermination camps were killed at once. Small working parties of inmates were used to sort the clothing and personal effects of the victims and to attend to the details of the mass exterminations. Killings were usually carried out in gas chambers using cyclon (hydrogen cyanide, HCN or HCy) or carbon monoxide (CO). In the beginning corpses were buried in mass graves, but afterward the bodies were burned in crematoria or upon platforms in the open. Mass exhumations were conducted in the spring of 1943, and previously buried corpses were burned so as to eliminate evidence of the crimes. Hundreds of thousands of persons were killed in each of the extermination centers. All property confiscated from the victims was sent regularly to Germany. This property included clothing, jewels, money, gold (removed from teeth of the dead), and human hair. At Belzec, Sobibor, and Treblinka only Jews were murdered. At Chelmno, other nationalities were also exterminated, particularly Poles and Russians.

According to the SS witness Morgen, the head of the four extermination centers in Poland was the same Kriminalkommissar Wirth who had set up the euthanasia establishments in Germany. Morgen testified to the killing methods used in these camps as they had been described to him by Wirth:

Wirth said that he had four extermination camps and that about 5,000 Jews were working at the extermination of Jews and the seizure of Jewish property.... Then I asked Wirth how he killed Jews with these Jewish agents of his. Wirth described the whole procedure that went off like a film every time. The extermination camps were in the east of the Government General, in big forests or uninhabited wastelands. They were built up like a Potemkin village. The people arriving there had the impression of entering a city or a township. The train drove into a dummy railroad station. After the escorts and the train personnel had left the area, the cars were opened and the Jews got out.

They were surrounded by these Jewish labor detachments, and Kriminal-kommissar Wirth or one of his representatives made a speech. He said, "Jews, you were brought here to be resettled, but before we organize this future Jewish State, you must of course learn how to work. You must learn a new trade. You will be taught that here. Our routine here is, first everyone must take off his clothes so that your clothing can be disinfected, and you can have a bath so that no epidemics will be brought into the camp."

After he had found such calming words for his victims, they started on the road to death. Men and women were separated. At the first place, one had to deliver the hat; at the next one, the coat, collar, shirt, down to the shoes and socks. These places were faked cloak rooms, and the person was given a check at each one so that the people believed that they would get their things back. The other Jews had to receive the things and hurry up the new arrivals so that they should not have time to think. The whole thing was like an assembly line. After the last stop they reached a big room, and were told that this was the bath. When the last one was in, the doors were shut and the gas was let into the room.

As soon as death had set in, the ventilators were started. When the air could be breathed again, the doors were opened, and the Jewish workers removed the bodies. By means of a special procedure which Wirth had invented, they were burned in the open air without the use of fuel....

When Wirth took over the extermination of the Jews, he was already a specialist in mass-destruction of human beings. He had previously carried out the task of getting rid of the incurably insane. By order of the Fuehrer himself, whose order was transmitted through the Chancellery of the Fuehrer, he had, at the beginning of the war, set up a detachment for this purpose, probably composed of a few officials of his, as I believe, the remainder being agents and spies of the Criminal Police.

Wirth very vividly described how he went about carrying out this assignment. He received no aid, no instructions, but had to do it all by himself. He was only given an old empty building in Brandenburg. There he made his first experiments. After much consideration and many individual experiments, he evolved his later system, and then this system was used on a large scale to exterminate the insane.

A commission of doctors previously investigated the files, and those insane who were listed by the asylums as incurable were put on a separate list. Then the asylum concerned was told one day to send these patients to another institution. From this asylum the patient was transferred again, often more than once. Finally he came to Wirth's institution, where he was killed by gas and cremated.

This system, which deceived the asylums and made them unknowing accomplices, enabled him with very few assistants to exterminate large numbers of people, and this system Wirth now employed with a few alterations and improvements for the extermination of Jews. He was also given the assignment by the Fuehrer's Chancellery to exterminate the Jews....

At first Wirth's description seemed completely fantastic to me, but in Lublin I saw one of his camps. It was a camp which collected the property or part of the property of his victims. From the piles of things —there were an enormous number of watches piled up—I had to realize that something frightful was going on here. I was shown the valuables. I can say that I never saw so much money at one time, especially foreign money—all kinds of coins, from all over the world. In addition, there was a gold-smelting furnace and really prodigious bars of gold.[24]

While objectives were of course the same, according to Polish reports methods used varied somewhat in the several installations.

Chelmno.[25] The extermination camp at Chelmno was established primarily for the liquidation of the Jewish population of Lodz, situated some thirty-seven and a half miles away. In 1939 Lodz, the second largest city of Poland, had a Jewish population of 202,000. Jews from other Polish cities, and even from outside Poland, were exterminated at Chelmno, the total number killed amounting to about 340,000.

The Chelmno camp was established in November, 1941, and the extermination of victims began on December 8 and continued until April 9, 1943. Thereafter, relatively few persons were killed at the camp until its final closing in January, 1945.

The Chelmno victims were all under the impression that they were being transferred for work in the eastern territories. They were removed from the train at Zawadki, a village about a mile and a quarter from Chelmno. They remained in Zawadki overnight. The next morning three lorries came for them, from 100 to 150 being taken in each load. The lorries proceeded to the extermination building. The victims were unloaded and told that they were going to work in the East but that first they must bathe and have their clothes disinfected. They undressed in the main building and then followed the signs along a corridor pointing "to the bath." When they came to the front door of the building they were told to get into a closed car which would take them to the bathhouse.

The car was in fact a gas wagon. As soon as the victims had been herded in, the engine was started, and the poisonous carbon monoxide entered the airtight chamber through an iron vent in the middle of the floor. A few minutes having been allowed for the asphyxiation, the van was driven to a wood about two and one-half miles away where the corpses were unloaded and disposed of.

Meanwhile the transportation lorries returned to Zawadki to bring another group. The process was continued until the entire trainload had been destroyed. Normally, a contingent of one thousand victims was disposed of by early afternoon.

Until the spring of 1942 corpses were buried in mass graves. But at that time two crematoria were built, and thereafter all corpses were burned. The entire camp was operated by a Sonderkommando of only about 150 Germans. Jewish workers were utilized to remove valuables from corpses and to burn the bodies.

Treblinka.[26] Treblinka was situated in the Polish countryside to the east of Warsaw. It was established primarily as the extermination center for Warsaw Jews. Work began on the camp in June, 1942, and the first railroad transports of victims arrived on July 23, 1942. The camp was closed in November, 1943. During that period, according to Polish estimates, about 730,000 persons, mostly Jews from Warsaw, Radom, and the central part of Poland, were exterminated at Treblinka.

The camp was surrounded by a barbed-wire fence, ten to thirteen feet high, interwoven with pine branches for purpose of disguise. The camp was divided into two sections, one for administration and the other for extermination. The latter consisted of a special killing room called the Lazarett, two buildings containing thirteen gas chambers, and pits for the burning of corpses.

This camp, too, was administered by a small staff of Germans, supplemented by Russian and Jewish prisoners. The victims arrived in trains at Treblinka. After the cars were emptied, the Jewish workers removed the baggage, and the corpses of those who had died en route. The victims were driven into the enclosure where the old, the sick, and abandoned children were separated and taken to the Lazarett. A Red Cross flag marked the entrance. A door led from the waiting room into a second area, in which there was a pit. Here the victims were killed by a shot through the back of the head.

After a small number of able-bodied men had been selected for labor in the camp, the remaining persons were required to deliver up their possessions and to disrobe for bathing. Barbers cut off the hair of the women. All were then taken to the gas chambers. In the beginning they were required to bring a coin as bath fee. Later this pretense was done away with. The street to the gas chambers was called the "Way to Heaven."[27]

Each gas chamber contained a number of small rooms with tiled floors sloping toward the outer wall. Openings in the ceilings of each room were connected to exhaust pipes coming from engines situated in adjoining buildings. As soon as a room was filled with its victims the carbon monoxide was pumped in until all were dead. The corpses were removed through a door in the outer wall. There was no crematorium, and the bodies were burned on an iron grate made of rails on concrete supports.

Auschwitz

Auschwitz was the Inferno of the Hitlerian *Commedia*. The most complete and awesome factory for murder ever designed, it surpassed in magnitude and in horror anything that Dante could imagine. In Auschwitz the same fate befell the pure and the wicked alike—the old man, the crippled woman, the tender child: all were cast into the gas chambers and burned in the furnaces.

The Nuremberg trial was nearing its close when the prosecution staff received a report that the British had captured the No. 1 murderer of the Hitler regime—Rudolf Hoess, the commandant of Auschwitz. He was brought to Nuremberg at once for questioning and during three days was interrogated by the writer. Hoess was a man of about forty-five years, short, rather heavy set, somewhat red of face, with close-cropped hair. He was quiet, unprepossessing, and fully co-operative. He had joined the Party in 1922. Shortly after, he was convicted of murder. Upon release from prison he renewed his activities in the NSDAP. In 1934 he became a member of a Death's Head Battalion of the SS and was assigned to duty as a guard in the Dachau concentration camp. From that time forward he made his career in the concentration camp system of Hitler's Germany. In 1940, he was sent to Auschwitz. It was Hoess who converted this camp into the primary extermination center of the Hitler regime. The material portions of his confession were faithfully reduced to affidavit form by the writer. The affidavit was carefully read by Hoess, both in German and in English, and was corrected by him in his own handwriting and signed.

Hoess made his confession, not in philosophical justification of what he had done, but simply as the explanation of a loyal member of the Party—a follower of Hitler and of Himmler. In 1941 he was called to Berlin to confer with Himmler. Himmler told him that a decision of the greatest importance had been reached at the highest level. That decision was to exterminate European Jewry. Himmler explained that Jews were the enemy of the German people, and that it was simply a question of survival. Either the Jews had to be destroyed or, in the end, they would destroy the Germans. Himmler explained that certain concentration camps had already been converted into extermination centers; that it had been decided to establish the greatest of them all at Auschwitz; and that he, Hoess, would be given the responsibility of constructing and operating the necessary gas chambers and crematoria. Funds would be supplied by the SS. To Hoess the order was authoritative—the explanation sufficient. In his mind, he had no alternative but to obey. He did so to the best of his ability, and his ability was such that he became the greatest killer of history. Devoid of moral principle, he reacted to the order to slaughter human beings as he would have to an order to fell trees. It was his "war task." And it was sufficient to him that someone higher in authority in the Party had given him "the order." As Hoess testified: "In view of all these doubts which I had, the only one and decisive argument was the strict order and the reason given for it by the Reichsfuehrer Himmler."[28]

This is the confession which was given to the writer by Rudolf Hoess:

I have been constantly associated with the administration of concentration camps since 1934, serving at Dachau until 1938; then as Adjutant in Sachsenhausen from 1938 to May 1, 1940, when I was appointed Commandant of Auschwitz. I commanded Auschwitz until 1 December 1943, and estimate that at least 2,500,000 victims were executed and exterminated there by gassing, and burning, and at least another half million succumbed to starvation and disease, making a total dead of about 3,000,000. This figure represents about 70 or 80 per cent of all persons sent to Auschwitz as prisoners, the remainder having been selected and used for slave labor in the concentration camp industries. Included among the executed and burned were approximately 20,000 Russian prisoners of war (previously screened out of Prisoner of War cages by the Gestapo) who were delivered at Auschwitz in Wehrmacht transports operated by regular Wehrmacht officers and men. The remainder of the total number of victims included about 100,000 German Jews, and great numbers of citizens, mostly Jewish, from Holland, France, Belgium, Poland, Hungary, Czechoslovakia, Greece, or other countries. We executed about 400,000 Hungarian Jews alone at Auschwitz in the summer of 1944....

The "final solution" of the Jewish question meant the complete extermination of all Jews in Europe. I was ordered to establish extermination facilities at Auschwitz in June 1941....I visited Treblinka to find out how they carried out their exterminations. The camp commandant at Treblinka told me that he had liquidated 80,000 in the course of one-half year. He was principally concerned with liquidating all the Jews from the Warsaw ghetto. He used monoxide gas and I did not think that his methods were very efficient. So when I set up the extermination building at Auschwitz, I used Cyklon B, which was a crystallized prussic acid which we dropped into the death chamber from a small opening. It took from three to fifteen minutes to kill the people in the death chamber depending upon climatic conditions. We knew when the people were dead because their screaming stopped. We usually waited about one-half hour before we opened the doors and removed the bodies. After the bodies were removed our special Kommandos took off the rings and extracted the gold from the teeth of the corpses.

Another improvement we made over Treblinka was that we built our gas chambers to accommodate 2,000 people at one time, whereas at Treblinka their 10 gas chambers only accommodated 200 people each. The way we selected our victims was as follows: We had two SS doctors on duty at Auschwitz to examine the incoming transports of prisoners. The prisoners would be marched by one of the doctors who would make spot decisions as they walked by. Those who were fit for work were sent into the camp. Others were sent immediately to the extermination plants. Children of tender years were invariably exterminated since by reason of their youth they were unable to work.

Still another improvement we made over Treblinka was that at Treblinka the victims almost always knew that they were to be exterminated and at Auschwitz we endeavored to fool the victims into thinking that they were to go through a delousing process. Of course, frequently they realized our true intentions and we sometimes had riots and difficulties due to that fact. Very frequently women would hide their children under the clothes but, of course, when we found them we would send the children in to be exterminated. We were required to carry out these exterminations in secrecy but, of course, the foul and nauseating stench from the continuous burning of bodies permeated the entire area and all of the people living in the surrounding communities knew that exterminations were going on at Auschwitz....[29]

After hearing Hoess confess to these facts in court, Hans Frank told prison psychologist Gilbert: "That was the low point of the entire trial—to hear a man say out of his own mouth that he exterminated 2½ million people in cold blood—that is something that people will talk about for a thousand years."[30]

Auschwitz (Oswiecim in Polish)[31] was built in the suburbs of the town of Auschwitz some 200 miles southwest of Warsaw. The camp was begun in June, 1940. At first it consisted of military barracks and buildings of the Polish Tobacco Monopoly. It was rapidly enlarged. By the end of 1941 the main camp could hold eighteen thousand prisoners, and in 1943 it accommodated thirty thousand. When the camp was evacuated on January 18, 1945, some fifty-eight thousand prisoners were removed. Five or six thousand additional sick and infirm were left for capture by the Russians.

Even before the gas chambers were established, large-scale killings took place at Auschwitz. Apart from the thousands who died of starvation, disease, and mistreatment, deaths were brought about by injections of phenol, shootings through the nape of the neck, and hanging. Extermination through gassing was first tried in the summer of 1941. About 250 hospital patients and 600 prisoners of war were herded into the coal-cellars of Block XI. The windows of the cellars were blocked with dirt, and the contents of a can of cyclon was spilled on the floor. The poison had to be twice administered before all died. Gassing methods were gradually improved until the summer of 1942, when it was decided to enlarge the facilities.

Four huge gas chambers were constructed at that time. Two of them were underground, one containing 480 square yards, and the other 250 square yards. The other two chambers, both of which were above ground, each contained 700 square yards. It was possible to pack as many as two thousand victims into a single chamber.

The gas chambers were called *Badeanstalt fuer Sonderaktion*— Baths for Special Action. Imitation bath fixtures were attached to the ceilings. Cans of cyclon were emptied through openings in the ceilings of the underground chambers and the sidewalls of the surface chambers.

As at Treblinka, upon the arrival of a trainload of prisoners, those selected for execution were marched directly to the gas chambers. Since labor was more widely used at Auschwitz, able-bodied men and women had a better chance of being sent to the labor camps. They were tattooed with a concentration camp number, given prison clothing, and assigned to barracks, from which they were sent out each day to work in the marshes or in factories established in the area. A sign, *"Arbeit Macht Frei"* (Work Makes Free), was affixed to the entrance of the base camp. Most of those assigned to labor died under the extreme conditions of semistarvation, mistreatment, and excessive work. Of the Jews brought to Auschwitz from all over Europe only about 10 per cent were given even this chance for life.

The doomed were told that they must be bathed and disinfected before being admitted into the camp. They were driven to the dressing room, marked *"Wasch und Desinfektionsraum,"* words which were repeated in their own languages. They hung their clothes on numbered pegs and were advised to remember the numbers carefully so that they could reclaim the clothing. They were then brought into the gas chamber, which had previously been heated to facilitate evaporation of the cyclon into deadly hydrogen cyanide. After the airtight doors had been closed, natural air was largely pumped out and the cyclon poured in through the special apertures. After several minutes all were dead.

In the beginning, the corpses were buried in mass graves in a near-by wood. A small crematorium, installed in 1940, proved entirely inadequate after gassing began in 1941, and eight open pits were constructed near the gas chambers. In the spring of 1943 four large crematoria were constructed with a total capacity of about twelve thousand bodies in twenty-four hours. Even these were not able to keep up with the corpses coming from the gas chambers in the summer of 1944, when great transports of Hungarian Jews and French insurgents arrived at Auschwitz. Six huge new pits were then dug in which thousands of corpses were burned each day. The costs of operating the crematoria under the conditions existing in August, 1944, when twenty-four thousand bodies had to be destroyed each day, were so great that thereafter the crematoria were abandoned and all corpses were burned in the open pits.

Horror

A French woman, Madame Vaillant-Couturier, testified to her experiences as an inmate of the women's section of Birkenau, the labor-camp at Auschwitz. She was a member of a convoy of 230 French women sent to Auschwitz on January 23, 1943. Only forty-nine of these women came back alive.

It was a terrible journey. We were 60 in a car and we were given no food or drink during the journey. At the various stopping places we asked the Lorraine soldiers of the Wehrmacht who were guarding us whether we would arrive soon; and they replied "If you knew where you are going you would not be in a hurry to get there."

We arrived at Auschwitz at dawn. The seals on our cars were broken and we were driven out by blows with the butt end of a rifle, and taken to the Birkenau Camp, a section of the Auschwitz Camp. It is situated in the middle of a great plain, which was frozen in the month of January. During this part of the journey we had to drag our luggage. As we passed through the door we knew only too well how slender our chances were that we would come out again, for we had already met columns of living skeletons going to work; and as we entered we sang "The Marseillaise" to keep up our courage.

We were led to a large shed, then to the disinfecting station. There our heads were shaved and our registration numbers were tattooed on the left forearm. Then we were taken into a large room for a steam bath and a cold shower. In spite of the fact that we were naked, all this took place in the presence of SS men and women. We were then given clothing which was soiled and torn, a cotton dress and jacket of the same material.

As all this had taken several hours, we saw from the windows of the block where we were, the camp of the men; and toward the evening an orchestra came in. It was snowing and we wondered why they were playing music. We then saw that the camp foremen were returning to the camp. Each foreman was followed by men who were carrying the dead. As they could hardly drag themselves along, every time they stumbled, they were put on their feet again by being kicked or by blows with the butt end of a rifle.[32]

Madame Vaillant-Couturier was asked whether she could describe the selection of victims for gassing at the time of the arrival of the convoys.

Yes, because when we worked at the sewing block in 1944, the block where we lived directly faced the stopping place of the trains. The system had been improved. Instead of making the selection at the place where they arrived, a side line now took the train practically right up to the gas chamber; and the stopping place about 100 meters from the gas chamber, was right opposite our block though, of course, separated from us by two rows of barbed wire. Consequently, we saw the unsealing of the cars and the soldiers letting men, women, and children out of them. We then witnessed heartrending scenes; old couples forced to part from each other, mothers made to abandon their young daughters, since the latter were sent to the camp, whereas mothers and children were sent to the gas chambers. All these people were unaware of the fate awaiting them. They were merely upset at being separated, but they did not know that they were going to their death. To render their welcome more pleasant at this time—June-July 1944—an orchestra composed of internees, all young and pretty girls dressed in little white blouses and navy blue skirts, played during the selection, at the arrival of the trains, gay tunes such as "The Merry Widow," the "Barcarolle" from "The Tales of Hoffman," and so forth. They were then informed that this was a labor camp and since they were not brought into the camp they saw only the small platform surrounded by flowering plants. Naturally, they could not realize what was in store for them. Those selected for the gas chamber, that is, the

old people, mothers, and children, were escorted to a red-brick building
... which bore the letters "Baden," that is to say "Baths." There, to begin
with, they were made to undress and given a towel before they went
into the so-called shower room. Later on, at the time of the large
convoys from Hungary, they had no more time left to play-act or to
pretend; they were brutally undressed, and I know these details as I
knew a little Jewess from France who lived with her family at the
"Republique" district....

She was called "little Marie" and she was the only one, the sole
survivor of a family of nine. Her mother and her seven brothers and
sisters had been gassed on arrival. When I met her she was employed
to undress the babies before they were taken into the gas chamber.
Once the people were undressed they took them into a room which
was somewhat like a shower room, and gas capsules were thrown
through an opening in the ceiling. An SS man would watch the effect
produced through a porthole. At the end of 5 or 7 minutes, when
the gas had completed its work, he gave the signal to open the doors;
and men with gas masks—they too were internees—went into the
room and removed the corpses. They told us that the internees must
have suffered before dying, because they were closely clinging to one
another and it was very difficult to separate them.

After that a special squad would come to pull out gold teeth and
dentures; and again, when the bodies had been reduced to ashes they
would sift them in an attempt to recover the gold.

At Auschwitz there were eight crematories, but, as from 1944,
these proved insufficient. The SS had large pits dug by the internees,
where they put branches, sprinkled with gasoline, which they set on
fire. Then they threw the corpses into the pits. From our block we
could see after about three-quarters of an hour or an hour after the
arrival of a convoy, large flames coming from the crematory, and the
sky was lighted up by the burning pits.[33]

At the beginning of 1943 all inmates were tattooed with a
number. Children born in the concentration camp were branded
with the same number as the mother. Jewish children "were immediately put to death."[34] Other children "were placed in a special
Block and after a few weeks, sometimes after a month, they were
taken away from the camp."[35]

The inmates of the concentration camps were frequently required to send postcards to their families and friends at home.

As for the Jewesses from Salonika, I remember on their arrival they were given picture postcards, bearing the post office address of "Waldsee," a place which did not exist; and a printed text to be sent to their families stating, "We are doing very well here; we have work and we are well treated. We await your arrival." I myself saw the cards in question; and...I know that whole families arrived as a result of these postcards.[36]

As to this practice SS witness Morgen testified: "Certain Jewish prisoners with connections abroad were selected and were made to write letters abroad telling how well-off they were in Auschwitz, so that the public got the impression that these well-known people were alive and could write that they were doing well."[37]

But the name "Auschwitz" came nonetheless to be known to inmates of other camps as a synonym for horror. The witness Victor du Pont, an inmate of Buchenwald, testified to the forbidding reputation of Auschwitz:

In 1944 a convoy of several hundred Gypsy children arrived at Buchenwald, by what administrative mystery we never knew. They were assembled during the winter of 1944 and were to be sent on to Auschwitz to be gassed. One of the most tragic memories of my deportation is the way in which these children, knowing perfectly well what was in store for them, were driven into the vans, screaming and crying.[38]

The Freed and the Slain

As the Allied armies pressed closer and closer upon Germany, Hitler and Himmler faced the problem of what disposition to make of the thousands of prisoners in police prisons, prisoner of war cages, and concentration camps. By all rules of international warfare and all standards of human decency they should have permitted the starving and wretched victims to remain in the camps and to be saved from death by the armies of liberation. But they were determined that all should die before any should be freed by the enemy.

On July 20, 1944, the Commander of the Gestapo and SD in the General Government issued the following order with respect to inmates of the police prisons:

Should the situation develop suddenly in such a way that it is impossible to evacuate the prisoners, the prison inmates are to be liquidated and their bodies disposed of as far as possible (burning, blowing up the building, *et cetera*). If necessary, Jews still employed in the armament industry or on other work are to be dealt with in the same way.

The liberation of prisoners or Jews by the enemy, be it the Western enemies or the Red Army, must be avoided under all circumstances. Nor may they fall into their hands alive.[39]

In the course of a situation report at Hitler's headquarters on January 27, 1945, the problem of the disposition of ten thousand air force officers imprisoned at Sagan, in eastern Poland, was discussed:

Goering: There are 10,000 captured air corps officers at Sagan; their custody is the responsibility of the Director General of Training [BDE]. Personnel for guarding or transporting them is said to be lacking. The thought has been expressed to leave the prisoners to their Soviet Allies. It would give them 10,000 flyers.

Fuehrer: Why did you not remove them earlier? This is unequalled bungling.

Goering: That's the BDE. We have nothing to do with it. I can only report it.

Fuehrer: They must go, even if they have to march afoot through the mud. The Volkssturm will be called out. Anyone who escapes, will be shot. This has to be done with all means available....

Goering: How many cattle-cars are required for 10,000 men?

Fuehrer: If we transport them according to German standards we will need at least 20 transport trains for 10,000 men. If we transport them according to Russian standards, we will need 5 or 3.[40]

Prisoners still living in the concentration camps in Poland were evacuated under conditions of extreme cruelty and suffering as the Soviet troops advanced from the east in the final months of the war. All but the seriously ill were evacuated from Auschwitz on January 18, 1945, four days before the camp was occupied by the Soviet Army. The evacuees were forced to walk. Those who were unable to keep up were shot. According to Polish reports, about fifty-eight thousand prisoners were evacuated. Some five or six thousand sick were left behind. A Pole, David Wajnapel, who escaped during the evacuation, described the plight of the inmates: "On the way, the SS escort machine-gunned exhausted prisoners and, later on, near Rybnik, the rest of the marching column. Several hundred people were killed at that time."[41]

A Norwegian, Hans Cappelen, testified to the manner in which the Gross-Rosen camp in Poland was evacuated, and the bulk of its prisoners brought to the work-camp Dora, which was part of the Buchenwald complex:

> The worst of it all was the evacuation of Gross-Rosen.... We were very feeble, all of us. We had hard work, little food, and all sorts of ill-treatment. Well, we started to walk in parties of about 2,000 to 3,000. In the party I was with, we were about 2,500 to 2,800. We heard so and so many when they took up the numbers.
>
> Well, we started to walk, and we had SS guards on each side. They were very nervous and almost like mad persons. Several were drunk. We couldn't walk fast enough, and they smashed in the heads of five who could not keep up. They said in German, "That is what happens to those who cannot walk." The others would have been treated in the same way if they had not been able to follow. We walked the best we could. We attempted to help one another, but we were all too exhausted. After walking for 6 to 8 hours, we came to a station, a railway station. It was very cold and we had only striped prison clothes on, and bad boots; but we said, "Oh, we are glad that we have come to a railway station. It is better to stand in a cow truck than to walk, in the middle of winter." It was very cold, 10 to 12 degrees below zero (centigrade). It was a long train with open cars. In Norway we call them sand cars, and we were kicked on to those cars, about 80 on each car. We had to sit together and on this car we sat for about 5 days without food, cold, and without water. When it was snowing we made like this (indicating) just to get some water into the mouth and, after a long, long time—it seemed to me years—we came to a place which I afterwards learned was Dora. That is in the neighborhood of Buchenwald.
>
> Well, we arrived there. They kicked us down from the cars, but many were dead. The man who sat next to me was dead, but I had no right to get away. I had to sit with a dead man for the last day. I didn't see the figures myself, naturally, but about one-third of us or half of us were dead, getting stiff. And they told us that one-third—I heard the figures afterwards in Dora—that the dead on our train numbered 1,447.[42]

The prisoners who survived evacuation from the east were brought to the already overcrowded camps in Germany. As the Allied forces advanced it was first decided to evacuate these camps as well. Such an order was given as to Buchenwald. But the problem of transporting and guarding the vast numbers of prisoners was so great that the order was countermanded. Instead it was agreed to remove only prominent inmates to other camps.

A Dutchman, Baron van Lamsweerde, averred that, having been arrested in 1943 while trying to cross the Spanish frontier, he was taken to Buchenwald concentration camp, and later to a camp at Rehmsdorff. At the approach of the Allied forces, the camp at Rehmsdorff was evacuated in great haste and the political prisoners were ordered removed to the Theresienstadt camp.

At first the prisoners were transported by train and in goods-vans. We arrived by train at Marienbad, where, for causes I do not know, we had a delay of about one week. The vans with the prisoners were kept standing at the station. In the course of that week Allied bombers attacked the Marienbad station and in the confusion some 1,000 prisoners escaped into the surrounding woods. Naturally the entire local service (the SS, Volkssturm, and Hitler Jugend) was set to work to recapture the escaped prisoners and practically all prisoners, who of course wore their camp clothes and could easily be recognized, were recaptured. These prisoners, about a thousand men, were led back in groups to Marienbad station and there they were killed by the SS guards by a shot in the neck. As both engines of the train had been wrecked during the air attack, the prisoners had to walk all the way from Marienbad to Theresienstadt. Many among them were unable to go so far, and fell down along the road, totally exhausted; without exception these prisoners were murdered by the guards by a shot in the neck.[43]

Another Dutchman, involved in the same evacuation, averred that out of some 2,900 men who left Rehmsdorff, only about 500 ultimately reached Theresienstadt alive. He stated that "the others were simply killed off during the transport by the so-called 'shot in the neck.' The corpses were thrown into mass graves which were filled up afterwards."[44]

Rudolf Hoess testified:

After Buchenwald had been occupied, it was reported to the Fuehrer that internees had armed themselves and were carrying out plunderings in the town of Weimar. This caused the Fuehrer to give the strictest order to Himmler to the effect that in the future no more camps were to fall into the hands of the enemy, and that no internees capable of marching would be left behind in any camp.[45]

There followed a series of erratic orders out of the Reich Main Security Office in Berlin to various camp commanders, directing liquidation of their camps and disposition of the inmates. The evacuations were made with utter disregard for human life. Rudolf Hoess testified to orders for the removal of inmates from Sachsenhausen:

The Gestapo chief, Gruppenfuehrer Mueller, called me in the evening and told me that the Reichsfuehrer had ordered that the camp at Sachsenhausen was to be evacuated at once. I pointed out to Gruppenfuehrer Mueller what that would mean. Sachsenhausen could no longer fall back on any other camp except perhaps on a few labor camps attached to the armament works that were almost filled up anyway. Most of the internees would have to be sheltered in the woods somewhere. This would mean countless thousands of deaths and, above all, it would be impossible to feed these masses of people. He promised me that he would again discuss these measures with the Reichsfuehrer. He called me back and told me that the Reichsfuehrer had refused and was demanding that the commanders carry out his orders immediately.[46]

If concentration camps had been adequately maintained to the moment of surrender great loss of life could have been avoided. Unfortunately, as the military situation deteriorated it became increasingly difficult to obtain the food and medical supplies required to support the large populations of the camps. The plight of the inmates was described by Rudolf Hoess:

The catastrophic situation at the end of the war was due to the fact that, as a result of the destruction of the railway network and the continuous bombing of the industrial plants, care for these masses—I am thinking of Auschwitz with its 140,000 internees—could no longer be assured. Improvised measures, truck columns, and everything else tried by the commanders to improve the situation were of little or no avail; it was no longer possible. The number of the sick became immense. There were next to no medical supplies; epidemics raged everywhere. Internees who were capable of work were used over and over again. By order of the Reichsfuehrer, even half-sick people had to be used wherever possible in industry. As a result, every bit of space in the concentration camps which could possibly be used for lodging was overcrowded with sick and dying prisoners.[47]

In the final days thousands of prisoners died in Dachau and the other concentration camps. Bodies could not be burned because there was neither fuel nor the personnel to operate the crematories. The quick and the dead lay side by side in the tiered barracks, the moaning of the dying and the stench of the corpses creating the mausoleums of horror discovered by the advancing armies of liberation.

Madame Vaillant-Couturier, one of the few women to survive the misery, degradation, and death of these institutions of horror, concluded her testimony in these words:

It is difficult to convey an exact idea of the concentration camps to anybody, unless one has been in the camp oneself, since one can only quote examples of horror; but it is quite impossible to convey any impression of that deadly monotony. If asked what was the worst of all, it is impossible to answer, since everything was atrocious. It is atrocious to die of hunger, to die of thirst, to be ill, to see all one's companions dying around one and being unable to help them. It is atrocious to think of one's children, of one's country which one will never see again, and there were times when we asked whether our life was not a living nightmare, so unreal did this life appear in all its horror.

For months, for years we had one wish only: The wish that some of us would escape alive, in order to tell the world what the Nazi convict prisons were like everywhere, at Auschwitz as at Ravensbrueck. And the comrades from the other camps told the same tale; there was the systematic and implacable urge to use human beings as slaves and to kill them when they could work no more.[48]

The murder marts were the result of a belief, a policy, and a method. The belief was that there is no intrinsic value to human life; the policy was that all persons who were unable to contribute positively to the material strength of the nation should be eliminated; and the method was the organized extermination of the unwanted.

Policy and method were first united in the program of euthanasia which Hitler ordered in Germany under cover of the war. The inmates of hospitals who were thought to be incurable, or unable presently or in the future to contribute through work to the strengthening of the Reich, and who were, to the extent of the food which they ate and the care which they required, a burden upon the nation, were ordered to be killed. This policy was applied to the insane, to feeble-minded, to epileptics, and even to the aged. In principle, no person was to be allowed to live in Germany who was not able to support and strengthen the nation.

The slaughter of Jews and other unwanted peoples was a simple extension of this policy. Those who could be used for labor were permitted to live in slavery. Those who were unable to work were killed.

The method by which these unwanted Jews, the intelligentsia of Poland, Soviet commissars, gypsies, and others, were exterminated was Hadamar and Grafeneck on the grand scale. Where death by injection was too time-consuming, the gas chamber was brought into operation. And where crematoria were unable to keep up with the output of corpses, bodies were consumed in great fires in open pits.

And so, to twentieth-century Christian civilization there came these monstrous instruments of extermination. They were the product of the philosophy of nihilism—of the negation of the worth of the individual—of the denial of soul—of the rejection of God.

CHAPTER 26

The Einsatz Groups

Einsatzgruppen were Special Action Groups, the function of which was bluntly and aptly described by the witness Bach-Zelewski in these words: "The principal task of the Einsatzgruppen ... was the annihilation of the Jews, gypsies and political commissars."[1] They were task forces of the Gestapo, SD, and SS, assigned to a mission of murder. Unlike their comrades in the murder marts, however, these bands carried out their executions in the field, working closely behind the German armies.

Formation of the Special Action Groups

The Special Action Groups of the Security Police and SD were first formed to follow the armies in the invasion of Poland. Their task at that time was primarily to round up Polish Jews and place them in ghettos. It was not until the invasion of the Soviet Union that the Einsatz groups engaged in organized extermination. The story of the formation and activities of these groups was first told to the writer by the witness Otto Ohlendorf.

In the course of the interrogation of Ohlendorf the writer asked him to describe in detail his activities during the war. He said that apart from one year he had served as chief of the SD. When asked what he had done during that year, he replied: "I was the chief of Einsatzgruppe D." Although this was prior to the commencement of the trial, enough information had been collected about the Special Action Groups to establish that their principal function was the killing of Jews and other racial "undesirables." The next question to Ohlendorf, therefore, was: "During the year you were chief of Einsatzgruppe D, how many men, women, and children did your group kill?" He shrugged and answered, with only the slightest hesitation: "Ninety thousand!"

Following the completion of this interrogation the writer reduced Ohlendorf's testimony to an affidavit which Ohlendorf corrected and signed, and which he confirmed under oath at the trial, just as Rudolf Hoess was to do later on. Ohlendorf had one thing in common with Rudolf Hoess—he, too, was a mass killer. But in other respects he differed markedly from the commandant of Auschwitz. Ohlendorf was the Chief of Amt III of the Reich Main Security Office. He was in charge of secret intelligence inside Germany. He had held that position, one of obvious responsibility in any police state, from its organization as a special office in the RSHA in 1939. And yet at the time he was interrogated by the writer in Nuremberg, Ohlendorf was only thirty-six years of age. Unlike Hoess, he sought no justification for his actions as Chief of Einsatzgruppe D in a plea of "superior orders." Ohlendorf explained his participation in the Nazi extermination system as essentially a basic duty connected with the improvement of the race through the elimination of unwanted peoples. He was one of those who saw an opportunity through the war to exterminate the undesirables in the European population, and thereby to strengthen the German race in Europe. It was an unpleasant task, he acknowledged, but one which had to be done. Ohlendorf felt that he had to assume his fair share of that responsibility. He was an intellectual killer.

Ohlendorf was questioned at length at the trial. He testified that the concept "Einsatzgruppe" was promulgated after a meeting between the Chiefs of the OKW and the OKH for the purpose of allowing the Security Police to have its own organizational units in the field. His testimony, under examination by Colonel John Harlan Amen, on the formation and activities of these Special Action Groups in the campaign against the Soviet Union was as follows:

Question: What position did you occupy with respect to this agreement?
Answer: From June 1941 to the death of Heydrich in June 1942,

I led Einsatzgruppe D, and was the representative of the Chief of the Sipo and the SD with the 11th Army....

Question: How much advance notice, if any, did you have of the campaign against Soviet Russia?

Answer: About 4 weeks.

Question: How many Einsatz groups were there, and who were their respective leaders?

Answer: There were four Einsatzgruppen, Groups A, B, C, and D. Chief of Einsatzgruppe A was Stahlecker; Chief of Einsatzgruppe B was Nebe; Chief of Einsatzgruppe C, Dr. Rasche, and later, Dr. Thomas; Chief of Einsatzgruppe D, I myself, and later Bierkamp....

Question: When did Group D commence its move into Soviet Russia?

Answer: Group D left Duegen on 21 June and reached Pietra Namsk in Romania in 3 days. There the first Einsatzkommandos were already being demanded by the Army, and they immediately set off for the destinations named by the Army. The entire Einsatzgruppe was put into operation at the beginning of July.

Question: You are referring to the 11th Army?

Answer: Yes.

Question: In what respects, if any, were the official duties of the Einsatzgruppe concerned with Jews and Communist commissars?

Answer: On the question of Jews and Communists, the Einsatzgruppen and the commanders of the Einsatzkommandos were orally instructed before their mission.

Question: What were their instructions with respect to the Jews and the Communist functionaries?

Answer: The instructions were that in the Russian operational areas of the Einsatzgruppen the Jews, as well as the Soviet political commissars, were to be liquidated.

Question: And when you say "liquidated" do you mean "killed"?

Answer: Yes, I mean "killed."...

Question: Do you know how many persons were liquidated by Einsatz Group D under your direction?

Answer: In the year between June 1941 to June 1942 the Einsatz-kommandos reported 90,000 people liquidated.

Question: Did that include men, women, and children?

Answer: Yes.

Question: On what do you base those figures?

Answer: On reports sent by the Einsatzkommandos to the Einsatz-gruppen.

Question: Were those reports submitted to you?

Answer: Yes....

Question: Do you know how those figures compare with the number of persons liquidated by other Einsatz groups?

Answer: The figures which I saw of other Einsatzgruppen are considerably larger....

Question: Did you personally supervise mass executions of these individuals?

Answer: I was present at two mass executions for purposes of inspection.

Question: Will you explain to the Tribunal in detail how an individual mass execution was carried out?

Answer: A local Einsatzkommando attempted to collect all the Jews in its area by registering them. This registration was performed by the Jews themselves.

Question: On what pretext, if any, were they rounded up?

Answer: On the pretext that they were to be resettled.

Question: Will you continue?

Answer: After the registration the Jews were collected at one place; and from there they were later transported to the place of execution, which was, as a rule an antitank ditch or a natural excavation. The executions were carried out in a military manner, by firing squads under command.

Question: In what way were they transported to the place of execution?

Answer: They were transported to the place of execution in trucks, always only as many as could be executed immediately. In this way it was attempted to keep the span of time from the moment in which the victims knew what was about to happen to them until the time of their actual execution as short as possible.

Question: Was that your idea?

Answer: Yes.

Question: And after they were shot what was done with their bodies?

Answer: The bodies were buried in the antitank ditch or excavation.

Question: What determination, if any, was made as to whether the persons were actually dead?

Answer: The unit leaders or the firing-squad commanders had orders to see to this and, if need be, finish them off themselves.

Question: And who would do that?

Answer: Either the unit leader himself or somebody designated by him.

Question: In what positions were the victims shot?

Answer: Standing or kneeling.

Question: What was done with the personal property and clothing of the persons executed?

Answer: All valuables were confiscated at the time of the registration or the rounding up and handed over to the Finance Ministry, either through the RSHA or directly. At first the clothing was given to the population, but in the winter of 1941-42 it was collected and disposed of by the NSV.

Question: All their personal property was registered at the time?

Answer: No, not all of it, only valuables were registered.

Question: What happened to the garments which the victims were wearing when they went to the place of execution?

Answer: They were obliged to take off their outer garments immediately before the execution.

Question: All of them?

Answer: The outer garments, yes....

Question: Was that true of not only your group but of the other Einsatz groups?

Answer: That was the order in my Einsatzgruppe. I don't know how it was done in other Einsatzgruppen.

Question: In what way did they handle it?

Answer: Some of the unit leaders did not carry out the liquidation in the military manner, but killed the victims singly by shooting them in the back of the neck.

Question: And you objected to that procedure?

Answer: I was against that procedure, yes.

Question: For what reason?

Answer: Because both for the victims and for those who carried out the executions, it was, psychologically, an immense burden to bear.[2]

Gas Vans

Ohlendorf was asked whether all victims, including the men, women, and children, were executed in the same manner.

Answer: Until the spring of 1942, yes. Then an order came from Himmler that in the future women and children were to be killed only in gas vans.

Question: How had the women and children been killed previously?

Answer: In the same way as the men—by shooting.

Question: What, if anything, was done about burying the victims after they had been executed?

Answer: The Kommandos filled the graves to efface the signs of the execution, and then labor units of the population leveled them.

Question: Referring to the gas vans which you said you received in the spring of 1942, what order did you receive with respect to the use of those vans?

Answer: These gas vans were in the future to be used for the killing of women and children.

Question: Will you explain to the Tribunal the construction of these vans and their appearance?

Answer: The actual purpose of these vans could not be seen from the outside. They looked like closed trucks, and were so constructed that at the start of the motor, gas was conducted into the van causing death in 10 to 15 minutes.

Question: Explain in detail just how one of these vans was used for an execution.

Answer: The vans were loaded with the victims and driven to the place of burial, which was usually the same as that used for the mass executions. The time needed for transportation was sufficient to insure the death of the victims.

Question: How were the victims induced to enter the vans?

Answer: They were told that they were to be transported to another locality.[3]

The functioning of the gas vans was described by the principal operator of them, SS Untersturmfuehrer Becker, in a letter to Walter Rauff, the head of the motor vehicles department of the Gestapo:

The place of execution is usually 10 to 15 kilometers away from the highway and is difficult of access because of its location; in damp or wet weather it is not accessible at all. If the persons to be executed are driven or led to that place, then they realize immediately what is going on and get restless, which is to be avoided as far as possible. There is only one way left: to load them at the collecting point and drive them to the spot.

I ordered the vans of group D to be camouflaged as housetrailers by putting one set of window shutters on each side of the small van and two on each side of the larger vans, such as one often sees on farm houses in the country. The vans became so well-known that not only the authorities but also the civilian population called the van "death van" as soon as one of the vehicles appeared. It is my opinion the van cannot be kept secret for any length of time, not even camouflaged....

I should like to take this opportunity to bring the following to your attention: Several commands have had the unloading, after the application of gas, done by their own men. I brought to the attention of the commanders of these special detachments concerned the immense psychological injury and damage to their health which that work can have for those men, even if not immediately, at least later on. The men complained to me about headaches which appeared after each unloading. Nevertheless they don't want to change the orders, because they are afraid prisoners called for that work could use an opportune moment to flee. To protect the men from such damage, I request orders to be issued accordingly. The application of gas usually is not undertaken correctly. In order to come to an end as fast as possible, the driver presses the accelerator to the fullest extent. By doing that the persons to be executed suffer death from suffocation and not death by dozing off as was planned. My directions now have proved that by correct adjustment of the levers death comes faster and the prisoners fall asleep peacefully. Distorted faces and excretions, such as could be seen before, are no longer noticed.[4]

Ohlendorf testified that he knew of Becker and Rauff, and that the Becker letter was genuine. He added that the gas vans were of various sizes, large enough to kill from fifteen to twenty-five persons at one time.

Special Actions

The Soviet member of the Tribunal, General Nikitchenko, asked the following questions of Ohlendorf:

Question: In your testimony you said that the Einsatz group had the object of annihilating the Jews and the commissars, is that correct?
Answer: Yes.
Question: And in what category did you consider the children? For what reason were the children massacred?
Answer: The order was that the Jewish population should be totally exterminated.
Question: Including the children?
Answer: Yes.
Question: Were all the Jewish children murdered?
Answer: Yes.[5]

The contention that these murders were carried out by subterfuge and without force and terror was belied by the account of two such mass murders witnessed by one Hermann Graebe, the German manager and engineer in charge of the branch office of the Solingen firm of Josef Jung in Sdolbunow, Ukraine, from September, 1941, until January, 1944. Graebe's interest in the mass executions derived from the fact that in addition to Poles, Germans, and Ukrainians, he employed Jews on the various construction projects under his supervision. He was personally acquainted with SS-Major Putz, the leader of the Security Police and SD in Rowno, who carried out the actions with the aid of SS-men and Ukrainian militia. Graebe negotiated with Major Putz for the release of about one hundred Jewish workers from the action which took place in Rowno on July 13, 1942.

On the evening of this day I drove to Rowno and posted myself with Fritz Einsporn in front of the house in the Bahnhofstrasse in which the Jewish workers of my firm slept. Shortly after 2200 the ghetto was encircled by a large SS detachment and about three times as many members of the Ukrainian militia. Then the electric arclights which had been erected in and around the ghetto were switched on. SS and militia squads of four to six men entered or at least tried to enter the house. Where the doors and windows were closed and the inhabitants did not open at the knocking, the SS-men and militia broke the windows, forced the doors with beams and crowbars, and entered the houses. The people living there were driven on to the street just as they were, regardless of whether they were dressed or in bed. Since the Jews in most cases refused to leave their houses and resisted, the SS and militia applied force. They finally succeeded, with strokes of the whip, kicks, and blows with rifle butts, in clearing the houses. The people were driven out of their houses in such haste that small children in bed had been left behind in several instances.

In the streets women cried out for their children and children for their parents. That did not prevent the SS from driving the people along the road at running pace, and hitting them, until they reached a waiting freight train. Car after car was filled, and the screaming of women and children and the cracking of whips and rifle shots resounded unceasingly. Since several families or groups had barricaded themselves in especially strong buildings and the doors could not be forced with crowbars or beams, the doors were now blown open with hand grenades. Since the ghetto was near the railroad tracks in Rowno, the younger people tried to get across the tracks and over a small river to get away from the ghetto area. As this stretch of country was beyond the range of the electric lights, it was illuminated by small rockets. All through the night these beaten, hounded, and wounded people moved along the lighted streets. Women carried their dead children in their arms, children pulled and dragged their dead parents by their arms and legs down the road toward the train. Again and again the cries, "Open the door! Open the door!" echoed through the ghetto.[6]

Graebe described a mass execution which he observed on October 5, 1943, at Dubno, Ukraine.

Thereupon I drove to the site, accompanied by my foreman, and saw near it great mounds of earth, about 30 meters long and 2 meters high. Several trucks stood in front of the mounds. Armed Ukrainian militia drove the people off the trucks under the supervision of an SS-man. The militia men acted as guards on the trucks and drove them to and from the pit. All these people had the regulation yellow patches on the front and back of their clothes and thus could be recognized as Jews.

My foreman and I went directly to the pits. Nobody bothered us. Now I heard rifle shots in quick succession from behind one of the earth mounds. The people who had got off the trucks—men, women, and children of all ages—had to undress upon the orders of an SS-man, who carried a riding or dog whip. They had to put down their clothes in fixed places, sorted according to shoes, top clothing, and underclothing. I saw a heap of shoes of about 800 to 1,000 pairs, great piles of under linen and clothing. Without screaming or weeping these people undressed, stood around in family groups, kissed each other, said farewells, and waited for a sign from another SS-man, who stood near the pit, also with a whip in his hand. During the 15 minutes that I stood near I heard no complaint or plea for mercy. I watched a family of about eight persons, a man and a woman both about 50 with some children of about 1, 8, and 10, and two grown-up daughters of about 20 and 24. An old woman with snow-white hair was holding the one-year-old child in her arms and singing to it and tickling it. The child was cooing with delight. The couple was looking on with tears in their eyes. The father was holding the hand of a boy about 10 years old and speaking to him softly; the boy was fighting his tears. The father pointed to the sky, stroked his head, and seemed to explain something to him. At that moment the SS-man at the pit shouted something to his comrade. The latter counted off about 20 persons and instructed them to go behind the earth mound. Among them was the family which I have mentioned. I well remember a girl, slim and with black hair, who as she passed close to me, pointed to herself and said, "23." I walked around the mound and found myself confronted by a tremendous grave. People were closely wedged together and lying on top of each other so that only their heads were visible. Nearly all had blood running over their shoulders from their heads. Some of the people shot were still moving. Some were lifting their arms and turning their heads to show that they were still alive. The pit was already two-thirds full. I estimated that it already contained about 1,000 people. I looked for the man who did the shooting. He was an SS-man, who sat at the edge of the narrow end of the pit, his feet dangling into the pit. He had a tommy gun on his knees and was smoking a cigaret. The people, completely naked, went down some steps which were cut in the clay wall of the pit and clambered over the heads of the people lying there, to the place to which the SS-man directed them. They lay down in front of the dead or injured people; some caressed those who were still alive and spoke to them in a low voice. Then I heard a series of shots. I looked into the pit and saw that the bodies were twitching or the heads lying motionless on top of the bodies which lay before them. Blood was running away from their necks. I was surprised that I was not ordered away but I saw that there were two or three guards in uniform nearby. The next batch was approaching already. They went down into the pit, lined themselves up against the previous victims and were shot. When I walked back around the mound I noticed another truck load of people which had just arrived. This time it included sick and infirm persons. An old, very thin woman with terribly thin legs was undressed by others who were already naked, while two people held her up. The woman appeared to be paralyzed. The naked people carried the woman around to the mound. I left with my foreman and drove in my car back to Dubno.[7]

Mass Exterminations

Two official reports submitted by the Chief of Einsatz Group A, Stahlecker, to Himmler were introduced in evidence. The first report, found in Himmler's personal files, stated that during the first four months of the campaign in the Soviet Union, Einsatz Group A murdered 135,000 Communists and Jews, and carried out widespread destruction of homes and villages and other vast crimes. This report disclosed that the Einsatz groups frequently enlisted the aid of the local population in the extermination program: "...In view of the extension of the area of operations and the great number of duties which had to be performed by the Security Police, it was intended from the very beginning to obtain the co-operation of the reliable population for the fight against vermin—that is mainly the Jews and Communists."[8]

As to the extermination of Jews the report stated:

From the beginning it was to be expected that the Jewish problem in the East could not be solved by pogroms alone. In accordance with the basic orders received, however, the cleansing activities of the Security Police had to aim at a complete annihilation of the Jews. Special detachments reinforced by selected units—in Lithuania partisan detachments, in Latvia units of the Latvian auxiliary police—therefore performed extensive executions both in the towns and in rural areas. The actions of the execution detachments were performed smoothly....[9]

Enclosure 8 to this report was a careful survey of the number of persons murdered during the four months covered by the report, classified as to each country, and whether the victim was Jew or Communist, with totals given for each category.[10]

The second report from Einsatz Group A disclosed the extermination of nearly 220,000 persons. With respect to Esthonia, it stated in part: "Only by the SIPO and SD were the Jews gradually executed as they became no longer required for work. Today there are no longer any Jews in Esthonia."

With respect to Latvia, the report stated in part: "Up to October, 1941 approximately 30,000 Jews had been executed by these Sonderkommandos."

With respect to Lithuania, the report stated in part: "Altogether 136,421 people were liquidated in a great number of single actions."

With respect to White Russia, the report stated in part: "In view of the enormous distances, the bad condition of the roads, the shortage of vehicles and petrol, and the small forces of Security Police and SD, it needs the utmost effort to be able to carry out shootings in the country. Nevertheless 41,000 Jews have been shot up to now."

Attached as an enclosure to this report was a map entitled "Jewish Executions Carried out by Einsatzgruppe A," on which, by the use of coffins as symbols, the number of Jews murdered in each area covered by Einsatz Group A was illustrated. The map showed thousands of Jews in ghettos, and an estimated 128,000 Jews "still on hand" in the Minsk area. The number murdered, according to figures beside the coffins, during the period covered by this report, was 218,050.[11]

Under each of the four Einsatz groups were smaller units called Einsatzkommandos or Sonderkommandos. On October 30, 1941, the German commissioner of the territory of Sluzk wrote a report to the commissioner general of White Ruthenia, in which he severely criticized the actions of the Einsatzkommandos operating in his area for the manner in which they murdered the Jews of Sluzk:

On 27 October, in the morning at about 8 o'clock, a first lieutenant of the Police Battalion Number 11, from Kovno, Lithuania, appeared and introduced himself as the adjutant of the battalion commander of the Security Police. The first lieutenant explained that the police battalion had received the assignment to effect the liquidation of all Jews here in the town of Sluzk within two days. The battalion commander with his battalion in strength of four companies, two of which were made up of Lithuanian partisans, was on the march here and the action would have to begin instantly. I replied to the first lieutenant that I had to discuss the action in any case first with the commander. About half an hour later the police battalion arrived in Sluzk. Immediately after the arrival a conference with the battalion commander took place according to my request. I first explained to the commander that it would not very well be possible to effect the action without previous preparation, because everybody had been sent to work and that it would lead to terrible confusion. At least it would have been his duty to inform me a day ahead of time. Then I requested him to postpone the action one day. However, he refused this with the remark that he had to carry out this action everywhere in all towns and that only two days were allotted for Sluzk. Within those two days the town of Sluzk had by all means to be cleared of Jews....

For the rest, as regards the execution of the action, I must point out, to my deepest regret, that the latter almost bordered on sadism. The town itself during the action offered a picture of horror. With indescribable brutality on the part of both the German police officers and particularly of the Lithuanian partisans, the Jewish people, and also with them White Ruthenians, were taken out of their dwellings and herded together. Everywhere in the town shots were to be heard, and in different streets the corpses of Jews who had been shot accumulated. The White Ruthenians were in the greatest anguish to free themselves from the encirclement. In addition to the fact that the Jewish people among whom were also artisans, were barbarously maltreated in sight

VON DER EINSATZGRUPPE A DURCHGEFÜHRTE
JUDENEXEKUTIONEN

PETERSBURG

KRASNOGWARDEISK

OSTSEE

REVAL

963

JUDENFREI

3600

RIGAER
BUCHT

RIGA
GHETTO 2500

35,238

GHETTO 4500
SCHAULEN

DUNABURG

GHETTO 950

136,421

KAUEN
GHETTO 15,000

41,828

MINSK

GESCHÄTZTE ZAHL DER NOCH VORHANDENEN JUDEN 128,000

Diagram in the Stahlecker report to Himmler showing by casket
symbols the number of Jews killed by Task Group A operating behind
the German lines in the Baltic area, and the number of Jews "still on
hand." Note that after 963 Jews had been exterminated, Esthonia was
marked "Free of Jews."

of the White Ruthenian people, the White Ruthenians themselves were also beaten with clubs and rifle butts. It was no longer a question of an action against the Jews. It looked much more like a revolution....

In conclusion, I find myself obliged to point out that the police battalion looted in an unheard-of-manner during the action and that not only in Jewish houses but equally in those of the White Ruthenians. Anything of use, such as boots, leather, cloth, gold and other valuables, was taken away. According to statements of the troops, watches were torn off the arms of Jews openly on the street and rings pulled off their fingers in the most brutal manner. A disbursing officer reported that a Jewish girl was asked by the police to obtain immediately 5,000 rubles to have her father released. This girl is said actually to have run about everywhere to obtain the money.[12]

This report was forwarded by the commissioner general of White Ruthenia to the defendant Rosenberg, the Reich Minister for the occupied Eastern Territories, on November 1, 1941, with the following comment:

I am submitting this report in duplicate so that one copy may be forwarded to the Reich Minister. Peace and order cannot be maintained in White Ruthenia with methods of that sort. To have buried alive seriously wounded people, who then worked their way out of their graves again, is such extreme beastliness that this incident as such must be reported to the Fuehrer and the Reich Marshal.[13]

On the same date by separate letter the commissioner general of White Ruthenia reported to the Reich commissioner for the Eastern Territories that he had received money, valuables, and other objects taken by the police in the action at Sluzk and other regions, all of which had been deposited with the Reich Credit Institute for the disposal of the Reich commissioner.

A report from the German prison administrator at Minsk as of May 31, 1943, to the commissioner general of White Ruthenia stated:

On 13 April 1943 the former German dentist Ernst Israel Tichauer and his wife, Elisa Sara Tichauer, née Rosenthal, were committed to the court prison by the Security Service.... Since that time all German and Russian Jews who were turned over to us had their gold bridgework, crowns, and fillings pulled or broken out. This happens always one to two hours before the respective action.

Since 13 April 1943, 516 German and Russian Jews have been finished off.[14]

This report was forwarded to the Reich Minister for the occupied Eastern Territories on June 1, 1943.

Recruiting of Forced Labor

As the war progressed to the disadvantage of Germany, greater emphasis was laid upon the forced recruitment of labor than upon extermination. A report of the chief of a Sonderkommando of Einsatz Group C, written on March 19, 1943, indicated such change of emphasis in the sector assigned to that subgroup:

It is the task of the Security Police and of the Security Service to discover all enemies of the Reich and fight against them in the interest of security, and in the zone of operations especially to guarantee the security of the army. Besides the annihilation of active opponents, all other elements who, by virtue of their opinions or their past, may appear active as enemies under favorable conditions, are to be eliminated through preventive measures. The Security Police carries out this task according to the general directives of the Fuehrer with all the required toughness. Energetic measures are especially necessary in territories endangered by the activity of hostile gangs. The competence of the Security Police within the zone of operations is based on the Barbarossa decrees. I deem the measures of the Security Police, carried out on a considerable scale during recent times, necessary for the two following reasons:

1. The situation at the front in my sector had become so serious that the population, partly influenced by Hungarians and Italians who streamed back in chaotic condition, took openly hostile positions against us.

2. The strong expeditions of hostile gangs, who came especially from the forest of Brvansk, were another reason. Besides that, other revolutionary groups, formed by the population, appeared suddenly in all districts. The providing of arms evidently provided no difficulties at all. It would have been irresponsible, if we had observed this whole activity without acting against it. It is obvious that all such measures bring about some harshness. I want to take up the significant points of harsh measures:

1. The shooting of Hungarian Jews.

2. The shooting of Agronoms.

3. The shooting of children.

4. The total burning down of villages.

5. The "shooting, while trying to escape," of Security Service prisoners.

Chief of Einsatz Group C confirmed once more the correctness of the measures taken, and expressed his recognition of the energetic actions.

With regard to the current political situation, especially in the armament industry in the fatherland, the measures of the Security Police have to be subordinated to the greatest extent to the recruiting of labor for Germany. In the shortest possible time, the Ukraine has to put at the disposal of the armament industry one million workers, 500 of whom have to be sent from our territory daily.

The work of the field groups has therefore to be changed as of now. The following orders are given:

1. Special treatment is to be limited to a minimum.

2. The listing of communist functionaries, activists and so on, is to take place by roster only for the time being without arresting anybody. It is, for instance, no longer feasible to arrest all the close relatives of a member of the communist party. Also, members of the Komsomolz are to be arrested only if they were active in a leading position.

3. The activity of the labor offices and of recruiting commissions, is to be supported to the greatest extent possible. It will not be possible always to refrain from using force. During a conference with the chief of the labor commitment staffs, an agreement was reached stating that wherever prisoners can be released, they should be put at the disposal of the commissioner of the labor office. While searching villages, when it has become necessary to burn down a village, the whole population will be put at the disposal of the commissioner by force.

4. As a rule, no more children will be shot.

5. The reporting of hostile gangs as well as drives against them is not affected hereby. All drives against these hostile gangs can only take place after my approval has been obtained.

6. The prisons have to be kept empty, as a rule. We have to be aware of the fact that the Slavs will interpret all soft treatment on our part as weakness and that they will act accordingly right away. If we limit our harsh measures of Security Police through above orders for the time being, that is only done for the following reason. The most important thing is the recruiting of workers. No check of persons to be sent into the Reich will be made. No written certificates of political reliability check or similar things will be issued.[15]

Activities and Situation Reports

The reports of the various Einsatz groups were summarized at Berlin headquarters of the Security Police and SD, and the summaries were then distributed to various interested departments, especially the regional offices of the Gestapo, the SD, and the Criminal Police. One such report covering the period of October 1-31, 1941, was entitled "Activity and Situation Report No. 6 of the Einsatz Groups of the Security Police and the SD in the USSR." This report described in summary the activities of all four Einsatz groups during the month of October, 1941. First given were the locations of the respective groups:

During the period covered by this report the stations of the Einsatz groups of the Security Police and the SD have changed only in the Northern Sector.

The present stations are:

Einsatz Group A: since 7 October 1941 Krasnowardeisk.

Einsatz Group B: continues in Smolensk.

Einsatz Group C: since 27 September 1941 in Kiew.

Einsatz Group D: since 27 September 1941 in Nikolajew.

The Action and Special Commandos which are attached to the Einsatz groups continue on the march with the advancing troops into the sectors which have been assigned to them.[16]

The report next discussed the activities of the Einsatz groups in the Baltic area, White Ruthenia, and the Ukraine. Under each section the work of the Einsatz groups in connection with the action taken against the partisans, Jews, and Communist officials was considered. With respect to the treatment of Jews in the Baltic area the report stated in part:

...However, the Estonian Protective Corps, formed at the time of the entry of the Wehrmacht, immediately started a *comprehensive arrest action of all Jews*. This action was under the direction of the task force of the Security Police and the SD.

The measures taken were:

1. Arrest of all male Jews over sixteen.

2. Arrest of all Jewesses from 16-20 years, who lived in Reval and environments and were fit for work, these were employed in peat cutting.

3. Comprehensive detention in the synagogue of all Jewesses living in Dorpot and its environments.

4. Arrest of the Jews and Jewesses fit for work in Pernau and environments.

5. Registration of all Jews according to age, sex, and capacity for work for the purpose of their detention in a camp is being prepared.

The male Jews over 16 were executed with the exception of doctors and the elders. At the present time this action is still in progress. After completion of this action, there will remain only 500 Jewesses and children in the Eastern territory....[17]

As to activities in White Ruthenia, the report stated:

All the more vigorous are the actions of the Einsatz groups of the Security Police and the SD against the Jews who make it necessary that steps be taken against them in different spheres.

In Gorodnia 165 Jewish terrorists and in Tschernigow 19 Jewish communists were liquidated. 8 more Jewish communists were shot at Beresna.

It was experienced repeatedly that the Jewish women showed an especially obstinate behavior. For this reason 28 Jewesses had to be shot in Krugoje and 337 at Mogilew.

In Borissow 321 Jewish saboteurs and 118 Jewish looters were executed.

In Bobruisk 380 Jews were shot who had engaged to the last in incitement and horror propaganda against the German army of occupation.

In Tatarsk the Jews had left the ghetto of their own accord and returned to their old home quarters, attempting to expel the Russians who had been quartered there in the meantime. All male Jews as well as 3 Jewesses were shot.

In Sadrudubs the Jews offered some resistance against the establishment of a ghetto so that 272 Jews and Jewesses had to be shot. Among them was a political commissar....

In Mogilew, too, the Jews attempted to sabotage their removal to the ghetto. 113 Jews were liquidated....

In Talka 222 Jews were shot for anti-German propaganda, and in Marina Gorka 996 Jews were shot because they had sabotaged orders issued by the German occupation authorities.

At Schklow 627 more Jews were shot, because they had participated in acts of sabotage....

On account of the extreme danger of an epidemic, a beginning was made to liquidate the Jews in the ghetto at Witebsk. This involved approximately 3,000 Jews....[18]

The situation for this month in the Ukraine was described:

The embitterment of the Ukrainian population against the Jews is extremely great, because they are thought responsible for the explosion in Kiev. They are also regarded as informers and agents of the NKVD, who started the terror against the Ukrainian people. As a measure of retaliation for the arson at Kiev, all Jews were arrested and altogether 33,771 Jews were executed on the 29th and the 30th September. Money, valuables and clothing were secured and put at the disposal of the National-Socialist League for Public Welfare (NSV), for the equipment of the National Germans (Volksdeutschen) and partly put at the disposal of the provisional city administration for distribution to the needy population....

In Shitomir 3,145 Jews had to be shot, because from experience they had to be regarded as bearers of Bolshevist propaganda and saboteurs....

In Cherson 410 Jews were executed as a measure of retaliation for acts of sabotage. Especially in the area east of the Dnjepr the solution of the Jewish question has been taken up energetically by the Einsatz groups of the Security Police and the SD. The areas newly occupied by the Commandos were purged of Jews. In the course of this action 4,891 Jews were liquidated. At other places the Jews were marked and registered. This rendered it possible to put at the disposal of the Wehrmacht for urgent labor, Jewish worker groups up to 1,000 persons.[19]

Subsequently monthly and weekly reports of the exterminations carried out by the Einsatz groups were distributed to almost all Higher SS and Police Leaders and Reich Defense Commissioners. Several of these reports were found in the files of the Nazi Youth Leader, the defendant Schirach.

Report No. 9, for the month of January, 1942, contained this entry on the activities of the Einsatz groups:

Now as ever the attitude of the Jews is unequivocally anti-German and criminal. It is attempted to purge the eastern territories as completely as possible of Jews. Executions by shooting are carried out everywhere in such a manner as not to attract public attention. The public and even the remaining Jews are mostly of the opinion that the Jews have only been transferred to a different domicile.

Esthonia is already free of Jews.

In Latvia the number of 29,500 Jews remaining in Riga was reduced to 2,500. Nine hundred sixty-two Jews still living in Dvinsk are urgently needed as workers.

In Lithuania the country and the smaller towns have been completely purged of Jews.... In Lithuania there are still 15,000 Jews in Kaunas, 4,500 in Shavli, and an additional 15,000 in Vilna who are also needed as workers.

In White Ruthenia the purge of Jews is under way. The number of Jews in the part up to now handed over to the civilian administration amounts to 139,000. In the meantime, 33,210 Jews were shot by the Einsatz group of the Security Police and the Security Service.[20]

Report No. 11 of the Einsatz groups, covering the month of March, 1942, stated:

Since the largest part of the eastern territory was free from Jews, and the few who remained and were needed for the most urgent labor projects, were located in ghettos, it was the main task of the Security Police and SD to get hold of the Jews who were mostly hiding in the country. Several times Jews were seized who had left the ghetto without permission or who were not wearing the Jewish star....

At Riga, among others, three Jews from the Reich, who had been assigned to the ghetto and had made a breakaway, were seized and publicly hanged in the ghetto.

In the course of some larger actions against the Jews, 3,412 of them were shot at Minsk, 302 at Vileyka, and 2,007 at Baranovitchi.

The population welcomed these actions since upon inspection of the residences, they found out that the Jews still had quite a supply of food, while the food situation of the population was extremely bad....

In the remaining territories of the eastern front, the duty of the Security Police and SD consisted in general clean up activities of larger villages, along with actions against individual Jews who put in a political or criminal appearance.

Thus in Rakow alone 15,000 Jews were shot and 1,224 in Artenowsk, so that these places are free from Jews.

In the Crimea 1,000 Jews and Gypsies were executed.[21]

Weekly summarizations of the activities of the Einsatz groups began on May 1, 1942. Excerpts from widely distributed reports are illustrative.

Report No. 4, dated May 22, 1942:

Of the Krimtschaks (approximately 6,000) who were generally counted to be Jews, about half lived for the greater part in Simferopol (2,500) and in Karasubarsar. Their annihilation together with that of the real Jews and the gypsies in the Crimea took place essentially until the beginning of December 1941. The fact that the Krimtschaks and the gypsies shared the fate of the Jews did not particularly excite the population.[22]

Report No. 7, dated June 12, 1942:

After the entry of the German troops into Latvia there were still about 70,000 Jews, while the others had fled with the retreating Bolshevist armies.

The acts of sabotage and arson which occurred in Latvia shortly after the entry of the German troops were caused or committed to the greatest extent by Jews. For example, in Dunaburg so many fires were laid by Jews that a large part of the town was destroyed thereby. The removal of 33,038 Latvians is also to be attributed to Jewish influence.

At the present time there are only a few Jews in the ghettos who are doing specialized work.

The figures are as follows:

In Riga about 2,500
Dunaburg about 950
Libau about 300

Aside from these Jews, Latvia has become free of Jews in the meantime.[23]

Report No. 9, dated June 26, 1942:

The measures taken by the Security Police and SD have caused basic changes also in White Ruthenia in regard to the Jewish question. In order to bring the Jews under an effective control, independent of the measures to be taken later, Jewish Councils of Elders were formed, who were responsible to the Security Police and the SD for the behavior of their racial comrades. Besides, the registration of the Jews was initiated and they were concentrated in ghettos. Finally the Jews had to wear yellow insignia in front and on their back to be recognized, in the manner of the Jewish star introduced in the territory of the Reich.... With these measures the foundation was laid for the later intended final solution of the European Jewish problem, for the White Ruthenian territory as well.[24]

Report No. 38, dated January 22, 1943, disclosed that in one action during that week 1,308 persons were seized for labor mobilization in the Reich.

Report No. 41, dated February 12, 1943, described several special actions. In one of them 1,165 persons received "special treatment," because they took sides with the guerrillas. In another action 1,510 persons "suspected" of belonging to the guerrillas were shot; and, in connection with the drive, 2,658 Jews and 30 gypsies "were taken." In another drive, 785 persons "suspected" of belonging to a band were shot, and 126 Jews and 24 gypsies "were taken."[25]

Report No. 46, dated March 19, 1943, described an action in the Pripet Swamps in which, in addition to 2,219 killed in fighting, 7,378 persons received "special treatment."[26] Destruction of dwellings amounted to 1,900 houses, 56 camps, and 1,064 shelters.

All reports on activities of the Einsatz groups were classified "secret," but they were widely distributed. Thus, Report No. 9 was sent to all chiefs of Einsatzgruppen and Einsatzkommandos, to eleven Higher SS and Police Leaders, to ten SS and Police Leaders, and to seven Reich Defense Commissioners. Many addressees had no direct interest in the territories in which the killings took place. Police leaders in Berlin, Dresden, Breslau, Stettin, Vienna, Warsaw, and Prague received copies of the reports. And the information was sent to Reich Defense Commissioners located in Koenigsberg, Stettin, Breslau, Vienna, and Danzig. There undoubtedly was, in addition, an internal distribution within the Reich Main Security Office, and certain higher echelons of the government.

Racial extermination was the worst of Hitler-ordered crimes. If it had been attempted in Germany itself, Hitler most assuredly would have been overthrown. He was able to accomplish it only under cover of the war, when the full energies of the German people were devoted to the war effort and the safety of their country. The action was directed by Heinrich Himmler and executed by small numbers of select members of the Gestapo and the SD. The officials of occupied countries complied with the orders of Eichmann and his immediate assistants to round up the Jews and put them upon transports to concentration camps. In the camps, a small number of SS-men directed the exterminations, which were largely performed by the inmates themselves, under duress of death. Four task forces composed principally of Gestapo and SD officials assisted by SS-men moved into the eastern territories behind the advancing German armies. They, too, impressed elements of the native populations into the actions. It was thus possible for Himmler to achieve the mass extermination of the Jewish people of Europe with a small number of select personnel drawn from the Gestapo, the SD, and the SS. Neither the military forces nor the general government administration had any responsibility for this program. For the sake of authentic history it was a misfortune that neither Hitler nor Himmler, who issued the orders, could be brought to trial at Nuremberg, there to explain and to answer for this greatest crime of modern times.

CHAPTER 27

We Are the Masters

"THE SLAVS ARE TO WORK FOR US. Insofar as we don't need them, they may die. They should not receive the benefits of the German public health system. We do not care about their fertility. They may practice abortion and use contraceptives; the more the better. We don't want them educated; it is enough if they can count up to 100. Such stooges will be the more useful to us. Religion we leave to them as a diversion. As to food, they will not get any more than is absolutely necessary. We are the masters; we come first."[1]

These were not the words of a hysterical SA-man, shouting propagandistic phrases at a Party rally. They were the instructions of the highest leader in the Party under Hitler, Reich Leader Bormann, the chief of the Party Chancery, in a formal letter of instructions to the commissioner of the Eastern Occupied Territories, Reich Leader Rosenberg; and they established the policy under which those territories were to be administered.

The Reich Commissioner for the Ukraine, Erich Koch, responded to these instructions in an expression of views at Kiev on March 5, 1943:

We are the master race and must govern hard but just.... I will draw the very last out of this country. I did not come to spread bliss. I have come to help the Fuehrer. The population must work, work, and work again ... for some people are getting excited that the population may not get enough to eat. The population cannot demand that. One has only to remember what our heroes were deprived of in Stalingrad. ... We definitely did not come here to give out manna. We have come here to create the basis for victory.... We are a master race, which

372

must remember that the lowliest German worker is racially and biologically a thousand times more valuable than the population here.[2]

Himmler, as the chief Nazi proponent of the master race idea—the idea which was the foundation of the SS elite corps—time and again reiterated the concept of the master race and its corollary, the degradation and subjugation of "inferior" peoples. In his speech to SS generals at Posen on October 4, 1943, Himmler said:

What happens to the Russians, to the Czechs, does not interest me in the slightest. What the nations can offer in the way of good blood of our type we will take, if necessary, by kidnapping their children and raising them here with us. Whether other nations live in prosperity or starve to death interests me only insofar as we need them as slaves for our culture; otherwise it is of no interest to me. Whether 10,000 Russian females fall down from exhaustion while digging an anti-tank ditch or not interests me only insofar as the anti-tank ditch for Germany is finished.[3]

Hitler had written in *Mein Kampf* that Germany should find "living space" in the East. The war was not begun by the Nazis as the final means of settling a dispute; it was begun and waged for the purpose of conquest—conquest of heavily populated countries, with cultures and traditions of their own, peoples who had the spirit of national pride and who sought to maintain their place in the community of nations. Hitler's conquest was no daring plunge into the wilderness, no intrepid search for new lands in uncivilized portions of the world; it was a calculated attempt to subjugate the civilized neighboring states of Germany, to seize their lands, despoil their properties, and enslave their peoples—the program of Germanization.

While this program could not, of course, be identical in every territory, basically it contemplated a gradual Germanic absorption of captured lands. Where there were persons of German ethnic origin in occupied territories they were to be given German status and used as the nucleus for subsequent control. In other territories, German island settlements were to be established as bases for future racial domination. Leadership of the native population was to be destroyed. Intelligentsia, propertied persons, and racial undesirables were to be liquidated. Thousands of others, able to work, were to be brought to Germany for forced labor, and were to be prevented from biological reproduction, thus weakening the future native population and permitting its eventual replacement by Germans at the upper levels.

Himmler discussed the settlement of Germans in occupied eastern territories in the course of a secret speech delivered at Cracow on March 30, 1942:

> The Reichsfuehrer SS developed additional trains of ideas to the effect that, in the first five-year plan for resettlement after the war, the new German eastern territories should first be filled; it is intended afterwards to provide the Crimea and the Baltic countries with a German upper class at least. Into the Government General, perhaps, further German island settlements should be newly transplanted from European nations. An exact decision in this respect, however, has not been issued. In any case, it is wished that at first a heavy colonization along the San and the Bug be achieved so that the parts of Poland with alien populations are encircled. Hitherto, it has been always proved that this kind of encircling leads most quickly to the desired nationalization.[4]

In a foreword to the *Deutsche Arbeit* issue of June/July, 1942, Himmler wrote: "It is our task to Germanize the East, not in the old sense—that is, to teach the people there the German language and German law—but to see to it that only people of purely German, Germanic blood live in the East."[5] And on another occasion, in a confidential publication of Himmler's Office for the Consolidation of German Nationhood, the basic objective of the program to Germanize these territories was stated in these words: "The removal of foreign races from the incorporated eastern territories is one of the most essential goals to be accomplished in the German East."[6]

In the quest for German blood, child stealing became an approved practice. On October 14, 1943, Himmler declared in a speech:

> I consider that in dealing with members of a foreign country, especially some Slav nationalities, we must not start from German points of view, and we must not endow these people with decent German thoughts and logical conclusions of which they are not capable,

but we must take them as they really are. Obviously in such a mixture of peoples, there will always be some racially good types. Therefore I think that it is our duty to take their children with us, to remove them from their environment, if necessary by robbing, or stealing them.[7]

The implacable will of Nazi leaders to seize the lands of their neighbors and resettle them with German nationals was expressed in terms of decades of German domination. On April 19, 1941, Hans Frank said in the course of an address delivered in Krakow: "Thanks to the heroic courage of our soldiers this territory has become German; and the time will come when the valley of the Vistula, from its source to its mouth at the sea will be as German as the valley of the Rhine."[8] And on January 14, 1944, even as the German military forces were falling in retreat before the Allied armies, he said: "Once the war is won, then, for all I care, mincemeat can be made of the Poles and Ukrainians and all the others who run around here; it doesn't matter what happens."[9]

Germanization of Poland

The colonization of Poland involved several features, some of which were antagonistic. Poland was to serve as dumping ground for the unwanted population elements from Germany until these people could be eliminated in the mass extermination centers established on Polish soil. Polish intelligentsia were to be liquidated. Inferior Poles were to be placed in concentration camps and sent to the Reich for forced labor. Germans were to be settled in evacuated areas of Poland. Ultimately the former Polish nation was to be reduced to a colony and Germanized.

Hans Frank was the governor general of Poland. His views on the administration of the occupied territory were disclosed in a report of October 3, 1939, made even as the German and Soviet armies were together completing the subjugation of free Poland:

... Frank explained the instruction which had been entrusted to him by the Fuehrer and the economic political directives according to which he intended to administer Poland. According to these directives, Poland could be administered only by utilizing the country by means of ruthless exploitation; removal of all supplies—raw materials, machines, factory installations, *et cetera*—which are important for the German war economy; availability of all workers for work within Germany; reduction of the entire Polish economy to the absolute minimum necessary for the bare existence of the population; closing of all institutions, especially technical schools and colleges in order to prevent the growth of a new Polish intelligentsia. Poland shall be treated as a colony; the Poles shall be the slaves of the Greater German World Empire.[10]

Frank added: "By destroying Polish industry its subsequent reconstruction after the war would become more difficult, if not impossible, so that Poland would be reduced to its proper position as an agrarian country which would have to depend upon Germany for importation of industrial products."[11]

The use of the Government General as a receptacle into which would be poured unwanted populations from Germany (including the Polish territories to be at once incorporated therein), and other occupied areas, was developed in a secret thesis, prepared in January, 1940, by the Academy of German Law, of which Frank was then president. The study concluded that the Government General could absorb from one to one and a half million persons to be made up of Jews from the liberated East, the remaining Jews of Germany, Austria, and the Protectorate, and the leaders of the part of Poland to be brought into the Reich, including intelligentsia, political leaders, large landowners, industrialists, and businessmen. To provide space in the Government General for these displaced persons, it would be necessary to remove equivalent numbers of Poles from the Government General. As to this, the report stated:

In order to relieve the living space of the Poles in the Government General as well as in the liberated East, one should remove cheap labor temporarily by the hundreds of thousands, employ them for a few years in the old Reich, and thereby hamper their native biological propagation. (Their assimilation into the old Reich must be prevented)....Strictest care is to be taken that secret circulars, memoranda, and official correspondence which contain instructions detrimental to the Poles are kept steadily under lock and key so that they will not some day fill the White Books printed in Paris or the U.S.A.[12]

About this time, Frank was writing in his diary: "The Reichsfuehrer SS wishes that all Jews be evacuated from the newly-gained Reich territories. Up to February approximately one million people are to be brought in this way into the General Government. The families of good racial extraction present in the occupied Polish territory (approximately four million people) should be transferred into the Reich and individually housed, thereby being uprooted as a people."[13]

On August 5, 1942, at Cracow, Frank said: "The situation in regard to Poland is unique insofar as on the one hand—I speak quite openly—we must expand Germanism in such a manner that the area of the General Government becomes pure German colonized land at some decades to come; and, on the other hand, under the present war conditions we have to allow foreign racial groups to perform here the work which must be carried out in the service of Greater Germany."[14]

Persons of German race living in occupied Poland were required to apply for Germanization. The penalty for refusal was commitment to a concentration camp. A decree of February 16, 1942, allowed persons listed in the "German Ethnic List" only eight days within which to prove to the local Gestapo office that they had applied for Germanization. "If such proof is not submitted, the person in question is to be taken in protective custody for transfer into a concentration camp."[15] So-called "Polanized Germans" who were of "inferior hereditary quality" or of "bad political record" were committed to concentration camps. A second decree of February 16, 1942, described the treatment of wives and children of such persons so confined:

The wives and children of such persons are to be resettled in old Reich territory and to be included in the Germanization measures. Where the wife also had a particularly bad political record, and cannot be included in the resettlement action, her name, too, is to be turned over to the competent State Police (superior) Office with a view to transferring her to a concentration camp. In such cases the children are to be separated from their parents....[16]

The deportations carried out under the Germanization program brought suffering and misery to hundreds of thousands. Families were frequently separated, friends and relations were lost, and homes were destroyed. The severity of the measures was recounted by Himmler in a speech to the officers of the SS-Leibstandarte "Adolf Hitler":

Now I would like to bring another matter to your attention. Very frequently the member of the Waffen SS thinks about the deportation of these people here. These thoughts came to me today when watching the very difficult work out there performed by the Security Police, supported by your men, who help them a great deal. Exactly the same thing happened in Poland in weather 40 degrees below zero, where we had to haul away thousands, ten thousands, a hundred thousands; where we had to have the toughness—you should hear this but also forget it again immediately—to shoot thousands of leading Poles, where we had to have the toughness, otherwise it would have taken revenge on us later. We also had to bring in, in this winter of 40 degrees below zero, ten thousands of Germans. . . . In many cases it is much easier to go into combat with a company than to suppress an obstructive population of low cultural level in some area with a company, or to carry out executions, or to haul away people, or to evict crying and hysterical women, or to return our German racial brethren across the border from Russia and to take care of them.[17]

Frank did not hesitate to admit the murder of thousands of people in connection with the expulsion of Poles from their homeland. In a conference held on January 21, 1943, he said:

I should like to state one thing: We must not be squeamish when we learn that a total of 17,000 people have been shot. After all, these people who were shot are also war victims. . . . We must remember that all of us who are gathered together here figure on Mr. Roosevelt's list of war criminals. I have the honor of being Number One. We have therefore become, so to speak, accomplices in the sense of world history.[18]

But deportations were too cruel even for Frank wholly to approve, as indicated by his report to Hitler of June 19, 1943, in which he commented upon the clearance of Polish farmers from the Lublin district of the Government General for the purpose of settling German nationals on their lands:

Moreover—as I have already reported separately—the pace at which it was carried out and the methods adopted caused immeasurable bitterness among the populace. At short notice families were torn apart; those able to work were sent to the Reich, while old people and children were directed to evacuated Jewish ghettos. This happened in the middle of the winter of 1942-43 and resulted in considerable loss of life, especially among members of the last mentioned group. The dispossession meant the complete expropriation of the movable and immovable property of the farmers. The entire population succumbed to the belief that these deportations meant the beginning of a mass deportation of the Poles from the region of the Government General. The general impression was that the Poles would meet a fate similar to that of the Jews.[19]

Frank had written in his diary: "We must annihilate the Jews, wherever we find them, and wherever it is possible." State Secretary Krueger confirmed to Frank that the Poles compared their deportation with the treatment of the Jews:

When we settled about the first 4,000 in Kreis Zamosc shortly before Christmas I had an opportunity to speak to these people.... It is understandable that in resettling this area ... we did not make friends of the Poles.... In colonizing this territory with racial Germans, we are forced to chase out the Poles.... We are removing those who constitute a burden in this new colonization territory. Actually, they are the asocial and inferior elements. They are being deported, first brought to a concentration camp, and then sent as labor to the Reich. From a Polish propaganda standpoint this entire first action has had an unfavorable effect. For the Poles say: After the Jews have been destroyed then they will employ the same methods to get the Poles out of this territory and liquidate them just like the Jews.[20]

Frank summarized the effect of the Germanization program in Poland in his June 19, 1943, report to Hitler:

In the course of time, a series of measures, or of consequences of the German rule, have led to a substantial deterioration of the attitude of the entire Polish people to the Government General. These measures have affected either individual professions or the entire population and frequently, also—often with crushing severity—the fate of individuals.
Among these are in particular:
1. The entirely insufficient nourishment of the population, mainly of the working classes in the cities, the majority of which are working for German interests. Until the war of 1939 their food supplies, though

not varied, were sufficient and were generally assured owing to the agrarian surplus of the former Polish State and in spite of the negligence on the part of their former political leadership.

2. The confiscation of a great part of the Polish estates, expropriation without compensation, and evacuation of Polish peasants from maneuver areas and from German settlements.

3. Encroachments and confiscations in the industries, in commerce and trade, and in the field of other private property.

4. Mass arrests and shootings by the German police who applied the system of collective responsibility.

5. The rigorous methods of recruiting workers.

6. The extensive paralyzing of cultural life.

7. The closing of high schools, colleges, and universities.

8. The limitation, indeed the complete elimination, of Polish influence from all spheres of State administration.

9. Curtailment of the influence of the Catholic Church, limiting its extensive influence—an undoubtedly necessary move—and, in addition, until quite recently, often at the shortest notice, the closing and confiscation of monasteries, schools, and charitable institutions.[21]

No country suffered greater hardships than Poland under Hitler's program of Germanization. And it suffered twice, for in the East it was subjected to Sovietization as well, until Germany occupied the entire country after the attack upon the Soviet Union.

Germanization of Czechoslovakia

On August 31, 1940, Von Neurath, Reich Protector of Bohemia and Moravia, submitted a memorandum to Hitler on the Germanization of Czechoslovakia:

... But as things are like that, a decision will have to be taken as to what is to be done with the Czech people in order to attain the objective of incorporating the country and filling it with Germans as quickly as possible and as thoroughly as possible. The most radical and theoretically complete solution to the problem would be to evacuate all Czechs completely from this country and replace them by Germans.[22]

The memorandum pointed out that, unfortunately, there were not enough Germans to carry out such an ambitious program immediately, so the following alternative was proposed:

It will, where the Czechs are concerned, rather be a case on the one hand, of keeping those Czechs who are suitable for Germanization by individual selective breeding, while on the other hand expelling those who are not useful from a racial standpoint or are enemies of the Reich, that is, the intelligentsia which has developed in the last twenty years. If we use such a procedure, Germanization can be carried out successfully.[23]

That Hitler approved the alternative last stated is disclosed by a top secret report dated October 15, 1940, which was written by General Friderici, Deputy General of the Wehrmacht in Bohemia and Moravia:

Since creation of the Protectorate of Bohemia and Moravia, Party agencies, industrial circles, as well as agencies of the central authorities of Berlin, have had difficulties about the solution of the Czech problem. After ample deliberation the Reich Protector expressed his view about the various plans in a memorandum. In this, three ways of solution were indicated:

a) German infiltration of Moravia and reduction of the Czech nationality to a residual Bohemia. This solution is considered unsatisfactory, because the Czech problem, even if in a diminished form, will continue to exist.

b) Many arguments can be brought up against the most radical solution, namely, the deportation of all the Czechs. Therefore, the memorandum comes to the conclusion that it cannot be carried out within a reasonable time.

c) Assimilation of the Czechs, i.e. absorption of about half of the Czech nationality by the Germans, insofar as this is of importance by being valuable from a racial or other standpoint. This will take place, among other things, also by increasing the work task of the Czechs in the Reich territory (with the exception of the Sudeten German border district), in other words, by dispersing the closed Czech nationality. The other half of the Czech nationality must be deprived of its power, eliminated, and shipped out of the country by all sorts of methods. This applies particularly to the racially mongoloid part and to the major part of the intellectual class. The latter can scarcely be converted ideologically and would represent a burden by constantly making claims for leadership over the other Czech classes and thus interfering with a rapid assimilation. Elements which counteract the planned Germanization are to be handled roughly and should be eliminated. The above development naturally presupposes an increased influx of Germans from the Reich territory into the Protectorate.

After a discussion, the Fuehrer has chosen solution (c) (assimilation) as a directive for the solution of the Czech problem and decided that, while keeping up the autonomy of the Protectorate on the surface, the Germanization will have to be carried out in a centralized way by the office of the Reich Protector for years to come.[24]

The adoption of the plan of gradual assimilation meant forced Germanization for one large segment of the Czech population and forced labor in Germany for another large segment. About half of the population, including the educated class, was to be harried out of the country, and "eliminated" through "rough handling," which meant confinement in concentration and labor camps.

Germanization of the U.S.S.R.

Although the incorporation of huge portions of Soviet territory into the Reich was envisioned at the beginning of the German depredations in the East, it was numerically impossible to spread the comparatively small German population into conquered Soviet territories as the German armies advanced. A preliminary plan was developed, therefore, to integrate the Ukraine with Europe and to reduce northern Russia to primitive status. All foodstuffs and raw materials produced in the Ukraine, above the requirements of the German armies in the field and the minimum needs of the Ukrainian people, were to be shipped to Germany. Since, in the past, the Ukraine had supplied most of the food for the "forest zone" of the Soviet Union, which included the principal industrial areas such as Moscow and Leningrad, it was clear that the plan would mean the certain starvation of millions of northern Russians. And this was openly contemplated and assumed.

The following order of priority was established for utilization of Soviet-produced food: first, the combat troops; second, the remainder of troops in enemy territory; third, troops stationed in Germany; fourth, the German civilian population; and fifth, the population of the occupied countries. All industry in the northern area of the Soviet Union was to be destroyed in order to make the remnants of the Soviet population completely dependent upon Germany for consumer goods.

Seven weeks before the attack upon Russia consideration was given in military circles to the feeding of German armies invading Soviet territory. A memorandum of May 2, 1941, reporting the result of a discussion with the State Secretaries about Barbarossa, contained these significant observations:

"1. The war can only be continued if all the armed forces are fed with stocks from Russia in the third year of war.

"2. There is no doubt that as a result many millions of people will die of starvation if we take out of this country everything that we need."[25]

Several days later, on May 23, 1941, Goering's "Economic Staff East" prepared detailed plans concerning the Soviet economy in the light of the planned attack upon Russia and the incorporation or colonization of its territories:

The surplus territories are situated in the black soil district (that is, the south and southeast) and in the Caucasus. The deficit areas are principally located in the forest zone of the north. Therefore, an isolation of the black soil areas must in any case place greater or lesser surpluses in these regions at our disposal. The consequences will be cessation of supplies to the entire forest zone, including the essential industrial centers of Moscow and Leningrad....

Germany is not interested in the maintenance of the productive power of these territories, except for supplying the troops stationed there. The population, as in the old days, will utilize arable land for growing its own food. It is useless to expect grain or other surpluses to be produced. Only after many years can these extensive regions be intensified to an extent that they might produce genuine surpluses. The population of these areas, particularly the urban population, will have to face most serious distress from famine. It will be necessary to divert the population into the Siberian spaces. Since rail transport is out of the question, this too, will be an extremely difficult problem....

In the future, southern Russia must turn its face toward Europe. Its food surpluses, however, can only be paid for if it purchases its industrial consumer goods from Germany, or Europe. Russian competition from the forest zone must, therefore, be abolished.

It follows from all that has been said that the German administration in these territories may well attempt to mitigate the consequences of the famine which undoubtedly will take place, and to accelerate the return to primitive agriculture conditions. An attempt might be made to intensify cultivation in these areas by expanding the acreage under potatoes or other important food crops giving a high yield. However, these measures will not avert famine. Many tens of millions of people in this area will become redundant and will either die or have to emigrate to Siberia. Any attempt to save the population there from death by starvation by importing surpluses from the black soil zone would be at the expense of supplies to Europe. It would reduce Germany's staying power in the war, and would undermine Germany's and Europe's power to resist the blockade. This must be clearly and absolutely understood....

In conclusion, the principles must be pointed out once more: Under the Bolshevik system Russia has, purely out of power motives, withdrawn from Europe and thus upset the European equilibrium based on division of labor. Our task is to reintegrate Russia with the European division of labor, and it involves, of necessity, the destruction of the existing economic equilibrium within the Soviet Union. Thus, it is not important, under any circumstances, to preserve what has existed, but what matters is a deliberate turning away from the existing situation and introducing Russian food resources into the European framework. This will inevitably result in an extinction of industry as well as of a large part of the people in what so far have been the food-deficit areas. It is impossible to state an alternative in sufficiently hard and severe terms.[26]

The Reich Minister for the Occupied Eastern Territories, the defendant Rosenberg, stated similar objectives to his subordinates in a secret speech which he delivered on June 21, 1941, the day before the German attack upon the Soviet Union:

The job of feeding the German people stands this year, without a doubt, at the top of the list of Germany's claims on the East; and here the southern territories and the northern Caucasus will have to serve as a balance for the feeding of the German people. We see absolutely no reason for any obligation on our part to feed also the Russian people with the products of that surplus territory. We know that this is a harsh necessity, bare of any feelings.[27]

The aim of a Reich Commissioner for Esthonia, Latvia, Lithuania, and White Russia, must be to strive to achieve the form of a German protectorate and then transform the region into part of the Greater German Reich by Germanizing racially possible elements, colonizing Germanic races, and banishing undesirable elements. The Baltic Sea must become a Germanic inland sea, under the guardianship of Greater Germany.[28]

At a meeting with his top advisers, Lammers, Goering, Keitel, Rosenberg, and Bormann, only a month later, on July 16, 1941, Hitler discussed future plans for the utilization and disposition of the territories of the Soviet Union.

"On principle," he said, "we have now to face the task of cutting up the giant cake according to our needs, in order to be able: first, to dominate it; second, to administer it; and third, to exploit it."[29]

Hitler called for the complete evacuation of the Crimea and its settlement by Germans, only. In the same way the former Austrian part of Galicia was to become Reich territory. Hitler stated that the entire Baltic country was to be incorporated into Germany, as well as the Crimea, including as large a hinterland as possible, the Volga Colony, and the district around Baku. Hitler noted that Finland wanted East Carelia, but he said, "The Kola Peninsula will be taken by Germany because of the large nickel mines there. The annexation of Finland as a federated state should be prepared with caution. The area around Leningrad is wanted by the Finns; the Fuehrer will raze Leningrad to the ground and then hand it over to the Finns."[30]

Hitler observed that "the Russians have now ordered partisan warfare behind our front. This partisan war again has some advantages for us; it enables us to eradicate everyone who opposes us."[31] He added: "Naturally this giant area would have to be pacified as quickly as possible; the best solution was to shoot anybody who looked sideways."[32] To this Keitel commented that "the inhabitants had to understand that anybody who did not perform his duties properly would be shot."[33]

The impoverishment of the peoples whose land they occupied and the gradual displacement of them with persons of "German blood" proceeded according to plan as the German armies advanced in the East. The rich granaries of the Ukraine, the great industries of Czechoslovakia, the lands of Poland—the accumulated resources of all nations overrun by the marauders—were converted to the enrichment of the conquerors and the service of their hungry war machine. But when the tide turned, and the displaced peoples regained their homes and lands, the Germans left only charred buildings, plundered houses, and devastated properties. The guiding rule, laid down in directives to the armed forces, was: "The enemy must take over a completely useless uninhabitable desert land where mine detonations will occur for months hence."[34]

On September 7, 1943, Goering issued this decree at Hitler's direction:

First. In the territories east of the line fixed by the highest military command, the following measures are to be taken gradually, according to the military situation at the time. The measures are to be determined by the commanders of the army groups:

(1) All agricultural products, means of production, and machinery of enterprises serving the agricultural and food economy are to be removed.

(2) The factories serving the food economy, both in the field of production and of processing, are to be destroyed.

(3) The basis of agricultural production, especially the records and establishments, storage plants, et cetera, of the organization responsible for the food economy, are to be destroyed.

(4) The population engaged in the agricultural and food economy is to be transported into the territory west of the fixed line.[35]

Where Germanization failed, devastation took its place.

Germanization in the West

The notes concerning a conversation of June 19, 1940, at the headquarters of Field Marshal Goering disclosed general plans for incorporation of western territories into Greater Germany: "Luxembourg is to be annexed by the Reich. Norway is to become German. Alsace-Lorraine is to be reincorporated into the Reich. An autonomous Breton state is to be created. Considerations are pending concerning Belgium, the special treatment of the Flemish in that country, and the creation of a State of Burgundy."[36]

It was proposed to Hitler that the territories in the north and east of France which, for any pretended historical, political, racial, geographical, or other reason, could be considered as belonging to central rather than to western Europe should be incorporated into the Reich. Hitler approved the initial draft of this plan in its entirety, but upon reconsideration decided that it was too moderate, and he ordered that it be extended to other territories as well, notably those along the coast of the Channel. In the final draft "the intended frontier followed approximately a course beginning at the mouth of the Somme, turning eastward along the northern edge of the Paris Basin and Champagne to the Argonne, then bent to the south crossing Burgundy, and westward of the Franche-Comté, reaching the Lake of Geneva."[37]

Alsace and Lorraine were at once incorporated into the civil administration of Germany. The frontier and customs police were placed on the western border of the territories; railroads were incorporated into the German network; the French language was eliminated in administration and public life; names of localities were Germanized; and German racial legislation was introduced. Some of the measures introduced were quite absurd. Inscriptions on tombstones and crosses were required to be written in German; "Heil Hitler" was to replace the French "Bonjour"; and the wearing of French berets was forbidden.[38]

During the period from July to December, 1940, 105,000 Alsatians were expelled or prevented from returning to their homes.

They were in the main Jews, Gypsies, and other foreign racial elements, criminals, asocial and incurably insane persons, and in addition Frenchmen and Francophiles. The Patois-speaking population was combed out by this series of deportations in the same way as the other Alsatians.

Referring to the permission the Fuehrer had given him to cleanse Alsace of all foreign, sick or unreliable elements, Gauleiter Wagner has recently pointed out the political necessity of new deportations which are to be prepared as soon as possible.[39]

With respect to Luxembourg, the president of the Chamber of Deputies, M. Reuter, testified:

The measures that were taken by the Germans in the Grand Duchy were obviously equivalent to a *de facto* annexation of that country. Shortly after the invasion the leaders of the Reich in Luxembourg stated in public and official speeches that the annexation by law would occur at a time which would be freely selected by the Fuehrer. The proof of this *de facto* annexation is shown in a clear manner by the whole series of ordinances which the Germans published in the Grand Duchy.[40]

In Luxembourg the Germans conscripted the youth into the Hitler Jugend and the young men into the armed forces. The witness Reuter estimated that about three thousand Luxembourgers lost their lives as a result of the decrees of conscription. Among the numerous "Germanization" orders introduced into Luxembourg was one dated June 16, 1941:

1. All pupils must stand up when the teacher enters to begin the lesson and when leaving the classroom at the end of the lesson.

2. The German salute will be given in the following manner:

a) Raise the outstretched right arm to shoulder level. b) Shout: "Heil Hitler."

3. The pupils must return the same salute which the teachers use at the beginning and end of the lessons.

4. I also expect all pupils to give the German salute in the street, especially to those gentlemen known to be enthusiastic partisans of the German salute.[41]

Germanization of portions of Yugoslavia was planned within a few months after German troops had invaded that country. On December 16, 1941, Frick spoke of instructions he had given to Gauleiter Dr. Friedrich Rainer. German was to be the only authorized language and the only one to be used officially. Instruction in the schools was to become exclusively German as soon as possible. Frick said that when "the Slovene language is replaced by German —only then will we be able to speak of the Germanization of the Upper Kranj."[42]

These measures were all part of Hitler's dream of a New Order in Europe in which the territories occupied by the German military forces were to become Germanic in fact or subject to German domination and control for the centuries to come.

CHAPTER 28

Plunder

IN A CONFERENCE with the Reich Commissioners for the Occupied Territories on August 6, 1942, Goering made the following remark: "It seemed to me to be a relatively simple matter in former days. It used to be called plundering. It was up to the party in question to carry off what had been conquered. But today things have become more humane. In spite of that, I intend to plunder and to do it thoroughly."[1] Goering then explained how in modern warfare plunder should be thoroughly organized and accomplished even at the cost of starvation of the peoples of the occupied territories:

At this moment Germany commands the richest granaries that ever existed in the European area, stretching from the Atlantic to the Volga and the Caucasus, lands more highly developed and fruitful than ever before, even if a few of them cannot be described as granaries. I need only remind you of the fabulous fertility of the Netherlands, the unique paradise that is France. Belgium too is extraordinarily fruitful, and so is the province of Posen. Then, above all, the Government General has to a great extent the rye and wheat granary of Europe, and along with it the amazingly fertile districts of Lemberg (Lvov) and Galicia, where the harvest is exceptionally good. Then there comes Russia, the black earth of the Ukraine on both shores of the Dnieper, the Don region, with its remarkably fertile districts which have scarcely been destroyed. Our troops have now occupied, or are in process of occupying, the excessively fertile districts between the Don and the Caucasus.

God knows, you are not sent out there to work for the welfare of the people in your charge but to squeeze the utmost out of them, so that the German people may live. That is what I expect of your exertions. This everlasting concern about foreign peoples must cease now, once and for all.

I have here before me reports on what you expect to be able to deliver. It is nothing at all when I consider your territories. It makes no difference to me if you say that your people are starving.

One thing I shall certainly do. I will make you deliver the quantities asked of you; and if you cannot do so, I will set forces to work that will force you to do so whether you want to or not....

All that interests me is what we can squeeze out of the territory now under our control with the utmost application and by straining every nerve; and how much of that can be diverted to Germany. I don't give a damn about import and export statistics of former years.

Now, regarding shipments to the Reich. Last year France shipped 550,000 tons of grain and now I demand 1.2 million tons. Two weeks from now a plan will be submitted for handling it. There will be no more discussion about it. What happens to the Frenchmen is of no importance. One million two hundred thousand tons will be delivered. Fodder—last year 550,000 tons, now one million; meat—last year 135,000 tons, now 350,000; fats—last year 23,000, this year 60,000.[2]

Goering continued to demand exorbitant confiscations of produce from every occupied country. And he insisted that the Wehrmacht be provisioned by each country in which units were stationed. The seizure of property in the occupied territories was related to this grand plan for spoliation.

Spoliation in the East

Hitler entered Prague at nightfall on March 15, 1939, and spent the night in the famous castle of Hradcany. When he left on the morning of the next day he took with him a number of valuable tapestries which he had hand-looted from the castle. The report of the Czechoslovak Government shows that these private thefts were incidental to the organized pillage of the country:

The German troops who invaded Prague brought with them a staff of German economic experts, that is, experts in economic looting.

Everything that could be of some value to Germany was seized, especially large stocks of raw materials, such as copper, tin, iron, cotton, wool, great stocks of food, et cetera.

Rolling stock, carriages, engines, and so on were removed to the Reich. All the rails in the Protectorate which were in good condition were lifted and sent to Germany; later they were replaced by old rails brought from Germany. New cars fresh from the factory which were on order for the Prague municipal tramways and had just been completed were deflected from their purpose and sent to the Reich.

The vessels belonging to the Czechoslovak Danube Steam Navigation Company (the majority of shares belonged to the Czechoslovak State) were divided between the Reich and Hungary.

Valuable objects of art and furniture disappeared from public buildings, without even an attempt at any legal justification of such robbery; pictures, statues, tapestries were taken to Germany. The Czech National Museum, the Modern Art Gallery, and public and private collections were plundered.

The German Reich Commissioner of the Czechoslovak National Bank stopped all payments of currency abroad and seized all the gold reserve and foreign currency in the Protectorate. Thus the Germans took 23,000 kilograms of gold of a nominal value of 737,000 million crowns (5,265,000 pounds sterling) and transferred the gold from the Bank of International Settlement to the Reichsbank.[3]

Less than a month after the commencement of the war with Poland the German military authorities, on September 27, 1939, issued a decree authorizing the sequestration and confiscation of Polish property in the western provinces. "The property of the Polish State, Polish public institutions, municipalities and unions, individuals, and corporations can be sequestered and confiscated."[4]

On October 19, 1939, Goering issued a directive in which he ordered removed from the territories of the Government General all raw materials, scrap, machines, and other property useful to the German war economy:

Enterprises which are not absolutely necessary for the meager maintenance of the bare existence of the population must be transferred to Germany, unless such transfer would require an unreasonably long period of time and would make it more practical to exploit those enterprises by giving them German orders to be executed at their present location.[5]

The plunder of property from the Government General was the responsibility of Frank, who made the following entries in his diary:

My relationship with the Poles resembles that between an ant and a plant louse. When I treat the Poles helpfully, tickle them in a friendly manner, so to speak, I do it in the expectation that I shall profit by their labor output. This is not a political, but a purely tactical and technical problem. In cases where, in spite of all measures, the output does not increase, or where I have the slightest reason to step in, I would not hesitate to take even the most Draconian action....

We must remember that notes issued by the Bank of Poland to the value of 540,000,000 zlotys were taken over in occupied eastern territory by the Governor General without any compensation being made by the Reich. This represents a contribution of more than 500 million exacted from the Government General by Germany, in addition to other payments.[6]

A report of May 22, 1940, disclosed the extent of the confiscation of privately owned Polish property:

The lack of agricultural laborers still exists in the old Reich. The transfer of the previous owners of the confiscated enterprises, together with their entire families, to the Reich is possible without any further consideration. It is only necessary for the labor office to receive the lists of the persons in time, in order to enable it to take the necessary steps (collection of transportation, distribution over the various regions in need of such labor). Furniture cannot be taken along under any circumstances; in the course of the confiscation the only things left to the Poles were, anyway, only the most vital items, like bedding, ample food, clothes and other such things.[7]

A typical operation was carried out at Alzen, where the mayor of the village was required to round up all Poles who possessed agricultural property in the areas surrounding the village. The report disclosed that farmers were dispossessed of their lands, their homes, furniture, livestock, and all their worldly belongings save what they could carry on their backs.

The confiscation of these Polish enterprises in Alzen will also be carried out within the next few days. The commandant of the concentration camp will furnish SS-men and a truck for the execution of the action. Should it not yet be possible to take the Poles from Alzen to Auschwitz, they should be transferred to the empty castle at Zator. The liberated Polish property is to be given to the needy racial German farmers for their use.[8]

The purposeful confiscation of private property was disclosed in a decree issued by Goering on September 17, 1940, which made mandatory the sequestration of movable and immovable property, stores, and intangible interests of Jews and "persons who have fled or who have absented themselves for longer than a temporary period," and which authorized the sequestration of property required "for the public good, especially for purposes of national defense or the strengthening of German folkdom."[9] The property of German nationals was expressly exempt from both sequestration and confiscation—leaving only the Jews, Poles, and other non-Germans to suffer loss of their belongings. Under this decree the lands and homes of all Poles were subject to confiscation. On April 15, 1941, a Himmler order construing the decree provided: "The objective conditions permitting seizure according to Section II, Subsection 2(a), are to be assumed whenever, for example, the property belongs to a Pole, for the Polish real estate will be needed without exception for the preservation of the German folkdom."[10] By May 31, 1943, four Estate Offices had completed the confiscation of over 700,000 Polish estates comprising over 6,300,000 hectares of land.

Frank recorded a statement made by a representative to a conference called by him on December 7, 1942, concerning measures for increasing Polish food shipments for the years 1942-43: "If the new food scheme is carried out, it would mean that in Warsaw and its suburbs alone 500,000 people would be deprived of food."[11]

Later, Frank recorded his own intentions in this entry:

I shall endeavor to squeeze out from the reserves of this province everything that is still possible to squeeze out.... If you recall that I was able to send to Germany 600,000 tons of grain and that an additional 180,000 tons were reserved for local troops, as well as many thousands of tons of seed, fats, vegetables, besides the export to Germany of 300 million eggs, *et cetera,* you will understand how important the work in this region is for Germany....

These consignments to the Reich had, however, one definite drawback to them, since the quantities we were responsible for delivering exceeded the actual food supplies required by the region. We now have to face the following problem. Can we, as from February, cut two million non-German inhabitants of the region out of the general rationing scheme?[12]

An excerpt from the minutes of a conference of April 14, 1943, which took place in Cracow, indicates the enormity of German demands for 1943-44: "One thousand five hundred tons of sweets for the Germans, 36 million liters of skimmed fresh milk; 15,100,-000 liters of full cream milk for the Germans."[13]

Frank further recorded the extent of these expropriations:

Last year, more than 20 percent of the total amount of livestock in the Government General was requisitioned. Cattle which were really required for the production of milk and butter were slaughtered last year so that the Reich and the armed forces could be supplied and the meat ration maintained to a certain extent. If we want 120,000 tons of meat, we must sacrifice 40 percent of the remaining live stock.[14]

And further:

In answer to a question by the Governor General, President Naumann replied that 383,000 tons of grain were requisitioned in 1940, 685,000 tons in 1941, and 1.2 million tons in 1942. It appears from these figures that requisitions have increased from year to year and have steadily approached the limits of possibility. Now they are preparing to increase the requisitions by another 200,000 tons which will bring them to the extreme bounds of possibility. The Polish peasant cannot be allowed to starve beyond the point where he will still be able to cultivate his fields and carry out any further tasks imposed upon him, such as carting wood for the forestry authorities.[15]

Plunder led to poverty in Yugoslavia. A report of February 12, 1944, concerning the effect of the seizure of cattle for the Wehrmacht and for the German people stated:

1. If they are deprived of so many cattle, the peasants will not be able to cultivate their fields. On the one hand, they are ordered to cultivate every inch of ground, on the other hand, their cattle are ruthlessly confiscated.

2. The cattle are purchased at such a low price that the peasants feel that they are hardly compensated at all for the loss of their cattle.[16]

Where the peasant resisted, or showed "an unfriendly attitude" toward the invaders, the orders were to confiscate everything essential to life—adding starvation to the Hitler armory of weapons. The order of Major General Kuebler to the German troops in Yugoslavia contained this passage: "Troops must treat these members of the population who maintain an unfriendly attitude toward the occupation forces in a brutal and ruthless manner, depriving the enemy of every means of existence by the destruction of localities which have been abandoned and by seizing all available stocks."[17]

The same policy of expropriation was applied in the case of Greece. The report of the Greek Government contained these entries:

> Owing to her geographical position, Greece was used by the Germans as a base of operations for the war in North Africa. They also used Greece as a rest center for thousands of their troops from the North African and Eastern fronts, thus concentrating in Greece much larger forces than were actually necessary for the purpose of occupation.
>
> A large part of the local supplies of fruit, vegetables, potatoes, olive oil, meat, and dairy products were confiscated to supply these forces. As current production was not sufficient for these needs, they resorted to the requisitioning of livestock on a large scale, with the result that the country's livestock became seriously depleted....
>
> Between August 1941 and December 1941 the sum of 26,206,-085,000 drachmas was paid to the Germans, representing a sum of 60 percent more than the estimated national income during the same period. In fact, according to the estimates of two Axis experts, Dr. Barberin, from Germany, and Dr. Bartoni, an Italian, the national income for that year amounted to only 23,000 million drachmas. In the following year, as the national income decreased, this money was taken from national funds.[18]

As in other occupied countries, the Germans flooded Greece with occupation currency, blocked prices of goods exported to Germany, and forced the Greeks to pay for imports at inflated prices. The report of the Greek Government stated: "In consequence, notwithstanding the fact that Greece exported the whole of her available resources to Germany, the clearing account showed a credit balance of 264,157,574.03 marks in favor of Germany when the Germans left. At the time of their arrival the credit balance in favor of Greece was 4,353,428.82 marks."[19]

The territories of the Soviet Union were from the beginning looked upon as great areas of spoliation. German agricultural leaders were sent into the conquered Soviet lands with instructions to carry out faithfully and diligently twelve commandments, among which were the following:

5th commandment: It is essential that you should always bear in mind the end to be attained. You must pursue this aim with the utmost stubbornness; but the methods used may be elastic to a degree. The methods employed are left to the discretion of the individual....[20]

6th commandment: The areas just opened up must be permanently acquired for Germany and Europe. Everything will depend upon your behavior. You must realize that you are the representatives of Greater Germany and the standard-bearers of the National Socialist Revolution and of the New Europe for centuries to come. You must, therefore, carry out with dignity even the hardest and most ruthless measures required by the necessities of the state....[21]

7th commandment: Do not ask, "How will this benefit the peasants?" but "How will it benefit Germany?"

8th commandment: Do not talk—act! You can never talk a Russian around or persuade him with words. He can talk better than you can, for he is a born "dialectic"....Only your will must decide, but this will must be directed to the execution of great tasks. Only in this case will it be ethical even in its cruelty. Keep away from the Russians— they are not Germans, they are Slavs.

9th commandment: We do not wish to convert the Russians to National Socialism; we wish only to make them a tool in our hands.[22]

The basic directive under which all plunder of Soviet lands was carried out was Goering's "Green File,"[23] compiled for the purpose of directing the exploitation of the Soviet economy. The main economic tasks were stated in these words:

According to the Fuehrer's order, it is essential in the interests of Germany that every possible measure for the immediate and complete exploitation of the occupied territories be adopted. Any measure liable to hinder the achievement of this purpose should be waived or cancelled.

The exploitation of the regions to be occupied immediately should be carried out primarily in the economic field controlling food supplies and crude oil. The main economic purpose of the campaign is to obtain the greatest possible quantity of food and crude oil for Germany. In addition, other raw materials from the occupied territories must be supplied to the German war economy as far as it is technically possible and as far as the claims of the industries to be maintained outside the Reich permit....

The idea that order should be restored in the occupied territories and their economic life re-established as soon as possible is entirely mistaken. On the contrary, the treatment of the different parts of the country must be a very different one. Order should only be restored and industry promoted in regions where we can obtain considerable reserves of agricultural products or crude oil.[24]

An order issued by Keitel on June 16, 1941, six days before the attack on the Soviet Union, instructed the military command on the need for conforming to the planned exploitation of the occupied territories. The order concluded with these words: "The exploitation of the country must be carried out on a wide scale, with the help of field and local headquarters, in the most important agricultural and oil-producing districts."[25]

It was already realized that removal of great quantities of food could be carried out only at the risk of starvation of the indigenous population. On December 2, 1941, the Inspector of Armaments for the Ukraine stated in a letter addressed to the Chief of the Army Armament Section:

The export of agricultural surpluses from the Ukraine for the purpose of feeding the Reich is only possible if the internal trade in the Ukraine is reduced to a minimum. This can be attained by the following measures:

1. Elimination of unwanted consumers (Jews; the populations of the large Ukrainian towns, which like Kiev, received no food allocation whatsoever).

2. Reduction as far as possible of food rations allocated to the Ukrainians in other towns.

3. Reduction of food consumption by the peasant population. If the Ukrainian is to be made to work, we must look after his physical existence, not for sentimental motives, but for purely business reasons.[26]

In a speech delivered on June 20, 1941, Rosenberg stated:

...The problem of feeding German nationals undeniably heads the German demands on the East just now, and here the southern regions and the northern Caucasus must help to balance the German food

situation. We certainly do not consider ourselves obliged to feed the
Russian people as well from the produce of these fertile regions. We
know that this is a cruel necessity, which has nothing to do with any
humane feelings. It will undoubtedly be necessary to carry out evacuation on a large scale and the Russians are doomed to live through
some very hard years.[27]

The Reich Commissioner for the Ukraine said in a conference
at Rowno in August, 1942, that he understood his duties in the
following terms:

There is no free Ukraine. We must aim at making the Ukrainians
work for Germany, and not at making the people here happy. The
Ukraine will have to make good the German shortages. This task must
be accomplished without regard for losses.... The Fuehrer has ordered
3 million tons of grain from the Ukraine for the Reich, and they must
be delivered....[28]

On October 17, 1944, Rosenberg reported to Bormann that in
the year preceding March 31, 1944, there had been shipped to
Germany from the Eastern Territories, among other commodities,
the following:

> Cereals ....9,200,000 tons
> Meat and meat products .... 622,000 tons
> Oil seed .... 950,000 tons
> Butter .... 208,000 tons
> Sugar .... 400,000 tons
> Fodder ....2,500,000 tons
> Potatoes ....3,200,000 tons

The Soviet prosecution offered a report of the Soviet Extraordinary Commission on spoliation:

The Extraordinary State Commission has undertaken the task of
estimating the damage done to the Soviet citizens by the occupation
authorities and has established that the German fascist invaders burned
down and destroyed approximately four million dwelling houses which
were the personal property of collective farmers, workers, and employees; confiscated one and a half million horses, nine million head
of cattle, twelve million pigs, thirteen million sheep and goats; and
took away an enormous quantity of household goods and chattels of
all kinds.[29]

Spoliation in the West

Hitler took the position that Denmark was not an occupied territory and hence was not required to pay the expenses of occupation of German troops. Instead, sums necessary to cover occupation expenses were placed at the disposal of the central administration of the Reichskreditkasse by the Central Danish Bank, through ordinary channels of credit, assured for the duration of the war. The end result was cash withdrawals of over 3,000,000,000 crowns. Levies in kind were made in substantial amounts. Requisitions of agricultural items alone were estimated at over 4,200,000,000 crowns. The total of all damages claimed preliminarily by Denmark was 11,600,000,000 crowns.

The pattern was the same in Norway. The Bank of Norway showed German debits of 1,450,000,000 crowns at the end of 1940; 3,000,000,000 crowns at the end of 1941; 6,300,000,000 crowns at the end of 1942; 8,700,000,000 crowns at the end of 1943; and 11,676,000,000 crowns after liberation. The Nazis systematically raised the prices of all products imported into Norway, which were used for the most part by the occupying forces; and, on the other hand, systematically drove down the prices of the products exported from Norway. Huge levies in kind were imposed.

In the Netherlands a total of 6,356,000,000 florins was exacted as indemnity for the maintenance of occupation troops. Clearing operations and imposition of excessive fines made possible the removal of huge quantities of produce and goods from Holland. Large levies in kind were imposed upon the Dutch. As of the end of 1943 the Nazis had seized 600,000 hogs, 275,000 cattle, and 30,000 tons of preserved meat. They took 490 locomotives out of a total of 890; 1,446 passenger coaches out of 1,750; 215 electric trains out of 300; and 36 diesel trains out of 37. The Nazis confiscated the greater part of the automobiles, motorcycles, and bicycles. They took all river vessels and a great quantity of telephone and telegraph equipment. Furniture, private archives, carriages, linen, silverware, paintings, tapestries, and art objects were taken from the Royal palaces.

Belgium paid a total of 64,181,000,000 Belgian francs to the army of occupation, a sum considerably in excess of the full cost of maintaining the German army in Belgium. Clearing transactions were used to permit taking out a further like sum. The Nazis organized a huge black market operation in Belgium and northern France. Seizure of vehicles and railroad equipment followed the pattern set in Holland.

The little country of Luxembourg lost about 33 per cent of its national wealth through plunder.

The armistice signed by France with Germany required the French government to pay the expenses of the maintenance of German troops of occupation. The word "maintenance" was soon interpreted "in the broadest possible sense."[30] Sums demanded as occupation costs included not only maintenance, equipment, and the armament of German troops in France, but also the cost of operations based in France. "Surpluses" were used "for purposes important to the Four Year Plan."[31] So extreme were the Hitler demands that on August 18, 1940, Hemmen, chief of the German economic delegation, reported to the Minister of Foreign Affairs: "These large payments would enable Germany to buy up the whole of France, including its industries and foreign investments, which would mean the ruin of France."[32]

The French Government repeatedly protested. A note of August 26, 1940, ended with the passage: "The French nation fears neither work nor suffering, but it must be allowed to live. This is why the French Government would be unable in the future to continue along the road to which it is committed if experience showed that the extent of the demands of the government of the Reich is incompatible with this right to live."[33]

In a final report on financial levies against France, Hemmen stated: "...during the four years which have elapsed since conclusion of the armistice, there has been paid for occupation costs and billeting 34,000 million Reichsmarks, or 680,000 million francs. France thus contributed approximately 40 per cent of the total cost of occupation and war contributions raised in all the occupied and Allied countries."[34]

Levies in kind corresponded to seizures in other occupied territories. The Nazis took 8,900,000 tons of cereals, 900,000 tons of meat, 690,000 horses and mules. They levied 75 per cent of oats produced, 80 per cent of the crude oil and motor fuel, 74 per cent of the iron ore, 75 per cent of the copper, 76 per cent of the tin, 100 per cent of the magnesium, 59 per cent of the wool, 67 per cent of the leather, and 67 per cent of the industrial soap. Millions of francs' worth of manufactured products were removed. Percentages showed: automobiles 70 per cent, industrial precision parts 100 per cent, heavy castings 100 per cent, lime and cement 68 per cent, rubber 60 per cent, naval construction 79 per cent, aeronautic construction 90 per cent. The total value of levies of manufactured goods and products amounted to 184,640 million francs.[35]

The Looting of Treasures of Art

The spoliation of occupied territories could be partially justified as necessary to supply and maintain the Hitler war machine. If the war had ended in Germany's favor, plunder of this sort might have been reduced or stopped. Incorporation of occupied territories into the Greater Reich could have resulted in quite different economic relationships. While the war continued, however, it was understandable, from the Hitler point of view, that the occupied territories were to be exploited in every way helpful to the strength of Germany and of its armies in the field. The crime of spoliation thus was really a part of the crime of initiating and waging wars of aggression.

Theft of art treasures was in quite a different category. No possible argument could be advanced to the effect that such treasures were required to enable Germany to prosecute its wars. The seizure of works of art was a result not of the requirements of the German armies, but of the avarice of Germany's leaders. In this game of grab, Hermann Goering was the principal player. During the war, Goering brought his private collection of paintings and works of art to a value, according to his own estimate, of fifty million Reichsmarks.

Scarcely a month after the attack upon Poland, Goering issued an order for the securing of all Polish art treasures. On December 16, 1939, Hans Frank, the Governor General of Poland, ordered

the confiscation of art objects in public possession. "Public possession" included ecclesiastical art properties and private art collections
taken under protection by the special commissioner for the seizure
and safekeeping of art and cultural treasures. Within six months,
the special commissioner could report seizure of "almost the entire
art treasure of the country" with the single exception of the Flemish
Gobelin series from the castle in Cracow. It was reported that these
were kept in France, "so that it will be possible to secure them
eventually."[36] They were, according to Himmler, "confiscated for
the benefit of the German Reich."[37]

In France, seizures were more directly for the cultural gratification of Hitler and Goering. On November 5, 1940, Goering issued
the following order to Alfred Rosenberg as director of the Einsatzstab Rosenberg, which had been established to carry out art seizures
in occupied territories:

In conveying the measures taken until now for the securing of
Jewish art property by the Chief of the Military Administration, Paris,
and the Einsatzstab Rosenberg...the art objects brought to the Louvre
will be disposed of in the following way:
1. Those art objects the decision as to the use of which the Fuehrer
will reserve for himself;
2. Those art objects which serve the completion of the Reich
Marshal's collection;
3. Those art objects and library materials which seem useful for
the establishment of the Hohe Schule and for the program of
Reichsleiter Rosenberg;
4. Those art objects which are suitable for sending to German
museums....
5. Those art objects that are suited to be given to French museums
or might be of use for the German-French art trade, will be auctioned
off at a date yet to be fixed; the profit of this auction will be given
to the French state for the benefit of those bereaved by the war.
6. The further securing of Jewish art property in France will be
continued by the special purpose staff Rosenberg in the same way as
heretofore in connection with the Chief of the Military Administration,
Paris.[38]

The corpulent leader of the German Air Force, to whom the
German people looked for protection from Allied bombings, found
time personally to inspect the collections of looted art and to select

the items to be shipped to Hitler and to himself. One of the
officials of Rosenberg's staff described a visit of the Reich Marshal
in the following words:

On Wednesday, 5 February 1941, I was ordered to the Jeu de
Paume by the Reich Marshal. At 1500 o'clock, the Reich Marshal,
accompanied by General Hanesse, Herrn Angerer, and Herrn Hofer,
visited the exhibition of Jewish art treasures newly set up there.

Then with me as his guide, the Reich Marshal inspected the
exhibited art treasures and made a selection of those works of art
which were to go to the Fuehrer, and those which were to be placed
in his own collection. During this confidential conversation, I again
called the Marshal's attention to the fact that a note of protest had
been received from the French Government against the activity of the
Einsatzstab Rosenberg, with reference to the Hague Rules on Land
Warfare recognized by Germany at the Armistice of Compiègne, and
I pointed out that General von Stuelpnagel's interpretation of the
manner in which the confiscated Jewish art treasures are to be treated
was apparently contrary to the Reich Marshal's interpretation. Thereupon, the Reich Marshal asked for a detailed explanation and gave
the following orders:

"First, it is my orders that you have to follow. You will act directly
according to my orders. The art objects collected in the Jeu de Paume
are to be loaded on a special train immediately and taken to Germany
by order of the Reich Marshal. Those art objects which are to go into
the Fuehrer's possession, and those art objects which the Reich Marshal
claims for himself, will be loaded on two railroad cars which will be
attached to the Reich Marshal's special train, and upon his departure
for Germany, at the beginning of next week, will be taken along to
Berlin. Feldfuehrer von Behr will accompany the Reich Marshal in his
special train on the journey to Berlin."

When I made the objection that the jurists would probably be of
a different opinion and that protests would most likely be made by the
military commander in France, the Reich Marshal answered saying
verbatim as follows, "Dear Bunjes, let me worry about that; I am the
highest jurist in the state."[39]

Most of the art treasures taken by Goering for his private
collection had been "confiscated" Jewish property. Further use
was made of these confiscations in trading for special objects of
art. The affiant M. Gustav Rochlitz told of a typical Goering
transaction:

Lohse came to see me in February 1941. He told me that he was looking for pictures for different highly placed persons, chiefly for Goering. I showed to him a painting by Wennix of which I was the owner and a "Portrait of a Man," by Titian, of which two-thirds belonged to Birchentski and one-third to me.... He showed me a certain number of paintings and offered me eleven of them in exchange for the two paintings. He prevented me from looking at the backs of the paintings....

I thought at that time that the paintings came from Germany. I found out shortly after that these paintings and those subsequently exchanged with Lohse were paintings confiscated from Jews. When I saw that these had been confiscated I protested and Lohse answered, "I am acting under Goering's orders, you have nothing to fear. These confiscations have been anticipated by the armistice convention and the exchanges are regular." As I still protested, he called me an enemy of the people.[40]

The quantity of treasures thus seized by the Nazi leadership was enormous. Thousands of precious art objects, taken from their owners, were stored in German salt mines to await the ending of the war. During the period from March, 1941, to July, 1944, 29 large shipments of pictorial art were brought into the Reich comprising 137 freight cars containing 4,174 cases of art works. One such shipment was reported by Rosenberg to Hitler in these words:

I report the arrival of the principal shipment of ownerless Jewish treasures of art at the salvage point Neuschwanstein by special train on Saturday the 15th of this month. It was secured by my Einsatzstab, in Paris. The special train, arranged for by Reich Marshal Hermann Goering, comprised 25 express baggage cars filled with the most valuable paintings, furniture, Gobelin tapestries, works of artistic craftsmanship, and ornaments. The shipments consisted mainly of the most important parts of the collection of Rothschild, Seligmann.... Besides this special train, the main art objects selected by the Reich Marshal—mainly from the Rothschild collection—had previously been shipped in two special cars to Munich and were there put into the air raid shelter of the Fuehrerhaus.[41]

By July, 1944, a total of 21,903 art objects of all types, removed from occupied territories to Germany, had been counted and inventoried. The value of this enormous loot could scarcely be estimated. As early as January 28, 1941, Rosenberg had declared that the value of art properties seized in France alone amounted to "close to a billion Reichsmarks."[42] As reported by a Rosenberg official:

The extraordinary artistic and material value of the seized art works cannot be expressed in figures. The paintings, period furniture of the 17th and 18th centuries, the Gobelins, the antiques and renaissance jewelry of the Rothschilds are objects of such a unique character that their evaluation is impossible, since no comparable values have so far appeared on the art market.... Among the seized paintings, pastels and drawings there are several hundred works of the first quality, masterpieces of European art, which could take first place in any museum. Included therein are absolutely authenticated signed works of Rembrandt van Rijn, Rubens, Frans Hals, Vermeer van Delft, Velasquez, Murillo, Goya, Sebastiano del Piombo, Palma Vecchio, *et cetera*.[43]

Twenty-five portfolios of the pictures of the most valuable art objects seized in the West were presented to Hitler. The treasures themselves were meticulously inventoried and stored away. It was not merely plunder; it was exquisite plunder. It was stolen sweets added to the stolen bread.

Goering was asked whether he gave the following instruction to the Reich Commissioners responsible for the plundering of the occupied territories: "Whenever you come across anything that may be needed by the German people, you must be after it like a bloodhound. It must be taken out ... and brought to Germany." And he answered: "I certainly assume that I did say it; yes."[44]

CHAPTER 29

Slave Labor

Not only the material, but also the human resources of the occupied territories were applied to the strengthening of the German economy. German youths taken into the armed forces created serious shortages of labor in the Reich. Their replacement was indispensable to the high level of industrial and agricultural production required for continuous prosecution of Hitler's aggrandizement by force.

Albert Speer was appointed Reich Minister for Armaments and Munitions on February 15, 1942. Subsequently his authority was enlarged to include all war production. He was undoubtedly a genius at organization, and he may have been responsible more than any other man for continued German resistance after Allied bombings shattered the Reich. For war production Speer required manpower. And he testified, frankly, that forced labor was used for this purpose. "The workers were brought to Germany largely against their will, and I had no objection to their being brought to Germany against their will. On the contrary, during the first period, until the autumn of 1942, I certainly also took some pains to see that as many workers as possible should be brought to Germany in this manner."[1]

Direct responsibility for recruitment of foreign labor fell to Fritz Sauckel, who was appointed Plenipotentiary General for the Utilization of Labor on March 21, 1942. Sauckel operated under Goering as Commissioner for the Four Year Plan. In a meeting of the Central Planning Board on March 1, 1944, Sauckel declared that "out of five million foreign workers who arrived in Germany, not even 200,000 came voluntarily."[2] Shortly after his appointment he described the labor mobilization program in a letter to Rosenberg under date of April 20, 1942:

> The aim of this new, gigantic labor mobilization is to use all the rich and tremendous resources, conquered and secured for us by our fighting armed forces under the leadership of Adolf Hitler, for the armament of the armed forces and also for the nutrition of the homeland. The raw materials as well as the fertility of the conquered territories and their human labor power are to be used completely and conscientiously to the profit of Germany and her allies.[3]

All the countries of Europe overrun by the German military forces were required to send workers to Germany. Poland, the Ukraine, France, Holland, Belgium—all gave up men, women, and even children to till the soil, to work the mines, to operate the machines, and even to man guns in Hitler's service. While the heaviest recruitment took place after Speer and Sauckel assumed their respective posts, the search for labor began immediately upon the seizure of Poland. Thus on January 25, 1940, Hans Frank, as Governor General of Poland, wrote to Goering that a particular objective of his administration was the "supply and transportation of at least one million male and female agricultural and industrial workers to the Reich—among them at least 750,000 agricultural workers of which at least 50 per cent must be women—in order to guarantee agricultural production in the Reich and as a replacement for industrial workers lacking in the Reich."[4]

Recruitment by force was used as early as May, 1940. In his diary Frank wrote on May 10, 1940: "Upon the pressure from the Reich it has now been decreed that compulsion may be exercised in view of the fact that sufficient manpower was not voluntarily available for service inside the German Reich. This compulsion means the possibility of arrest of male and female Poles."[5] Frank wrote that "generally speaking, he had no objections at all to the rubbish, capable of work yet often loitering about, being snatched from the streets. The best method for this, however, would be the organization of a raid...."[6]

The confiscation of Polish farms made it relatively simple to seize Polish farmers for labor in Germany. An SS report issued on May 22, 1940, stated:

It is possible without difficulty to accomplish the confiscation of small agricultural enterprises in the villages in which larger agricultural enterprises have already been confiscated and are under the management of the East German Corporation for Agricultural Development. ... The former owners of Polish farms together with their families will be transferred to the old Reich by the employment offices for employment as farm workers. In this way many hundreds of Polish agricultural workers can be placed at the disposal of agriculture in the old Reich in the shortest and simplest manner.[7]

The Hitler regime was a pattern of paradoxes. Jews, stripped of property and of freedom, were used as slave labor in Reich factories. Yet even the desperate requirements of Germany for manpower did not prevent their deportation for extermination, thus further aggravating the already serious labor shortages. On November 26, 1942, Sauckel wrote about this difficulty to the Land employment offices:

In agreement with the Chief of the Security Police and the SD, these Jews who are still in employment are also, from now on, to be evacuated from the territory of the Reich and are to be replaced by Poles, who are being evacuated from the Government General.... The Poles who are to be evacuated as a result of this measure will be put into concentration camps and put to work, insofar as they are criminal or asocial elements. The remaining Poles, so far as they are suitable for labor, will be transported—without family—into the Reich, particularly to Berlin, where they will be put at the disposal of the labor allocation offices to work in armament factories instead of the Jews who are to be replaced.[8]

Slave-Raiding in the East

Poland was but the testing ground for the mass deportations from the Ukraine, the Balkan countries, and other eastern occupied territories. Minutes of the Central Planning Board, recording a conference with Hitler in August, 1942, disclosed the following:

Gauleiter Sauckel promises to make Russian labor available for the fulfillment of the iron and coal program and reports that, if required, he will supply a further million Russian laborers for the German armament industry up to and including October, 1942. So far he has already supplied one million for industry and 700,000 for agriculture. In this connection the Fuehrer states that the problem of providing labor can be solved in all cases and to any extent. He authorizes Gauleiter Sauckel to take all necessary measures. He would agree to any compulsory measures in the East as well as in the occupied western territories if this question could not be solved on a voluntary basis.[9]

On October 3, 1942, in a letter to the Reich Minister for the occupied eastern territories, Sauckel declared further demands for labor to be levied upon the Ukraine:

The Fuehrer has worked out new and most urgent plans for armaments which require the quick mobilization of two million more foreign workers. The Fuehrer therefore has granted me, for the execution of his decree of 21 March 1942, new powers for my new duties, and has especially authorized me to take whatever measures I think are necessary in the Reich, the Protectorate, the Government General, as well as in occupied territories, in order to assure, at all costs, an orderly mobilization of labor for the German armament industry. The additional required labor forces will have to be drafted, for the most part, from the recently occupied eastern territories, especially from the Reichskommissariat Ukraine. Therefore, the Reichskommissariat Ukraine must furnish 225,000 workers by 31 December 1942 and 225,000 more by 1 May 1943.[10]

One of Rosenberg's deputies complained to him, in a top secret memorandum of October 25, 1942, of the methods used in recruiting workers from the occupied eastern territories:

We now experienced the grotesque picture of having to recruit, precipitately, millions of laborers from the occupied eastern territories, after prisoners of war had died of hunger like flies, in order to fill the gaps that have formed within Germany. Now suddenly the food question no longer existed. In the customary limitless disregard for the Slavic people, "recruiting" methods were used which probably have their precedent only in the blackest periods of the slave trade. A regular manhunt was inaugurated. Without consideration of health or age, the people were shipped to Germany where it turned out immediately that more than 100,000 had to be sent back because of serious illness and other incapacity for work.[11]

Rosenberg wrote to Sauckel on December 21, 1942, protesting against slave raiding as inciting the native population to resistance:

The reports I have received show that the increase of the guerrilla bands in the occupied eastern territories is largely due to the fact that the methods used for procuring laborers in these regions are felt to be forced measures of mass deportations, so that the endangered persons prefer to escape their fate by withdrawing into the woods or going to the guerrilla bands.[12]

In the same letter Rosenberg enclosed an extract from a secret report on morale prepared by the Foreign Mail Censorship Post in Berlin:

In the letters from the Ukraine a further sharp decline in the morale is pictured, and under the impact of an increased requisition of labor forces for the Reich, the Ukrainian population has been seized by a terrible fear.

Horrifying pictures of *compulsory measures* by the administrative authorities for the seizure of Eastern laborers form a major part of the news from home to their relatives working in Germany. The disinclination to answer the call to work in the Reich has evidently grown steadily....In order to secure the required number for the labor transport, men and women including youngsters from 15 years on up, are allegedly taken from the street, from the market places and village festivals, and carried off. The inhabitants therefore hide themselves in fear and avoid any appearance in public. After public beatings during the month of October, so available letters state, came the burning down of homesteads, and of whole villages as retribution for failure to comply with the demand for the appropriation of labor forces directed to the communities. The execution of the latter measures is being reported from various villages.[13]

The report contained extracts from two censored letters:

At our place, new things have happened. People are being taken to Germany. On October 5 some people from the Kowkuski district were scheduled to go, but they did not want to and the village was set on fire. They threatened to do the same thing in Borowytschi, as not all who were scheduled to depart wanted to go. Thereupon three truck-loads of Germans arrived and set fire to their houses. In Wrasnytschi twelve houses and in Borowytschi three houses were burned.

On October 1 a new conscription of labor forces took place. Of what happened, I will describe the most important to you. You cannot imagine the bestiality. You probably remember what we were told about the Soviets during the rule of the Poles. At that time we did

not believe it and now it seems just as incredible. The order came to
supply 25 workers, but no one reported. All had fled. Then the German
police came and began to ignite the houses of those who had fled. The
fire burned furiously, since it had not rained for two months. In addition the grain stacks were in the farm yards. You can imagine what
took place. The people who had hurried to the scene were forbidden
to extinguish the flames, were beaten and arrested, so that six homesteads were burned down. The policemen meanwhile ignited other
houses. The people fall on their knees and kiss their hands, but the
policemen beat them with rubber truncheons and threaten to burn
down the whole village. I do not know how this would have ended
if Sapurkany had not intervened. He promised that there would be
laborers by the next morning. During the fire the police went through
the adjoining villages, seized the laborers, and brought them under
arrest. Wherever they did not find any laborers, they detained the
parents until the children appeared. This is how they raged throughout
the night in Bielosersk . . .

The workers who had not yet appeared by then were to be shot.
All schools were closed and the married teachers were sent to work
here, while the unmarried ones go to work in Germany. They are now
catching humans as the dogcatchers used to catch dogs. They are already
hunting for one week and have not yet enough. The imprisoned workers
are locked in the schoolhouse. They cannot even go to perform their
natural functions, but have to do it like pigs in the same room. People
from many villages went on a certain day to a pilgrimage to the
Poczajow Monastery. They were all arrested, locked in, and will be
sent to work. Among them there are lame, blind, and aged people.[14]

Problems increased as the war progressed unfavorably for the
Germans. It became harder to convince people by propaganda that
they should leave their homes, and Germany's need for labor became
greater. In February, 1943, the chairman of the Ukrainian main
committee at Cracow described the methods used by the labor
recruiters:

The general nervousness is still further increased by the wrong
methods of labor mobilization which have been used more and more
frequently in recent months.

The wild and ruthless manhunt as practiced everywhere in towns
and country, in streets, squares, stations, even in churches, as well as
at night in homes, has shaken the feeling of security of the inhabitants.
Every man is exposed to the danger of being seized suddenly and
unexpectedly, anywhere and at any time, by the police, and brought

into an assembly camp. None of his relatives knows what has happened to him, and only weeks or months later one or another gives news of his fate by a postcard....

In November of last year an inspection of all males of the age-classes born in 1910 to 1920 was ordered in the area of Zaleszcyti (district of Czortkow). After the men had appeared for inspection, all those who were selected were arrested at once, loaded into trains, and sent to the Reich. Similar recruitment of laborers for the Reich also took place in other areas of this district. Following some interventions, the action was then stopped.[15]

A month later, on March 17, 1943, Sauckel demanded, in a letter to Rosenberg, a million more workers from the eastern territories:

Especially the labor allocation for German agriculture and likewise the most urgent armament production programs ordered by the Fuehrer, make the fastest importation of approximately one million men and women from the eastern territories within the next four months, a necessity. Starting 15 March the daily shipment must reach 5,000 female or male workers, while from the beginning of April this number has to be stepped up to 10,000, if the most urgent programs and the spring tillage and other agricultural tasks are not to suffer to the detriment of food and of the armed forces.

I have provided for the allotment of the draft quotas for the individual territories, in agreement with your experts for labor supply, as follows:

Daily quota starting 15 March 1943: From General Kommissariat, White Ruthenia—500 people; Economic Inspection, Center—500 people; Reichkommissariat, Ukraine—3,000 people; Economic Inspection, South—1,000 people; total—5,000 people.

Starting 1 April 1943, the daily quota is to be doubled corresponding to the doubling of the entire quota.[16]

Two days later, on March 19, 1943, the SS-leader of the special detachment of the Security Police and SD was issuing the following instructions to the leaders of his auxiliary groups:

The activity of the labor offices, particularly of recruiting commissions, is to be supported to the greatest extent possible. It will not be possible always to refrain from using force. During a conference with the chief of the labor commitment staffs, an agreement was reached

stating that wherever prisoners can be released, they should be put at
the disposal of the commissioner of the labor office. When searching
villages, or when it has become necessary to burn down a village, the
whole population will be put at the disposal of the commissioner by
force.... The most important thing is the recruiting of workers. No
check of persons to be sent into the Reich will be made.[17]

The use of force was almost universal by the summer of 1943.
A secret report of a conference between Rosenberg and the Commissioner General of Shitomir of June 17, 1943, stated:

The symptoms created by the recruiting of workers are, no doubt,
well known to the Reich Minister through reports and his own observations. Therefore I shall not repeat them. It is certain that a recruitment
of labor in the true sense of the word can hardly be spoken of. In most
cases it is nowadays a matter of actual conscription by force.[18]

The effect of the labor drives was described by an office of the
High Command in a report of June 28, 1943, to one of Rosenberg's
top officials:

Thus recruitment of labor for the Reich, however necessary, had
disastrous effects, for the recruitment measures in the last months and
weeks were absolute manhunts, which have an irreparable political and
economic effect.... From White Ruthenia approximately 50,000 people have been obtained for the Reich so far. Another 130,000 are to
be taken. Considering the 2,400,000 population...the fulfillment of
these quotas is impossible.... Owing to the sweeping drives of the
SS and police in November 1942, about 115,000 hectares of farmland
...are not used, as the population is not there and the villages have
been razed....[19]

A secret organization order of Army Group South, dated August
17, 1943, disclosed that inhabitants of occupied territories were
called up by age groups for forced labor in the Reich:

According to this order by the Plenipotentiary General for Allocation of Labor [GBA] you have to recruit and to transport to the Reich
immediately all labor forces in your territory born during 1926 and
1927. The decree of 6 February 1943 relative to labor duty and labor
employment in the theater of operations of the newly occupied eastern
territory and the executive orders issued on this subject are the authority

for the execution of this measure. Enlistment must be completed by 30 September 1943 at the latest.[20]

A top secret memorandum dated June 12, 1944, disclosed a plan for kidnapping children in the occupied countries and deporting them to Germany for labor. This wicked practice was carried out under the code name "Heu-Aktion" (Hay Action). The memorandum began:

The Army Group "Center" has the intention to apprehend 40-50,000 youths at the ages of 10 to 14 who are in the Army territories, and to transport them to the Reich. This measure was originally proposed by the 9th Army. These youths cause considerable inconvenience in the theatre of operations. To the greater part these youths are without supervision of their parents since men and women in the theatres of operations have been and will be conscripted into labor battalions to be used in the construction of fortifications.... It is intended to allot these juveniles primarily to the German trades as apprentices to be used as skilled workers after two years' training. This is to be arranged through the Organization Todt which is especially equipped for such a task through its technical and other set-ups. This action is being greatly welcomed by the German trade since it represents a decisive measure for the alleviation of the shortage of apprentices.[21]

In the beginning Rosenberg entertained considerable misgivings about the plan: "The Minister feared that the action would have most unfavorable political consequences, that it would be regarded as abduction of children, and that the juveniles did not represent a real asset to the enemy's military strength anyhow. The Minister would like to see the action confined to the 15-17 year olds."[22]

His arguments were answered as follows:

1. This action is not only aimed at preventing a direct reinforcement of the enemy's military strength but also at a reduction of his biological potentialities as viewed from the perspective of the future. These ideas have been voiced not only by the Reichsfuehrer of the SS but also by the Fuehrer. Corresponding orders were given during last year's withdrawals in the southern sector.

2. A similar action is being conducted at the present time in the territory of the Army Group Ukraine—North (General Field Marshal Model). Even in this politically especially preferred Galizian territory

recruiting measures were being taken with the aim to collect 135,000 laborers to be organized in battalions for the construction of fortifications. The youths over 17 were to be detailed to the SS Division and those under 17 to the SS Auxiliary. This action which has been going on for several weeks has not led to any political disturbances. While it is true that the population has to be recruited by force, they do show a certain understanding, later on, for this measure of purely military necessity. Provided, of course, that they receive correct treatment, good food and lodging, et cetera.[23]

On June 14, 1944, Rosenberg approved "Hay Action."[24] By July 20, 1944, he reported to the chief of the Reich Chancellery, Dr. Lammers, the seizing and turning over of youths between the ages of ten and fourteen into Reich territories, as suggested by the military offices, with the aim of "placing them in the Reich Youth Movement and the training of apprentices for the German economy...."[25]

Man-Catching in the West

In the West, the slave-labor program involved the recruitment of workers to be shipped to Germany for forced labor and also the recruitment of workers for German war production in the occupied territories themselves. On June 27, 1943, in reporting to Hitler on the labor recruitment program in France, Sauckel concluded: "I therefore beg you, my Fuehrer, to approve my suggestion of making available one million French men and women for German war production in France proper in the second half of 1943 and, in addition, of transferring 500,000 French men and women to the Reich before the end of the current year."[26] Hitler approved the requests, and Sauckel proceeded to fill the quotas thus established by himself.

On August 13, 1943, Sauckel reported to Hitler that the deportations were to be kept secret, and that similar actions were to take place in Belgium and the Netherlands:

A program was established in Belgium for the employment of 150,000 workers in the Reich and, with the approval of the military commander in Belgium, an organization for compulsory labor corresponding to that in France was decided upon....

A program has likewise been prepared for. Holland, providing for the transfer of 150,000 workers to Germany and of 100,000 workers, men and women, from Dutch civilian industries to German war production.[27]

In February, 1944, the Central Planning Board called for the recruiting of 1,500,000 Italian workers, 1,000,000 French workers, and 250,000 workers each from Belgium and the Netherlands.

At a meeting of the Central Planning Board on March 1, 1944, Sauckel complained of what he considered to be unjust criticisms of the efficiency of his recruitment organization. "The most abominable point against which I have to fight," he said, "is the claim that there is no organization in these districts properly to recruit Frenchmen, Belgians, and Italians, and to dispatch them to work. So I have even proceeded to employ and train a whole staff of French and Italian agents of both sexes who for good pay, just as was done in olden times for 'shanghaiing,' go hunting for men and dupe them, using liquor as well as persuasion in order to dispatch them to Germany."[28] But shanghaiing was the exception rather than the general method of obtaining workers for forced labor.

The report of the Netherlands government concerning deportation of Dutch workmen to Germany stated:

Many big and reasonably large business concerns, especially in the metal industry, were visited by German commissions who selected workmen for deportation. This combing-out was called the "Sauckel action," so named after its leader, who was charged with procurement of foreign workers for Germany.

The employers had to cancel the contracts with the selected workmen; and the latter were forced to register at the labor offices, which then took charge of the deportation under supervision of German "Fachberater."

Workmen who refused—relatively few—were prosecuted by the Sicherheitsdienst—the SD. If captured by this service, they were mostly lodged for some time in one of the infamous prisoners' camps in the Netherlands and eventually put to work in Germany....

At the end of April 1942 the deportation of workers started on a grand scale. Consequently, in the months of May and June the number of deportees amounted to not less than 22,000 and 24,000 respectively, of which many were metal workers.

After that the action slackened somewhat, but in October 1942 another peak was reached (26,000). After the big concerns, the smaller ones had, in their turn, to give up their personnel....

This changed in November 1944. The Germans then started a ruthless campaign for manpower, passing by the labor offices. Without warning they lined off whole quarters of the towns, seized people in the streets or in the houses and deported them.

In Rotterdam and Schiedam where these raids took place on 10 and 11 November, the number of people thus deported was estimated at 50,000 and 5,000 respectively.[29]

In speaking of these raids, an officer of the Wehrmacht noted that "there had been some difficulties with the Arbeitseinsatz, that is, during the man-catching action, which became very noticeable because it was unorganized and unprepared. People were arrested in the streets and taken out of their homes...."[30]

The Exploitation of Labor

Recruitment and deportation were steps toward the ultimate objective—exploitation. The workers brought to Germany were treated as well as, but no better than, other tools and machines. As Sauckel said on April 20, 1942, shortly after he had taken control of the labor mobilization program: "All the men must be fed, sheltered, and treated in such a way that they produce to the highest possible extent at the lowest conceivable degree of expenditure."[31]

Even this minimum standard of life sometimes was not accorded to foreign workers. A report to a director of the Krupp locomotive factory in Essen, dated March, 1942, long before any threat of starvation came to Germany itself, disclosed that in one of the Krupp plants Russian workers were not given enough food to be able to work:

During the last few days we established that the food for the Russians employed here is so miserable that the people are getting weaker from day to day. Investigations showed that single Russians are not able to place a piece of metal for turning into position, for instance, because of a lack of physical strength. The same conditions exist in all other places of work where Russians are employed.[32]

On May 17, 1944, the Polish Main Committee submitted the

following report to the General Government, describing the working conditions of Poles deported to Germany for forced labor:

The call for help which reaches us brings to light privation and hunger, severe stomach and intestinal trouble, especially in the case of children, resulting from insufficiency of food which does not take into consideration the needs of children. Proper medical treatment or care for the sick is not available in the mass camps.... There are cases of 8-year-old, delicate, and undernourished children put to forced labor and perishing from such treatment....

The fact that these bad conditions dangerously affect the state of health and the vitality of the workers is proved by the many cases of tuberculosis found in very young people returning from the Reich to the General Government as unfit for work. Their state of health is usually so bad that recovery is out of the question. The reason is that a state of exhaustion resulting from overwork and a starvation diet is not recognized as an ailment until the illness betrays itself by high fever and fainting spells.

Although some hostels for unfit workers have been provided as a precautionary measure, one can only go there when recovery may no longer be expected (Neumarkt in Bavaria). Even there the incurables waste away slowly, and nothing is done even to alleviate the state of the sick by suitable food and medicines. There are children there with tuberculosis whose cure would not be hopeless and men in their prime who, if sent home in time to their families in rural districts, might still be able to recover.... No less suffering is caused by the separation of families when wives and mothers of small children are taken away from their families and sent to the Reich for forced labor.[33]

Dr. Wilhelm Jaeger, a senior camp doctor in Krupp's workers' camps, gave this statement on the basis of his personal knowledge of conditions in the labor camps:

My first official act as senior camp doctor was to make a thorough inspection of the various camps.... Conditions in all of these camps were extremely bad. The camps were greatly overcrowded. In some camps there were twice as many people in a barrack as health conditions permitted. At Kramerplatz, the inhabitants slept in treble tiered bunks, and in other camps they slept in double tiered bunks. The health authorities prescribed a *minimum* space between beds of 50 cm., but the bunks in these camps were separated by a *maximum* of 20-30 cm.

The diet prescribed for the eastern workers was altogether insufficient. They were given 1,000 calories a day less than the minimum prescribed for any German. Moreover, while German workers engaged in the heaviest work received 5,000 calories a day, the eastern workers in comparable jobs received only 2,000 calories. The eastern workers were given only two meals a day and their bread ration....

Sanitary conditions were exceedingly bad. At Kramerplatz, where approximately 1,200 eastern workers were crowded into the rooms of an old school, the sanitary conditions were atrocious in the extreme. Only ten children's toilets were available for the 1,200 inhabitants. At Dechenschule, fifteen children's toilets were available for the 400-500 eastern workers. Excretion contaminated the entire floors of these lavatories. There were also few facilities for washing. The supply of bandages, medicine, surgical instruments, and other medical supplies at these camps was likewise altogether insufficient. As a consequence, only the very worst cases were treated. The percentage of eastern workers who were ill was twice as great as among the Germans. Tuberculosis was particularly widespread among the eastern workers.... These workers were likewise afflicted with spotted fever. Lice, the carrier of the disease, together with countless fleas, bugs and other vermin tortured the inhabitants of these camps. As a result of the filthy conditions of the camps nearly all eastern workers were afflicted with skin disease....

With the onset of heavy air raids in March 1943, conditions in the camps greatly deteriorated. The problem of housing, feeding, and medical attention became more acute than ever. The workers lived in the ruins of their former barracks. Medical supplies which were used up, lost, or destroyed, were difficult to replace. At times, the water supply at the camps was completely shut off for periods of 8-14 days. We installed a few emergency toilets in the camps, but there were far too few of them to cope with the situation.

During the period immediately following the March 1943 raids many foreign workers were made to sleep at the Krupp factories in the same rooms in which they worked. The day workers slept there at night, and the night workers slept there during the day despite the noise which constantly prevailed. I believe that this condition continued until the entrance of American troops into Essen....

In my report to my superiors at Krupps dated 2 September 1944, I stated:

"Camp Humboldstrasse had been inhabited by Italian prisoners of war. After it had been destroyed by an air raid, the Italians were removed and 600 Jewish females from Buchenwald Concentration Camp were brought in to work at the Krupp factories. Upon my first visit at Camp Humboldstrasse, I found these females suffering from open festering wounds and other diseases. I was the first doctor they had seen for at least a fortnight. There were no doctors in attendance at the camp. There were no medical supplies in the camp. They had no shoes and went about in their bare feet. The sole clothing of each consisted of a sack with holes for their arms and head. Their hair was shorn. The camp was surrounded by barbed wire and closely guarded by SS guards."[34]

Forced laborers assigned to work on German farms, outside the labor camps, were given better food and care, but were similarly degraded. Regulations issued on March 6, 1941, to govern farm workers of Polish nationality assigned to German farmers for labor, provided in part:

2. The farm workers of Polish nationality may no longer leave the localities in which they are employed, and have a curfew from 1 October to 31 March from 2000 hours to 0600 hours and from 1 April to 30 September from 2100 hours to 0500 hours.

3. The use of bicycles is strictly prohibited. Exceptions are possible for riding to the place of work in the field if a relative of the employer or the employer himself is present.

4. The visit to churches, regardless of faith, is strictly prohibited, even when there is no service in progress. Individual spiritual care by clergymen outside the church is permitted.

5. Visits to theaters, motion pictures, or other cultural entertainment are strictly prohibited for farm workers of Polish nationality.

6. The visit to restaurants is strictly prohibited to farm workers of Polish nationality, except for one restaurant in the village, which will be selected by the Regional Commissioner's Office and then only 1 day per week. The day which is allowed for visiting the restaurant will also be determined by the Regional Commissioner's Office. This regulation does not change the curfew regulation mentioned above under "2."

7. Sexual intercourse with women and girls is strictly prohibited; and wherever it is discovered, it must be reported.

8. Gatherings of farm workers of Polish nationality after work is prohibited, whether it is on other farms, in the stables, or in the living quarters of the Poles.

9. The use of railroads, buses, or other public conveyances by workers of Polish nationality is prohibited....

11. ...The farm workers of Polish nationality have to work daily as long as it is to the interests of the enterprise and is demanded by the employer. There are no limits to the working hours.

12. Every employer has the right to give corporal punishment to farm workers of Polish nationality if persuasion and reprimand fail. The employer may not be held accountable in any such case by an official agency.

13. Farm workers of Polish nationality should, if possible, be removed from the household; and they can be quartered in stables, *et cetera*. No consideration whatever should restrict such action....[35]

In his speech of April 20, 1942, Sauckel said:

In order to relieve considerably the German housewife, especially the mother with many children and the extremely busy farmwoman, and in order to avoid any further danger to their health, the Fuehrer also has charged me with the procurement of 400,000 to 500,000 selected, healthy, and strong girls from the territories of the East for Germany.[36]

His orders for the treatment of female household workers imported from the occupied territories were:

There is no claim for free time. Female domestic workers from the East may, on principle, leave the household only to take care of domestic tasks. As a reward for good work, however, they may be given the opportunity to stay outside the home without work for three hours once a week. This leave must end with the onset of darkness, at the latest at 2000 hours. It is prohibited to enter restaurants, movies, or other theaters, and similar establishments provided for German or foreign workers. Attending church is also prohibited.... The recruiting of Eastern domestics is for an indefinite period.[37]

Slave labor was exploited in the factories, on the fields, and in the homes. In all, five million people were brought from their native lands into Germany and held there for labor. It cannot be imagined that all were mistreated, or that individual employers to whom they were assigned adhered to the extreme "rules" for their "discipline." Employers did have the right to inflict corporal punishment upon workers. And they were expected to report instances of unwillingness to work, impertinent behavior, or slowing down of work, even in minor cases, to the authorities. The consequence for the employee in such circumstances was usually incarceration in Gestapo work camps. But the employer did not suffer loss of his worker, for he was given top preference for a replacement from the competent labor office. It may be suspected that the threat of turning employees over to the Gestapo was in itself an excellent means of discipline. And it provided a convenient way for employers to rid themselves of incompetent or disagreeable workers.

The Gestapo maintained its own standards of discipline for eastern workers. On February 20, 1942, Himmler issued a secret order providing in part:

> In keeping with the equal status of laborers from the original Soviet Russian territory with prisoners of war, a strict discipline must be maintained in quarters and in workshops. Violations against discipline, including refusal to work and loafing at work, will be dealt with exclusively by the secret state police. ... In serious cases, that is, in such cases where the measures at the disposal of the leader of the guard do not suffice, the state police is to step in. In such instances, as a rule, severe measures will be taken, that is, transfer to a concentration camp or special treatment. ... Sexual intercourse is forbidden to laborers of the original Soviet Russian territory. ... For every case of sexual intercourse with German men or women application for special treatment is to be made for male labor from the original Soviet Russian territory, transfer to a concentration camp for female labor. ... Fugitive workers from the original Soviet Russian territory are to be announced on principle in the German search book. Furthermore, search measures are to be decreed locally. When caught the fugitive must in principle be proposed for special treatment.[38]

"Special treatment," of course, meant death.

In a telegram to Hitler dated April 20, 1943, Sauckel said: "I shall devote my entire strength with fanatical determination to the accomplishment of my task, and to justify your confidence."[39]

When confronted with this statement on cross-examination, Sauckel explained: "I saw in Hitler, whom at that time I revered, a man who was the leader of the German people. ... I was unable to see a criminal in Hitler at that time, and I never felt he was one...."[40]

The fanaticism of Sauckel was the fanaticism which brought millions of enslaved persons to Germany—persons required to work in the fields and factories, supplying the food and manufacturing the munitions to support Hitler's armies and to strengthen his hold upon their native lands.

CHAPTER 30

Experiments in Sadism

WHEN INTERROGATED about his knowledge of medical experiments conducted on concentration camp inmates, Goering defended himself by stating: "In 1934 I strictly forbade experiments and tortures to be carried out on living animals; kindly do not expect me to have permitted them to be carried out on human beings."[1]

To this the British prosecutor, Sir David Maxwell Fyfe, rejoined: "It is not for me to comment. Plenty of people have standards with regard to animals which they do not apply to fellow-men. But this is a matter of comment and I do not wish to pursue it."[2]

The experiments conducted upon human beings by Hitler's pseudo scientists were not, for the most part, scientific studies at all—they were simply experiments in sadism. These experiments caused the most atrocious suffering to innocent and helpless human beings who were forcibly exposed to the surgeon's knife, to venomous injections, to extreme heat and cold, and to various acts of mistreatment which often resulted in pitiful infirmities or convulsive death.

Experiments for the Air Force

Experiments were conducted on human beings at Dachau on behalf of the Air Force. A medical officer of the Luftwaffe, Dr. Sigmund Rascher, requested permission of Himmler to utilize concentration camp inmates for research on the effect of high altitudes upon flyers. On May 15, 1941, Rascher wrote to Himmler:

For the time being I have been assigned to the Luftgaukommando

VII, Munich, for a medical course. During this course where research on high-altitude flights plays a prominent part (determined by the somewhat higher ceiling of the English fighter planes), considerable regret was expressed at the fact that no tests with human material had yet been possible for us, as such experiments are very dangerous and nobody volunteers for them. I put, therefore, the serious question: Can you make available two or three professional criminals for these experiments? ... The experiments, by which the subjects may, of course, die, would take place with my co-operation. They are essential for research on high-altitude flight and cannot be carried out, as has been tried, with monkeys, who offer entirely different test-conditions. I have had a very confidential talk with the deputy of the Surgeon of the Air Force, who makes these experiments. He is also of the opinion that the problem in question could only be solved by experiments on human persons. (Feeble-minded could also be used as test material.)[3]

On May 22, 1941, Dr. Rascher received a reply to this letter from Himmler's adjutant, SS Sturmbannfuehrer Karl Brandt:

Shortly before flying to Oslo, the Reichsfuehrer SS gave me your letter of 15 May 1941 for partial reply. I can inform you that prisoners will, of course, be made available gladly for the high-flight research. I have informed the Chief of the Security Police of this agreement of the Reichsfuehrer SS, and requested that the competent official be instructed to get in touch with you.[4]

Field Marshal Milch expressed the appreciation of the Supreme Commander of the Air Force, Goering, to the SS for the co-operation given in making possible such low-pressure experimentations on human beings at Dachau. The method used was to place the victim in a chamber in which the air pressure was quickly reduced. An affiant, Pacholegg, described the effect of the experiments upon the men subjected to them.

I have personally seen, through the observation window of the chamber, when a prisoner inside would stand a vacuum until his lungs ruptured. Some experiments gave men such pressure in their heads that they would go mad and pull out their hair in an effort to relieve the pressure. They would tear their heads and faces with their fingers and nails in an attempt to maim themselves in their madness. They would beat the walls with their hands and head and scream in an effort to relieve pressure on their eardrums. These cases of extremes of vacuums generally ended in the death of the subject. An extreme experiment was so certain to result in death that in many instances the chamber was used for routine execution purposes rather than as an experiment.[5]

This testimony was confirmed by the witness Franz Blaha, a Czech, who was a prisoner in Dachau concentration camp from April, 1941, until the liberation of the camp in April, 1945.

In 1942 and 1943 experiments on human beings were conducted by Dr. Sigmund Rascher to determine the effects of changing air pressure. As many as 25 persons were put at one time into a specially constructed van in which pressure could be increased or decreased as required. The purpose was to find out the effects on human beings of high altitude and of rapid descents by parachute. Through a window in the van I have seen the people lying on the floor of the van. Most of the prisoners used died from these experiments, from internal hemorrhage of the lungs or brain. The survivors coughed blood when taken out. It was my job to take the bodies out and as soon as they were found to be dead to send the internal organs to Munich for study. About 400 to 500 prisoners were experimented on. The survivors were sent to invalid blocks and liquidated shortly afterward. Only a few escaped.[6]

In addition to high-altitude pressure experiments, Dr. Rascher conducted experiments on rewarming persons who had been subjected to extreme cold. In some instances the victims were submerged in very cold water for long periods of time. In other cases they were exposed without clothing to icy winter nights. On September 10, 1942, Dr. Rascher submitted an interim report on freezing experiments.

The experimental subjects (VP) were placed in the water dressed in complete flying uniform, winter or summer combination, and with an aviator's helmet. A life-jacket made of rubber or kapok was used to prevent submerging.... Fatalities occurred only when the brain stem and the back of the head were also chilled. Autopsies of such fatal cases always revealed large amounts of free blood, up to a half liter, in the cranial cavity. The heart invariably showed extreme dilation of the right chamber. As soon as the temperature in these experiments reached 28° the experimental subjects (VP) were bound to die despite all attempts at resuscitation....

During attempts to save severely chilled persons, it was evident that rapid rewarming was in all cases preferable to a slow rewarming because, after removal from the cold water, the body temperature continued to sink rapidly. I think that for this reason we can dispense with the attempt to save intensely chilled subjects by means of animal warmth. Rewarming by animal warmth—animal bodies or women's bodies—would be too slow.[7]

In spite of this preliminary report that rewarming by women's bodies would be too slow, female inmates were nonetheless made available for subsequent experiments. They were required to lie with the half-frozen men until the men either revived or became corpses by their sides. On November 16, 1942, Himmler took note of the assignment of women to this ghoulish duty:

The following struck me during my visit to Dachau on the 13th of November 1942 regarding the experiments conducted there for the saving of people whose lives are endangered through intense chilling in ice, snow, or water, and who are to be saved by the employment of every method or means:

I had ordered that suitable women are to be set aside from the concentration camp for these experiments for the warming of those who were exposed. Four girls were set aside who were in the concentration camp for loose morals and because as prostitutes they were a potential source of infection.[8]

The witness Blaha likewise described these experiments:

Rascher also conducted experiments on the effect of cold water on human beings. This was done to find a way for reviving airmen who had fallen into the ocean. The subject was placed in ice cold water and kept there until he was unconscious. Blood was taken from his neck and tested each time his body temperature dropped one degree. This drop was determined by a rectal thermometer. Urine was also periodically tested. Some men stood it as long as 24 to 36 hours. The lowest body temperature reached was 19 degrees centigrade, but most men died at 25 or 26 degrees. When the men were removed from the ice water attempts were made to revive them by artificial sunshine, with hot water, by electro-therapy, or by animal warmth. For this last experiment prostitutes were used and the body of the unconscious man was placed between the bodies of two women. Himmler was present at one such experiment. I could see him from one of the windows in the street between the blocks. I have personally been present at some of these cold water experiments when Rascher was absent, and I have seen notes and diagrams on them in Rascher's laboratory. About 300 persons were used in these experiments. The majority died. Of those who survived, many became mentally deranged. Those who did not die were sent to invalid blocks and were killed just as were the victims of the air pressure experiments. I know only two who survived, a Yugoslav and a Pole, both of whom are mental cases.[9]

The witness Von Eberstein was interrogated concerning his knowledge of the Rascher experiments. He testified that he knew that Rascher had been carrying out experiments on humans and that in the course of these experiments he had been killing them. Von Eberstein said that no charges were ever brought against Rascher on this account because "Himmler was the only one who could accuse him as he was the competent judge at the court."[10]

Why Himmler would never charge Rascher with murder for experimentation on human beings is indicated by a letter which he wrote to Field Marshal Milch in November, 1942, in which he sought to obtain the transfer of Rascher from the Air Force to the SS:

This research which deals with the reaction of the human organism at great heights, as well as with manifestations caused by prolonged chilling of the human body in cold water, and similar problems which are of vital importance to the Air Force, in particular, can be performed by us with particular efficiency because I personally assumed the responsibility for supplying asocial individuals and criminals, who only deserve to die, from concentration camps for these experiments.[11]

Himmler recommended that for purposes of liaison Milch appoint a "non-Christian" physician who could be informed of the results of the sadistic experiments. Even Himmler realized that Christians could not be expected to participate in cruelties of this type inflicted upon human beings.

Poison Bullets

One of the most wicked experiments conducted upon concentration camp inmates was the testing of the effectiveness of poison bullets. A report of September 12, 1944, prepared in the office of the Reich Surgeon of the SS and Police, reviewed some of these experiments:

On 11 September 1944, in the presence of SS Sturmbannfuehrer Dr. Ding, Dr. Widmann, and the undersigned, experiments with aconite nitrate bullets were carried out on five persons who had been sentenced to death. The caliber of the bullets used was 7.65 millimeters, and they were filled with poison in crystal form. Each subject of the experiment received one shot in the upper part of the left thigh, while in a horizontal position. In the case of two persons, the bullets passed clean through the upper part of the thigh. Even later no effect from the poison could be seen. These two subjects were therefore rejected....

The symptoms shown by the three condemned persons were surprisingly the same. At first, nothing special was noticeable. After 20 to 25 minutes, a disturbance of the motor nerves and a light flow of saliva began, but both stopped again. After 40 to 44 minutes, a strong flow of saliva appeared. The poisoned persons swallowed frequently; later the flow of saliva is so strong that it can no longer be controlled by swallowing. Foamy saliva flows from the mouth. Then a sensation of choking and vomiting starts.[12]

The report continued to describe in cold scientific language the death agony of the victims.

At the same time there was pronounced nausea. One of the poisoned persons tried in vain to vomit. In order to succeed he put four fingers of his hand, up to the main joint, right into his mouth. In spite of this, no vomiting occurred. His face became quite red.

The faces of the other two subjects were already pale at an early stage. Other symptoms were the same. Later on the disturbances of the motor nerves increased so much that the persons threw themselves up and down, rolled their eyes, and made aimless movements with their hands and arms. At last the disturbance subsided, the pupils were enlarged to the maximum, the condemned lay still. Rectal cramps and loss of urine was observed in one of them. Death occurred 121, 123, and 129 minutes after they were shot.[13]

Collecting Skeletons

A particularly gruesome crime was the anthropological measuring of living persons and then the killing of them for further pseudoscientific study. Assistance in obtaining victims for this purpose was provided by Wolfram Sievers, as Reich manager of the Ahnenerbe, or Ancestral Heritage Society. The anatomical research for which victims were required was conducted by Professor Hirt of the Anatomical Institute of the University of Strasbourg.

On December 22, 1941, Sievers forwarded to Himmler's adjutant, Brandt, a request of Professor Hirt for skulls of Jewish-Bolshevik commissars "for the purpose of scientific research at the Reich University at Strasbourg."[14] The report stated:

We have large collections of skulls of almost all races and peoples at our disposal. Of the Jewish race, however, only very few specimens of skulls are available, with the result that it is impossible to arrive at precise conclusions from examination. The war in the East now presents us with the opportunity to overcome this deficiency. By procuring the skulls of the Jewish-Bolshevik commissars, who represent the prototype of the repulsive, but characteristic, subhuman, we have the chance now to obtain scientific material.

The best practical method for obtaining and collecting this skull material could be followed by directing the Wehrmacht to turn over alive all captured Jewish-Bolshevik commissars to the Feldpolizei. The Feldpolizei, in turn, would be given special directives to inform a certain office at regular intervals of the numbers and places of detention of these captured Jews, and to give them close attention and care until a special delegate arrives. This special delegate, who will be in charge of securing the material (a junior physician of the Wehrmacht or the Feldpolizei, or a student of medicine equipped with a motor car and driver), will be required to take a previously stipulated series of photographs, make anthropological measurements, and, in addition, determine as far as possible descent, date of birth, and other personal data.

Following the subsequently induced death of the Jew, whose head should not be damaged, the physician will sever the head from the body and will forward it to its proper point of destination in a hermetically sealed tin can especially made for this purpose and filled with a conserving fluid. Having arrived at the laboratory, the comparison tests and anatomical research on the skull, as well as determination of the race membership of the pathological features of the skull form, the form and size of the brain, *et cetera,* can be undertaken by photos, measurements, and other data supplied on the head and the skull itself.[15]

Subsequently, on November 2, 1942, in connection with a

request for additional human materials, Sievers noted in a letter to Brandt that Himmler had directed that Professor Hirt "be supplied with everything needed for his research work."[16]

Experiments in the Concentration Camps

Similar experiments were conducted in most of the concentration camps. Human beings could be obtained for experimentation, even though death were certain to follow, by simple letter request to Himmler. Thus on June 16, 1943, Himmler gave permission for eight Jews of the Polish resistance movement confined in Auschwitz to be used for experiments into the cause of contagious jaundice. He agreed that such experiments might be conducted at Sachsenhausen.[17] One hundred prisoners were made available for experiments at Natzweiler on typhus serum, and when these had been used up, a new request was submitted for two hundred more victims. Wherever there was an infirmary in a concentration camp, and a sufficiently sadistic pseudo scientist, experiments were sure to be made upon helpless victims of the camp.

The witness Blaha described a series of malaria experiments conducted by Dr. Klaus Schilling on about 1,200 people at Dachau:

Schilling was personally ordered by Himmler to conduct these experiments. The victims were either bitten by mosquitoes or given injections of malaria sporozoites taken from mosquitoes. Different kinds of treatment were applied.... Thirty to forty died from the malaria itself. Three hundred to four hundred died later from diseases which were fatal because of the physical condition resulting from the malaria attacks.[18]

Blaha averred that the persons used in these experiments were never volunteers but were forced to submit to the inoculations. The witness discussed other experiments at Dachau, including the following:

Phlegmone experiments were conducted by Dr. Schutz, Dr. Babor, Dr. Kieselwetter and Professor Lauer. Forty healthy men were used at a time, of which twenty were given intramuscular and twenty intravenous injections of pus from diseased persons. All treatment was forbidden for three days, by which time serious inflammation and in many cases general blood poisoning had occurred. Then each group was divided again into groups of ten. Half were given chemical treatment with liquid and special pills every ten minutes for 24 hours. The remainder were treated with sulfanamide and surgery. In some cases all the limbs were amputated. My autopsy also showed that the chemical treatment had been harmful and had even caused perforations of the stomach wall. For these experiments Polish, Czech, and Dutch priests were ordinarily used. Pain was intense in such experiments. Most of the 600 to 800 persons who were used finally died. Most of the others became permanent invalids and were later killed.[19]

The witness Vaillant-Couturier described sterilization experiments and abortions at Auschwitz:

As to the experiments, I have seen in the infirmary, because I was employed at the infirmary, the queue of young Jewesses from Salonika who stood waiting in front of the X-ray room for sterilization. I also know that they performed castration operations in the men's camp. Concerning the experiments performed on women I am well informed because my friend, Doctor Hade Hautval of Montbeliard, who has returned to France, worked for several months in that block nursing the patients; but she always refused to participate in those experiments. They sterilized women either by injections or by operation or with rays. I saw and knew several women who had been sterilized. There was a very high mortality rate among those operated upon.... They said that they were trying to find the best method for sterilizing so as to replace the native population in the occupied countries by Germans after one generation, once they had made use of the inhabitants as slaves to work for them....

The Jewish women, when they arrived in the first months of pregnancy, were subjected to abortion. When their pregnancy was near the end, after confinement, the babies were drowned in a bucket of water. I know that because I worked in the infirmary and the woman who was in charge of that task was a German midwife, who was imprisoned for having performed illegal operations. After a while another doctor arrived and for two months they did not kill the Jewish babies. But one day an order came from Berlin saying that again they had to be done away with. Then the mothers and their babies were called to the infirmary. They were put in a lorry and taken away to the gas chamber.[20]

She also described the "rabbit girls" at Ravensbrueck:

On leaving Auschwitz we were sent to Ravensbrueck. There we were escorted to the "NN" block—meaning "Nacht and Nebel," that is, "The Secret Block." With us in that block were Polish women with the identification number "7,000." Some were called "rabbits" because they had been used as experimental guinea pigs. They selected from the convoys girls with very straight legs who were in very good health, and they submitted them to various operations. Some of the girls had parts of the bone removed from their legs, others received injections; but what was injected, I do not know. The mortality rate was very high upon the women operated upon. So when they came to fetch the others to operate on them they refused to go to the infirmary. They were forcibly dragged to the dark cells where the professor, who had arrived from Berlin, operated in his uniform, without taking any aseptic precautions, without wearing a surgical gown, and without washing his hands. There are some survivors among these "rabbits." They still endure much suffering. They suffer periodically from suppurations; and since nobody knows to what treatment they had been subjected, it is extremely difficult to cure them.[21]

The witness Balachowsky described the medical experiments carried out on concentration camp inmates in Block 46 at Buchenwald:

The experiments carried out in Block 46 did without a doubt serve a medical purpose, but for the greater part they were of no service to science. Therefore, they can hardly be called experiments. The men were used for observing the effects of drugs, poisons, bacterial cultures, et cetera....

We could ascertain in Block 46 twelve different cultures of typhus germs.... A constant supply of these cultures was kept in Block 46 by means of the contamination of healthy individuals through sick ones; this was achieved by artificial inoculation of typhus germs by means of intravenous injections of 0.5 to 1 cubic centimeters of infected blood drawn from a patient at the height of the crisis. Now, it is well-known that artificial inoculation of typhus by intravenous injection is invariably fatal. Therefore all these men who were used for bacterial culture during the whole time such cultures were required (from October 1942 to the liberation of the camp) died, and we counted 600 victims sacrificed for the sole purpose of supplying typhus germs....

Now I come back to the typhus and vaccine experiments.... The 150 prisoners were divided into two groups: those who were to be used as tests, and those who were to be the subjects. The latter only received (ordinary) injections of the different types of vaccine to be tested. Those used for testing were not given any injections. Then, after the vaccination of the subjects, inoculations were given (always by means of intravenous injections) to everybody selected for this experiment, those for testing as well as the subjects. Those used for tests died about two weeks after the inoculation as such is approximately the period required before the disease develops to its fatal issue. As for the others, who received different kinds of vaccines, their deaths were in proportion to the efficacy of the vaccines administered to them. Some vaccines had excellent results, with a very low death rate—such was the case with the Polish vaccines. Others, on the contrary, had a much higher death rate. After the conclusion of the experiments, no survivors were allowed to live, according to the custom prevailing in Block 46. All the survivors of the experiments were "liquidated" and murdered in Block 46, by the customary methods which some of my comrades have already described to you, that is by means of intracardiac injections of phenol. Intracardiac injections of ten cubic centimeters of pure phenol was the usual method of extermination in Buchenwald.[22]

Balachowsky described experiments with phosphorus burns:

I now come to experiments with phosphorus, particularly made on prisoners of Russian origin. Phosphorus burns were inflicted in Block 46 on Russian prisoners for the following reason. Certain bombs dropped in Germany by the Allied aviators caused burns on the civilians and soldiers which were difficult to heal. Consequently, the Germans tried to find a whole series of drugs which would hasten the healing of the wounds caused by these burns. Thus, experiments were carried out in Block 46 on Russian prisoners who were artificially burned with phosphorus products and then treated with different drugs supplied by the German chemical industry.[23]

Experiments of this kind led ultimately to acts of utter depravity. Collections were made of human skin and skulls. Blaha testified to these terrible practices at Dachau:

It was common practice to remove the skin from dead prisoners. I was commanded to do this on many occasions. Dr. Rascher and Dr. Wolter in particular asked for this human skin from human backs and chests. It was chemically treated and placed in the sun to dry. After that it was cut into various sizes for use as saddles, riding breeches, gloves, house slippers, and ladies' handbags. Tattooed skin was especially valued by SS men. Russians, Poles, and other inmates were used in this way, but it was forbidden to cut out the skin of a German. This skin had to be from healthy prisoners and free from defects. Sometimes we did not have enough bodies with good skin and Rascher would say, "All right, you will get the bodies." The next day we would receive 20 or 30 bodies of young people. They would have been shot in the neck or struck on the head so that the skin would be uninjured. Also we frequently got requests for the skulls or skeletons of prisoners. In those cases we boiled the skull or the body. Then the soft parts were removed and the bones were bleached and dried and reassembled. In the case of skulls it was important to have a good set of teeth. When we got an order for skulls from Oranienburg the SS men would say, "We will try to get you some with good teeth." So it was dangerous to have good skin or good teeth.[24]

Balachowsky testified to the same actions at Buchenwald.

There were always tattooed human skins in Block 2. I cannot say whether there were many, as they were continuously being received and passed on, but there were not only tattooed human skins, but also tanned human skins—simply tanned, not tattooed. I know from my comrades who worked in pathological Block 2 that there were orders for skins, and these tanned skins were given as gifts to certain guards and to certain visitors, who used them to bind books....[25]

The affiant Pfaffenberger attested further to this Buchenwald barbarism:

In 1939 all prisoners with tattooing on them were ordered to report to the dispensary. No one knew what the purpose was; but after the tattooed prisoners had been examined, the ones with best and most artistic specimens were kept in the dispensary and then killed by injections administered by Karl Beigs, a criminal prisoner. The corpses were then turned over to the pathological department where the desired pieces of tattooed skin were detached from the bodies and treated. The finished products were turned over to SS Standartenfuehrer Koch's wife, who had them fashioned into lamp shades and other ornamental household articles.[26]

The War Crimes Section, Judge Advocate General, United States Army, delivered to the office of the United States Chief of Counsel specimens of tattooed human skin found at Buchenwald and in addition a human head with the skull bone removed, shrunken, stuffed, and preserved. In introducing this exhibit, the American prosecutor, Thomas J. Dodd, stated: "The Nazis had one of their many victims decapitated, after having had him hanged, apparently for fraternizing with a German woman, and fashioned this terrible ornament from his head."[27]

Medical experiments of this type performed upon human beings were a product of the pseudo science of the master race. Though some Nazis, like Goering, would not tolerate the infliction of cruelties upon dumb animals, it was perfectly consistent with Hitler dogma for others—in the name of scientific study—to perform sadistic experiments upon humans of "inferior" race.

CHAPTER 31

The Third Degree

A PRINCIPAL witness for the Gestapo, Dr. Werner Best, testified that Reinhard Heydrich, Chief of the Reich Main Security Office, informed him in 1937 that the Gestapo had been authorized to use third degree measures "to prevent conspiracy activities on the part of organizations hostile to the State and thus prevent actions dangerous to the State."[1] This was followed by an order issued to all Gestapo offices on October 26, 1939, under the signature of Gestapo chief Mueller, concerning punishment to be inflicted upon persons taken into protective custody by the Gestapo:

> In certain cases the Reichsfuehrer SS and Chief of the German Police will order flogging in addition to detention in a concentration camp. Orders of this kind will, in the future, also be transmitted to the State Police district office concerned. In this case, too, there is no objection to spreading the rumor of this increased punishment....[2]

By June 12, 1942, the chief of the Gestapo had decided that third degree methods used by the Gestapo should be regularized, and he accordingly issued an order authorizing the use of such methods where the preliminary investigation indicated that the prisoner could give information on important facts, such as subversive activities, but not to extort confessions of the prisoner's own crimes. The order stated in part:

> Third degree may, under this supposition, only be employed against Communists, Marxists, Jehovah's Witnesses, saboteurs, terrorists, members of resistance movements, parachute agents, asocial elements, Polish or Soviet Russian loafers, or tramps. In all other cases my permission must first be obtained....

Third degree can, according to the circumstances, consist amongst other methods of: very simple diet (bread and water); hard bunk; dark cell; deprivation of sleep; exhaustive drilling; also in flogging (for more than 20 strokes a doctor must be consulted).[3]

The official approval of third degree methods for Gestapo interrogations, whatever the stated limitations, gave rise to a number of tortures, consisting mainly of "other methods." On February 24, 1944, for example, the commander of the Gestapo and SD for the district Radom in occupied Poland acknowledged in an order that there had been a great "variety of methods used to date" in third degree interrogations. That acknowledgment came one year before the end of the Hitler tyranny. Torture had been used by many Gestapo offices for a very long time before then.

Third degree methods were widespread in the occupied eastern territories, reflecting Hitler's general treatment of the eastern peoples as racially inferior. But cruel measures were taken against persons interrogated by the Gestapo in western occupied countries, as well. Whenever a resistance movement gained strength the Gestapo countered with extreme actions, including whatever methods seemed necessary to obtain information required to identify members of the movement.

The prison "Pierre Levee" was used by the Gestapo in France. A report on treatment of persons in this prison contained these entries:

Another prisoner weighed 120 kilograms and lost 30 kilograms in a month. Was in isolation cell for a month. Was tortured there and died of gangrene of legs due to wounds caused by torture. Died after 10 days of agony alone and without help....

Victim was kept bent up by hands attached around right leg. Was then thrown on the ground and flogged for 20 minutes. If he fainted, they would throw a pail of water in his face. This was to make him speak. M. Francheteau was flogged like that four days out of six....

One torture consisted in hanging up the victims by the hands, which were tied behind the back, until the shoulders were completely dislocated. Afterwards, the soles of the feet were cut with razor blades and then the victims were made to walk on salt.[4]

A report upon methods employed by the German police in

northern France and Belgium set forth these instances of torture:

A prisoner captured while trying to escape was delivered in his cell
to the fury of police dogs who tore him to pieces....

Commander Grandier, who had had a leg fractured in the war of
1914, was threatened by those who conducted the interrogations with
having his other leg broken and this was actually done. When he had
half revived, as a result of a hypodermic injection, the Germans did
away with him.[5]

M. Vanessche told this story:

I was arrested the 22 February 1944 at Mouscron in Belgium by
men belonging to the Gestapo who were dressed in civilian clothing.
During the interrogation they were wearing uniforms....I was interrogated for the second time at Cand in the main German prison
where I remained 31 days. There I was locked up for 2 or 3 hours in a
sort of wooden coffin where one could breathe only through three
holes in the top.[6]

M. Remy described torture endured by him:

Arrested 2 May 1944 at Armentieres, I arrived at the Gestapo, 18
Rue François Debatz at La Madelaine, about 3 o'clock the same day.
I was subjected to interrogation on two different occasions. The first
lasted for about an hour. I had to lie on my stomach and was given
about 120 lashes. The second interrogation lasted a little longer. I was
lashed again, lying on my stomach. As I would not talk, they stripped
me and put me in the bath tub. The 5th of May I was subjected to a
new interrogation at Loos. That day they hung me up by my feet and
rained blows all over my body. As I refused to speak, they untied me
and put me again on my stomach. When pain made me cry out, they
kicked me in the face with their boots....[7]

The testimony of M. Guerin was:

...as I would not admit anything, one of the interrogators put my
scarf around my mouth to stifle my cries. Another German policeman
took my head between his legs, and two others, one on each side of
me, beat me with clubs over the loins. Each of them struck me 25
times....This lasted over two hours. The next morning they began
again and it lasted as long as the day before. These tortures were
inflicted upon me because, on 11 November, I with my comrades of

the resistance had taken part in a demonstration by placing a wreath on the monument to the dead of the 1914-18 war....[8]

M. Delltombe told this story:

Thursday, 15 June, at 8 o'clock in the morning, I was taken to the torture cellar. There they demanded that I should confess to the sabotage which I had carried out with my groups and denounce my comrades as well as name my hiding places. Because I did not answer quickly enough, the torture commenced. They made me put my hands behind my back. They put on special handcuffs and hung me up by my wrists. Then they flogged me, principally on the loins, and in the face. That day the torture lasted three hours.

Friday, 16 June, the same thing took place; but only for an hour and a half, for I could not stand it any longer; and they took me back to my cell on a stretcher.

Saturday the tortures began again with even more severity. Then I was obliged to confess my sabotage, for the brutes stuck needles in my arms. After that they left me alone until 10 August; then they had me called to the office and told me I was condemned to death. I was put on a train of deportees going to Brussels, from which I was freed on 3 September by Brussels patriots.[9]

M. Alfred Deudon recounted the following ill-treatment: "18 August, sensitive parts were struck with a hammer. 19 August, was held under water; 20 August, my head was squeezed with an iron band; 21 and 24 August, I was chained day and night; 26 August, I was chained again day and night, and at one time hung up by the arms."[10]

A Madame Bondoux, supervisor at the prison in Bourges, certified that nine men, most of them youths, were chained, their hands tied behind their backs, for from fifteen to twenty days. She said that it was impossible for them to eat in a normal way. When other prisoners sought to pass them portions of their own small rations the police supervisor threw the bread in a corner of the cell. All of the young men were shot.

The deposition of M. Dommergues, a professor at Besançon, disclosed that he was made to believe that a woman suffering from torture was his own wife. He saw a comrade hung up with a weight of over a hundred pounds on each foot. "Another had his eyes pierced with pins."[11]

A traitor to France, who assisted the Gestapo, described the torture inflicted upon a Major Madeline which resulted in his death: "He was beaten with a whip and a bludgeon; blows on his fingernails crushed his fingers. He was forced to walk barefooted on tacks. He was burned with cigarettes. Finally, he was beaten unmercifully and taken back to his cell in a dying condition."[12]

Occasionally, complaints were made of such acts of mistreatment. Thus a French medical doctor wrote to the chief medical officer of the Feldkommandantur in Besançon on September 11, 1943:

Quite recently I had to treat a Frenchman who had wounds and multiple ecchymosis on his face and body, as a result of the torture apparatus employed by the German security service. He is a man of good standing, holding an important appointment under the French Government; and he was arrested because they thought he could furnish certain information. They could make no accusation against him as is proved by the fact that he was freed in a few days, when the interrogation to which they wanted to subject him was finished. He was subjected to torture, not as a legal penalty or in legitimate defense; but for the sole purpose of forcing him to speak under stress of violence and pain.[13]

The response to this letter was a request that the complainant be identified so that he could be visited and an appropriate meeting date made. The consequences of such a "visit" were sufficiently obvious to the doctor, and he declined to divulge the identity of his patient.

M. Labussiere, a captain of the reserve and a teacher at Marseilles-les-Aubigny, was dreadfully abused. The floggings were so severe as to have necessitated surgical treatment. Labussiere was told that his wife would be continuously tortured until he gave the names of his comrades in the resistance movement. He concluded his testimony with a general summary of the third degree methods:

1. The lash: Flogging was the most common punishment.

2. The bath: The victim was put in a tub full of cold water until he was almost drowned. He was then revived by artificial respiration. If he would not talk the process was repeated.

3. Electric current: The victim was subjected to repeated nonlethal shocks.

4. Pressing: Parts of the body were painfully squeezed in presses specially made for the purpose.

5. Hanging: The victim's hands were handcuffed together behind his back. A hook was slipped through the handcuffs and he was lifted off his feet by a pulley. At first he might be jerked up and down; later he would be left suspended for varying, fairly long, periods. The arms were often dislocated.

6. Burning: Parts of the body would be seared by a soldering lamp or matches.

A witness who testified for the Gestapo, Karl Hoffman, admitted that while he held office in Denmark he knew that third degree methods were used whenever it was deemed necessary to obtain information to counter acts of violence by resistance organizations, as in the case of attacks upon German soldiers, or sabotage of means of transportation. He acknowledged, moreover, that such methods were authorized "to forestall those dangers. . . ."[14] Of course, when the third degree is authorized "to forestall" possible acts of sabotage it may be used in *any* interrogation. In Denmark the most common forms of mistreatment consisted in lashing with sticks or beating with rubber truncheons.

Gestapo torture in Belgium left some men disfigured for life. In one district of Oslo, Norway, fifty-two persons died from cruel treatment suffered during interrogations. A witness in the Netherlands saw with his own eyes a priest beaten to death with a rubber truncheon.

Gestapo third degree methods were not isolated acts by individual members of the secret state police. They were partly the result of express authorization of the state. Under an order which directed Gestapo officials, "among other methods," to flog the persons arrested by them, there not only was no effective prohibition against cruel interrogations but in fact a clear permission to use brutality where the interrogator believed that vital information was being withheld. These orders led to the systematic torture of persons arrested by the Gestapo and held for investigation in Germany and in the occupied territories. They made the Gestapo the most feared, because it thereby became the most brutal, of the repressive agencies of the Hitler police state.

Insofar as justification could be pleaded for these extreme measures, it had to be based upon the necessity to obtain facts about resistance organizations so as to preserve order in the occupied territories and prevent the possibility of effective sabotage. The resistance movements were themselves an inevitable consequence of the acts of aggression upon neighboring nations. There would have been no Maquis in France if France had not been invaded and occupied by Hitler's armies. The crime of Gestapo torture inflicted upon persons of the occupied territories thus arose out of the greater crime of aggressive war.

In examining a former Gestapo official, Mr. Justice Jackson asked: "I am asking you as to the crimes committed by the Gestapo and I am asking if it included the torturing of thousands of persons?"

And the witness replied: "Yes."[15]

CHAPTER 32

Hitler Before God

A CERTAIN Major Meinel, who opposed the selection of Soviet prisoners of war for "special treatment," that is, for killing in concentration camps, was investigated by the SD for his loyalty to Hitler. An unfavorable report was submitted in which Meinel was criticized for having allegedly shown aversion to the National Socialist creed. "For example," said the report, "he mentioned God but not the Fuehrer in an order of the day."[1]

The New Faith

Christianity and Hitlerism were wholly incompatible. The only member of Hitler's cabinet to resign because of ideological differences, Baron von Eltz-Ruebenach, did so because he could not conscientiously become a member of the Nazi Party and remain a Christian. When invited to join the Party, Von Eltz-Ruebenach wrote to Hitler under date of January 30, 1937:

I thank you for the confidence you have placed in me during the few years of your leadership and for the honor you do me in offering to admit me into the Party.

My conscience forbids me, however, to accept this offer. I believe in the principles of positive Christianity and must remain faithful to my God and to myself. Party membership, however, would mean that I should have to countenance, without protest, the increasingly violent attacks by Party officers on the Christian confessions and on those who wish to remain faithful to their religious convictions....I ask to be permitted to resign.[2]

The attack upon the churches was related to the purpose of

Hitler to achieve a monolithic state and to subvert the German people to the criminal objectives which he had set out for himself, including the initiating and waging of aggressive wars, the extermination of the Jews, and the enslavement of eastern European peoples. No such program could have been accepted and supported by people who believed in the teachings of Christ.

The leader of this new Nazi cult which was to replace Christianity in Germany was Martin Bormann, the chief of the Party Chancery. On June 7, 1941, he expressed his views on this subject in a letter which he sent to all Gauleiter:

> Our National Socialist ideology is far loftier than the concepts of Christianity, which in their essential points have been taken over from Jewry.... More and more the people must be separated from the churches and their organs, the pastors.... Not until this has happened does the state leadership have influence on the individual citizens. Not until then are people and Reich secure in their existence for all the future.[3]

Rosenberg advocated a German religion in his book, *The Myth of the 20th Century*.[4] He argued that the Catholic and Protestant churches represented "negative Christianity" and did not correspond to the soul of "the people designated as a Nordic race."[5] He wrote: "The idea of honor—national honor—will be for us the beginning and end of all our thoughts and deeds." And he concluded that this national honor did not permit besides itself "Christian love" or any other "equivalent center of power."[6]

In a letter to Rosenberg on February 22, 1940, in which he proposed a National Socialist catechism to provide the basis for a National Socialist religion to replace Christianity, Bormann wrote:

> Christianity and National Socialism are phenomena which originated from entirely different basic causes. Both differ fundamentally, so strongly that it will not be possible to construct a Christian teaching which would be completely compatible with the point of view of the National Socialist ideology; just as the communities of Christian faith would never be able to stand by the ideology of National Socialism in its entirety.... The churches cannot be conquered by a compromise between National Socialism and Christian teachings, but only through a new ideology, whose coming you, yourself, have announced in your writings.[7]

Hitler, too, realized that his aims were in direct conflict with the moral teachings of Christianity. It was necessary to subvert the morals of the German people if they were to be united in his projected criminal enterprises; and it was essential to eliminate the influence of the churches so far as could safely be done if the moral principles of the German people were to be thus subverted.

The Struggle Against the Churches

The attack upon the Christian churches had a twofold objective. During the war every effort was to be made to harass and weaken the churches without, however, causing widespread opposition among the people. After the war the churches were to be destroyed upon evidence collected to show opposition of church leaders to Hitler's aggressions.

In the forefront of the struggle against the churches were the SS and the Gestapo. The organization book of the Nazi Party contained this description of the activities of the SS-man: "He openly and unrelentingly fights the most dangerous enemies of the State— Jews, Freemasons, Jesuits, and political clergymen."[8]

So important was the church problem to the Gestapo that a special department was established within the secret state police organization for the handling of church questions. On September 22 and 23, 1941, a conference of Gestapo church specialists was held in Berlin. The purpose of the meeting was to inspire those present with a determination to destroy the Christian churches by the best means available to them. One of the lecturers concluded with these remarks:

Each one of you must go to work with your whole heart and a true fanaticism. Should a mistake or two be made in the execution of this work, this should in no way discourage you, since mistakes are made everywhere. The main thing is that the adversary should be constantly opposed with determination, will and effective initiative.[9]

The executive measures to be applied by the Gestapo were discussed at the conference. It was stated that it was impractical to deal with political offenses under normal legal procedure because of the lack of political perception which prevailed among the legal authorities. The so-called agitator priests, preachers, and lay leaders of the various Protestant and Catholic churches, therefore, had to be handled by Gestapo measures, and where necessary removed to a concentration camp. The following punishments were to be applied to them according to individual circumstances: warning, fining, forbidden to preach, forbidden to remain in the parish, forbidden all activities as a priest, short term arrest, protective custody. Retreats, youth and recreational camps, evening services, processions, and pilgrimages were all to be forbidden on grounds of interfering with the war effort. The purpose of this work by the Gestapo was expressed as follows:

The immediate aim: The church must not regain one inch of the ground it has lost.

The ultimate aim: Destruction of the confessional churches, to be brought about by the collection of all material obtained through Nachrichtendienst activities, which will, at a given time, be produced as evidence against the church of its treasonable activities during the German fight for existence.[10]

Among the measures which were taken by the Gestapo against the churches were the imprisonment of outspoken clergymen and lay leaders, the dissolution of church groups and societies, the prohibition of religious meetings and demonstrations, the closing of monasteries and orders and seizure of their properties, the suppression of religious publications and education, and a constant propaganda designed to discredit the churches and religion and to lead the German youth away from God.

The Gestapo arrested and imprisoned the Protestant leader, Pastor Niemoeller, because he dared to speak against Hitler. The Munich priest, Rupert Mayer, was confined in Oranienburg-Sachsenhausen concentration camp. The Guild of the Virgin Mary of the Bavarian Diocese was dissolved and its property confiscated because it engaged in "worldly" activities, such as community games and social evenings, and because the members were allegedly trained and mobilized for "political and seditious tasks."[11] Members of small religious groups—the Freemasons and the Bible Students, particularly—were systematically rounded up and sent to concentration camps. By September, 1941, the Gestapo had closed about one hundred monasteries in the Reich, and many theological faculties had been shut down or shifted so as to impede religious training and education.

As early as 1934 denominational youth groups had been prohibited from public activities outside the church, especially from appearances in groups, such as hikes, holiday outings, and camping trips. Promptly after the beginning of the war with Poland the Gestapo prohibited evening church meetings because of blackout regulations, and forbade processions on grounds of overburdened transport facilities. One official even prohibited a procession on the excuse that it would unnecessarily wear out shoe leather. Bormann gave instructions that rations of printing paper to churches should be strictly curtailed so as to restrict production of religious publications.

The attack upon religious education was based upon the following concepts as expounded by Bormann:

National Socialist and Christian concepts are irreconcilable....No human being would know anything of Christianity if it had not been drilled into him in his childhood by pastors. The so-called dear God in no wise gives knowledge of his existence to young people in advance, but in an astonishing manner, in spite of his omnipotence, leaves this to the efforts of the pastors. If, therefore, in the future our youth learns nothing more of this Christianity, whose doctrines are far below ours, Christianity will disappear by itself.[12]

Promptly upon gaining control of the state, Hitler sought and obtained a concordat with the Catholic Church, in which the German Reich guaranteed freedom of profession and public practice of the Catholic religion, and the Vatican pledged loyalty by the clergy to the Reich government and emphasis in religious instruction on the patriotic duties of the Christian citizen. But by 1937 the Pope had become completely disillusioned about the intention of the Hitler government to live up to its part of the agreement. In an Encyclical of March 14, 1937, Pope Pius XI described the Hitler program in these words:

It discloses intrigues which from the beginning had no other aim than a war of extermination. In the furrows in which we had labored to sow the seeds of pure peace, others, like the enemy in Holy Scripture (Matt. xiii, 25), sowed the tares of suspicion, discord, hatred, calumny, of secret and open fundamental hostility to Christ and His Church, fed from a thousand different sources and making use of every available means.... Anyone who has even a grain of a sense of truth left in his mind and even a shadow of a feeling of justice left in his heart will have to admit that, in the difficult and eventful years which followed the concordat, every word and every action of ours was ruled by loyalty to the terms of the agreement; but also he will have to recognize with surprise and deep disgust that the unwritten law of the other party has been arbitrary misinterpretation of agreements, circumvention of agreements, weakening of the force of agreements and, finally, more or less open violation of agreements.

In the occupied territories direct methods of suppression were more readily employed. At the outbreak of the war, 487 Catholic priests were among the thousands of Czech citizens arrested and sent to concentration camps as hostages. Religious orders were dissolved and their members expelled or sent to Germany for compulsory labor. All religious instruction in Czech schools was suppressed, and most religious publications were prohibited.

The persecution of the churches was similar and even more severe in Poland, where, according to the report of the Polish Government, by January, 1941, about seven thousand priests had been killed, and three thousand more sent to prison or put into concentration camps. The petition of the Vatican that the church leaders be permitted to emigrate to neutral countries of Europe or to America was answered by the concession that they would all be collected in one concentration camp—Dachau.

In his Allocution of June 2, 1945, Pope Pius XII described the conditions of the churchmen in Dachau:

In the forefront, for the number and harshness of the treatment meted out to them, are the Polish priests. From 1940 to 1945, 2,800 Polish ecclesiastics and religious were imprisoned in that camp; among them was the Auxiliary Bishop of Wloclawek, who died there of typhus. In April last there were left only 816, all the others being dead except for two or three transferred to another camp. In the summer of 1942, 480 German-speaking ministers of religion were known to be gathered there; ... Nor should we pass over in silence those belonging to occupied territories, Holland, Belgium, France (among whom the Bishop of Clermont), Luxembourg, Slovenia, Italy. Many of those priests and laymen endured indescribable sufferings for their faith and for their vocation. In one case the hatred of the impious against Christ reached the point of parodying on the person of an interned priest with barbed wire, the scourging and the crowning with thorns of our Redeemer.[13]

Like the extermination of the Jews, the struggle against the churches was a secondary war in Hitler's design for conquest and tyrannous rule. And just as the extermination actions in the eastern territories gave rise to resentment and resistance which contributed to the defeat of German military forces in the field, so the assaults upon the churches, disguised as they might be, caused a lessening of confidence in Hitler by German Christians and led to the undermining of Hitler's strength at home. In his political testament, written in prison shortly before he took his own life, Robert Ley asked himself why catastrophe had fallen upon Germany; and, answering, said: "We deserted God, and so God deserted us."[14]

Hans Frank, who had so readily confessed to the guilt he felt within himself for the crimes committed against humanity by Hitler's Germany, declared in his final remarks to the Tribunal:

At the beginning of our way we did not suspect that our turning away from God could have such disastrous deadly consequences and that we would necessarily become more and more deeply involved in guilt. At that time we could not have known that so much loyalty and willingness to sacrifice on the part of the German people could have been so badly directed by us.

Thus, by turning away from God, we were overthrown and had to perish. It was not because of technical deficiencies and unfortunate circumstances alone that we lost the war, nor was it misfortune and treason. Before all, God pronounced and executed judgment on Hitler and the system which we served with minds far from God. Therefore, may our people, too, be called back from the road on which Hitler—and we with him—have led them.

I beg our people not to continue in this direction, be it even a single step; because Hitler's road was the way without God, the way of turning from Christ, and, in the last analysis, the way of political foolishness, the way of disaster, and the way of death. His path became more and more that of a frightful adventurer without conscience or honesty, as I know today at the end of this trial.[15]

Perhaps Frank was thinking then of those who suffered under that "frightful adventurer"—of the enslaved Ukrainian peasant, the brutalized Pole, or the beaten and harried Jew, of whom it could be said, in Markham's ageless words:

> Thru this dread shape humanity betrayed,
> Plundered, profaned and disinherited,
> Cries protest to the Judges of the World,
> A protest that is also prophecy.[16]

But Frank gave thought, too, to others who had departed from God's laws and who had committed wrongs against the German people, and he asked: "Who shall ever judge these crimes against the German people?"[17] The world well understands that wrong was not all upon the German side in World War II. And yet others who were guilty have never been, and will never be, brought to the bar of justice.

Those who, through fortuitous circumstance, escape the judgment of man will yet answer to the judgment of God. Indeed, the judgment of man against man for crimes against the very laws of God is but a palliative to public conscience. We do not expiate the slaughter of millions of innocent men, women, and children by hanging a few men chiefly responsible for the crime. Nor do we cleanse our own consciences by casting blame upon Hitler, or upon Hitler's staff, or upon Hitler's Germany. The commission of crimes against humanity, as they were proved at Nuremberg, is a responsibility of humanity itself.

In the first public meeting held in Nuremberg after the end of the war Lutheran Bishop Hans Lilje, who had spent nine months in Nazi jails, part of the time in chains, said to hundreds of people gathered in the little church and churchyard where he spoke:

If all of us would understand the real reason for our tragedy, this could become the source of new hope. Though I do not presume to know all the historical details leading to our catastrophe, I do know, as a Christian, that the only way out of darkness and misery is the road of obedience to God.[18]

And Frank's final words were:

We call upon the German people, whose rulers we were, to return from this road which, according to the law and justice of God, had to lead us and our system into disaster and which will lead everyone into disaster who tries to walk on it, or continue on it, everywhere in the whole world.[19]

World War II, which brought Hitler's Germany to destruction, was a dreadful calamity. If the world is to be saved from greater wars and worse catastrophes, the peoples of every continent, and of every nation, must seek the guidance of God, and heed His word:

> In all thy ways acknowledge Him and
> He shall direct thy paths.[20]

If men will believe, and believing, manifest their faith in God, He will direct their paths along the way to peace and the brotherhood of man.

PART FIVE

The End

CHAPTER 33

Flames

B ENEATH THE GARDEN to the rear of the Reich Chancellery an underground bunker had been built during the war. It consisted of two levels, a servants' area of twelve rooms and, below it, a Fuehrer-bunker of eighteen rooms. Hitler spent his fifty-sixth birthday, April 20, 1945, in its sunless chambers. Thenceforward he knew no other home.

On that day Hitler was saluted by the architect of the Reich Chancellery, Albert Speer, and by the architects of the Nazi state —Himmler, Goering, Goebbels, Bormann, Ribbentrop, Doenitz, Keitel, and Jodl. He was remembered by a delegation of Hitler Youth whom he decorated in the garden of the Chancellery. He was entreated to leave beleaguered Berlin; but for the time being he said he wished to remain. Not so the architects, who already saw their handiwork crumbling about them. On the evening of that day, or shortly after, many departed—Speer for Hamburg, Himmler for Ziethen castle, and Goering for Obersalzberg. Only Goebbels and Bormann were to remain with Hitler until the end.

The plans for the final defense of Germany had been based upon two centers of command, one in the north under Admiral Doenitz, and the other in the south which Hitler himself was to direct with the aid of his top military advisers. It had been planned to leave Berlin by plane for Berchtesgaden. But after the situation report on April 22, Hitler called Keitel and Bormann to him and abruptly announced, "I will never leave Berlin, never."[1] This was the first indication of any such radical change of plans. It created an entirely new situation for Keitel, Jodl, and the other military leaders. For instead of a fight for Germany, the last days of the war were to be turned into a struggle for Berlin.

Even so, Hitler ordered Keitel and Jodl to Berchtesgaden. Keitel protested: "If you have made the statement once that you will fight before Berlin, in Berlin, and behind Berlin, then that is the way you will have to do it; but it is simply impossible that, after all this time that you have been directing and leading us, all of a sudden you should send your staff away and let them lead themselves."[2] The plea was to no avail. "I have taken a position," Hitler said, "I have taken a fixed position, and I can't leave it."[3] On the twenty-third, Keitel and Jodl left Berlin. Neither was able, thereafter, to return to the Reich Chancellery.

Meanwhile, Hitler's decision to remain in Berlin had been announced over the radio and word of it had come to Goering, who was in the far less vulnerable and far more comfortable site of Berchtesgaden. By an order of June 29, 1941, Hitler had decreed that in the hierarchy of the Nazi state Goering should have first right of succession. Upon learning of Hitler's decision to remain in Berlin, Goering sent him a telegram asking whether Hitler agreed that under the circumstances Goering should take over the leadership of the Reich in accordance with the decree of June 29, 1941. Speer had returned to Berlin and was present in the Fuehrer-bunker when Hitler received Goering's telegram. He described Hitler's reaction in these words:

Hitler was unusually excited about the contents of the telegram, and said quite plainly what he thought about Goering. He said that he had known for some time that Goering had failed, that he was corrupt, and that he was a drug addict. I was extremely shaken, because I felt that if the head of the state had known this for such a long time, then it showed a lack of responsibility on his part to leave such a man in office, when the lives of countless people depended upon him.[4]

Hitler's reply to the telegram was a communication informing Goering that his action was treasonable, and that unless he immediately resigned from all his offices he would be shot. By separate orders Hitler then arranged to have Goering arrested for high treason. On the following day it was announced that for reasons of health the Reichsmarshal had resigned. Hitler then ordered Air Force General Ritter von Greim to report to him from Munich.

Von Greim was flown to Reichlin by the famed woman pilot, Hanna Reitsch. A sergeant-pilot flew them to Gatow airport in Berlin. From there Von Greim personally brought the plane over troops fighting in the streets to a safe landing on the East-West Axis. Greim was seriously wounded in the course of the flight, but he and Hanna Reitsch made their way safely to the Chancellery, arriving at the bunker in the evening of April 26.

At their first meeting Hitler asked Greim if he knew why he had been called to Berlin. When Greim answered in the negative, Hitler, according to Hanna Reitsch, replied:

Because Hermann Goering has betrayed and deserted both me and his Fatherland. Behind my back he has established connections with the enemy. His action was a mark of cowardice. And against my orders he has gone to save himself at Berchtesgaden. From there he sent me a disrespectful telegram. He said that I had once named him as my successor and that now, as I was no longer able to rule from Berlin, he was prepared to rule from Berchtesgaden in my place. He closes the wire by stating that if he had no answer from me by nine-thirty on the date of the wire he would assume my answer to be in the affirmative.

An ultimatum! A crass ultimatum! Now nothing remains. Nothing is spared me. No allegiances are kept, no "honor" lived up to, no disappointments that I have not had, no betrayals that I have not experienced, and now this above all else. Nothing remains. Every wrong has already been done me.

I immediately had Goering arrested as a traitor to the Reich, took from him all his offices, and removed him from all organizations. That is why I have called you to me. I hereby declare you Goering's successor as Oberbefehlshaber der Luftwaffe. In the name of the German people I give you my hand.[5]

Goebbels was especially infuriated to learn of Goering's demand for power. Reitsch recalled that Goebbels hobbled about his quarters, talking to himself, accusing Goering of treachery and treason, and pouring verbal abuse upon the absent object of his wrath:

That swine, who has always set himself up as the Fuehrer's greatest support now does not have the courage to stand beside him. As if that were not enough, he wants to replace the Fuehrer as head of the State. He, an incessant incompetent, who has destroyed his Fatherland with his mishandling and stupidity, now wants to lead the entire nation. By this alone he proves that he was never truly one of us, that at heart he was always weak and a traitor.[6]

In the evening of the first day, Reitsch said that Hitler called her to him. "Hanna," he said, "you belong to those who will die with me."[7] Handing her two vials of poison, one for herself and one for Greim, he explained: "Each of us has a vial of poison such as this. I do not wish that one of us falls to the Russians alive, nor do I wish our bodies to be found by them. Each person is responsible for destroying his body so that nothing recognizable remains. Eva and I will have our bodies burned. You will devise your own method. Will you please so inform Von Greim?"[8]

After a further scene in which she begged Hitler to leave Berlin and "live so that Germany can live,"[9] Reitsch returned to Greim and handed him the poison. They agreed then that should the Soviets take the Reich Chancellery they would each drink the contents of a poison vial and then pull the pin from a heavy grenade held tightly against their bodies.

The Soviet bombardment increased in intensity as the Russian troops drove relentlessly into the heart of dying Berlin. Early in the morning hours of April 27 the first heavy Soviet barrage struck the Reich Chancellery. Reitsch spent most of the night tending the wounded Greim, who was in great pain.

In the morning she learned that besides Hitler, Eva Braun, Reichsleiter Martin Bormann, and Reichsminister Goebbels and his wife and their six children, the remaining occupants of the bunker were State Secretary Naumann (secretary of state in the ministry for propaganda), Hevel (representing Foreign Minister Ribbentrop), Vice-admiral Voss (representing Doenitz), General Krebs (chief of the general staff of the Army), General Burgdorf (chief adjutant of the Wehrmacht), Hansel Bauer (Hitler's personal pilot), Baetz (another pilot), SS-Gruppenfuehrer Fegelein (representing Himmler), Dr. Stumpfegger (Hitler's personal physician), Oberst von Buelow (adjutant of the Luftwaffe), Dr. Lorenz (representing Dr. Dietrich for the German press), Frau Christian and Fraulein Kreuger (two of Hitler's secretaries), and various SS orderlies and messengers.

If the thought of sudden death was stunning to most of these remaining inhabitants of the bunker, it at least offered an exciting diversion to the frenetic Goebbels who, having vicariously garrotted Goering, turned agreeably to thought of the suicide of himself, his wife, and his six children.

"We are teaching the world how men die for their 'honor.' Our deaths shall be an eternal example to all Germans, to all friends and enemies alike. One day the whole world will acknowledge that we did right, that we sought to protect the world against Bolshevism with our lives. One day it will be set down in the history of all time."[10]

After Goering, the next betrayal was that of SS-Gruppenfuehrer Fegelein. Not only was Fegelein the personal representative of Himmler at Fuehrer headquarters, he was also the husband of Eva Braun's sister. His desertion was, therefore, a disgrace as well as an act of personal cowardice. He disappeared late in the afternoon of April 27. Shortly thereafter he was captured in the suburbs of Berlin, disguised in civilian clothes. Fegelein was brought to the Reich Chancellery and questioned by Gestapo chief Mueller. Hitler ordered him shot at once. Thus disposed of was deserter number two. And, then, there was Himmler.

Walter Schellenberg, chief of the foreign political intelligence service, had become convinced during 1943 that Germany was going to lose the war and "that it was necessary to reach a compromise."[11] He commenced scheming to turn Himmler against Hitler. To accomplish this he convinced Himmler that he should receive an astrologer whom Schellenberg had previously instructed "to influence Himmler in favor of taking matters into his own hands...."[12] In spite of this resort to astrological influence, Schellenberg was unable to induce Himmler to take positive action until the last days of the war. Finally, however, he obtained Himmler's permission to enter into negotiations with Count Bernadotte of Sweden for the capitulation of the German forces to the Western Powers. The refusal of the Allies to accept this offer was broadcast on April 28, and in this way Hitler learned of the treachery of his loyal Heinrich. It was the bitterest blow of all. Goering, Fegelein, and now Himmler—in adversity even the most faithful had proven disloyal.

Meanwhile the Soviet armies pressed ever closer upon the center of Berlin. The time of survival had passed from numbered days to numbered hours. Hitler prepared to die. But before death he wished to make Eva Braun his wife, and to write his personal and political testaments.

The marriage ceremony was performed by Municipal Counselor Walter N. Wagner in the Fuehrer-bunker on the evening of April 28. The witnesses were Goebbels and Bormann. According to the marriage certificate Eva Braun was then thirty-five years of age, and Hitler fifty-six. She gave the names of her parents, but Hitler, who had been an illegitimate child, left those spaces in the certificate unfilled. For her identification, Eva Braun referred to the special pass issued by the chief of the German police. Hitler's identification was "publicly known." The certificate recited that the principals to the marriage "declared that they are of complete Aryan descent," and "in view of war developments, they requested a war marriage under exceptional circumstances and requested further that the publication of the banns be done orally and all delays be avoided." The requests were granted, and the banns were approved as in good order. After the parties stated their desire to enter into the marriage, the official "declared the marriage concluded legally before the law."[13]

Hitler dictated his political testament and his personal will in the early morning hours of the next day—April 29. The political testament was witnessed by Dr. Joseph Goebbels, Wilhelm Burgdorf, Martin Bormann, and Hans Krebs. The personal will was witnessed by Martin Bormann, Dr. Joseph Goebbels, and Nicolaus von Buelow.

In his political testament, Hitler began by saying: "More than thirty years have passed since I made my modest contribution as a volunteer in the First World War, which was forced upon the Reich."[14] He did not suggest who was the aggressor of World War I, but he did not leave unplaced the blame for World War II: "It is untrue that I or anybody else in Germany wanted war in 1939. It was wanted and provoked exclusively by those international statesmen who either were of Jewish origin or worked for Jewish interests."[15]

Hitler contended that he had "never wished that after the appalling First World War there should be a second one against either England or America."[16] His failure to include Czechoslovakia, Poland, and the Soviet Union in that wish was, of course, a tacit admission of his purpose to conquer the eastern territories. He contended that his proposal to the British ambassador in Berlin to solve the German-Polish difficulty was "rejected only because the ruling political clique in England wanted war, partly for commercial reasons, partly because it was influenced by propaganda put out by the international Jewry."[17]

The most striking feature of the testament was the implied confession of the slaughter of the Jews of Europe.

I also made it quite plain that... the Jews, the race that is the real guilty party in this murderous struggle, would be saddled with the responsibility for it. I left no one in doubt that this time not only would millions of children of European Aryan races starve, not only would millions of grown men meet their death, and not only would hundreds of thousands of women and children be burned and bombed to death in cities, but this time the real culprits would have to pay for their guilt even though by more humane means than war.[18]

The "more humane means" were, of course, the gas chambers of the extermination centers, though Hitler did not say so.

Hitler declared that he had elected to die in Berlin so as not to "fall into the hands of the enemy, who requires a new spectacle, presented by the Jews, to divert their hysterical masses."[19] At the same time he called upon the soldiers at the front, the women at home, the peasants, the workers, and the Hitler Youth not to give up the struggle but to "carry it on wherever they may be against the enemies of the Fatherland...."[20] For, he declaimed, "from the sacrifice of our soldiers and from my own comradeship with them to death itself, the seed has been sown that will grow one day in the history of Germany to the glorious rebirth of the National Socialist movement and thereby to the establishment of a truly united nation."[21]

He then declared the expulsion of Goering and Himmler from

the Party and the revocation of all their respective offices. "Apart altogether from their disloyalty to me," he complained, "Goering and Himmler have brought irreparable shame on the country and the whole nation by secretly negotiating with the enemy without my knowledge and against my will, and also by illegally attempting to seize control of the State."[22]

In place of the deposed Goering, Hitler named Admiral Doenitz to succeed him as President of the Reich and as Supreme Commander of the Armed Forces. He named the members of the new cabinet, omitting therefrom such former comrades as Ribbentrop, Keitel, and Speer.

Finally, he asked all Germans "to be loyal and obedient to the new government and its president until death. Above all, I enjoin the government of the nation and the people to uphold the racial laws to the limit and to resist mercilessly the poisoner of all nations, international Jewry."[23]

In his personal will Hitler declared that he had "decided to take as my wife the woman who, after many years of true friendship, came to this city, almost already besieged, of her own free will in order to share my fate."[24] And he said that "she will go to her death with me at her own wish as my wife."[25] He left all his possessions to the Party or, if it should no longer exist, to the state. "If the state, too, is destroyed, there is no need for any further instructions on my part."[26] He said that the paintings "bought by me during the years"[27] had been assembled for a picture gallery in his home town of Linz. He named Martin Bormann the executor of his will, and authorized Bormann to give to his relatives personal mementos of value and to provide a modest living standard for them, especially for his wife's mother and his faithful fellow-workers of both sexes, chief among them his former secretaries. But how Bormann was to fulfil this bequest he did not trouble to explain.

At the end, he declared: "My wife and I choose to die in order to escape the shame of overthrow or capitulation. It is our wish for our bodies to be cremated immediately on the place where I have performed the greater part of my daily work during twelve years of service to my people."[28]

In his political testament, Hitler ordered Bormann and Goebbels, and others unnamed, to leave Berlin and to continue the cause of National Socialism. Bormann was only too ready to do so—perhaps, in his view, because a dead man would be little able to serve as the executor of the Fuehrer's will. But with Goebbels it was a different story. For Goebbels, the master of propaganda, could not resist the opportunity to share with Hitler, for the glory of posterity, the final dramatic act in the story of National Socialism. Such was his fervor for immortal fame that he coolly committed his children to die with him for a cause for which they had never lived themselves.

Shortly after Hitler completed his testament, Goebbels drafted a personal codicil. Noting that Hitler had commanded him to leave Berlin, Goebbels declared that "for the first time in my life I must categorically refuse."[29] He added: "In the nightmare of treason that surrounds the Fuehrer in these most critical days of the war, there must be at least some people to stay with him unconditionally until death, even if this contradicts the formal and, from a material point of view, entirely justifiable order that he gives in his political testament."[30] He said that this sacrifice was made to inspire the people by "examples that are clear and easily understandable." He concluded:

For this reason, together with my wife and on behalf of my children, who are too young to be able to speak for themselves, and who if they were sufficiently old would agree with this decision without reservation, I express my unalterable decision not to leave the Reich capital even if it falls, and at the side of the Fuehrer to end a life that for me personally will have no further value if I cannot spend it at the service of the Fuehrer and at his side.[31]

The next day three messengers were dispatched, each carrying a copy of Hitler's political testament and will, with instructions to pass through the enemy lines and deliver the instruments to named addressees. Although none of the documents was actually delivered, British and American intelligence agents succeeded in obtaining original copies of all of them after the capitulation.

Prophetically, on that day, too, came the news of the death of Mussolini. Whether or not Hitler learned of the ignominious hanging of the Fascist chief and his mistress head-downward in the market place of Milan, the fact that Mussolini had been captured and killed must have confirmed Hitler's determination to avoid any such fate. The hour for death was near.

The first to go was neither man nor woman, but Hitler's dog, which was poisoned. Poison, too, Hitler handed his two secretaries, to be taken by them as they might desire. In the first hours after midnight, Hitler called his coterie about him. Silently, he shook hands with them, and retired to his chambers. But Hitler did not die that night.

By noon of the next day, April 30, the military situation had reached a point of utter crisis. The Tiergarten had been overrun by Soviet troops and they had reached Potsdamer Platz. At any moment they would enter the grounds of the Reich Chancellery.

About 2:30 in the afternoon SS-Sturmbannfuehrer Guensche telephoned Erich Kempka, Hitler's chauffeur, and told him to bring two hundred liters of gasoline to the bunker. With the aid of others, Kempka brought the gasoline to the entrance of the bunker in the garden of the Reich Chancellery. The other men went back but Kempka entered the bunker where he was told by Guensche that Hitler was dead. Guensche told Kempka that Hitler had ordered that his body be burned at once after his death, "so that he would not be exhibited at a Russian freak-show."[32] In a few moments SS-Sturmbannfuehrer Linge, Hitler's valet, came from the Fuehrer's private room carrying Hitler's body wrapped in a blanket. Reichsleiter Martin Bormann came from the living room of the bunker carrying in his arms the body of Mrs. Hitler. He turned her corpse over to Kempka. Linge and the orderly went upstairs with the corpse of the Fuehrer, and Kempka followed, carrying the body of Mrs. Hitler. They were followed by Bormann, Goebbels, and Guensche.

It was then about 3:00 P.M. The two corpses were placed in a small depression in the sandy ground of the Reich Chancellery garden. The gasoline was poured over them and ignited. Bormann, Goebbels, Guensche, Linge, the orderly, and Kempka "stood in the bunker entrance, looked towards the fire and all saluted with raised hands."[33]

When they re-entered the bunker Kempka went into the private rooms of the Fuehrer. He noted two pistols upon the floor. He had previously observed a dampness in the region of Mrs. Hitler's heart. From these observations he concluded "that the Fuehrer and Miss Eva Braun shot themselves."[34] Nothing was done to remove traces of the corpses at the place of their burning. "This also was not necessary, because the traces had been wiped out by the uninterrupted artillery-fire...."[35] Adolf Hitler thus died by his own hand on April 30, 1945.

In the evening of that day Doenitz received a radio message from headquarters to the effect that Hitler had designated him as head of the German state. And, in Doenitz' words: "I was authorized to take at once all measures which I considered necessary."[36] On the following morning, May 1, Doenitz received a second message which informed him that he was to be Reich President, that Goebbels was to be Reich Chancellor, that Bormann was to be Party Minister, and that Seyss-Inquart was to be Foreign Minister. Doenitz refused to respect the instructions in the second telegram. He had not, however, been apprised of Hitler's political testament.

During the same day Goebbels prepared to comply with the grand gesture of his codicil to Hitler's testament. First, he poisoned his six children. Then, in the evening, with his wife he walked up the stairs, out of the bunker, and into the garden. There they met death by gunshot. There they, too, were cremated, but imperfectly, for when the Soviets entered the Chancellery grounds they found the half-burned bodies of Hitler's faithful mouthpiece and his pitiful wife.

At nine o'clock that evening the bunker itself was set on fire. The handful who remained behind attempted to flee Berlin. Some succeeded; but most did not. Among those believed killed while trying to break through the Soviet lines was Martin Bormann. Even as the few left alive at Fuehrer headquarters in Berlin were thus seeking to escape with their lives, the German radio gave warning to the German people of an announcement of grave importance. At 9:30 and 9:45 and 9:57 listeners were alerted by the following statement:

"Attention, attention! The German radio will broadcast a serious and important announcement to the German people."[37]

There was portent of what was to come in the rendition after each announcement of the drama-laden music of Hitler's favorite composers, Wagner and Bruckner.

At 10:26 the warning was repeated, followed by a ruffle of drums. Then:

It has been reported from the Fuehrer's Headquarters, that our Fuehrer Adolf Hitler has died this afternoon in his Battle Headquarters at the Reich Chancellery fighting to the last breath for Germany against Bolshevism.

On the 30th April the Fuehrer nominated Grand Admiral Doenitz to be his successor. The Grand Admiral and Fuehrer's successor will speak to the German nation.

Hitler's successor, Admiral Doenitz, then spoke:

German men and women, soldiers of the German armed forces. Our Fuehrer Adolf Hitler is dead. The German people bow in deepest sorrow and respect. Early he had recognized the terrible danger of Bolshevism and had dedicated his life to the fight against it. His fight having ended, he died a hero's death in the capital of the German Reich, after having led a straight and steady life.

His life was dedicated to the service of Germany. His devotion in the fight against the Bolshevist flood was in the interest not only of Europe but of the entire civilized world. The Fuehrer has nominated me as his successor. Fully conscious of the responsibility, I am taking over the leadership of the German nation in this fateful hour. My first task is to save German men from being destroyed by the advancing Bolshevist enemy. For this reason only do the armies continue fighting. As far and as long as the achievement of this task is being prevented by the British and Americans, we have to defend ourselves against them too and must go on fighting. Thus the Anglo-Americans are no longer carrying on the fight for their own peoples but only for the spreading of Bolshevism in Europe. What the German people have achieved in this war through fighting and sufferings they have undergone at home are unique in history. In the coming emergency arising for our people I shall to the best of my ability make it my business to secure for our brave women, men and children the most tolerable conditions essential to life.

In order to do this, I need your help. Give me your confidence, as your road is also my road. Uphold order and discipline in towns and country. Let everybody remain at his post doing his duty. Only thus will we be able to mitigate the suffering, which the future will bring for everyone of us, and prevent the collapse. If we do all that is in our power, God will not forsake us after so much suffering and sacrifice.[38]

After this announcement, "Deutschland, Deutschland ueber Alles" and the "Horst Wessel Song" were played. A radio silence of three minutes was broken by Doenitz' order of the day:

German armed forces, my comrades. The Fuehrer is dead. Faithful to his great idea to save the people of Europe from Bolshevism, he has devoted his life and has died the death of a hero. *With him one of the greatest heroes of German history has gone.* With proud respect and sorrow we lower the flags for him.

The Fuehrer has designated me to be his successor as head of state and as Commander in Chief of the armed forces. I am taking over the supreme command of all branches of the German armed forces with the will to carry on the struggle against the Bolshevists until the fighting forces and until hundreds of thousands of families of the German eastern area have been saved from slavery and destruction....

The situation requires from you, who have achieved such great historic deeds, and who are longing for the end of this war, further unconditional devotion. I demand discipline and obedience. Only by carrying out my orders unconditionally will chaos and destruction be avoided. He is a coward and traitor who, especially at this time, evades his duties and thus brings death or slavery to German women and children.

The oath sworn by you to the Fuehrer is now owed to me by everyone of you as the successor appointed by the Fuehrer.

German soldiers do your duty. The life of our nation is at stake.[39]

On the night of February 27, 1933, Adolf Hitler, the newly-appointed Chancellor of the German Reich, had stood with Goering watching the flames leap from the Reichstag into the blackness. The red glow flickered in the Fuehrer's face and cast a beacon into the Berlin sky. Germany's freedom went up in flames that night. Hate, bigotry, and racial oppression succeeded faith, tolerance, and personal dignity as the controlling principles of the Greater German Reich. Twentieth-century Germany passed into the Dark Ages. Twelve years later, as though fired by the small torch of Hitler's pyre in the garden of the Reich Chancellery, all of Berlin was set ablaze, consuming the evil which Hitler and his collaborators had conceived in Germany and inflicted upon the world.

CHAPTER 34

Ashes

The BLACK SWASTIKA of Hitler's Germany was shattered—as Germany itself was crushed. The noble city of Nuremberg had become a somber mass of crumbled buildings, of scattered bricks and twisted girders, of people without homes and without families, of the fatherless child and the legless soldier. And the people of Nuremberg, like the people of all the other smashed and ruined cities of Germany, asked themselves over and over again, "Why have our country, our cities, and our homes thus been reduced to ashes?" Their cry was echoed throughout the bruised world.

Where lay the guilt for all this agony?

The defendant Frank confessed to the Tribunal:

"I, myself, speaking from the very depths of my feelings and having lived through the five months of this trial, want to say that now after I have gained a full insight into all the horrible atrocities which have been committed, I am possessed by a deep sense of guilt."[1]

Keitel, the leader of Hitler's military forces, said this:

In the course of the trial, my defense counsel submitted two fundamental questions to me, the first one already some months ago. It was: "In case of a victory, would you have refused to participate in any part of the success?"

I answered: "No, I should certainly have been proud of it."

The second question was: "How would you act if you were in the same position again?"

My answer: "Then I would rather choose death than to let myself be drawn into the net of such pernicious methods."

From these two answers the High Tribunal may see my viewpoint.

I believed, but I erred, and I was not in a position to prevent what ought to have been prevented. That is my guilt.

It is tragic to have to realize that the best I had to give as a soldier, obedience and loyalty, was exploited for purposes which could not be recognized at the time, and that I did not see that there is a limit set even for a soldier's performance of his duty. That is my fate.

From the clear recognition of the causes, the pernicious methods, and the terrible consequences of this war, may there arise the hope for a new future in the community of nations for the German people.[2]

Von Schirach, the man who trained the youth of Germany to follow Hitler, concluded:

I have educated this generation in faith and loyalty to Hitler. The youth organization which I built up bore his name. I believed that I was serving a leader who would make our people and youth of our country great and happy. Millions of young people believed this, together with me, and saw their ultimate ideal in National-Socialism. Many died for it. Before God, before the German nation and before my German people I alone bear the guilt of having trained our young people for a man whom I for many long years had considered unimpeachable, both as a leader and as the head of the State, of creating for him a generation who saw him as I did. The guilt is mine in that I educated the youth of Germany for a man who murdered by the millions.[3]

The Fuehrer Principle

This has been the story of Hitler's Germany—a great nation ruled and ruined by one man. This man, the world now knows, was not only a despot, he was a common criminal. And because he held the absolute power of the state within his personal control, his criminality was imposed on Germany. Might it have been otherwise? Might Germany have had the benefit of totalitarian efficiency under a despot who would live by the book of God rather than by the principle of strife? Was the evil which came to Germany merely the evil of a man, or was it the evil of the system which gave the tyrant unlimited power?

That question was answered by the man to whose hands Hitler left the power of state when he deserted the German people in their last dark moment of despair. Admiral Doenitz, in reflecting upon the causes which led to Germany's disaster, told the International Military Tribunal that "the Fuehrer principle as a political principle is wrong."[4] And he added:

In the military leadership of all armies in this world, the Fuehrer principle has proved itself in the best possible way. On the strength of this experience I considered it also right with regard to political leadership, particularly in the case of a nation in the hopeless position in which the German people found itself in 1932. The great successes of the new government and a feeling of happiness such as the entire nation had never known before seemed to prove it right. But, if in spite of all the idealism, all the decency, and all the devotion of the great majority of the German people, no other result has been achieved through the Fuehrer principle, in the last analysis, than the misfortune of this people, then this principle as such must be wrong, wrong because apparently human nature is not in a position to use the power of this principle for good, without falling victim to the temptation of this power.[5]

And Fritzsche, who next to Goebbels best knew the power of propaganda in the totalitarian state, said this: "After the totalitarian form of government has brought about the catastrophe of the murder of five millions, I consider this form of government wrong even in times of emergency. I believe any kind of democratic control, even a restricted democratic control, would have made such a catastrophe impossible."[6]

Although Hitler was eager to claim the privileges of authority as German dictator, in the end he shifted his responsibility back to the German people. Speer commented on this aspect of the Fuehrer principle:

I, personally, when I became Minister in February 1942, placed myself at the disposal of this Fuehrer principle. But I admit that in my organization I soon saw that the Fuehrer principle was full of tremendous mistakes, and so I tried to weaken its effect. The terrible danger of the authoritarian system, however, became really clear only at the moment when we were approaching the end. It was then that one could see what the principle really meant, namely, that every order should be carried out without criticism. Everything that has become known during this trial, in the way of orders carried out without any consideration, finally proved—for example the carrying-out of the order to destroy the bridges in our own country—to be a mistake or a consequence of this authoritarian system.... The combination of Hitler and this system, then, brought about these terrible catastrophes in the world.[7]

But in no modern state can a dictator rule alone. And Hitler, absolute ruler that he was, nonetheless required the support of fanatical followers—men of little conscience, willing to execute his orders without question. Hitler found his top conspirators in the band of men who helped him to power, and in others who were willing to forego principle for position. The strutting Goering, the blatant Goebbels, and the heinous Himmler were allowed to touch the scepter of unlimited power. Others, who could not share that thrill, supported Hitler because of personal prestige, advancement, and gain. The German people, believing in Hitler as the savior of Germany, fed with the falsehoods of Bormann and Himmler, excited by the promises of Goering and Goebbels, followed him, fearfully and hopefully, into the valley of death.

If Hitler's career was crime, his talent was deception. Schacht said that whatever Hitler promised to the German people he afterward denied to them.

He promised equal rights for all citizens, but his adherents, regardless of their capabilities, enjoyed privileges before all other citizens. He promised to put the Jews under the same protection which foreigners enjoyed, yet he deprived them of every legal protection. He had promised to fight against political lies, but together with his Minister Goebbels he cultivated nothing but political lies and political fraud. He promised the German people to maintain the principles of positive Christianity yet he tolerated and sponsored measures by which institutions of the Church were abused, reviled, and damaged. Also, in the foreign political field he always spoke against a war on two fronts—and then later undertook it himself. He despised and disregarded all laws of the Weimar Republic, to which he had taken the oath when he became Chancellor. He mobilized the Gestapo against personal liberty. He gagged and bound all free exchange of ideas and information. He pardoned criminals and enlisted them in his service. He did everything to break his promises.[8]

Hitler deceived neighboring states which relied upon his statements of good intentions; he deceived the German youth, who sang

"Yes, the Flag is more than Death" and died before the gates of Stalingrad; and in the end he deceived the people of Germany who trusted and sacrificed for him. As Speer said:

This war has brought an inconceivable catastrophe upon the German people, and indeed started a world catastrophe. Therefore it is my unquestionable duty to assume my share of the responsibility for this disaster before the German people. This is all the more my obligation, all the more my responsibility, since the head of the Government has avoided responsibility before the German people and before the world....

From January 1945 onward, a very unpleasant chapter begins: The last phase of the war and the realization that Hitler had identified the fate of the German people with his own; and from March 1945 onward, the realization that Hitler intended deliberately to destroy the means of life for his own people if the war were lost....

At a Gauleiter meeting in the summer of 1944 Hitler had already stated—and Schirach is my witness for this—that if the German people were to be defeated in the struggle it must have been too weak, it had failed to prove its mettle before history and was destined only to destruction. Now, in the hopeless situation existing in January and February 1945, Hitler made remarks which showed that these earlier statements had not been mere flowers of rhetoric. During this period he attributed the outcome of the war in an increasing degree to the failure of the German people, but he never blamed himself. He criticized severely this alleged failure of our people who made so many brave sacrifices in this war....

The sacrifices which were made on both sides after January 1945 were senseless. The dead of this period will be the accusers of the man responsible for the continuation of that fight, Adolf Hitler. The same is true of the ruined cities, which in this last phase had to lose tremendous cultural values and where innumerable dwellings suffered destruction. Many of the difficulties under which the German nation is suffering today are due to the ruthless destruction of bridges, traffic installations, trucks, locomotives, and ships. The German people remained loyal to Adolf Hitler until the end. He betrayed them with intent. He tried to throw them definitely into the abyss.[9]

Fritzsche confirmed Speer's view:

The fact was that Hitler tried to use this defeat for the extermination of the German people, as Speer has now horribly confirmed, and as I was able to observe during the last phase of the conflict in Berlin when, through deceit by rousing false hopes, boys of 15, 14, 13 and 12 years of age were equipped with small arms to fight against tanks and called into battle, boys who otherwise might have been the hope for future reconstruction.[10]

Hitler had led the German people down the highway to hell. As Frank said: "His path became more and more that of a frightful adventurer without conscience or honesty, as I know today at the end of this trial."[11] It is hard to believe that a man of criminal instincts could gain absolute power in a modern state, and it is difficult to comprehend how he could direct the energy of a great people into the fulfilment of the objectives to which those instincts impelled him. But Hitler's genius was not at first recognized as evil. He gained power at a time when the morale of the German people was completely shattered. He poured salt upon their wounded pride. He inflamed them into fury against other peoples over fancied wrongs. He kept the truth from them and distorted the facts into grotesque falsehoods. He created a false environment, gave them false ideals, and instilled into them false hopes. When he led them into war they fought at first because they thought the cause was righteous. Later, when disillusionment cooled their passions and common sense exposed the wicked fantasy, they fought on for their country, their families, their lives, and their personal honor. Who can blame the German soldier who stood his ground in Saxony against the Russian hordes, or the German woman who labored in the ammunition factory until the end?

The ordinary man of Germany was not motivated by any desire to harm his fellow-man. He wanted only to do that which was right and just for his family and for his country. For that purpose alone he risked his life in Hitler's war. To charge the ordinary citizen with the intention to commit, or the responsibility for the commission of, the crimes of Hitler's Germany, would be to negate the meaning of the judgment of the International Military Tribunal which placed that responsibility upon the tyrant and his tyrannous crew.

In his final remarks to the International Military Tribunal the defendant Speer left both a word of warning to the peoples of the world and a message of hope to the people of Germany:

Hitler and the collapse of his system have brought a time of tremendous suffering upon the German people. The useless continuation of this war and the unnecessary destruction make the work of reconstruction more difficult. Privation and misery have come to the German people. After this trial, the German people will despise and condemn Hitler as the proven author of its misfortune. But the world will learn from these happenings not only to hate dictatorship as a form of government, but to fear it.

Hitler's dictatorship differed in one fundamental point from all its predecessors in history. His was the first dictatorship in the present period of modern technical development, a dictatorship which made complete use of all technical means in a perfect manner for the domination of its own nation....

Hitler not only took advantage of technical developments to dominate his own people—he almost succeeded, by means of his technical lead, in subjugating the whole of Europe. It was merely due to a few fundamental shortcomings of organization such as are typical in a dictatorship because of the absence of criticism, that he did not have twice as many tanks, aircraft, and submarines before 1942.

But, if a modern industrial state utilizes its intelligence, its science, its technical developments, and its production for a number of years in order to gain a lead in the sphere of armament, then even with a sparing use of its manpower it can, because of its technical superiority, completely overtake and conquer the world, if other nations should employ their technical abilities during that same period on behalf of the cultural progress of humanity....

Will there ever again be a nation which will use the technical discoveries of this war for the preparation of a new war, while the rest of the world is employing the technical progress of this war for the benefit of humanity, thus attempting to create a slight compensation for its horrors? As a former minister of a highly developed armament system, it is my last duty to say the following:

A new large-scale war will end with the destruction of human culture and civilization. Nothing can prevent unconfined engineering and science from completing the work of destroying human beings, which it has begun in so dreadful a way in this war.

Therefore this trial must contribute towards preventing such degenerate wars in the future, and towards establishing rules whereby human beings can live together.

Of what importance is my own fate, after everything that has happened, in comparison with this high goal?

During the past centuries the German people have contributed much towards the creation of human civilization. Often they have made these contributions in times when they were just as powerless and helpless as they are today. Worthwhile human beings will not let themselves be driven to despair. They will create new and lasting values, and under the tremendous pressure brought to bear upon everyone today these new works will be of particular greatness.

But if the German people create new cultural values in the unavoidable times of their poverty and weakness, and at the same time in the period of their reconstruction, then they will have in that way made the most valuable contribution to world events which they could in their position.

It is not the battles of war alone which shape the history of humanity, but also, in a higher sense, the cultural achievements which one day will become the common property of all humanity. A nation which believes in its future will never perish. May God protect Germany and the culture of the West.[12]

However much he tried, the tyrant Hitler could not destroy the spirit of Germany or the faith of the German people. Their right to existence could not be forfeited by their failure to bring him Humanity's head on a bloody tray. Nor was Hitler able, with the means in his hands, to conquer all the nations he attacked. He began the war with conventional weapons. At the end, his technicians had developed flying bombs and rockets. What would the outcome have been if Hitler had taken five more years to prepare his attempt at conquest, and other nations had spent those years in peaceful pursuits?

While tyranny holds sway anywhere in the world, democratic nations must make whatever sacrifice is necessary to provide the technological means for national defense. As Speer forewarned, despots other than Hitler may secretly plan and prepare for aggression. A sleeping free world could be destroyed through a surprise assault. The tyrant of tomorrow can strike with devastating forces unavailable to yesterday's despot. He may be deterred by the certainty that democracy will retaliate with greater power. He may be deterred, too, by the knowledge that he will be held to answer in a court of law for his crime.

CHAPTER 35

Judgment

In his final address to the Tribunal, Mr. Justice Jackson said:

It is common to think of our own time as standing at the apex of civilization, from which the deficiencies of preceding ages may patronizingly be viewed in the light of what is assumed to be "progress." The reality is that in the long perspective of history the present century will not hold an admirable position, unless its second half is to redeem its first. These two-score years in the twentieth century will be recorded in the book of years as one of the most bloody in all annals. Two World Wars have left a legacy of dead which number more than all the armies engaged in any war that made ancient or medieval history. No half-century ever witnessed slaughter on such a scale, such cruelties and inhumanities, such wholesale deportations of peoples into slavery, such annihilations of minorities. The terror of Torquemada pales before the Nazi Inquisition. These deeds are the overshadowing historical facts by which generations to come will remember this decade. If we cannot eliminate the causes and prevent the repetition of these barbaric events, it is not an irresponsible prophecy to say that this twentieth century may yet succeed in bringing the doom of civilization.[1]

The Tribunal adjourned to weigh these facts and to pass upon the guilt of the individual defendants and the criminality of the organizations. On the morning of September 30, 1946, the Tribunal reconvened for the reading of its judgment. This masterful judicial opinion was read during all of that day and most of the following day. Each member and each alternate member of the Tribunal read some portion of the judgment.

Following a historical introduction, the opinion dealt successively with the preparation, planning, and initiating of wars of aggression, the commission of crimes against the laws of war, and the perpetration of crimes against humanity. The Tribunal then considered the responsibility of each of the named organizations and the accused defendants for the basic crimes it found to have been committed.

The Leadership Corps of the Party was defined to include Hitler, the Reichsleitung, the Gauleiter and their staff officers, the Kreisleiter and their staff officers, the Ortsgruppenleiter, the Zellenleiter and the Blockleiter, a group estimated to contain at least 600,000 people. This organization was declared criminal by reason of its use in "the Germanization of incorporated territory, the persecution of the Jews, the administration of the slave labor program, and mistreatment of prisoners of war."[2]

The Gestapo and SD were first united in their functions and activities on June 26, 1936, when Heydrich took charge of both organizations. The Tribunal declared them criminal upon a finding that they were used for "the persecution and extermination of the Jews, brutalities and killings in concentration camps, excesses in the administration of occupied territories, the administration of the slave labor program, and the mistreatment and murder of prisoners of war."[3]

The SS was established as an elite corps in the period of the Nazi struggle for power. After Hitler had gained control of Germany the SS became a semiautonomous quasi-military body under the control of Himmler. Its Death's Head Battalions supplied personnel for concentration camps; and the Waffen SS furnished forces for clearing ghettos, fighting partisans, and even engaging in ordinary military actions. The Tribunal found that the SS was utilized for the same criminal activities as the Gestapo and the SD.

The other organizations named in the indictment, the SA, Reich Cabinet, and the General Staff and High Command, were not declared by the Tribunal to be criminal organizations.

The Tribunal found that of the twenty-two defendants on trial before it, three were not guilty under any count. All the other defendants, including Martin Bormann who had been tried *in absentia*, were found guilty on at least one count of the indictment for participation in some aspect of the activities of the Hitler regime which the Tribunal had declared to be criminal.

The Soviet member of the Tribunal dissented from the exculpation of the Reich Cabinet and the General Staff and High Command and from the acquittals of Schacht, Papen, and Fritzsche, and he felt that the Tribunal erred in not giving Hess a death penalty. In other respects he concurred—by his failure to dissent—with the opinion, the determinations of guilt, and the awarding of punishments.

The Sentences

The Tribunal completed the reading of the judgment early in the afternoon of October 1. When it reconvened, after a short recess, every chair in the courtroom was occupied except the twenty-one chairs in the prisoners' dock. The accused were to be brought into the courtroom one at a time, each to hear his sentence alone.

At ten minutes before three, the paneled door in the back of the prisoners' dock slid silently open. The defendant Goering stepped out of the elevator which had brought him from the ground floor where the defendants waited. Goering put on a set of headphones which had been handed to him by one of the white-helmeted guards. The president of the Tribunal began to speak. Goering signaled that he was unable to hear through the headphones, and there was an awkward delay while the technicians sought to correct the mechanical difficulty. A new set of headphones was produced, and once again Goering quietly awaited the words which were to decide his fate.

"Defendant Hermann Wilhelm Goering, on the counts of the indictment on which you have been convicted, the International Military Tribunal sentences you to death by hanging."[4]

The No. 2 Nazi turned on his heel, passed through the paneled door into the waiting elevator. The door closed; and there was a hum of whispered voices in the courtroom as those present awaited the arrival of the next defendant, Hess.

The sallow-faced, beetle-browed former Deputy Fuehrer stepped through the door briskly and cast a nervous glance toward the visitors' gallery. He cocked his head as he heard the words:

"Defendant Rudolf Hess, on the counts of the indictment on

which you have been convicted, the Tribunal sentences you to imprisonment for life."[5]

The gaunt, stooped, worn Ribbentrop next entered the prisoners' dock and nervously fixed the headphones over his ears. His pale face became a chalky white when he heard the sentence:

"Defendant Joachim von Ribbentrop, on the counts of the indictment on which you have been convicted, the Tribunal sentences you to death by hanging."[6]

Ribbentrop was followed by the first of the soldiers. Erect and proud in his green unadorned Wehrmacht uniform, his mouth set and firm, Keitel displayed no emotion at the words:

"Defendant Wilhelm Keitel, on the counts of the indictment on which you have been convicted, the Tribunal sentences you to death by hanging."[7]

The hulking Kaltenbrunner blinked in the bright kleig lights as he stepped into the dock.

"Defendant Ernst Kaltenbrunner, on the counts of the indictment on which you have been convicted, the Tribunal sentences you to death by hanging."[8]

Kaltenbrunner bowed deeply and respectfully to the Tribunal as though he had been awarded a military honor rather than a sentence of death. Rosenberg followed him.

"Defendant Alfred Rosenberg, on the counts of the indictment on which you have been convicted, the Tribunal sentences you to death by hanging."[9]

Frank appeared, the cruel-faced Frank, who once had slashed his throat and wrists in an effort to escape this day of fate but who had in the end confessed his crimes and found composure in religious faith. He knew only one sentence could expiate his wrongs.

"Defendant Hans Frank, on the counts of the indictment on which you have been convicted, the Tribunal sentences you to death by hanging."[10]

Frick, red-faced, square-jawed, his close-cropped hair the whiter in the bright lights, turned away in quiet anger after he heard the President say:

"Defendant Wilhelm Frick, on the counts of the indictment on which you have been convicted, the Tribunal sentences you to death by hanging."[11]

The vicious Streicher stepped into the prisoners' dock and almost defiantly picked up the headphones. He seemed surprised when the sentence was read:

"Defendant Julius Streicher, on the count of the indictment on which you have been convicted, the Tribunal sentences you to death by hanging."[12]

Little, pudgy Funk, looking as frightened as he was, sighed when he heard the words:

"Defendant Walter Funk, on the counts of the indictment on which you have been convicted, the Tribunal sentences you to imprisonment for life."[13]

Doenitz, slender and defiant, awaited sentence.

"Defendant Karl Doenitz, on the counts of the indictment on which you have been convicted, the Tribunal sentences you to ten years imprisonment."[14]

He had received the first sentence less than life imprisonment, yet Doenitz pursed his lips, seemingly stung by the words of the President.

The former Grand Admiral, Raeder, oldest of all the defendants, accepted his fate without show of emotion.

"Defendant Erich Raeder, on the counts of the indictment on which you have been convicted, the Tribunal sentences you to imprisonment for life."[15]

None suspected that Raeder would have preferred a sentence of death.

Schirach, youngest of the defendants, listened quietly to his fate.

"Defendant Baldur von Schirach, on the count of the indictment on which you have been convicted, the Tribunal sentences you to twenty years imprisonment."[16]

The stubby Sauckel, trembling with fear, heard the bitter words:

"Defendant Fritz Sauckel, on the counts of the indictment on which you have been convicted, the Tribunal sentences you to death by hanging."[17]

Jodl clicked his heels together in military fashion. He accepted the sentence against him without flinching.

"Defendant Alfred Jodl, on the counts of the indictment on which you have been convicted, the Tribunal sentences you to death by hanging."[18]

The scholarly-looking, tall, bespectacled Seyss-Inquart listened impassively to the President:

"Defendant Arthur Seyss-Inquart, on the counts of the indictment on which you have been convicted, the Tribunal sentences you to death by hanging."[19]

Speer retained his objectivity to the last. He looked directly at the President while his sentence was being read:

"Defendant Albert Speer, on the counts of the indictment on which you have been convicted, the Tribunal sentences you to twenty years imprisonment."[20]

The aged and ailing Neurath, once lauded as an aristocrat, now convicted as a common criminal, looked nonetheless the nobleman when his turn came:

"Defendant Konstantin von Neurath, on the counts of the indictment on which you have been convicted, the Tribunal sentences you to fifteen years imprisonment."[21]

When the door closed on Neurath, all but one of the convicted had received his sentence. That one, the absent Bormann, was then sentenced to death by hanging.

The Appeals

Article 29 of the Charter provided that, in case of guilt, sentences should be carried out in accordance with the orders of the Control Council for Germany, which might at any time reduce or otherwise alter the sentences, but might not increase the severity thereof. Control Council Directive No. 35 provided that a petition for clemency filed by any person condemned to death by the Tribunal must be addressed to the Control Council and lodged with the Secretariat of the Tribunal within four days from the day on which sentence was passed. The sentences on all the defendants were passed on October 1, 1946, and the four-day period therefore expired on October 5, 1946. Directive No. 35 also provided that the executions would be carried out on the fifteenth day after the pronouncement of sentence in open court unless otherwise ordered by the Tribunal or the Control Council within said period.

Petitions for clemency were filed on behalf of the following individual defendants: Bormann, Frick, Rosenberg, Streicher, Raeder, Goering, Funk, Doenitz, Frank, Keitel, Von Neurath, Jodl, Seyss-Inquart, Von Ribbentrop, Hess, and Sauckel. Counsel for Von Schirach filed a letter purporting to reserve his right to petition for clemency on behalf of Schirach at a later date. No petitions were filed on behalf of Kaltenbrunner and Speer.

Counsel for Bormann contended that the Tribunal, despite explicit authority of the Charter, lacked jurisdiction to try Bormann *in absentia.*

Frick's lawyer argued that by a special directive Hitler ordered subordinates of Frick to perform the killings in the insane asylums and that Frick was powerless to protest or prevent execution of the order.

Counsel for Rosenberg pleaded that Rosenberg was of weak personality and character, a man who followed Hitler with blind loyalty and who was used by Hitler as a tool.

Streicher's attorney stated that Streicher had requested that no plea for mercy be submitted on his behalf and that he did not want the judgment pronounced against him contested. He argued that Streicher's offenses against humanity were not connected with aggressive war, as required by the Tribunal's construction of the Charter.

Raeder, sentenced to life imprisonment, filed his petition with only one purpose, stated in these words: "I request the Allied Control Council for Germany to commute this sentence to death by shooting, by way of mercy."[22] Raeder stated that in view of his age he considered that execution by shooting would be a mitigation of his sentence of life imprisonment.

The petition filed on behalf of Goering disclosed that Goering had requested that no petition be submitted for him. His counsel asked that the death sentence be commuted to one of life imprisonment or, in the alternative, that the mode of execution be altered from hanging to shooting. One of the three main points of appeal was that Goering had been a brave officer in World War I and had been highly respected then by the enemy on account of his chivalry.

Counsel for Frank stated that the petition on Frank's behalf was filed against his express wish but at the request of his family, and asked that the death sentence be commuted to life imprisonment.

Attached to the petition filed on behalf of Keitel, which asked that the death sentence be changed from hanging to shooting, was a letter signed by Keitel. The letter stated that Keitel would gladly give his life in atonement in the hope that his sacrifice might prove beneficial to the German people and an exoneration of the German Wehrmacht. He recited his attitude and training as a soldier, his feeling of unconditional obedience, and his realization that it was this tragic mistake which had led to his downfall. He asked that he be permitted to atone for his mistake "by a death which is granted to a soldier in all armies in the world should he incur the supreme penalty"—death by shooting.[23]

The petition filed by counsel for Von Neurath urged annulment of the judgment pronounced or at least postponement of the sentence in view of the advanced age of the accused, seventy-four years, and his poor health.

Counsel for Jodl contended that Jodl, a soldier, acted only in accordance with the orders of his superiors. He asserted that Jodl believed that only political leaders were competent to make a decision to wage war and that the members of the General Staff did not have either the duty or the right to judge the legality of such a decision. He asked that the death sentence be set aside, or that, alternatively, Jodl be permitted to meet a soldier's death before a firing squad.

The petition filed on behalf of Seyss-Inquart claimed that the policies enforced in the occupied territories were not of his making, and that he had no control over the police, who were responsible only to Himmler. It asked that the sentence be commuted to life imprisonment or a term of years.

Von Ribbentrop's petition was accompanied by a statement of his own and a plea for mercy from his wife. The petition asked that the sentence be commuted to life imprisonment or death by shooting. His counsel contended that Ribbentrop was not inhumane, but that he was merely the tool and follower of Hitler. Ribbentrop personally attacked the judgment against him. The plea of his wife stated that he was a decent and capable man, full of love and solicitude for his family and for Germany.

The petition filed on behalf of Hess pointed out that Hess was the only one of the defendants who had been convicted solely of initiating and waging aggressive war and not also of war crimes or crimes against humanity. It asked that no punishment be imposed on Hess or that a term less than life imprisonment be considered sufficient.

Funk's attorney stressed the fact that Schacht had been acquitted and argued that Funk had only carried out measures which "Schacht had for years introduced and carried out." It asked that the sentence of life imprisonment be commuted to imprisonment for ten years.

Counsel for Doenitz filed a petition asking that the sentence of ten years' imprisonment be commuted in its entirety or to the period already served. A letter was submitted on his behalf by former Admiral Albrecht of the German Navy, attesting to his good character and personal integrity.

The petition filed on behalf of Sauckel asked that the death sentence be commuted to a prison sentence. It contended that Sauckel did not have supreme authority in the labor program, and that he always attempted to act humanely toward the foreign workers. It asked for mercy in the name of Sauckel's nine living children.

Petitions for revision of the judgment were also filed on behalf of the four organizations which had been declared criminal, the SS, the SD, the Gestapo, and the Leadership Corps of the Nazi Party.

The Control Council considered the various petitions filed on behalf of the defendants at its meeting of October 10, 1946. The petitions, without exception, were denied. It was felt that Raeder's plea that his sentence should be changed from life imprisonment to death by shooting was, in fact, whatever Raeder's wishes in the premises, an increase in the severity of the sentence which the Control Council was unable to grant under the Charter. It held that the petitions filed on behalf of the four organizations were not admissible in view of the Charter provision that the judgment of the Tribunal as to guilt or innocence should be final and not subject to review. It rejected the reservations submitted by the counsel for Schirach.

At the conclusion of the meeting, the Soviet member, Marshal Sokolovsky, read the following statement:

The International Military Tribunal in Nuremberg has examined a case of exceptional importance, a case of criminal aggression which drew humanity into the catastrophe of World War, a case of war crimes without precedent in magnitude and cruelty, of the murder of millions of peace-loving people, organized by Hitler's Government. As a member of the Control Council, I must state that the Tribunal, in the course of ten months' careful consideration of all evidence, passed sentences which give a complete picture of the crimes committed by the Nazis.

I am strongly convinced that the major war criminals convicted by the Tribunal, to whose sentences we have just given our assent, have richly deserved the punishments meted out to them by the Tribunal. At the same time, I consider it my duty to state that I completely share the views expressed by General Nikitchenko, U.S.S.R. member of the Tribunal, and I consider that there was sufficient evidence to convict Schacht, Papen and Fritzsche, to pass the death sentence on Hess, and to pronounce the Nazi Government and the General Staff and High Command, criminal organizations.[24]

The Executions

The writer had been designated by Mr. Justice Jackson to represent him at the executions and, while not admitted to the death chamber, was present in the Palace of Justice on the fateful night of October 15-16, 1946. Shortly before midnight the electrifying word was released that Goering, the No. 2 Nazi, had cheated the hangman by taking poison while lying, apparently asleep, upon the bed in his humble cell. Death thus came to Goering by his own hand, as it had come to Hitler and Himmler before him, even as the prison officer was walking to the cell block to announce the final action by the Control Council on the sentences and to give formal notice of the executions which were to take place that night.

How Goering succeeded in obtaining and keeping hidden the vial of poison is still unknown. He left three letters, all of which were turned over to the Allied Control Council and have not been published. An independent investigator, Ben Swearingen, believes that Goering had hidden a poison vial in his possessions and clothing held in a storage room away from his cell and was aided in recovering it by an American military officer shortly before the time of the executions.[25]

The other defendants prepared to die.

At eleven minutes past one o'clock in the morning of October 16, the white-faced former Foreign Minister, Joachim von Ribbentrop, stepped through the door into the execution chamber and faced the gallows on which he and the others condemned to die by the Tribunal were to be hanged. His hands were unmanacled and bound behind him with a leather thong. Ribbentrop walked to the foot of the thirteen stairs leading to the gallows platform. He was asked to state his name, and answered weakly, "Joachim von Ribbentrop." Flanked by two guards and followed by the chaplain, he slowly mounted the stairs. On the platform he saw the hangman with the noose of thirteen coils and the hangman's assistant with the black hood. He stood on the trap, and his feet were bound with a webbed army belt. Asked to state any last words, he said: "God protect Germany, God have mercy on my soul. My last wish is that German unity be maintained, that understanding between East and West be realized and there be peace for the world." The trap was sprung and Ribbentrop died at 1:29.

In the same way, each of the remaining defendants to receive capital sentences approached the scaffold and met the fate of common criminals. All, except the wordy Nazi philosopher, Rosenberg, uttered final statements. Keitel spoke as a Prussian soldier: "I call on the Almighty to be considerate of the German people, provide tenderness and mercy. Over 2,000,000 German soldiers went to their death for their Fatherland before me. I now follow my sons. All for Germany." Gestapo Chief Kaltenbrunner declared apologetically: "I served the German people and my Fatherland with willing heart. I did my duty according to its laws. I am sorry that in her trying hour she was not led only by soldiers. I regret that crimes were committed in which I had no part. Good luck Germany." Frank said quietly: "I am thankful for the kind treatment which I received during this incarceration and I pray God to receive me mercifully." Frick spoke only the phrase, "Let live the eternal Germany." Streicher shouted, "Heil Hitler!" as he climbed the stairs and followed with the words: "Now I go to God, Purim Festival 1946. And now to God." Turning to the hangman, he prophesied, "The Bolshevists will one day hang you." His last words were: "I am now by God, my Father. Adele, my dear wife." Sauckel protested: "I die innocently. The verdict was wrong. God protect Germany and make Germany great again. Let Germany live and God protect my family." Jodl spoke in the manner of an officer addressing his troops: "I salute you my Germany." Seyss-Inquart climaxed the final statements when he said: "I hope that this execution is the last act of the tragedy of the second World War and that a lesson will be learned so that peace and understanding will be realized among the nations. I believe in Germany." Seyss-Inquart died at 2:57, less than two hours after Von Ribbentrop had entered the execution chamber.

After the executions the body of each man was placed upon a simple wooden coffin. A tag with the name of the deceased was pinned to coat, shirt, or sweater. With the hangman's noose still about the neck, each hanged man was photographed. The body of Hermann Goering was brought in and placed upon its box, there to be photographed with the others.

In the early morning hours two trucks, carrying the eleven caskets, left the prison compound at the Palace of Justice. They were bound for a Munich crematory. There, during all of that day, the bodies were burned, one after the other. It was reported that in the evening the eleven urns containing the ashes were taken away to be emptied into the river Isar. The dust of the dead was carried along in the currents of the stream to the Danube—and thence, to the sea.

The other seven, who were sentenced to varying terms of imprisonment, were brought to Spandau prison in the British sector of Berlin, under constant revolving guard by the four major powers— the only prisoners in a prison built to house six hundred inmates. The first to be released was Hitler's successor, Admiral Karl Doenitz;

the last was Rudolf Hess, who managed somehow to commit suicide on August 17, 1987, forty-one years after the final judgment of the Tribunal. With his death the Hitler tyranny ended.

The tyrant and his chief cohorts were gone. They had sought to achieve greatness in history. But they inscribed their names in sand, and clean waters fell upon the beach and washed them out. They had intended to establish a new order for Europe. But they built upon pillars of hate; and what they stood for, could not stand.

Hitler had taken the best that was Germany, and that was in Germany, and corrupted it to his evil purposes. He took the loyalty of the German people and led them into endless, hopeless wars; he took the creativeness of the German mind and set it to devising horrible instruments of mass murder; he took the bravery of youth and commanded them to die upon far and frozen battlefields; he took the nobility of the German spirit and sullied it with wicked persecutions.

In all this he was aided and abetted by men eager to share his hours of triumph. They shared, too, his guilty ways and his personal shame. With Hitler, they erred, and for their errors they paid a just and deserved penalty. Because they turned from truth the final result could not have been otherwise.

> Truth, crushed to earth, shall rise again;
> Th' eternal years of God are here;
> But Error, wounded, writhes in pain,
> And dies among his worshipers.[26]

The tyrant is dead, and dead the evil of his reign. Germany, crushed to earth, shall nobly rise again.

PART SIX

The Law of the Case

CHAPTER 36

The Judicial Process

THERE ARE two requisites to the judicial process—an extant body of law to be applied, and a judiciary to apply that law. Executive action proceeds in quite another way. The decree both declares the law and determines the issue. Under the judicial process the law is first pronounced and subsequently enforced.

Every free modern society uses the judicial process to determine guilt and to affix individual punishments. And, in most cases, the law applied has previously been promulgated in legislative form, not so much to avoid entrapment of the accused as to provide restraints upon the accuser. The enactment of criminal statutes does not serve so importantly the function of informing the public of what is, and what is not, criminal conduct. Every person is presumed to know the law; yet no one knows the hundreds of criminal statutes in modern legal systems, and private conscience continues to govern the conduct of most persons. But there is much less danger of oppression when laws are promulgated for future general effect and enforced by independent judges.

Public offenses grew out of private wrongs. The development was from self-help, through the blood-feud, to the concept of crime as an offense against society punished by society. Wrongs became crimes when the community undertook to try and to punish the offender. And the community took interest in those offenses, such as murder and robbery upon the highways, which threatened its own security. These actions had always been recognized as wrongs. No legislation was needed for that purpose. They became crimes simply by the fact of their enforcement in the courts of the king. Hence crimes began as unwritten common laws.

The principle that the king's courts could thus punish individuals for unwritten crimes was perfectly proper so long as these crimes were of a type accepted by everyone in the community. But it afforded the possibility of oppression if abused. In England, the Star Chamber began as a high court of criminal equity, and it served a vital purpose in preserving order in the nation. Under the Stuarts, however, it became an instrument of political control and thus outlived its usefulness. And so in municipal law reformers called for reducing all public offenses to written form, so that the judges might be restrained by codes and the unwary might not be trapped by unspecified and hence unknown laws.

In the eighteenth century this movement was reflected in demands for codes of criminal law and of criminal procedure. In 1787 such a code was promulgated by Joseph II of Austria. After the French Revolution the greatest contribution of France to law was achieved in codifying the existing body of law. And in the field of crimes this was accomplished by the Criminal Code of 1810 and the Code of Criminal Procedure of 1818. Under this stimulus, almost every nation of the world has now reduced the bulk of its criminal law to statutory form. This process has not eliminated the common law basis of crimes, nor in some nations—and particularly in England—the judge-declared, as distinguished from the statutory, criminal offense. It has been primarily a process of codification possible only in highly developed societies with established, competent, and authoritative legislative bodies to restate old law, and to promulgate new laws according to the needs of society.

Nullem crimen, nulla poena sine lege (no crime, no punishment, without law) is a postulate of the developed municipal criminal law. It was the concept of Feuerbach who considered that in modern legal systems it was not permissible to find a crime, or to impose a punishment, except upon the basis of declared law. While it marked the trend toward codification of the penal law, it did not in England, at any rate, replace the time-tested crimes of the common law. As Holmes said, "The life of the law has not been logic, it has been experience."[1] And experience had confirmed judicial decisions that certain conduct is criminal. Only in relatively modern times in England have statutes largely replaced judicially declared crimes.

In the relations of nations there has been no similar possibility of legislation, or of codification. When Jeremy Bentham coined the phrase "international law" he expressed thereby the problem of law outside the perimeters of nations. Here, too, experience had proved a superior teacher. The needs of the community of nations could not be restrained by definitions of law which would render it powerless to serve justice beyond national boundaries. Long before Bentham, Hugo Grotius had observed "that there is a common law among nations, which is valid alike for war and in war."[2] A common international law of crimes has grown up in response to the "felt necessities" of the world community, haltingly and imperfectly, to be sure, but marking progress from ill-defined custom to law. The legislative stage has not yet been reached.

Piracy has long been recognized in the international law of crimes and has been, it is said, "far better enforced than any major prohibition of any municipal criminal code."[3] Whether this is so or not, the readiness of courts to punish pirates for felonies upon the high seas has had its part in eliminating piracy as a serious problem in world affairs. Yet as Brierly has noted, "there is no authoritative definition of international piracy,"[4] and the concept of the pirate has changed in the law as the pirate's activities have changed in fact. The picture of the pirate as a swashbuckler who captures vessels for their loot has given way to the criminal who engages in felonious acts upon the high seas. Explaining the judicial enlargement of the common law definition, a British jurist has said: "A careful examination of the subject shows a gradual widening of the earlier definition of piracy to bring it from time to time more in consonance with situations either not thought of or not in existence when the older jurisconsults were expressing their opinions."[5]

The common law concept of the international crime of piracy has been adopted in the United States. In *United States* v. *Smith,* the Supreme Court observed that "whatever may be the diversity of definitions in other respects, all writers concur in holding that robbery or forcible depredations upon the sea, *animo furandi,* is piracy."[6]

And Congress, itself, has based the statutory definition of piracy upon the common law of nations. "Whoever, on the high seas, commits the crime of piracy *as defined by the law of nations,* and is afterwards brought into or found in the United States, shall be imprisoned for life."[7] (Italics added.) The Supreme Court of the United States, speaking through Mr. Chief Justice Stone, has held that "An act of Congress punishing 'the crime of piracy, as defined by the law of nations' is an appropriate exercise of its constitutional authority."[8]

Piracy is a crime against the law of nations. Its meaning is derived from the decisions of judges, the facts of each new situation being tested against the precedents of past judgments. The concept of piracy has been modified according to changes in the world community. The punishment of individuals for the crime of piracy does not depend upon there being a previously established international tribunal with statutory authority to proceed against pirates; nor is it affected by the absence of a statute prescribing the procedure for trial, or the penalty which may be imposed upon conviction. While municipal law may provide procedures and penalties for municipal courts hearing piracy cases, the pirate has no choice of forum, for his offense is against the law of nations. In the words of Blackstone: "As therefore he has renounced all the benefits of society and government, and has reduced himself afresh to the savage state of nature, by declaring war against all mankind, all mankind must declare war against him. . . ."[9]

There is a clear distinction between the crime of piracy, long recognized in the common law of nations, and the crime of initiating and waging aggressive war. The pirate acts outside, rather than under, the authority of the state. Despoliations committed in the name of a sovereign are not acts of piracy, but acts of war. The Nuremberg defendants were accused of subverting German sovereignty to their criminal purposes. They acted under that sovereignty, nonetheless, and what they did was war, and not piracy. But the basic juridical principle underlying the Nuremberg proceeding was that the accused had offended against the common law of nations; and for this, the punishment of individuals for piratical actions is a firm legal precedent.

International law, as Mr. Justice Cardozo has so eloquently stated, "has at times, like the common law within states, a twilight existence during which it is hardly distinguishable from morality or justice, till at length the *imprimatur* of a court attests its jural quality."[10] Civilized peoples have long realized that aggressive war is against the moral law. In holding that the initiating and waging of aggressive war is criminal, the International Military Tribunal placed its *imprimatur* upon that principle and attested its jural quality. The Tribunal did not seek thereby to bridge over, but only to set a stepping stone within the turbulent stream of international strife. It found the legal authority for its action in juridical principles which comprise the common law of nations, growing from decade to decade and from century to century, even as the universal conscience of mankind itself responds to new facts and relationships in the world about us. "International law is not a body of authoritative codes or statutes," wrote Mr. Henry L. Stimson, "it is the gradual expression, case by case, of the moral judgments of the civilized world. As such, it corresponds precisely to the common law of the Anglo-American tradition."[11]

In his historic opinion in *United States* v. *La Jeune Eugenie,* Mr. Justice Story wrote:

Now the law of nations may be deduced, first from the general principles of right and justice, applied to the concerns of individuals, and thence to the relations and duties of nations; or, secondly, in things indifferent or questionable, from the customary observances and recognitions of civilized nations; or lastly, from the conventional or positive law, that regulates the intercourse between states. What, therefore, the law of nations is, does not rest upon mere theory, but may be considered as modified by practice, or ascertained by the treaties of nations at different periods. It does not follow, therefore, that because a principle cannot be found settled by the consent or practice of nations at one time it is to be concluded that at no subsequent period the principle can be considered as incorporated into the public code of nations. Nor is it to be admitted that no principle belongs to the law of nations which is not universally recognized, as such, by all civilized communities or even by those constituting, what may be called, the Christian states of Europe.[12]

This profound analysis of the common law of nations was

formulated by Mr. Justice Story in arriving at his decision that the slave traffic, which even then was widely practiced in certain areas of the world, had become illegal in international law. In a similar way, the Nuremberg judges declared against aggressive war and related acts which they considered to have been morally condemned by the majority of nations. In the Tribunal's view these acts, like piracy, could no longer be tolerated in a civilized world, and the Tribunal concluded that the responsible individuals could be punished for their actions just as earlier courts had resolved upon the punishment of men for acts of piracy.

In his report of June 6, 1945, to the President of the United States, Mr. Justice Jackson stated:

International Law is more than a scholarly collection of abstract and immutable principles. It is an outgrowth of treaties or agreements between nations and of accepted customs. But every custom has its origin in some single act, and every agreement has to be initiated by the action of some state. Unless we are prepared to abandon every principle of growth for International Law, we cannot deny that our own day has its right to institute customs and to conclude agreements that will themselves become sources of a newer and strengthened International Law.[13]

The historic trial at Nuremberg was grounded in the common law of nations. That common law, as codified in international treaties and conventions, and as interpreted and applied by scholars and judges, provided its juridical basis. Correlatively, the trial contributed a powerful new precedent to the growing body of international law. It was a proceeding conducted by lawyers, and it constitutes an important step in the long struggle of the legal profession to replace the role of force by the rule of law. Mr. Justice Jackson said recently that "the conception of law as a brake on power is one of the chief contributions to civilization made by our profession."[14] At Nuremberg, for the first time in history, men who had abused power were held to answer in a court of law for crimes committed in the name of war.

At the Teheran Conference during November and December, 1943, Premier Joseph Stalin proposed to Prime Minister Winston Churchill that at the end of the war the German military strength should be extirpated by liquidation of the German General Staff, its officers and technicians—some fifty thousand men in all. Mr. Churchill responded: "The British Parliament and public will never tolerate mass executions. Even if in war passion they allowed them to begin, they would turn violently against those responsible after the first butchery had taken place. The Soviets must be under no delusion on this point." When Stalin persisted, Churchill said in anger: "I would rather be taken out into the garden here and now and be shot myself than sully my own and my country's honor by such infamy."[15]

No mass punishments by decree followed the war. Executive action was not used at all. For the first time in the long history of warring nations the judicial process was effectively applied to determine guilt and to assess punishment. In his opening address, Mr. Justice Jackson had said: "That four great nations, flushed with victory and stung with injury stay the hand of vengeance and voluntarily submit their captive enemies to the judgment of the law is one of the most significant tributes that Power has ever paid to Reason."[16] That no general reprisals were taken against the German people at the end of the war is proof of the wisdom—and of the humanity—of utilizing the judicial process to determine war guilt.

Not fifty thousand—not even fifty—persons were executed as the result of this first trial of alleged major war criminals. It cannot be doubted that resort to "the judgment of the law" saved the lives of hundreds of persons who, in the hour of high passion at war's end, would have been executed to requite demands for vengeance. Instead of a trial in the Palace of Justice at Nuremberg a guillotine might have been set up in Adolf Hitler Platz in the center of the Old City, and "executive action" substituted for the "judicial process." In the words of Judge John J. Parker, "... History shows that when this sort of program is entered upon, the hand of the executioner is not stayed until the public becomes sick of the slaughter."[17]

Doubtless a victorious nation may, by executive action, isolate the leader of the defeated state, as Napoleon was exiled to Elba, to prevent him from inciting his people once again to war. But it does not follow that the heads of a defeated state may be executed for crimes against peace or war crimes, without trial. Undoubtedly the victorious nation has the power to deal as it will with the political and military leaders of the vanquished state. Dr. Sheldon Glueck has written: "The fact that the victorious United Nations could, if they chose, impose any conditions on the Axis States—including the surrender for execution *without trial* of a long list of leading militarists, politicians and industrialists believed to be involved in the murders, lootings and other crimes—is of basic importance."[18] It does not follow that any such exercise of arbitrary power would be right, or might not itself contravene developed international law. As Dr. Glueck himself later stated: "But the common law of nations probably requires a fair trial of offenders against war law as a prerequisite to punishment for alleged offenses; and the Geneva Convention so prescribes in the case of prisoners of war."[19]

The state of war, if recognized as lawful, implies the right, in the course of active fighting, to kill the enemy. But not every person on the other side may be killed with impunity. Children may not, nor the infirm or aged, nor for that matter noncombatants generally. Even combatants, once taken captive, cannot be killed out of hand. It follows that when active fighting stops, even upon the basis of unconditional surrender, the victorious nations—which now hold, as it were, the entire military forces of the enemy as prisoners of war—cannot execute enemy persons in pursuance of the right to kill derived from the state of war. Any further taking of life must be based upon law.

Under principles universally prevailing in free nations the life of no man, however suspect of crime, can be forfeited unless he is first allowed a hearing, with opportunity for his defense according to due process of law. The conviction, when entered, must be supported by the evidence received. The hearing can never be the excuse for a previous political decision to execute the prisoner. As Mr. Justice Jackson stated in his 1945 address to the American Society of International Law: "We must not use the forms of juridical proceedings to carry out or rationalize previously settled political or military policy."[20] The process must be juridical and the proceeding must be fair.

Several persons who had leading responsibility for drafting the London Agreement and the Charter of the International Military

Tribunal subsequently took important parts in the trial itself. Mr. Justice Jackson, who was the chief United States representative at London, became the United States Chief of Counsel at Nuremberg. Sir David Maxwell Fyfe had similar dual responsibilities for the United Kingdom. General Nikitchenko, who conducted negotiations for the Soviets, became the U.S.S.R. member of the Tribunal. And M. Falco, who was a principal French negotiator, became the alternate member of the Tribunal for France. Furthermore, the United States member of the Tribunal, Mr. Francis Biddle, had been a signatory to the Yalta memorandum which led to the London Agreement and the use of the judicial process for the trial of the major Axis war criminals.

There was nothing improper in this. One who serves as a legislator may later be called to act in the capacity of prosecutor or judge. There is no reason why, in any such subsequent status, he should not apply the law which he helped to draft and to enact. The prosecutor seeks to prove facts under the law. The judge has the duty of determining facts in accordance with law. Neither function demands any previous dissociation from that law. The only impropriety which could arise out of the circumstance that some of the principals in the Nuremberg proceeding likewise assisted in the drafting of the Charter of the International Military Tribunal would be if they did so under orders to establish special law for the defendants and to convict them, under that law, irrespective of evidence. Neither proposition is sustainable under any impartial evaluation of what took place in London and in Nuremberg. The law laid down in the Charter applies in terms to all states notwithstanding the limitations upon the jurisdiction of the International Military Tribunal. And the judgment of the Tribunal was fully supported by substantial and convincing evidence.

The Nuremberg Tribunal was composed of judges appointed by the heads of nations which were victorious in the war. This circumstance would not create a condition of partiality so long as the judges were left uncontrolled in their decisions by superior political authority and were objective in their determinations of guilt or innocence according to the evidence. However, the remarks of the Soviet member of the Tribunal, General Nikitchenko, during the course of the London negotiations, to the effect that the purpose of the trial was primarily to determine the punishment to be given individuals whose guilt had already been declared by heads of state, indicated a bias upon his part which, if carried with him into the trial which followed, would have impaired the integrity of the proceeding.

This circumstance could not have affected the actual outcome of any particular case so long as the Soviet member did not influence other members of the Tribunal in arriving at their decisions, since under the Charter no person could be convicted or sentenced except upon a vote of three of the four members. Consequently, the secret purpose of one of them to convict without regard to the evidence could not, in and of itself, have determined the conviction or sentence of an accused person. Two out of the remaining three votes would have had to be against the accused. Moreover, a vote of at least one member representing the common law and one member representing the civil law systems was required for each conviction and sentence.

No published record of the proceedings indicates that the remarks of General Nikitchenko in the course of the London negotiations reflected the disposition on his part, after having been named the Soviet member of the Tribunal, to decide the case upon any basis other than the proven facts. With the other members of the Tribunal, he had made the following declaration at the opening session of the Tribunal, in Berlin, on October 18, 1945: "I solemnly declare that I will exercise all my powers and duties as a Member of the International Military Tribunal honorably, impartially, and conscientiously."[21] And he joined in the opinion of the Tribunal which carefully pointed out the factual basis for each part of its decision. In his personal dissent, differences with the Tribunal were supported upon the evidence and not upon revealed political considerations. As can now be seen, however, it was unfortunate that General Nikitchenko should have been named to the Tribunal.

The circumstances prevailing at the close of World War II did not afford a simple means for creating a Tribunal composed of members other than those drawn from the victorious powers. The International Military Tribunal was an *ad hoc* instrumentality. It was established in the pattern of traditional military commissions, which are always staffed by personnel of the victorious nation. There was no juridical basis upon which it could be insisted that neutral nations appoint judges to the Tribunal. Nor, realistically, could it be said that there were neutral nations in World War II. Sympathies were strong for each side, even if not supported by effective military action. Spain favored the Axis; Switzerland and Sweden favored the Allies. If a German jurist had agreed to serve as a member of such an *ad hoc* body, would German public opinion have considered him impartial or traitorous, on the basis of an opinion against Hitler and Hitler's Germany? If a dissenting opinion had been the other way, could that have affected the verdict of a Tribunal the majority of the members of which were drawn from the victorious nations?

There was no international criminal court in existence at the end of World War II. The Tribunal, therefore, had to be created. Judges had to be selected after the event they were to try, rather than before. This was unfortunate, but it was unavoidable. The difficulty was met by placing the confidence of mankind in the personal integrity of judges who had solemnly promised to uphold the law, to determine guilt upon evidence, and to try accused persons fairly and in accordance with due process of law. The decision was vindicated by the manner in which the trial was conducted, and by the verdict of the Tribunal so clearly based upon the evidence. While many eminent lawyers have differed with the Tribunal upon various points of law, no serious challenge has yet been offered to the basic factual record of the Hitler regime as developed in the trial. Nor can the opinion of the International Military Tribunal be impugned as grounded in vengeance. The period was one of high temper against the leaders of Hitler's Germany. There may be those who, in the still waters of afteryears, look back upon the trial with misgivings and doubts, but none who were there in the fury of the storm can doubt that the judicial process accorded the best assurance of justice to men accused of such high crimes and misdemeanors.

CHAPTER 37

The Law and Crimes in War

I T WAS written of old that the prophet Samuel said unto Saul that he should gather the people of Israel together and should smite the Amalekites and utterly destroy all that they had, and spare them not, "but slay both man and woman, infant and suckling, ox and sheep, camel and ass." And Saul gathered the people to him and warred against the Amalekites, "and utterly destroyed all the people with the edge of the sword."[1]

If in ancient times Carthaginian policies were practiced, they have long since been rejected as the legitimate end of war. In Clausewitz' view war was merely "a continuation of politics by other means." Assuredly it is more than that. It is the use of force by nations, or groups of nations, against each other to vindicate a cause or to achieve a goal. Initiating and waging aggressive war is now undoubtedly criminal. But war need not be waged in a criminal manner.

The fact that wars have been going on almost constantly in some area of the world in recent centuries has given war a positive juridical standing. Concepts have arisen with respect to belligerents and neutrals, combatants and noncombatants. Rights have been recognized in individuals involved in war. Rules have been agreed upon and stated, to assure that neither fighting men nor civilians shall be hurt or harmed or killed save as an inevitable consequence of legitimate military action. And if inexcusable mistreatment is perpetrated, it is now beyond cavil that the perpetrators may be held to answer for their misdeeds before military courts and commissions.

There is a common law of war crimes. The Congress of the

United States gave effect to it in the 15th Article of War which speaks of "offenders or offenses that ... by the law of war may be triable by such military commissions." In referring to this Article in *Ex parte Quirin,* Mr. Chief Justice Stone stated:

> Congress had the choice of crystallizing in permanent form and in minute detail every offense against the law of war, or of adopting the system of common law applied by military tribunals so far as it should be recognized and deemed applicable by the courts. It chose the latter course.[2]

The judgment of the International Military Tribunal contributed to the common law of crimes in war. To be sure, in most instances in which the Tribunal found and declared actions to have been war crimes it did no more than apply well-established legal principles to new fact situations. But in certain cases, and particularly in respect to the offenses which it recognized as crimes against humanity, it added importantly to this area of the common law of nations.

Traditional War Crimes

All crimes in war are founded upon the laws and customs of war. Traditional war crimes are those which have been defined in international conventions or have long been recognized in trials conducted by military courts and commissions.

Persons who commit war crimes may not excuse their actions as in accord with municipal law except as they are entitled to invoke the defense of superior orders. And those who actually sponsor or promulgate legislation or decrees which authorize or direct the commission of crimes in war can claim no protection for their own wrongful acts. Moreover, in thus leading others to the commission of such crimes, they likewise share the culpability.

War crimes must be committed in the course of war, and must be related to war prosecution. Prior to the attack upon Poland, the SD murdered several men for the purpose of giving color to feigned Polish border depredations. These offenses may have been evidence of a conspiracy to wage aggressive war, or even of aggression itself, but they were not conventional war crimes. The fact that many of the attacks by Germany upon other nations were undeclared is not important. It is not necessary that a state of war be declared; it is sufficient that it exist. Even forcible resistance, *animo belligerendi*, may constitute war in this sense. Where a *de jure* state of war did not exist in World War II based upon the customary formal exchange of declarations of war, there was nevertheless a *de facto* state of war between Germany and the nation attacked or invaded by it.

The primary written source of the laws of humane warfare has long been the Hague convention on land warfare of 1907, and the regulations issued pursuant thereto. Of comparable importance is the Geneva convention on prisoners of war of 1929. These two instruments constituted the basic conventional law of land warfare in effect during World War II. A question of applicability of these conventions in the East, where the major war crimes occurred, arose out of the circumstance that the Soviet Union had not considered itself bound by the Hague conventions ratified by the Czarist government and had never adhered to the Geneva convention.

This circumstance was of particular significance with respect to the Hague convention because of the general participation clause which provided that the provisions of the convention did not apply except between contracting powers, and then only if all the belligerents were parties to the convention. The reason for this clause, which was inserted in nine of the conventions adopted at the Second Hague Peace Conference in 1907, as stated by Louis Renault, Legal Advisor to the Ministry of Foreign Affairs of France, was "that a belligerent should not be under a restraint which is not imposed upon the enemy."[3]

Literally applied, the Hague convention would have ceased to be applicable in any area of the last war after the German invasion of the Soviet Union, since not all of the belligerents were then parties to the convention. But any such construction would have subverted the purpose of the clause, which was merely to permit a belligerent the equivalent freedom from legal restraint claimed by an enemy not bound by the convention. A similar point was raised during World War I when it was argued that the convention of 1899 was binding only until August, 1917, when a nonsigner, Liberia, entered the war. It would be ridiculous to permit a belligerent to invoke the general participation clause by deliberately attacking, and thereby creating a state of war with, a nonsigner, and it could hardly be seriously contended that the German assault upon the Soviet Union released Germany from the obligations of Hague Convention IV as to the other belligerents.

The International Military Tribunal held that the underlying principles of the Hague convention respecting land warfare were applicable even between Germany and the Soviet Union. The Tribunal noted that many of the customary laws of war were not codified in the Hague convention. Indeed, the preamble to Hague Convention IV states expressly that it does not purport to constitute a complete statement of the laws of land warfare. The Hague and Geneva conventions were largely acts of codification. They reduced to specific language certain rules relating to land warfare and the treatment of prisoners of war which already had been recognized by most civilized nations. In this sense, the conventions were merely a definite expression of the customs of war binding upon the belligerents in every armed conflict. The Tribunal concluded that by 1939 the rules set out in the Hague convention were recognized by all civilized nations, "and were regarded as being declaratory of the laws and customs of war...."[4] Nor was this an innovation.

When, in February, 1945, a question was raised whether Germany should then renounce the several international agreements relating to war, the top secret report of the International Bureau of the Operational Staff of the German armed forces stated:

> On the basis of the practice of states in the wars of the last centuries, there exists the "international law of usage" which cannot be done away with unilaterally. It comprises the latest principles of a humane conduct of war; it is not laid down in writing.... Consequently Germany will by no means free herself from this essential obligation of the laws of war by a renunciation of the conventions on the laws of war.[5]

The Tribunal applied this reasoning, and it held the defendants responsible for complying with the standards of humane warfare as they had evolved in judicial decisions, in international conventions, and in the common experience of military men and the common judgment of mankind, notwithstanding the nonadherence by the Soviet Union to these basic conventions.

The war in the East was not conducted on either side in strict accordance with conventional international law. The failure of Soviet Russia to adhere to the Hague and Geneva conventions gave Hitler a pseudolegal justification for the extreme cruelties which he directed to be inflicted upon the eastern peoples. But Hitler was not in good faith, for he had ordered similar measures to be taken against Poland, although Poland had adhered to Hague Convention IV in 1925. Hitler's war in the East was one of conquest and extermination. Rules of humane warfare could scarcely be observed under such circumstances.

Hitler's Chief of Military Intelligence, Admiral Canaris, stated his objections to the harsh measures proposed to be taken against prisoners of war in the East in a memorandum which he sent to Keitel as Chief of the OKW. After taking note of the contention that the rules of the Geneva convention were not binding between Germany and the Soviet Union, Canaris declared:

Since the 18th century these have gradually been established along the lines that war captivity is neither revenge nor punishment, but solely protective custody the only purpose of which is to prevent the prisoners of war from a further participation in the war. This principle was developed in accordance with the view held by all armies that it is contrary to military tradition to kill or injure helpless people; this is also in the interest of all belligerents in order to prevent mistreatment of their own soldiers in case of capture.[6]

War crimes in the East could not be justified on the basis that the Soviet Union was not bound by conventional law. Nor would Soviet violations of customary rules of humane warfare entitle the defendants to escape responsibility for those acts of cruelty which they, in the first instance, had ordered against Soviet civilians and prisoners of war.

Where it was established by the evidence before the Tribunal that conduct on both sides departed from a previously applicable rule of war, however, the Tribunal did not assess liability under that rule against the defendants even though it had previously been recognized as a cognizable war crime. During World War I Germany had engaged in submarine warfare against neutral merchant vessels in proclaimed operational zones, and the practice had been adopted in retaliation by Great Britain. The Washington Conference of 1922, the London Naval Agreement of 1930, and the Naval Protocol of 1936 were all directed against unrestricted submarine warfare, and the Protocol made no exception for operational zones. Doenitz was accused of proclaiming operational zones and ordering the sinking of neutral merchant vessels which entered them. But the evidence disclosed that on May 8, 1940, the British Admiralty announced that all vessels found in the Skagerrak at night would be sunk; and Admiral Nimitz, in response to defense interrogatories, stated that unrestricted submarine warfare was carried on in the Pacific by the United States from and after December 7, 1941. Under this evidence, the Tribunal held that notwithstanding proof that Doenitz violated the Protocol by orders which he issued for submarine warfare against neutrals in operational zones and for the sinking of merchant vessels without attempt at rescue, he could not be held accountable for such crimes in view of the fact that Great Britain and the United States did not themselves comply with the Naval Protocol of 1936. The Tribunal excused Doenitz on this charge even though the actions taken by the United States and Great Britain might have been justified as necessary measures of defense against aggression.

The Charter defined war crimes as violations of the laws or customs of war. Count Three of the indictment specified in detail the categories of war crimes charged to the defendants. Especially notorious were the killing of hostages, the reprisal actions behind the lines, the Night and Fog Decree, the commando order, the Sagan incident, special treatment of Soviet prisoners of war, and the Bullet Decree against escaped Soviet war prisoners. The top echelon of Nazi leaders was responsible for the most serious war crimes committed by German forces during the war.

The killing of hostages was charged as a war crime at Nuremberg. In former times it was not unusual in the course of war to take and hold hostages against the threat of treachery by the enemy. But as early as the seventeenth century Grotius had written that hostages "should not be put to death unless they have themselves done wrong."[7] His words were echoed by President Roosevelt on October 15, 1941: "Civilized peoples long ago adopted the basic principle that no man should be punished for the deed of another."[8] The Hague convention was silent on this subject, and it was not until the Geneva convention of 1949 on the protection of civilians that the taking of hostages was prohibited by international convention. The preamble of Hague Convention IV did provide, however, that in cases not covered by rules adopted by the high contracting parties "the inhabitants and the belligerents remain under the protection and the rule of the principles of the law of nations, as they result from the usages established among civilized peoples, from the laws of humanity, and the dictates of the public conscience."[9] The taking and holding in custody of hostages may not have been unlawful during the last war, but the killing of hostages is contrary to the Grotian concept of international law and is certainly against the laws of humanity. It was therefore prohibited by the general language of the preamble to Hague Convention IV. In the words of Lord Wright such killings are "terroristic murder."[10] The practice of killing hostages was criminal under international law during World War II.

Many of the crimes for which the defendants were indicted were committed as acts of reprisal. The Geneva convention of 1929 on the treatment of prisoners of war and the 1949 Geneva convention on the same subject prohibit the use of reprisals against prisoners of war. The mistreatment of war prisoners could not, therefore, be justified on the ground of reasonable reprisal. But there was no express conventional restriction upon reprisals against the persons or property of noncombatants in the last war. Such reprisals were not prohibited by the Hague conventions or by customary law. Indeed, they had been extensively employed in World War I where towns and villages were sometimes destroyed for the alleged ambushing of occupation troops. Obviously, however, even if reprisals had been recognized as permissible under the laws of war, they could not be so far in excess of the stated cause as to amount to arbitrary destruction and killing. Reprisals must be reasonably related to the acts of provocation. Lidice, Oradour-sur-Glane, Kalavryta, and Warsaw undoubtedly were excessive retaliatory actions, not justifiable under the doctrine of reprisals as it existed at the time the communities were razed and their populations decimated.

Of course, there is no defense to the murder of prisoners of war, whether it is the murder of one, as in the case of General Mesny, or of fifty, as in the case of the Sagan incident, or of thousands of escaped and recaptured war prisoners under the Bullet Decree, or of tens of thousands of politically and racially undesirable prisoners of war screened out of prison camps for "special treatment." Mass murder was employed by Hitler's Germany against prisoners of war, not for fault or in reprisal, but as part of the extermination of the unwanted.

The Tribunal found that Nazi war crimes were excessive and widespread. It declared:

> The evidence relating to War Crimes has been overwhelming, in its volume and its detail. It is impossible for this Judgment adequately to review it, or to record the mass of documentary and oral evidence that has been presented. The truth remains that War Crimes were committed on a vast scale, never before seen in the history of war.[11]

Crimes Against Humanity

No clear-cut distinction exists between war crimes and crimes against humanity committed in the course of war. Some atrocities perpetrated upon civilian populations have long been recognized as war crimes. And most war crimes would fall within any generally accepted definition of crimes against humanity. The idea of crimes against humanity raises no difficulty insofar as such crimes likewise constitute violations of the laws of war. But, as Goodhart says, "novel considerations arise when the acts charged cannot be brought within this category."[12]

The Commission of Fifteen appointed by the Preliminary Peace Conference in January, 1919, to inquire into breaches of the laws and customs of war during World War I concluded that Germany and her allies had conducted war in violation of established laws and customs of war and elementary "laws of humanity," and further held that persons guilty of offenses against the "laws of humanity" should be subject to criminal prosecution. The American members, Robert Lansing and James Brown Scott, dissented from the report and particularly from the use of the phrase "laws of humanity." In their dissent they stated:

War was and is, by its very nature inhuman, but acts consistent with the laws and customs of war, although these acts are inhuman, are nevertheless not the object of punishment by a court of justice. A judicial tribunal only deals with existing law and only administers existing law, leaving to another forum infractions of the moral law and actions contrary to the laws and principles of humanity.[13]

The London Agreement and the judgment of the International Military Tribunal rejected this approach to the law insofar as acts against humanity were committed in connection with aggressive war or traditional war crimes. The Tribunal construed the Charter as being coextensive with the preamble of Hague Convention IV in which the contracting parties recognized the validity of "the laws of humanity" as a source of international law governing humane warfare.[14]

Most of the crimes against humanity committed by the defendants were in pursuance of decrees of Hitler which were the then effective municipal law of Germany. The defendants could not, therefore, have been tried by the Allied powers under Nazi law on the theory that the victorious nations had succeeded to the sovereign authority of Germany upon unconditional surrender, for the defendants could have interposed as a bar to prosecution on the most severe counts, including slave labor and extermination of racial groups, the orders of Hitler directing that these things be done. Indeed, the gravamen of the indictment was that the decrees of Hitler, binding though they may have been as the technical law of Germany under National Socialism, were the source of the major crimes against humanity committed by the defendants. Instead of "leaving to another forum infractions of the moral law and actions contrary to the laws and principles of humanity," the International Military Tribunal accepted such infractions as a legal basis for trial of the war leaders of Nazi Germany.

Dangers implicit in introducing into international law a concept as vaguely conceived as crimes against humanity should not be discounted. The only crimes considered by the Tribunal to fall within this category, however, were the murder and ill-treatment of prisoners of war and civilian populations, the pillage of public and private property, slave labor, and racial persecution carried to the point of extermination, all of which had to be committed in connection with, or in execution of, aggressive war. The judgment of the Tribunal thus helped to make specific the indefinite concept of crimes against humanity. It has, in a sense, applied the conscience of humanity to a fact situation. And, while accepting the general idea of crimes against humanity as cognizable in international law, the Tribunal has restricted it to principles acceptable to all civilized peoples. As thus construed, the Charter gains strength from the judgment of the Tribunal; and the judgment itself becomes the primary measure of what may, or may not, constitute a crime against humanity within the permissible cognizance of any future international tribunal.

In conferring jurisdiction upon the International Military Tribunal over crimes against humanity, as well as over offenses against the laws of war, the drafters of the London Agreement intended the Tribunal to have juristic authority beyond the limits of traditional war crimes. As originally drafted, Article 6, Section (c) of the Charter defined crimes against humanity as:

Murder, extermination, enslavement, deportation, and other inhumane acts committed against any civilian population, before or during the war; or persecutions on political, racial or religious grounds in execution of or in connection with any crime within the jurisdiction of the Tribunal, whether or not in violation of the domestic law of the country where perpetrated.[15]

Use of the semicolon opened the definition to the construction that inhumane acts committed against any civilian population before the war were criminal without regard to connection with any other crime within the jurisdiction of the Tribunal. After the Charter had been signed it was discovered that in the Russian text a comma had been used instead of the semicolon, and by a special protocol of October 6, 1945, the English and French texts were revised to conform with the Russian text.[16] On the basis of this change the Tribunal construed the Charter to mean that crimes against humanity were not actionable unless committed in connection with a crime otherwise within the jurisdiction of the Tribunal.

The Tribunal stated that insofar as inhumane acts committed after the beginning of the war did not constitute recognized war crimes, they were all committed in execution of or in connection with aggressive war, and were properly subject to the jurisdiction of the Tribunal as crimes against humanity. But the Tribunal declined to take jurisdiction over crimes and persecutions committed by the defendants against the German people or other civilian populations before September 1, 1939. Much of the mistreatment of German peoples by the Hitler regime, and particularly the persecution of German Jewry, occurred prior to the outbreak of the war with Poland. In restricting the concept of crimes against humanity to the war period the Tribunal removed such mistreatment from its jurisdiction, save as it had probative value in proving the conspiracy to wage aggressive war.

This limitation was a proper one in view of the status of the Tribunal as an international military body, charged with determining responsibility for war and crimes related thereto. If the Tribunal had assumed jurisdiction to try persons under international law for crimes committed by them which were not related to war it would have wholly disregarded the concept of sovereignty and subjected to criminal prosecution under international law individuals whose conduct was lawful under controlling municipal law in times of peace. Such jurisdiction should never be assumed by an *ad hoc* military tribunal established to adjudicate crimes of war.

This is not to say that the individual held accountable for a crime against humanity must have been personally involved in the commission of a war crime or of participation in aggressive war. It is sufficient that his act against humanity be related to war crimes or to aggressive war. The defendants Streicher and Von Schirach were charged only with conspiracy and with crimes against humanity. Both were acquitted of the former charge and yet both were convicted of the latter. And Streicher was sentenced to hang. The same rule is applied to war crimes. It is not necessary that a defendant have been personally implicated in an act of aggression to be held accountable either for crimes against the laws of war or against the precepts of humanity.

The limitation, stated by the International Military Tribunal, that inhumane acts which are not connected directly with war crimes must have been committed in connection with *aggressive* war was derived from the Tribunal's construction of the Charter. As a matter of legal logic there is no more reason to require crimes against humanity to be related to *aggressive* war than to require war crimes to be so related. War crimes, of course, may be committed by the defensive as well as by the aggressive side. If the last war had started through an act of aggression by the Soviet Union and Hitler had established mass extermination centers for the liquidation of the Jewish population of Europe under cover of the ensuing conflict, it would have been a travesty upon justice to excuse him from accountability for that crime solely because he was engaged in a defensive war. Furthermore, any such restriction of crimes against humanity to the aggressor in war would impose different standards of conduct upon belligerents. Such a distinction is not permitted as to ordinary war crimes; and crimes against humanity should not be otherwise treated. The International Military Tribunal did not have to meet this issue because only German defendants were on trial and the Tribunal was satisfied from the evidence that the war was the result of German aggression.

Recognition of the concept of crimes against humanity was an important contribution of the International Military Tribunal to world law. It is surprising that the significance of the punishment of the top leaders of the Nazi regime for such crimes has not caused reaction in any degree comparable to the idea of individual liability for initiating and waging aggressive war. The principle thus enunciated will hold individuals liable for atrocities connected with, or committed in execution of, war. The judgment of the Tribunal, which may limit this concept to aggressive war, has nonetheless enlarged upon the doctrine of traditional war crimes. Conventional law now states a minimum standard of conduct in war. Individuals may be held personally accountable for other actions committed by them which may not be proscribed by existing conventions.

CHAPTER 38

The Law and Aggressive War

THE FIRST two thousand years of Christian civilization have constituted an Age of War. War has been a tolerated, even an accepted, method of adjusting differences among nations. Like the plague, it has come, men have suffered and died, and it has passed temporarily away. Science has found remedies for the plague, but to this day no certain cure has been found for war. There is no greater challenge to modern man than to find that cure and to bring humanity into the Age of Peace.

If such a modern challenge overthrows the reign of force it probably will succeed because of two primary factors—one derived from the physical sciences, the other from the realm of law. In the first few years of the thermonuclear age there has been placed in the hands of men a new power potential capable of such destructiveness as to threaten the users of the power as well as the intended victims. War has always been homicidal; now it has become suicidal. Civilization may see the end to war, because it cannot survive a renewal of war. The second factor is the universal condemnation of aggressive war, of which the Nuremberg judgment is both source and reflection. For many years prior to World War II the peoples of the world had thought of aggressive war as wrongful and wicked. The Nuremberg judgment gave expression to that feeling by punishing the individuals responsible for launching World War II.

"Aggressive war" has not yet been, and perhaps never will be, adequately defined, and it has been contended that the very indefiniteness of the concept makes difficult its prohibition. Dr. George A. Finch has written: "An indefinable act cannot be prohibited in advance unless we are willing to acknowledge our constitutional heresy with regard to *ex post facto* legislation."[1] Yet the same writer found no fault with the concept of "crimes against humanity,"[2] which is equally difficult to define. Aggressive war may be incapable of a definition which is comprehensive enough to cover every act of war which should be punished and yet flexible enough to permit every act of self-defense which should be permitted. But it does not follow that so elusive a concept may not afford an adequate juridical basis for criminal prosecution. Neither treason nor piracy has been defined in the precise terms common to most municipal criminal statutes, but they are well-established crimes, and their extent and meaning have been developed through the many judicial decisions in which they have been employed. And even in municipal law our courts deal successfully with such hard-to-define concepts as "due process" and "equal protection."

In the Nuremberg trial the phrase "aggressive war" was construed and applied to a relatively clear fact situation. A case may arise in the future in which a war will be found to lie close to the border between aggression and defense. But that can be true of any killing in alleged self-defense. The difficulty of applying the concept in close cases does not mean that courts are powerless to recognize inexcusable aggressive action when it clearly occurs. The problem of applying an abstract principle in its narrowest range does not impair its application in broad gauge.

No fair-minded person could read the record of the Nazi regime and fail to conclude that the attacks by Germany commencing with the assault upon Poland were clear cases of aggression. A small group of conspirators plotted each act of war and directed its execution. Even provocation was simulated. If initiating and waging aggressive war is criminal it is indisputable that the leaders of Hitler's Germany were properly convicted on that count.

Under the Charter of the International Military Tribunal the planning or waging of a war of aggression was declared to be a crime in international law. While the Tribunal might have based its judgment upon that declaration, it was sensitive to the charge that the Charter itself might be regarded as *ex post facto* in this respect, and the Tribunal therefore heard arguments on the question whether, at the time of Hitler's aggression, the initiating and waging of aggressive war was an international crime. Upon mature deliberation the Tribunal concluded that the Charter stated existing law and was not *ex post facto* legislation. The United States alternate member of the Tribunal has declared: "The charter did not create the crimes or make criminal what was not criminal beforehand; it merely defined the crimes which the Tribunal was authorized to punish and set up machinery for their punishment."[3]

The *ex post facto* principle is of general applicability in municipal law where legislatures exist to state the law in statutory form. But even in municipal law courts frequently reverse a previously accepted rule of judge-made law or construe a statute in a way not anticipated by an accused person. Legislatures "make" law and courts "declare" law. A person accused of crime may rely upon the statutes in effect at the time the crime was committed; he cannot be certain that the courts will construe the statutes in just the way he thinks they should be interpreted. Of course, it is *ex post facto* to enact a statute making criminal that which was not a crime when committed. But it is not *ex post facto* for a court to declare that an act, when committed, was a crime, even though no previous judicial declaration had been made to that effect—or even if a previous judicial decision had held to the contrary.

The International Military Tribunal declared that at the time the Nuremberg defendants conspired to initiate and wage aggressive war such conduct was criminal in international law. One may disagree with that conclusion; but it is no more *ex post facto* for the Tribunal to have made that declaration than it would be for a municipal court so to declare in the absence of legislation. If the conclusion was wrong, it was an error of judgment, not a violation of legal principle. In construing the same charter language, and arriving at the same result, the Tokyo Tribunal, which conducted the trial of the Japanese war criminals, ruled expressly that unless under international law existing at the time the alleged acts of aggression were committed such acts were criminal, the victorious nations would have been without legal authority to subject the accused to trial upon this count. The International Military Tribunal at Nuremberg and the Tokyo Tribunal both concluded that the charter provisions which declared criminal the initiating of wars of aggression were not *ex post facto* but were statements of subsisting international law.

The defendants claimed surprise. At the outset of the trial all defense counsel joined in a plea in bar based in part upon the contention that it was not a crime in international law to initiate and wage aggressive war when these acts were allegedly committed by the defendants. It was suggested that the Tribunal confine itself to fact findings upon this issue on the basis of which "the states of the international legal community would then create a new law under which those who *in the future* would be guilty of starting an unjust war would be threatened with punishment by an International Tribunal."[4] (Italics added.)

The defendants could not have been surprised as to the moral aspects of their conduct. No one sends millions to die without a qualm of conscience. The doctrine that no man shall be punished save in accordance with law in effect at the time of his act presupposes that there could be a question of criminal conduct in his mind at that time. In commenting upon this matter, the noted philosopher, Ralph Barton Perry, has written:

When a defendant is found guilty of transgressing precepts recognized by the community of which he is a member and held to be vital to its well-being, it is reasonable to suppose that he anticipates the possibility of retribution from the community which he injures. In terms of the *ex post facto* maxim, literally and rigidly construed, it would be impossible to explain either the latitude of the judicial process, or the first steps in the development of the common law. Positive law is forever being generated from custom or conscience by application to cases deemed of sufficient importance to warrant the intervention of society as a whole.

Suppose a pioneer community in which there is no established legal system. A horse thief is caught red-handed. Shall he be expelled, hanged, confined, or otherwise punished? Or shall he be exonerated on the ground that at the time of his theft there was no law against stealing horses? No such community has ever hesitated in its answer. The horse thief was aware that his action so violated the common interest that every man's hand would be against him. He has no excuse for being surprised that having declared war on society, society in turn should protect itself against him. Such procedures of the community express the collective interest against its internal enemies; and at the same time its aspiration to become an organized community, in which justice shall prevail over vindictiveness, and cool reflection over passion. They are not manifestations of disorder but beginnings of order.

The criminals of Nuremberg were like that horse thief, taken red-handed in conduct intolerable to the wider complex of human interests. None of those convicted at Nuremberg, despite their air of injured innocence and their legalistic protests, could have been unaware of the opinion and sentiment of the world in which they lived—repeatedly, and solemnly affirmed in countless treaties and agreements, publicly professed by heads of state, and voiced by the most authentic exponents of the western and modern conscience.[5]

For centuries, kings acted above the law and directed acts to be done which, if caused by others, would have been punishable by death. When Lord Coke challenged the prerogatives of James I and asserted that the king, as every other man, was "under God and the law," it was not contended that James was wrongly attacked because earlier kings had never been so judged. Perhaps James was surprised at Coke's pronouncement, although he should not have been, since Bracton had similarly challenged "divine right" four centuries before. The International Military Tribunal declared that leaders of Nazi Germany who led the world into war should answer to law, as well as to God. Nor should they have been heard to challenge that declaration as something unknown, for three centuries ago Hugo Grotius proclaimed the wickedness of the unjust war. And Plato had proclaimed as much, twenty-one centuries before Grotius.

The guilty mind of the Nazis is evidenced by the elaborate measures which Hitler took to place blame for war upon his victims. In the case of Czechoslovakia he charged intolerable provocations against the German minority. In Poland it was the brutal mistreatment of the Germans in Danzig. And to pretend to the world that Poland was aggressive Hitler staged the fake border attacks at Gleiwitz and other towns. He instructed his commanders that full-scale military action in the West should be made to appear as having been started by the British and the French. The leaders of Hitler's Germany knew full well that in waging aggressive war they were committing great wrongs. They sought to justify their actions in other alleged wrongs, such as the limitations of Versailles, which they laid to their enemies. And Hitler rationalized that the death and suffering which his wars would bring to present generations would be redeemed in the greater Germanic empire which would be created in the heartland of Europe.

What the defendants at Nuremberg really were complaining about was not that they were not guilty of the crime of initiating and waging aggressive war, but that they were the *first* men in history to be adjudged, and punished, for that crime. Dr. Hans Ehard, the Minister President of Bavaria, expressed the same thought when, after criticizing the aggressive war charge as contrary to the maxim, *nullum crimen, nulla poena sine lege,* he stated that the Nuremberg trial nevertheless "represents a tremendous advance of the law of nations if, *in the future,* war of aggression is prosecuted as an international crime without regard to the nation or the person, and if the responsible statesmen are personally taken to account."[6] (Italics added).

There was none of the spirit of Von Moltke in this. Von Moltke contended that war was ordained by God and could not be adjudged at all by earthly judges. Having these views, he could quite logically assert that launching and waging aggressive war is not criminal and that no tribunal should declare it so or find aggressors guilty of that crime, at least until some international covenant had so provided. But the Nuremberg defendants could not accept this cynical and amoral position. And so they sought refuge in the legal defense, borrowed from municipal law, that they could not be punished for acts which had not been specified as criminal by legislation. This argument ignores the common law of nations. Having in effect conceded the moral wrong in initiating and waging aggressive war, the defendants could not deny to a properly constituted tribunal the authority to give a jural quality to that wrong if it could do so consistently with applicable principles of international law.

The Charter of the International Military Tribunal defined crimes against peace as the planning, preparation, initiating, or waging of wars of aggression, or wars in violation of international treaties, agreements, or assurances. In holding that certain of the defendants planned and waged aggressive war, the Tribunal deemed it unnecessary to consider the extent to which the wars of aggression in which they were implicated may likewise have been wars "in violation of international treaties, agreements, or assurances."[7] The initiating and waging of aggressive war, rather than the violation of specific treaties and agreements, constituted the basis for the conviction of the defendants of the commission of crimes against peace. The finding that it was a crime in international law for the defendants to have initiated and waged aggressive war, at the time these actions were taken by them, may be tested against the three primary sources of the laws of nations: convention, custom, and universal conscience.

The principal instrument of conventional international law applicable to the aggressions of Adolf Hitler was the General Treaty for the Renunciation of War of August 27, 1928, more commonly known as the Pact of Paris, or the Briand-Kellogg Pact. It consists of two Articles:

Article I. The High Contracting Parties solemnly declare in the names of their respective peoples that they condemn recourse to war for the solution of international controversies, and renounce it as an instrument of national policy in their relations with one another.

Article II. The High Contracting Parties agree that the settlement or solution of all disputes or conflicts of whatever nature or of whatever origin they may be, which may arise among them, shall never be sought except by pacific means.[8]

Sixty-three nations, including Germany, Italy, and Japan, adhered to the Briand-Kellogg Pact. Their signatures evidenced more than a multilateral declaration that war is an evil thing and should be shunned. Had that been the sole purpose of the Pact, Article I would have ended with the condemnation of recourse to war for the solution of international controversies. But the Pact does not stop there. It further states that the contracting parties *renounce* war as an instrument of national policy in their relations to one another. And Article II gives additional emphasis to this second aspect of the treaty by providing that the settlement or solution of all disputes or conflicts of whatever nature or origin shall *never* be sought except by pacific means. Since, under the Pact, war was renounced by the contracting parties, recourse to war by Pact signatories as an instrument of national policy thereafter clearly was illegal. As Secretary of State Stimson declared in 1932, by the Briand-Kellogg Pact war had become "an illegal thing."[9]

The Pact did not outlaw defensive warfare. It speaks only of renouncing war as an instrument of national policy. That is one way of describing aggressive war. Dr. Jahrreis, in his argument on the law for all the defendants, asserted that in the comments about the Pact after its promulgation there was complete agreement only to the proposition that a war of self-defense is an undeniable right of all states, without which sovereignty does not exist. He further contended that every state is alone competent to judge whether in a given case it is waging a war of defense. As to this proposition, it is certainly within the province of each nation, under the Pact, to determine under what circumstances it will commit itself to a war of defense. But, obviously, aggressive war does not become defensive war by the simple act of calling it such.

Dr. Jahrreis submitted that the Pact could not be construed as denying to states recourse to war when necessary to rectify a grave injustice which could not otherwise be remedied. He contended that no effective international procedure had been established after the adoption of the Pact, "by which the community of states, even against the will of the possessor, can change conditions that have become intolerable, in order to provide life with the safety valve it must have if it is to be spared an explosion."[10] The argument was a major one in the Nazi scheme of things.

It had been contended by Hitler from the beginning that the "chains" of Versailles must be broken. This was asserted not as a basis of negotiation for the establishing of a community of European nations, but rather as a matter of right to which German power had to be dedicated. It is certainly true, as Dr. Jahrreis contended, that after the Briand-Kellogg Pact no federation of nations was established in Europe, offering to Germany an alternative to the Hitler idea of rectifying the "disgrace" of Versailles. But while diplomatic channels are open, and statesmen meet and discuss their differences, the hope of correcting real injustice, and not merely prideful claims, certainly exists. If no effective international body was established in Europe during the thirties with promise of greater equality for Germany in world affairs, it could not have been claimed by Germany that any effort was made by Hitler in that direction. Furthermore, although Hitler's initial claims were for rectification of the Versailles Treaty, his true goal at all times was aggression for purposes far more extensive than that—the conquering and colonization of all of eastern Europe. And so, even if in the extreme case the lack of possibility of rectification of grave injustice by any peaceful means might warrant a signatory to the Briand-Kellogg Pact to renounce the Pact and gain its point by war, that argument could not justifiably have been asserted by the Nuremberg defendants in defense of the aggressions of Adolf Hitler in which they were implicated.

In the years of indecision prior to the outbreak of war in 1939, signatories to the Briand-Kellogg Pact did not apply effective sanctions against nations who repeatedly violated the Pact. Japan in Manchuria and Italy in Ethiopia were clear examples of the utilization of war as an instrument of national policy. From this failure of the signatories to the Pact to take effective action against Japan and Italy, Dr. Jahrreis concluded that "in the actual relations between states there existed—quite a number of years prior to 1939—no effective general ruling of international law regarding prohibited warfare."[11] The argument was thus based upon a theory of estoppel. But the Pact had not been discarded or renounced. It simply had not been enforced in those cases. The fact that signatories to the Briand-Kellogg Pact failed to take effective measures against these aggressors could be construed neither as a promise to tolerate any violation of the Pact in the future nor as an implied understanding that the Pact no longer stated a rule of international law. What Japan and Italy and the Soviet Union did in their cases was illegal. The illegality simply was never adjudicated, nor the perpetrators thereof brought to justice. In the words of Sir Hartley Shawcross, "That was a failure of the policeman, not of the law."[12]

The Briand-Kellogg Pact clearly made aggressive war illegal. While the Pact remained in force rights claimed as a result of aggression could be denied recognition by the other signatories. The United States, for example, refused to recognize the validity of the Soviet seizure and absorption of the Baltic states. Moreover, under the Pact, not only may an attacked nation take action in its self-defense, but other nations may grant it assistance without themselves violating international law. It was upon this theory that prior to its direct involvement in World War II the United States granted aid to Great Britain. The Pact provides a legal basis for effective collective action against an aggressor if the signatories are able to agree upon the collective measures to be taken. These sanctions are permissible because the Pact declared aggressive war illegal. But illegality is one thing, and criminality another.

The International Military Tribunal construed the Briand-Kellogg Pact as making aggressive war criminal, as well as illegal, and as affording the juridical basis for the punishment of individuals who initiated and waged wars of aggression in violation of its terms. In placing this construction upon the Pact, the Tribunal referred particularly to custom as a subsidiary source of international law. While many lawyers have disagreed with this construction of the Briand-Kellogg Pact, most would concede that—granting the validity of the premise that (as Grotius said) there is a common law of nations for war—the Tribunal's interpretation does have support in law. The Pact might have been construed the other way. But the Tribunal was not arbitrary or capricious in this conclusion on the law.

As a source of law, custom must be continuous and permanent. It need not have been accepted by all nations, but it must have been recognized and respected by the parties to the dispute or by nations generally. It may be found, in part, in the declarations of responsible international authorities. Writing in 1946, Dr. Sheldon Glueck expressed doubt that the launching and conducting of aggressive war constituted an international crime, but on the basis of a more extensive research he concluded two years later that various international covenants, statements, and resolutions, made after World War I, might "be regarded as evidence of a sufficiently developed *custom* to be acceptable as international law."[13]

Among these pronouncements were four of which the Tribunal itself took particular notice. Article I of the unratified 1923 draft Treaty of Mutual Assistance provided that aggressive war is an international crime; the preamble to the 1924 Geneva Protocol for the Pacific Settlement of International Disputes declared that "a war of aggression...is...an international crime";[14] the 1927 resolution of the Assembly of the League of Nations concerning wars of aggression stated the conviction that "a war of aggression can never serve as a means of settling international disputes, and is, in consequence, an international crime...";[15] and in 1928 the Sixth International Conference of American States declared at Havana in the preamble to a resolution against aggression that "war of aggression constitutes a crime against the human species."[16] While these declarations may have been made to express the moral condemnation of aggressive war, they do constitute, in connection with the Pact of Paris of 1928 which outlawed the use of war as an instrument of national policy, imposing evidence of customary international law under which, as of the close of the third decade of the twentieth century, the initiating and waging of aggressive war might be held criminal.

There is, of course, nothing remarkable in any such change in customary law which may thus have taken place after World War I. If it be conceded that prior to the first world conflict of this century the custom was to tolerate aggressive war, or at least to accept it as noncriminal, the dreadful experiences of that conflict quite obviously led to the several subsequent pronouncements condemning war as a crime. For many, many years slave trading was tolerated in customary international law. But there came a time when, in response to the increasing condemnatory statements against the practice, the custom in law changed accordingly.

If, therefore, it were permissible to look only to these post World War I pronouncements as evidence of a change in custom with respect to aggressive war it might reasonably, indeed necessarily, be concluded that when Hitler commenced his series of aggressions the initiating and waging of such wars was criminal in customary international law. But pronouncements are not the sole, or even the primary, source of customary international law. They must be tested, too, by the actual practice of nations. And in this respect, grave doubts arise as to the validity of custom as a basis for the interdiction of the Hitler aggressions. For, while the third decade of the twentieth century showed a rather general acceptance of the proposition that aggressive war may and should be condemned as criminal, in the fourth decade of the century national actions indicated that this proposition was not to be universally observed or supported consistently by effective sanctions. Including the wars begun by Hitler, in a period of ten years following 1930 four major world powers committed undeniable acts of military aggression. Japan in China, Italy in Ethiopia, Germany in Poland, and Soviet Russia in Finland involved military actions inconsistent with the developing custom that aggression is criminal.

The case of the Soviet Union is one in point. The Soviets entered into a nonaggression pact with Lithuania in 1926, and signed similar pacts in 1932 with Poland, Finland, Latvia, and Esthonia. Yet on September 17, 1939, in pursuance of the Black Pact of August 23, 1939, Stalin invaded Poland from the east less than three weeks after Hitler had attacked from the west. Two months later, on November 30, 1939, the Soviet Union attacked Finland and forced its tiny neighbor to cede over sixteen thousand square miles of territory by a treaty of peace imposed in March, 1940. In June, 1940, Stalin seized the Baltic states of Latvia, Esthonia, and Lithuania, and incorporated them into the U.S.S.R.

The seizure of these territories cannot be excused as measures of defense even though it may be true, as Sir Winston Churchill has written, that the actions were initiated "to block the lines of entry into the Soviet Union from the west."[17] There is no concept in international law of "preventive war." Grotius wrote: "But that the possibility of being attacked confers the right to attack is abhorrent to every principle of equity."[18] Even if, under extreme conditions, a nation might be justified in attacking another nation to forestall the certain assault of the latter, such a rule could not be applied in favor of the Soviet aggressions, for their attacks were not upon the enemy—Germany—but upon Poland, Finland, Lithuania, Esthonia, and Latvia, none of which had offered the slightest threat to the U.S.S.R.

The problem in its simplest relationship is this: prior to World War I there was no generally accepted custom in international law making the initiating and waging of aggressive war a crime; in the first decade after that war such a custom developed in the expressions of responsible leaders in international affairs; in the second decade after that war those pronouncements were belied, ignored, and violated by the leaders of four of the major nations of the world.

Of course a custom, to be valid, need not be universally accepted or respected. It is not necessary that every nation in the world community acknowledge the wrongfulness of slave trading to permit a custom against slave trading to be recognized as valid international law. If there was a custom against aggression before Japan attacked in Manchuria, the custom was not destroyed by the Japanese violation of it. Nor was it lost because all other nations did not instantly come to the aid of Manchuria with military force. Every act of aggression after World War I led to condemnation and in many cases to the application, or the attempted application, of sanctions against the aggressor. There was, therefore, no loss of custom by implied assent to, or approval of, these first acts of aggression.

World War II began as a German attack upon Poland. But Hitler and the world knew that when he attacked Poland a general European conflict would necessarily follow. The British and French mutual assistance pacts with Poland were made to stop aggression, if aggression could thus be prevented. They were in vindication of the principle that aggression is wrongful and is criminal. They resulted in a pledge of British and French lives to preserve that principle. And as such they constituted the application of the most powerful sanctions against aggression.

The spirit of this custom was demonstrated during the Soviet attack upon Finland, and the gallant defense of their country by the Finns. Even while committed in war themselves, the French and British people sought to aid the Finns with scarce war goods. Volunteers to fight with the Finns against their oppressors came from the free nations of Europe and the United States of America. The condemnation of the Soviet Union led to its expulsion from the League of Nations. The world applauded the heroic Finns and hated the Russians for their deeds.

It cannot be contended that there was any general disregard of the custom against aggression merely because certain major powers from time to time had found it to their own advantage to break the custom. Moreover, the excuses offered by the aggressors and the condemnation of their conduct added support to its continued vitality. None of these nations denied that aggression was criminal, but each sought to prove in world opinion that its own actions were fully justifiable measures of self-protection or for the advancement of civilization. Under such rationalizations, Japan attacked China to protect the lives and property of its citizens in Manchuria and elsewhere; Mussolini attacked Ethiopia to bring the blessings of modern civilization to the savages of Abyssinia; Hitler attacked Poland to forestall a Polish attack upon Germany; and Soviet Russia attacked Finland to strengthen its defenses against expected assaults from western Europe. The fact that these justifications may have been entirely cynical is quite beside the point. The very making of them constituted an acknowledgment that at that time, in customary international law, the initiating and waging of aggressive war was wrongful. That is why these protestations of innocence had to be made.

Even so, in view of these several acts of aggression, it is doubtful whether custom alone could be looked to as providing a sufficient legal basis for the proposition that the leaders of states which were signatories to the Briand-Kellogg Pact committed crime in initiating and waging wars of aggression at the time Hitler began his conquest of Europe. But universal conscience likewise may be referred to for this purpose.

Established principles of law recognized by all civilized nations constitute a valid source of international law. Among these are the sanctity of life and the right to property. Killing, mayhem, despoliation, and destruction—the inevitable consequences of war—are criminal in every society, unless justified under law. The taking of a human life is forgiven when necessary to self-defense. Property may be destroyed to stop an onrushing fire. But in the absence of such justifications, every legal system declares these acts to be criminal, and the individuals who perpetrate them to be subject to the penalties of the law. Murder is the supreme crime in every jurisdiction. And inexcusable war is mass murder.

Dr. Jahrreis contended: "What the Prosecution is doing when,

in the name of the world community as a legal entity, it desires to
have individuals legally sentenced for their decisions regarding war
and peace is...destroying the spirit of the state."[19] Yet he would
not deny that if a group of men should form a conspiratorial body
to achieve an insurrection in a state, and in the course thereof
should destroy life and property, they should be subject to prosecution and punishment for such crimes committed in the course of
the insurrection. If the same men gain control of the political
machinery of the state and carry out the same depredations, why
should they escape similar treatment when brought to trial before
a court of competent jurisdiction?

The answer in previous years had been the bar of sovereignty
upon which Dr. Jahrreis based his defense. The killings of war
could not be laid to individual aggressors because war was a
tolerated method of adjusting disputes among nations, even when
resorted to in violation of specific treaties and assurances. Perhaps
this should not have been the law, for the conscience of mankind
is shocked by callous killings even when ordered in accordance with
national policy. But if it was, the Briand-Kellogg Pact undercut
any such defense by declaring that war was no longer to be recognized as an instrument of national policy. A leader of a signatory
state who directed his country into aggressive military action could
not, thereafter, plead in justification of the consequent killings and
devastation that the war was a matter of state policy. He could be
held accountable for the deaths which he ordered, because the
Briand-Kellogg Pact had swept away whatever justification might
previously have been asserted by him, as the responsible head of
the state, upon the ground of sovereignty.

This theory of individual responsibility for initiating and waging
an aggressive war may be related to the personal accountability of
heads of states for crimes against humanity. The slaughter of
civilians in concentration camps, ordered by Hitler, was a crime of
Hitler, even though he directed this mass killing as head of the
German state. In quite the same way, Hitler ordered the killing of
men called to the defense of countries which German armies
invaded at Hitler's command. Insofar as these invasions were acts
of pure aggression, and wholly without legal justification, the

resultant killings offended the conscience of mankind just as the slaughter of persons in concentration camps offended universal conscience. It is, after all, moral condemnation which underlies legal prosecution. The killing of innocent human beings by order of heads of states is subject to substantially the same moral blame whether it is the killing of civilian populations in connection with war or the killing of troops resisting unlawful aggression.

A very great judge made a similar analysis of slave trading more than a hundred years ago:

We are not to be told that war is lawful, and slavery lawful, and plunder lawful, and the taking away of life is lawful, and the selling of human beings is lawful. Assuming that they are so under circumstances, it establishes nothing. It does not advance one jot to the support of the proposition that a traffic that involves them all, that is unnecessary, unjust, and inhuman, is countenanced by the eternal law of nature on which rests the law of nations.... It is not, as the learned counsel for the government have justly stated, on account of the simple fact that the traffic necessarily involves the enslavement of human beings, that it stands reprehended by the present sense of nations; but that it necessarily carries with it a breach of all the moral duties, of all the maxims of justice, mercy and humanity, and of the admitted rights, which independent Christian nations now hold sacred in their intercourse with each other.[20]

It is not the fact of initiating and waging aggressive war which reprehends it, but that it is necessarily a course of killings and of brutality which is attained in no other relationship of man or nation. Even apart from the slaughter of soldiers and the destruction of cities, particular cruelties result inevitably from aggressive war. The conqueror takes hostages to maintain order, and imposes reprisals to prevent uprisings. His police agencies invoke the third degree to discover members of resistance movements. Individual rights are lost in the struggle of nations. The worst conduct of men may be overlooked, sanctioned, or even rewarded. These are the things that make war criminal. Not the moving of armies against each other. But the slain, and the halt, and the blind; Lidice and Malmedy; the Night and Fog Decree; and the crimes against humanity perpetrated in every war.

In discussing the importance of the Pact of Paris in providing the legal support for the judgment of the Nuremberg Tribunal, the United States alternate member, Judge Parker, wrote:

> The Kellogg-Briand Pact was thus not the expression of a mere pious hope, but a definite statement of positive law. Thereafter those guilty of making such wars were violating a definite provision of international law relating to warfare; and it has long been settled that a violation of the laws of warfare is a crime for which punishment may be imposed upon the guilty. It is immaterial that violation of the pact was not defined as a crime or that no punishment therefor was specifically provided; for it is not necessary that violation of the law relating to warfare be defined as a crime or that punishment be prescribed therefor to render it punishable criminally. Violation of the Rules of Land Warfare laid down by the Hague Convention is not defined as a crime and no punishment is prescribed for such violation; but no lawyer would contend that there may not be a trial and punishment for such violation. If crime may be predicated of an incident of warfare because forbidden by international agreement, *a fortiori* it may be predicated of the war itself if international agreement forbids the war.[21]

The comparison between individual responsibility for commission of war crimes and for initiating and waging aggressive wars extends, of course, only to heads of states. Every individual is accountable for committing specific crimes against the laws of war, subject only to mitigation for action taken in accordance with superior orders. But persons who have no responsibility for the initiating and waging of aggressive war cannot be punished for what they do in legitimate furtherance of the war. However begun, war does create a status. It brings into effect entirely new legal relationships, including rules of humane warfare and proper treatment of prisoners of war. And it protects the ordinary citizens of nations at war in whatever actions, permissible under the rules of humane warfare, they may take to further their country's cause. Heads of states, on the other hand, may be held criminally accountable for the consequences of initiating and waging aggressive war because they may not assert their own illegal acts in defense of conduct which otherwise would be criminal.

This distinction is easily applied as between political leaders and draftees. But the responsibility of top military personnel is more difficult to assess. It is almost inevitable that military leaders know something of plans for aggressive war. Yet they are under a positive duty to protect the nation and to execute the orders of its political leadership. It would be intolerable to permit military leaders individually to evaluate each political decision as to whether it was or was not aggressive; and it would be wrong to hold such leaders criminally accountable for failing individually to reach a correct evaluation of such decisions.

Of course, no one should be heard to assert absolute immunity for acting in accordance with the orders of anyone else, even in such a fundamental matter as war. Conceivably, a plan of aggression might be so obvious, and so wicked, as to impose upon military leaders who share knowledge of the plans a duty to retire rather than to aid in their fulfillment. But this would, indeed, be the extreme case. On the other hand, military leaders who actually participate in political decisions, and support plans for aggression, should not be heard to plead in defense simply that they acted while in uniform. If this were not so, the military dictator would have freedom of action denied to civilian heads of states. The liability of the military leaders of Nazi Germany for engaging in Hitler's aggressions must turn, therefore, upon evidence of free and active participation by them in the political decisions for aggressive war.

Five such leaders were indicted at Nuremberg. They were: Goering, Commander in Chief of the Air Force; Keitel, Chief of the High Command of the Armed Forces; Jodl, Chief of Staff of the High Command; Doenitz, Chief of the Submarine Command until January 30, 1943, and thereafter Commander in Chief of the German Navy; and Raeder, Commander in Chief of the German Navy until January 30, 1943. All were convicted of initiating and waging wars of aggression except Doenitz, who was convicted solely of waging aggressive war.

Insofar as these military leaders assumed the prerogatives of political leadership which led to acts of armed aggression, they could fairly be required to share the responsibility for such decisions with the purely political officers of the state. Goering, of course, was primarily a politician and only incidentally a military leader. But Keitel, Jodl, Raeder, and Doenitz were professional soldiers, and positive evidence was required to show their participation in political decisions. Keitel and Jodl were both active in the political maneuvers which led to the absorption of Austria and Czechoslovakia, but these operations were not charged as acts of aggressive war. Keitel was constantly at Hitler's side in framing the assault upon Poland, but Jodl was not. Both of them participated in planning aggressive actions thereafter. Raeder was present at the discussions leading to the attack on Poland, and he urged the assault upon Norway and the military occupation of Greece. In all of these cases there was some evidence from which the Tribunal could conclude that the mentioned military leaders joined willingly, and even enthusiastically, with Hitler in formulating and executing many of the acts of aggression for which the political leaders of the state were held accountable. Doenitz, however, presents a special case.

The Tribunal did not find Doenitz guilty of *initiating* aggressive war, but it did find him guilty of *waging* aggressive war. During the period of planning the attacks upon other states Doenitz held a relatively minor position in the German military organization. The Tribunal found:

> Although Doenitz built and trained the German U-boat Arm, the evidence does not show he was privy to the conspiracy to wage aggressive wars or that he prepared and initiated such wars. He was a line officer performing strictly tactical duties. He was not present at the important conferences when plans for aggressive wars were announced, and there is no evidence he was informed about the decisions reached there.[22]

The later political triumphs of Admiral Doenitz, resulting in his ultimate designation as the successor of Adolf Hitler as head of the German state, tended to show his sympathy with the aims of aggression, and evidence that he had joined the conspiracy after its commencement would, of course, support his conviction. Had the finding that Doenitz waged aggressive war been based solely upon his activities as a naval officer, however, his conviction on this count would not, in the writer's view, have been warranted in law.

The activities of these generals may be contrasted with the case of Field Marshal von Rundstedt. Speaking to Keitel of Von Rundstedt, Hitler once said:

> I know perfectly well that Rundstedt is a general of the old Prussian royalist tradition, but he is an awfully good general and he is not a National Socialist, and he is not a Party man, and he doesn't want to have anything to do with us. I know that perfectly well. But, Keitel, history must know this, and

I want to say this right here, history will know that that thing will never have prevented me from selecting the best man for such a purpose.[23]

Von Rundstedt was not a collaborator on the political level with Hitler and with Keitel. He was not sympathetic to National Socialism, at all. And yet when Hitler placed the Western Front in his hands, Von Rundstedt replied: "Whatever your order, I shall do to my last breath."[24] The entirely nonpolitical activities of Field Marshal von Rundstedt would have excused him from liability for waging aggressive war. If that were not so, where would patriotism end and criminality begin?

If the soldier so far lays aside his military immunity as to participate actively in political discussions and maneuvers leading to aggressive war, he may quite properly be held responsible for his share in launching and continuing that war. But if he adheres strictly to his professional duty to conduct war, when declared by others without his participation or connivance, only the most extreme circumstances ought to require him, at the risk of being adjudged a criminal, to resign from the military service and his country's cause in time of peril.

The waging of aggressive war in its purely military aspects should not be cognizable as an international crime even as to a military leader who has reason to suspect that the war is an aggressive one. Nor did those who participated in the drafting of the Charter of the International Military Tribunal intend to make the mere military waging of war an international crime. In commenting upon the language of the Charter in this respect, Mr. Justice Jackson stated: "It never occurred to me, and I am sure it occurred to no one else at the conference table, to speak of anyone as 'waging' a war except topmost leaders who had some degree of control over its precipitation and policy."[25] Properly considered, the crime of initiating and waging aggressive war is the crime of starting and continuing to prosecute an aggressive war. This crime cannot reach beyond the heads of states and those who knowingly join with them in making the political decisions for war. Military leaders, and others who do not share in that responsibility, should not be charged with crime for doing their part in support of their country at war, even if the war was commenced wrongfully and is in fact illegal.

Under the Charter of the International Military Tribunal, leaders, organizers, instigators, and accomplices participating in the formulation or execution of a common plan or conspiracy to commit any of the crimes defined in the Charter could be held responsible for all acts performed in pursuance thereof. Proving this common plan and the participation of each indicted individual in it was the principal responsibility of the American prosecution staff which sought to include within the conspiracy the formative period of the National Socialist movement, the rise to power, and the consolidation of rule in which minority groups were ruthlessly oppressed in Germany. The prosecution claimed not only the existence of a conspiracy to wage aggressive war but also a conspiracy to commit war crimes and crimes against humanity, and it treated the development of National Socialism itself, in the light of its avowed objectives to establish the paramountcy of a master race and to despoil the eastern peoples, as a part of that conspiracy.

The Tribunal, however, construed the Charter as restricting the common plan to the initiating and waging of aggressive war, and it held that to incur such liability the conspirators must have plotted aggression within a short period prior to the actual commencement of hostilities. The Tribunal wholly disregarded the portions of Count One of the indictment charging that the defendants conspired to commit war crimes and crimes against humanity. Whether a provable conspiracy to commit such crimes would be cognizable under customary international law, or whether any such conspiracy had in fact been proved by the prosecution, was not considered. The Tribunal simply held the concept of conspiracy under the Charter to a much more restricted definition than that set forth in the indictment which the prosecution sought to prove. The Tribunal declared that the conspiracy to wage aggressive war must not be too far removed from the time of decision and action and must be clearly proved. It found that a conspiracy to wage aggressive war did exist at least as early as November 5, 1937, the date of the first of the four secret meetings, attended by top military and political leaders, at which Hitler unequivocally stated his intention to attack neighboring nations with arms.

This concept of criminal conspiracy did not go beyond the doctrine of conspiratorial crimes recognized in the ordinary criminal law of the Anglo-American legal system. The judgment of the Tribunal did no more than to hold that men meeting furtively together to plot the overthrow of a friendly nation, with action pursuant thereto following quickly thereafter, are as guilty of criminal conspiracy in international law as men who meet under similar circumstances to rob a bank or kidnap a child are guilty under municipal law. There was no departure from established legal principle in this result, although, to be sure, the prosecution had claimed the right to prove a conspiracy of wider scope under the Charter.

In finding the Nuremberg defendants guilty of the crime of initiating and waging aggressive war and conspiring to that end, the International Military Tribunal helped to develop the international law of crimes in a way similar to the growth and development of the common law of crimes in English law. The absence of legislators and criminal statutes did not deter the English judges in the formative period of English law from creating a great body of criminal law through the case-by-case prosecution of persons whose conduct offended public conscience. Neither did the Tribunal, in this formative era of international law, hesitate to add aggressive war to the body of crimes against the laws of nations, and thereby contribute to the growth of international law.

Law is but the means to justice. The first world-wide conflict had led to the conviction that civilization could no longer accept war as a legal method of settling international disputes. But it took a second war to turn that conviction into law. The Nuremberg judgment marks the acceptance, at last, of the Grotian philosophy of law. "The law on the subject has now undergone a fundamental change. War has ceased to be a supreme prerogative of states. The Grotian distinction between just and unjust war is once more part of positive international law."[26] Aggressive war has long been morally condemned; it has now been adjudged criminal in law.

Few persons living in a thermonuclear age will disagree with this statement of the International Military Tribunal:

War is essentially an evil thing. Its consequences are not confined to the belligerent States alone, but affect the whole world. To initiate a war of aggression, therefore, is not only an international crime; it is the supreme international crime differing only from other war crimes in that it contains within itself the accumulated evil of the whole.[27]

This statement is law, and what is more, "This law applies for all times, in all places and for everyone, victor and vanquished."[28] The initiating and waging of aggressive war is now indisputably criminal. No more important decision was ever made by any court.

PART SEVEN

Justice After Nuremberg

CHAPTER 39

Principles and Precedent

We have an obligation to carry forward the lessons of Nuremberg.
Those accused of war crimes against humanity and genocide must
be brought to justice. There must be peace for justice to prevail, but
there must be justice when peace prevails.

President William Jefferson Clinton

THE MOST significant thing about Nuremberg is that it happened.
More important than the punishment of the defendants, or the pronouncements of law, is the simple fact that for the first time in history the judicial process was brought to bear against those who had
offended the conscience of humanity by committing acts of military
aggression and related crimes.

No one would deny that what was done by Hitler and his
confederates, as recounted in these pages, was morally wrong.
Nuremberg marked the transition of these wrongs from the moral to
the legal plane. Crimes against humanity, and the initiating and
waging of aggressive war, are now juridical concepts. International
law, in this vast area, has passed from conscience to precept. We have,
in the words of Mr. Henry L. Stimson, brought "our law in balance
with the universal moral judgment of mankind."[1] As to this contribution of Nuremberg, Dr. Ralph Barton Perry wrote:

Had those responsible for the aggressions and inhumanities of the Nazi
regime been allowed to go unpunished, mankind would have lost a
supreme opportunity to crystallize in legal form a recognized and pressing
moral necessity. The time was ripe to step across the line from conscience
to a legal order; and to create a legal precedent for future time. Those who

would have preferred exoneration, or assassination, or summary execution, were not the friends of law in principle, but the defenders of outmoded law or of the perpetuation of lawlessness.[2]

Principles of Law

The Nuremberg trial emerged as a new legal process in which effect was given to developing standards of just and unjust behavior in international law. The vanquished were brought before the bar of justice by the victors, to be sure, but the principles applied were *sui generis*. In addition to the use of the judicial process to determine guilt and assess penalties for crimes committed against international law, the Nuremberg process established and applied seven basic legal principles:

1. *The initiating and waging of aggressive war is a crime.* The Tribunal held that leaders of a state, including military commanders when they act in a political capacity, who initiate and wage an aggressive war, are guilty of a crime for which they may be tried by a duly constituted international tribunal. Those who initiate and wage aggressive war must answer for the killings and devastation inevitably resulting therefrom to the extent of their participation in the planning and prosecution of the war. They may not exculpate themselves by a plea that such killings and devastation are the unavoidable incidents of war.

2. *Conspiracy to wage aggressive war is a crime.* The Tribunal construed the Charter as conferring jurisdiction upon it to find that a conspiracy to initiate and wage aggressive war is a crime. The Tribunal did not find authority for charging the defendants with a separate count of conspiracy to commit war crimes or crimes against humanity. The crime of conspiring to commit aggressive war must be closely related to the actual outbreak of armed conflict and extend only to those who meet conspiratorially to plan specific acts of aggression.

3. *The violation of the laws or customs of war is a crime.* The specifications of war crimes in the Hague and Geneva conventions are declaratory of the laws and customs of war which forbid the mistreatment of prisoners of war, or killings and spoliation in war not justified by military necessity. The concept of total war has not made obsolete the rules of humane warfare.

4. *Inhumane acts upon civilians in execution of, or in connection with, aggressive war constitute a crime.* The Tribunal limited the charge of crimes against humanity under the Charter to acts of barbarism against civilians committed in execution of, or in connection with, aggressive war. Such limitations would not apply to the charge of crimes against humanity before a permanent International Criminal Court.

5. *Individuals may be held accountable for crimes committed by them as heads of state.* The Nuremberg judgment is a positive precedent for holding the leaders of a state, who formulate its policy and direct its actions into channels which are criminal under international law, personally responsible for such crimes. They cannot plead that what they did was state, rather than individual, accountability. The Tribunal said: "Crimes against international law are committed by men, not by abstract entities, and only by punishing individuals who commit such crimes can the provisions of international law be enforced."[3]

6. *Individuals may be held accountable for crimes committed by them pursuant to superior orders.* Only by holding individuals accountable for the consequences of their own acts, even when carried out in pursuance of higher authority, can war crimes be restrained. As the Tribunal said:

> That a soldier was ordered to kill or torture in violation of the international law of war has never been recognized as a defense to such acts of brutality, though, as the Charter here provides, the order may be urged in mitigation of the punishment. The true test, which is found in varying degrees in the criminal law of most nations, is not the existence of the order, but whether moral choice was in fact possible.[4]

7. *An individual charged with crime under international law is entitled to a fair trial.* The Tribunal's judgment makes clear that persons accused of crime in international law must be given a fair trial. They are entitled to a presumption of innocence which can only be overcome by evidence which establishes guilt beyond a reasonable doubt. In the acquittal of Schacht the Tribunal said: "The Tribunal has considered the whole of this evidence with great care, and comes to the conclusion that this necessary inference has not been established *beyond a reasonable doubt.*"[5] And in acquitting Von Papen it stated:

"But it is not established *beyond a reasonable doubt* that this was the purpose of his activity. . . ."[6] Confessions may not be used when taken under duress, as in the case of Hans Fritzsche whose admission of guilt to his Soviet captors was disregarded by the Tribunal.

The Nuremberg trial affords no precedent for a drumhead court-martial of the leaders of a vanquished state. It stands for a fair trial in which the rights of the accused are respected, an adequate defense is assured, and convictions are based upon evidence establishing guilt beyond a reasonable doubt. Nuremberg fulfilled the unique opportunity presented at the end of World War II to convert vital moral principles into valid rules of law.

Pre-war Proceedings

Legal scholars had long distinguished the just from the unjust war, finding in the former a moral permissibility totally absent in the latter. But war, even aggressive war, came to be accepted as an effective and seemingly indispensable means of adjusting the conflicting claims of nations. Its participants were professional soldiers who engaged in combat as a means of livelihood or were inducted serfs who had no choice in the matter. The general population was not involved in combatant roles. And the winners and losers were kings and nobles. Ordinary people were often victims but they were usually observers rather than participants. The moral judgment of society therefore was addressed to principles of proper conduct *in* war rather than to the outlawry *of* war. But as Mr. Henry L. Stimson wrote: "The attempt to moderate the excesses of war without controlling war itself was doomed to failure by the extraordinary scientific and industrial developments of the nineteenth and twentieth centuries."[7] Efforts to "humanize" war could not suffice when war became "total."

In the effort to prevent the outbreak of war in this period nations sought allies. When a *causus belli* occurred, however, military alliances designed to prevent war sometimes had the effect of escalating the conflict. That was the outcome of the assassination of Archduke Francis Ferdinand, heir to the Habsburg throne, and his wife, in Sarajevo, then the seat of Bosnia-Hercegovina, on June 28, 1914. At that time the uneasy peace of Europe hinged on the balance of the triple alliance—Germany, Austria-Hungary, and Italy, and the triple entente—Great Britain, France, and Russia. When Austria-Hungary declared war on Serbia to avenge the Sarajevo murders, Russia came to the aid of Serbia, and the skein of treaties upon which the peace of Europe depended, unraveled. Germany sided with Austria-Hungary, France supported Russia, and Great Britain aligned herself with France.

The war that began in 1914 involved more nations and combatants than any previous war in history. It was the first armed conflict between nations able to command the energies of all their subjects and the products and resources of industrial technology; and it was the first war which demanded virtually universal conscription.

After that terrible conflict the efforts of political leaders were directed less to ameliorating the lot of those involved *in* war and more to the elimination *of* war. The moral judgment of humankind came to be applied not merely to excesses not justified by military necessity but to the justification of military action in the first place. The Briand-Kellogg Pact restated in positive terms the condemnation of war, while recognizing the right of nations to defend against aggression.

World War II proved again the terrible cost of total war. While that conflict raged, decisions were made to establish that aggressive war is criminal. These decisions resulted in the Nuremberg trial in which legal effect was given to Grotian concepts of the just and unjust war, and through which the perpetrators of war and war crimes and of crimes against humanity committed in the course of war were justly punished. That proceeding led to other war crimes trials after World War II.

Post-war Proceedings

The effect of the Nuremberg trial varied according to the several types of war crimes proceedings. In the Far East the Tokyo Military Tribunal conducted a trial of major Japanese war criminals in which the Nuremberg pattern was closely followed. On the other hand, special military tribunals, before which persons accused of ordinary war crimes were tried, were only slightly influenced by the Nuremberg trial. Denazification proceedings were instituted against thousands of former Nazis by special German tribunals which applied some of the findings of the International Military Tribunal. And, pursuant to legislation of the Control Council for Germany, some of the occupying powers brought other Nazi leaders to trial for the same categories of crime charged against the Nuremberg defendants.

TOKYO TRIAL. An international military tribunal was established in the Far East pursuant to a proclamation of January 19, 1946, issued by General Douglas MacArthur as the Supreme Commander

---

TABLE I

United States, *et al.*, v. Tojo, *et al.*

The "Tokyo War Crimes Trial" charged that certain Japanese political and military leaders had, over a period of seventeen years prior to 1945, engaged in criminal acts against the law of nations comprising crimes against peace, conventional war crimes, and crimes against humanity.

The judges were: Sir William F. Webb (Australia), E. Stuart McDougall, K.B. (Canada), Mei Ju-ao (China), Lord Patric (Great Britain), Judge Bernard V. A. Roling (The Netherlands), Mr. Justice Northcroft (New Zealand), Major General I. M. Zaryanov (Soviet Union), Judge John P. Higgins and, after July 22, 1946, Major General Myron C. Cramer (United States), Judge Henri Bernard (France), Judge R. M. Pal (India), and Justice Delfin Jaranilla (Philippines). Of twenty-eight defendants charged in the indictment the case proceeded to judgment against twenty-five. Sentences imposed were as follows:

Kenji Dohihara	Death	Koki Hirota	Death
Seichiro Itagaki	Death	Heitaro Kumura	Death
Iwane Matsui	Death	Akira Muto	Death
Hideki Tojo	Death	Sadao Araki	Life
Kingaro Hashimoto	Life	Shunroku Hata	Life
Kiichiro Hiranuma	Life	Naoki Hoshino	Life
Koichi Kido	Life	Juniaki Koiso	Life
Jior Minami	Life	Hiroshi Oshima	Life
Takazumi Oka	Life	Shigetaro Shimada	Life
Kenryo Sato	Life	Okinori Kaya	Life
Teiichi Suzuki	Life	Yoshijiro Umezu	Life
Toshio Shiratori	Life	Mamoru Shigemitsu	7 years
Shigenori Togo	20 years		

of the Allied Powers in the Pacific. The tribunal of eleven members convened on April 29, 1946, to receive the indictment. The trial opened for the taking of evidence on June 4, 1946, and judgment was handed down during the period November 4–11, 1948. The Charter of the Tokyo Tribunal incorporated the same definitions of crime that had been set forth in the Charter of the International Military Tribunal, and the specifications of charges closely followed the Nuremberg indictment. While procedures applied by the tribunals were dissimilar in some respects, the Tokyo Tribunal followed the rulings of the International Military Tribunal on the law of the case. It held specifically that crimes against humanity and the initiating and waging of aggressive war are cognizable offenses against international law for the commission of which individuals may be tried and punished by a competent international military tribunal. The chief of counsel for the United States at the Tokyo trial, Mr. Joseph B. Keenan, wrote that the Tokyo case "confirmed and reinforced the massive achievements of the Nuremberg Tribunal in these matters."[8] Seven defendants received the death sentence at Tokyo; sixteen were sentenced to be confined in prison for life, one for twenty years, and one for seven years.

MILITARY COMMISSIONS. The Nuremberg proceeding constituted a limited precedent for the trial of persons charged with the commission of conventional war crimes. In Germany, these trials were conducted by occupying powers through their own military commissions. Special military tribunals were established at Dachau for this purpose by order of the United States Commander, European Theater. Of the 1,672 individuals brought to trial, 1,090 ultimately were sentenced, 426 receiving the death penalty. These trials, which were completed on December 30, 1947, were based upon acts which occurred during the course of the war, and which fell within the definition of traditional war crimes.

DENAZIFICATION PROCEEDINGS. On March 5, 1946, the three German Laender in the United States zone of occupation joined in the enactment and promulgation of the Law for Liberation from National Socialism and Militarism (more commonly known as the denazification law). The purpose of this law was not primarily to punish, but rather to remove from leadership, Germans who had taken a leading role in the Nazi conspiracy. Accused persons were subject to classification as major offenders, offenders, lesser offenders, and followers. Major offenders were subject to permanent exclusion from public office, confiscation of property, and detention for as long as ten years. The law called for the registration of over thirteen million persons in the United States zone of occupation. Of these, approximately three million were found to be subject to classification under the law. Ultimately, about 545 tribunals, employing a personnel of 22,000, were engaged in the task of classifying offenders in the United States zone. In spite of amnesties granted by the Military Governor, over 930,000 individuals were actually tried by these tribunals. Only 1,549 were classified as major offenders, but 21,000 were denominated as offenders, 104,000 as lesser offenders, and 475,000 as followers. Over 500,000 persons were fined, 122,000 suffered restrictions upon employment, 25,000 were subjected to property confiscation, 22,000 were declared ineligible to hold public office, 30,000 were required to perform special labor, and 9,000 were sentenced to terms in prison.

SUBSEQUENT PROCEEDINGS. On December 20, 1945, the Control Council for Germany enacted Law No. 10 for the purpose of establishing "a uniform legal basis in Germany for the prosecution of war criminals and other similar offenders, other than those dealt with by the International Military Tribunal."[9] Both the Moscow Declaration of October 30, 1943, and the London Agreement of August 8, 1945, were made integral parts of the law. Cognizable crimes included crimes against peace, war crimes, and crimes against humanity, as defined in the Charter of the International Military Tribunal. But in addition, "membership in categories of criminal groups or organizations declared criminal by the International Military Tribunal"[10] was specified as a separate crime. The law provided that any person found guilty of any of the crimes listed might be punished with imprisonment or even the death penalty. Each occupying authority within its zone of operations was empowered to arrest persons suspected of having committed a crime or crimes as defined in the law and to cause all persons so arrested and charged to be brought to trial before an appropriate tribunal.

The authority to impose heavy criminal penalties under Control Council Law No. 10 was alarming to the members of the International Military Tribunal who foresaw as a possible consequence of any declaration they might make of the criminality of organizations a widespread series of prosecutions based solely upon membership in such organizations. And they were further concerned that any such declaration of organizational criminality might result in heavy punishments imposed upon members who joined involuntarily, or without knowledge of the criminality of the organization, or who took no active part in its criminal activities. Mr. Justice Jackson shared this concern.

Accordingly, the Tribunal recommended in its judgment that punishment of individuals for membership in organizations declared criminal by it should be standardized throughout the four zones of occupation in Germany, that double punishments should be avoided, and that penalties should not exceed the sanctions provided by the Law for Liberation. In declaring the Leadership Corps of the Party, the SS, the SD, and the Gestapo to be criminal organizations, moreover, the Tribunal expressly excluded persons who had ceased to belong to them prior to the commencement of hostilities on September 1, 1939.

The Tribunal observed that criminal guilt is personal, and it warned that mass punishments should never be inflicted It recognized that an organization may be criminal if it consists of a group formed for, and engaged in, a common criminal purpose. But the Tribunal held that no member of such a group could be held personally liable by reason of membership if the member had no knowledge of the criminal purposes or acts of the organization, or joined it under compulsion, unless the member was personally implicated in the commission of specific acts.

The judgment of the International Military Tribunal constituted a direct precedent for the trials authorized by Control Council Law No. 10. In the United States zone these trials were prosecuted under the direction of Brigadier General Telford Taylor, who had been responsible for preparing and presenting to the International Military Tribunal the case against the German High Command. Mr. Justice Jackson had exercised his authority under direct orders of the President of the United States. On October 24, 1946, the Office of Chief of Counsel for War Crimes was transferred to the Office of Military Government for Germany (United States), and General Taylor was named to that post. His authority to try "second-line" leaders of Hitler's Germany in United States custody was provided by Military Government Ordinance No. 7, which became effective on October 18, 1946.

The purpose of Ordinance No. 7 was "to provide for the establishment of military tribunals which shall have power to try and punish persons charged with offenses recognized as crimes in Article II of Control Council Law No. 10, including conspiracies to commit any such crimes."[11] The tribunals were to have three or more members. The Chief of Counsel for War Crimes was empowered to determine the persons to be tried by the tribunals and to prepare and file the indictments with the secretary general of the tribunals.

Article X of Ordinance No. 7 provided that findings of the International Military Tribunal "that invasions, aggressive acts, aggressive wars, crimes, atrocities or inhumane acts were planned or occurred"[12] were to be binding on the tribunals and not subject to question "except insofar as the participation therein or knowledge thereof by any particular person may be concerned."[13] And it further provided that statements of the International Military Tribunal in the judgment should "constitute proof of the facts stated, in the absence of substantial new evidence to the contrary."[14] In the Flick Case, Presiding Judge Sears declared that his tribunal would "indulge no implications therefrom to the prejudice of the defendants against whom the judgment [of the International Military Tribunal] would not be *res judicata* except for this article."[15] Other judges referred to the fact findings of the International Military Tribunal primarily for background information and not as proof of guilt of the individuals on trial before them. Thus, in the Pohl Case, Presiding Judge Toms stated: "The whole sordid history of the SS and its criminal activities has been told in detail in the judgment of the International Military Tribunal."[16] For the most part references to the opinion of the International Military Tribunal in the subsequent trials were on undisputed facts and on points of law.

In all, twelve trials, most of which involved several defendants, were completed in the subsequent proceedings conducted at Nuremberg under the authority of Military Government Ordinance No. 7. After taking into consideration the commutation of sentences ordered by the High Commissioner for Germany on January 31,

1951, thirteen defendants received the death penalty, eight were imprisoned for life, seventy-seven served terms of imprisonment, thirty-three were released on the basis of time already served, and one received a medical parole.

In eight of the trials some of the defendants were charged with membership in one or more of the organizations which had been declared criminal by the International Military Tribunal. All individuals charged with this offense were likewise accused of specific crimes. Ten were acquitted of the charge; sixty-four who were found guilty of membership in a criminal organization were also convicted of specific crimes; only nine were convicted solely of membership in a criminal organization. Of these nine, two received sentences of ten years, one of five years, and the other six were discharged on the basis of time served awaiting and during trial. The two ten-year sentences were subsequently commuted to time served.

The tribunals were careful to comply with the limitations imposed by the International Military Tribunal in finding individuals guilty of crimes because of membership in a criminal organization. In acquitting the defendant Rudolf Scheide of this charge in the Pohl Case, for example, the tribunal observed that while the defendant had admitted membership in the SS, "the prosecution has offered no evidence that the defendant had knowledge of the criminal activities of the SS, or that he remained in said organization after September, 1939 with such knowledge, or that he engaged in criminal activities while a member of such organization."[17]

The adjudication of the criminality of the SS, SD, Gestapo, and Leadership Corps of the Party was not of major importance in the subsequent proceedings conducted at Nuremberg against Nazi leaders remaining in United States custody, nor did it lead to any widespread action against members of the organizations as seems to have been feared by the International Military Tribunal. The principal value of the declaration was in the assistance it gave to the denazification tribunals in arriving at classifications of offenders under the denazification law, and in the finding, for historical purposes, that these four agencies of the Hitler government were the primary instrumentalities through which crimes of that regime, especially crimes against humanity, were perpetrated.

TABLE II

Case No. 1

United States v. Brandt, *et al.*

The "Medical Case" charged twenty-four defendants with responsibility for medical experiments upon concentration camp inmates and other living human subjects, without their consent, in the course of which murders, tortures, and other inhuman acts were committed.

The members of the Tribunal were: Judge Walter B. Beals, presiding judge, Judges Harold L. Sebring and Johnson T. Crawford, members, and Judge Victor C. Swearingen, alternate member.

Eight of the defendants were acquitted. Sentences imposed upon the other defendants were:

Defendant	*Sentence*	*Commutation*
Karl Brandt	Death	
Siegfried Handloser	Life	20 years
Oskar Schroeder	Life	15 years
Karl Genzken	Life	20 years
Karl Gebhardt	Death	
Rudolf Brandt	Death	
Joachim Mrugowsky	Death	
Helmut Poppendick	10 years	Time served
Wolfram Sievers	Death	
Gerhard Rose	Life	15 years
Viktor Brack	Death	
Hermann Becker-Freyseng	20 years	10 years
Waldemar Hoven	Death	
Wilhelm Beiglboeck	15 years	10 years
Herta Oberheuser	20 years	10 years
Fritz Fischer	Life	15 years

TABLE III

CASE No. 2

United States v. Erhard Milch

The "Milch Case" charged the defendant Erhard Milch with the exploitation of slave labor and the perpetration of medical experiments upon inmates of concentration camps.

The members of the Tribunal were: Judge Robert M. Toms, presiding judge, Judges Fitzroy D. Phillips and Michael A. Musmanno, members, and Judge John J. Speight, alternate member. Milch was convicted and sentenced to imprisonment for life. His sentence was commuted to fifteen years.

TABLE IV

CASE No. 3

United States v. Josef Altstoetter, et al.

The "Justice Case" charged sixteen defendants with the commission of war crimes and crimes against humanity through abuse of the judicial process and the administration of justice.

The members of the Tribunal were: Judge Carrington T. Marshall, presiding judge (to June 19, 1947), Judge James T. Brand, presiding judge (after June 19, 1947), Judge Mallory B. Blair, member, and Judge Justin W. Harding, alternate member, and member (from June 19, 1947).

Of the fourteen defendants who remained in the trial through judgment four were acquitted. Sentences imposed upon the other defendants were:

Defendant	Sentence	Commutation
Franz Schlegelberger	Life	Medical parole
Herbert Klemm	Life	20 years
Curt Rothenberger	7 years	
Ernst Lautz	10 years	Time served
Wolfgang Mettgenberg	10 years	
Wilhelm von Ammon	10 years	Time served
Guenther Joel	10 years	Time served
Oswald Rothaug	Life	20 years
Rudolf Oeschey	Life	20 years
Josef Altstoetter	5 years	

TABLE V

CASE NO. 4

United States v. Pohl, *et al.*

The "Pohl Case" charged eighteen defendants with the administration of the concentration camps or of economic enterprises of the
SS conducted with slave labor.

The members of the Tribunal were: Judge Robert M. Toms, presiding judge, Judges Fitzroy D. Phillips and Michael A. Musmanno,
members, and Judge John J. Speight, alternate member.

Three of the defendants were acquitted. Sentences imposed upon
the other defendants were:

Defendant	*Sentence*	*Commutation*
Oswald Pohl	Death	
Franz Eirenschmalz	Death	9 years
Karl Sommer	Life	20 years
Karl Mummenthey	Life	20 years
August Frank	Life	15 years
Heinz Karl Fanslau	20 years	15 years
Georg Loerner	Life	15 years
Hans Loerner	10 years	Time served
Hans Baier	10 years	Time served
Hans Bobermin	15 years	Time served
Hermann Pook	10 years	Time served
Leo Volk	10 years	8 years
Erwin Tschentscher	10 years	Time served
Max Kiefer	20 years	Time served
Hans Hohberg	10 years	Time served

TABLE VI

CASE NO. 5

United States v. Friedrich Flick, *et al.*

The "Flick Case" charged six defendants, who were leading officials in the Flick concern, with criminal conduct relating to slave labor, the spoliation of property in occupied France and the Soviet Union, and the "Aryanization" of Jewish industrial and mining properties.

The members of the Tribunal were: Judge Charles B. Sears, presiding judge, Judges Frank N. Richman and William C. Christianson, members, and Judge Richard D. Dixon, alternate member.

Three of the defendants were acquitted. Sentences imposed upon the other defendants were: Friedrich Flick, 7 years; Otto Steinbrinck, 5 years; Bernhard Weiss, 2½ years. None of the sentences were commuted.

TABLE VII

CASE NO. 6

United States v. Carl Krauch, *et al.*

The "I. G. Farben Case" charged 24 defendants, who were the leaders of the I. G. Farben concern, with spoliation of property in invaded countries and participation in Hitler's slave labor program.

The members of the Tribunal were: Judge Curtis Grover Shake, presiding judge, Judges James Morris and Paul M. Herbert, members, and Judge Clarence F. Merrill, alternate member.

The case proceeded to judgment against 23 defendants. Of these, ten were acquitted. Sentences imposed upon the other defendants were:

Defendant	Sentence	Defendant	Sentence
Carl Krauch	6 years	Hermann Schmitz	4 years
Georg von Schnitzler	5 years	Fritz ter Meer	7 years
Otto Ambros	8 years	Ernst Buergin	2 years
Heinrich Buetefisch	6 years	Paul Haefliger	6 years
Max Ilgner	3 years	Friedrich Jaehne	1½ years
Heinrich Oster	2 years	Walter Duerrfeld	8 years
Hans Kugler	1½ years		

None of the sentences of these defendants were commuted.

TABLE VIII

CASE NO. 7

United States v. Wilhelm List, *et al.*

The "Hostage Case" charged 12 defendants, who were generals assigned to southeastern Europe, with criminal disregard of the civilized rules of warfare in respect to the treatment of hostages and civilians.

The members of the Tribunal were: Judge Charles F. Wennerstrum, presiding judge, and Judges Edward F. Carter and George J. Burke, members.

The case proceeded to judgment against 10 defendants. Of these, two were acquitted. Sentences imposed upon the other defendants were:

Defendant	Sentence	Commutation
Wilhelm List	Life	
Walter Kuntze	Life	
Lothar Rendulic	20 years	10 years
Wilhelm Speidel	20 years	Time served
Helmuth Felmy	15 years	10 years
Ernst von Leyser	10 years	Time served
Hubert Lanz	12 years	Time served
Ernst Dehner	7 years	Time served

TABLE IX

CASE NO. 8

United States v. Ulrich Griefelt, *et al.*

The "RuSHA Case" charged 14 defendants, who were the high officials in the Race and Settlement Office of the SS Elite Guard and related offices, with carrying out systematic programs of genocide.

The members of the Tribunal were: Judge Lee B. Wyatt, presiding judge, and Judges Daniel T. O'Connell and Johnson T. Crawford, members.

One of the defendants was acquitted. Five defendants were discharged as having served sufficient time before and during the trial. Sentences imposed upon the other defendants were:

Defendant	Sentence	Commutation
Ulrich Griefelt	Life	
Rudolf Creutz	15 years	10 years
Herbert Huebner	15 years	Time served
Werner Lorenz	20 years	15 years
Heinz Brueckner	15 years	Time served
Otto Hofmann	25 years	15 years
Richard Hildebrandt	25 years	
Fritz Schwalm	10 years	Time served

TABLE X

CASE No. 9

United States v. Otto Ohlendorf, *et al.*

The "Einsatzgruppen Case" charged 23 defendants, who were officers of the SS Elite Guard and in charge of the extermination squads, with responsibility for the murder, as the International Military Tribunal found, of 2,000,000 people.

The members of the Tribunal were: Judge Michael A. Musmanno, presiding judge, Judges John J. Speight and Richard D. Dixon, members.

The case proceeded to judgment against 22 defendants. One defendant was discharged as having served sufficient time before and during the trial. Sentences imposed upon other defendants were:

Defendant	Sentence	Commutation
Paul Blobel	Death	
Ernst Biberstein	Death	Life
Walter Blume	Death	25 years
Werner Braune	Death	
Walter Haensch	Death	15 years
Waldemar Klingelhoefer	Death	Life
Erich Naumann	Death	
Otto Ohlendorf	Death	
Adolf Ott	Death	Life
Martin Sandberger	Death	Life
Heinz Hermann Schubert	Death	10 years
Willy Seibert	Death	15 years
Eugen Steimle	Death	20 years
Heinz Jost	Life	10 years
Gustav Nosske	Life	10 years
Waldemar von Radetzky	20 years	Time served
Erwin Schulz	20 years	15 years
Franz Six	20 years	10 years
Lothar Fendler	10 years	8 years
Feliz Ruehl	10 years	Time served
Eduard Strauch	Death	

TABLE XI

CASE NO. 10

United States v. Alfred Krupp, *et al.*

The "Krupp Case" charged 12 defendants, who were among the highest executives in the Krupp industrial empire, with slave labor and spoliation for the aggrandizement of the concern.

The members of the Tribunal were: Judge H. C. Anderson, presiding judge, and Judges Edward James Daly and William J. Wilkins, members.

The case proceeded to judgment against 11 defendants. One defendant was discharged as having served sufficient time before and during the trial. Sentences imposed upon the other defendants were:

Defendant	*Sentence*	*Commutation*
Alfred Felix Alwyn Krupp von Bohlen und Halbach	12 years and confiscation of all property	Time served and no confiscation
Ewald Oskar Loeser	7 years	
Eduard Houdremont	10 years	Time served
Erich Mueller	12 years	Time served
Friedrich Wilhelm Janssen	10 years	Time served
Werner Wilhelm Heinrich Lehmann	6 years	Time served
Max Otto Ihn	9 years	Time served
Karl Adolf Ferdinand Eberhardt	9 years	Time served
Heinrich Leo Korschan	6 years	Time served
Friedrich von Buelow	12 years	Time served

TABLE XII

CASE NO. 11

United States v. Ernst von Weizsaecker, *et al.*

The "Ministries Case" charged 21 defendants, who were high-ranking officials, with playing an important part in the political and diplomatic preparation for initiation of aggressive wars, violation of international treaties, economic spoliation, and diplomatic implementation of the extermination program.

The members of the Tribunal were: Judge William C. Christianson, presiding judge, and Judges Leon W. Powers and Robert F. Maguire, members.

The case proceeded to judgment against 19 defendants. Sentences imposed were:

Defendant	Sentence	Commutation
Ernst von Weizsaecker	7 years	Time served
Ernst Bohle	5 years	
Ernst Woermann	7 years	
Karl Ritter	4 years	
Edmund Veesenmayer	20 years	10 years
Hans Lammers	20 years	10 years
Richard Darre	7 years	
Otto Dietrich	7 years	
Wilhelm Keppler	10 years	Time served
Walter Schellenberg	6 years	
Gottlob Berger	25 years	10 years
Schwerin von Krosigk	10 years	Time served
Emil Puhl	5 years	
Karl Rasche	7 years	
Paul Koerner	15 years	10 years
Paul Pleiger	15 years	9 years
Hans Kehrl	15 years	Time served
Gustav Adolf Steengracht von Moyland	7 years	
Wilhelm Stuckart	3 yrs., 10 mos., 20 days	

TABLE XIII

Case No. 12

United States v. Wilhelm von Leeb, *et al.*

The "High Command Case" charged 14 defendants, who held lead-ing command or staff positions in the German Armed Forces, with personal responsibility for ordering the killing and mistreatment of prisoners of war and fostering and participating in a program involving the deportation and abuse of civilians in occupied areas.

The members of the Tribunal were: Judge John C. Young, presid-ing judge, and Judges Winfield B. Hale and Justin W. Harding, members.

The case proceeded to judgment against 13 defendants. Two were acquitted. One was discharged as having served sufficient time before and during the trial. Sentences imposed upon the other defendants were:

Defendant	*Sentence*	*Commutation*
Wilhelm von Leeb	3 years	
Georg Karl Friedrich-Wilhelm von Kuechler	20 years	12 years
Hermann Hoth	15 years	
Hans Reinhardt	15 years	
Hans von Salmuth	20 years	12 years
Karl Hollidt	5 years	
Karl von Roques	20 years	
Hermann Reinecke	Life	
Walter Warlimont	Life	18 years
Otto Woehler	8 years	
Rudolf Lehmann	7 years	

POST-NUREMBERG TRIALS. Great Britain and France held post-Nuremberg trials under the authority of Control Council Law No. 10 after the Nuremberg proceeding. The Soviet Union did not. For over half a century trials were conducted of German war criminals and non-German collaborators in the courts of the nations in which the crimes had been committed in accordance with the Moscow Declaration of October 30, 1943, or in the courts of nations with sufficient legal interest to conduct the prosecutions. Two of these trials arose out of the Final Solution.

No record has ever been found of a specific written order by Adolf Hitler directing the annihilation of the Jews of Europe. But he had called for their elimination in *Mein Kampf* and in public addresses, and it is certain that he intended their total destruction as part of his plan for Germanization of the Eastern territories and eventual Germanic rule over the European continent. The Final Solution could not have been initiated and carried out without Hitler's direct order. Heinrich Himmler, Chief of the German Police and the SS, was responsible for the execution of this secondary war against the Jews. Himmler would have been a defendant at Nuremberg had he not committed suicide while in British custody. Second to him was Reinhard Heydrich, the chief of the Reich Main Security Office before Kaltenbrunner. Heydrich disclosed the true meaning of the "Final Solution," the extermination of the Jews of Europe, to Nazi functionaries at the Wannsee Conference on January 20, 1942. Two individuals who had primary responsibility for the fulfillment of this incredible crime were Rudolf Hoess, the commandant of Auschwitz concentration camp, and Adolf Eichmann, the head of the Jewish Section of the Reich Main Security Office.

After completion of his testimony as a witness at Nuremberg, Hoess was delivered to Polish authorities. He was brought to trial in Warsaw for the crime of genocide against the inmates of Auschwitz. The affidavit which the writer had obtained from him at Nuremberg was introduced into evidence at his trial. Hoess recanted the portion of his confession in which he asserted that two and a half million persons had been destroyed at Auschwitz. He stated that the figure had been supplied to him by Adolf Eichmann and that he regarded the total as far too high. He declared that even Auschwitz had limits to its destructive possibilities. If so, why had Hoess given this figure to his British captors and again to me at Nuremberg? There may have been a macabre twist to Hoess's testimony. Since he was to be labeled the world's supreme murderer, in any case, he may have thought, in his twisted mind, to establish a record of mass killings never to be surpassed by anyone. This seems a reasonable supposition when it is remembered that Eichmann had bragged that he would jump laughing into his grave remembering the killing of five million Jews of Europe. Hoess was convicted of the commission of crimes against humanity and was hanged on the grounds of Auschwitz in 1947. The gallows still stand there as silent remembrance of the Auschwitz massacres and the man who directed the killing of innocents in that tomb of terror.

Adolf Eichmann escaped to Argentina where he lived under the pseudonym Ricardo Klement. In May, 1960, fifteen years after the end of the war, Eichmann was captured by Israeli agents and spirited to Israel where he was brought to trial for his role in the extermination of European Jews. In the first televised trial of history, Eichmann testified from a bullet-proof glass booth. His defense that he merely carried out orders to bring European Jews to Auschwitz and other destinations in Poland and was not responsible for what happened to them upon arrival fell upon deaf ears. "The man in the glass booth" was convicted and executed for his role in the Nazi program of genocide.

Two major war criminals who were never brought to trial were Joseph Mengele and Walter Rauff. Mengele was an SS pseudo-doctor at Auschwitz concentration camp who conducted macabre experiments upon inmates, principally twins, using them as laboratory animals in an effort to discover a basis for racial superiority. For more than 34 years after the war he eluded both German and Israeli pursuers. In 1949 he escaped to Argentina, where he lived until moving to Paraguay and finally to Brazil. On February 7, 1979, he drowned in the sea off Bertioga, 25 miles south of Sao Paulo. Walter Rauff was responsible for the development and production of mobile gas vans used to kill thousands of Jews and Communist functionaries on the Eastern front. He escaped to Chile and successfully evaded several attempts to obtain his extradition to Germany. He died of lung cancer in Santiago in May, 1983.

As the years passed other persons were brought to trial in national courts upon discovery of their complicity in Nazi crimes. Former Nazis who had fled to Canada, the United States, and other nations were returned to the countries from which they had emigrated, in accordance with the Moscow declaration of 1943, to be held for trial long after the crimes had been committed. Many individuals were charged with the commission of war crimes in German and Italian courts, and in the courts of nations which had been under Nazi occupation.

On August 9, 1993, the Supreme Court of Israel overturned the conviction of John Demjanjuk, who had been extradited from the United States and charged with crimes against humanity allegedly committed at Treblinka concentration camp by a guard known as "Ivan the Terrible," upon the ground that the evidence was insufficient to overcome conflicting evidence that the crimes had been committed by Ivan Marchenko, a different person.

The longest trial in modern French history, involving six months of testimony, concluded in Bordeaux, France, in 1998 with the conviction of Maurice Papon, 87 years of age, of ordering the arrest and deportation of 1,690 French Jews during the Nazi occupation, the great majority of whom were murdered at Auschwitz. The conviction was particularly significant since Papon was a refined and highly educated member of the French elite who rose to become a Cabinet minister after the war. Papon was the first and the last Vichy official to be prosecuted for the deportation of Jews from France. Addressing the jury of nine civilians and three judges Papon argued that it would be a humiliation for France to be linked with Nazi Germany in its responsibility for Jewish genocide. The jury accepted the implications of that humiliation by finding Papon guilty of complicity in the deportation of the victims while absolving him of their deaths at Auschwitz, accepting his plea that while he had reason to believe that the deportees would meet a cruel fate he did not know that they would be killed under a program of extermination instituted against the Jews by the Nazis. Papon was sentenced to ten years in prison rather than the twenty-year sentence sought by the prosecution. At his age it was, in fact, a life sentence.

The trial of Maurice Papon was in many ways a continuation of the 1987 trial of Klaus Barbie, the "Butcher of Lyon," who as head of the Gestapo in Lyon from 1942 to 1944 was found responsible for the deaths of 4,000 persons and the deportation of 7,500 others. For these crimes against humanity Barbie had been sentenced to life imprisonment.

One of the war crimes proved at Nuremberg was the massacre of 335 civilians, including 71 Jews, in the Ardeatine Caves outside Rome, ordered by Hitler to avenge the ambush killing of 32 German soldiers. Former SS Capt. Erich Priebke, 84 years of age, was extradited to Italy from the southern Andean resort of Bariloche, in Argentina, where he had been under house arrest since June, 1994, to stand trial for his participation in this crime. He did not deny his involvement in the murders, and was found guilty by the military court and sentenced to ten years. In 1998 the Italian military appeals court upheld the conviction and raised his sentence, at age 85, to life. Former SS Major Karl Hass, also 85, likewise received a life sentence for his participation in the massacre. The sentences were confirmed by Italy's highest appeal court.

Arrests and trials of Nazi war crime suspects became increasingly rare toward the end of the century in Germany. In 1992 Josef Schwammberger, the Nazi commander of a Jewish ghetto and slave labor camp in Poland, was convicted of crimes against humanity and sentenced to life imprisonment. On November 26, 1998, Alfons Goetzfried, a former low-ranking Gestapo officer at Majdanek concentration camp, near Lublin, Poland, was charged with taking part in systematic killings at the camp in November, 1943. Goetzfried admitted personally shooting to death 500 people, including women and children, during a two-day killing spree, called Operation Harvest Festival. The Majdanek camp was built in 1941 and became a principal site for Jewish extermination. By 1944, 360,000 of the camp's inmates had perished in its seven gas chambers or from brutal treatment by prison guards.

In 1991 Great Britain enacted a War Crimes Act which for the first time extended British jurisdiction over war crimes committed by non-British nationals in German-controlled territory during World War II. The legislation was passed after heated debates pitting those who contended that alleged war criminals could not expect a fair trial so many years after the alleged crimes were committed against those who argued that Britain should not become a hiding place for former Nazis. The first trial under the Act began on May 29, 1998, when a British magistrate ordered Anthony Sawoniuk held for the first World War II war crimes trial in Great Britain. Sawoniuk, aged 77 and deaf, was charged with killing four unnamed Jews in late 1942 in his home town of Domachevo in what is now Belarus but was then German-occupied Poland.

On June 16, 1998, Dinko Sakic, 76, was taken from his cell in Argentina and extradited to Croatia on a charge of commanding the Jasenovac concentration camp in Croatia from December, 1942, until October, 1944, where thousands of Serbs, Jews and Gypsies died under the Nazi puppet regime. His wife, Nada Sakic, suspected of carrying out torture, terror and intimidation of inmates in the women's block of the camp, was released for lack of evidence. The Sakic family had lived quietly in Argentina for nearly half a century until April, 1998, when Dinko Sakic admitted during an Argentine television interview that he had been the commandant of the notorious Jasenovac camp.

These were residual trials of minor World War II war criminals. Prosecutors were seldom able to locate reliable witnesses to crimes committed fifty or more years ago. And the accused were old, frequently in ill health, and scarcely able to defend themselves. The judicial inquest of Nazi Germany had ended. The world turned from punishing aggressions and related crimes of the past to preventing aggressions and related crimes in the future.

Nuremberg in History

Recognition of the validity of the Nuremberg principles was not sufficient to assure peace through law in the post–World War II era. In his final address to the Tribunal, Mr. Justice Jackson had warned that if humankind failed to eliminate the causes and prevent the repetition of the barbaric events proved at Nuremberg it would not be irresponsible to prophesy that the twentieth century might yet witness the doom of civilization. After Nuremberg the opponents abruptly changed and the capacity for world destruction vastly multiplied. Nazism was destroyed, and its evil philosophy discredited, but the democratic nations of the West faced the growing power and truculence of Soviet Russia and its allies in the East.

The dropping of the first atomic bomb upon Hiroshima on

August 6, 1945, assured the end of World War II, and brought into reality the incredible destructive power of nuclear weaponry. On October 4, 1956, the Soviet Union put *Sputnik,* the first manmade satellite, into orbit around the earth, and the opening of the atomic age, with its potential for the total destruction of humankind, brought reality to Justice Jackson's prophecy. The world was facing Armageddon at the end of only the twentieth century after the birth of Christ.

Thus began the period of the Cold War in which democratic nations of the West opposed the Communist system of the Soviet Union and its allies. It was a frightening period of modern history in which localized military actions threatened to escalate into nuclear war among great powers. Germany, once the aggressor, seemed destined to become the battleground in a new war between former Allies. Berlin marked the dividing line between East and West.

November ninth may be considered Germany's date with destiny in the twentieth century. On November 9, 1923, the aspiring dictator, Adolf Hitler, marched with his supporters into the center of Munich with the objective of seizing the Chancellorship of Germany. On November 9, 1938, Hitler, who by then had become both Chancellor and dictator of Germany, initiated *Kristallnacht,* the first major physical assault upon the Jews of Germany. And it was on November 9, 1989, that East and West Berliners openly breached the Berlin Wall, ending the division of Germany which had been central to the Cold War. At the Brandenburg Gate, on the eastern side of the wall, thousands burst into the old square that once was the center of an undivided Berlin. East Berliners scaled the fences and crossed the no-man's-land that had trapped so many of their comrades seeking to escape in the past. West Berliners climbed the wall and dropped into the welcoming arms of those below. Elsewhere, people passed freely through crossing points, without call for identity papers or search of cars. At Checkpoint Charlie the mood was especially buoyant. As midnight approached, young West Berliners stood upon the barricades, raising bottles of champagne which they sprayed on the crowds milling below. At 3:30 A.M. a man raced across the border waving a freshly printed edition of the *Berliner Zeitung.* "The Wall Is Gone," proclaimed the enormous headline, "Berlin Is Berlin Again." "Remember the ninth of November," shouted a middle-aged man over the roar of the jubilant crowd. He was thinking, of course, of November 9, 1989. But Germany, and the world, should never forget those other November ninths of the Hitler tyranny. Each marked a turn in Germany's destiny in the twentieth century.

Throughout the years of the Cold War, which did not end until the dramatic events of that November ninth, the world was apprehensive of the possibility of a third World War in this century between the Soviet Union and the United States, and their respective allies. The wars in Korea and Vietnam, in which the United States was directly involved, demonstrated the dangers inherent in the developing discord between communist and capitalist societies. In the international setting which then prevailed there was no possibility of a judicial assessment of aggression or of individual responsibility for crimes committed in the course of these confrontations.

The turn toward peace was initiated by the rise to power in the Soviet Union of Mikhail Gorbachev, who succeeded Konstantin Chernenko as general secretary of the Communist Party in 1985 and as president of the Soviet Union in 1988. His political acumen and skill enabled him to gain support for his plans of restructuring (*perestroika*), openness (*glasnost*), and democratization of the Soviet Union. In December, 1988, Gorbachev announced in a major speech to the United Nations a unilateral reduction of 500,000 Soviet troops over the ensuing two years and the withdrawal of 10,000 tanks from Eastern Europe. It was the beginning of the end of Soviet domination in Europe. On October 3, 1990, East Germany was unified into the Federal Republic of Germany. The Cold War in Europe was over.

The promise of peace among great powers did not reflect a world without conflict. Petty tyrants continued to commit crimes in the pattern of the German dictator. The urgency of establishing legal controls over post-Hitler tyrants became clear when on August 2, 1990, Iraqi military forces under orders of the Iraqi dictator, Saddam Hussein, attacked Kuwait with the declared objective of incorporating it as the nineteenth province of Iraq, in direct violation of a 1963 agreement in which Iraq recognized the independence of Kuwait. In addition to waging aggressive war, Saddam was responsible for the commission of war crimes in the launching of Scud missiles against civilian centers in Israel and Saudi Arabia, and the despoliation of oil properties in Kuwait by emptying tanks into the Persian Gulf and burning wells, refineries, and other oil facilities, and with crimes against humanity in the killing, torturing, raping, and forcible removal of Kuwaiti civilians. The war of aggression waged by Saddam Hussein against Kuwait was repulsed by a coalition formed under authority of the Security Council of the United Nations. But no criminal charges were brought against Saddam because an international criminal court was not in existence and the world community was unwilling to try him *in absentia* before an *ad hoc* tribunal (as Martin Bormann had been tried at Nuremberg), despite a resolution of former Nuremberg prosecutors published in the Congressional Record, which the writer had initiated, calling for his trial.

In 1991 Yugoslavia disintegrated into the political and ethnic groups from which it had been formed, leading to armed clashes. The following year reports of acts of genocide and inhumanity led to the establishment by the Security Council on May 25, 1993, of the International Criminal Tribunal for the Former Yugoslavia with the mission of bringing to an end the commission of war crimes by ensuring that persons guilty of atrocities would be brought to justice. The tribunal was authorized to prosecute individuals responsible for war crimes, genocide, crimes against humanity, and serious violations of international humanitarian law in the former Yugoslavia after January, 1991. The first president of the tribunal, Antonio Cassese, declared that the purposes of the tribunal were threefold: to do justice, to deter further crimes, and to contribute to the restoration and maintenance of peace.

Reports of incredible mass murders in Rwanda caused the Security Council on November 8, 1994, to establish a second tribunal to deal with genocide, war crimes, and crimes against humanity in Rwanda. Later in November the European Parliament urged that the United Nations prepare a convention establishing a permanent International Criminal Court. At a conference on the Nuremberg Trial at the University of Connecticut in 1995 President Clinton declared his personal support of these two war crimes tribunals. "By successfully prosecuting war criminals in the former Yugoslavia and Rwanda," he said, "we can send a strong signal to those who would use the cover of war to commit terrible atrocities that they cannot escape the consequences of such actions."[18] Of even greater significance was the President's endorsement of the creation of a permanent International Criminal Court by the United Nations. He declared that the establishment of such a court would be the ultimate tribute to the people "who did such important work at Nuremberg."[19]

The Commitment to Law

The victorious powers of World War II tried and convicted the leaders of Germany of crimes against peace, and the laws of war, and the principles of humanity itself. What they charged to others they cannot deny as binding upon themselves. It has become a test of faith that the victors now live by the rules of law they used to condemn and to punish the leaders of Hitler's Germany.

While with some plausibility the accused at Nuremberg could complain that no precedent existed in international law for holding the leaders of a state criminally responsible for initiating and waging aggressive war and committing concomitant crimes against humanity, no future aggressors may claim that defense. The precedent now stands, for the victors of World War II as well as for the vanquished in that war, that initiating and waging wars of aggression is criminal, and that those responsible for aggressive wars and related crimes may be held personally accountable in law. As Mr. Justice Jackson said, "While this law is first applied against German aggressors, the law includes, and if it is to serve a useful purpose it must condemn, aggression by any other nations, including those which sit here now in judgment."[20]

That the Nuremberg trial established a precedent for the judicial prosecution and punishment of those men who, through the instrumentality of a state subservient to their commands, engage in aggressive war, there can be no doubt. If Nuremberg stands for anything, it stands for that. If it has validity as a precedent for any purpose, it is that leaders of states can never again with impunity employ national power for aggressive war and related crimes. Of course a triumphant nation may wrongly accuse and corruptly convict. But the victor may dispose of the leaders of the vanquished state by other means, as well. The precedent is there, and what it stands for cannot be controverted. To initiate a war of aggression is *"the supreme international crime."*21

The principles of the Nuremberg trial have been accepted by the people of Germany and incorporated in their basic law. Article 24 of the Bonn Constitution stated that sovereign powers may be transferred by legislation to international institutions; Article 25 provided that the general rules of international law shall form a part of, *and shall take precedence over, federal law, creating rights and duties directly for the inhabitants of federal territory;* and Article 26 provided specifically that activities tending to disturb the peaceful relations between nations, *and especially the preparing for aggressive war,* shall be unconstitutional and shall be made subject to punishment. If Germany, defeated in World War II, could so readily accept these principles of law, how ill it would have been for the victors in that war to fail to honor them.

Responsible representatives of the United States have acknowledged that the Charter and the judgment of the International Military Tribunal are both binding precedents for the future. The chief delegate to the United Nations placed his endorsement on the principles of the Charter thirty days after the judgment of the International Military Tribunal had been handed down. In his opening address to the General Assembly, Mr. Warren R. Austin declared: "Besides being bound by the law of the United Nations Charter, twenty-three nations, members of this Assembly, including the United States, Soviet Russia, the United Kingdom, and France, are also bound by the law of the Charter of the Nuremberg Tribunal."22 The President of the United States in whose term of office the case was tried, Hon. Harry S. Truman, said of the trial and judgment:

I have no hesitancy in declaring that the historic precedent set at Nuremberg abundantly justifies the expenditure of effort, prodigious though it was. This precedent becomes basic in the international law of the future. The principles established and the results achieved place International Law on the side of peace as against aggressive warfare.23

On November 9, 1946, Mr. Francis Biddle, who had served as the United States member of the International Military Tribunal, recommended in a report to the President of the United States that the principles of the Charter should be reaffirmed by the United Nations. A few days later the American delegation proposed a resolution to that effect. On December 11, 1946, the General Assembly took note of the London Agreement of August 8, 1945, and the annexed Charter, and of the Charter of the Tokyo Tribunal, and affirmed "the principles of international law recognized by the Charter of the Nuremberg Tribunal and the judgment of the Tribunal."[24] This action of the General Assembly of the United Nations constituted recognition by the constituent members of that organization of the principles of the Charter and of the judgment. In the words of Dr. C. A. Pompe, "The resolution signified a recognition that judicial not political action had been taken, that Nuremberg did not signify an ephemeral, opportunistic deviation from the established rules, but a permanent, irrevocable change, and that it was not a unilateral provision but general law, binding the whole community, which had been applied."[25]

This world in which we live is subject to the overwhelming fact of force. Nature speaks to us in that idiom. The hurricane that rises from the sea and spreads havoc on the land; the earthquake that shatters the stillness of the day and brings buildings tumbling to the ground; the erupting volcano that sends boiling lava over green fields and quiet homes are forces which Nature may unleash in angry mood. Against these forces mortals have yet to prove their greater power. No one has shown the way to still the voice of the mighty hurricane or quell the mysterious shifts of underlying mountains, or stop the red lava in its flow to the sea. And yet, these forces of destruction do not possess the power to destroy humankind which human beings themselves have devised. The atomic age burst in fury upon the world. We are caught in the peril of that age. Manmade forces can now destroy man. Perhaps civilization is in its decline— and barbarism, its due. That will depend upon whether force or law triumphs in tomorrow's world.

Speaking to the Sixth International Congress on Penal Law on October 3, 1953, Pope Pius XII declared that "unjust war is to be accounted one of the very gravest crimes that international law must proscribe," and he called upon all civilized nations to elaborate a code of international law that would provide punishment for persons who initiate unjust wars or wage them with excessive cruelty. He called, too, for tribunals, impartially constituted, to pass judgment upon "unprincipled criminals who, in order to realize their ambitious plans, are not afraid to unleash total war."[26] The security of nations, like the security of individuals, is best preserved by impartial judges applying fair laws.

A civilized world must be a law-ordered world. Sir David Maxwell Fyfe wisely wrote:

> Most men at the close of the war wanted a better world. They approached the desire from different standpoints of national tradition and religious and political thought. Yet almost all are convinced that justice between man and man and between the individual and the State, based on an ordered system of law, is an essential prerequisite of comfort and security in a civilized community. The majority of mankind hoped to see an effective system of international justice set up to regulate the relations between States, and be a crown and unifying principle of municipal systems of law.[27]

In an address to the American Society of International Law, Mr. Justice Jackson offered this challenge: "If aggression is so wrong that international law calls upon our youth to die in remote parts of the world to stop it, these innocents have, I submit, a moral right to ask, 'What will you do about those persons guilty of it?'"[28] We must have the courage to find the way to make law supreme in international affairs, or we shall live forever in a world of force under a pall of fear.

Hitler and his confederates who led Germany in his regime are dead. They were the principal actors in a fearsome drama. But as Prospero foretold, they "were all spirits, and melted into air, into thin air. . . ."[29] The tyrant Hitler and his associates in crime will some day be forgotten; forgotten, too, may be their crimes. It is enough that tomorrow's world remember what today's world has learned through the bitter experience of this fallen regime—that tyranny leads to inhumanity, and inhumanity is death.

CHAPTER 40

The International Criminal Court

ALTHOUGH CRIMINAL JUSTICE is dispensed in almost every domestic society, by king or court, international criminal courts are a historical rarity. In 1474 a court comprised of judges from Austria, Germany, Switzerland and Alsace was convened, *ad hoc*, to try a certain Peter de Hagenbach for crimes allegedly committed by him during occupation of the town of Breisach. Four centuries later, in 1872, Gustav Moynier, a founder of the International Committee of the Red Cross, proposed the establishment of an international criminal court to have jurisdiction over war crimes. His proposal failed to gain the support of international lawyers and proposed states parties, and was never implemented.

At the end of World War I a commission of inquiry recommended that an *ad hoc* international criminal tribunal be established with jurisdiction over war crimes and crimes against humanity committed during the war. The Treaty of Versailles of June 28, 1919, called for the prosecution of Kaiser Wilhelm II, under Article 227, and of German war criminals, under Articles 228 and 229. The proposed trials did not materialize. The Netherlands refused to surrender Wilhelm for trial and the Allies ultimately acceded to a German proposal to conduct its own war crimes trials at Leipzig. These were less than a success. Of the 896 persons accused of war crimes by the Allies, only twelve were tried. Six were convicted and given small sentences. The Treaty of Peace between the Allied Powers and Turkey of August 10, 1920, called for the prosecution of Turkish officials responsible for the Armenian massacre of 1915. This, too, failed, and a general amnesty was granted on adoption of the Treaty of Lausanne of July 24, 1923.

The failure of the Allied Powers to establish an international tribunal to try German war criminals at the end of World War I provided a regrettable precedent for the German leaders in World War II. Punishment having been entrusted to the national courts of the defeated state in the first World War, who could anticipate the convening of an international court for the second? Indeed, it was argued by German defense counsel that although justice required the dismissal of the accused before the International Military Tribunal, the precedent of a postwar international criminal proceeding having been established at Nuremberg, defendants at the end of any *future* war could no longer interpose this defense!

The creation of the International Military Tribunal for the trial of the major German war criminals at the end of World War II was an innovation in international criminal law. Each of the victorious powers might have brought German defendants in its custody to trial before its own military tribunals. But to establish an international court, applying the rules and principles of international law, was novel. The thrust of the Nuremberg trial was to reach the architects of war, as well as violators of the laws of war, and the instigators and planners of crimes in war and against humanity, as well as simple executioners. The convening of an international military tribunal for this purpose was a distinct contribution of Nuremberg to international law.

The accused complained that a trial of this scope and magnitude should not have been brought before a special tribunal established for that purpose by the victors in the war. It would have been preferable to have held such a trial before a preexisting international judicial instrumentality. But none existed on November 20, 1945, at the commencement of the trial.

When the trial ended on October 1, 1946, a long struggle began to establish a permanent International Criminal Court competent to adjudicate crimes against peace, and related offenses, in the future. Shortly after the judgment was handed down an international congress was convened in Paris under sponsorship of the *Mouvement National Judiciaire Francais.* The congress, which consisted of lawyers from twenty-two countries, including all of the prosecuting powers before the International Military Tribunal, called for the establishment of an international criminal court. Judge Henri Donnedieu de Vabres, the French judge on the International Military Tribunal, proposed the following year that a criminal chamber of the International Court of Justice should be empowered to hear certain cases and that in addition a permanent international criminal court should be established. The General Assembly considered this proposal when drafting the Convention on the Prevention and Punishment of the Crime of Genocide, but failed to approve it. On the day it adopted the Genocide Convention, December 18, 1948, however, the General Assembly requested the International Law Commission to undertake a study of the proposal to create a permanent international criminal court. This was in addition to a directive of the General Assembly of November 21, 1947, requesting the International Law Commission to formulate the principles of international law which it considered to have been promulgated by the Charter of the International Military Tribunal as construed by the Tribunal.

In August, 1951, a Committee on International Criminal Jurisdiction, composed of representatives of seventeen member states, submitted a draft statute to the General Assembly calling for the formation of a court to try persons accused of crimes under international law. The committee submitted a revised Draft Statute in 1953, review of which was delayed pending consideration of the draft Code of Offenses by the International Law Commission. Review of the draft Code of Offenses was in turn delayed until consideration could be given to the report of a special Committee on the Question of Defining Aggression. It was not until 1974 that the General Assembly adopted a definition of aggression by consensus resolution. In the Cold War atmosphere then prevailing, however, there was no real disposition on the part of leading world states to adopt a statute establishing a permanent international criminal court or a code of international criminal law.

In 1989 the climate began to change. Trinidad and Tobago reintroduced in the General Assembly a proposal for a permanent international criminal court, and the General Assembly requested the International Law Commission to prepare a draft statute for a court. The International Law Commission considered the matter from its forty-second session, in 1990, to its forty-sixth session, in 1994, when its completed draft statute for an international criminal court was submitted to the General Assembly. By resolution 49/53 of December 9, 1994, the General Assembly decided to establish an *ad hoc* committee to review the major substantive and administrative issues arising out of the draft statute prepared by the International Law Commission and, in light of that review, to consider arrangements for the convening of an international conference of plenipotentiaries.

The Ad Hoc Committee on the Establishment of an International Criminal Court met in April and in August, 1995, to review the issues arising out of the draft statute prepared by the International Law Commission and to consider arrangements for the convening of an international conference. By resolution 50/46 of December 11, 1995, the General Assembly established a Preparatory Committee on the Establishment of an International Criminal Court to give further consideration to the major substantive and administrative issues arising out of the draft statute prepared by the International Law Commission and to prepare a consolidated text of a convention for an international criminal court in anticipation of the calling of a conference of plenipotentiaries. The Preparatory Committee, under leadership of Adriaan Bos of the Netherlands, held two sessions in 1996 and began the preparation of a consolidated text of an agreement for an international criminal court.

By resolution 51/207 of December 17, 1996, the General Assembly decided to hold a diplomatic conference of plenipotentiaries in 1998 with a view of finalizing and adopting a convention on the establishment of an international criminal court, and it directed the Preparatory Committee to complete the drafting of the text for submission to the conference. The Preparatory Committee met in three sessions during 1997. This directive was renewed by General Assembly resolution 52/160 of December 15, 1997. The Preparatory Committee met once in 1998, completing a draft Convention on the Establishment of an International Criminal Court which was transmitted to the United Nations Diplomatic Conference of Plenipotentiaries on the Establishment of an International Criminal Court which convened in Rome on June 15, 1998.

The General Assembly, by resolution 52/160, requested the Secretary-General to invite all States Members of the United Nations or members of specialized agencies and the International Atomic Energy Agency to participate in the Conference and also invited, as observers, representatives of organizations that held a standing invitation from the Assembly as well as representatives of regional intergovernmental organizations and other international bodies including the International Tribunals for the former Yugoslavia and Rwanda.

For more than fifty years major non-governmental organizations had supported the creation of an international criminal court. This objective had been a priority issue for many leading human rights and peace organizations. In February 1995 approximately thirty of these NGOs formed a Coalition for an International Criminal Court. Three years later the coalition consisted of eight hundred member organizations, approximately two hundred of which were invited by United Nations Secretary-General Kofi Annan to participate in the conference. Among them was the Committee of Former Nuremberg Prosecutors for an International Criminal Court, of which the writer was the organizer and coordinator. The objective of this committee was to support the establishment of a permanent international criminal court capable of adjudicating and enforcing the categories of crime first applied against the German defendants at Nuremberg.

The conference convened in Rome on June 15, 1998, under the chairmanship of Phillip Kirsch of Canada. Giovanni Conso of Italy was elected President. M. Cherif Bassiouni was appointed chairman of the Drafting Committee. In opening the conference Secretary-General Kofi Annan declared:

> After the defeat of Nazism and fascism in 1945, the United Nations was set up in an effort to ensure that world war could never happen again. The victorious powers also set up international tribunals, at Nuremberg and Tokyo, to judge the leaders who had ordered and carried out the worst atrocities. And they decided to prosecute Nazi leaders not only for "war crimes"—waging war and massacring people in occupied territories—but also for "crimes against humanity" which included the slaughter of their own fellow citizens and others in the tragedy we now know as the Holocaust.
>
> Was it enough to make an example of a few arch-criminals in two states that had waged aggressive war, and leave it at that? The General Assembly of the United Nations did not think so. In 1948 it adopted the Convention on

the Prevention and Punishment of the Crime of Genocide. And it requested the International Law Commission to study the possibility of establishing a permanent international criminal court. In this area, as in so many, the Cold War prevented further progress at that time. . . .

Events in the former Yugoslavia and in Rwanda overtook the slow processes by which the world was considering the creation of a permanent international criminal court. *Ad hoc* tribunals had to be set up for these two countries. . . . These tribunals are showing, however imperfectly, that there is such a thing as international criminal justice, and that it can have teeth. But *ad hoc* tribunals are not enough. People all over the world want to know that humanity can strike back—that whatever and whenever genocide, war crimes or other such violations are committed, there is a court before which the criminal can be held to account. . . .[1]

On June 17, the United States Ambassador to the United Nations, Bill Richardson, addressed the conference. After pointing to United States support of the establishment of the *ad hoc* tribunals for the former Yugoslavia and Rwanda, he introduced a note of caution into the coming deliberations. He endorsed the inclusion of serious violations of international humanitarian law—genocide, large-scale war crimes and crimes against humanity—but declared it premature "to attempt to define a crime of aggression for purposes of individual criminal responsibility." He opposed the concept of a self-initiating prosecutor and called for a dominant role by the Security Council in referring cases to the court. Within such limitations he advocated bringing to justice individuals "responsible for genocide, crimes against humanity, and war crimes" and preventing "the recurrence of such unspeakable acts in the future."[2]

The conference deliberated on the proposed Statute for an International Criminal Court over a period of five weeks. The Statute was adopted by consensus on July 17, 1998. United States Ambassador David Scheffer, the head of the U.S. delegation, held fast to limitations suggested by Ambassador Richardson and opposed adoption of the Statute at the end of the conference. The United States called for a roll call and the unrecorded vote showed 120 in favor to 7 against, with 21 abstentions. Voting against the statute were Iraq, Libya, Qatar, Yemen, China, Israel, and the United States. The Arab countries opposed the Statute primarily because it omitted the death penalty. China was concerned with the possibility of charges of offenses against human rights. Israel believed that the shifting of population into occupied territory should not have been included as a war crime. The United States feared that its role as a primary peace-keeper with American military forces deployed around the world might be adversely affected by spurious charges of war crimes. The United States championed, while India deprecated, the significant role of the Security Council in the initiating of cases before the Court. But the overwhelming majority of the nations represented at the Rome Conference approved the statute as the principal international document of peace and justice of the latter half of the twentieth century. Chairman Kirsch declared: "This is an extraordinary moment, a historical moment. I am not sure to what extent those present here know how important this is for the future of mankind."[3]

A ceremony was held at the Campidoglio on the afternoon of July 18 to celebrate the adoption of the Rome Statute of the International Criminal Court. Secretary-General Kofi Annan transmitted the Statute to the Italian Government, observing that it would remain in Italy's hands until October 17, 1998, after which it would remain open for signature at the headquarters of the United Nations in New York until December 31, 2000. "It is my fervent hope that by then a large majority of United Nations Member States will have signed and ratified it, so that the Court will have unquestioned authority and the widest possible jurisdiction," he declared.[4]

The Foreign Minister of Italy, Lamberto Dini, observed that the new Court complemented the Universal Declaration of Human Rights which had been adopted by the General Assembly of the United Nations fifty years before and which had declared that "recognition of the inherent dignity and of the equal and inalienable rights of all members of the human family is the foundation of freedom, justice and peace in the world."[5] He added, "Thanks to this Court, United Nations credibility has now been further enhanced."[6]

The mayor of Rome, the host of the ceremony, observed that the representatives of the United Nations had gathered at the end of the century to give to the world a crucial instrument to fight against crime, violence and genocide and to establish law, justice and peace in the "spirit of Rome." Professor Gerhard Hafner, speaking on behalf of the European Union, declared that the delegates to the Conference could justifiably say: *Roma locuta, causa finita* (when Rome has spoken the task is finished).

The Rome Statute for an International Criminal Court is a very long and detailed document, the product of many years of study by experts in criminal and international law. The following summary indicates the depth and comprehensiveness of this first attempt by treaty to bring the rule of law into force in international criminal proceedings.

ROME STATUTE OF THE INTERNATIONAL CRIMINAL COURT

PREAMBLE

The Preamble recalls the millions of children, women and men who were victims of the "unimaginable atrocities" of the twentieth century, observing that "such grave crimes threaten the peace, security and well-being of the world." It declares that these crimes of concern to the international community must not go unpunished. It reaffirms that all States must refrain from the threat or use of force against the territorial integrity or political independence of any State. And it calls for the establishment of an independent permanent International Criminal Court, complementary to national criminal jurisdictions and in relationship with the United Nations system, to take jurisdiction over the most serious crimes of concern to the international community.

PART 1. ESTABLISHMENT OF THE COURT

The International Criminal Court is established with jurisdiction over persons for the most serious crimes of international concern, complementary to national criminal jurisdictions. The Court, which is created by treaty and not by amendment of the Charter of the United Nations, is brought into relationship with the United Nations by an agreement approved by the Assembly of States Parties

and concluded by the President of the Court. The seat of the Court
is at The Hague in the Netherlands.

PART 2. JURISDICTION, ADMISSIBILITY
AND APPLICABLE LAW

The Court is given the right to exercise its functions and powers
on the territory of States Parties and by special agreement on the
territory of other States. Its jurisdiction is limited to the most serious crimes which are of concern to the international community as a
whole, namely: (a) genocide, (b) crimes against humanity, (c) war
crimes, and (d) the crime of aggression.

Jurisdiction over the crime of aggression is abated until a provision is adopted defining the crime and setting out the conditions under which the Court shall exercise jurisdiction with respect
thereto. In his remarks to the Conference, United States Ambassador
Bill Richardson had observed that the International Law Commission
had struggled for many years to find an adequate definition of
aggression, without success. Yet the International Military Tribunal
had no difficulty in finding Nuremberg defendants guilty of this
crime. And on December 14, 1974, the General Assembly by
Resolution 3314 (XXIX) adopted a consensus definition of aggression as "the use of armed force by a State against the sovereignty, territorial integrity or political independence of another State, or in any
other manner inconsistent with the Charter of the United Nations."
The consensus definition further specified acts of aggression, such as
invasion or attack, bombardment, blockade, and similar acts. The
United States, as the world's major peace-keeping nation, was con
cerned that its military personnel, stationed strategically in many
foreign countries, might be called into account, unjustly and un-
fairly, on charges of aggression, based upon peace-keeping missions.
The Statute provides protection against such eventuality since no
investigation or prosecution may be commenced or undertaken for a
period of twelve months after a request to that effect, subject to right
of renewal, is made by the Security Council under Chapter VII of the
Charter of the United Nations.

Aggressive war is subject to future definition, but the other core
crimes—genocide, crimes against humanity, and war crimes—are

specified in detail. In some cases the definitions are too detailed. Thus Israel declined to sign the Statute because the transfer of population into occupied territory is defined as a war crime. Since the thrust of the Statute is to reach only the "most serious" crimes of international concern, leaving to national jurisdictions the handling of relatively minor crimes, it might have been better to omit excessive detailing of some crimes, such as, for example, "outrages upon personal dignity, in particular humiliating and degrading treatment." Under the Statute the Court will be required to determine whether any such "outrage" qualifies as a "most serious" crime.

Of particular importance is the fact that crimes against humanity qualify as a crime within the jurisdiction of the Court whether or not incurred during an external or internal military conflict. The International Military Tribunal was restricted to finding that crimes against humanity were cognizable under the Tribunal's Charter solely when committed in connection with aggressive war or war crimes. In defining crimes against humanity as crimes in and of themselves, without regard to war or crimes of war, the international legal community has taken a tremendous step toward recognition of the inalienable rights of humanity.

The Court may exercise jurisdiction only with respect to crimes committed after the Statute enters into force. If a State becomes a Party to the Statute after it becomes operative the Court may take jurisdiction for that State only over crimes committed after it becomes a Party. The Court may exercise jurisdiction only if the State on the territory of which the alleged crime occurred, or the State of which the accused is a national, is a Party to the Statute or has accepted its jurisdiction.

The Court may exercise jurisdiction if a State Party has referred the case to the Prosecutor, the Security Council has referred the case to the Prosecutor under Chapter VII of the UN Charter, or the Prosecutor has initiated an investigation *proprio motu.* The Prosecutor may proceed *proprio motu* only upon authorization of the Pre-Trial Chamber. No investigation or prosecution may be undertaken for a period of twelve months after the Security Council has requested abeyance under Chapter VII. The Court shall determine that a case is inadmissible where the case is being investigated or prosecuted in good faith by a State which has jurisdiction over it. No person shall be tried for a crime of which that person has been convicted or acquitted in a prior judicial proceeding.

PART 3. GENERAL PRINCIPLES OF
INTERNATIONAL LAW

This Part sets forth basic principles of criminal law including the doctrines of *nullum crimen sine lege, nulla poena sine lege, mens rea,* and nonretroactivity *ratione personae.* Persons who commit or order the commission of crimes are to be held individually responsible and are not exempt because of official capacity. Military commanders are responsible for crimes committed by forces under their command as a result of failure to exercise proper control over such forces. The Statute sets out normal grounds for excluding criminal responsibility such as mental incapacity, duress, and self-defense. Acting pursuant to superior orders will not relieve a person of liability if he or she knew that the order was unlawful or the order was manifestly unlawful, as in the case of orders to commit genocide or crimes against humanity.

PART 4. COMPOSITION AND ADMINISTRATION
OF THE COURT

The branches of the Court are (a) the Presidency, (b) the Appeals, Trial and Pre-Trial Divisions, (c) the Office of the Prosecutor, and (d) the Registry. All judges serve as full-time members of the Court. There are eighteen judges, subject to increase according to need. Judges are chosen from among persons of high moral character, impartiality and integrity who possess the qualifications required in their respective States for appointment to the highest judicial offices. Judges are nominated by States Parties and elected by the Assembly of States Parties, taking into account the need for representation of the principal legal systems of the world, equitable geographical representation, and a fair balance of female and male judges. Judges hold office for a term of nine years and are not subject to reelection.

The President and the First and Second Vice-Presidents are elected by an absolute majority of the judges, serving for a term of three years, and are eligible for reelection for a single additional term. They collectively constitute the Presidency, responsible for the administration of the Court, except the Office of the Prosecutor.

The Appeals Division is composed of the President and four other judges, the Trial Division of not less than six judges, and the Pre-Trial Division of not less than six judges. The judicial functions of the Court are carried out in each Division by Chambers. The Appeals Chamber is composed of all judges of the Appeals Division, the Trial Chamber by three judges of the Trial Division, and the Pre-Trial Chamber by either three judges, or in some cases by one judge, of the Pre-Trial Division.

Judges may not engage in any activity which is likely to interfere with their judicial functions, and full-time judges may not engage in any other occupation of a professional nature. They may not participate in any case in which impartiality might reasonably be doubted on any ground. Either the Prosecutor or the accused may challenge a judge whose possible disqualification will be decided by an absolute majority of the judges.

The Office of the Prosecutor functions as a separate organ of the Court. It is responsible for conducting investigations and prosecutions before the Court. The Prosecutor is elected by secret ballot by an absolute majority of the members of the Assembly of States Parties. Deputy Prosecutors are elected in the same way from a list of candidates provided by the Prosecutor. The Prosecutor and the Deputy Prosecutors hold office for a term of nine years and are not eligible for reelection. They may not engage in any other occupation of a professional nature. Any question as to the disqualification of the Prosecutor or a Deputy Prosecutor is decided by the Appeals Chamber.

The Registry is responsible for the nonjudicial aspects of the administration and servicing of the Court. The judges elect the Registrar by an absolute majority by secret ballot. The Registrar holds office for a term of five years, is eligible for reelection once, and serves on a full-time basis. The Registrar appoints qualified staff personnel for the Court, and the Prosecutor appoints staff for his office, including investigators.

The compensation of the judges, Prosecutor, Deputy Prosecutors, Registrar and Deputy Registrar are fixed by the Assembly of States Parties. The official languages of the Court are Arabic, Chinese, English, French, Russian and Spanish, and the working languages are English and French.

The Rules of Procedure and Evidence enter into force upon adoption by a two-thirds majority of the members of the Assembly of States Parties. Amendments may be proposed by a State Party, the judges acting by an absolute majority, or the Prosecutor.

PART 5. INVESTIGATION AND PROSECUTION

The Prosecutor makes the initial determination whether to initiate an investigation. If the Prosecutor concludes that there is a reasonable basis to believe that a crime within the jurisdiction of the Court has been committed but that an investigation would not serve the interest of justice, he or she so informs the Pre-Trial Chamber.

If the Prosecutor determines that there is not a sufficient basis for prosecution or that prosecution is not in the interests of justice, the Prosecutor so advises the Pre-Trial Chamber and the State or the Security Council which referred the case. The Pre-Trial Chamber may request the Prosecutor to reconsider his or her decision.

In conducting an investigation the Prosecutor must consider incriminating and exonerating circumstances equally. The person under investigation may not be compelled to incriminate him- or herself or be subject to any form of coercion. The person under investigation is to be informed that there are grounds to believe that he or she committed a crime within the jurisdiction of the Court and that he or she has the right to remain silent, to have legal counsel of his or her choosing, and to be questioned in the presence of counsel.

The Pre-Trial Chamber may take appropriate measures to preserve evidence for subsequent proceedings. It shall issue an arrest warrant upon application of the Prosecutor where there are reasonable grounds to believe that the person has committed a crime within the jurisdiction of the Court, or the arrest of the person appears necessary to ensure his or her appearance at trial, that he or she does not obstruct the investigation or court proceedings, or to prevent continuation of the commission of the crime charged. As an alternative to seeking a warrant of arrest, the Prosecutor may request the Pre-Trial Chamber to issue a summons for the person to appear.

A State Party which has received a request for the arrest of a person shall bring the person before competent judicial authority to determine that the warrant applies to him or her, that the person has been arrested in accordance with due process, and that his or her rights have been respected. The person arrested may be given interim release, but once ordered to be surrendered by the custodial State he or she is to be delivered to the Court as soon as possible.

Upon appearance before the Court, the Pre-Trial Chamber satisfies itself that the person has been informed of the crimes which he or she is alleged to have committed and of his or her legal rights. Within a reasonable time after the accused person's appearance before the Court, the Pre-Trial Chamber holds a hearing to confirm the charges on which the Prosecutor intends to seek trial. The accused person is entitled to be present with counsel. He or she is provided a document containing the charges and informed of the evidence on which the Prosecutor intends to rely. At the hearing the Prosecutor is required to support each charge with sufficient evidence to establish substantial grounds to believe that the person committed the crime charged. The accused person may object to the charges, challenge the evidence presented by the Prosecutor, and present evidence in his or her own behalf. The Pre-Trial Chamber determines whether there is sufficient evidence to establish substantial grounds to believe that the accused committed each of the crimes charged. If the charges are confirmed the Presidency constitutes a Trial Chamber for the conduct of subsequent proceedings.

PART 6. THE TRIAL

The accused is present during the trial. The Trial Chamber ensures that the trial is fair and expeditious and is conducted with full respect for the rights of the accused. The Trial Chamber requires the attendance and testimony of witnesses and the production of documents and other evidence. At the commencement of the trial the Trial Chamber has read to the accused the charges previously confirmed by the Pre-Trial Chamber, affording the accused the right to plead guilty or not guilty to the charges.

If the accused pleads guilty the Trial Chamber determines whether the accused understands the nature and consequences of the admission of guilt, and that the admission is voluntary and is supported by the facts of the case. The Trial Chamber may consider an admission of guilt as not having been made and order the case to proceed under ordinary trial procedures.

Every accused person is presumed to be innocent with the burden on the Prosecutor to prove the guilt of the accused beyond a reasonable doubt. The accused is entitled to a public hearing and to be informed of the nature, cause and content of the charge against him or her in a language which he or she fully understands; to have adequate time to prepare a defense and to communicate freely with counsel of his or her choice in confidence; to be tried without delay; to conduct his or her defense in person or through counsel of his or her choice or counsel assigned and, if necessary, compensated by the Court; to examine witnesses against him or her and to present witnesses in his or her behalf; to have, free of cost, the assistance of competent interpreters and translators; to remain silent without such silence being a consideration in the determination of guilt or innocence; and to make an unsworn oral or written statement in his or her defense. And, finally, the Prosecutor must disclose to the defense evidence in the prosecution's possession which shows or tends to show the innocence of the accused, or to mitigate the guilt of the accused, or which may affect the credibility of the prosecution's evidence. The Court is required to take appropriate measures to protect the safety, physical and psychological well-being, dignity and privacy of victims and witnesses.

The Court may rule on the relevance or admissibility of any evidence, taking into account the probative value of the evidence and any prejudice that it may cause to a fair trial or to a fair evaluation of the testimony of a witness. The Court may take jurisdiction over offenses against the administration of justice, when committed intentionally, such as giving false testimony, presenting evidence known to be false, corruptly influencing a witness or an official of the court, or soliciting or accepting a bribe as an official of the Court.

If a State learns that information or documents of the State may be disclosed during the proceedings, and is of the opinion that disclosure would prejudice its national security interest, it may intervene in order to obtain resolution of that issue by the Court.

All of the judges of the Trial Chamber must be present at each stage of the trial and throughout the deliberations. The decision is based on the entire proceedings. It may not exceed the facts and circumstances set out in the charges and must be based solely on the evidence submitted at the trial. The decision is required to be in writing and must contain a full and reasoned statement of the Trial

Chamber's findings on the evidence and its conclusions. In the absence of unanimity the decision must contain the views of the majority and the minority. The decision or a summary thereof is delivered in open court.

The Court must establish principles relating to reparations to victims, including restitution, compensation and rehabilitation.

In the event of a conviction, the Trial Chamber considers the appropriate sentence to be imposed, taking into account the evidence presented and submissions made during the trial that are relevant to the sentence.

PART 7. PENALTIES

The Court may impose a penalty of imprisonment for a specified number of years, not to exceed a maximum of thirty years, or a term of life imprisonment when justified by the extreme gravity of the crime and the individual circumstances of the convicted person. In addition, the Court may impose a penalty of fine and forfeiture of proceeds, property and assets derived from the crime. A Trust Fund is to be established by decision of the Assembly of States Parties for the benefit of victims of crimes within the jurisdiction of the Court, and of the families of such victims.

PART 8. APPEAL AND REVISION

The decision of the Trial Chamber may be appealed by the Prosecutor or the convicted person for procedural error or error of fact or law. In addition, the convicted person may appeal upon any other ground that affects the fairness or reliability of the proceedings or the decision. The sentence may be appealed by the Prosecutor or the convicted person on the ground of disproportion between the crime and the sentence. If the Appeals Chamber finds that the proceedings appealed from were unfair in a way that affected the reliability of the decision or sentence, or that the decision or sentence appealed from was materially affected by error of fact or law or procedural error, it may reverse or amend the decision or sentence, or order a new trial before a different Trial Chamber.

The convicted person or the Prosecutor may apply to the Appeals Chamber to revise a final judgment of conviction or sentence on the ground that new evidence has been discovered that was not available at time of trial which, had it been proved at the trial, would have been likely to result in a different verdict, or it has been discovered that evidence upon which the conviction depended was false, or that one or more of the trial judges had committed an act of serious misconduct or breach of duty. Where miscarriage of justice has occurred the victim of the miscarriage may be awarded compensation.

PART 9. INTERNATIONAL COOPERATION AND JUDICIAL ASSISTANCE

States Parties are required to cooperate fully with the Court in its investigation and prosecution of crimes within the jurisdiction of the Court. If a State Party fails to comply with a request to cooperate by the Court the matter may be referred to the Assembly of States Parties or, if the Security Council has submitted the matter to the Court, to the Security Council.

The Court may transmit a request for the arrest and surrender of a person, together with the material supporting the request, to any State in which the person may be found. States Parties must comply with requests for arrest and surrender. The Court shall request the cooperation of a non-State Party in the arrest and surrender of any such person. A request for arrest and surrender is made in writing and contains or is supported by information describing the person sought sufficient to identify the person and his or her probable location, a copy of the warrant of arrest, and such additional information as may be necessary to meet the requirements for the surrender process in the requested State. In the case of a request for the arrest and surrender of a person already convicted the request is supported by a copy of any warrant of arrest, a copy of the judgment of conviction, information establishing that the person sought is the one referred to in the judgment of conviction, and a copy of any sentence imposed including a statement of the time served and time remaining to be served. In urgent cases the Court may ask for the provisional arrest of the person sought pending presentation of the formal request for surrender with supporting documents. States Parties are expected to comply with requests by the Court to provide assistance in relation to investigations or prosecutions.

PART 10. ENFORCEMENT

A sentence of imprisonment is served in a State designated by the Court from a list of States which have declared willingness to accept sentenced persons. The State of enforcement must notify the Court of any circumstances which could materially affect the terms of the imprisonment. The Court may at any time transfer a sentenced person to a prison in another State, and a sentenced person may at any time apply to the Court to be transferred to a prison of another State. The enforcement of a sentence of imprisonment is subject to the supervision of the Court and must be consistent with generally accepted standards governing the treatment of prisoners. A sentenced person in custody of the State of enforcement may not be subject to prosecution, punishment or extradition for any conduct engaged in prior to his or her delivery to the State of enforcement unless approved by the Court at the request of the State of enforcement.

The State of enforcement may not release the convicted person before expiration of the sentence pronounced by the Court which has the sole right to pass upon any reduction of sentence. When the convicted person has served two-thirds of the sentence, or twenty-five years in the case of life imprisonment, the Court must review the sentence to determine whether it should be reduced.

PART 11. ASSEMBLY OF STATES PARTIES

The Statute establishes an Assembly of States Parties. Each State Party has one representative in the Assembly who may be accompanied by alternates and advisers. Other States which have signed the Statute or the Final Act may be observers in the Assembly. The Assembly considers recommendations of the Preparatory Commission, provides management oversight to the Presidency, the Prosecutor and the Registrar regarding the administration of the Court, passes upon the budget for the Court, decides whether to change the number of judges, and performs other functions consistent with the Statute.

The Assembly has a Bureau consisting of a President, two Vice-Presidents and eighteen members elected by the Assembly for three-year terms. The Bureau meets as often as necessary, but at least once a year, to assist the Assembly in the discharge of its responsibilities.

The Assembly meets once a year at the seat of the Court or at the headquarters of the United Nations and holds special sessions when circumstances require. Special sessions are convened by the Bureau or at the request of one-third of the States Parties. Each State Party has one vote. Every effort is made to reach decisions by consensus. Where this is not possible matters of substance are decided by a two-thirds majority of those present with an absolute majority constituting the quorum for voting. Matters of procedure are decided by a simple majority of States Parties present and voting. If a State Party is in arrears of its financial obligations for the preceding two years it may lose its vote in the Assembly and the Bureau.

PART 12. FINANCING

The expenses of the Court and the Assembly of States Parties, including its Bureau and subsidiary bodies, are paid from assessed contributions of States Parties and funds provided by the United Nations, subject to approval of the General Assembly, covering especially expenses incurred due to referrals by the Security Council.

The Court may receive and utilize voluntary contributions from Governments, international organizations, individuals, corporations and other entities, in accordance with relevant criteria adopted by the Assembly of States Parties.

Contributions of States Parties are assessed in accordance with an agreed scale of assessment based upon the scale adopted by the United Nations for its regular budget.

PART 13. FINAL CLAUSES

Any dispute concerning the judicial functions of the Court are settled by decision of the Court. Any other dispute between two or more States Parties which is not settled through negotiations is referred to the Assembly of States Parties which may seek to settle the dispute itself or recommend further means of settlement including possible referral to the International Court of Justice.

After the expiration of seven years from the entry into force of the Statute any State Party may propose amendments thereto. The text of any proposed amendment must be submitted to the Secretary-General of the United Nations, who promptly circulates it to all States Parties. The Assembly of States Parties decides by majority vote of those present whether to take up the proposal. The adoption of an amendment at a meeting of the Assembly of States Parties on which consensus cannot be reached requires a two-thirds majority of States Parties. Except for the definition of crimes within the jurisdiction of the Court, an amendment enters into force for all States Parties one year after instruments of ratification or acceptance have been deposited with the Secretary-General of the United Nations by seven-eighths of the States Parties, provided that any State Party which has not accepted the amendment may withdraw from the Statute with immediate effect by giving notice no later than one year after the entry into force of the amendment.

Amendments affecting crimes within the jurisdiction of the Court enter into force for those States Parties which have accepted the amendment one year after deposit of their instruments of ratification or acceptance. If a State Party has not accepted the amendment, the Court may not exercise jurisdiction over a crime covered by the amendment when committed by the State Party's nationals or on its territory.

Amendments to the Statute which are of an exclusively institutional nature may be proposed at any time. The text of the proposed amendment is submitted to the Secretary-General of the United Nations or such other person designated by the Assembly of States Parties who promptly circulates it to all States Parties and to others participating in the Assembly. Amendments on which consensus cannot be reached are adopted by a two-thirds majority vote of States Parties. Such amendments enter into force six months after adoption.

Seven years after the entry into force of the Statute the Secretary-General of the United Nations is required to convene a Review Conference to consider any amendments to the Statute. Such review may include, but is not limited to, the list of crimes set out in the Statute. The Conference is open to those participating in the Assembly of States Parties. At any time thereafter, the Secretary-General of the United Nations, at the request of a State Party and with the approval of a majority of States Parties, is required to convene a Review Conference. The adoption of an amendment on which consensus cannot be reached requires a two-thirds majority of States Parties. Except for jurisdiction over crimes, an amendment enters into force for all States Parties one year after instruments of ratification or acceptance have been deposited with the Secretary-General of the United Nations by seven-eighths of the States Parties. Any amendment to the Statute affecting the definition of crimes enters into force for those States Parties which have accepted the amendment one year after the deposit of their instruments of ratification or acceptance. With respect to a State Party which has not accepted the amendment, the Court may not exercise jurisdiction regarding a crime covered by the amendment when committed by that State Party's nationals or on its territory. If an amendment has been accepted by seven-eighths of the States Parties, a State Party which has not accepted the amendment may withdraw from the Statute with immediate effect by giving notice no later than one year after the entry into force of the amendment.

The Statute enters into force on the first day of the month after the sixtieth day following the date of the deposit of the sixtieth instrument of ratification, acceptance, approval or accession with the Secretary-General of the United Nations.

A State Party may, by written notification addressed to the Secretary-General of the United Nations, withdraw from the Statute effective one year after the date of receipt of notification.

Over eighty nations have signed the Rome Statute including such leading states as Argentina, Australia, Austria, Belgium, Canada, Denmark, France, Germany, Greece, Ireland, Italy, the Netherlands, New Zealand, Norway, South Africa, Spain, Sweden, Switzerland, and the United Kingdom. Whether the Treaty will become operative in the year 2000 remains to be seen, but there is little doubt that it will take effect early in the third millennium.

The Rome Statute of the International Criminal Court is the initial treaty document establishing for the first time in world history an international criminal court, complementary to national criminal law jurisdictions and capable of bringing to justice persons guilty of aggressive war, war crimes, and crimes against humanity including genocide. It recognizes that crimes occur in the world which require the availability of an international judicial forum for resolution.

It is fitting that this great legal document should have been adopted in Rome. For as Virgil observed two thousand years ago:

> The Greeks shape bronze statues so real they seem to breathe,
> And carve cold marble until it almost comes to life.
> The Greeks compose great orations, and measure
> The heavens so well they can predict the rising of the stars.
> But you, Romans, remember your great arts:
> To govern the peoples with authority,
> To establish peace under the rule of law,
> To conquer the mighty, and show them mercy once they are conquered.
> —*Aeneid* VI, 847–853

The Rome Statute was the product of the efforts of many persons, beginning with the drafting of the Charter of the International Military Tribunal more than half a century before the Rome Conference. But even fifty years is just an hour in history's struggle for justice. Revision of the Rome Statute must be considered after seven years of trial with its law and procedures. Seven hundred years may pass before humankind is able to eliminate war in the world and establish a system of universal justice. Rome was the beginning. The end may never come. For like Rome itself, the struggle for peace, law and justice in the world is eternal.

If an H. G. Wells should write an *Outline of History* some thousands of years from now, the first chapter might be entitled "Prehistoric Civilization." In all likelihood the second chapter would be "The Age of War." Succeeding chapters would describe, in a period of enduring peace, the achievements which the free spirit of human beings can attain when their efforts are directed towards the search for truth and the betterment of life—rather than when applied to war and acts of inhumanity.

We have yet to close that second chapter on the history of the world. And mankind was never in greater peril. The lance is now a missile, the arrow is a rocket, and the cannon has become a nuclear bomb. Caesar's legions conquered primitive tribes. Today's armies can destroy the world.

It is in this context that the Rome Conference of 1998 assumes such great significance. It brought international law, its precepts and procedures, to a new standard of enforceability, and gave not only the hope, but the promise, of a future world in which criminal conduct is impermissible under international law. It marked the beginning of the end of "The Age of War."

Virgil's Rome is to be distinguished from the Rome of nineteen hundred ninety-eight. When Virgil speaks of the rule of law he is referring to Roman law, imposed upon the conquered territories. But the rule of law of Nuremberg, and of modern Rome, is universal, binding large states and small, victor and vanquished in any future war. The principle was most forcefully expressed by Mr. Justice Jackson when he declared that international law condemned aggression by every nation, "including those which sit here now in judgment."[7] Virgil's law of yesterday was the law of Rome. Rome's law of today is universal.

Many nations, and alliances of nations, have tried to follow the precedent of ancient Rome. France, under Napoleon; Spain in the New World; and the British Empire—all have failed. No single tyrant, no nation or alliance of nations, has been able to impose its rule, indefinitely, upon the world. There must be universal consensus for universal peace. At Rome, in 1998, such a consensus was reached upon a legal basis for an end to war and to crimes committed in the name of war. This was not the law of Rome imposed upon the world, but world-law endorsed and adopted by nations seeking an end to war and inhumanity.

Nuremberg, in 1946, and Rome, in 1998, stood fast against the pressures of the precedents of the past. Nuremberg refused to apply executive punishment against its vanquished enemies, according them the rights of accused persons under the law. Rome ruled that every person is subject to the law. The twentieth century, which spawned the gravest wars *of* history, found redemption in these greatest achievements of international law *in* history.

Nuremberg and Rome stand against the resignation of humankind to its self-debasement and its self-destruction. The achievements of that great trial and historic conference in elevating justice and law over inhumanity and war give promise for a better tomorrow. We may enter the atomic age determined that tyranny shall not extend its sway, nor war become its game—placing our faith in the cause of justice, in the freedom of man, and in the mercy of God.

This book began with Exodus. It shall end with Revelation:

"And God shall wipe away all tears from their eyes; and there shall be no more death, neither sorrow nor crying, neither shall there be any more pain; for the former things are passed away."

Notes

Abbreviations

NCA: *Nazi Conspiracy and Aggression* (Washington, D.C.: Office of the United States Chief of Counsel for the Prosecution of Axis Criminality [Government Printing Office], 1946).

TMWC: *Trial of the Major War Criminals* (Nuremberg: International Military Tribunal, 1947-49).

ICMT: *Report of Robert H. Jackson, United States Representative to the International Conference on Military Trials, London, 1945* (Washington, D. C.: Department of State Publication 3080 [Government Printing Office], 1949).

PREFACE

1. Lucius D. Clay, *Decision in Germany* (New York: Doubleday & Co., 1950), p. 250.
2. *NCA*, VI, 703.
3. *War Crimes Trials*, I, "The Peleus Trial" (London: William Hodge & Co.), Foreword.
4. Hans Ehard, "The Nuremberg Trial Against the Major War Criminals and International Law," *American Journal of International Law*, XLIII (1949), 224.
5. Whitney J. Oates and Eugene O'Neill, Jr., *The Complete Greek Drama* (New York: Random House, 1938), I, 930.

CHAPTER 1

1. *New York Times*, October 26, 1941, p. 1, col. 3.
2. *TMWC*, V, 412.
3. *New York Times*, August 22, 1942, p. 4, col. 4.
4. *TMWC*, VIII, 417; *ICMT*, p. 9.
5. *New York Times*, October 16, 1942, p. 1, cols. 5-6; p. 8, col. 2.
6. *ICMT*, p. 10.
7. *Ibid.*, p. 10.
8. *Ibid.*, pp. 10, 11.
9. *Ibid.*, p. 12.
10. *Vital Speeches of the Day* (New York: City News Publishing Co.), X (Dec. 1, 1943), 108.

11. Michael Sayers and Albert E. Kahn, *The Plot Against the Peace* (New York: Dial Press, 1945), p. 155.
12. *Ibid.*, p. 123.
13. *ICMT*, pp. 12, 13.
14. Henry L. Stimson and McGeorge Bundy, *On Active Service in Peace and War* (New York: Harper & Bros., 1948), p. 577.
15. *Ibid.*, p. 578.
16. *Ibid.*, p. 584.
17. *Ibid.*, p. 584.
18. *ICMT*, p. 6.
19. *Ibid.*, p. 6.
20. *Ibid.*, p. 6.
21. *Ibid.*, p. 6.
22. James F. Byrnes, *Speaking Frankly* (New York: Harper & Bros., 1947), p. 21.
23. *Ibid.*, p. 44.
24. *The Axis in Defeat* (Washington, D. C.: Department of State Publication No. 2423, 1945), p. 7.
25. *ICMT*, p. 46.
26. *Ibid.*, p. 47.
27. *Ibid.*, p. 48.
28. *Ibid.*, pp. 104-6.
29. *Ibid.*, p. 107.
30. *Ibid.*, p. 115.
31. *Ibid.*, p. 303.
32. *Ibid.*, p. 327.
33. *Ibid.*, p. 330.
34. *Ibid.*, p. 387.
35. *Ibid.*, p. 422.
36. *Ibid.*, pp. 381-82.
37. *Ibid.*, pp. 383-84.

38. *Ibid.,* p. 385.
39. *The Axis in Defeat,* p. 17.
40. *TMWC,* I, 10.

CHAPTER 2

1. *Negotiating with the Russians* (Boston: World Peace Foundation, 1951), p. 83.
2. *TMWC,* II, 496.
3. *Ibid.,* I, 166.
4. *Ibid.,* p. 170.
5. *Ibid.,* p. 168.
6. *Ibid.,* II, 30.
7. *Ibid.,* I, 94.
8. *Ibid.,* II, 98-99.
9. *Ibid.,* p. 104.
10. *Ibid.,* p. 102.
11. *Ibid.,* p. 105.
12. *Ibid.,* pp. 154-55.

CHAPTER 3

1. *NCA,* V, 272.
2. *TMWC,* XXII, 428; IV, 521.
3. *Ibid.,* IV, 521.
4. *Ibid.,* p. 522.
5. *Ibid.,* p. 523.
6. *Ibid.,* p. 524.
7. *Ibid.,* p. 523.
8. *Ibid.,* p. 524.
9. *Ibid.,* p. 524.
10. *Ibid.,* p. 524.
11. *Ibid.,* p. 525.
12. *Ibid.,* XXII, 456; IV, 525.
13. *Ibid.,* XXII, 428-29.
14. *Ibid.,* IV, 526.
15. *NCA,* I, 205.
16. *TMWC,* XVI, 258.

CHAPTER 4

1. *TMWC,* IV, 45-46.
2. *Ibid.,* II, 112.
3. Willi Frischauer, *The Rise and Fall of Hermann Goering* (Boston: Houghton Mifflin Co., 1951), pp. 88-90.
4. *Manchester Guardian* (Daily), December 5, 1934, p. 6, col. 6.
5. *TMWC,* IX, 434.
6. *Ibid.,* II, 110.
7. *Ibid.,* pp. 189-90.
8. *Dokumente der Deutschen Politik,* I.
9. *TMWC,* IX, 253.
10. *NCA,* I, 219.
11. *Ibid.,* p. 212.
12. *TMWC,* II, 195.
13. *Ibid.,* pp. 196-97; *NCA,* I, 223.

14. *TMWC,* II, 197; *NCA,* I, 223.
15. *TMWC,* I, 178.
16. *Ibid.,* p. 179.
17. *Ibid.,* p. 179.
18. *Ibid.,* IV, 233; *NCA,* II, 250.
19. *NCA,* II, 260.
20. *Ibid.,* pp. 262-63.
21. *Ibid.,* V, 654.
22. *TMWC,* IV, 278-79, IX, 521; *NCA,* V, 854.
23. *NCA,* IV, 432.
24. *TMWC,* IX, 538; *NCA,* IV, 439.
25. *TMWC,* IV, 67; *NCA,* V, 869.
26. *NCA,* V, 871.
27. *Ibid.,* p. 871.
28. *Ibid.,* pp. 874-76.

CHAPTER 5

1. *TMWC,* IV, 524; *NCA,* VII, 167.
2. *TMWC,* XIX, 408; *NCA,* VII, 333.
3. *NCA,* VII, 455.
4. *Ibid.,* IV, 994-95.
5. Winston Churchill, *The Gathering Storm* (Boston: Houghton Mifflin Co., 1948), p. 638.
6. *TMWC,* IV, 537.
7. *Ibid.,* XIX, 409; *NCA,* III, 887-89.
8. *TMWC,* IV, 538; *NCA,* VII, 465.
9. *TMWC,* IX, 280-81.
10. *Ibid.,* II, 263, 266, 268, 269; *NCA,* III, 295-301.
11. *TMWC,* IV, 539; *NCA,* VIII, 227-29.
12. *TMWC,* III, 389; *NCA,* VIII, 235.
13. *NCA,* III, 901-4.
14. *TMWC,* XIX, 410; *NCA,* IV, 828-29.
15. *TMWC,* XIX, 411; *NCA,* VI, 726.
16. *TMWC,* II, 258-59; *NCA,* III, 572-73.
17. *TMWC,* XIX, 436-37.
18. *Ibid.,* XIII, 22-23.
19. *Ibid.,* IX, 477.

CHAPTER 6

1. *TMWC,* II, 349.
2. *Ibid.,* p. 381.
3. *Ibid,* p. 356.
4. *Ibid.,* p. 361.
5. *Ibid.,* p. 361.
6. *Ibid.,* VI, 95; *NCA,* IV, 317.
7. *TMWC,* II, 378; *NCA,* II, 943.
8. *TMWC,* II, 400.
9. *Ibid.,* p. 403.
10. *Ibid.,* IX, 300.
11. *Ibid.,* XVI, 89-90.

12. *Ibid.*, II, 406-7.
13. *Ibid.*, p. 407.
14. *Ibid.*, XVI, 168, 170.
15. *Ibid.*, II, 405.
16. *Ibid.*, p. 408.
17. *Ibid.*, p. 410.
18. *Ibid.*, p. 409.
19. *Ibid.*, p. 411.
20. *Ibid*, pp. 415-16.
21. *Ibid.*, p. 416.
22. *Ibid.*, p. 418.
23. *Ibid*, pp. 419-20; *NCA*, V, 638.
24. *TMWC*, II, 420-21.
25. *Ibid.*, p. 421.
26. *Ibid.*, pp. 421-22.
27. *Ibid.*, pp. 422-23.
28. *Ibid.*, p. 424.
29. *Ibid.*, p. 425.
30. *Ibid.*, p. 426.
31. *Ibid.*, IX, 297.
32. *Ibid*, p. 300.
33. *Ibid.*, II, 427.
34. *Ibid.*, p. 425.
35. *Ibid.*, XIV, 410.
36. *Ibid.*, p. 429.

CHAPTER 7

1. *TMWC*, III, 38, 189.
2. *Ibid.*, p. 38.
3. *Ibid.*, pp. 39-40.
4. *Ibid.*, II, 269.
5. *Ibid.*, p. 270.
6. *Ibid.*, p. 270.
7. *Ibid.*, III, 40-41; *NCA*, V, 419.
8. *TMWC*, III, 192.
9. *Ibid.*, II, 275-76; *NCA*, III, 306-7.
10. *TMWC*, III, 43-44; *NCA*, III, 316-18.
11. *TMWC*, III, 55-56; *NCA*, III, 332-33.
12. *TMWC*, III, 50-51; *NCA*, V, 426.
13. *TMWC*, III, 53; *NCA*, V, 432.
14. *TMWC*, III, 52; *NCA*, V, 431.
15. *NCA*, III, 352.
16. *TMWC*, III, 86-87; *NCA*, IV, 1100-1.
17. *TMWC*, III, 87.
18. *Ibid.*, pp. 87-88.
19. *Ibid.*, p. 89.
20. *Ibid.*, p. 90; *NCA*, V, 430.
21. *TMWC*, III, 149.
22. *Ibid.*, p. 149; *NCA*, V, 426.
23. *TMWC*, III, 155.
24. *Ibid.*, p. 155.
25. *Ibid.*, pp. 158-59; *NCA*, V, 433-34.
26. *NCA*, V, 435.

27. *TMWC*, III, 159; *NCA*, V, 435-36.
28. *TMWC*, III, 160-61; *NCA*, V, 437-38.
29. *TMWC*, III, 162; *NCA*, V, 438-39.
30. *TMWC*, IX, 303.
31. *Ibid.*, X, 346-47.
32. *Ibid.*, III, 165.
33. *Ibid.*, p. 165.
34. *Ibid.*, p. 168.

CHAPTER 8

1. *TMWC*, III, 197.
2. *Voelkische Beobachter*, XLVIII (1935), 121-51.
3. *TMWC*, III, 204; *NCA*, VIII, 481.
4. *TMWC*, III, 207; *NCA*, VIII, 516.
5. *TMWC*, III, 207.
6. *Ibid.*, p. 212.
7. *Ibid.*, p. 213.
8. *NCA*, VIII, 488.
9. *TMWC*, III, 215.
10. *Ibid.*, p. 215.
11. *Ibid.*, p. 216.
12. *Ibid.*, pp. 216-17.
13. *Ibid.*, p. 248.
14. *Ibid.*, p. 220.
15. *Ibid.*, p. 221.
16. *Ibid.*, II, 279.
17. *Ibid.*, p. 280.
18. *Ibid.*, p. 280.
19. *Ibid.*, p. 280.
20. *Ibid.*, p. 280.
21. *Ibid.*, p. 281.
22. *Ibid.*, p. 281.
23. *Ibid.*, III, 223.
24. *Ibid.*, p. 224.
25. *Ibid.*, pp. 226-28; *NCA*, VIII, 518-29.
26. *TMWC*, III, 228.
27. *Ibid.*, p. 230.
28. *Ibid*, p. 230.
29. *Ibid.*, p. 231.
30. *Ibid.*, X, 267-69.
31. *Ibid.*, II, 287-89.
32. *NCA*, III, 585.
33. *TMWC*, III, 232-33; *NCA*, III, 665.
34. *TMWC*, III, 236.
35. *Ibid.*, p. 237.
36. *NCA*, VIII, 456.
37. *TMWC*, III, 238.
38. *Ibid.*, p. 242.
39. *Ibid.*, p. 243.
40. *Ibid.*, pp. 239-40.
41. *Ibid.*, p. 249.
42. *Ibid.*, p. 249.
43. *Ibid.*, p. 249.

44. *Ibid.*, p. 249.
45. *Ibid.*, pp. 249-50.
46. *Ibid.*, p. 250.
47. *Ibid.*, p. 251.
48. *Ibid.*, pp. 252-53.
49. *Ibid.*, pp. 254-55.
50. *Ibid.*, p. 255.
51. *Ibid.*, pp. 255-56.
52. *Ibid.*, IX, 476.
53. *Ibid.*, IV, 242-44.
54. *Ibid.*, III, 257.
55. *Ibid.*, p. 257.
56. *Ibid.*, p. 258.
57. *Ibid.*, p. 260.

CHAPTER 9

1. *TMWC*, III, 261.
2. *Ibid.*, p. 263.
3. *Ibid.*, p. 262.
4. *Ibid.*, p. 263.
5. *Ibid.*, p. 264.
6. *Ibid.*, p. 266.
7. *Ibid.*, p. 265.
8. *Ibid.*, p. 269.
9. *Ibid.*, p. 270.
10. *Ibid.*, pp. 270-71.
11. *Ibid.*, p. 272.
12. *Ibid.*, pp. 272-73.
13. *Ibid.*, p. 273.
14. *Ibid.*, p. 275.
15. *Ibid.*, p. 276.
16. *Ibid.*, pp. 277-78.
17. *Ibid.*, p. 278.
18. *Ibid.*, p. 280.
19. *Ibid.*, p. 280.
20. *Ibid.*, p. 280.
21. *Ibid.*, p. 281.
22. *Ibid.*, p. 281.
23. *Ibid.*, p. 283.
24. *Ibid.*, p. 283.
25. *Ibid.*, p. 287.

CHAPTER 10

1. *TMWC*, III, 132; *NCA*, VIII, 381.
2. *TMWC*, III, 292; *NCA*, VIII, 381-82.
3. *TMWC*, III, 294; *NCA*, III, 287-88.
4. *TMWC*, III, 263; *NCA*, VIII, 379-80.
5. *TMWC*, III, 295; *NCA*, VII, 850.
6. *TMWC*, III, 296; *NCA*, VII, 850.
7. *TMWC*, III, 296.
8. *Ibid.*, p. 298; *NCA*, VIII, 384.
9. *TMWC*, III, 298.
10. *Ibid.*, pp. 298-99.
11. *Ibid.*, p. 299.
12. *NCA*, III, 578-79.
13. *TMWC*, III, 302.

14. *Ibid.*, p. 304; *NCA*, III, 422-23.
15. *TMWC*, III, 303; *NCA*, III, 422.
16. *TMWC*, III, 303-4; *NCA*, III, 422.

CHAPTER 11

1. *TMWC*, III, 307-8.
2. *Ibid.*, p. 308; *NCA*, VIII, 536-37.
3. *TMWC*, IX, 604.
4. *Ibid.*, III, 309, IX, 604.
5. *Ibid.*, III, 310.
6. *Ibid.*, p. 311.
7. *Ibid.*, p. 314.
8. *Ibid.*, pp. 314-15.
9. *Ibid.*, p. 316.
10. *Ibid.*, pp. 318-19.
11. *Ibid.*, XV, 476.
12. *Ibid.*, p. 476.
13. *Ibid.*, III, 319.
14. *Ibid.*, pp. 320-21.

CHAPTER 12

1. *TMWC*, III, 371.
2. *New York Times*, October 7, 1939, p. 8, col 8.
3. *TMWC*, III, 329.
4. *Ibid.*, p. 330.
5. *Ibid.*, p. 331.
6. *Ibid.*, p. 332.
7. *Ibid.*, p. 333.
8. *Ibid.*, pp. 333-34.
9. *Ibid.*, II, 294-95.
10. *Ibid.*, IX, 427.
11. *Ibid.*, III, 339.
12. *Ibid.*, p. 340.
13. *Ibid.*, p. 342.
14. *Ibid.*, p. 364.
15. *Ibid.*, p. 364.
16. *Ibid.*, p. 344, VI, 858.
17. *Ibid.*, III, 344.
18. *Ibid.*, pp. 143, 362.

CHAPTER 13

1. *TMWC*, III, 369-70.
2. *Ibid.*, pp. 373-74, 392.
3. *Ibid.*, pp. 376-77.
4. *Ibid.*, p. 378.
5. *Ibid.*, pp. 379-80.
6. *Ibid.*, II, 298-300.
7. *Ibid.*, III, 383.
8. *Ibid.*, pp. 384-85.
9. *Ibid.*, p. 385.
10. *Ibid.*, pp. 395-96.
11. *Ibid.*, pp. 396-97.
12. *Ibid.*, p. 397.
13. *Ibid.*, p. 397.
14. *Ibid.*, p. 398.
15. *Ibid.*, p. 399.

CHAPTER 14

1. *TMWC*, II, 146.
2. *Ibid.*, XX, 611.
3. *Ibid.*, III, 144.
4. *Ibid.*, VII, 417.
5. *NCA*, IV, 59-60.
6. *Ibid.*, VII, 411-14.
7. *Ibid.*, p. 414.
8. *TMWC*, VII, 347.
9. *Ibid.*, XV, 546; *NCA*, III, 127-29.
10. *TMWC*, VII, 430.
11. *Ibid.*, p. 431.
12. *Ibid.*, XXII, 230; *NCA*, IV, 578.
13. *TMWC*, VI, 376-77.
14. *Ibid.*, III, 458.
15. *Ibid.*, p. 459.
16. *Ibid.*, p. 460.
17. *NCA*, VIII, 178.
18. *TMWC*, III, 460.
19. *Ibid.*, p. 456.
20. *Ibid.*, XIX, 478.

CHAPTER 15

1. *TMWC*, IV, 456.
2. *Ibid.*, pp. 458-59; *NCA*, VI, 961-62.
3. *TMWC*, X, 617, 620-21.
4. *Ibid.*, IV, 459-61.
5. *Ibid.*, IX, 609; *NCA*, VII, 177.
6. *TMWC*, IX, 609.
7. *Ibid.*, p. 567; *NCA*, IV, 262-63.
8. *TMWC*, IX, 567.
9. *Ibid.*, IV, 217; *NCA*, IV, 562.
10. *TMWC*, IV, 221; *NCA*, VIII, 207.
11. *TMWC*, IV, 479.
12. *Ibid.*, p. 480.
13. *Ibid.*, IX, 563; *NCA*, III, 452.
14. *TMWC*, IV, 481-82, 494.
15. *Ibid.*, XV, 407.
16. *Ibid.*, X, 390.
17. *Ibid.*, p. 391.
18. *NCA*, IV, 369-70.
19. *TMWC*, IV, 474.
20. *Ibid.*, VII, 530-31.
21. *Ibid.*, XVII, 158.
22. *Ibid.*, VIII, 122.
23. *Ibid.*, VI, 130.
24. *Ibid.*, p. 401.
25. *Ibid.*, pp. 401-2.
26. *Ibid.*, IX, 566.
27. *Ibid.*, VI, 405-11.
28. *Ibid.*, pp. 411, 412.
29. *Ibid.*, IX, 222-23.
30. *Time Magazine*, January 26, 1953, p. 33.
31. *TMWC*, VIII, 118.
32. *German Crimes in Poland* (Warsaw: Central Commission for Investigation of German Crimes in Poland, 1946), p. 187.

33. *Ibid.*, pp. 200-3; *TMWC*, XX, 379-82.
34. *TMWC*, XX, 199-200.
35. *Ibid.*, pp. 205-6.
36. *Ibid.*, pp. 212-13.
37. *Ibid.*, pp. 215-16.
38. *TMWC*, VIII, 116-17.
39. *Ibid.*, XII, 22.
40. *Ibid.*, p. 76.

CHAPTER 16

1. *TMWC*, V, 87; *NCA*, IV, 917.
2. *TMWC*, VI, 121.
3. *Ibid.*, IV, 458; *NCA*, VI, 961.
4. *TMWC*, X, 645; *NCA*, IV, 127.
5. *TMWC*, VI, 121-22.
6. *Ibid.*, p. 122.
7. *Ibid.*, p. 125.
8. *Ibid.*, p. 127.
9. *Ibid.*, p. 127.
10. *Ibid.*, p. 128.
11. *Ibid.*, p. 137.
12. *Ibid.*, p. 129.
13. *Ibid.*, p. 131.
14. *Ibid.*, pp. 146-47.
15. *Ibid.*, p. 132.
16. *Ibid.*, p. 133.
17. *Ibid.*, p. 147.
18. *Ibid.*, p. 148.
19. *Ibid.*, IX, 221.
20. *Ibid.*, p. 221.
21. *Ibid.*, p. 232.
22. *Supra*, pp. 199-206.
23. *TMWC*, VI, 150.
24. *Ibid.*, pp. 151-52.
25. *Ibid.*, X, 647.
26. *Ibid.*, p. 647.
27. *NCA*, III, 626.
28. *Ibid.*, VII, 782.
29. *TMWC*, VII, 47.
30. *Ibid.*, p. 48.
31. *Ibid.*, XX, 145.
32. *Ibid.*, VII, 45.
33. *Ibid.*, p. 46.
34. *Ibid.*, XX, 145-46.
35. *Ibid.*, VII, 45.

CHAPTER 17

1. *TMWC*, X, 626.
2. *Ibid.*, p. 627.
3. *Ibid.*, p. 627.
4. *Ibid.*, IV, 272; *NCA*, VII, 873.
5. *TMWC*, IV, 273; *NCA*, VII, 872.
6. *TMWC*, IV, 274; *NCA*, III, 477.
7. *TMWC*, X, 628.
8. *Ibid.*, p. 630; *NCA*, VII, 222.
9. *TMWC*, X, 631; *NCA*, VII, 266.
10. *TMWC*, X, 634.

11. *Ibid.*, p. 634.
12. *Ibid.*, p. 634.
13. *Ibid.*, pp. 634-35.
14. *Ibid.*, p. 633.
15. *Ibid.*, p. 633.
16. *Ibid.*, VI, 282-83.

CHAPTER 18

1. *TMWC*, IV, 441-42.
2. *Ibid.*, pp. 443-44.
3. *Ibid.*, p. 446.
4. *Ibid.*, XIV, 338.
5. *Ibid.*, IV, 449.
6. *NCA*, III, 856.
7. *Ibid.*, p. 438.
8. *TMWC*, IV, 453-54.
9. *Ibid.*, X, 639.
10. *Ibid.*, p. 639.
11. *Ibid.*, IV, 454; *NCA*, III, 439.
12. *TMWC*, IV, 301-2; *NCA*, VII, 799

CHAPTER 19

1. *TMWC*, IX, 115.
2. *Ibid.*, p. 586.
3. *Ibid.*, XI, 158-59.
4. *Ibid.*, X, 566.
5. *Ibid.*, XI, 160.
6. *Ibid.*, p. 11.
7. *Ibid.*, IX, 593.
8. *Ibid.*, XV, 496.
9. *Ibid.*, IV, 49; *NCA*, VIII, 108.
10. *TMWC*, IV, 305.
11. *Ibid.*, VI, 369.
12. *NCA*, III, 531.
13. *Ibid.*, p. 532.
14. *TMWC*, VI, 364; *NCA*, III, 533.
15. *NCA*, III, 535.
16. *Ibid.*, p. 529.
17. *TMWC*, XI, 19.
18. *Ibid.*, VI, 366; *NCA*, III, 533.
19. *TMWC*, VI, 185-86.
20. *Ibid.*, p. 236.
21. *Ibid.*, p. 342.
22. *Ibid.*, p. 343.
23. *Ibid.*, p. 355, XI, 19.
24. *Ibid.*, XI, 19, XIX, 474.

CHAPTER 20

1. *TMWC*, XIX, 474, XI, 19.
2. *Ibid.*, XI, 19, XIX, 474.
3. *NCA*, V, 550.
4. *Ibid.*, p. 343.
5. *TMWC*, IV, 258-59; *NCA*, III, 423-25.
6. *TMWC*, VII, 406.

7. *Ibid.*, pp. 407-8.
8. *Ibid.*, XIX, 474-75.
9. *Ibid.*, XX, 148.
10. *Ibid.*, p. 149.
11. *Ibid.*, X, 616.

CHAPTER 21

1. *TMWC*, III, 505-6; *NCA*, IV, 158.
2. *TMWC*, III, 506; *NCA*, IV, 159.
3. *NCA*, V, 230.
4. *TMWC*, IV, 263-64.
5. *Ibid.*, VI, 186.
6. *Ibid.*, VII, 376-77.

CHAPTER 22

1. *TMWC*, I, 54.
2. Statement of Robert H. Jackson before Select Committee of House of Representatives to Investigate the Katyn Massacre, November 11, 1952, p. 3.
3. *Ibid.*, p. 3.
4. *Ibid.*, p. 4.
5. *Ibid.*, p. 3.
6. *TMWC*, VII, 426-28.
7. *Ibid.*, XVII, 282-84.
8. *Ibid.*, pp. 301-2.
9. *Ibid.*, pp. 313-14.
10. *Ibid.*, pp. 324-26.
11. *Ibid.*, pp. 335-38.
12. *Ibid.*, p. 350.
13. *Ibid.*, p. 353.
14. *Ibid.*, pp. 353-54.
15. *Ibid.*, p. 355.
16. *Ibid.*, p. 356.
17. *Ibid.*, p. 358.
18. *Ibid.*, p. 361.
19. *Ibid.*, p. 365.
20. *Ibid.*, p. 365.
21. Hearings before the Select Committee to Conduct an Investigation of the Facts, Evidence, and Circumstances of the Katyn Forest Massacre, Part 3 (March 13-14, 1952), 340 ff.
22. *Ibid.*, pp. 338 ff.
23. *Ibid.*, Part 4 (April 16-19, 1952), 731.
24. *Ibid.*, Part 3, 379.
25. *Ibid.*, p. 387.
26. *Ibid.*, pp. 391-94.
27. *Ibid.*, p. 328.
28. *Ibid.*, Part 4, 553; *Ibid.*, Final Report (December 22, 1952), p. 20.
29. *Ibid.*, Part 4, 555; Final Report, p. 20.

30. *Ibid.*, Part 3, 491.
31. *Ibid.*, Final Report, pp. 37-38.
32. *TMWC*, XIV, 513.
33. *Ibid.*, III, 577.
34. *Ibid.*, XI, 23.
35. *Ibid.*, VII, 468-69.
36. *Ibid.*, XXIX, 447-48.
37. *NCA*, II, 643; IV, 911.
38. Hearings . . . Katyn Forest Massacre, Part 3, 427.
39. *Ibid.*, p. 379.

CHAPTER 23

1. *TMWC*, XX, 150; *NCA*, Supp. A, 808-9.
2. *NCA*, Supp. A, 811.
3. *Ibid.*, p. 807.
4. *Ibid.*, p. 808.
5. *TMWC*, XX, 563.
6. *Ibid.*, p. 564.
7. *Ibid.*, p. 564; *NCA*, Supp. A, 833-34.
8. *TMWC*, XX, 563.

CHAPTER 24

1. *TMWC*, III, 522; *NCA*, V, 366.
2. *TMWC*, III, 527; *NCA*, V, 367.
3. *NCA*, VII, 191.
4. *TMWC*, X, 411; *NCA*, VII, 191.
5. *TMWC*, X, 412.
6. *Ibid.*, XII, 347-48; *NCA*, VIII, 21, 23.
7. *TMWC*, V, 97.
8. *Ibid.*, pp. 105-6.
9. *Ibid.*, p. 96.
10. *Ibid.*, p. 100.
11. *NCA*, VIII, 9.
12. *Ibid.*, Supp. A, 959.
13. *Ibid.*, p. 959.
14. *Ibid.*, pp. 959-60.
15. *Ibid.*, p. 960.
16. *Ibid.*, p. 960.
17. *Ibid.*, p. 961.
18. *Ibid.*, p. 961.
19. *Ibid.*, p. 961.
20. *Ibid.*, p. 962.
21. *Ibid.*, p. 962.
22. *Ibid.*, p. 962.
23. *Ibid.*, p. 962.
24. *Ibid.*, p. 963.
25. *TMWC*, V, 109.
26. *NCA*, VIII, 28-29.
27. *TMWC*, V, 111.
28. *Ibid.*, p. 110.
29. *Ibid.*, p. 113.
30. *Ibid.*, p. 113.
31. *Ibid.*, p. 117.
32. *Ibid.*, pp. 117-18.
33. *NCA*, II, 1046.

34. *TMWC*, III, 528; *NCA*, V, 367.
35. *TMWC*, III, 528; *NCA*, V, 367.
36. *TMWC*, V, 205.
37. G. M. Gilbert, *Nuremberg Diary* (New York: Farrar, Straus and Co., 1947), p. 269.
38. *TMWC*, XII, 13.
39. *Ibid.*, p. 13.
40. *Ibid.*, IV, 116.
41. *NCA*, IV, 425-27, 430.
42. *Ibid.*, pp. 432-34.
43. *Ibid.*, pp. 436-38, 445, 450.
44. *TMWC*, IX, 519-20; *NCA*, III, 525-26.
45. *TMWC*, III, 529; *NCA*, III, 223-24.
46. *TMWC*, III, 530-31.
47. *Ibid.*, p. 538; *NCA*, IV, 891-92.
48. *NCA*, VII, 756, 758, 760, 763.
49. *Ibid.*, pp. 766, 767, 770.
50. *TMWC*, XIV, 426; *NCA*, V, 776-77.
51. *TMWC*, VI, 492.
52. *Ibid.*, VII, 40.
53. *Ibid.*, p. 42.
54. *Ibid.*, p. 42.
55. *Ibid.*, IV, 361-64, 366, 369.
56. *Ibid.*, III, 502-3; *NCA*, V, 316, 319, 320, 323, 324.
57. *TMWC*, XX, 385-86; *NCA*, Supp. A, 1146-47.
58. *TMWC*, III, 555; *NCA*, III, 718.
59. *NCA*, III, 720-21.
60. *Ibid.*, pp. 721-26.
61. *Ibid.*, pp. 732-33.
62. *Ibid.*, p. 734.
63. *Ibid.*, p. 737.
64. *Ibid.*, pp. 740-41.
65. *Ibid.*, p. 743.
66. *Ibid.*, p. 745.
67. *Ibid.*, p. 771.
68. *Ibid.*, p. 772.
69. *TMWC*, XX, 316.
70. *NCA*, IV, 892.
71. *Ibid.*, p. 902.
72. *TMWC*, III, 500-1; *NCA*, IV, 563-66.
73. *TMWC*, IV, 371.
74. *NCA*, V, 381.
75. *Ibid.*, pp. 381-82.
76. *TMWC*, XXI, 235.
77. *Ibid.*, XII, 371; *NCA*, Supp. A, 407.
78. *TMWC*, XVII, 231.
79. *Ibid.*, p. 181.
80. *Life Magazine*, XXXVI (May 10, 1954), 119.

CHAPTER 25

1. *TMWC*, II, 194.

2. *Ibid.*, III, 461.
3. *Ibid.*, pp. 461-62.
4. *Ibid.*, p. 462.
5. *Ibid.*, pp. 463-64.
6. *NCA*, II, 289.
7. *TMWC*, III, 466-67.
8. *Ibid.*, XIII, 342.
9. *Ibid*, XX, 353.
10. *Ibid.*, III, 512; *NCA*, IV, 1001.
11. *TMWC*, V, 183.
12. *Ibid.*, VI, 184.
13. *Ibid.*, p. 244.
14. *Ibid.*, XIX, 513.
15. *NCA*, Supp. A. 1218, 1219, 1222, 1223.
16. *Ibid.*, pp. 1223-24.
17. *Ibid.*, pp. 1216-17.
18. *Ibid.*, III, 449-51.
19. *TMWC*, XX, 490.
20. *Ibid.*, p. 491.
21. *Ibid.*, pp. 500-1.
22. *Ibid.*, VI, 271.
23. *Ibid.*, p. 184.
24. *Ibid.*, XX, 493-95.
25. *German Crimes in Poland* (Warsaw: Central Commission for Investigation of German Crimes in Poland, 1946), pp. 109 ff.
26. *Ibid.*, pp. 95 ff.
27. *TMWC*, VIII, 325.
28. *Ibid.*, XI, 401.
29. *Ibid.*, pp. 414, 416, 417.
30. Gilbert, *op. cit.*, p. 266.
31. *German Crimes in Poland*, pp. 27 ff.
32. *TMWC*, VI, 205-6.
33. *Ibid.*, p. 216.
34. *Ibid.*, VIII, 318.
35. *Ibid.*, p. 318.
36. *Ibid.*, VI, 218.
37. *Ibid.*, XX, 506.
38. *Ibid.*, VI, 244.
39. *Ibid.*, XIX, 514; *NCA*, VII, 815.
40. *NCA*, VI, 676.
41. *TMWC*, XX, 386.
42. *Ibid.*, VI, 284-85.
43. *NCA*, Supp. A, 1115-16.
44. *Ibid.*, p. 1114.
45. *TMWC*, XI, 407.
46. *Ibid.*, p. 407.
47. *Ibid.*, p. 404.
48. *Ibid.*, VI, 228.

CHAPTER 26

1. *TMWC*, IV, 477.
2. *Ibid.*, pp. 315-21.
3. *Ibid.*, p. 322.
4. *Ibid.*, III, 560-61; *NCA*, III, 418-19.

5. *Ibid.*, IV, 337-38.
6. *Ibid.*, pp. 255-56; *NCA*, V, 701-2.
7. *TMWC*, XIX, 507-9; *NCA*, V, 697-98.
8. *TMWC*, II, 122; *NCA*, VII, 983.
9. *TMWC*, II, 123-24; *NCA*, VII, 985.
10. *NCA*, VII, 992.
11. *TMWC*, VIII, 294-96; *NCA*, II, 271-72.
12. *TMWC*, IV, 247-48; *NCA*, III, 785-88.
13. *TMWC*, IV, 248; *NCA*, III, 784-85.
14. *TMWC*, III, 562, IV, 293-94; *NCA*, VIII, 208.
15. *TMWC*, IV, 249-51; *NCA*, V, 731-32.
16. *NCA*, VIII, 97.
17. *Ibid.*, p. 98.
18. *Ibid.*, pp. 99-102.
19. *Ibid.*, p. 103.
20. *Ibid.*, Supp. A, 619-20.
21. *TMWC*, XI, 373; *NCA*, Supp. A, 623-24.
22. *NCA*, Supp. A, 662.
23. *Ibid.*, pp. 663-64.
24. *Ibid.*, p. 665.
25. *Ibid.*, p. 667.
26. *Ibid.*, p. 668.

CHAPTER 27

1. *TMWC*, V, 332-33.
2. *Ibid.*, III, 406.
3. *Ibid.*, p. 406.
4. *Ibid.*, p. 589.
5. *Ibid.*, pp. 583-84.
6. *Ibid.*, p. 584.
7. *Ibid.*, pp. 584-85.
8. *Ibid.*, p. 590; *NCA*, IV, 905.
9. *TMWC*, V, 78.
10. *Ibid.*, III, 576-77.
11. *Ibid.*, p. 577.
12. *Ibid.*, p. 580.
13. *Ibid.*, p. 580.
14. *NCA*, II, 633.
15. *TMWC*, III, 587.
16. *Ibid.*, p. 588.
17. *Ibid.*, p. 582; *NCA*, IV, 553-54.
18. *TMWC*, XIX, 609-10; *NCA*, IV, 917.
19. *TMWC*, XII, 126.
20. *NCA*, IV, 916.
21. *TMWC*, V, 79-80.
22. *Ibid.*, XVII, 61; *NCA*, Supp. A, 601.
23. *TMWC*, V, 61; *NCA*, Supp. A, 601.
24. *NCA*, III, 618.
25. *TMWC*, XI, 570; *NCA*, V, 378.

26. *TMWC*, IV, 5-8; *NCA*, VII, 297-300.
27. *TMWC*, IV, 14.
28. *Ibid.*, p. 12.
29. *Ibid.*, pp. 10-11; *NCA*, VII, 1087.
30. *NCA*, VII, 1089.
31. *TMWC*, IV, 11; *NCA*, VII, 1087.
32. *TMWC*, IV, 11; *NCA*, VII, 1091.
33. *NCA*, VII, 1092.
34. *TMWC*, VIII, 110.
35. *Ibid.*, IX, 558-59.
36. *Ibid.*, VI, 428.
37. *Ibid.*, p. 431.
38. *Ibid.*, p. 440.
39. *Ibid.*, III, 596-97; *NCA*, VIII, 122.
40. *TMWC*, VI, 463.
41. *Ibid.*, pp. 480-81.
42. *Ibid.*, XX, 107.

CHAPTER 28

1. *TMWC*, IX, 633.
2. *Ibid.*, VIII, 46, 49.
3. *Ibid.*, pp. 2-3.
4. *Ibid.*, p. 7.
5. *Ibid.*, IV, 548.
6. *Ibid.*, VIII, 9.
7. *Ibid.*, III, 591; *NCA*, III, 917-18.
8. *TMWC*, III, 591; *NCA*, III, 919.
9. *TMWC*, IV, 549.
10. *Ibid.*, III, 592.
11. *Ibid.*, VIII, 9.
12. *Ibid.*, p. 9.
13. *Ibid.*, p. 10.
14. *Ibid.*, p. 10.
15. *Ibid.*, p. 10.
16. *Ibid.*, p. 13.
17. *Ibid.*, p. 15.
18. *Ibid.*, p. 16.
19. *Ibid.*, p. 18.
20. *Ibid.*, p. 20.
21. *Ibid.*, VII, 445.
22. *Ibid.*, VIII, 20-21.
23. *Ibid.*, p. 19.
24. *Ibid.*, pp. 23-24.
25. *Ibid.*, p. 27.
26. *Ibid.*, p. 36.
27. *Ibid.*, p. 22.
28. *Ibid.*, p. 22.
29. *Ibid.*, p. 42.
30. *Ibid.*, VI, 28.
31. *Ibid.*, p. 28.
32. *Ibid.*, p. 26.
33. *Ibid.*, p. 27.
34. *Ibid.*, p. 31.
35. *Ibid.*, pp. 36-39.
36. *NCA*, I, 1109.
37. *Ibid.*, p. 1108.
38. *TMWC*, IV, 82; *NCA*, III, 188-89.

39. *TMWC*, IX, 547-48; *NCA*, V, 260-61.
40. *Ibid.*, VII, 66.
41. *Ibid.*, IX, 549; *NCA*, III, 40.
42. *NCA*, I, 1105.
43. *Ibid.*, p. 1105.
44. *TMWC*, IX, 634.

CHAPTER 29

1. *TMWC*, XVI, 521.
2. *Ibid.*, III, 435.
3. *Ibid.*, p. 405.
4. *Ibid.*, p. 409.
5. *Ibid.*, p. 409.
6. *Ibid.*, p. 409.
7. *Ibid.*, p. 412.
8. *Ibid.*, p. 413.
9. *Ibid.*, p. 422.
10. *Ibid.*, p. 418; *NCA*, III, 60.
11. *TMWC*, III, 422; *NCA*, III, 248.
12. *TMWC*, III, 423; *NCA*, III, 62.
13. *NCA*, III, 63-64.
14. *TMWC*, III, 423-24; *NCA*, III, 64-65.
15. *TMWC*, III, 416-17; *NCA*, IV, 80, 87.
16. *TMWC*, III, 419, 420; *NCA*, III, 66.
17. *TMWC*, III, 430; *NCA*, V, 732.
18. *TMWC*, III, 430; *NCA*, III, 236.
19. *TMWC*, III, 431; *NCA*, V, 726.
20. *TMWC*, III, 421; *NCA*, V, 729.
21. *TMWC*, III, 407; *NCA*, III, 71-72.
22. *NCA*, III, 72.
23. *Ibid.*, p. 72.
24. *TMWC*, III, 408.
25. *NCA*, Supp. A, 337.
26. *TMWC*, V, 491.
27. *Ibid.*, p. 492.
28. *Ibid.*, III, 432-33; *NCA*, VIII, 148.
29. *TMWC*, III, 433-34; *NCA*, IV, 227.
30. *TMWC*, III, 434; *NCA*, V, 726-27.
31. *TMWC*, III, p. 440.
32. *Ibid.*, p. 441; *NCA*, VII, 20.
33. *TMWC*, III, 447-48; *NCA*, VIII, 105-6.
34. *TMWC*, III, 442-45; *NCA*, VII, 2-6.
35. *TMWC*, III, 450; *NCA*, VII, 260-61.
36. *TMWC*, III, 451; *NCA*, III, 52.
37. *TMWC*, III, 452; *NCA*, V, 765.
38. *TMWC*, III, 452-53; *NCA*, V, 748-50.
39. *TMWC*, XV, 150.
40. *Ibid.*, p. 150.

CHAPTER 30

1. *TMWC*, XXI, 315.
2. *Ibid.*, p. 315.
3. *Ibid.*, IV, 203.
4. *Ibid.*, p. 204.
5. *Ibid.*, XX, 536.
6. *Ibid.*, V, 169.
7. *Ibid.*, IV, 205-6.
8. *Ibid.*, p. 206.
9. *Ibid.*, V, 170.
10. *Ibid.*, XX, 328.
11. *Ibid.*, IV, 206-7.
12. *Ibid.*, p. 208.
13. *Ibid.*, pp. 208-9.
14. *Ibid.*, XX, 518.
15. *Ibid.*, p. 519.
16. *Ibid.*, p. 520.
17. *Ibid.*, p. 545.
18. *Ibid.*, V, 169.
19. *Ibid.*, p. 171.
20. *Ibid.*, VI, 211-12.
21. *Ibid.*, p. 220.
22. *Ibid.*, pp. 307-9.
23. *Ibid.*, p. 309.
24. *Ibid.*, V, 171.
25. *Ibid.*, VI, 311-12.
26. *Ibid.*, III, 515.
27. *Ibid.*, III, 516.

CHAPTER 31

1. *TMWC*, XX, 134.
2. *Ibid.*, III, 511; *NCA*, IV, 94.
3. *TMWC*, IV, 277; *NCA*, II, 295.
4. *TMWC*, VI, 167.
5. *Ibid.*, pp. 168-69.
6. *Ibid.*, p. 169.
7. *Ibid.*, p. 169.
8. *Ibid.*, pp. 169-70.
9. *Ibid.*, p. 170.
10. *Ibid.*, p. 170.
11. *Ibid.*, p. 174.
12. *Ibid.*, p. 178.
13. *Ibid.*, pp. 174-75.
14. *Ibid.*, XX, 164.
15. *Ibid.*, XII, 251.

CHAPTER 32

1. *TMWC*, XX, 148.
2. *Ibid.*, IV, 111; *NCA*, IV, 95-96.
3. *TMWC*, IV, 58-59.
4. *Ibid.*, V, 45.
5. *Ibid.*, p. 44.
6. *NCA*, V, 559.
7. *Ibid.*, III, 153-54.
8. *TMWC*, IV, 182; *NCA*, V, 347.
9. *TMWC*, IV, 281; *NCA*, IV, 418.
10. *TMWC*, IV, 281; *NCA*, IV, 421.
11. *NCA*, I, 270.

12. *TMWC*, II, 199; *NCA*, II, 899.
13. *New York Times*, June 3, 1945, p. 22, cols. 4-5.
14. *NCA*, VIII, 743.
15. *TMWC*, XXII, 384.
16. Edwin Markham, "The Man With The Hoe."
17. *TMWC*, XXII, 385.
18. *Life Magazine*, XXXVI (May 10, 1954), 116.
19. *TMWC*, XXII, 384.
20. Proverbs 3:6.

CHAPTER 33

1. *NCA*, Supp. B, 1275.
2. *Ibid.*, p. 1277.
3. *Ibid.*, p. 1277.
4. *TMWC*, XVI, 531-32.
5. *NCA*, VI, 554-55.
6. *Ibid.*, p. 558.
7. *Ibid.*, p. 555.
8. *Ibid.*, pp. 555-56.
9. *Ibid.*, p. 556.
10. *Ibid.*, p. 558.
11. *Ibid.*, Supp. B, 1629.
12. *Ibid.*, p. 1630.
13. *New York Times*, December 31, 1945, p. 6, cols. 6, 7, 8.
14. *Ibid.*, p. 6, col. 3.
15. *Ibid.*
16. *Ibid.*
17. *Ibid.*
18. *Ibid.*
19. *Ibid.*
20. *Ibid.*
21. *Ibid.*
22. *Ibid.*, p. 6, col. 4.
23. *Ibid.*
24. *Ibid.*, p. 6, col. 5.
25. *Ibid.*
26. *Ibid.*
27. *Ibid.*
28. *Ibid.*, p. 6, col. 6.
29. *Ibid.*, p. 6, col. 5.
30. *Ibid.*
31. *Ibid.*
32. *NCA*, VI, 575.
33. *Ibid.*, p. 576.
34. *Ibid.*, p. 576.
35. *Ibid.*, p. 577.
36. *TMWC*, XIII, 306.
37. *NCA*, VII, 55.
38. *Ibid.*, pp. 55-56.
39. *Ibid.*, pp. 56-57.

CHAPTER 34

1. *TMWC*, XII, 8.
2. *Ibid.*, XXII, 377-78.
3. *Ibid.*, XIV, 433.

4. *Ibid.*, XXII, 390.
5. *Ibid.*, pp. 390-91.
6. *Ibid.*, XVII, 150.
7. *Ibid.*, XVI, 533.
8. *Ibid.*, XII, 454.
9. *Ibid.*, XVI, 483, 490, 492, 493, 504.
10. *Ibid.*, XVII, 186.
11. *Ibid.*, XXII, 384.
12. *Ibid.*, pp. 405-7.

CHAPTER 35

1. *TMWC*, XIX, 397.
2. *Ibid.*, I, 261.
3. *Ibid.*, p. 267.
4. *Ibid.*, XXII, 588; *NCA*, Opinion and Judgment, p. 189.
5. *TMWC*, XXII, 588; *NCA*, Opinion, p. 189.
6. *TMWC*, XXII, 588; *NCA*, Opinion, p. 189.
7. *TMWC*, XXII, 588; *NCA*, Opinion, p. 189.
8. *TMWC*, XXII, 588; *NCA*, Opinion, p. 189.
9. *TMWC*, XXII, 588; *NCA*, Opinion, p. 189.
10. *TMWC*, XXII, 588; *NCA*, Opinion, p. 189.
11. *TMWC*, XXII, 588; *NCA*, Opinion, p. 189.
12. *TMWC*, XXII, 588; *NCA*, Opinion, p. 189.
13. *TMWC*, XXII, 588; *NCA*, Opinion, p. 189.
14. *TMWC*, XXII, 588; *NCA*, Opinion, p. 189.
15. *TMWC*, XXII, 588; *NCA*, Opinion, p. 189.
16. *TMWC*, XXII, 589; *NCA*, Opinion, p. 189.
17. *TMWC*, XXII, 589; *NCA*, Opinion, p. 190.
18. *TMWC*, XXII, 589; *NCA*, Opinion, p. 190.
19. *TMWC*, XXII, 589; *NCA*, Opinion, p. 190.
20. *TMWC*, XXII, 589; *NCA*, Opinion, p. 190.
21. *TMWC*, XXII, 589; *NCA*, Opinion, p. 190.
22. Cf. *New York Times*, October 11, 1946, p. 1, cols. 2-3; p. 2, cols. 3-6.
23. Cf. *New York Times*, October 10, 1946, p. 4, col. 2.
24. Cf. *New York Times*, October 11, 1946, p. 2, cols. 3-4.
25. Ben Swearingen, *The Mystery of Hermann Goering's Suicide* (San Diego: Harcourt Brace, 1985).

26. William Cullen Bryant, "The Battle-Field."

CHAPTER 36

1. Oliver Wendell Holmes, *The Common Law* (Boston: Little, Brown & Co., 1951), p. 1.
2. Hugo Grotius, *De Jure Belli ac Pacis, Libre Tres* (Carnegie Endowment for International Peace, Oxford University Press, 1925), II, 20, para. 28.
3. William Seagle, *The History of Law* (New York: Tudor Publishing Co., 1946), p. 366.
4. J. L. Brierly, *Law of Nations*, 4th Edition (Oxford: Clarendon Press), p. 227.
5. *In re Piracy Jure Gentium* (1934 A. C.), pp. 586, 600.
6. 5 Wheat. 153, 161 (1820).
7. 18 U.S.C.A. sec. 1651.
8. *Ex parte Quirin*, 317 U.S. 1, 29 (1942).
9. Blackstone, *Commentaries on the Laws of England*, Ed. Chase, 4th Edition (1922), p. 882.
10. *New Jersey v. Delaware*, 291 U.S. 383 (1933).
11. Henry L. Stimson, "The Nuremberg Trial, Landmark in Law," *Foreign Affairs*, XXV (1946-47), 180.
12. *United States* v. *La Jeune Eugenie*.
13. *ICMT*, p. 51-52.
14. Robert H. Jackson, Address delivered at the American Bar Center Cornerstone Ceremony, International House Assembly Hall, Chicago, November 2, 1953.
15. Winston Churchill, *Closing the Ring* (Boston: Houghton Mifflin Co., 1951), p. 374.
16. *TMWC*, II, 99.
17. John J. Parker, "International Trial at Nuremberg: Giving Vitality to International Law," *American Bar Association Journal*, XXXVII (1951), 496.
18. Sheldon Glueck, *War Criminals: Their Prosecution and Punishment* (New York: Knopf, 1944), p. 13.
19. *Ibid.*, p. 77.
20. Robert H. Jackson, "The Rule of Law Among Nations," *American Bar Association Journal*, XXXI (1945), 292.
21. *TMWC*, II, 24.

CHAPTER 37

1. I Samuel 15: 3, 8.
2. Mr. Chief Justice Stone, *Ex parte*

Quirin, 317 U.S. 1 (1942).
3. James Brown Scott, *The Hague Peace Conferences of 1899 and 1907* (Baltimore: The Johns Hopkins University Press, 1909), I, 338.
4. *TMWC,* I, 254.
5. *NCA,* Supp. A, 895.
6. *Ibid.,* VII, 412.
7. Grotius, *op. cit.,* p. 742.
8. *TMWC,* VIII, 416.
9. Scott, *op. cit.,* II, 369-71.
10. Robert Alderson Wright (Lord), "The Killing of Hostages as a War Crime," *British Year Book of International Law,* XXV (1948), 302.
11. *TMWC,* I, 226.
12. A. L. Goodhart, "The Legality of the Nuremberg Trials," *Juridical Review,* LVIII (April, 1946), 15.
13. *Violations of the Laws and Customs of War,* Carnegie Endowment for International Peace, Division of International Law (Pamphlet No. 32, 1919), p. 73.
14. Scott, *op. cit.,* II, 371.
15. *ICMT,* p. 423.
16. *Ibid.,* p. 429.

CHAPTER 38

1. George A. Finch, "The Nuremberg Trial and International Law," *American Journal of International Law,* XLI (1947), 36.
2. *Ibid.,* p. 22.
3. Parker, *op. cit.,* p. 496.
4. *TMWC,* I, 169.
5. Ralph B. Perry, *Realms of Value* (Cambridge: Harvard University Press, 1945), pp. 245-46.
6. Hans Ehard, "The Nuremberg Trial Against the Major War Criminals and International Law," *American Journal of International Law,* XLIII (1949), 244.
7. *TMWC,* I, 11.
8. 46 Stat. 2343; 2345-2346; Hackworth, *Digest of International Law* (Department of State Publication No. 1961 [Washington, D.C., 1943]), VI, 9.
9. *ICMT,* p. 52.
10. *TMWC,* XVII, 470.
11. *Ibid.,* p. 475.
12. *Ibid.,* XIX, 460.
13. Sheldon Glueck, *The Nuremberg Trial and Aggressive War* (New York: Knopf, 1946), p. 5.
14. Max Habicht, *Post-War Treaties for the*

Pacific Settlement of International Disputes (Cambridge: Harvard University Press, 1931), p. 929.
15. Hersh Lauterpacht, *Oppenheim's International Law,* 7th ed. (New York: Longmans, Green & Co., 1952), II, 180.
16. *American Journal of International Law,* XXII (1928), 356-57.
17. Winston Churchill, *The Gathering Storm* (Boston: Houghton Mifflin Co., 1948), p. 538.
18. Grotius, *op. cit.,* II, 184.
19. *TWMC,* XVII, 478, 479.
20. Story, J., *United States* v. *La Jeune Eugenie,* 26 Fed. Cas. 832, 846 (Case No. 15,551) (1822).
21. Parker, *op. cit.,* p. 550.
22. *TMWC,* I, 310.
23. *NCA,* Supp. B, 1286.
24. *Ibid.,* p. 1285.
25. Robert H. Jackson, "The United Nations Organization and War Crimes," Address delivered at the American Society of International Law, April 26, 1952, Washington, D.C., p. 4.
26. Hersh Lauterpacht, "The Grotian Tradition in International Law," *British Year Book of International Law,* XXIII (1946), 39.
27. *TMWC,* I, 186.
28. Ehard, *op. cit.,* p. 244.

CHAPTER 39

1. Stimson, *op. cit.,* p. 185.
2. Perry, *op. cit.,* p. 246.
3. *TMWC,* I., 223.
4. *Ibid.,* p. 244.
5. *Ibid.,* p. 310.
6. *Ibid.,* p. 327.
7. Stimson, *op. cit.,* p. 182.
8. Keenan and Brown, *Crimes Against International Law* (Washington, D.C.: Public Affairs Press, 1950), p. 1.
9. *Trials of War Criminals* (Washington, D.C.: U.S. Government Printing Office, 1950), I, xvi.
10. *Ibid.,* p. xxii.
11. *Ibid.,* p. xxi.
12. *Ibid.,* p. xxiv.
13. *Ibid.,* p. xxiv.
14. *Ibid.,* p. xxiv.
15. *Ibid.,* VI, 1189.
16. *Ibid.,* XV, 552, 553.
17. *Ibid.,* V, 1018.
18. *White House,* 1995, WL 608247.
19. *Ibid.*

20. *Trials of War Criminals* (Washington, D.C.: U.S. Government Printing Office, 1950), II, 154.
21. *Ibid.,* I, 186.
22. *New York Times,* October 4, 1953, sec. 1, p. 1, col. 5.
23. *Department of State Bulletin,* XV (October 27, 1946), p. 776.
24. Plenary Meeting of the General Assembly, Verbatim Records of Meetings (October 23-December 16, 1946), p. 1144.
25. C. A. Pompe, *Aggressive War An International Crime* (The Hague: Martinus Nijhoff, 1953), p. 317.
26. Kenny, *Moral Aspects of Nuremberg,* Dominican House of Studies, 1949, Washington, D.C., p. viii.
27. *New York Times,* October 4, 1953, sec. 1, p. 1, col. 5.
28. American Society of International Law, April 26, 1952, Washington, D.C., p. 2.
29. Shakespeare, *The Tempest,* Act IV, Scene I.

CHAPTER 40

1. United Nations Press Release, Dept. Pub. Info., L/ROM/6/Rev. 1, June 14, 1998.
2. United Nations Press Release, Dept. Pub. Info., L/ROM/8, June 17, 1998.
3. Terraviva, No. 26, Rome, July 18, 1998, p. 1.
4. United Nations Press Release, Dept. Pub. Info., L/ROM/23, July 18, 1998.
5. General Assembly Resolution 21/A (III), December 10, 1948.
6. United Nations Press Release, Dept. Pub. Info., L/ROM/23, July 18, 1998.
7. *Trials of War Criminals.* Washington, D.C.: U.S. Government Printing Office, 1950, II, 154.

Select Bibliography

Relating to the Proceedings of
The International Military Tribunal

Bibliographical Materials

NEWMANN, INGE S. (compiler). *European War Crimes Trials.* New York: Carnegie Endowment for International Peace, 1951.

SCANLON, HELEN L. (compiler). *War Crimes.* Washington: Carnegie Endowment for International Peace, 1945.

CONOVER, HELEN F. (compiler). *The Nazi State, War Crimes and War Criminals.* Washington, D.C.: Library of Congress, General Reference and Bibliography Division, 1945.

Books on Persecution, Terror and Resistance in Nazi Germany. London: Wiener Library, 1941.

Documentary Materials

Report of Robert H. Jackson, United States Representative to the International Conference on Military Trials, London, 1945. Washington, D.C.: Government Printing Office, 1949.

The Trial of German Major War Criminals (Proceedings of the International Military Tribunal Sitting at Nuremberg, Germany). London: H.M. Stationery Office, 1946.

Trial of the Major War Criminals Before the International Military Tribunal, Nuremberg, 14 November 1945–1 October 1946. 42 vols. Nuremberg: International Military Tribunal, 1947–49.

Trials of War Criminals Before the Nuernberg Military Tribunals Under Control Council Law No. 10. 15 vols. Washington, D.C.: Government Printing Office, 1946–49.

Law Reports of Trials of War Criminals, selected and prepared by the United Nations War Crimes Commission. 15 vols. London: H.M. Stationery Office, 1947–49.

UNITED STATES CHIEF OF COUNSEL FOR THE PROSECUTION OF AXIS CRIMINALITY. *Nazi Conspiracy and Aggression.* 8 vols. Washington, D.C.: Government Printing Office, 1946. Supplement, 2 vols., 1947–48.

609

Special Collection

The Whitney Robson Harris Collection on the Third Reich of Germany, Olin Library, Washington University, St. Louis, Missouri. A compilation of over 3,000 current titles, continuously enlarged, in German, Russian, French, English and other languages, accessible through the Internet at http://library.wustl.edu. Current catalogues available through Olin Library.

Select Books and Articles Published in English

ABEL, THEODORE FRED. *Why Hitler Came into Power.* Cambridge: Harvard University Press, 1986.

ALDERMAN, SIDNEY S. *Negotiating the Nuremberg Trial Agreements.* Denner, R., and Johnson, J. E., eds. *Negotiating with the Russians.* World Peace Foundation, 1951.

ALLEN, WILLIAM SHERIDAN. *The Nazi Seizure of Power.* Chicago: Quadrangle Books, 1965.

ANDRUS, BURTON C. *I Was the Nuremberg Jailer.* New York: Coward, McCann & Geoghegan, 1969.

APPEL, BENJAMIN. *Hitler: From Power to Ruin.* New York: Grosset & Dunlap, 1964.

ARENDT, HANNAH. *Eichmann in Jerusalem.* New York: Penguin Books, 1964.

———. *The Origins of Totalitarianism.* New York: Harcourt, Brace, 1951.

BASSIOUNI, M. CHERIF. *The Statute of the International Criminal Court.* Ardsley, NY: Transnational Publishers, 1998.

BENDERSKY, JOSEPH W. *A History of Nazi Germany.* Chicago: Nelson-Hall, 1985.

BERNADOTTE, FOLKE. *The Curtain Falls: Last Days of the Third Reich.* Trans. by Count Eric Lewenhaupt. New York: A. A. Knopf, 1945.

BERNAYS, MURRAY C. "Legal Basis of the Nuremberg Trials," *Survey Graphic,* XXXV (January, 1946), 4–9.

BIDDLE, FRANCIS. *In Brief Authority.* New York: Doubleday, 1962.

———. "The Nuernberg Trial," *American Philosophical Society, Proceedings,* XCI (1947), 294–302.

BIRKETT, SIR NORMAN. "International Legal Theories Evolved at Nuremberg," *International Affairs,* XXIII (July, 1947), 317–25.

BOLDT, GERHARD. *Hitler: The Last Ten Days.* New York: Coward, McCann & Geoghegan, 1973.

BORKIN, JOSEPH. *The Crime and Punishment of I. G. Farben.* New York: Free Press, 1978.

BOSCH, WILLIAM J. *Judgment on Nuremberg.* Chapel Hill: University of North Carolina Press, 1970.

BRACHER, KARL DIETRICH. *The German Dictatorship: The Origins, Structure, and Effects of National Socialism.* Trans. by Jean Steinberg. New York: Praeger Publishers, 1970.

BRADY, ROBERT A. *The Spirit and Structure of German Fascism.* New York: Fertig, 1970.

BREITMAN, RICHARD. *The Architect of Genocide: Himmler and the Final Solution.* New York: Knopf: Distributed by Random House, 1991.

BROSZAT, MARTIN. *German National Socialism, 1919–1945.* Santa Barbara: Clio Press, 1966.

————. *The Hitler State: The Foundation and Development of the Internal Structure of the Third Reich.* New York: Longman, 1981.

BROWNING, CHRISTOPHER R. *Ordinary Men.* New York: Aaron Asher Books, 1992.

BRUCE, GEORGE LUDGATE. *The Nazis.* London; New York: Hamlyn, 1974.

BUCHHEIM, HANS, et al. *Anatomy of the SS State.* New York: Walker & Co., 1968.

BULLOCK, ALAN LOUIS CHARLES. *Hitler: A Study in Tyranny.* New York: Harper, 1952.

BUSCHER, FRANK M. *The U.S. War Crimes Trial Program in Germany, 1946–1955.* New York: Greenwood Press, 1989.

BUTLER, ROHAN D'OLIER. *The Roots of National Socialism.* New York: Dutton, 1942.

CALVOCORESSI, PETER. *Nuremberg: The Facts, the Law and the Consequences.* New York: Macmillan, 1948.

CARR, WILLIAM. *Hitler: A Study in Personality and Politics.* New York: St. Martin's Press, 1979.

CECIL, ROBERT. *Hitler's Decision to Invade Russia, 1941.* New York: David McKay, 1975.

————. *The Myth of the Master Race: Alfred Rosenberg and Nazi Ideology.* New York: Dodd, Mead & Co., 1972.

CHILDS, MARQUIS WILLIAM. *Witness to Power.* New York: McGraw-Hill, 1975.

CHURCHILL, WINSTON. *The Gathering Storm.* Boston: Houghton Mifflin, 1948.

CIANO, COUNT GALEAZZO. *Ciano's Diary.* London and Toronto: Heinemann, 1947.

CLARK, ALAN. *Barbarossa.* New York: William Morrow & Co., 1965.

CLAY, LUCIUS D. *Decision in Germany.* New York: Doubleday, 1950.

COHN, NORMAN. *Warrant for Genocide.* New York: Harper & Row, 1967.

CONOT, ROBERT E. *Justice at Nuremberg.* New York: Harper & Row, 1983.

COOPER, R. W. *The Nuremberg Trial.* Harmondsworth and New York: Penguin Books, 1947.

CROSS, COLIN. *Adolf Hitler.* London: Hodder and Stoughton, 1973.

CYPRIAN, TADEUSZ. *Nuremberg in Retrospect: People and Issues of the Trial.* Warsaw: Western Press Agency, 1967.

DAHLERUS, BIRGER. *The Last Attempt.* London: Hutchinson, 1948.

DAVIDSON, EUGENE. *The Trial of the Germans.* New York: Macmillan, 1967.

DAWIDOWICZ, LUCY. *The War Against the Jews.* New York: Holt, Rinehart & Winston, 1975.

DELARUE, JACQUES. *The History of the Gestapo.* London: Macdonald, 1964.

DODD, T. J. "The Nuremberg Trials," *Journal of Criminal Law and Criminology,* XXXVII (January, 1947), 357-67.

DOENITZ, KARL. *The Doenitz Memoirs.* Cleveland and New York: World Publishing Co., 1959.

DOUGLAS-HAMILTON, JAMES. *Motive for a Mission.* London: Macmillan-St. Martin's Press, 1971.

EHARD, JANS. "The Nuremberg Trial Against the Major War Criminals and International Law," *American Journal of International Law,* XLIII (April, 1949), 223–45.

ELLIOT, GIL. *Twentieth Century Book of the Dead.* London: Allen Lane, 1972.

FEST, JOACHIM C. *The Face of the Third Reich.* Trans. by Michael Bullock. New York: Pantheon Books, 1970.

————. *Hitler.* Trans. by Richard and Clara Winston. New York: Harcourt, Brace, Jovanovich, 1974.

FINCH, GEORGE A. "The Nuremberg Trial and International Law," *American Journal of International Law,* XLI (January, 1947), 20–37.

FITZGIBBONS, LOUIS. *Katyn.* London: Tom Stacey, 1971.

FLEMING, GERALD. *Hitler and the Final Solution.* Berkeley: University of California Press, 1984.

FLOOD, CHARLES BRACELEN. *Hitler: The Path to Power.* Boston: Houghton Mifflin, 1989.

FREI, NORBERT. *National Socialist Rule in Germany: The Fuehrer State, 1933–1945.* Oxford: Blackwell, 1993.

FRISCHAUER, WILLI. *The Rise and Fall of Hermann Goering.* Boston: Houghton Mifflin, 1951.

FRITSCHE, HANS. *The Sword in the Scales.* London: Allan Wingate, 1953.

FYFE, MAXWELL (EARL OF KILMUIR). *Political Adventure: The Memoirs of the Earl of Kilmuir.* London: Weidenfeld & Nicolson, 1964.

GALLO, MAX. *The Night of Long Knives.* Trans. by Lily Emmet. New York: Harper & Row, 1972.

GASKIN, HILARY. *Eyewitnesses at Nuremberg.* London: Arms and Armour, 1990.

GERHART, EUGENE C. *Robert H. Jackson, America's Advocate.* Indianapolis and New York: Bobbs-Merrill, 1958.

GILBERT, GUSTAVO M. *Nuremberg Diary.* New York: Farrar, Straus, 1947.

GLASER, HERMANN. *The Cultural Roots of National Socialism.* Trans. by Ernest A. Menze. London: Croon Helm, 1978.

GLUECK, SHELDON. *War Criminals: Their Prosecution and Punishment.* New York: Knopf, 1944.

GLUECK, SHELDON. *The Nuremberg Trial and Aggressive War.* New York: Knopf, 1946.

GOEBBELS, JOSEPH. *The Goebbels Diaries, 1942–1943.* Trans. by Louis P. Lochner. New York: Doubleday, 1948.

———. *Final Entries 1945: The Diaries of Joseph Goebbels.* Trans. by Richard Barry. Ed. by Hugh Trevor-Roper. New York: Putnam, 1978.

GOLDHAGEN, DANIEL J. *Hitler's Willing Executioners.* New York: Knopf, 1996.

GOLDSTON, ROBERT C. *The Life and Death of Nazi Germany.* Indianapolis: Bobbs-Merrill, 1967.

GORDON, HAROLD J. *Hitler and the Beer Hall Putsch.* Princeton: Princeton University Press, 1972.

GRABER, G. S. *The History of the SS.* New York: McKay, 1978

———. *The Life and Times of Reinhard Heydrich.* New York: McKay, 1980.

GRUNBERGER, RICHARD. *The Twelve Year Reich.* New York: Holt, Rinehart & Winston, 1971.

HAFFNER, SEBASTIAN. *The Meaning of Hitler.* Trans. by Ewald Osers. London: Weidenfeld and Nicolson, 1979.

HAIGH, R. H., D. S. MORRIS, AND A. R. PETERS. *Years of Triumph: German Military and Diplomatic History, 1933–1941.* Tutowa, NJ: Barnes & Noble Books, 1986.

HALDER, FRANZ. *Hitler as Warlord.* London, Putnam, 1950.

HANSER, RICHARD. *Prelude to Terror: The Rise of Hitler, 1919–1923.* London: Hart-Davis, 1971.

HARRIS, WHITNEY R. "The Nuremberg Trial," *State Bar Journal of California,* XXII (March-April, 1947), 97–121.

———. "Justice Jackson at Nuremberg," *The International Lawyer,* Vol. 20, No. 3 (Summer, 1986), 867–96.

———. "A Call for an International War Crimes Court: Learning from Nuremberg," *University of Toledo Law Review.* Vol. 23, No. 2 (Winter, 1992), 229–52.

HEIDEN, KONRAD. *Der Fuehrer: Hitler's Rise to Power.* Trans. by Ralph Manheim. Boston: Beacon Press, 1969.

HERZSTEIN, ROBERT EDWIN. *Adolf Hitler and the Third Reich, 1933–1945.* Boston: Houghton Mifflin, 1971.

HEYDECKER, JOE JULIUS. *The Nuremberg Trial.* Cleveland: World Publishing Co., 1962.

HIDEN, JOHN. *Explaining Hitler's Germany: Historians and the Third Reich.* Totowa, NJ: Barnes & Noble Books, 1983.

HILBERG, RAUL. *The Destruction of the European Jews.* Chicago: Quadrangle Books, 1967.

HILDEBRAND, KLAUS. *The Third Reich.* Trans. by P. S. Falla. London: Allan & Unwin, 1984.

HITLER, ADOLF. *Main Kampf.* Boston: Houghton Mifflin, 1943.

HITLER, ADOLF. *Hitler's Secret Book*. Trans. by S. Attanasio. New York: Grove Press, 1962.

————. *Secret Conversations, 1941–1944*. Trans. by N. Cameron and R. H. Stevens. New York: Farrar, Straus and Young, 1953.

————. *The Speeches of Adolf Hitler, April 1922–August 1939*. Ed. by N. H. Baynes. London: Oxford University Press, 1942.

HOESS, RUDOLF. *Commandant of Auschwitz*. London: Weidenfeld and Nicolson, 1953.

HOETTL, WILHELM. *The Secret Front*. London: Weidenfeld and Nicolson, 1953.

HOFFMAN, HEINRICH. *Hitler Was My Friend*. London: Burke, 1955.

HOFFMAN, PETER. *German Resistance to Hitler*. Cambridge, MA: Harvard University Press, 1988.

HOLDEN, MATTHEW. *Hitler*. New York: St. Martin's Press, 1975.

HOYT, EDWIN PALMER. *Hitler's War*. New York: McGraw Hill, 1988.

HUTTON, J. BERNARD. *Hess, the Man and His Mission*. New York: Macmillan, 1971.

JACKSON, ROBERT H. *Nuernberg Case, as Presented by Robert H. Jackson*. New York: Knopf, 1947.

————. "Nuernberg in Retrospect," *American Bar Association Journal*, XXXC (October, 1949), 813–16, 881–87.

JACKSON, WILLIAM E. "Putting the Nuremberg Law to Work," *Foreign Affairs*, XXV (1946–47), 550–65.

JAECKEL, EBERHARD. *Hitler in History*. Hanover, NH: University Press of New England, 1984.

JANECZEK, HANS HEINRICH. *Nuremberg Judgment in the Light of International Law*. Geneva: Imprimeries Populaires, 1949.

JONES, ELWYN. *In My Time: Autobiography of Lord Elwyn-Jones*. London: Weidenfeld & Nicolson, 1983.

KEENAN, J. B. AND BROWN, F. B. *Crimes Against International Law*. Washington: Public Affairs Press, 1950.

KELSON, HANS. *Peace Through Law*. Chapel Hill: University of North Carolina Press, 1944.

KENNY, JOHN P. *Moral Aspects of Nuremberg*. Washington: Pontifical Faculty of Theology, Dominican House of Studies, 1949.

KERSHAW, IAN. *Hitler*. London: Longman, 1991.

————. *Hitler, 1889–1936: Hubris*. New York: W. W. Norton, 1999.

KLAFKOWSKI, ALFONS. *The Nuremberg Principles and the Development of International Law*. Warsaw: Zachodnia Agencja Prasowa, 1966.

KNIERIEM, AUGUST VON. *The Nuremberg Trials*. Trans. by E. D. Schmitt. Chicago: H. Regnery, 1959.

KRAUSNICK, HELMUT, et al. *Anatomy of the SS State*. New York: Walker, 1968.

LACHS, MANFRED. *War Crimes: An Attempt to Define the Issues*. London: Stevens & Sons, 1945.

LANG, JOCHEN VON. *The Secretary: Martin Bormann.* New York: Random House, 1979.

LANGER, WALTER C. *The Mind of Adolf Hitler: The Secret Wartime Report.* New York: Basic Books, 1972.

LAWRENCE, GEOFFREY (LORD OAKSEY). "The Nuremberg Trial," *International Affairs,* XXIII (April, 1947), 151–59.

LEVIN, NORA. *The Holocaust Years: The Nazi Destruction of European Jewry, 1933–1945.* Malabar, FL: R. E. Krieger Pub. Co., 1990.

LOCHNER, LOUIS P., Ed. *The Goebbels Diaries.* New York: Doubleday, 1948.

LUCAS, JAMES. *Third Reich.* London: Arms and Armour, 1990.

MANCHESTER, WILLIAM. *The Arms of Krupp.* New York: Bantam Books, 1970.

MANVELL, ROGER. *Goering.* New York: Simon & Schuster, 1962.

———. *The Hundred Days to Hitler.* New York: St. Martin's Press, 1974.

MANVELL, ROGER AND FRAENKEL, HEINRICH. *Dr. Goebbels.* New York: Simon & Schuster, 1960.

———. *Himmler.* New York: G. P. Putnam's Sons, 1965.

———. *Hess.* London: McGibbon & Kee, 1971.

MASER, WERNER. *Hitler: Legend, Myth and Reality.* Trans. by P. Ross and B. Ross. New York: Harper & Row, 1973.

———. *Nuremberg: A Nation on Trial.* Trans. by Richard Barry. New York: Charles Scribner's Sons, 1977.

MCGOVERN, JAMES. *Martin Bormann.* New York: Morrow, 1968.

MCKAY, MARIA. *Germany, 1919–1945.* New York: Longman, 1989.

MIALE, FLORENCE R. *The Nuremberg Mind: The Psychology of the Nazi Leaders.* New York: Quadrangle, 1975.

MITCHELL, OTIS C. *Hitler over Germany: The Establishment of the Nazi Dictatorship, 1919–1934.* Philadelphia: Institute for the Study of Human Issues, 1983.

———. *Hitler's Nazi State: The Years of Dictatorial Rule (1934–1945).* Frankfurt: Peter Lang, 1987.

MITSCHERLICH, ALEXANDER. *Doctors of Infamy.* New York: Schuman, 1949.

MORELL, THEODOR GILBERT. *Secret Diaries of Hitler's Doctor.* New York: Macmillan, 1983.

MORGAN, JOHN HARTMANN. *Great Assize: An Examination of the Law of the Nuremberg Trials.* London: J. Murray, 1948.

MOSLEY, LEONARD. *The Reich Marshal.* Garden City, NY: Doubleday, 1974.

MYERSON, MOSES HYMAN. *Germany's War Crimes and Punishment: The Problem of Individual and Collective Criminality.* Toronto: Macmillan, 1944.

NEAVE, AIREY. *Nuremberg.* London: Hodder & Stoughton, 1978.

NEUMANN, FRANZ L. *Behemoth: The Structure and Practice of National Socialism.* New York: Harper & Row, 1963.

NICHOLLS, ANTHONY JAMES. *Weimar and the Rise of Hitler.* New York: St. Martin's Press, 1979.

NOAKES, JEREMY. *Documents on Nazism, 1919–1945.* New York: The Viking Press, 1974.

O'DONNELL, JAMES PRESTON. *The Bunker.* Boston: Houghton Mifflin, 1978.

ORLOW, DIETRICH. *The History of the Nazi Party: 1919–1945.* 2 vols. Pittsburgh, PA: University of Pittsburgh Press, 1969–1973.

OVERY, RICHARD J. *The Road to War.* New York: Random House, 1990.

PADFIELD, PETER. *Doenitz: The Last Fuehrer.* London: Collancz, 1984.

————. *Himmler: Reichsfuehrer-SS.* New York: Holt, 1991.

PAPEN, FRANZ VON. *Memoirs.* New York: E. P. Dutton & Co., 1953. G. P. Putnam's Sons, 1940.

PARKER, JOHN J. "International Trial at Nuremberg: Giving Vitality to International Law," *American Bar Association Journal,* XXXVII (July, 1951), 493–96, 549–55.

PAYNE, PIERRE STEPHEN ROBERT. *The Life and Death of Adolf Hitler.* New York: Praeger, 1973.

PERSICO, JOSEPH E. *Piercing the Reich.* New York: Viking, 1979.

————. *Nuremberg: Infamy on Trial.* New York: Viking, 1994.

PROCKTOR, RICHARD. *Nazi Germany.* New York: Holt, Rinehart & Winston, 1972.

RAUSCHNING, HERMANN. *The Voice of Destruction.* New York: G. P. Putnam's Sons, 1940.

REITLINGER, GERALD. *The Final Solution.* New York: A. S. Barnes, 1961.

————. *The SS, Alibi of a Nation.* New York: Viking Press, 1968.

————. *The House Built on Sand.* New York: Viking Press, 1960.

RENOUVIN, PIERRE. *World War II and Its Origins.* New York: Harper & Row, 1969.

REUTH, RALF GEORG. *Goebbels.* New York: Harcourt Brace, 1993.

RIBBENTROP, JOACHIM VON. *The Ribbentrop Memoirs.* London: Weidenfeld & Nicolson, 1953.

RICE, EARLE. *Nazi War Criminals.* San Diego: Lucent Books, 1998.

RICH, NORMAN. *Hitler's War Aims.* New York: Norton, 1974.

RUTHERFORD, WARD. *Hitler's Propaganda Machine.* New York: Grosset & Dunlap, 1978.

SCHACHT, HJALMAR. *Account Settled.* London: Weidenfeld & Nicolson, 1948.

————. *Confessions of the Old Wizard.* Boston: Houghton Mifflin, 1956.

SCHELLENBERG, WALTER. *The Schellenberg Memoirs.* London: Andre Deutsch, 1956.

SCHLABRENDORFF, FABIAN VON. *The Secret War Against Hitler.* New York: G. P. Putnam's Sons, 1965.

SCHLEUNES, KARL A. *The Twisted Road to Auschwitz.* Urbana: University of Illinois Press, 1970.

SCHLICK, FRANZ B. "The Nuremberg Trial and the International Law of the Future," *American Journal of International Law,* XLI (October, 1947), 770–94.

SCHMIDT, MATTHIAS. *Albert Speer: The End of a Myth.* Trans. by J. Neugroschel. New York: St. Martin's Press, 1984.

SCHMIDT, PAUL. *Hitler's Interpreter.* London: Heinemann, 1951.

SHIRER, WILLIAM L. *The Rise and Fall of the Third Reich.* New York: Simon & Schuster, 1960.

SIMPSON, WILLIAM. *Hitler and Germany.* Cambridge; New York: Cambridge University Press, 1991.

SMITH, BRADLEY. *Reaching Judgment at Nuremberg.* New York: Basic Books, 1977.

———. *The Road to Nuremberg.* New York: Basic Books, 1981.

SMITH, WOODRUFF D. *The Ideological Origins of Nazi Imperialism.* New York: Oxford University Press, 1986.

SNYDER, LOUIS LEO. *National Socialist Germany: Twelve Years That Shook the World.* Malabor, FL: Krieger Pub. Co., 1984.

SPEER, ALBERT. *Inside the Third Reich.* New York: Avon Books, 1971.

———. *Spandau.* New York: Pocket Books, 1977.

SPIELVOGEL, JACKSON. *Hitler and Nazi Germany: A History.* Englewood Cliffs, NJ: Prentice Hall, 1988.

SPRECHER, DREXEL. *Inside the Nuremberg Trial.* Lanham, MD: University Press of America, 1999.

STEINERT, MARLIS G. *Hitler's War and the Germans.* Athens: Ohio University Press, 1977.

STIMSON, HENRY L. *On Active Service in Peace and War.* New York: Harper, 1948.

———. "The Nuremberg Trial, Landmark in Law," *Foreign Affairs,* XXV (January, 1947), 179–89.

STONE, NORMAN. *Hitler.* New York: Little, Brown, 1980.

STOREY, ROBERT. *The Final Judgment.* San Antonio: Naylor Co., 1958.

TAYLOR, SIMON. *Prelude to Genocide: Nazi Ideology and the Struggle for Power.* New York: St. Martin's Press, 1985.

TAYLOR, TELFORD. *Sword and Swastika.* New York: Simon & Schuster, 1952.

———. *Guilt, Responsibility and the Third Reich.* Cambridge: Heffer, 1970.

———. *The Anatomy of the Nuremberg Trials.* New York: A. A. Knopf, 1992.

THOMPSON, HAROLD K. *Doenitz at Nuremberg.* New York: Amber, 1977.

THORNTON, M J *Nazism, 1918–1945.* New York: Pergamon, 1968.

TOBIAS, FRITZ. *The Reichstag Fire.* New York: G. P. Putnam's Sons, 1964.

TOLAND, JOHN. *Adolf Hitler.* Garden City, NY: Doubleday, 1976.

TOLAND, JOHN. *The Last 100 Days.* New York: Random House, 1966.

TREVOR-ROPER, HUGH. *The Last Days of Hitler.* New York: Macmillan, 1947.

TUSA, ANN AND JOHN. *The Nuremberg Trial.* New York: Atheneum, 1983.

TUTOROW, NORMAN E. *War Crimes, War Criminals, and War Crimes Trials.* New York: Greenwood Press, 1986.

WAITE, ROBERT GEORGE LEESON. *Hitler and Nazi Germany.* New York: Holt, Rinehart & Winston, 1969.

WARLIMONT, WALTER. *Inside Hitler's Headquarters.* New York: Frederick A. Praeger, 1964.

WECHSLER, HERBERT. *Principles, Politics, and Fundamental Law.* Cambridge: Harvard University Press, 1961.

WIESENTHAL, SIMON. *Justice, not Vengeance: Recollections.* New York: Grove Weidenfeld, 1989.

WIGHTON, CHARLES. *Heydrich.* London: Oldham, 1962.

WOETZEL, ROBERT K. *The Nuremberg Trials in International Law.* London: Stevens, New York: Praeger, 1962.

WRIGHT, QUINCY. "The Law of the Nuremberg Trial," *American Journal of International Law,* XLI (January, 1947), 38–72.

Index of Names

619

Index of Subjects

627

In addition to serving as trial counsel at Nuremberg, WHITNEY R. HARRIS was an officer in the U.S. Navy throughout World War II, professor of law at Southern Methodist University, executive director of the American Bar Association, Solicitor General for Southwestern Bell Telephone Company, and a practicing lawyer in Los Angeles, Dallas, and St. Louis.

Lieutenant Commander Whitney R. Harris at the Nuremberg Trial.